WILLOW WARE

Ceramics in the Chinese Tradition

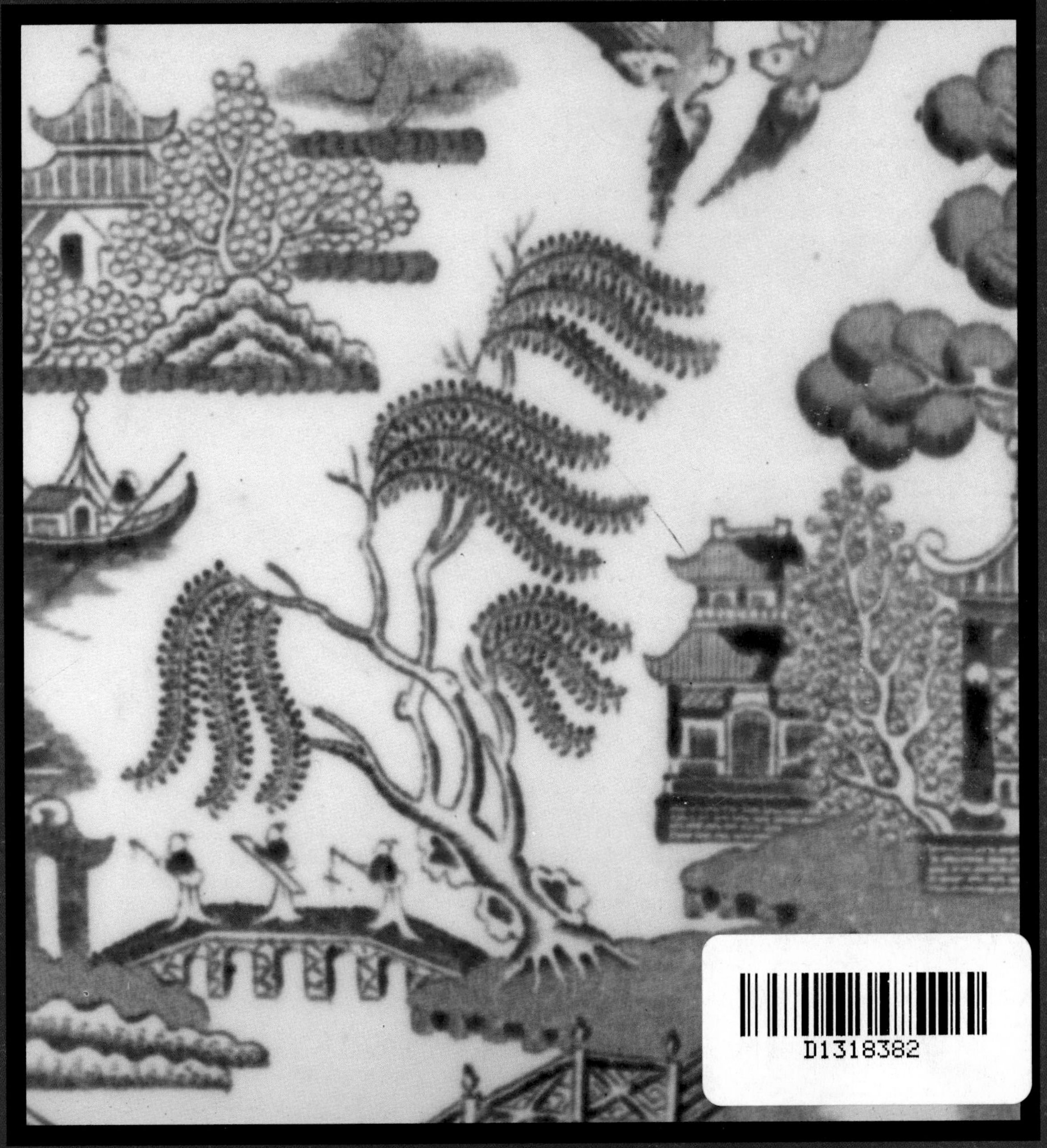

With Price Guide

Leslie Bockol

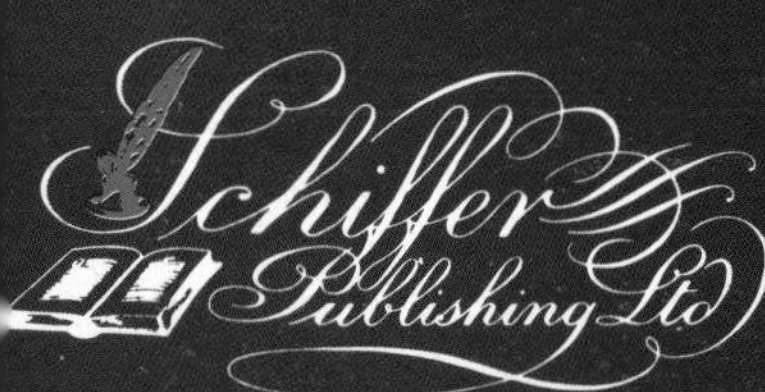

77 Lower Valley Road, Atglen, PA 19310

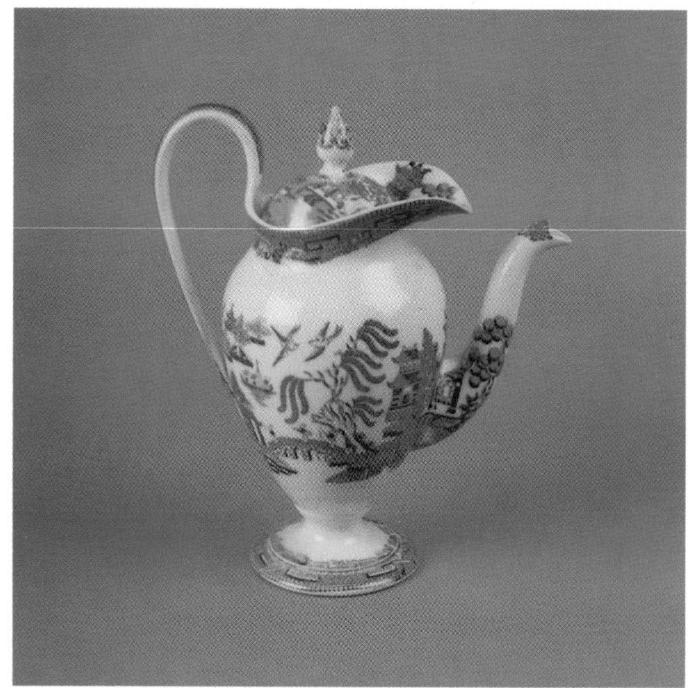

Printed in Hong Kong

Library of Congress Cataloging-in-Publication Data

Bockol, Leslie.
Willow Ware: ceramics in the Chinese tradition: with price guide/
Leslie Bockol.
p. cm.
Includes bibliographical references (p.) and index.
ISBN: 0-88740-720-X
1. Willow Ware--Collectors and collecting--Catalogs. I. Title.
NK4277.B63 1995
738.3'7--dc20 94-42662
CIP

We are interested in hearing from authors
with book ideas on related topics.

Published by Schiffer Publishing Ltd.
77 Lower Valley Road
Atglen, PA 19310
Please write for a free catalog.
This book may be purchased from the publisher.
Please include $2.95 postage.
Try your bookstore first.

Contents

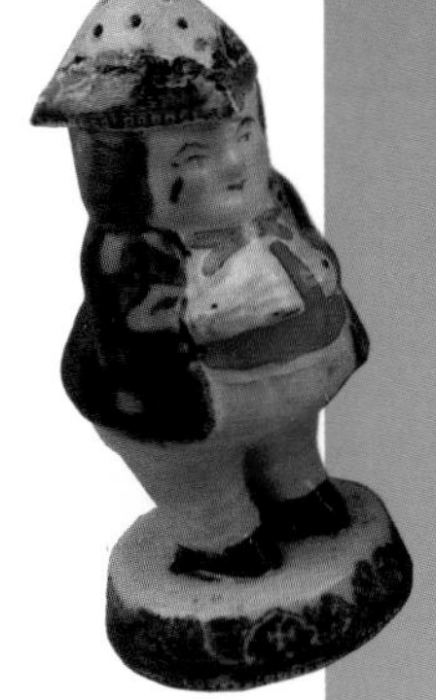

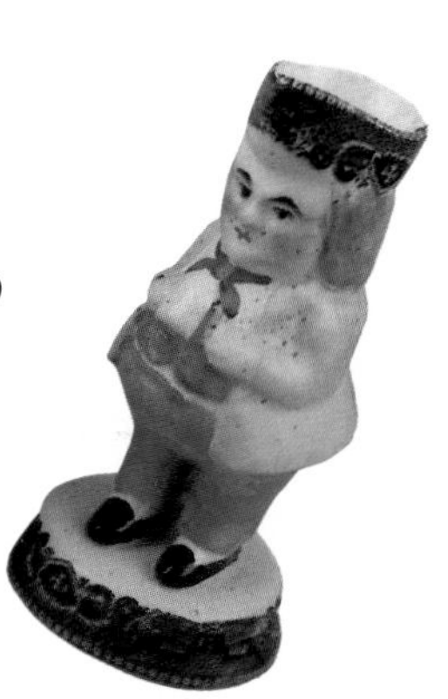

Acknowledgments

In the process of completing this book, I have become hopelessly indebted to a great many collectors, dealers, and other Willow enthusiasts from around the country and around the world. I extend my gratitude to Rita Entmacher Cohen (P.O. Box 708, Closter, NJ 07624) and to Arnold Kowalski, whose introductions were indispensible; to Phillip M. Sullivan, Peter and Susan Steelman, and Charles and Louise Loehr (Louise's Old Things, P.O. Box 208, Kutztown, PA 19530), who graciously opened their homes and shops to me, no matter how busy they were. Thanks also to Bobbie Jarrow (142 Main St., Nyack, NY) for going out of her way.

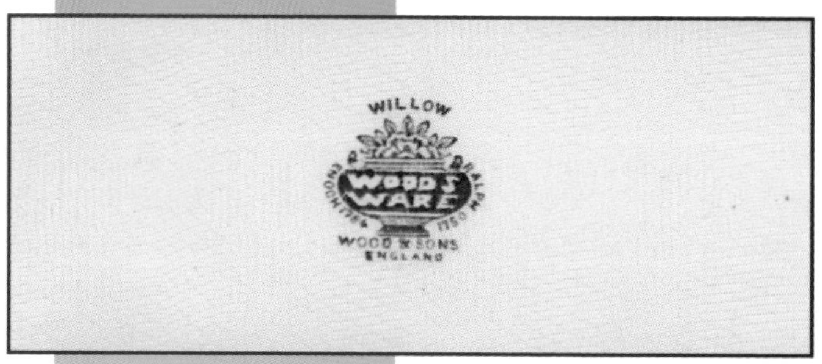

The 1993 International Willow Collectors convention in Hyannis, Massachussetts, provided the largest assembly of Willow I had ever seen, and more Willow enthusiasts than I could have hoped to have met. I am grateful to all those who allowed me to photograph their 'pride and joy' pieces that fantastic weekend, including Eva Lee Revels (Country Accents, Bandera, TX), Wendy Arbogast (Wendy's Willow, 7162 Mahoning NW, Warren, OH 44481), Marguerite and Bud Smith (Small World Antiques, Warren, IN), Joyce LaFont (My Wife's Antiques, Jackson, TN), Shirley Hagerty (Edgehill Antiques, Chardon, OH 44024), Loretta DeMarco, Ron and Linda Steed (Plattsburg, NY), and Loren Zeller. I would also like to thank speaker Gene Ellison. The members of the IWC and the organizers of the convention were friendly and helpful beyond the call of duty. Names and addresses of the club officers are provided at the back of this book, and I recommend calling upon them for any questions about the community of Willow dealers and collectors.

This book would never have been completed (or even started) without the help of the team at Schiffer Publishing. I would like to thank my publisher, Peter Schiffer; my editor (and sometime photo assistant), Nancy Schiffer; layout designer Mark Balbach; research assistant Audrey Whiteside; and moral supporters and advisors Jeff Snyder and Alison Levie.

My final thanks go to my family—Ann, Jeff, Matt and Marcia Bockol, and Gertrude and Daniel Perlov. Special thanks to Mom, who has a job as my photo assistant whenever she wants one.

Introduction

Willow pattern wares began their development in England at the end of the 18th century, with a delicate arrangement of Chinese-style trees, a pagoda, a bridge, and a pair of doves. Even today, the Willow pattern's gracefully placid landscape, most often transfer-printed in a soothing blue and white, can prompt modern collectors to lapse into a reverie of nostalgia for the earlier eras of Willow manufacture, if not for the days of China's antiquity.

The Willow pattern was inspired by hand-painted blue and white Chinese export porcelain, sometimes called 'Canton Ware'. Increasing quantities of Chinese porcelain were sent to England in 16th, 17th, and 18th century sailing ships,[1] weighing down shipments of even more expensive commodities like tea and silk. Due to the vagaries of international trade, changes in Western culture, and the development of the English potting industry, Chinese export porcelain lost favor in the second half of the 18th century. However, its derivative—English transfer-printed Willow ware decorated with underglaze cobalt blue—quickly found its own market and audience.

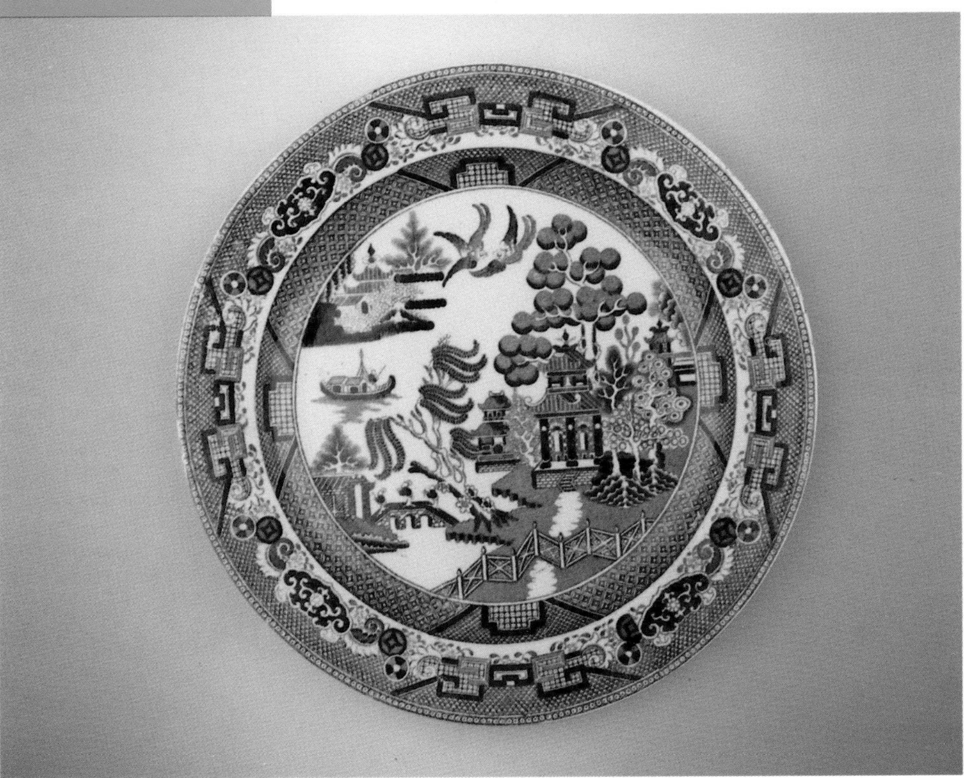

Pearlware plate, 9.75". Marked "F [anchor] 9". Courtesy of Rita Entmacher Cohen.

While not as pricey or refined as the earlier Chinese imports, Willow ware had a similar visual appeal. It soon became *de riguer* among the working and professional classes, just as Chinese blue and white porcelain had been among the elite. By 1800 there were approximately two hundred potters making Willow pattern wares in England.[2] At first, broad variations on the pattern abounded, but before long a 'Standard' Willow pattern emerged, with a prescribed set of oriental motifs arranged in a pre-determined pattern. Because each of the two hundred potters used this well-established design, a mere glance at the face of a Standard Willow plate is rarely sufficient to determine the piece's maker. Printed or impressed maker's marks are the only sure way to attribute a piece, and unfortunately, many early makers did not leave them for our reference today.

The dinnerware's original owners, unlike modern collectors, were largely untroubled by the lack of marks; they bought plates because of their reliable cheerfulness and tasteful front view, not for the back marks. This led to the application of the desirable pattern on a wide range of wares, in an even wider range of qualities; Willow can be found in porcelain, hybrid-paste, pearlware, earthenware, ironstone, and bone china.

Willow was made in an equally wide range of locations. It has been made by potters not only in England and the United States, but also in Scotland, Ireland, Holland, France, Japan, and—returning to its origins—in China. These pieces have appeared everywhere, from the most elegant dining rooms to the most homespun. On the 'elegant' end (at least by American standards) was the White House dining room under President Martin Van Buren; his purchase of "twenty-four 'willow' plates introduced [a] popular English decorative pattern...into the presidential pantry" between 1837 and 1841.[3] On the more humble end of the spectrum were 18th century English criminals imprisoned in Australia. Their favorite escape fantasy was of a land trip north; they misguidedly believed that this route would land them directly in "the back part of China," where they presumed they would be surrounded by "yellow girls and tea, opium and silk, queer-looking blue bridges and willows just like the ones on the plates."[4] In America, the television show "Gunsmoke" featured Willow dishes, suggesting that a hardy version of the pattern was widely available to American settlers in the 'Wild West' of the late 1800s.[5] Later, American restaurants and hotels relied on affordable, durable sets of the respectable ware for their dining rooms, prompting the phrase "Blue Plate Special."[6]

Willow was featured outside of the dining room as well, appearing in the theater—providing background scenery, a story line, or even a design for theater curtains[7]—and in every aspect of the home. It was no less pervasive in British everyday life, prompting one Englishwoman to write that she felt as if she "had absorbed with [her] National Health orange juice a knowledge and a secret love of this domestic manifestation of English orientalism" (see boxed section).[8]

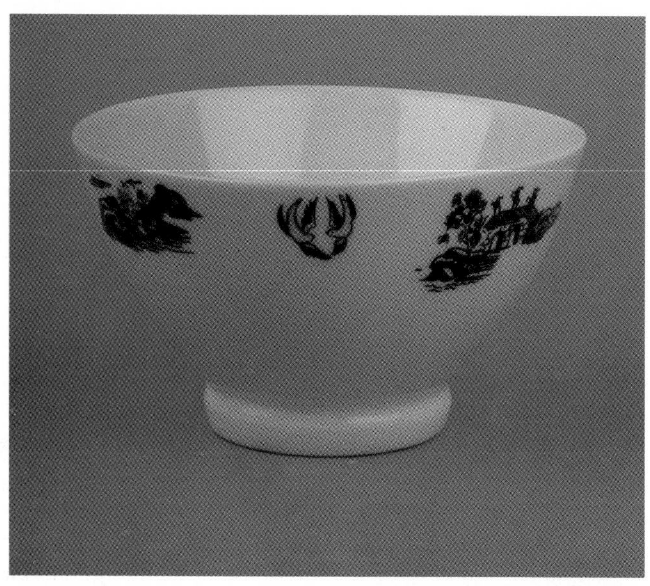

A small modern bowl made in China, decorated with some of the individual willow elements, 4" diam. Courtesy of Rita Entmacher Cohen.

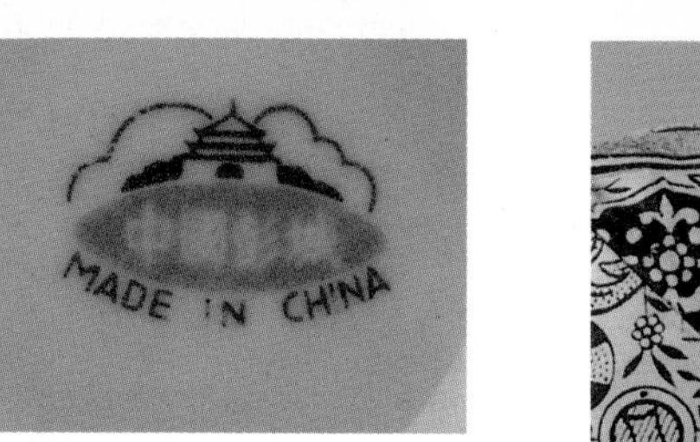

A pound package of tea and a tea tin, from Glasgow. Courtesy of Wendy's Willow.

Like many products faced with the unfortunate challenge of widespread popularity, Willow pattern dishware has often been accused of becoming commonplace, hackneyed, and trite due to over-production and broad distribution. As early as 1845, a *Punch* magazine cartoonist took a stab at Willow while attacking a new school of design in a cartoon entitled "The School of Bad Design," which shows a student copying the Standard Willow pattern from a hanging dish.[9] Moreover, the ease with which cobalt blue could be used in transfer-printing left it open to charges of overuse, and when ink suitable for transfer printing in other colors was developed around 1825, the traditionally blue Willow pattern was dealt a significant blow, at least among its trendier consumers. "Owing to the Blue printing having become so common," reports Geoffrey Godden, "the other [colors are] now obtaining a decided preference in most genteel circles."[10]

A coffee pot from Portugal, 8" high. Courtesy of Charles and Louise Loehr, Louise's Old Things, Kutztown, PA.

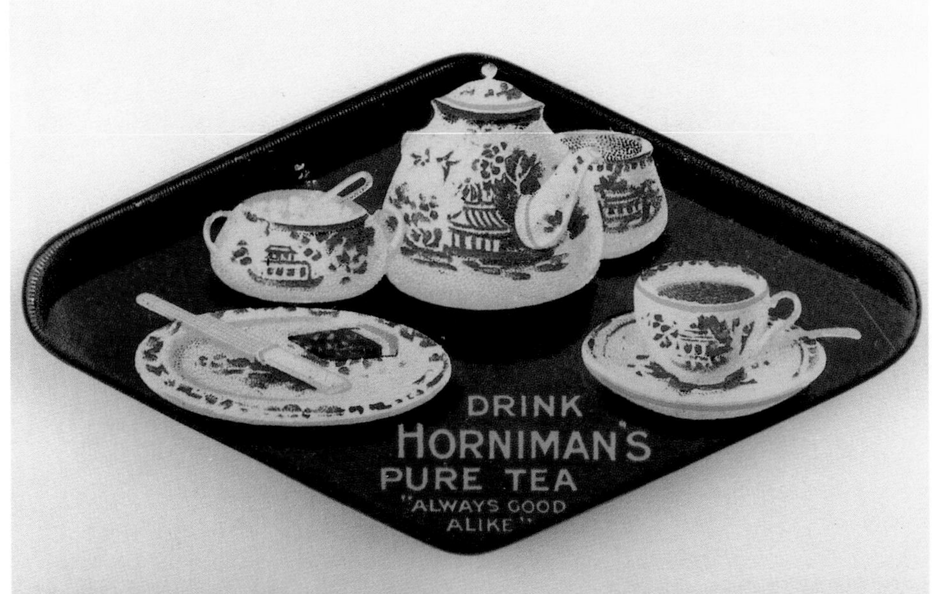

A tin box with a Willow element. Courtesy of Rita Entmacher Cohen.

Despite criticisms of this ilk, Willow has remained a consistently popular pattern with a broad range of consumers. 'Genteel circles' of past eras may have abandoned the pattern for newer and more glamorous dishware, but the pattern has outlived those who scorned it. The popular image of Willow's restrained and delicate elegance has kept it in high regard throughout the decades—if not in the eyes of the fickle dictators of taste and high fashion, then at least in the eyes of those who find its detail intriguing, its history and legend a delight, and its cheerful appearance a pleasant addition to everyday life. Willow's chinoiserie design and the romantic tales attached to it retain their charm even today, and the blue and white remains clear and crisp, refreshing in the face of more sophisticated techniques for coloration and printing. Today, it is not only antique collectors who seek out Willow; American supermarket customers can purchase newly-manufactured pieces offered as inexpensive premiums, while the makers of fine china continue to produce Willow as a matter of course. Judging from the loyalty of consumers over the past two hundred years, the lifelong enthusiasm of modern collectors, and the many creative applications of the pattern on everything from paper cups to sofa upholstery, Willow has stood the test of time.

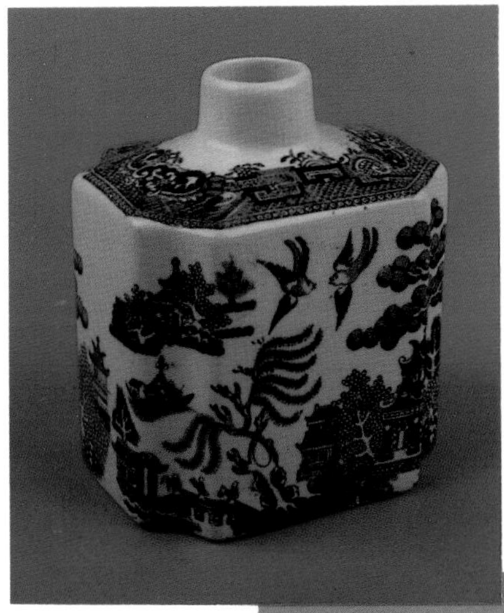

A tea cannister from 1820, 5". Courtesy of Rita Entmacher Cohen.

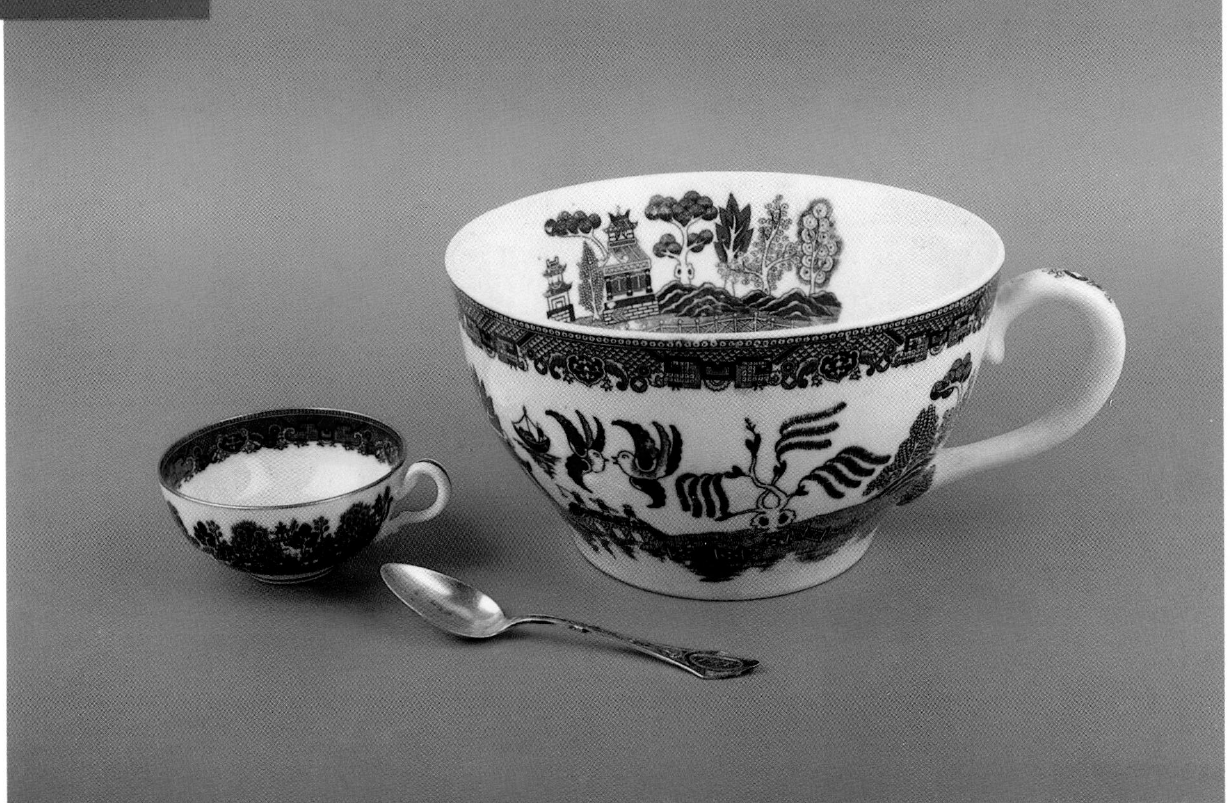

A Japanese waste bowl or large cup, 8.75", shown with a normal cup and spoon for comparison. Unmarked. Courtesy of Rita Entmacher Cohen.

The Smallest Pieces

Ruth Richardson, a writer from the outskirts of London, discovered that a great many unidentifiable blue and white pottery shards were strewn through her backyard garden beds. She could distinguish many different bodies—some pure white, others grey or cream-colored, with varying degrees of porosity—and shades of transfer-printed blue "from pale grays and the softest forget-me-nots, azures, aquamarines, ultramarines, and ceruleans to frank royal blues, cobalts, midnight blues, navy and blackish blues." She could also make out fragments of their original patterns, including landscapes, floral designs, Grecian temples, and Asiatic pheasants. After sorting and cleaning them, she realized that none seemed to match any others—a great mystery until she learned that broken crockery collected from dustyards (junkyards) were smashed into even smaller shards to be used in the foundations of buildings and roads.

Despite the broad range of unmatched shards Richardson found in her garden, she wrote that "the variety of these designs was entirely outdone by the ubiquity of willow-pattern ware. It was easy to identify these pieces. Somehow, even the smallest pieces seemed intimately familiar, as if I had absorbed with my National Health orange juice a knowledge and a secret love of this domestic manifestation of English orientalism. The largest pile of crocks—nearly half my collection—was inscribed with some aspect of the tale, from the tips of the lovebirds' wings or the pagoda, to the catkins dangling in curious curves from diminutive willows. Its characteristic scaly, geometric borders called up vague memories of a half-understood story, involving the familiar figures on boat and bridge...Now, when I take tea in the garden on fine summer days, it seems only right for it to be served upon blue-and-white willow-pattern china. I feel at home in the knowledge that dishes break, and that broken crocks get buried."[11]

Chapter 1

The Roots of Willow:
The Chinese Connection

"And why abroad our money fling,
To please our fickle fair.
No more from China, china bring,
Here's English china ware."
— from a song in the play
Alladin, or the Wonderful Lamp,
Covent Garden, 1788.[1]

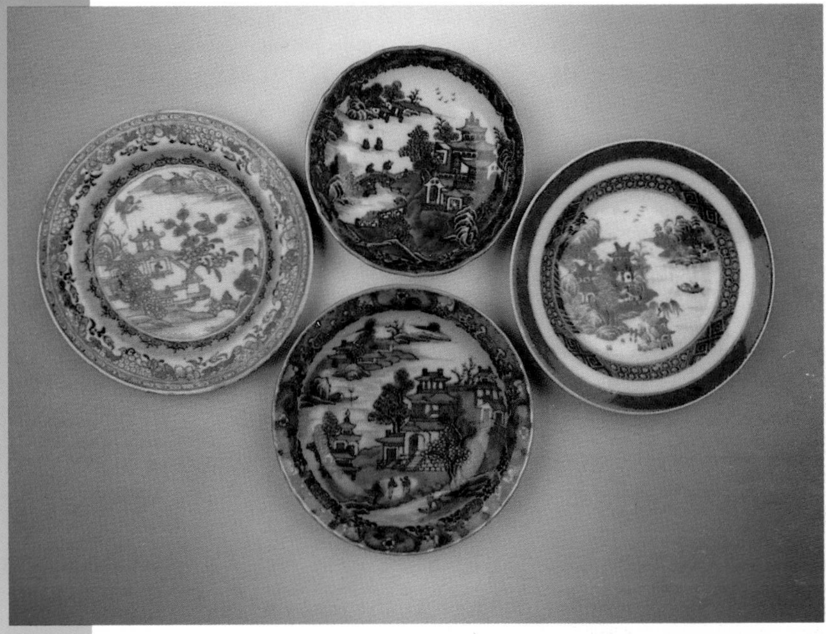

Four small Chinese export porcelain plates, c. 1770-1800, 6.25" to 5" diam. Courtesy of Rita Entmacher Cohen.

Long before England first produced Willow—indeed, long before they first tried to replicate porcelain, used cobalt, or attempted transfer printing—China had established itself as a center of sophisticated pottery, with advanced glazing and porcelain-making techniques as well as a well-grounded aesthetic standard. The West learned to draw inspiration from Eastern ceramic technology and artistic principles, but not before spending a great deal of time and money importing original Chinese porcelain from Canton, the majority of it hand-painted in blue over a pure white body. Since Willow ware was crafted as a competitor and a replacement for Canton ware, a look at the art (and business) of Chinese blue and white porcelain is useful in the discussion of Willow's development.

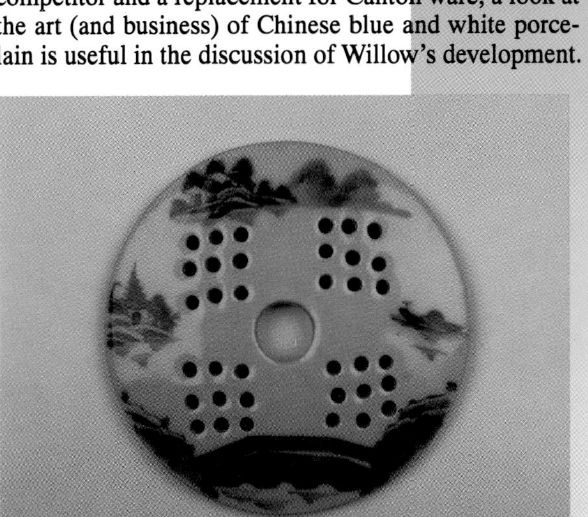

A round strainer in Chinese export porcelain, 4. 75" diam. Courtesy of Rita Entmacher Cohen.

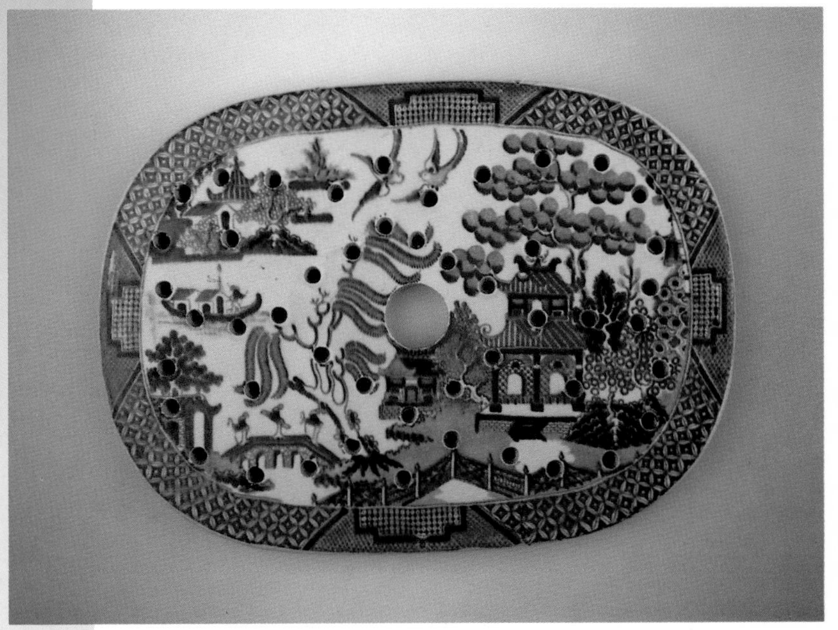

Pearlware drainer, 10" x 7.125".

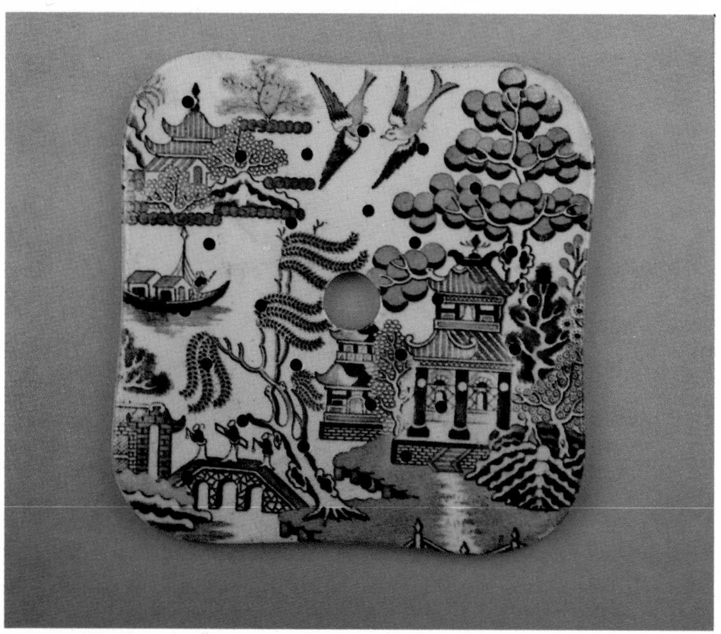

An English drainer in the Standard Willow pattern, 6.125" sq. Courtesy of Rita Entmacher Cohen.

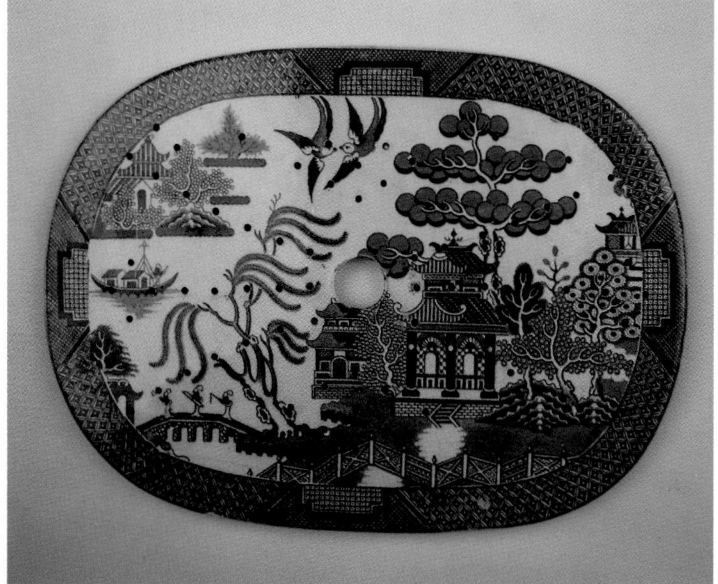

An English drainer, 12" wide. Courtesy of Rita Entmacher Cohen.

An English drainer, 13.625" wide. Courtesy of Rita Entmacher Cohen.

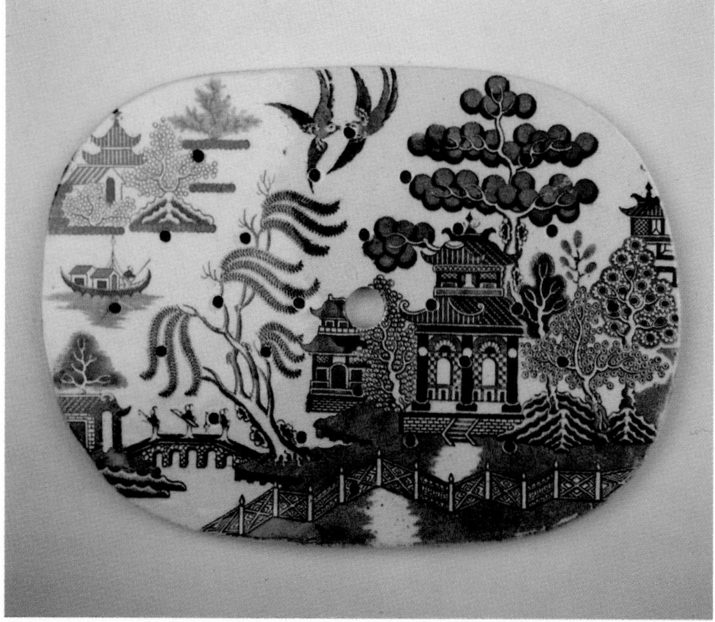

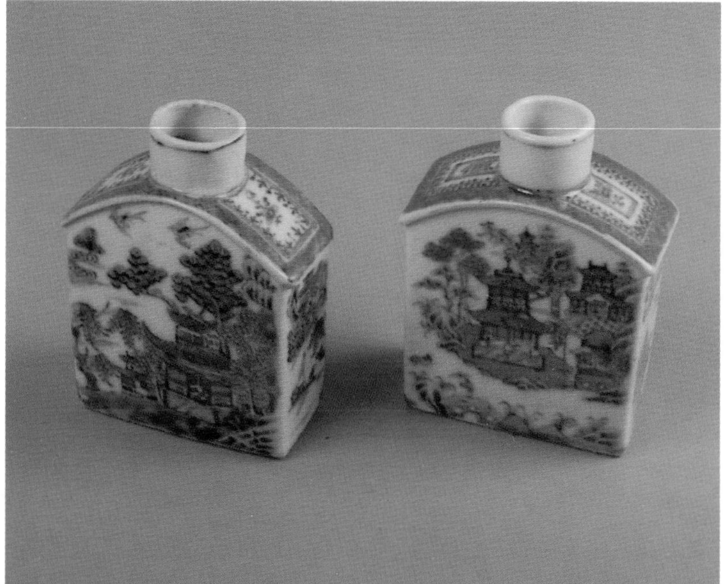

Two tea caddies, probably Nanking. Courtesy of Charles and Louise Loehr, Louise's Old Things, Kutztown PA.

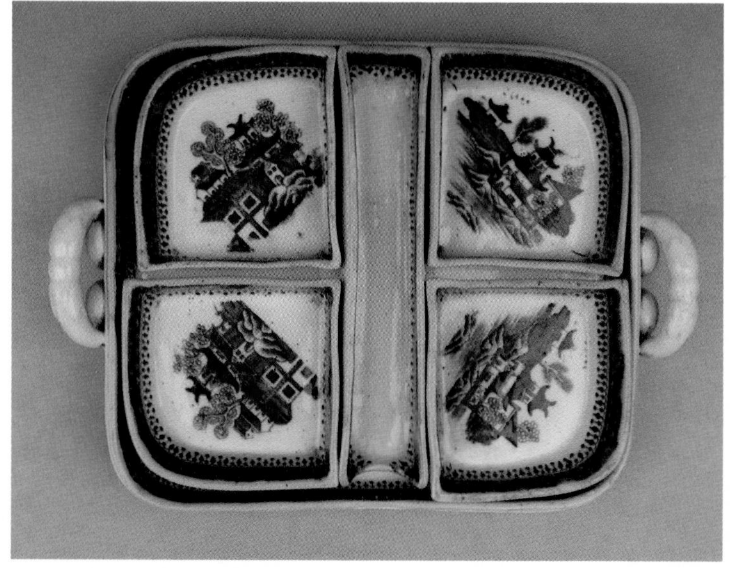

A hybrid hard paste porcelain relish set, with a tray and five dishes, 11.25" wide at the handles. Made by Coalport. Courtesy of Rita Entmacher Cohen.

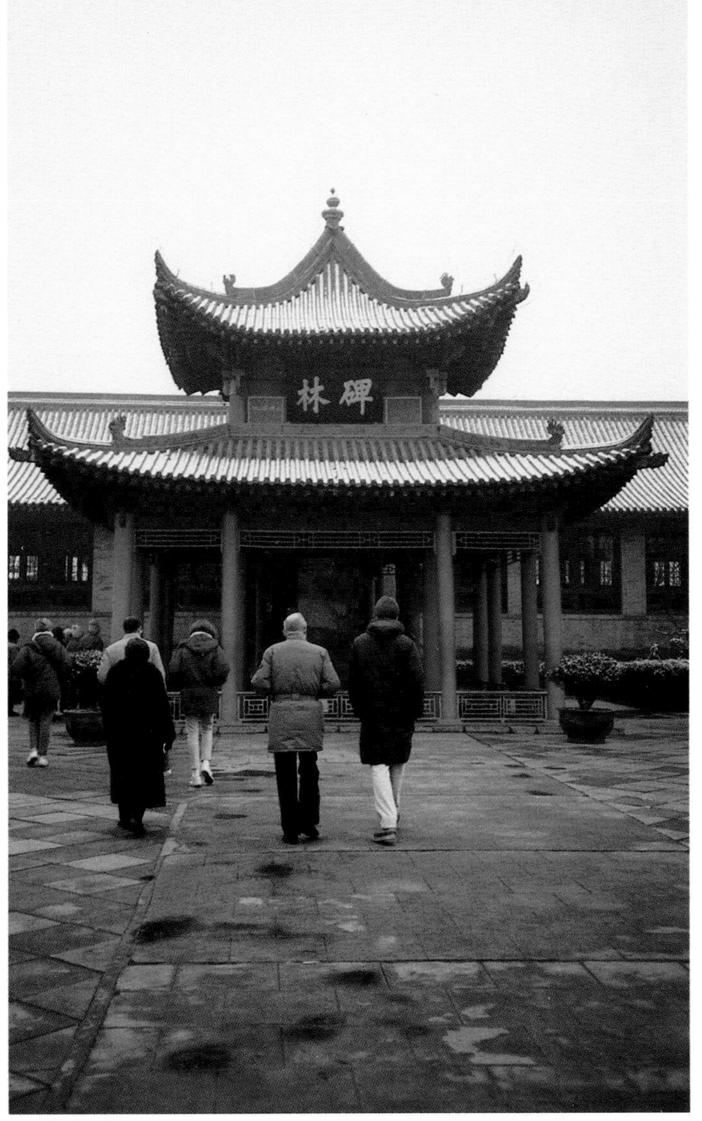

This pagoda is typical of the Chinese architecture echoed in both authentic Chinese landscape design and in English reproductions. Photo courtesy of Gertrude & Daniel Perlov.

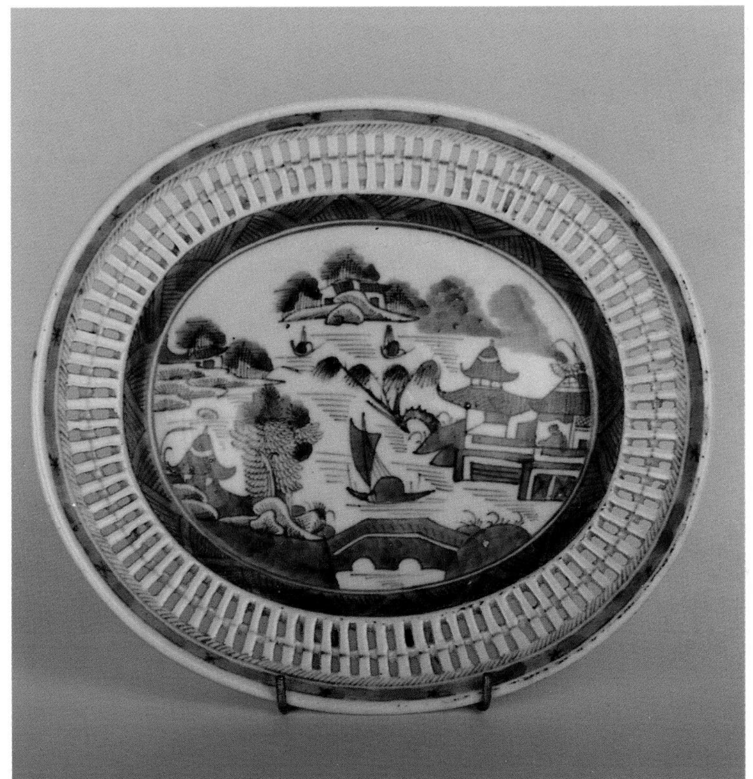

A piece of Chinese 'Canton' ware porcelain, in a typical landscape pattern like those Willow sought to imitate.

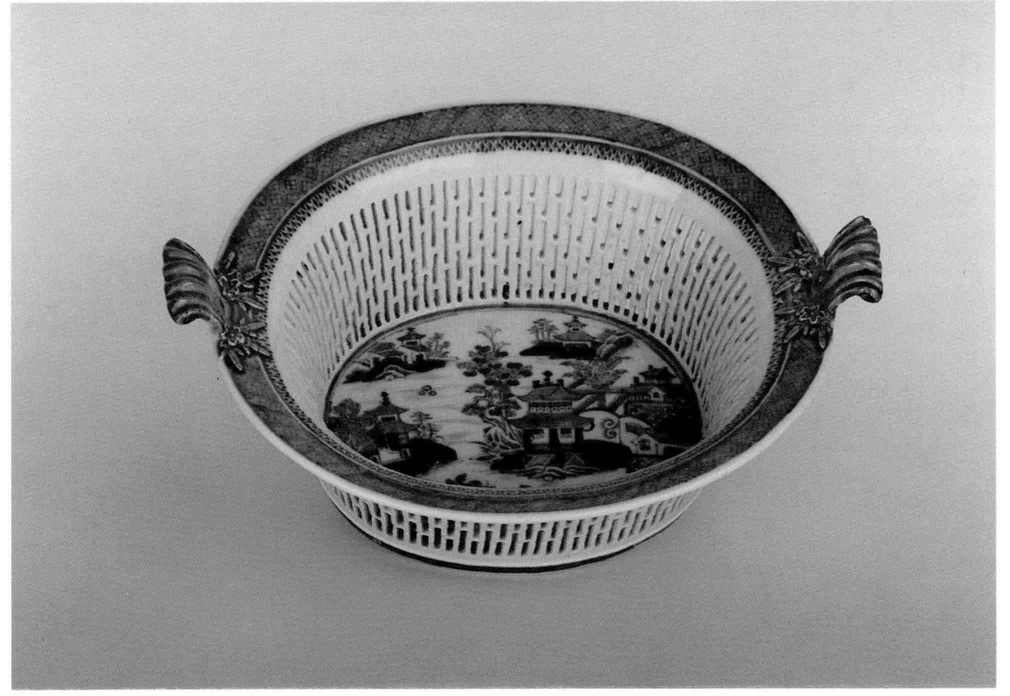

This chestnut basket is an example of Chinese export 'Nankin' ware, in porcelain.

Chinese Pottery: The Rise and Fall of Blue and White

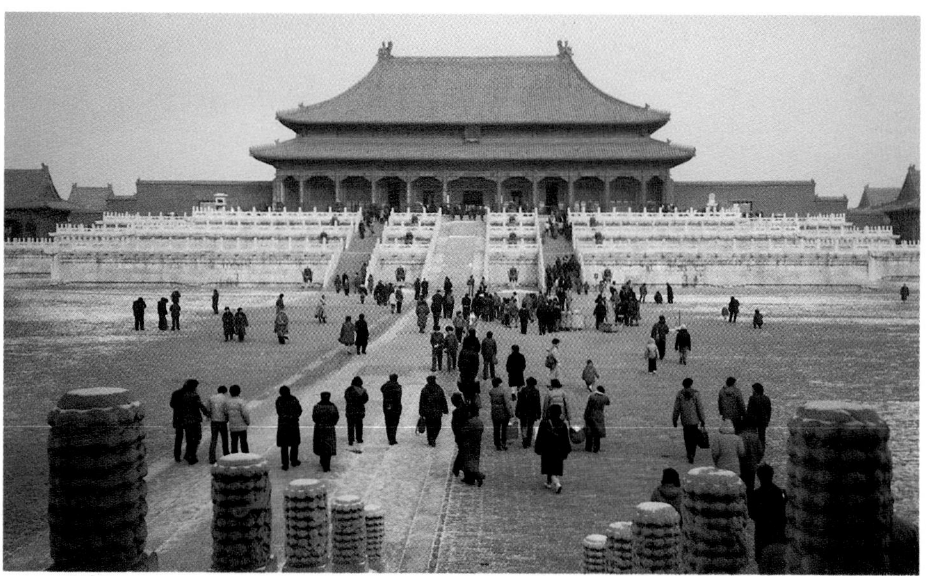

Today, tourists walk with impunity through the ancient heart of the Chinese empire—the Forbidden City. British traders and diplomats, blocked at every turn by the Chinese bureaucracy, were not so fortunate. Photograph courtesy of Jeffrey L. Bockol.

For centuries, traditional native Chinese pottery looked nothing like the smooth blue and white painted dishware that is now considered typical of the East. Early Chinese potters were not concerned with painted decoration, "taking far more interest in the form, graceful proportion, and texture" of their wares,[2] both porcelain and earthenware. Early in the 14th century, however, the country was swept up in a flurry of changes; the Mongols had taken over the south of China, opening the country to more extensive trade with the outside world. A significant number of Muslim merchants from the Near East began to live lavishly in Canton, bringing with them a pigment with properties and a color unlike anything Chinese potters had ever seen—cobalt.[3] (For further discussion of cobalt's history and uses, see Chapter 4)

While cobalt had been used for painting pottery wares to great advantage for centuries in the Near East, the pigment posed quite a threat to the tradition of "subdued tones and subtle textures" in Chinese pottery. Indeed, the new possibilities presented by cobalt were considered by China's cultural elite "to open up the rocky road to ruin, since the danger was that the vessel would become a vehicle for decoration rather than a pot valued for its form and function."[4] Today, the appeal of blue-painted ware seems hard to resist, but "the revolutionary twist towards visual elaboration of the surface without taking account of texture must have done violence to the aesthetic standards and sensibilities of the literati" in China at the time of its introduction.

Fortunately for modern blue and white enthusiasts, the "literati"—an aristocracy steeped in the traditional standards—were not the only consumers in the market for well-made pottery, nor, since the conquest of the Mongols, were the potteries controlled by the aristocracy through the earlier imperial patronage system.[5] The new techniques of cobalt decoration found a receptive audience in a rising class of merchants, and many of the new blue painted decorations were anecdotal scenes from legends and dramas "catering to (and popular with) the populace,"[6] in addition to the familiar landscapes from which Willow was eventually derived. In a sudden and drastic social change, the "ordinary people, the merchants, the shopkeepers and the fellow in the street stimulated the potters to produce what *they* wanted and what *they* would use"—much as the demand of the common man in England centuries later would sustain the production of great quantities of Willow ware long after the blue and white of expensive imported Chinese porcelain had disappeared from the dining rooms of the upper class.[7]

For their part, the Chinese potters have been described as "ready and receptive" to the imported Near Eastern techniques and technologies, "confident of their ability and prepared to try anything," just as their later English counterparts were. And as England would later discover (to its chagrin as much as to its delight), the Chinese potters were "certainly...happy to try to satisfy foreign taste"[8] in using the new cobalt glaze. Over the centuries a well-organized pottery industry developed in China, partly in response to the demands of the international market—first the Arabs and Persians in the 15th century, then the Japanese and Portuguese in the 16th and 17th centuries, and finally the Dutch and the English in the 17th and 18th centuries. In 1983 a sunken ship was discovered in the South China Sea; its cargo included "a mass of blue-and-white and other export wares" possibly dating to as early as 1643.[9]

Blue and white maintained its domestic popularity in China during the Ming dynasty, from 1368-1644, considered by some to be the last age of fine Chinese porcelain.[10] Though blue and white continued to be manufactured throughout the subsequent Qing dynasty, enthusiasm for it began to fade as other decorative techniques were discovered and developed. Still, it maintained an important presence in the domestic Chinese market through the first decade of the 18th century. After that, however, quality began to decline, in keeping with its waning popularity.[11] In the Yongzheng period (1723-1735), blue and white "began to become stereotyped and mechanical in execution," characterized by "a dry efficiency in the execution, which is only redeemed by the extraordinary technical perfection of body material, colour and glaze quality, and the apparently faultless firing"[12]—a criticism some might apply to the slickly-produced modern reproductions of Willow.

This did not mark the end of Chinese blue and white production or profitability. Chinese potters knew a trick that British potters would discover in their own time: when domestic popularity declines, taking quality with it, one last market always remains—export. While the blue and white of the later periods may not have met Chinese standards, its exotic novelty and inherent elegance were certainly good enough to take Europe by storm.

Europe's Fascination with China

In the 18th century, Europe went crazy over Chinese porcelain—as well as Chinese fabrics, Chinese fashions, Chinese fragrances, Chinese architecture, and Chinese furniture. This was Europe's era of chinoiserie, marked by an intense fascination with all aspects of that country's culture ("even to the pigtail," according to 1862 journalist George Godwin). This "cult of China" was started by the French missionaries who had been stationed in China, where they found that the natives were not the savages they had expected. The missionaries developed and relayed to Europe a healthy respect for China's ancient culture—from the industrious population, rich philosophy, and sophisticated bureaucracy to the monotheistic inclination that convinced Catholic and Jesuit missionaries that China would not be hard to bring into the fold of Christianity.[13]

Europe's regard for China's philosophical and political history fell off during the mid-18th century, as the French Enlightenment's new ideals of equality, religious freedom, and free speech made China's ritualized hierarchy and aristocracy seem outdated and oppressive. However, the fascination with China continued to grow in Europe's popular culture and decorative arts, providing some relief from neoclassical architecture's strict geometry and from Baroque's heavy ornamentation. Popular manifestations of chinoiserie, writes Chinese historian Jonathan Spence, "could be found everywhere in Europe, from the 'Chinese' designs on the new wallpapers and furnishings that graced middle-class homes to the pagodas in public parks, the sedan chairs in which people were carried on the streets, and the latticework that surrounded ornamental gardens."[14]

Pottery and porcelain figured largely in Europe's fascination with Chinese decorative arts. Companies like the British East India Company became deeply involved in the business of importing dinner services, tea services, and individual pieces of pottery. Much of this was newly-crafted Canton ware, primarily in the blue and white that had gone out of fashion in China. Many books on the subject were published, some "serious works written by travelers who had made the long and arduous journey to the East," while others "were written and illustrated by men who had neither left Europe, nor studied the works of those who had first hand experience."[15] Judging from the proliferation of books alone, Chinese ceramic wares had developed an enthusiastic audience of European collectors, laying the foundation for later collectors of (and books about) blue and white Willow ware.

English Trade with China: Kowtows and 'Foreign Devils'

China was not as thrilled with this interaction as the Europeans were. In the early 1700s, English merchants and traders were surprised by the reception they received from Qing dynasty Chinese officials, as they sought to negotiate trade agreements in the tea, silk, and porcelain industries. While Chinese merchants were happy to do business, the Chinese court was an active impediment, slandering the traders as "foreign devils."[16] The English businessmen stated their purposes in restrained terms—"We have no view but commerce, to be protected by the Chinese Government, subject to its Laws and Regulations, and formed upon a permanent Principle mutually beneficial," wrote one[17]—but the "Laws and Regulations" of the Chinese government required that prospective merchants from foreign countries submit themselves to an elaborate procedure of supplication and entreaty before they might be granted the right to trade and export Chinese goods.

This "complex and exasperating procedure" involved the use of subservient language, ritual prostrations ('kowtow'), and formal acknowledgment of China's cultural prestige, and was "far from the kind of diplomatic and commercial equality among nations that Western powers were beginning to take for granted." Based on the Chinese government's assumption that their kingdom was central and all others were peripheral, this belittling system of petitioning was bound to try the patience of Britain and other European nations, especially as each expanded its own overseas empire and became the center of another periphery. In 1760, after a number of unhappy incidents, the Chinese government restricted all European trade to the months of October through March in a single port, Canton—thus explaining the name "Canton ware."[18]

The British East India Co. in China

After wending his way through a heirarchy of underlings and sailing north to reach the capital, British East India Co. emissary James Flint finally reached the emperor, to whom he hoped to present a petition to enlarge the scope of British trading in China. The emperor was a sympathetic listener, and agreed to allow research to be undertaken on the matter. Flint, pleased, began his return trip south to report the good news. Unfortunately for Flint, the emperor quickly changed his mind; Flint was apprehended and arrested, and imprisoned for three years. His offenses? Flint had broken regulations by sailing north, by petitioning improperly, and by learning to speak the Chinese language.[19]

From China to England: "Utterly Routine"

Unconcerned with the difficulties of Far East trade relations, European consumers were thrilled with the translucence and lightness of Chinese porcelain (as were European potters, whose struggles to duplicate it are discussed in Chapter 4). Marco Polo (1254?-1324?) was the first European to report seeing the stuff, but even in the time of the Renaissance (c. 1400-1600) porcelain was still so rare in Europe that it was considered a suitable gift for princes to exchange.[20] While legend has it that in the 1600s the Medicis discovered (and then lost) the secret for making true hard-paste porcelain just like the Chinese version, later potters in England, Germany and France struggled for years to come up with an acceptable replacement. European consumers (if not the potters) resigned themselves, not unhappily, to the continued use of Chinese imports.

Porcelain was sent by ship from China, around the Cape of Good Hope to Europe in a round trip that could take as long as twenty-two months. The holds of these sailing ships were packed tightly; porcelain filled the bottom, while more water-sensitive (and expensive) commodities like tea and silk were packed above it. A great deal of porcelain was lost to breakage en route, and porcelain garnered no great profits even for an operation as large as the British East India Company.[21]

Still, the quantities imported increased dramatically between the early days in the 1600s and the pre-Willow days of the 1700s. East India Company records indicate that in 1637 their ship *Catherine* carried 53 tubs of china; in 1724 the *Macciesfield* carried 150 chests; and in 1734 the *Howard Grafton* carried 240 chests, with a total of 240,000 individual pieces of porcelain.[22]

The European traders in China during the 1600s had been forced to buy whatever already-manufactured and readily available wares they thought they could sell to European consumers, despite some unusual forms that were not well-suited to European dining habits. As the Western market became more important to Chinese manufacturers, however, and as European traders began to understand their customers' preferences in Chinese porcelain, the system changed. Importers started to commission wares geared for European tables and tastes, in Western forms and with painted copies of Western designs. The Chinese manufacturers were happy (and shrewd) to cooperate.[23] Chinese misinterpretations of Western patterns and scenes can be quite amusing—just as early British sketches for chinoiserie patterns sent to Cantonese decorating workshops must have been amusing to the Chinese artisans who painted copies of them.

After European traders started this system of consigning wares in European styles, the volume of trade accelerated, and in 1722 Britain received about 400,000 individual pieces of porcelain.[24] By the middle of the 18th century, most of England's wealthy class used Chinese porcelain dinner sets. The wares' designs became more uniform (one popular pattern was the 'Nankin', which may be the most direct inspiration for Willow). Those imported by the East India Company were, for the most part, blue and white painted wares produced in bulk. "This steady stream," writes one historian, "became a torrent later in the century, and in 1755 a single consignment brought to England on board the East India Company's *Prince George* included 26,000 blue and white cups and saucers, nearly that number of single plates, 402 complete dinner services, and 200 tea sets."[25]

The porcelain wares that British merchants consigned to have decorated with Western prints were most likely manufactured far from the site of the decorating workshops, at inland pottery centers like Ching-tê-Chên. These plain wares were sent to Canton to be decorated under the supervision of the British consigners, not just because Canton had been an artistic center for centuries,[26] but because in 1760 the Chinese government had forbidden foreign traders to conduct business anywhere but within the borders of that city.

As a result, Canton grew crowded with well-established decorating workshops by 1769. This industrial growth altered the way that artisans approached their decorating tasks, inevitably prompting the development of mass-production techniques.[27] One British merchant who toured the facilities reported that "we were shown the different processes used in finishing the chinaware. In one long gallery we found upwards of a hundred persons at work in sketching or finishing the various ornaments upon each particular piece of ware."[28] It goes without saying that the quality of these wares was no longer the same as it had been in the past, when finer wares of porcelain were exchanged as tributary gifts amongst the royalty of Europe.

Hand in hand with this artistic decline, however, came an overall improvement in technical skill. Western potters, especially those pursuing the elusive recipe for porcelain, could only envy "the utterly routine ability of the Chinese potters" to produce vast quantities of cheap and attractive porcelain after 1700, with a "thinness that had no commercially viable equivalent in Europe."[29]

The Decline

British potters were making great strides, however, and by the mid-1700s their 'soft-paste' porcelain (see Chapter 4 for further discussion) had captured a creditable part of the home market. In the 1770s and 1780s the import of Chinese wares to England suffered a noticeable decline; in the 1790s the East India Company stopped importing Chinese porcelain altogether,[30] and in 1810, only a few thousand pieces were brought into each European country by various other companies.[31] A 1934 thesis on the Staffordshire potteries asserts that "the potteries of North Staffordshire became so expert in imitating the original China tea and table ware that they were able to oust it from the home market,"[32] but the eradication of China from the market was not solely the result of technological growth among the English potteries. An intricate combination of economics, trade relations, and the winds of fashion also played a major part.

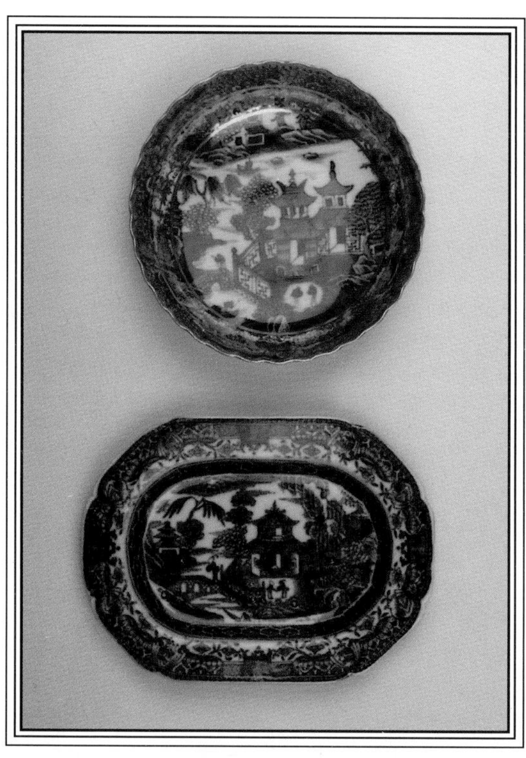

English chinoiserie sometimes drew directly from Chinese export merchandise. Compare the patterns in these two pieces: a round, painted Chinese export dish with gold trim, and a small, rectangular transfer-ware platter from England. Courtesy of Rita Entmacher Cohen.

Economically, consumer demand for the Chinese commodities of porcelain, tea, and silk was a national disaster in 18th century England. While boatload after boatload of Chinese merchandise was bought with English silver bullion, there was not much reciprocal demand in China for Western export items like fur, cotton and woolen goods, tin, lead, clocks, and "other mechanical curiosities"—resulting in a trade deficit that greatly alarmed the British government. Three million taels of silver were traded into the Qing purse during the 1760s; 7.5 million in the 1770s; and 16 million in the 1780s.[33]

England was not reassured by the edict with which the emperor Qianlong responded to George III's petition for more equitable trade relations: "We have never valued ingenious articles, nor do we have the slightest need of your country's manufactures. Therefore, O king, as regards to your request to send someone to remain at the capital, while it is not in harmony with the regulations of the Celestial Empire, we also feel very much that it is of no advantage to your country."

Despite shows of confidence (or bravura) like this, China ended up on the losing side of the trade war. While the Chinese people could well do without England's domestic products, they developed quite an affinity for England's illicit new cash crop, opium. In 1790, Britain sold over four thousand chests of opium (130 to 160 lbs. each) in China; by 1832, they sold almost 24,000 chests, draining nine million taels of silver from the Qing coffers, and six years later the count was up to over 40,000 chests.[34] Chinese-English trade relations grew less and less friendly as the Chinese government tried to curb the importation of opium, a political and economic conflict contributing significantly to the dwindling of Chinese imports in the British Isles.

Among other economic blows to English merchants who imported Chinese goods, the United States started to trade directly with China, ousting the English traders from their profitable positions as middlemen. The Napoleonic Wars, too, were quite damaging, since they resulted in increased taxation of Chinese imports from 47.5% in 1787 to 109% in 1799.[35]

Inroads being made by British ceramicists into the art of porcelain during the mid-18th century (see Chapter 4 for a further discussion) posed another challenge to Chinese imported porcelain. English potters modeled their wares after Far Eastern porcelain (not the Continental wares, made as early as 1715 by Sevrés and Meissen but prohibited from being imported into England), and were the beneficiaries of the long popularity of Chinese blue and white imports, which had "firmly established the market and set the fashion—especially for porcelain decorated in underglaze blue."[35a] By 1745 if not earlier, the Chelsea pottery was producing soft-paste (artificial) porcelain, and by 1747 the Bow factory was marketing its "New Canton" line of soft-paste porcelain, much of it blue and white. In 1768 Plymouth produced the first known English hard-paste porcelain, and by 1789 the first bone china (an intermediate between hard- and soft-paste porcelain, with a much stronger body than either) was made, further undermining the market for Chinese imports. As one scholar of Oriental ceramics writes,

> So it was that home ceramic products were displacing those of China commercially. A growing, mass-consumer market awaited products of the Industrial Revolution like ceramics, and skilful promotion and advertising made them desirable. At this date, it is not certain that the home products were less expensive to purchase than those of China...Not only that, but home producers did not always deliberately aim to be cheapest in price. On the contrary, Josiah Wedgwood believed in high prices, and got them by offering goods of quality, and by making them desirable. "A great price is at first necessary," he wrote, "to make the vessels esteemed 'Ornaments for Palaces'."[36]

Early domestic blue and white porcelain was expensive; even without the exorbinant taxes, so were the imports. As the wealthy classes became distracted by competing dishware styles and color schemes, the remaining customers from the middle and professional classes required that blue and white find another, less costly, medium. It did, of course—ironically, using the technology developed to make one of the 'distracting competitors', creamware. The creamware body, only briefly fashionable, became the basis for pearlware, which would prove the perfect body for Willow and the other blue underglaze transfer patterns which were fast approaching. A look at the changes in blue and white's popularity should provide some insights into this evolution.

Changes in English Style

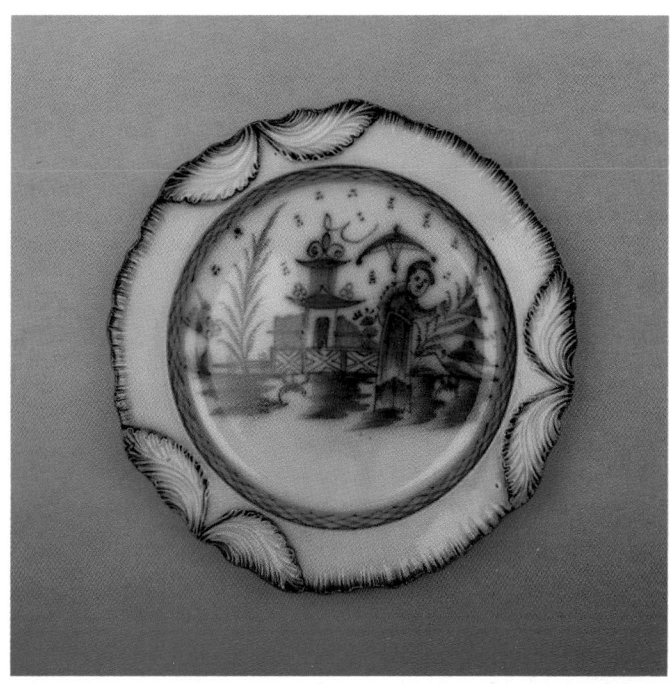

A pearlware plate with the "Swag and Shell" edge border, 9.5" diam. The plate is decorated in the "Long Eliza" pattern in underglaze blue. Early pearlware was often decorated with painted blue and white Chinese designs. Courtesy of Rita Entmacher Cohen.

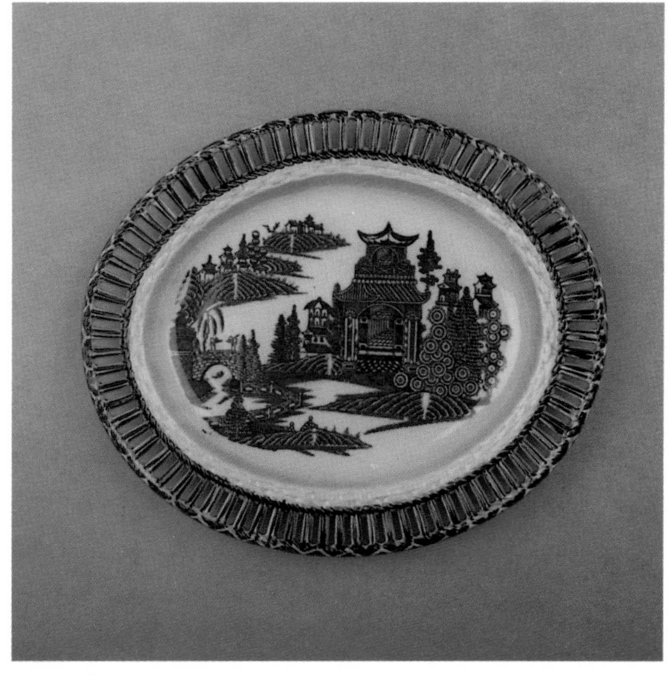

A basket stand, c. 1790, 8.5" wide. The decoration is line-engraved, with a reticulated edge. Courtesy of Rita Entmacher Cohen.

British fashion and culture had a major hand in Chinese blue and white porcelain's decline and the eventual development of a number of English varieties. The chinoiserie designs of early and mid-18th century imports had become rather standardized, and as previously discussed, the quality of many of the designs had become mechanical. In a statement to which Willow collectors might be inclined to take exception, one ceramics historian wrote that "the repetitious character of the designs, too, must have contributed something to the declining favor in which blue-and-white was held."[37] England's fashionable elite began to grow bored with blue and white for exactly the same reasons that the original Chinese customers had, and wealthy English consumers were no longer so ardent to own expensive Chinese imports.

The middle and lower classes still equated blue and white porcelain with elegance and wealth, however, so rather than closing, the market simply changed its target audience.[38] As Robert Copeland so aptly observes, "what the nobility found acceptible yesterday, the next lower level of society favours today."[39] The professional and merchant class adopted blue and white enthusiastically, and though their budgets were not quite so liberal, at least the market for the wares continued with substantial vigor. Of course, this adoption of Chinese blue and white by 'commoners' did nothing to sustain or revive its popularity with the fashionable elite.

For this 'elite', neoclassicism ousted chinoiserie as the style of choice in the late 1700s. Chinese porcelain decorators in Canton attempted to keep up with the trend, and while they still produced pieces "decorated with the well-worn forerunner of the willow-pattern design...other porcelains...were being designed and decorated to appeal to the new classical taste."[40] By 1804, however, England's attention had shifted to its own potteries; in that year, England's comptroller of the embassy in China wrote that Chinese porcelain lacked "elegance and form," and was inferior to "those inimitable models from Greek and Roman vases brought into modern use by the ingenious Mr. Wedgwood."[41]

It is possible that the comptroller was referring to Wedgwood's creamware, an earthenware body that was lighter and less expensive than English porcelain,[42] in a creamy color that, though not suited for clear blue and white chinoiserie, was ideal for neoclassicism. In the opinion of many blue and white aficianados, cobalt blue applied to creamware results in a muted, flat or muddy look; it certainly lacks the crispness that makes blue and white so appealing. Thus, the blue-printing that had begun to be used on imports and on domestic soft-paste porcelain found a less-than-satisfactory match with this off-white body.

Creamware did not ruin the blue and white market, however; indeed, as Robert Copeland explains, creamware "was destined not to have a very lengthy uninterrupted regieme."[43] Its most significant effects on the blue and white market were actually beneficial. First, creamware's initial fashionability with the upper classes in the 1760s ousted more Chinese export from the dining rooms of the wealthy and from the shop shelves of the merchants who catered to them.[44] More importantly, with a few adjustments, the creamware body and glaze were transformed into pearlware, which was ideal in color for the transfer-printing of new (and old) blue and white designs. First marketed as 'Pearl White' by Josiah Wedgwood c. 1775,[45] pearlware had the sturdiness and affordability of earthenware, perfect for the new consumers of blue and white, who wanted the elegant pure-white look of imported and domestic porcelain without the prohibitive price.

Concurrent with the development of pearlware in England was that of transfer printing. Overglaze transfer printing was used as early as 1753, and in 1756 Sadler & Green of Liverpool applied for a patent for the process.[46] The underglaze technique was first noticed on Worcester porcelain wares in 1757,[47] and was not perfected until 1781.[48] (For an explanation of the technique, see Chapter 4.) Transfer printing changed the nature of chinoiserie images in England. Unlike the hand-painted Canton wares, transfer-printed patterns could be intricately detailed and reproduced exactly in great quantities,[49] finally allowing customers to purchase large matching sets.

English potters had been carefully attentive to the designs of their Chinese competitors for years; with the advent of transfer printing and the discovery of suitable pottery bodies they were more than ready to reap the benefits. The English potters had many Chinese designs to draw upon; English customers had often asked domestic potters to make copies of imported Chinese wares as replacements for broken pieces, giving the potters opportunities to examine them in detail and record the patterns. Thomas Turner manufactured his own versions of four or five designs he had copied from import porcelain into his rag book. Josiah Spode I made over twenty-two faithful reproductions of original import patterns, and many other less faithful ones. Among these latter was the first official Willow pattern.[50]

For the first twenty years of its transfer-printing activity (1780-1800), Staffordshire was "largely experimental," and most patterns were derived Chinese ceramic designs.[51] Some of the maker's marks were similarly derived; many English potters copied Chinese seals and characters for their marks, even disguising simple Arabic numerals with slashes and dots to make them look Chinese, hoping to capitalize on the lingering glamor of imported porcelain.[52] Far from 'out of style', blue and white chinoiserie was about to hit its stride for the second time—and much to the English potter's satisfaction, this time *they* would control the market.

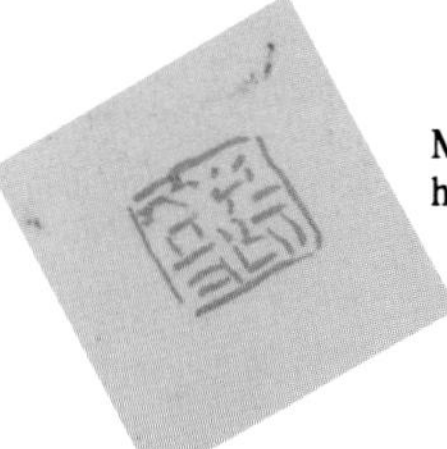

Many English potters used Chinese-type marks on the backs of their domestic ware, hoping to dupe the least wary of their customers.

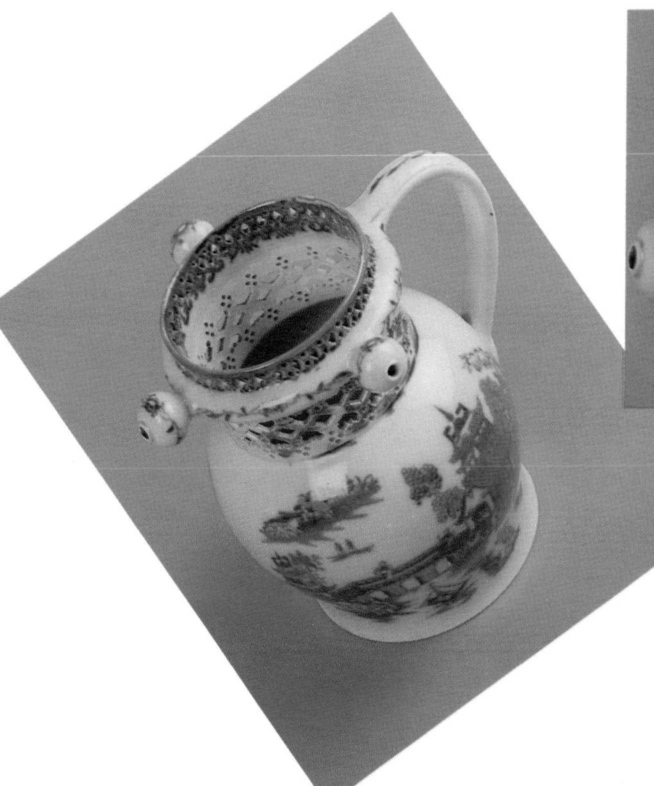

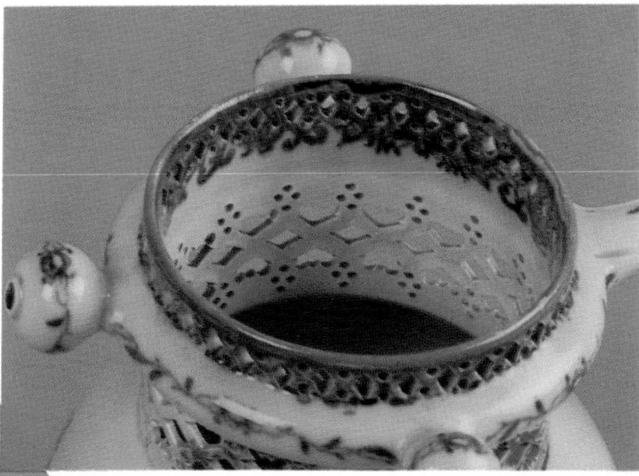

An unmarked puzzle jug, 6.75" high. Note the beautiful detailing in the reticulated areas. Courtesy of Peter and Susan Steelman, Mystic, CT.

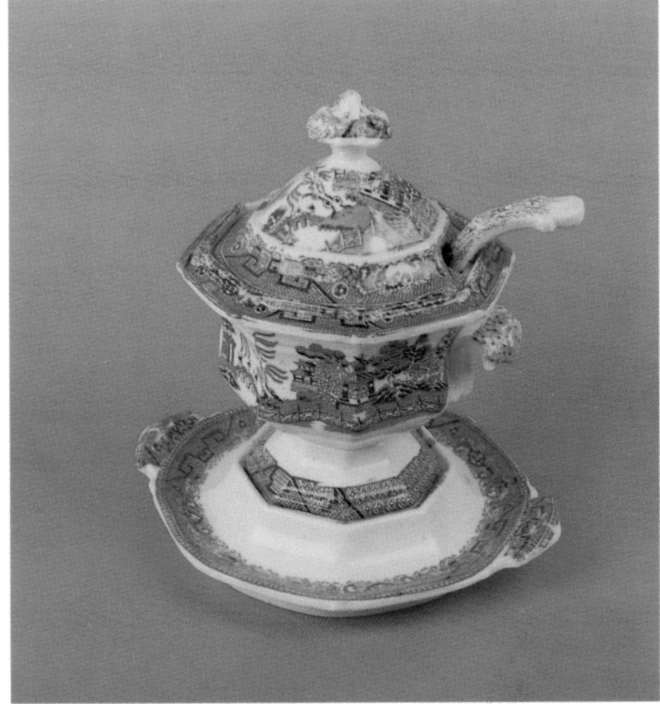

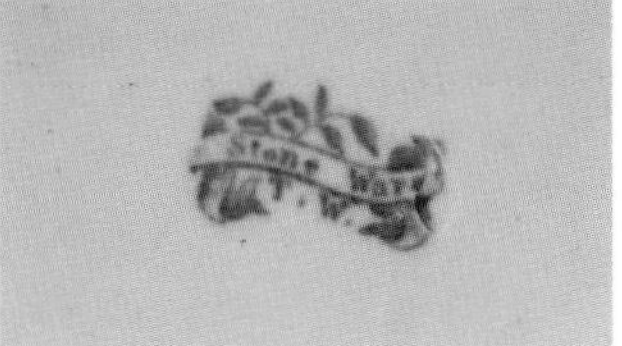

A sauce tureen marked "Stoneware TW", 8.5" high. From the collection of Peter and Susan Steelman, Mystic, CT.

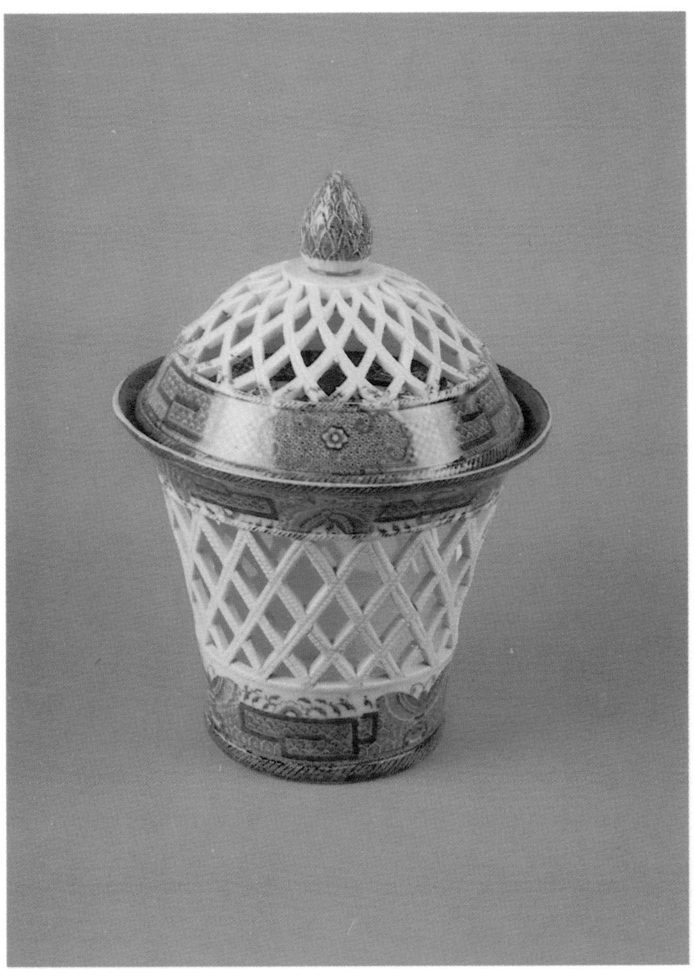

A pearlware potpourri keeper, 8.5" high x 6.5" diam. From the collection of Peter and Susan Steelman, Mystic, CT.

Chapter 2
The First Willow

The shift of English chinoiserie from imported Chinese porcelain to domestic blue and white was a gradual process, prompted by the developments of creamware in 1775 and underglaze transfer printing in 1781. Because the Willow pattern is a composite of a number of stock Chinese motifs, there are many opinions about which elements a piece must have to qualify as Willow. Just a Chinese-style landscape? Just a willow tree? The entire standard Willow design? The question has been answered differently by many dealers, collectors, and other authorities. As a result, no two collections look exactly alike—each collector's holdings reflect the range, focus, and flexibility of his or her interests and intrigues. There are those who gladly include the Chinese prototypes in their collections, and those who seek out only British or American Willow, only early or only late pieces, or sometimes only a particular pattern by a single maker; to each, his own Willow. For some collectors, establishing the credentials of the "first" Willow may not be critical, but the debate can not help but be an entertaining investigation into the early history of Willow, and it may serve to broaden (or to narrow) your definitions.

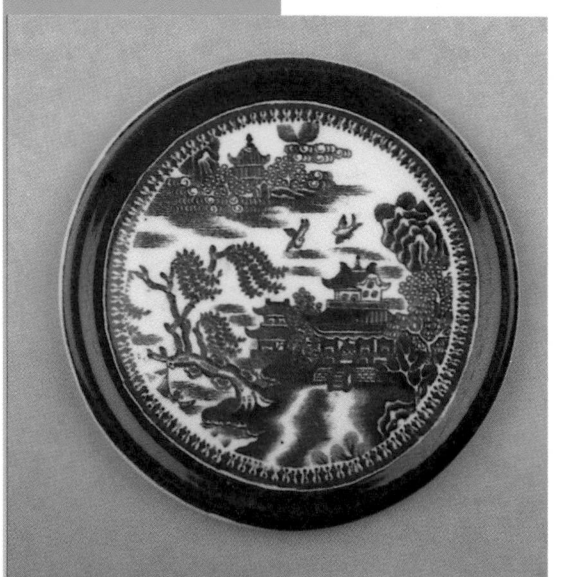

A round trivet, 5.75" diam. This Copeland Spode design, featuring a dark blue border with a Nankin band surrounding a willow center, is called the "Mandarin" pattern. Courtesy of Rita Entmacher Cohen.

The long-waged debate over the origins of English Willow focuses around a Caughley chinoiserie landscape pattern from 1780, and the Spode series of three patterns entitled Willow I from c. 1790, Willow II from c. 1800, and Willow III (or Standard Willow) from c. 1810.

Caughley and Willow

The first underglaze transfer-print on earthenware, made by Thomas Turner at Caughley in 1780, was a chinoiserie design called Willow Nankin, considered by some to be the first Willow.[1] Copper plates (marked "T.T.") from this pattern are now in the British Museum, showing a pagoda on the right side surrounded by six traditional trees including a willow tree and a tree bearing thirty-two apples.[2] Also prominent are a zig-zag fence, and a typical bridge. It should be noted that this pattern does not feature the three familiar pedestrians crossing the bridge, nor the two doves aloft above them, which were later established as necessary elements in the Standard Willow pattern. Also notable is the fact that the Caughley Rag Book of patterns and other Caughley records make no mention of a pattern officially titled "Willow."[3] Willow-Nankin was the first and most faithful version of the authentic Chinese pattern Mandarin, which had been established as one of England's most popular hand-painted Chinese import patterns.

It is commonly accepted that Thomas Minton, apprenticed as an engraver at Caughley during this time period, is responsible for the copper plates found in the British Museum and subsequent similar ones (though sometimes many engravers worked together to complete the different-sized pieces of one set). After his time at Caughley, Minton established himself as a freelance engraver. He made other chinoiserie landscapes for many other potters, generally maintaining the same central-willow arrangement with a few variations.[4] Among other Minton Willow-type patterns are Temple (a.k.a. Brosely Nankin or Pagoda), Striped Temple, Pagoda, Fence, Fenced Garden, Full Nankin, Conversation, Uninhibited Pagoda, Cottage, and Bandstand.[5] While these patterns do not conform to the Standard Willow arrangement, it should be remembered that the standard had not yet been established at the time that most of them were engraved and manufactured. Rather than being "variants" on an already-accepted norm, these pieces were its predecessors, and are considered by many collectors to be crucial components of a well-rounded collection.

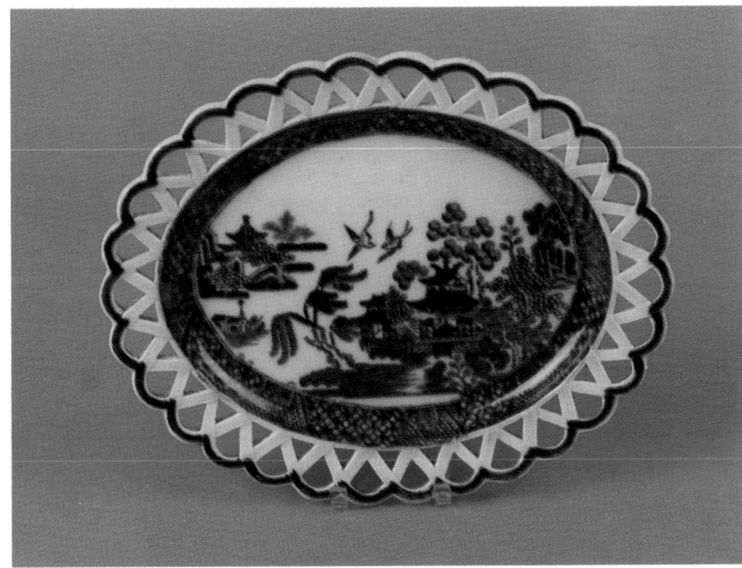

Spode's reticulated pearlware platter in the "Mandarin" pattern, 9" x 7.25". From the collection of Peter and Susan Steelman, Mystic, CT.

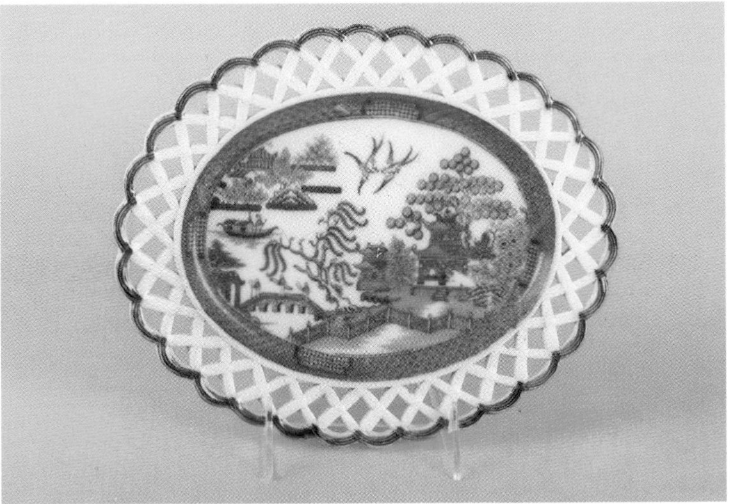

An oval pearlware platter in Spode's Willow I pattern, 10.75" wide. Courtesy of Rita Entmacher Cohen.

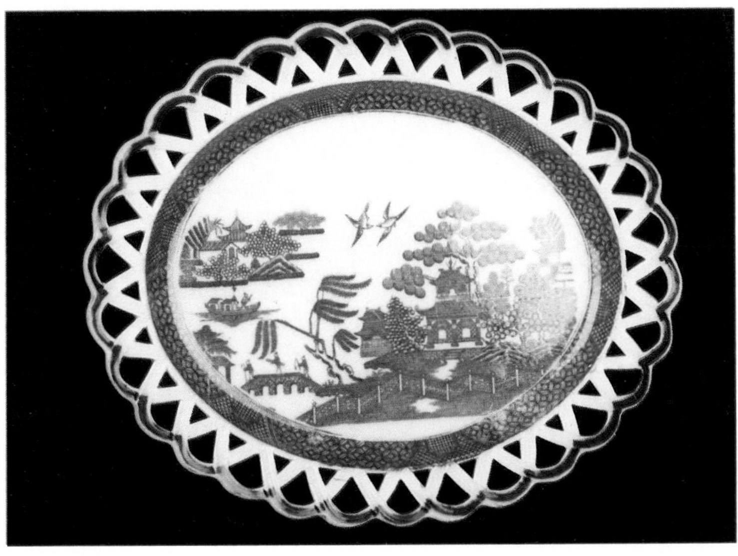

Spode and Willow

Spode, which would later set the standard with Willow I, Willow II, and Willow III, first jumped into the fray in 1784, with their line-engraved Two Figures I pattern. This pattern, like all of the others, capitalized on the well-grounded popularity of blue and white chinoiserie, and drew from both Chinese porcelain originals and from previous English imitations. Willow I's precursor within the Spode repertoire was the printed pattern they had engraved and called Mandarin, a reasonably faithful interpretation of the original hand-painted Chinese pattern of the same name. Spode's Mandarin lacked the bridge and fence of Willow I, and differed in a few other aspects,[6] but used the Nankin border later adopted for Willow.[7] It remained in production until 1950.[8]

Spode's most significant contribution to the world of Willow, however, was not to happen until 1790,[9] when they introduced an earthenware pattern now known as "Willow I," the first use of all the same Chinese elements in the same general arrangement as today's Standard Willow pattern: the central willow, the bridge, a three-pillar'd teahouse, an orange tree, a bridge with three figures hurrying to the left, an island, a boat carrying a man, a zig-zag fence in the foreground, and two birds soaring above. This design was line-engraved except for stippling on the oranges, and was printed in a bright, clear dark blue.[10]

The pattern now known as Willow II was their second effort, made during the same period with the same design. Its color is a softer, paler blue (considered more desirable), and though completely line-engraved it has much finer detailing.[11]

Spode's final version has become known as Willow III, or Standard Willow, and was produced from copper plates that may have been made after 1810 (20 years after Willow I). The line-engraving varied in depth to create subtle shade differences, and the quality of the engraving was further enhanced by a significant amount of stipple-work (the engraver's version of pointilism). The cobalt dyes used on Willow III sets range from a clear, bright blue to a non-flowing, sharp blue. It is this version which has been copied and imitated by countless other potters, in England, America, Europe and (coming full circle) in Asia.

An early English reticulated platter, unmarked, 10" x 8". Courtesy of Eva Lee Revels, Country Accents, Bandera, TX.

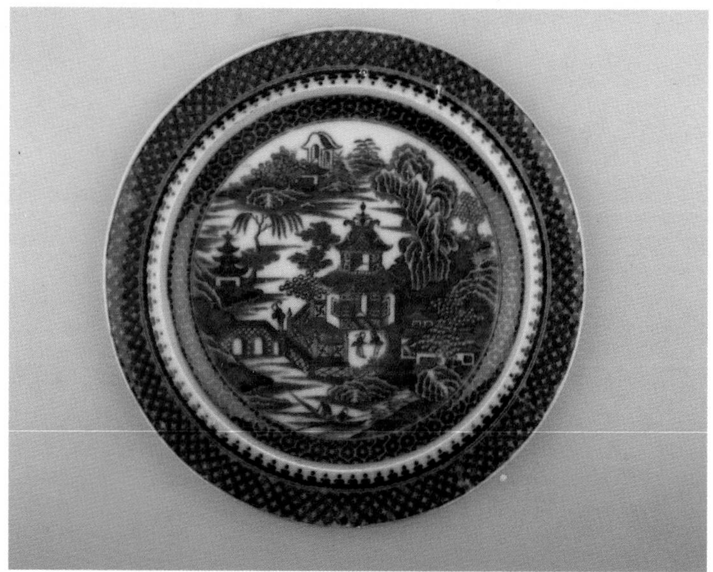

Pearlware plate in the "Conversation" pattern, 10". Unmarked. Courtesy of Rita Entmacher Cohen.

The Debate: "Willow in Any Pattern"?

The strictest definition of Willow, articulated (appropriately) by Robert Copeland of Spode, asserts that "the only design which should be called the Willow pattern [is] the bridge with three persons crossing it, the willow tree, the boat, the main tea house, the two birds, and a fence across the foreground of the garden"—Standard Willow.[12] As far as similar pattterns are concerned, one scholar wrote,

> Some of the English designs, erroneously called Willow, have but two men on the bridge, or one man, or they have no boat or birds, being in reality mere arrangements of oriental motifs—trees, pagodas, fences bridges, etc.—to suit the fancy of individual potters."[13]

A teacup in the "Conversation" pattern, 2" high, marked "S" on the bottom—possibly Salopian. Courtesy of Charles and Louise Loehr, Louise's Old Things, Kutztown PA.

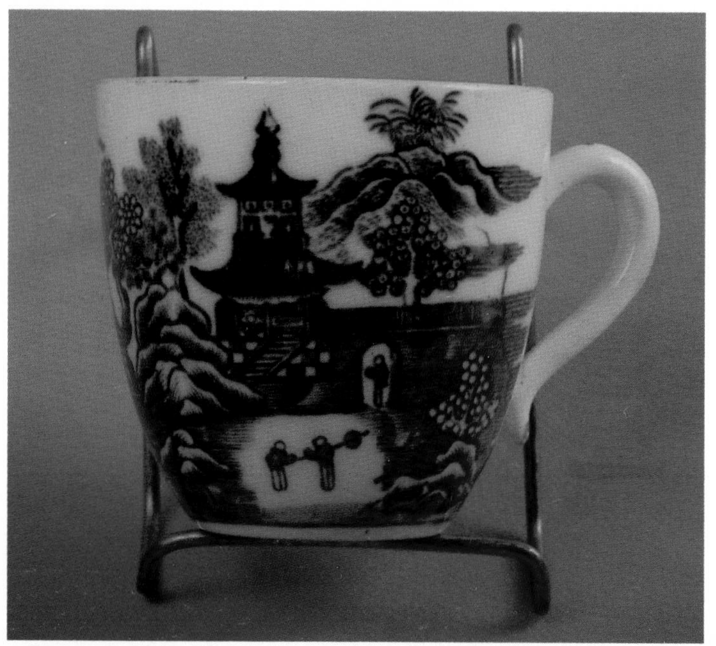

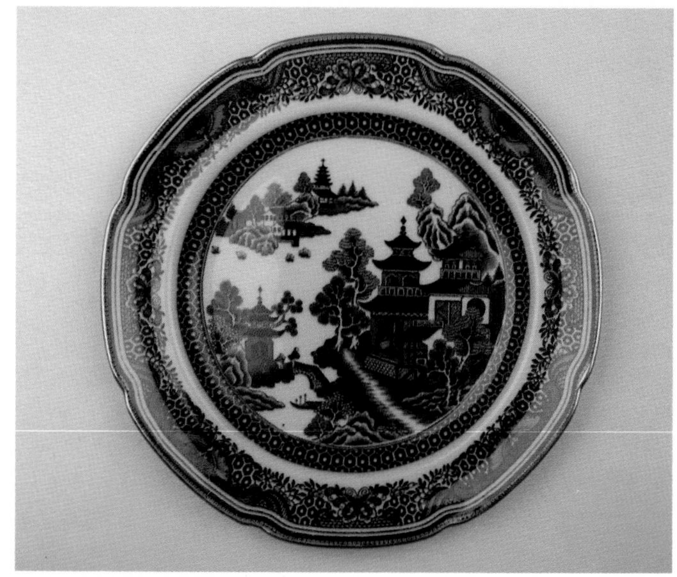

A Spode plate in the "Queen Charlotte" pattern, with a gold rim, 9.75" diam. The back shows the impressed year mark "08". Courtesy of Rita Entmacher Cohen.

This critique belies the fact that Standard Willow itself was "in reality [a] mere arrangement...of oriental motifs;" as Coysh and Henrywood wrote, it was "not a direct copy of a Chinese design but a composite picture drawn from Chinese sources," which happened to gain "immense popularity, probably because various legends grew up around it."[14] (Even had the Willow pattern been drawn directly from a Chinese export pattern, it should be noted that the landscapes hand-painted for export in Cantonese factories were fairly arbitrary 'arrangements' themselves, made for a largely undiscerning export market.) In another work, Coysh wrote that "the term 'Willow pattern' is commonly applied to a whole range of wares with chinoiserie patterns," which he concedes is often done "quite wrongly." Still, he is much less stringent in his categorization than Copeland, as is clear from his working definition of Willow:

An unmarked "Stag" pattern pearlware dish, 6.5" diam. Courtesy of Rita Entmacher Cohen.

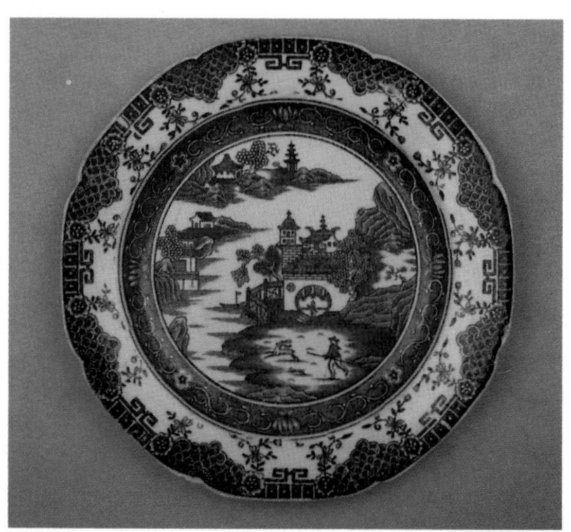

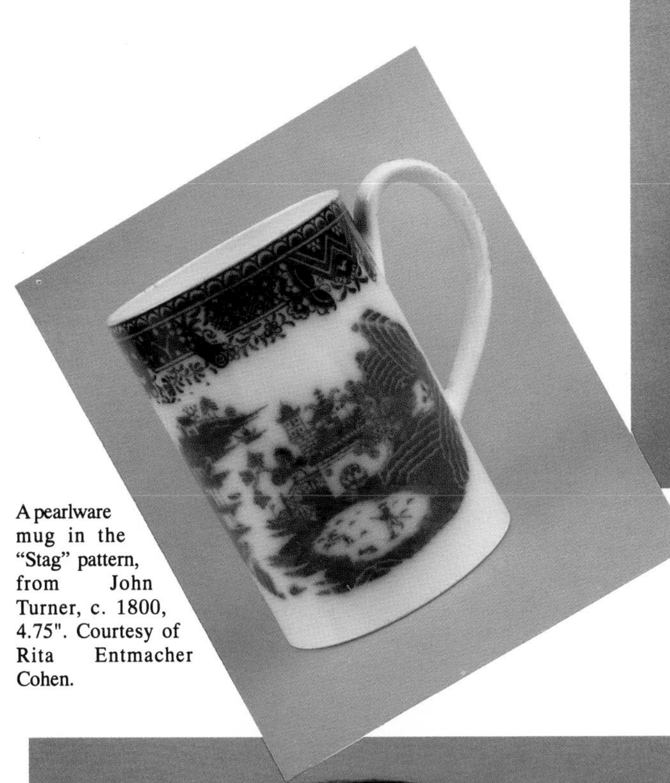

A pearlware mug in the "Stag" pattern, from John Turner, c. 1800, 4.75". Courtesy of Rita Entmacher Cohen.

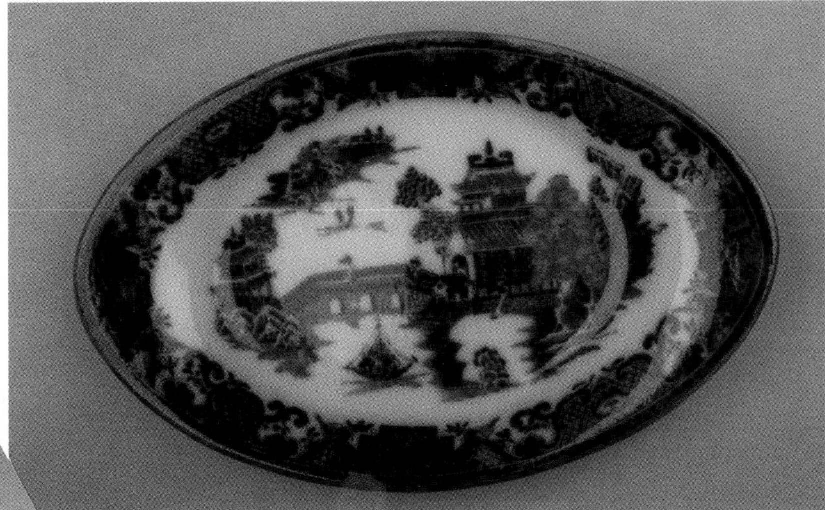

An oval "Long Bridge" dish with a brown edge, c. 1800, 8.5" wide. Courtesy of Rita Entmacher Cohen.

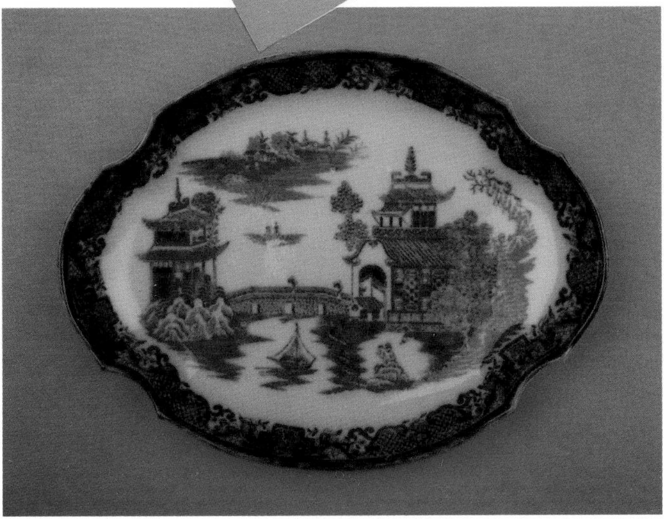

Swansea's oval-shaped pearlware platter with the "Long Bridge" pattern, c. 1800, 10.875" wide. Courtesy of Rita Entmacher Cohen.

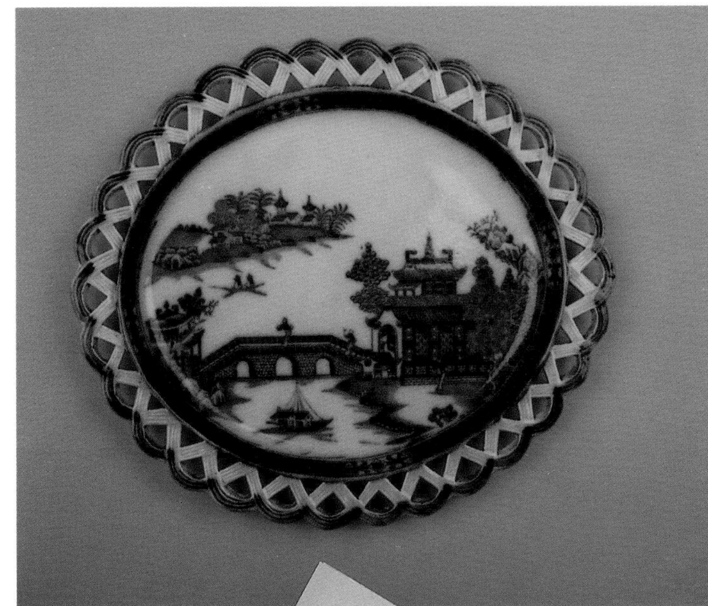

An unmarked, pierced-rim pearlware platter in the "Long Bridge" pattern, c. 1790, 10" wide. Courtesy of Rita Entmacher Cohen.

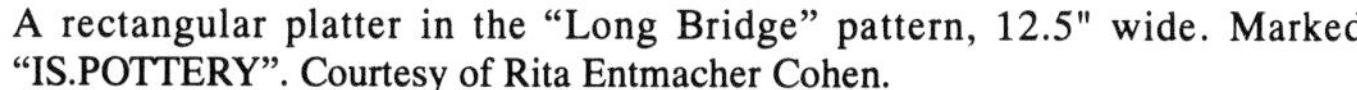

A rectangular platter in the "Long Bridge" pattern, 12.5" wide. Marked "IS.POTTERY". Courtesy of Rita Entmacher Cohen.

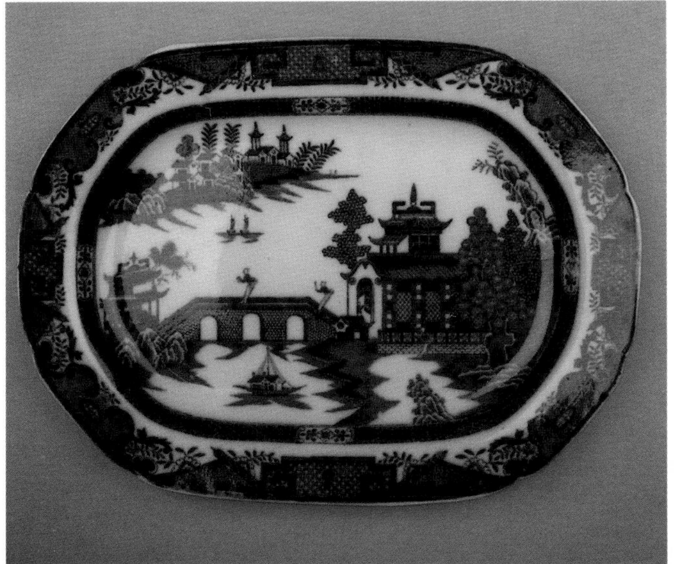

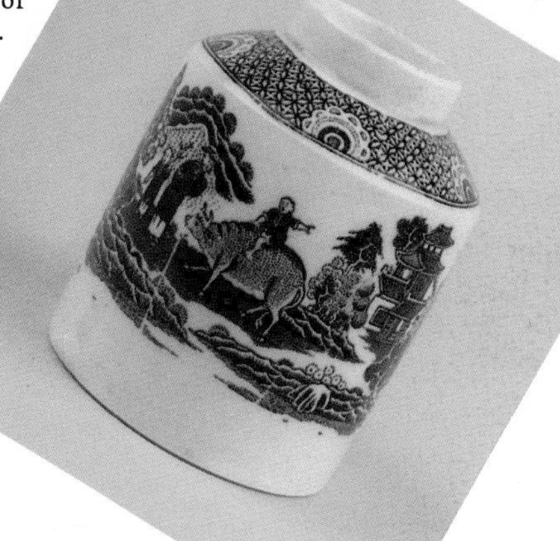

A pearlware tea caddy (lid missing) with the "Boy on a Buffalo" pattern transfer-printed in black, 3.75" high. Courtesy of Rita Entmacher Cohen.

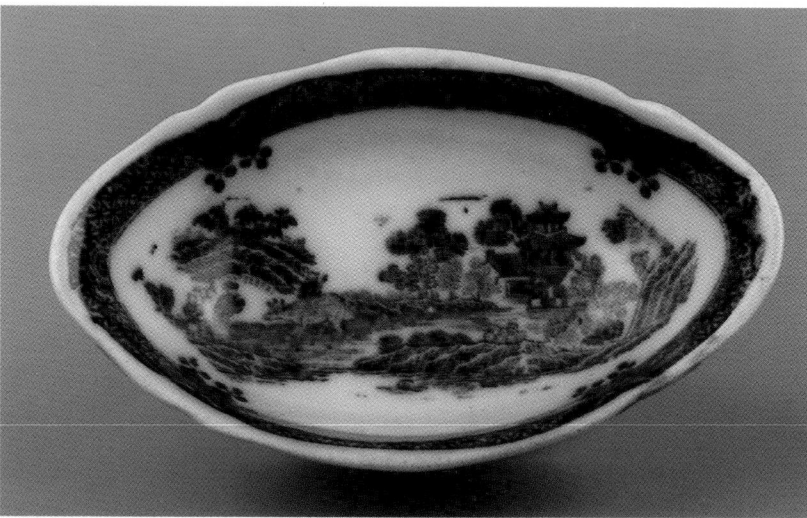

An oval footed bowl in the "Boy on a Buffalo" pattern, 1.5" x 5.125". Courtesy of Rita Entmacher Cohen.

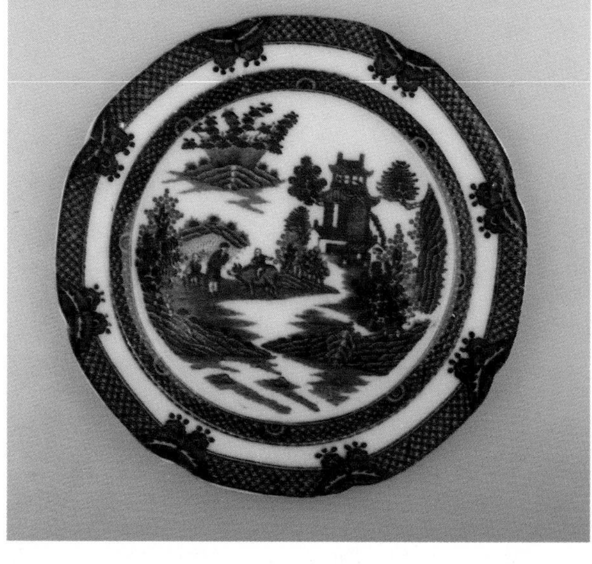

Pearlware plate in the "Boy on a Buffalo" pattern, 9.5". Unmarked. Courtesy of Rita Entmacher Cohen.

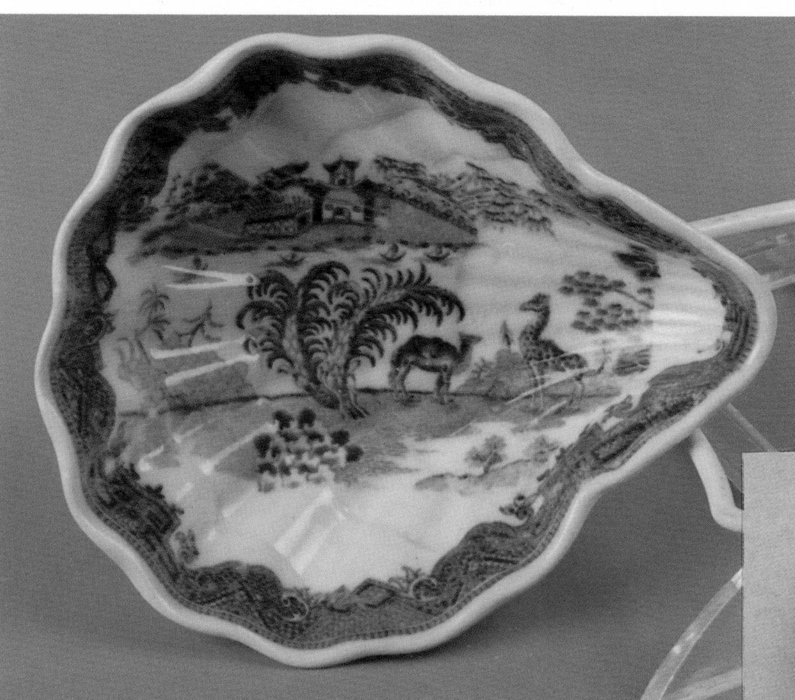

A three-footed scalloped candy dish in pearlware, 1.5" high x 5" x 4.25". This pattern is the variant giraffe and camel scene. From the collection of Peter and Susan Steelman, Mystic, CT.

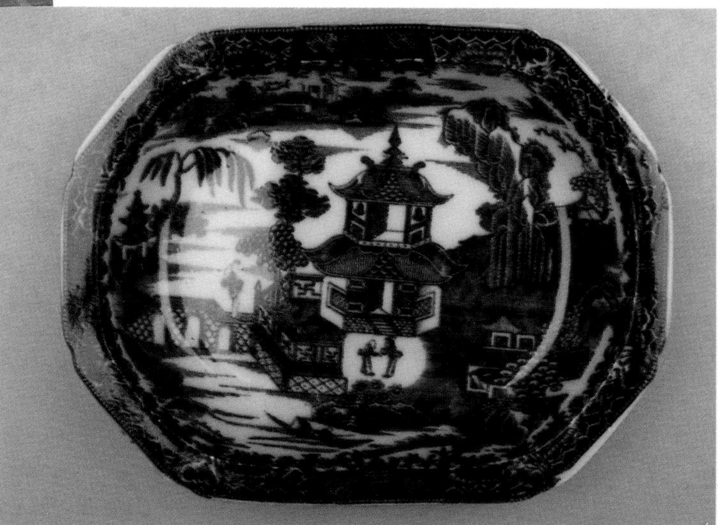

Swansea's oval-shaped pearlware platter with the "Long Bridge" pattern, c. 1800, 10.875" wide. Courtesy of Rita Entmacher Cohen.

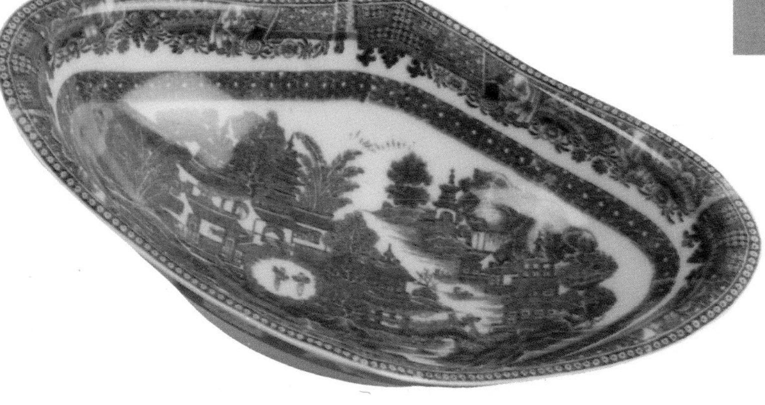

A large banana boat serving dish in the "Conversation" pattern, c. 1775, 3.5" high x 12" long. An "S" appears on the bottom , possibly indicating Salopian or Caughley. The pattern circles the outside of the bowl as well. Courtesy of Charles and Louise Loehr, Louise's Old Things, Kutztown PA.

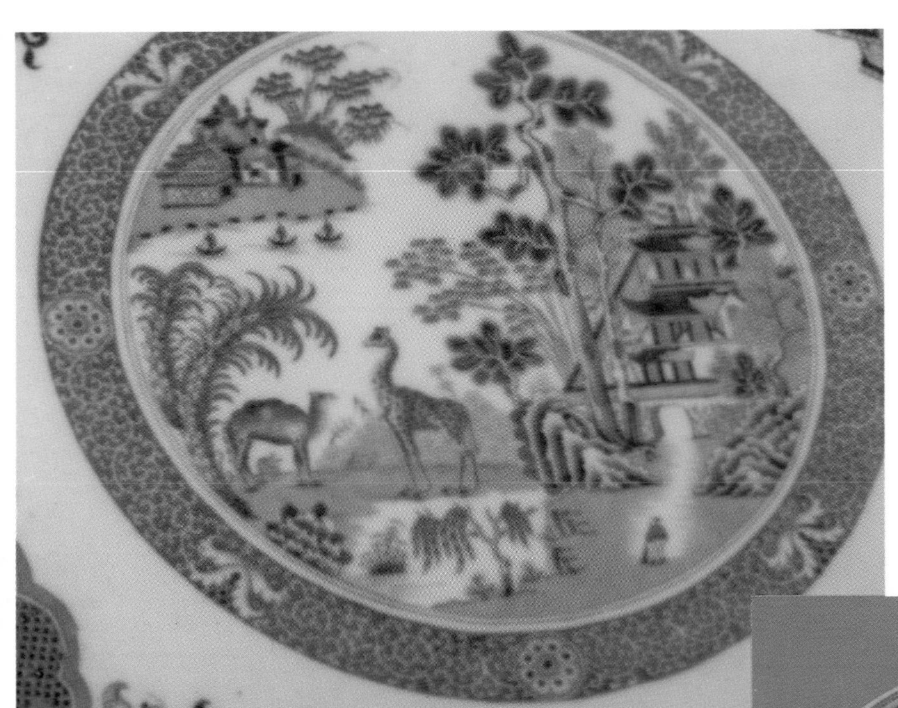

A pearlware cheese platter with the giraffe and camel variant scene, 2.5" high x 11" diam. From the collection of Peter and Susan Steelman, Mystic, CT.

> There are hundreds of patterns which have a willow tree but in many of them it is not a prominent feature...No chinoiserie design is described in this book *Willow Ware* as a willow pattern unless it has a prominent willow tree.[15]

Despite the Standard Willow elements missing in many early willow-type chinoisere designs, most Willow collectors are happy to grant these pieces a place on their display shelves, as Coysh was in his book. Collectors frequently call these pieces 'variants', but using that label for the earliest examples is problematic. Since many of them were in production long before the Spode standard pattern was designed, they had nothing from which to vary. If a collector does not accept these early pieces outright within the definition of Willow, he or she may more accurately call them predecessors than anything else.

Do not be distressed by the ambiguity; the term "Willow" has been used loosely since the 18th century, and confusion has always surrounded it. Copeland reports that a pottery merchant's bill from 1799 lists tea ware printed in "brown edge Willow"[16]—indicating that the term was used to refer to the pattern (even with color variations!) even before the Standard Willow pattern established itself as the predominant strain. A typical order from as late as 1824, more than ten years after Willow III was introduced, requested "blue willow in any pattern"—clear evidence that the earliest purchasers accepted many individual designs as falling into the Willow category.[17] "Country people," wrote Wedgwood's chief traveller in 1817, "do not understand anything about Pagodas or Chinese Temples."[18] Modern students of Willow, however, do understand, and do note the distinctions; the question each must ask is "Which ones matter?" Each collector must define for him or herself what parameters their collection will embrace, and how strictly to the "Standard" their definition of Willow will adhere.

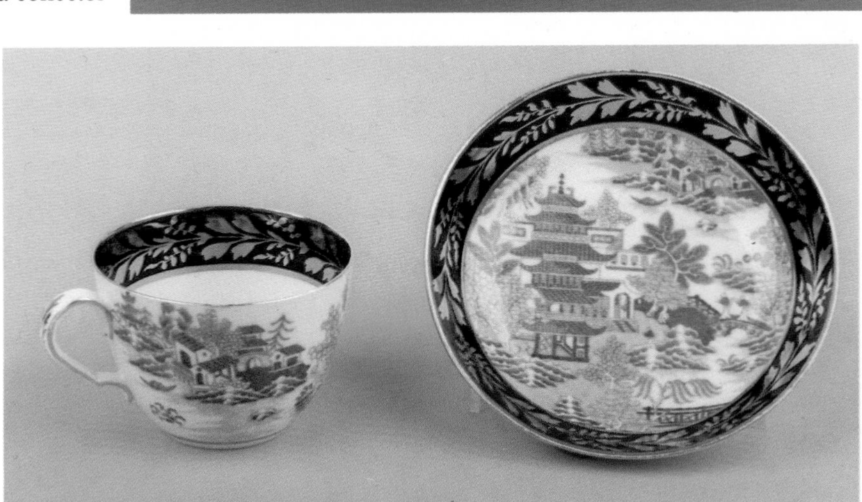

A Spode cup and saucer, c. 1810. Marked with the pattern number 1482. Courtesy of Rita Entmacher Cohen.

Spode

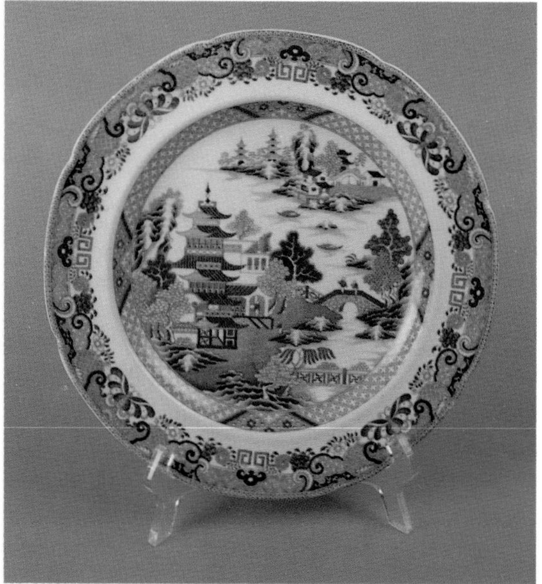

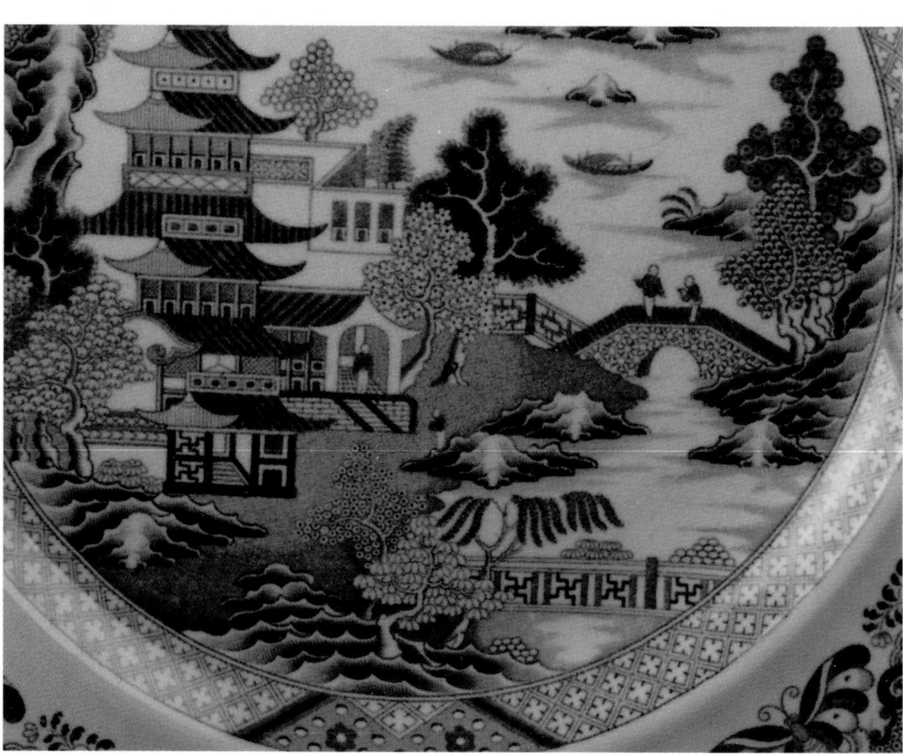

A plate in the rare Two Temples I pattern, with four figures. 10" diam., unknown maker. From the collection of Peter and Susan Steelman, Mystic, CT..

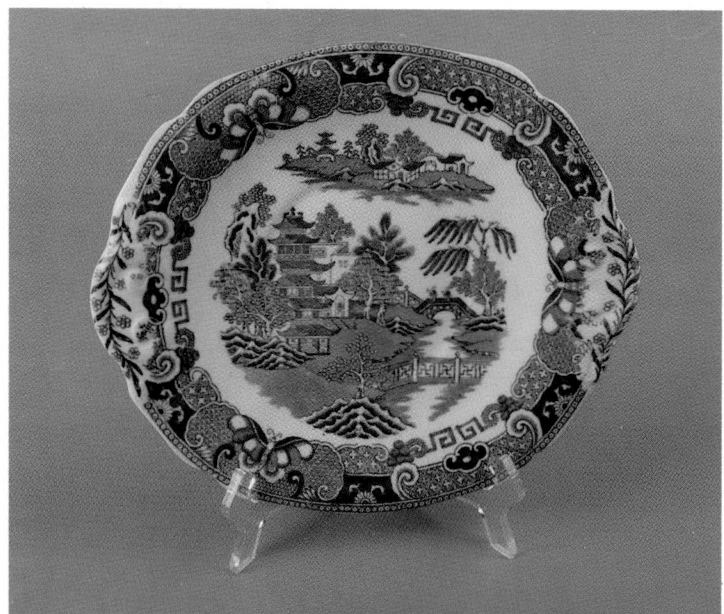

A platter in the more common Two Temples II pattern, with three figures. Semi-china, from 1927, with Ridgway's quiver and diamond mark, 10.5" diam. From the collection of Peter and Susan Steelman, Mystic, CT.

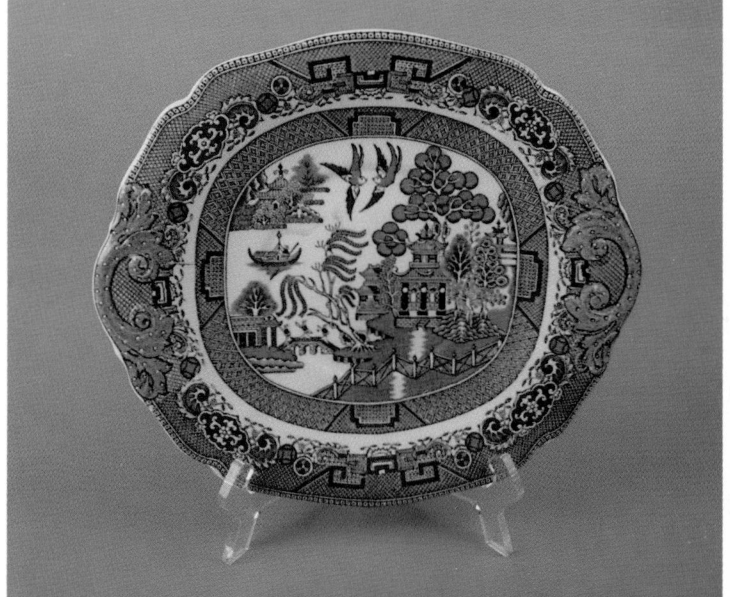

A handled Standard Willow platter from Ridgway, printed on the same body as used for the Two Temples II platter. Also marked with the quiver and diamond mark. From the collection of Peter and Susan Steelman, Mystic, CT.

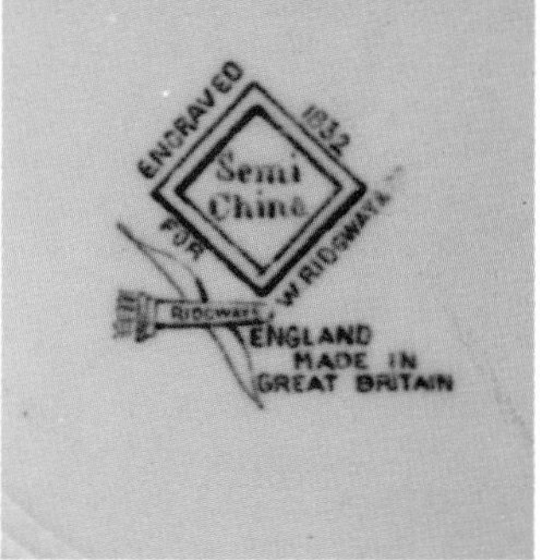

Chapter 3

The Story of Willow

The makers of early 14th and 15th century Chinese blue and white pottery catered to popular taste by portraying scenes from legends and dramas on their dishware; with similar marketing savvy, 18th and 19th century English potters encouraged the development of a brand new legend, a sentimental romance created especially to order for the new blue and white pattern called Willow. The Willow story, beloved to all who admire and collect these dishes, was not based on a Chinese original. Like the pattern itself, the story was fabricated on English soil, and like the pattern, it has many slight variations. Each version of the story accommodates different elements of the Willow pattern, some incorporating the bridge or the fence, the tiny boat or the island, and most importantly the birds. The romantic story that developed around these 'stage props' fascinated the original purchasers of the wares just as it fascinates collectors today.

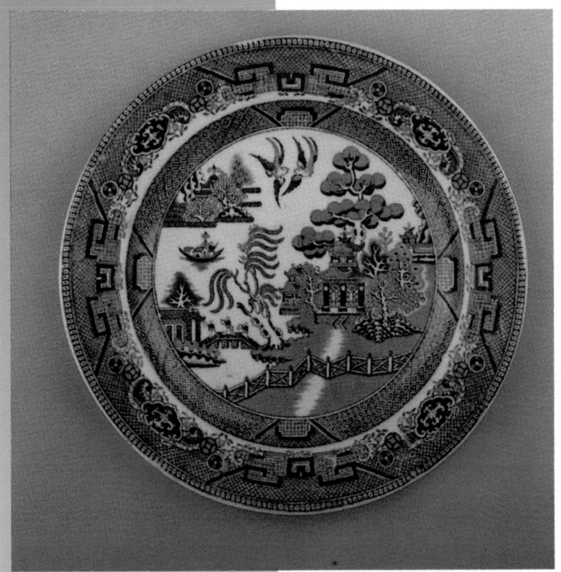

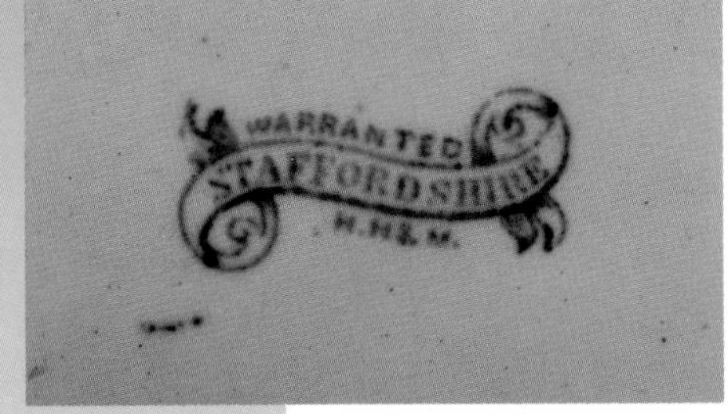

Plate by H.H. + M., 9.5". Blue mark reads "Staffordshire." Courtesy of Rita Entmacher Cohen.

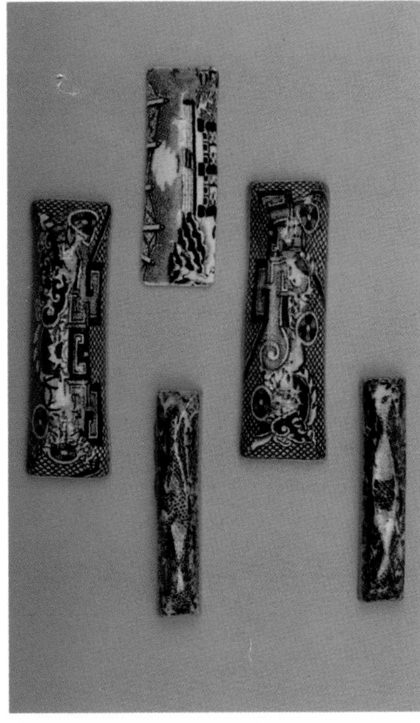

Five pearlware knife rests, c. 1820. Courtesy of Rita Entmacher Cohen.

Set in ancient China, the most frequently heard story describes a wealthy mandarin (nobleman) named Li-Chi and his daughter Koong-Shee; their home was the pagoda, set under the apple (or orange) tree on the right of the plate. Koong-Shee and her father's secretary Chang fell secretly in love; when their love was discovered, Li-Chi dismissed Chang, and betrothed his daughter to the wealthy and elderly Ta Jin. Koong-Shee and Chang then eloped, fleeing across the bridge. They were chased by the whip-brandishing Li-Chi, who followed after them. The lovers boarded a boat (see the upper left of the plate), and travelled to their new home, an island pagoda. After landing on the island, however, they were overtaken by their pursuers, and killed. In pity, the gods turned the two lovers into doves, those two birds which may be seen flying together, forever, at the top of every Willow plate.

Variations on this story have appeared for the past two hundred years. The names of the characters vary, as do the details of the plot, much as the borders, colors and details of the pattern itself do, though they all adhere to the basic Willow scheme. Some of the story variations that have arisen over the years are included in this chapter for your delight.

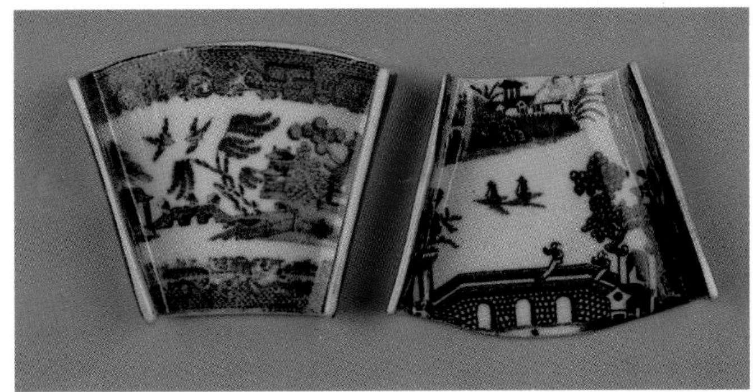

Two pearlware asparagus dishes, c. 1820, 3.5" wide. Courtesy of Rita Entmacher Cohen.

The Willow Story in Any Media

Once it became popular, the Willow story expanded from its dishware origins to become a favorite childrens' bedtime story, in "delightful bits of verse which formerly were taught to children along with their nursery rhymes."[1] From there it entered the theaters, as an exciting romance tale or as a blue and white backdrop for other Oriental tales. This commentary appeared in an 1890 edition of the *Pottery Gazette,* after the willow story had been ingrained on both sides of the Atlantic for almost a hundred years:

> How often has the willow-pattern plate done duty at the theatre both as to scenery as well as to its love tale, and it is to the fore again. One theatre has spent a lot of money on it to attract its audiences during this festive season. Then who can say that the willow plate is out of fashion? Good old willow plate! We remember it in our childhood and we love to see it yet—yes even if only in as pantomime![2]

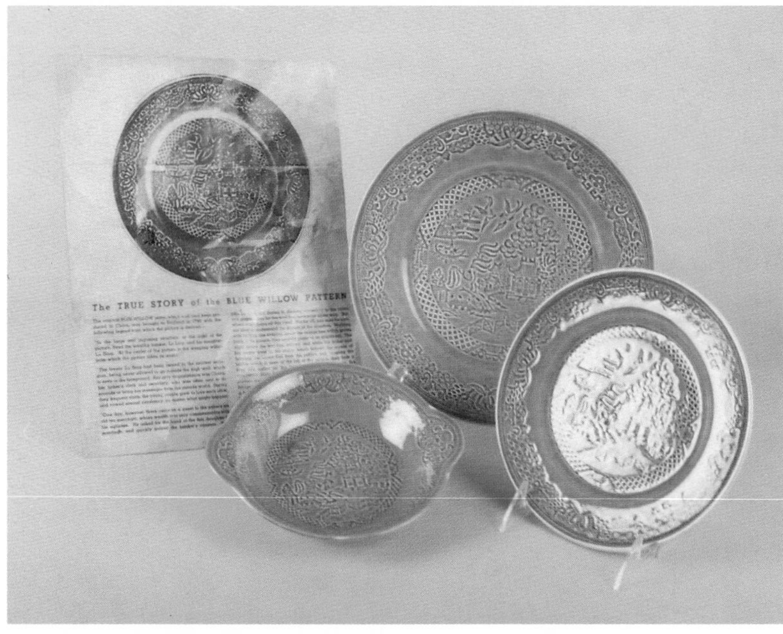

A setting in a Paden Pottery earthenware pattern. This set was offered as a premium to theater attendees in the 1930s. Courtesy of Wendy's Willow.

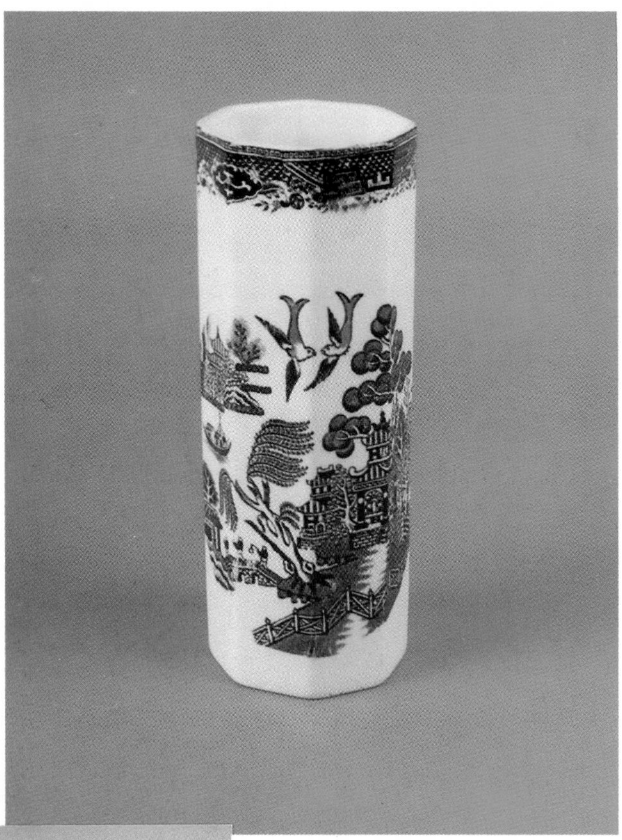

A vase, 7.5" high, marked in dark blue "Old Willow, S - Ltd H England." From the collection of Peter and Susan Steelman, Mystic, CT.

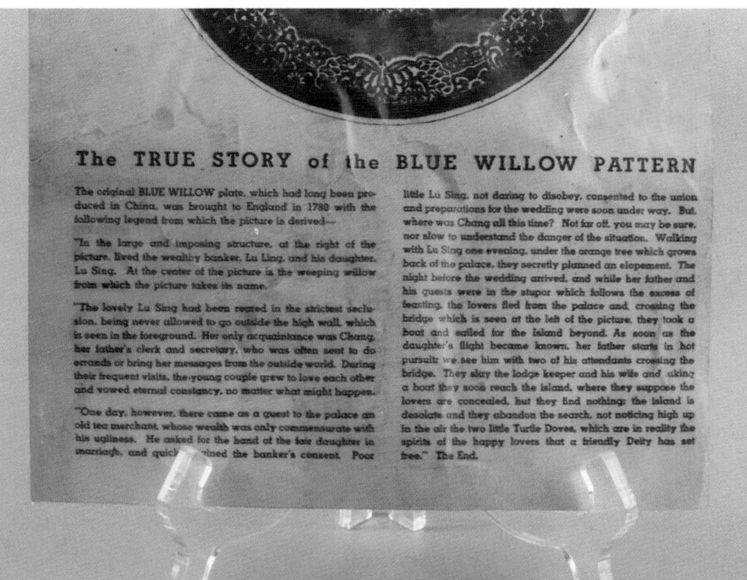

The TRUE STORY of the BLUE WILLOW PATTERN

The original BLUE WILLOW plate, which had long been produced in China, was brought to England in 1780 with the following legend from which the picture is derived—

"In the large and imposing structure, at the right of the picture, lived the wealthy banker, Lu Ling, and his daughter, Lu Sing. At the center of the picture is the weeping willow from which the picture takes its name.

"The lovely Lu Sing had been reared in the strictest seclusion, being never allowed to go outside the high wall, which is seen in the foreground. Her only acquaintance was Chang, her father's clerk and secretary, who was often sent to do errands or bring her messages from the outside world. During their frequent visits, the young couple grew to love each other and vowed eternal constancy, no matter what might happen.

"One day, however, there came as a guest to the palace an old tea merchant, whose wealth was only commensurate with his ugliness. He asked for the hand of the fair daughter in marriage, and quick[illegible]ined the banker's consent. Poor little Lu Sing, not daring to disobey, consented to the union and preparations for the wedding were soon under way. But, where was Chang all this time? Not far off, you may be sure, nor slow to understand the danger of the situation. Walking with Lu Sing one evening, under the orange tree which grows back of the palace, they secretly planned an elopement. The night before the wedding arrived, and while her father and his guests were in the stupor which follows the excess of feasting, the lovers fled from the palace and, crossing the bridge which is seen at the left of the picture, they took a boat and sailed for the Island beyond. As soon as the daughter's flight became known, her father starts in hot pursuit; we see him with two of his attendants crossing the bridge. They slay the lodge keeper and his wife and taking a boat they soon reach the island, where they suppose the lovers are concealed, but they find nothing; the island is desolate and they abandon the search, not noticing high up in the air the two little Turtle Doves, which are in reality the spirits of the happy lovers that a friendly Deity has set free." The End.

The story that accompanied the Paden premium.

When theater came to mean the *movies,* Willow again found its place. Thomas Edison's movie studio, established in 1893,[3] produced a motion picture of the Willow story. The traditional Willow border was used as trim around each frame, a pretty finishing touch to this film.

A Children's Nursery Rhyme[4]

So she tells me a legend centuries old
Of a Mandarin rich in lands and gold,
Of Koong-Shee fair and Chang the good,
Who loved each other as lovers should.
How they hid in the gardener's hut awhile,
Then fled away to the beautiful isle.
Though a cruel father pursued them there,
And would have killed the hopeless pair,
But kindly power, by pity stirred,
Changed each into a beautiful bird.

Here is the orange tree where they talked,
Here they are running away,
And over all at the top you see
The birds making love alway.

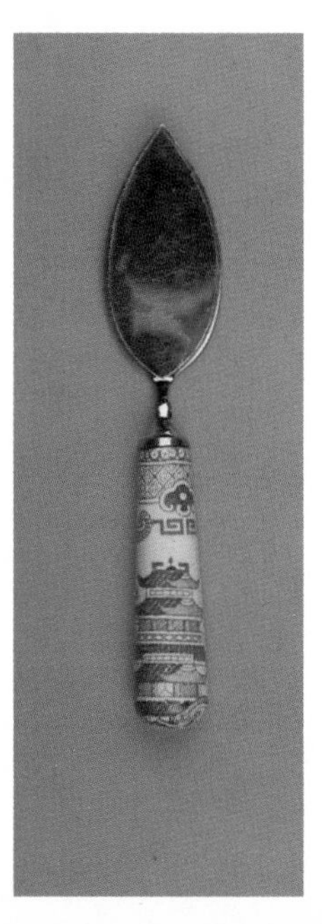

Cheese trowel. Courtesy of Rita Entmacher Cohen.

The Willow Pattern Plate[5]

Betty in her kitchen broke a willow pattern plate.
I spoke to her severely, but I spoke a moment late
To save those little people from a very dreadful fate
Whose fortune's told in blue upon the willow pattern plate.

> Two blue little people come running, together
> Across a blue bridge, in the sunshiny weather,
> They run from a garden, where stands a blue tree
> Above the house of a wealthy Chinee.
> The one is maiden, the other her lover—
> A blue weeping willow hang half the bridge over.
> Behind, in pursuit, comes papa with a whip,
> But they're over the bridge, and aboard the blue ship
> That her lover has moored by the strand of the sea—
> With a shove off the shore, from his wrath they are free.
> Now deep in the water their oars they are plying,
> While high in the heaven the blue doves are flying.
> To his blue island home her lover with waft her,
> And there they will happily live ever after.

This is the story of the willow pattern plate,
So please be very careful—though it's only one and eight—
And remember that you have in hand a very precious freight
When you carry from the kitchen a willow pattern plate.

— by Horace Hutchinson, Westminster Gazetter, Jan 1, 1912.

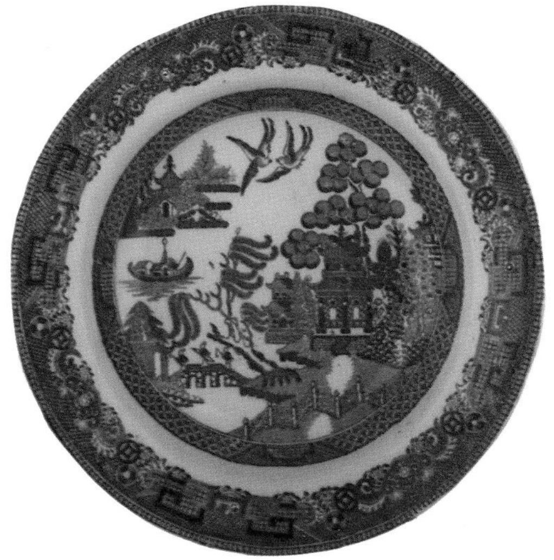

Pearlware soup dish, c. 1820, 9". Unmarked. Courtesy of Rita Entmacher Cohen.

An Old Staffordshire Rhyme[6]

Two pigeons flying high,
Chinese vessels sailing by,
Weeping willows hanging o'er,
Bridge with three men, if not four,
Chinese temple, there it stands,
Seems to take up all the land.
Apple tree with apples on,
A pretty fence to end my song.

The Legend of the Plate[7]

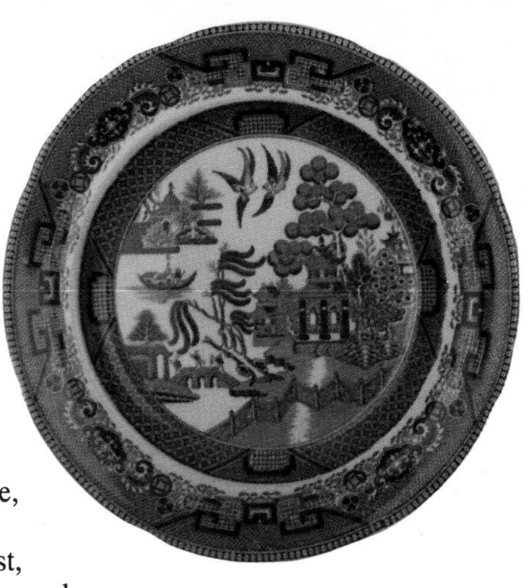

A light blue plate with a gold edge and a fluted rim, 8" diam. Unmarked. Courtesy of Bobbie Jarow, 142 Main St., Nyack, NY.

My Willow ware plate has
a story,
Pictorial, painted in blue
From the land of the tea
and the tea plant
And the little brown man
with the queue.
What ever the food you serve,
daughter
Romance enters into the feast,
If you only pay heed to the legend,
On the old china ware plate from the East.
Koong Shee was a mandarin's daughter
And Chang was her lover, ah me,
For surely her father's accountant
Might never wed pretty Koong Shee
So Chang was expelled from the compound,
The lovers' alliance to break,
And pretty Koong Shee was imprisoned
In a little blue house by the lake.
The doughty old mandarin reasoned
It was time that his daughter should wed,
And the groom of his choice should banish
That silly romance from her head.
For years had great artists been stitching
In symbols the dress she should wear,
Her headband of scarlet lay waiting,
She should ride in a gold wedding chair.
He was busily plotting and planning,
When a message was brought him one day,
Young Chang had invaded the palace,
And taken his sweetheart away.
They were over the bridge when he saw them,
They were passing the big willow tree,
And a boat at the edge of the water
Stood waiting for Chang and Koong Shee.
The furious mandarin followed
The Groom with revenge in his eyes,
But the little boat danced on the water
And traveled away with the prize.
But vengeance pursued to their shelter
And burned the pagoda, they say
From out of the flames rose the lovers
A pair of doves winging away.
They flew toward the western heaveens
The pretty Koong Shee and her Chang
Or so says the famous old legend
From the land of the Yangtse Kiang,
I wouldn't be one to deny it,
For the little blue dove and her
mate
Forever are flying together
Across my Willow ware
plate.

—Anonymous

An earthenware plate with a crackle glaze, 10" diam. Impressed with the mark "Best Goods." Courtesy of Rita Entmacher Cohen.

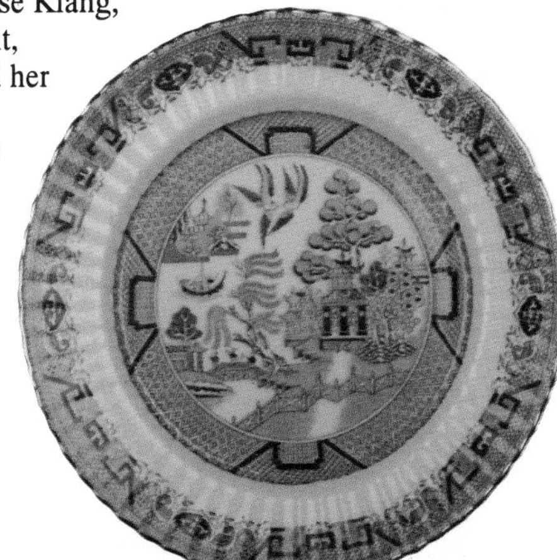

"The Willow Legend"[8]

—from the International Willow Collectors 1993 pamphlet.

"Long ago in China, in a magnificent pavilion surrounded by fruit trees, lived a Mandarin, his daughter Koong-shee and his young secretary, Chang. Chang and Koong-shee fell in love, but Chang was only a commoner, and she the daughter of a noble. Still, their love grew, and they met beneath a willow tree in the garden. But the Mandarin discovered their secret. Enraged, he banished Chang, and imprisoned Koong-shee by circling the pavilion with a zig-zag fence. Then he promised her hand to the Ta-Jin, a noble man far older than she. Not long afterward, the Ta-Jin arrived in pomp and the wedding feast began. Wine flowed frely. When all grew sleepy with the wine, Chang crept into the pavilion, and he and Koong-shee fled through the hushed rooms, carrying a casket of her jewels. But just as they reached the outer door the Mandarin awoke, and in a drunken rage pursued them across the little bridge that spans the river. Koong-shee carried her distaff, a symbol of virginity; Chang carried the jewels; and the Mandarin followed, brandishing a whip. But the lovers escaped the Mandarin, hiding in the small pavilion at the far side of the bridge.

Here lived Koong-shee's maid with her husband, the Mandarin's gardener. They hated the tyrant, and welcomed the lovers in their home. But the Mandarin discovered them, and Chang and Koong-shee were forced to flee once more. They poled a tiny boat down the Yang-Tze until they came to a small island. Here, they thought they would be safe. Selling the casket of jewels, they bought the island, and built a lovely pavilion on it. Chang tilled the land unitl it blossomed with every kind of fruit and vegetable. So successful were his agricultural ventures, Chang wrote a book about how to cultivate the land. This book became so well-known throughout Chinam that even the Ta-Jin heard of it. Guessing who the author was, he sent his soldiers to the island, determined to avenge himself on the man who had stolen his bride-to-be.

The Ta-Jin's soldier came upon Chang as he was working his fields and slew him. Koong-shee, who had watched the entire scene from afar, rushed into their pavilion and set it afire, determined to be with Chang in death as she had been in life.

The gods, looking down on the tragedy, took pity on the lovers and transformed them into a pair of earthly but immortal lovebirds. Until this day, we can see the faithful Chang and Koong-shee, flying high over the willow tree where they first pledged their love. And their story lives forever on the Willow-pattern plate."

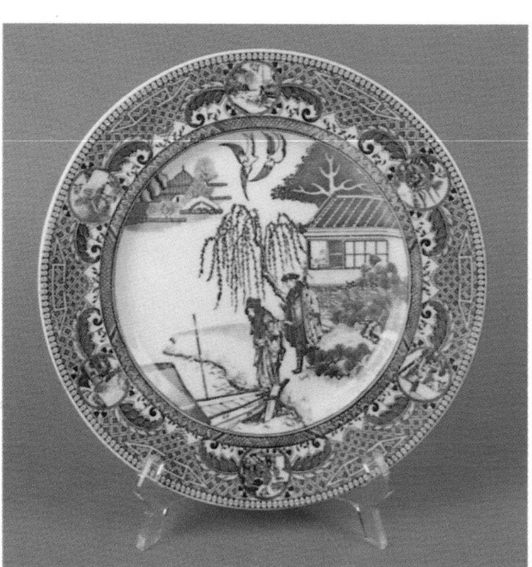

A Royal Doulton plate, 10.5" diam., possibly from 1925. This piece is one of a series of six illustrating various scenes from the Willow story; the central panel here shows the lovers cautiously boarding Chang's boat. Medallions in the border show miniatures versions of the scenes pictured on the other plates. Impressed "Doulton 10—25" mark. From the collection of Peter and Susan Steelman, Mystic, CT.

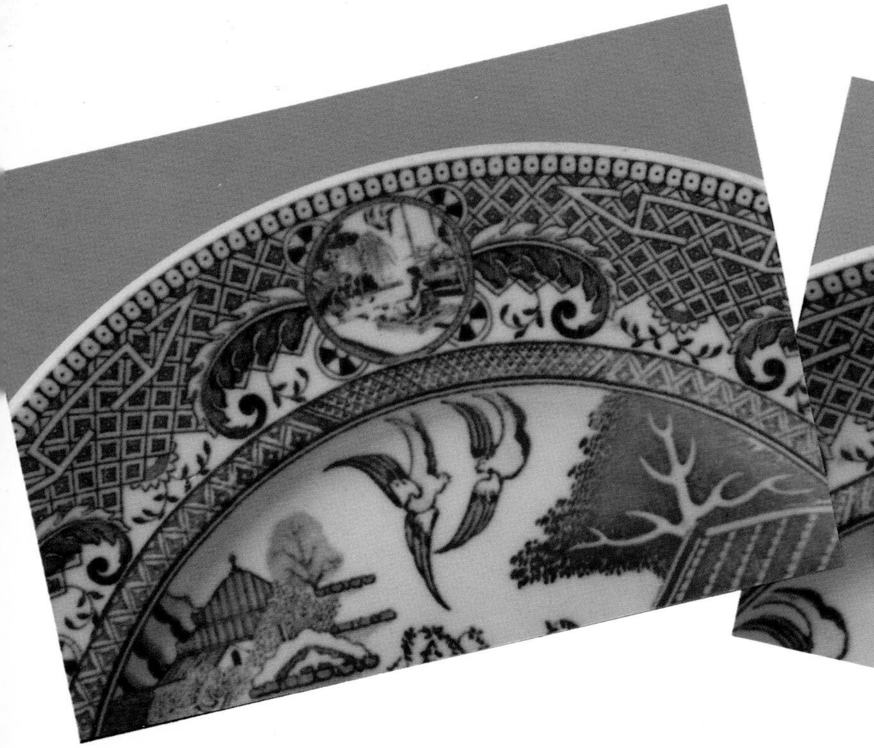

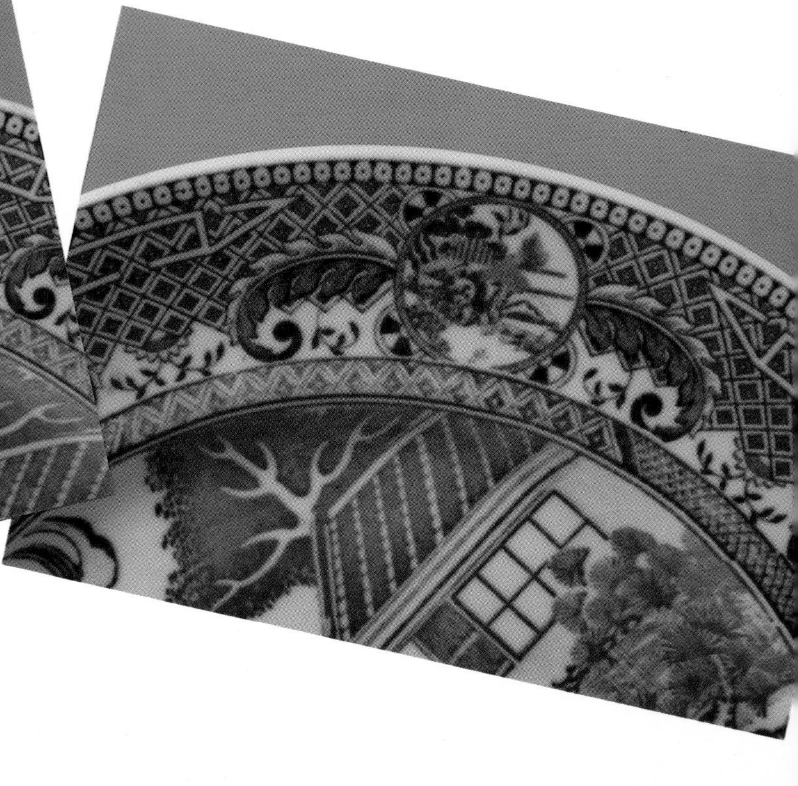

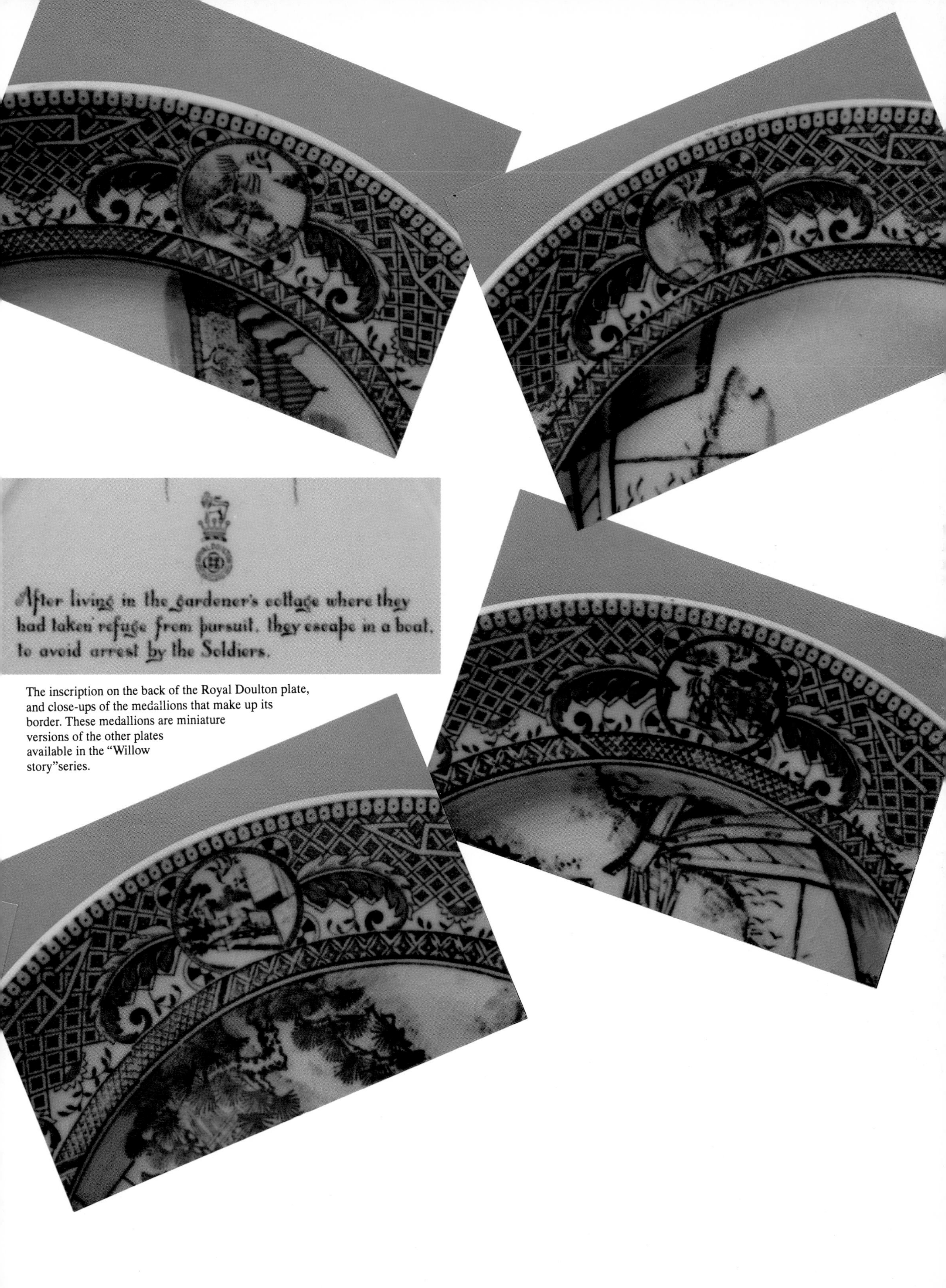

The inscription on the back of the Royal Doulton plate, and close-ups of the medallions that make up its border. These medallions are miniature versions of the other plates available in the "Willow story" series.

The Buffalo Version[9]

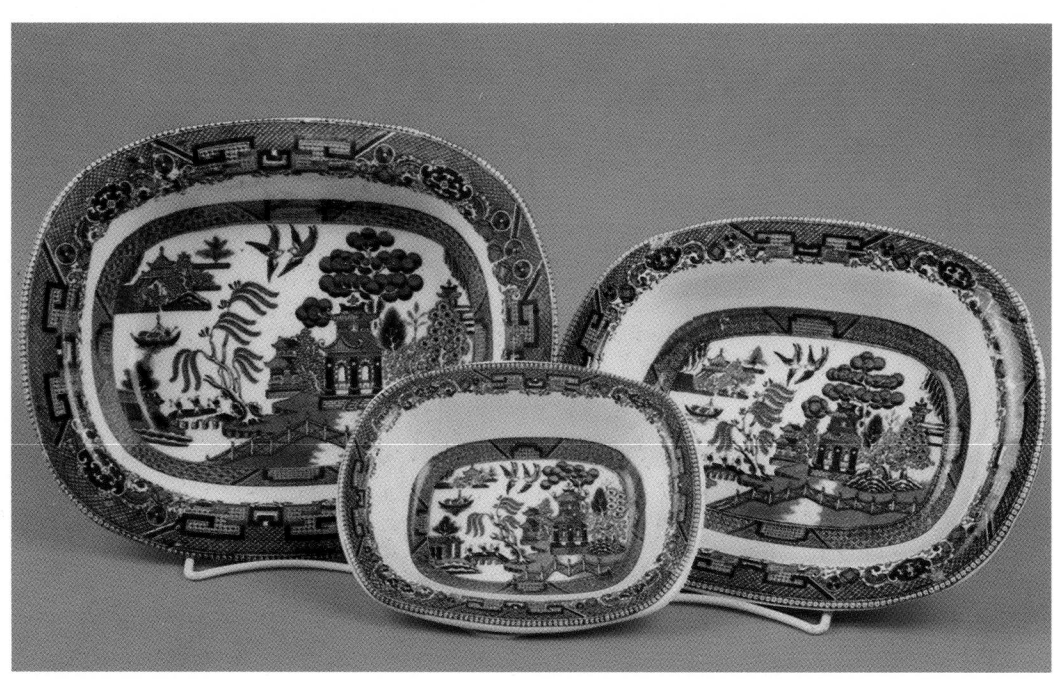

Three oblong vegetable serving bowls from the Buffalo Pottery: small, 1916; medium, 1911; large, 1916, 9.5" long. The small example is particularly difficult to find. From the collection of Phillip M. Sullivan, South Orleans, MA.

Once upon a time there was a rich old Mandarin who had an only daughter named Li-Chi. She and her father lived in a beautiful home, two stories in height, a rare thing in China.

If you look at a Willow pattern plate, you will see that not only is the house a two-storied one, but there are outbuildings (to the right) at the back, and large trees, of a rare and costly kind, surrounding it, showing that the owner was a man of great wealth.

Li-Chi was a very pretty girl, and as her father was a rich man, she was always dressed in the softest, brightest silks money could buy.

Her favorite dresses were of peach-colored silk, embroidered with silver, and if you could have seen her sitting on her balcony on a moonlight night, with flowers entwined in her hair, and the shimmering peach-colored silk falling in soft folds about her feet, you would have thought her worthy to marry a prince. But Li-Chi did not want to marry a prince. She had fallen in love with Chang, her father's secretary, who lived in the island cottage you will find at the top of the plate.

The Mandarin was very angry about this, and had forbidden the young man to come to the house, at the same time forbidding Li-Chi to leave it, so that the lovers might have no chance of meeting. He went still further—he betrothed his daughter to a Ta-jin, or Duke, who was rich, but many years older than Li-Chi. Li-Chi had never seen the Ta-jin, but her father came to her one evening as she was sitting on her balcony, which overhung the river, and told her that he had made arrangements for her marriage.

"Oh, no! no!" sobbed Li-Chi. "I love Chang! I cannot marry anyone else."

"Chang shall never be your husband," replied the Mandarin sternly. "I have promised the Ta-jin that you shall be married to him when the peach tree blossoms."

The willow tree was in bloosom then, for it was quite early in the year.

The peach tree would not bloom until the spring, but every day after this Li-Chi watched the buds of the peach tree, which grew close to her window, unfolding, and she watched them with dread and sorrow in her heart. "Is Chang dead or has he forgotten all about me?" she wondered to herself.

But Chang was not dead, neither had he forgotten; he thought of her night and day, and at last one evening he sent her a message.

She was sitting on her balcony as usual, when a little boat made out of half a coconut shell, and fitted with a tiny sail, floated right to her feet. Inside it she found a colored bead she had given her lover, a sure proof that the boat came from Chang; and also a piece of bamboo paper on which these words were writeen:

"When the willow fades away,
And the peach tree groweth gay
Tell me, sweetheart, can it be
They will steal my love from me?"

Li-Chi took her ivory tablets from the bosom of her dress and wrote an answer to his letter in the same strain:

"When the peach tree blooms, sweetheart,
Thou and I must weep and part.
Hasten then to take the prize
Ere 'tis seen by robber's eyes."

She knew that her lover would understand this flowery language, and she put the tablets in the boat, and lighted a stick of frankincense and placed it in the bow.

And leaning over the balcony, she watched it sail away into the darkness of the night.

"He will come for me before my wedding day," she said softly to herself.

The night air was full of the scent of flowers, and everything was still. Li-Chi half imagined she could hear the blossoms on the willow tree sighing faintly, and saying, "It will be too late—we are dying!" For Chang had promised, the last ime they met, that he would come for her while the willow was still in blossom.

And she thought she heard the blossoms on the peach tree replying, "We are nearly ready to open. Then she will marry the Ta-jin!"

Chang, on the farther bank of the river, waited to draw his frail little bark to land, and when he read the verse on the ivory tablets, his smile went up to the corners of his eyes, as Chinese smiles generally do; and he walked into the gardener's cottage where he was stopping, and called the gardener and his wife.

"Do you know when the Ta-jin is coming?" he said.

"The betrothal feast is fixed for next Thursday, for the moon will then be lucky," replied the old man. "The Mandarin has ordered his gardeners to take six dozen carp out of the fish ponds, and there are to be golden and silver pheasants on the table, and boar's head and roast peacock."

"And six casks of wine to be broached," continued his wife. "And as many oysters as his guests can eat."

"The servants say the Ta-jin is bringing his bride such a casket of jewels as never was seen," said the gardener. "A necklace of pearls—each pearl as big as a sparrow's egg—"

"Pigeon's egg, stupid!" interrupted the wife.

"Sparrow's egg, imbecile!" he retorted.

"Pigeon's egg, idiot!" repeated the old woman angrily.

"It doesn't matter which," Chang broke in. "What I want to know is whether you could borrow me one of the servant's dresses and smuggle me into the banqueting room that night?"

"It is impossible," replied the gardener, shaking his head.

The old couple knew all about Chang's love story, but they were afraid of helping him. Neither of them dared to risk the displeasure of such a rich and powerful Mandarin as Li-Chi's father.

The next few days passed in preparation for the betrothal feast.

Servants were running hither and thither all the time; the Mandarin never stopped giving orders from morning to night; the banqueting hall was swept and strewn with sweet-scented leaves and the walls and roof hung with colored-silk lanterns and fans.

Everyone was happy and busy except Li-Chi, who sat on her balcony, with her embroidery lying idle on her lap, and her eyes gazing wistfully across the river that separated her from her lover.

On the morning of the betrothal feast the peach tree was covered with lovely pink blossoms, while the willow blossoms hung faded and drooping on the tree.

This made Li-Chi so sad she could not stay on the balcony; she went into her room and sat on a couch, with her head resting on her hands, watching her attendants as the spread out on the floor the rich silk dresses the Ta-jin had sent as a present to his bride.

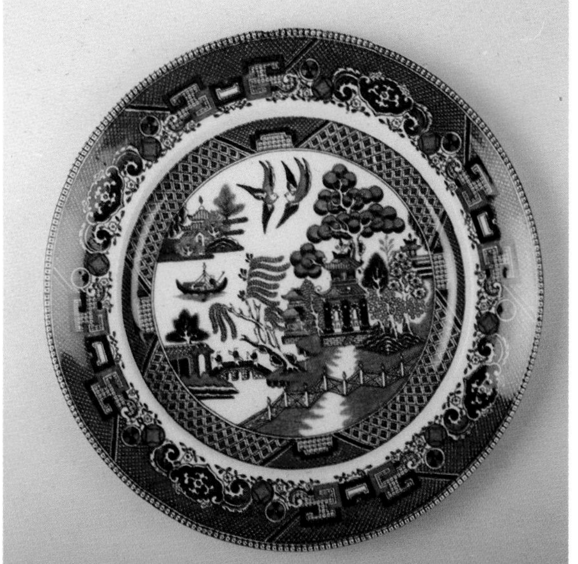

A round plate from the Buffalo Pottery, 1916, 10" diam. From the collection of Phillip M. Sullivan, South Orleans, MA.

They were all colors of the rainbow, pale blue, and pink, and yellow, and purple, embroidered in gold and silver, and one of them was peach-colored silk, embroidered with pearls.

"This is just the dress for a bride," said the women.

But Li-Chi shook her head. "'I will not wear peach-color anymore," she said.

At noon the Ta-jin sent her by his servant the box of jewels of which the gardener and his wife had spoken. There were diamonds and rubies in it of such size that the Emperor himself would not have despised them. And the necklace of pearls went twice around Li-Chi's neck, and nearly to her waist.

At last her attendants persuaded her to allow them to dress her for her betrothal and they chose a beautiful blue-silk dress, embroidered all over with golden butterflies; because in China butterflies are looked upon as a symbol of married happiness. And they fastened the pearls around her throat, and put some shining jewels in her hair.

"For she is going to be a great lady—the wife of a duke," they said. "Flowers in the hair are only for conmon people."

"Now leave me quite alone," commanded Li-Chi, when they had finished.

She was tired of all their foolish talk about the Ta-jin, and wanted to step out once more and see if the willow blossoms were quite faded, and if there was no message frm Chang sailing to her across the water. The women went away, but came back in a moment to tell her that one of the servants wished to speak to her. "Let him come in," said Li-Chi impatiently. The young man who entered wore a long blue cotton robe, and a broad straw hat that half-concealed his face, but as soon as they were alone he took off the hat, making her a low-sweeping bow, and Li-Chi saw that it was Chang himself. For a moment she could not believe it, but when he took her in his arms and kissed her, crumpling up all the golden butterflies is his eagerness, she knew it was really her lover, who had come to save her from marrying the Ta-jin.

"How did you get here?" she asked, sobbing for joy.

"I disguised myself as a beggar," said Chang, showing her the rags he wore under his blue robe. "But when I came to the banqueting room, to ask for alms, everybody was too busy to listen to me. So I managed to slip behind the screen they had spread across the lower end of it and find my way to your room."

"And this?" said Li-Chi, touching his servant's dress.

"One of the servants happened to have left it behind the screen. And now, Li-Chi, how can I disguise you? For we must pass behind the screen again, and through the banqueting room door into the garden, and across the bridge to the gardener's cottage."

He looked quickly around the room, and found a garment belonging to Li-Chi's old nurse, which covered all her bridal finery, except her pretty little gold-embroidered shoes.

"Never mind my shoes," she said. "I shall run so fast no one will see them."

She took her distaff in her hand because she did not want to be an idle, useless wife to Chang, and she gave him the box of jewels to carry.

I do not think they ought to have taken the jewels, although the Ta-jin had given them to Li-Chi. but perhaps Chang did not know what was in the box, and he was in to great a hurry to ask.

"The willow blossoms droop upon the bough, my darling! We must delay no longer," he said.

And indeed, as the lovers crept behind the screen a light breeze shook the last blossoms of the willow to the ground.

"If my father should see us!" whispered Li-Chi, holding her lover's hand very tightly.

"Don't be afraid," said Chang. "I have prayed to the good Genii not to let him catch us. If he comes near they will change us into two stars, shining together, or, perhaps, two turtle doves. You would not mind that, would you?"

"I do not mind anything, except parting from you," replied Li-Chi.

They reached the garden in safety, and Chang led his sweetheart toward the bridge.

But Li-Chi's pretty little shoes would not allow her to run very fast, after all, and when they got to the foot of the bridge, the Mandarin came running down the garden path, with a whip in his hand.

"Stop! stop!" he cried furiously. "Will no one stop the thief who has stolen my daughter?"

Chang put Li-Chi in front of him, and she ran across the bridge first, with her distaff, while he followed her with the casket of jewels. Behind them both came the Mandarin, brandishing his whip. But the good Genii, who were watching over the lovers, saw that the Mandarin gained quickly on Chang, and there was no chance of their escaping.

"He will flog Chang to death, and shut Li-Chi up for the rest of her life. What shall we do?" they asked each other.

Then the Genii said, "Let us change them into two turtle doves, that they may be happy together after all." Just as the Mandarin, therefore, put his hand out to seize the young man by the shoulder, the box of jewels fell splash! splash! into the water, and Chang and Li-Chi were changed into two beautiful doves. They at once flew away, out of the Mandarin's reach, and he was left with the whip in his hand, and the Ta-jin's jewels at the bottom of the river.

The story does not tell us any more about him—how he got home, or what the Ta-jin said when he arrived.

It only tells us that Chang and Li-Chi were as happy as two turtle doves could be.

And the next time you come across a willow-pattern plate, you must look for them, hovering in the air above the bridge.

On the bridge itself you will see three figures, Li-Chi with her distaff, Chang with the jewels, and the Mandarin with his whip.

At one end is the famous willow tree which shed its blossoms the day of the elopement; at the other is the gardener's cottage and at the top of the pate an island, with another on it, in which Chang had hoped to live with Li-Chi.

But instead of that they built a cozy nest in the garden, from which they could watch the willow and the peach tree bloom and fade without any fear of being parted from each other.

Chapter 4

Making Willow

The Methods and Materials

PART I: THE CERAMIC BODY

Once it was established, the Standard Willow pattern did not vary much over the years; the same can not be said about the bodies on which and the manufacturing processes by which the pattern was applied. Though the technique of transfer printing is not much different today from its earlier versions, much of today's new Willow is printed with other, more mechanical (and less detailed) techniques. Furthermore, the world of ceramics and pottery has always been one of change—sometimes gradual, sometimes sudden. As technology advanced, Koong-Shee and Chang found themselves fleeing across surfaces of earthenware, pearlware, stoneware, stone china, ironstone, crockery, and a variety of hard- and soft-paste porcelains (to say nothing of the metal, cloth, paper, and now plastic surfaces that have borne the pattern). A look at the manufacturing processes and materials used to make Willow can be helpful in deepening an understanding of the pieces.

The Roots of English Potting: Earthenware

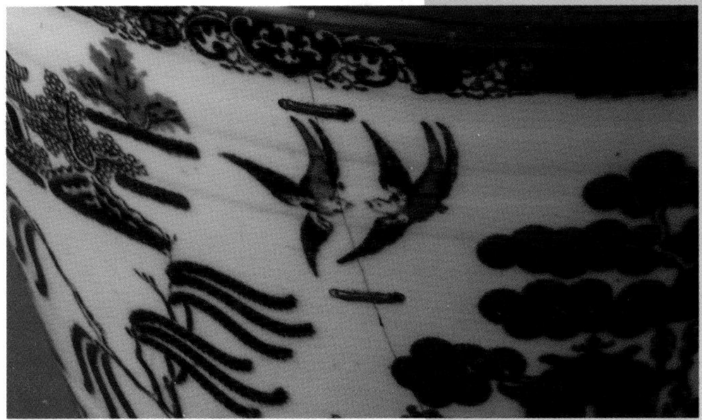

Repairs to an earthenware milk pail. Modern glueing methods have made staples like these unnecessary.

English potters were well-versed in the making of earthenware ceramics long before the Willow pattern arose in the 18th century. Earthenwares are made from clays, flint, stone and other silica compounds. Different types of clay and silica compounds result in varying colors of pottery, from reds and yellows to greys and near-whites. They are fired at 1000-1200 degrees Celcius, which leaves them opaque (except, on rare occasion, when an edge or surface is dangerously thin, allowing some light to shine through).

Earthenwares are porous, and need to be coated with a vitreous (glass-like) glaze to make them watertight.[1] Experimentation with glazes eventually allowed English potters to have a great deal of freedom in decorating earthenwares. For example, tin-glazing and lead-glazing allowed bright, opaque painted decorations, while glaze barely tinted with blue, green, or yellow could enhance or neutralize the shade of the clay—most significantly, for our purposes, the blueish-white pearlware achieved by adding a tinge of cobalt to the glaze. Despite this ever-growing flexibility, the glamour of 'blanc-de-Chine'—the pure, clean white of Chinese porcelain—made many potters (and consumers) dissatisfied with the more humble local earthenwares.

In Pursuit of Porcelain

Though most Willow found today has been applied to earthenware, the story of Willow originated in the English pursuit of Chinese porcelain, and porcelain Willow is particularly prized by some collectors. Porcelain, unlike earthenware, is translucent; hold a flashlight or a bare light bulb behind a piece, and you will see a glow shining through, sometimes faint and sometimes strong, depending on the thickness and the composition of the piece. It makes a clear, metallic ringing sound when tapped, quite unlike the dull sound of earthenware. These qualities entranced English and Continental consumers, who bought boatloads of the imported Chinese porcelain that had previously been considered "first a myth and then a rarity."[2]

Far from mythical, porcelain was being made by technically-minded Chinese potters by 620 C.E.,[3] using kaolin (white aluminum silicate clay or 'china clay'), and a feldspathic clay called "pentuntse."[4] These ingredients are mixed together to be 'matured' or 'weathered' outdoors. They are heaped in piles no more than three feet high, shaped to allow rain to run off easily, removing impurities from the clay; over the course of each year, winter's frost breaks down and begins to disintegrate the separate ingredients, and the summer sun gradually dries the clay to a useable consistency.[5] Since aging the mixture increases the strength and whiteness of the finished pieces, Chinese potters generally store their clay for decades before using it to make pieces for firing.[6]

When these ingredients are finally put through their single firing, at extremely high temperatures between 1300 and 1400 degrees Celcius, they vitrify like a natural glass, melting to form a smooth-textured body. They break with a clean, smooth fracture, normally in glass-like facets,[7] revealing what has been described as "a fine sparkling grain of compact texture."[8] The glaze is not a separate coat fired on top of the ceramic body, but is a thin layer arising from the clay mixture itself, blending almost imperceptibly with the surface of the piece.

As early as 1575, European potters in Venice and Florence were attempting to capture in their own works the color, texture, weight and refinement of Chinese porcelain.[9] By the end of that century, the Medicis are said to have discovered the secret of making an artificial but nonetheless translucent porcelain. That formula was lost, however, and the technique was not rediscovered until 1673 in France.

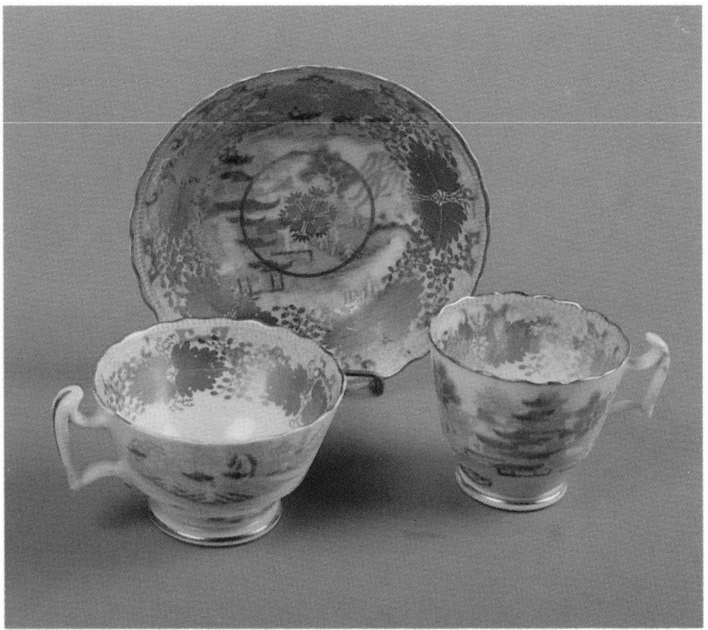

A teacup, saucer, and demitasse cup in gilded porcelain. The pattern, printed in pale blue, has been almost completely obscured by the gilding. The saucer in 5.5" diam. Courtesy of Charles and Louise Loehr, Louise's Old Things, Kutztown PA.

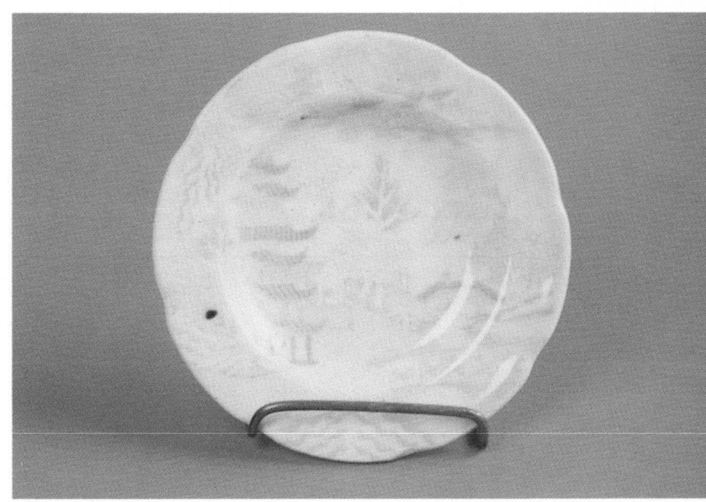

A porcelain saucer by Podmore Walker & Co., c. 1834, 4" diam. Courtesy of Charles and Louise Loehr, Louise's Old Things, Kutztown, PA.

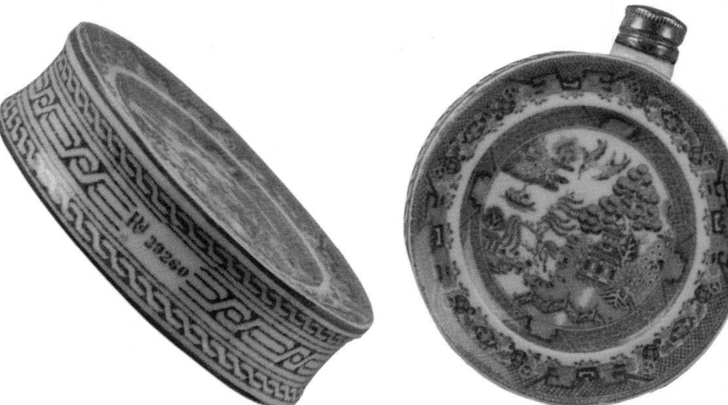

A porcelain perfume bottle, 2.25" diam., with the registered design number 29260. From the collection of Peter and Susan Steelman, Mystic, CT.

These new Western porcelains are called 'artificial' or 'soft-paste' (pâte tendre) porcelain, to distinguish them from the Chinese original now called 'true' or 'hard paste'. The artifical porcelain body was made from varying combinations of white clays, powdered glass, talcum powder, magnesium, white sand, gypsum, soda, alum, salt, and nitre—essentially white clay mixed with powdered glass— which resulted in "at best a creamy or ivory white tint."[10] Soft-paste porcelains are not self-glazing, and thus required two firings—the first, in the biscuit stage, at a temperature somewhat lower than that used for hard-paste porcelain, and the second, for glazing, at a lower temperature still. This results in a rather granular, porous body; to test a piece, check for an unglazed spot on the base, and try to scratch it with your fingernail. If the paste is marked by this scratching—or if it is "almost possible to feel the paste crumbling away"[11]—then it is soft-paste; hard-paste will roughen your fingernail. The surface of soft-paste porcelain is coated with a thick layer of glaze, which "lies more obviously on the top" than hard-paste's, as is apparent when a piece is broken.[12] In the early years, artificial porcelain's glaze was so soft that the inside of a teacup could be scratched by the stirring of a metal teaspoon.

In 1707, two alchemists in Dresden, Saxony finally discovered how to make hard-paste porcelain. In 1710 the Meissen factory was established in Saxony,[13] and thereafter most Continental porcelain was hard-paste.

England, however, was busily developing its porcelain industry independently, and rather more slowly. Importing Continental porcelain wares was prohibited before 1740, so the English potters had only Chinese and Japanese porcelains on which to base their speculation and experimentation.[14] By 1747—forty years after a hard-paste formula was finally developed by two Continental alchemists in Saxony—English potters began making their first soft-paste wares. These English artificial porcelains have been described as "relatively warm and 'friendly' to the touch," with overglaze enameled colors mellowing into the glaze, unlike true porcelains that "tend to appear cold and glittery."[15]

Many varieties of soft-paste porcelain were developed as the English pursued their own porcelains, displaying "a considerable degree of independence, even on the technical level."[16] By 1768 the first English hard-paste formula was in production at Plymouth, with Bristol close on their heels in c. 1770-1781.[17] As the experimentation continued, a hybrid soapstone-based stearite porcelain was developed. The Bow factory began using a formula with a high percentage of bone ash, making their wares hold their shapes better than earlier pastes did; this formula was adapted for use by many potteries, both domestic and abroad. "Research was clearly developing along a number of different lines," wrote one pottery scholar, "and experimentation was flourishing."[18] This growth would later lead to many interesting hybrid porcelain varieties, providing alternatives to pearlware as bodies for the transfer-printed Willow pattern.

Pearlware's Place

While English potters were experimenting with porcelain to compete with Chinese imports, they were also adressing a new market—those less-than-affluent customers who could afford neither foreign nor domestic porcelains, but who nonetheless desired the elegant look of blue-and-white. As the upper-crust's fascination with the color scheme began to fade in favor of neoclassical cream-colored wares and multi-colored pieces, this new merchant- and working-class market became more and more important for blue-and-white's survival. It was crucial that the potters develop an inexpensive earthenware with color white enough to imitate porcelain. Among Staffordshire's early efforts were experiments to coat red earthenware with a white-burning slip (a thin layer of wet clay), and tin-glazing; the challenge prompted what Robert Copeland called "a time of great commercial growth and explorations."[19]

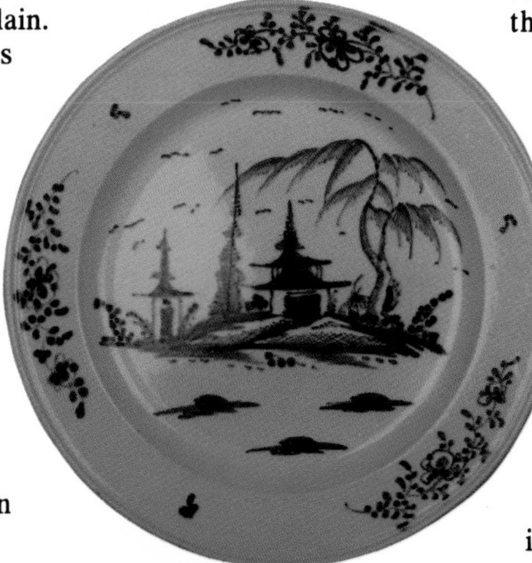

In the 1750s, the earthenware called 'creamware' was developed—white clay with a smooth flint-based glaze, which fired into a light cream-colored body. Unfortunately, it was not light enough to be an acceptible replacement for porcelain. While creamware was, as Robert Copeland put it, "destined not to have a very lengthy uninterrupted regieme,"[20] it provided a short-lived diversion for those customers who were ready to switch from traditional blue-and-white styles to a more neo-classical look. And while it indulged the neo-classical tastes of the upper classes, it really did not distract significantly from the pervasive popular demand for chinoiserie and an export porcelain look-alike. Indeed, creamware helped the blue-and-white market more than it hurt: the techniques developed and used for creamware (including transfer printing and tinted glazes) were soon to be adapted even more effectively in the manufacture of 'pearlware', a current term for the earthenware approximation of porcelain finally released by English potters in the 1770s.

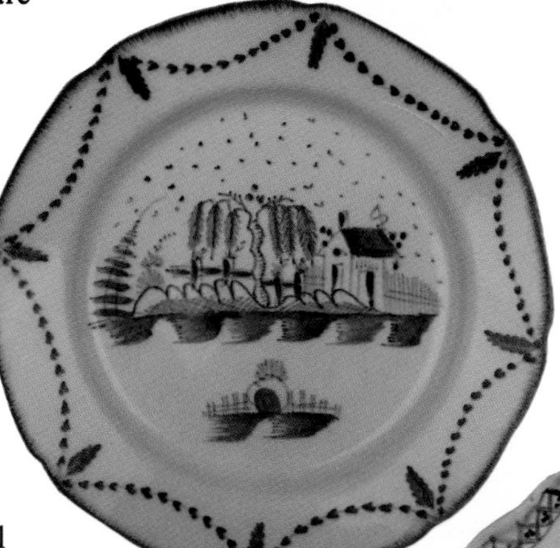

Pearlware was made by increasing the percentage of white clay and flint in the body formula, and by making a minor change in the usual creamware glaze: a small amount of cobalt frit was added to the clear glaze.[21] The pottery took on a blueish-white cast, which appeared much whiter than creamware, especially when decorations of dark cobalt blue were applied. This was precisely what was necessary to satisfy the demand for blue-and-white in the middle and lower classes—a relatively inexpensive, sturdy earthenware that nonetheless had a crisp, bright clarity akin to that of porcelain. To determine whether a piece is pearlware, check inside the footrims, or other areas where the glaze might have "pooled" or "puddled" thickly; if the glaze appears to have a definite blue tint, the piece is pearlware. Creamware frequently has a pale yellow or green tint in similar areas.

It has become generally accepted now that pearlware, though first marketed and popularized by Josiah Wedgwood in 1779, was preceded by a technically similar ware called 'China Glaze', developed around 1775 by other Staffordshire potters. This is supported by the discovery of almost a hundred and fifty pearlware or China Glaze shards on a British military camp in America which had already been shut down in 1779. These fragments appeared to have white bodies with a cobalt-tinged glaze. Over 60% of the pieces bear underglaze blue decoration, and those designs which can be discerned seem to be chinoiserie.[22]

It is uncertain whether the difference between these early China Glaze wares and Wedgwood's later pearlwares is a matter of quality or of simple marketing. In a 1779 letter, Wedgwood wrote to his partner Thomas Bentley about choosing a trade name for his own new cobalt-whitened ware, suggesting that "to give the brat a name you may set a cream-colour plate and one of the best blue and white ones before you, and suppose the one you are to name another degree white and finer still."[23] By June 19 the ware had a name: 'Pearl White'.[24] But was pearlware really 'white and finer still'? The description of the China Glaze wares found on the pre-1779 American site says that they looked "just like the pearlwares which are present in contexts from the 1780s." It is not impossible that Pearl White was distinguished not by superior looks but by the shrewd marketing for which Josiah Wedgwood is renowned. Understanding the nature of his customers, Wedgwood knew that he had to present his wares "as qualitatively different and better than the products of others"—and even more importantly, as something brand new. He was well aware, as he discussed the subject with Bentley, of the danger of "the pearl white being consider'd as an imitation of the blue and white fabriques, either earthenware or porcelain."[25] He was also aware that Pearl White must be differentiated from creamware, the preceding fashion. In another letter, Wedgwood pondered (in his own inimitable style) the fickle taste of his customers and the marketing potential of his new product. :

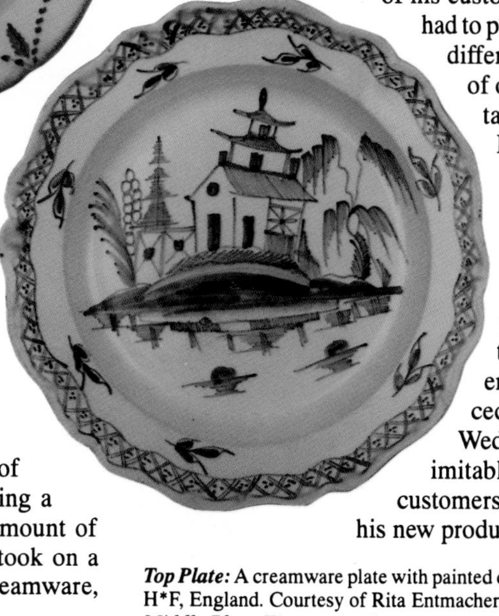

Top Plate: A creamware plate with painted decoration, c. 1790, 9.5" diam. Made by H*F, England. Courtesy of Rita Entmacher Cohen.

Middle Plate: The contrast between creamware and pearlware bodies is unmistakable. The tinge of cobalt added to pearlware's clear glaze (for accentuating the body's whiteness) leaves the 'pooling' in the edges noticably blue.

Bottom Plate: A creamware plate, c. 1780, painted in the pattern known as "Tree Fence House Fence Tree." $295. Courtesy of Rita Entmacher Cohen.

"I should not hesitate a moment in prefering [creamware] if I consulted my own taste and sentiments: but you know what Lady Dartmouth told us, that she and her friends were tired of creamcolor, and so they would be of Angels if they were shewn for sale in every chandlers shop through the town. The pearl white must be considered as a *change* rather than as an *improvement,* and I must have something ready to succeed it when the public eye is pall'd."[26]

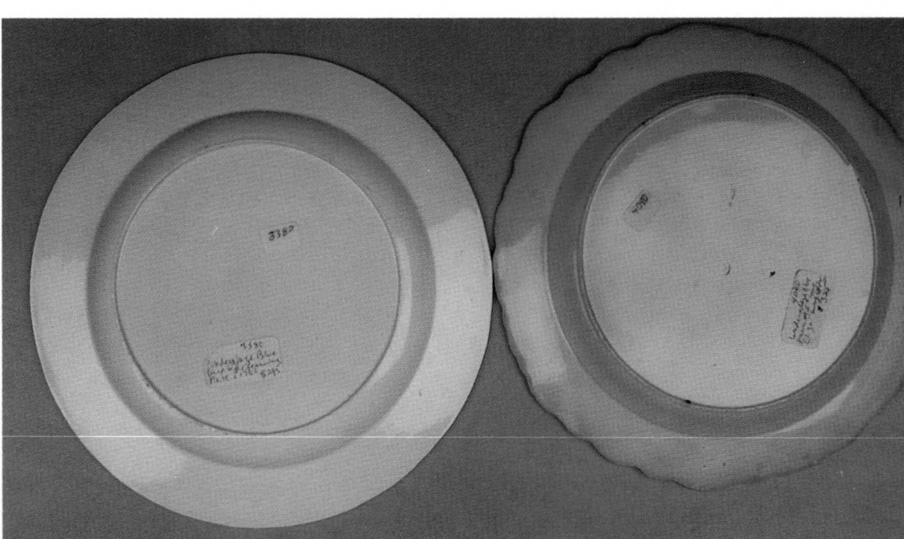

Pearlware and creamware: an unmistakable difference.

Wedgwood's 'Pearl White' line had more stamina than creamware had, however, perhaps because of the long-established tradition of desirable, high-quality blue-and-white from China. Wedgwood's version of pearlware became so popular that its origins were forgotten; earlier makers of identical or similar wares were forgotten, and the name 'China Glaze' became obsolete.

Creamware had made transfer-printing practical for the first time, and while it was sometimes used for chinoiserie patterns painted in cobalt, the first transfer-printing of the Willow pattern waited for pearlware. When customers saw how perfectly pearlware's blueish-white background set off delicate, fine-lined chinoiserie patterns like Willow, its market was assured. By 1802, the Staffordshire potteries were producing more pearlware than any other type of earthenware, and by 1810 pearlware was the dominant tableware in the United States.[27]

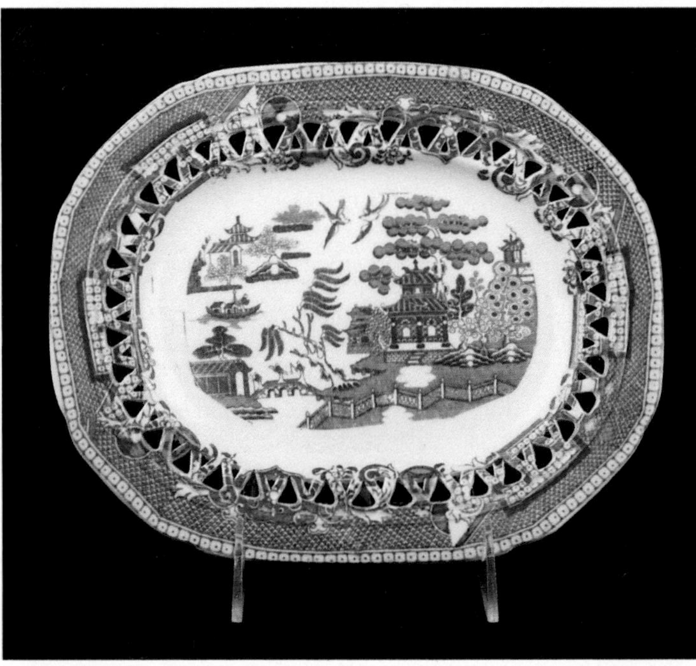

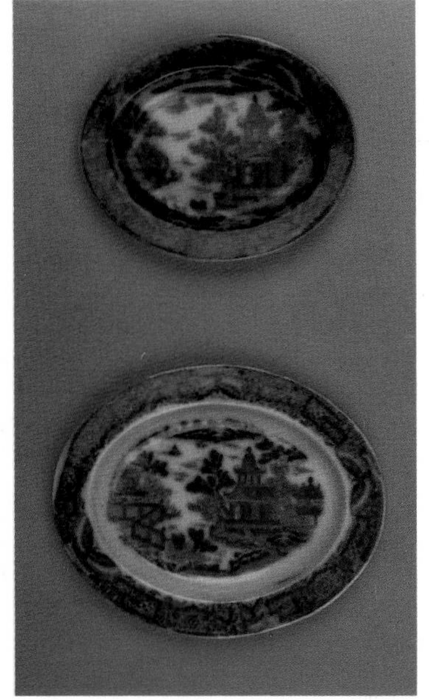

Two children's pearlware service platters, c. 1820, 4.125" long and 5" long. Unmarked. Courtesy of Rita Entmacher Cohen.

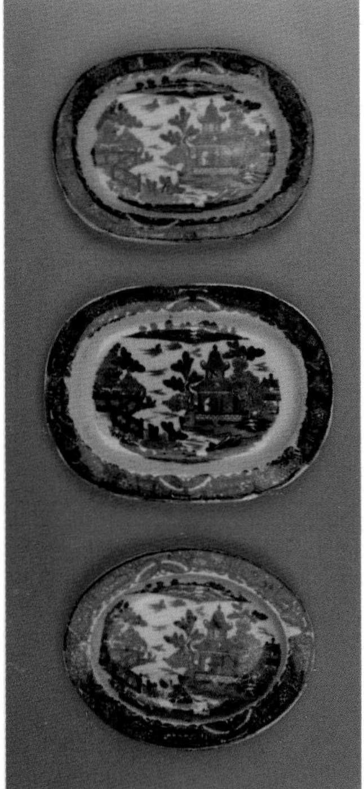

Three children's service platters in pearlware: 4.75" long, 5" long, and 5.5" long. Courtesy of Rita Entmacher Cohen.

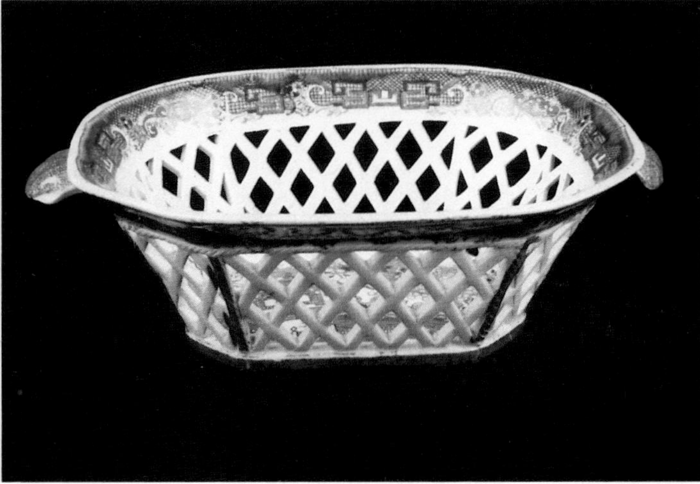

A pearlware chestnut basket with its stand, c. 1820. Courtesy of Rita Entmacher Cohen.

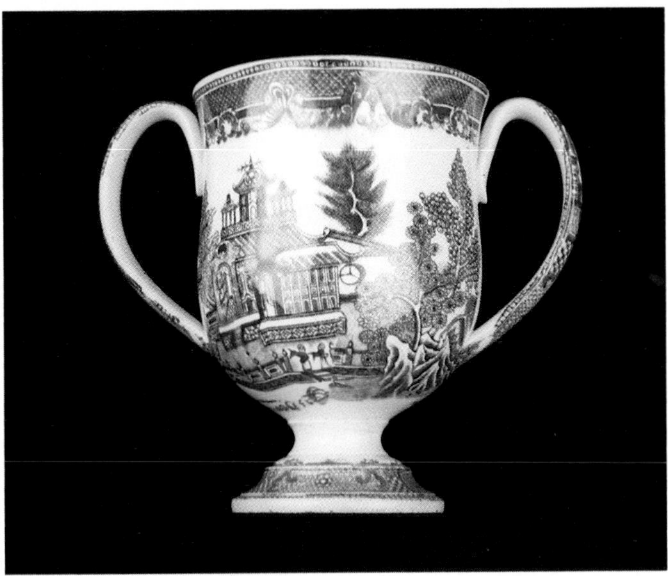

A pearlware loving cup, c. 1800. Unmarked, but initialed S I * E Courtesy of Rita Entmacher Cohen.

Porcelain Hybrids: Bone China and Stone China

While pearlware was dominating the earthenware market, English potters continued improving their porcelains with hybrid formulas. This research and development led to such important products as bone china and stone china.

While animal or fish bone was used at Bow as early as the 1740s, Josiah Spode is reputed to have developed the first actual bone china around 1789, using at least 50% bone ash. The result was a translucent, vitreous, compact body that was stronger than most hard-paste porcelains, with a less brilliant white color. Spode's timing was perfect; in the 1790s, imported Chinese porcelain was burdened with heavy tariffs, reaching over 100% by 1799.[28] After 1815, English porcelains were almost exclusively bone chinas, and "for all practical purposes," wrote Geoffrey Godden, "it can be said that all English tablewares of the post-1815 period are bone china."[29]

Many marks were devised to advertise new types of wares.

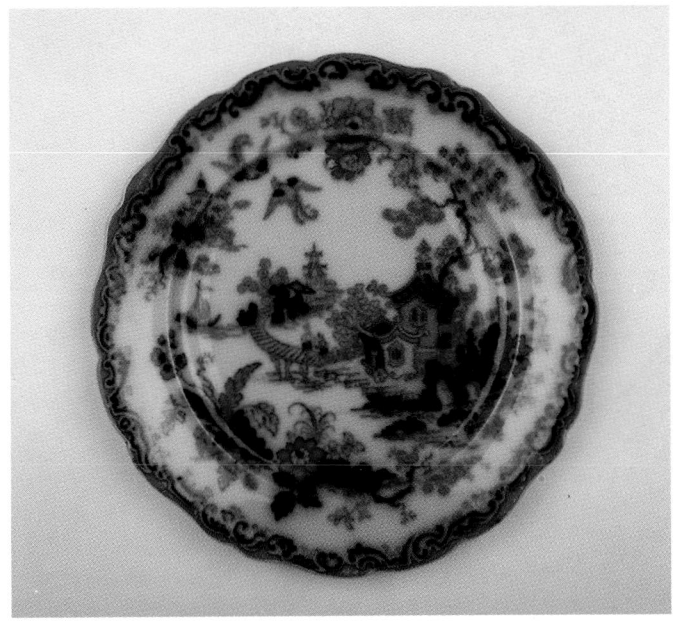

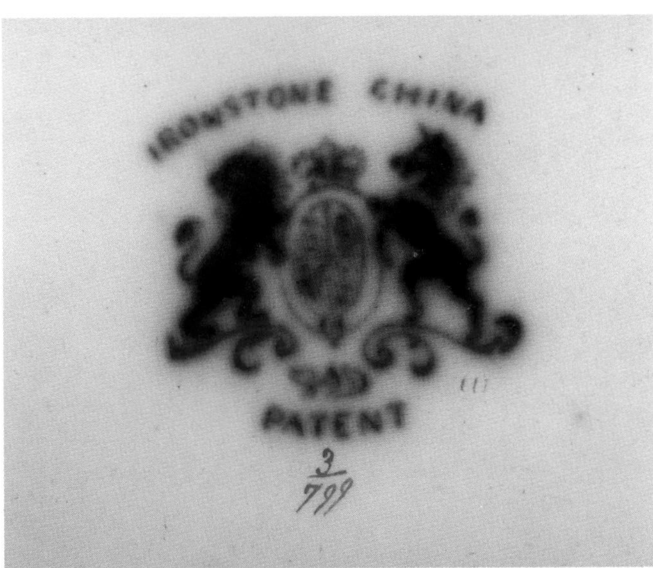

An ironstone polychrome plate with a lion and unicorn crest mark, 10.25" diam. Courtesy of Rita Entmacher Cohen.

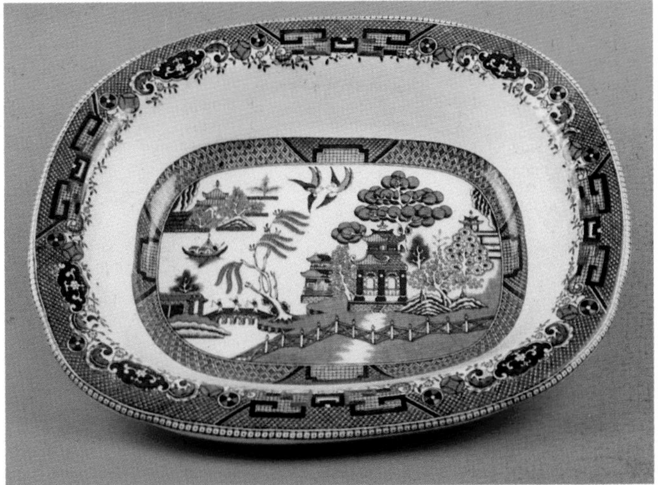

An oblong earthenware serving bowl from the Buffalo Pottery, 1909, 2" high x 11.5" x 9.5". From the collection of Phillip M. Sullivan, South Orleans, MA.

In 1800, John and William Turner of Lane End introduced the first of the stone chinas, a porcelain/stoneware hybrid they called 'Turner's Patent' (Pat. No. 2367).[30] A fine, grayish-white body, stone china was dense and sometimes translucent. The Turners declared bankruptcy in 1806, however, and in 1807 their assets were auctioned off. Josiah Spode II bought the rights to the Turner stone china patent and reintroduced it around 1812-1813.[31] They usually decorated their new 'Spode Stone China' or 'New China' wares with chinoiserie patterns in transfer-printed blue to compete with the "coarse contemporary Chinese export porcelain".[32]

Other stone chinas, particularly that developed by Miles Mason at his Staffordshire pottery in 1804, led to the introduction of yet another hybrid, ironstone. Miles Mason's 1804 stone china was advertised as "more beautiful and more durable than Indian Nanking china, and not so liable to snip at the edges, and more difficult to break." In 1813, a patent (No. 3724) was granted to his son Charles J. Mason for 'Ironstone', so named for its exceptional hardness and clear ring, though it was opaque.[33] The Mason's Ironstone patent alleged that their wares contained an amazing 25% iron slag; this is now considered to be a falsification, since to all appearances the ware is "similar, of not identical" to standard stone china. One difference remains certain, however; most stone china faded in popularity after a peak in the 1820s, but Mason's Ironstone stayed high in public favor until the middle of the century.[34] The term 'ironstone' was used by other makers, but by the 1840s it was being used simply to describe mid- to low-quality earthenwares.[35]

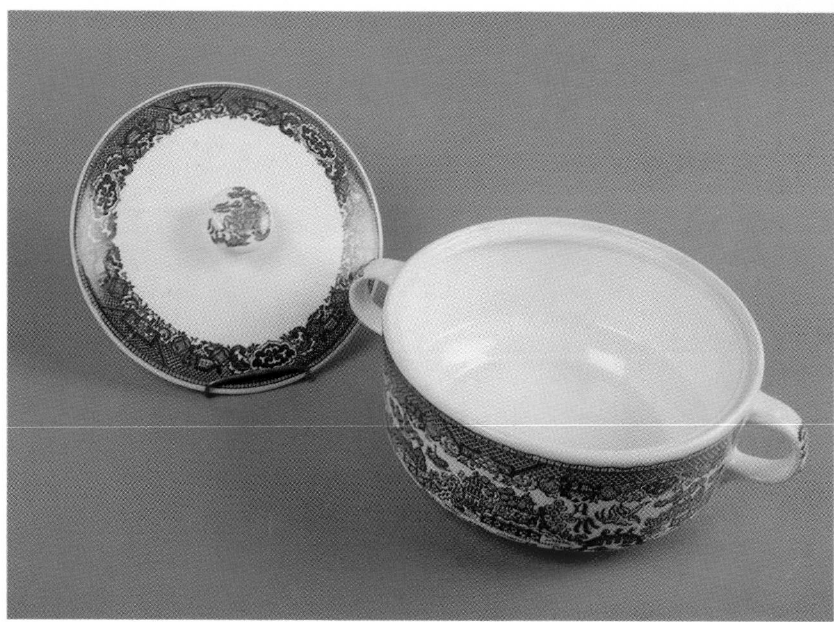

An earthenware covered vegetable server by Royal, 7" diam. (lid). Courtesy of Charles and Louise Loehr, Louise's Old Things, Kutztown PA.

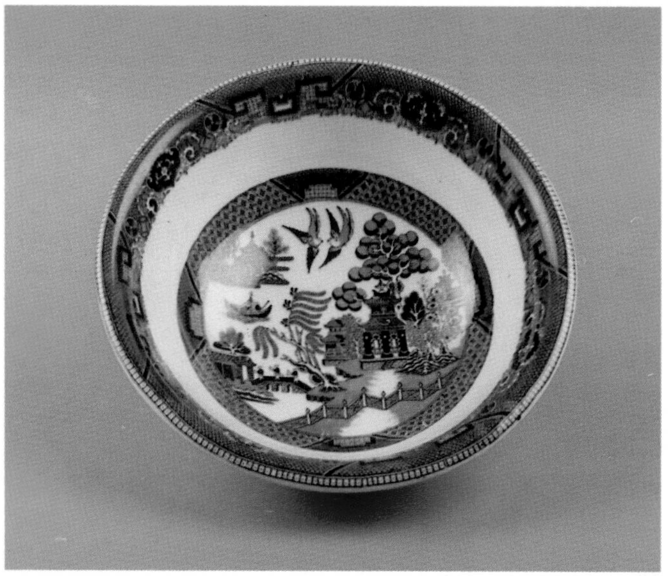

A round china compote bowl from Buffalo China, undated, 3.5" high x 9.5" diam. From the collection of Phillip M. Sullivan, South Orleans, MA.

Whitewares

As English potters became proficient at manufacturing their various porcelain hybrids, the market for pearlware—the earthenware substitute for porcelain—was beginning to fade. By the 1820s-1830s, the new clear-glazed 'whiteware' body was beginning to replace pearlware as the dominant earthenware.[36] Whitewares were widely mass-produced in the late 19th century, and can be identified simply as earthenwares of such light-colored composition that they do not require cobalt-enhanced glazes to give a clear, white impression. Later Willow pieces frequently fall into this category of earthenware.

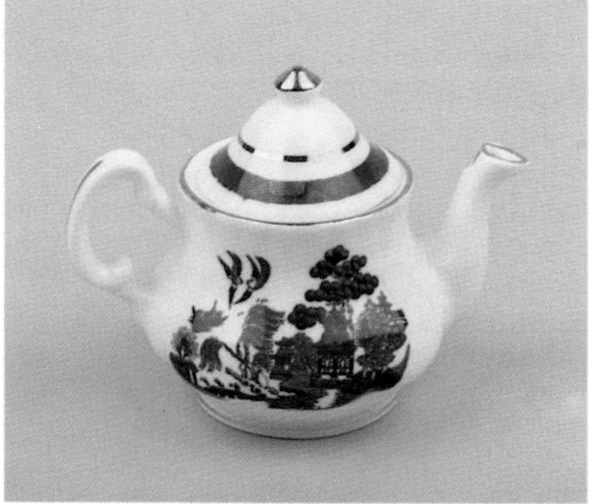

A modern miniature teapot, made by Wren, 3.25" high. Courtesy of Rita Entmacher Cohen.

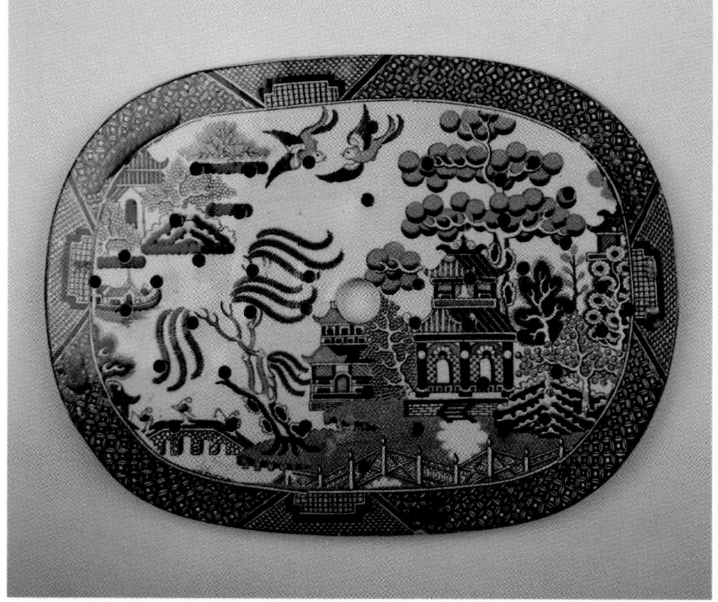

A drainer in Standard Willow, 14.5" wide, from Spode's New Stone line. Courtesy of Rita Entmacher Cohen.

Part II: The Decoration

No matter what ceramic body a pottery chose to use for its Willow, they all took advantage of a mass-production technique that was developed concurrently with pearlware in the mid-1700s—transfer printing. In this method of decoration, paper is used to lift a wet ink print from an engraving, and press it onto a ceramic surface. Transfer printing made it possible for potters to mass-produce tea or dinner sets in matching patterns, a luxury impossible or prohibitively expensive in the days of hand-painted decoration. Though it was invented by the Irish engineer John Brooks, transfer printing has been called England's "principal contribution" to the decoration of porcelain,[37] and it was to prove critical to the development and the popularization of the English Willow pattern.

Engraving

Every transfer-printed design begins with the engraver. The engraver's first step is to draw a paper pattern for the standard 10" dinner plate, from which an engraving is made. Then the design is drawn by hand directly onto other vessel forms—pitchers, teacups, etcetera—whose curves and angles will make distortions of the flat pattern necessary. Paper tracings are then carefully made from these round-surfaced drawings. When viewed on the flat paper, the pattern will appear to be laid out in unusual shapes, but the correct proportions will have been maintained. Until about 1810, only plates, cups, and saucers had specially-drawn and fitted patterns, since they were the biggest sellers; items produced in smaller runs were decorated with cut-outs from a variety of center patterns that had been prepared in different sizes, and border strips of various widths.[38]

The engravings themselves are made on copper plates, using tools called 'gravers' or 'burrins'. These steel instruments have angled tips that make V-shaped trenches, an ideal shape for transfer printing. Acid-etching or engraving with flat tools makes trenches that are flat-bottomed, with corners that are hard to fill with ink (and harder to get ink out of); lines printed from this type of engraving tend to have a ragged look in spots where ink did not completely fill or come out of the trench corners. V-shaped trenches, on the other hand, are easy to fill with ink, and easily print smooth, crisp lines.[39]

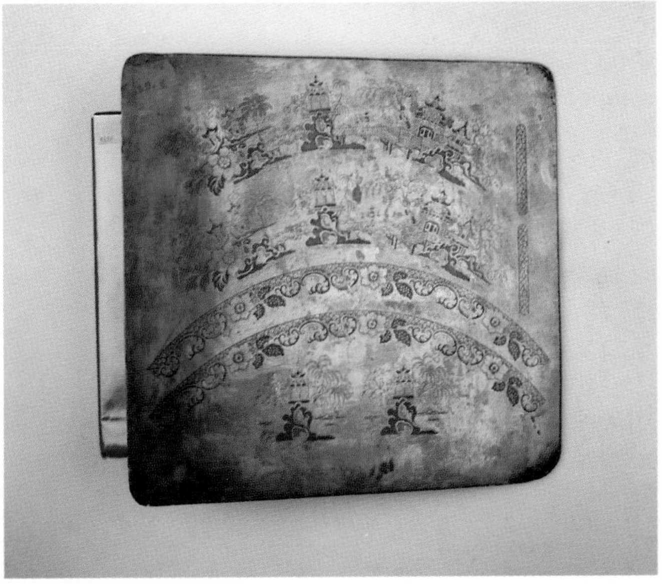

A copper engraving plate showing details of the Willow pattern and border, 12.75" x 13.5". Courtesy of Rita Entmacher Cohen.

An engraved plate for printing the Willow pattern.

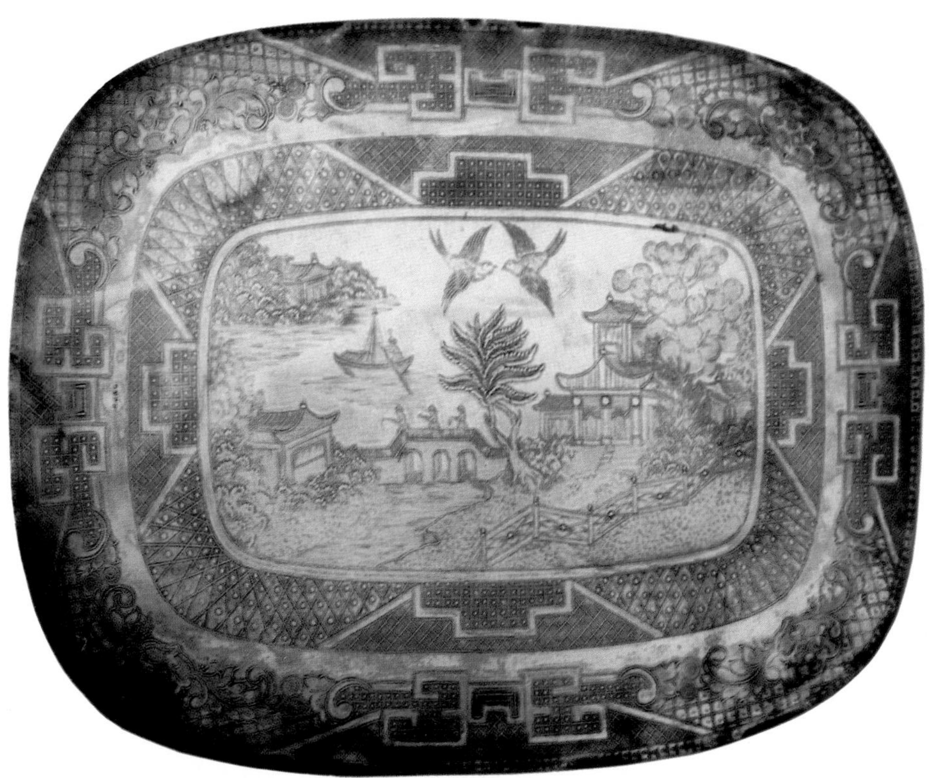

Affectionately known to its owners as 'The Dome', this huge unmarked piece is almost too heavy to lift without help. It is thought that it must have come with a serving tray and a rolling cart. Otherwise, specualtes owner Peter Steelman, the Dome with a tray and a turkey would have required "three men and a boy" to carry it to the dining room. Many different border strips, of varying widths, were used to build up the design on the sides of the dome, which stands 11" high x 22" long x 17" wide, c. 1860. From the collection of Peter and Susan Steelman, Mystic, CT.

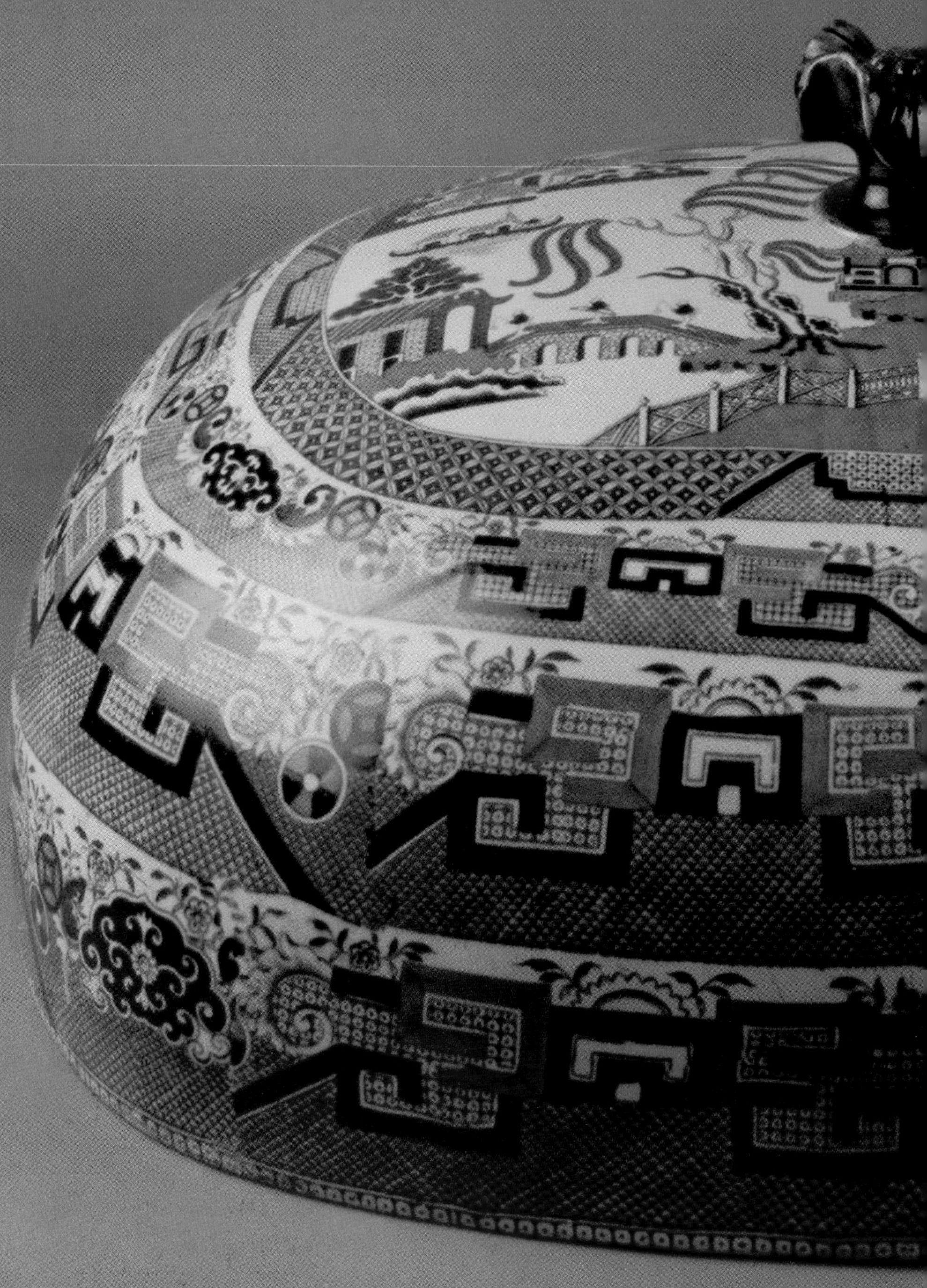

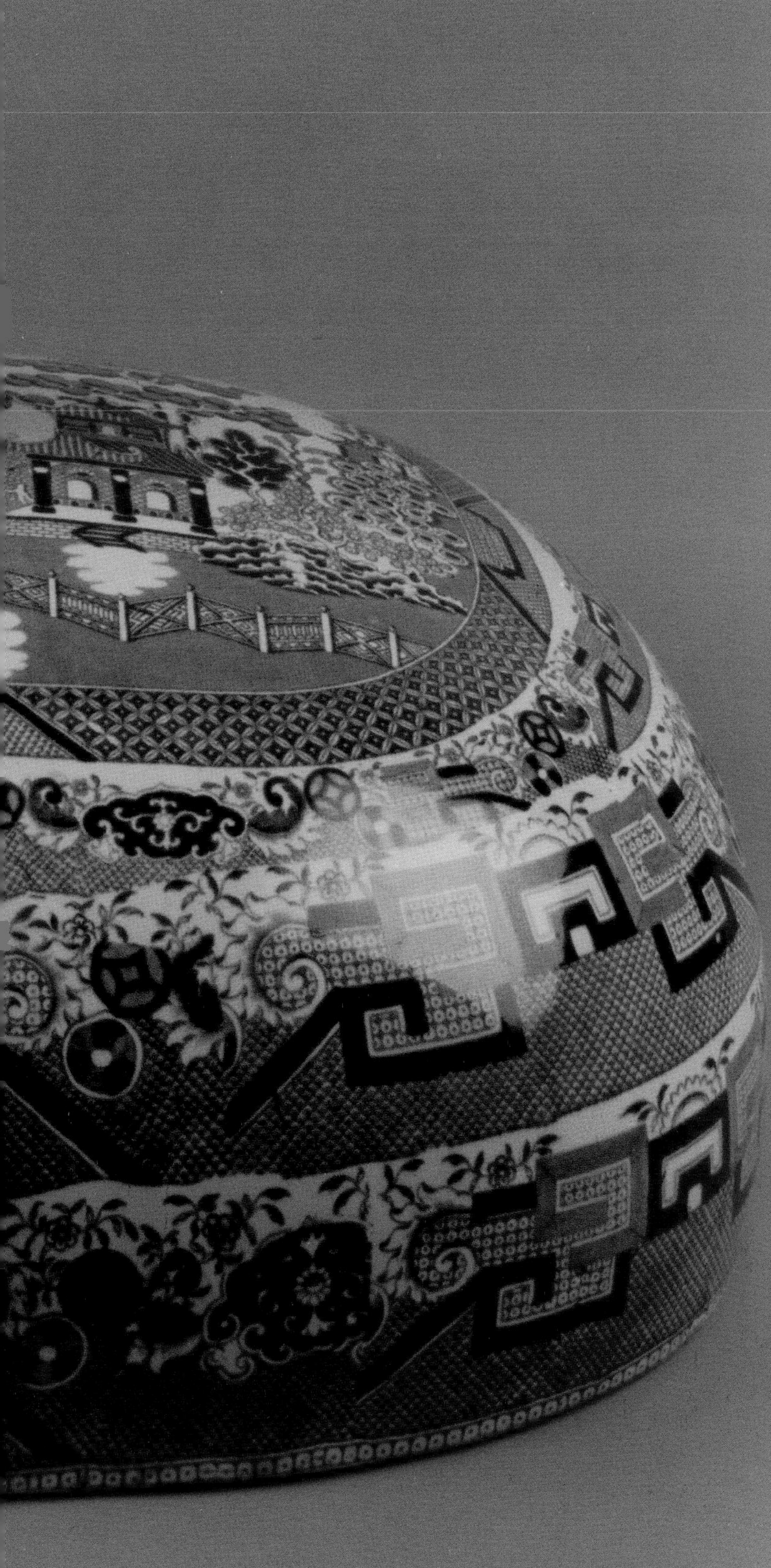

Three cow-shaped cream pitchers, decorated with small scraps cut from the Willow pattern transfer sheets. From the collection of Peter and Susan Steelman, Mystic, CT.

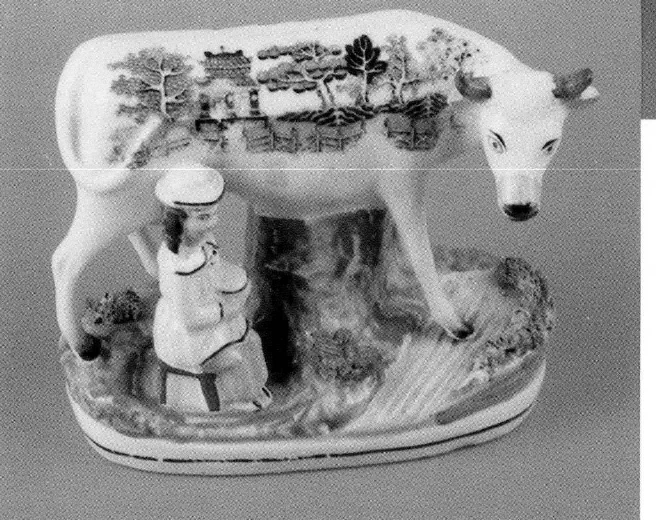

An unmarked figurine with Willow details, 6" x 8". From the collection of Peter and Susan Steelman, Mystic, CT.

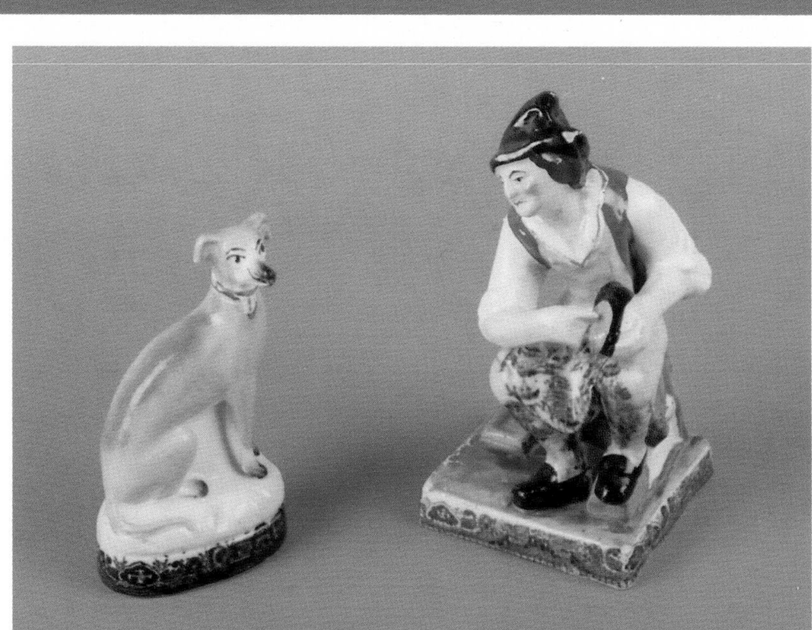

Two unmarked figurines with Willow details; the man is 6.5" high, the dog is 5" high. From the collection of Peter and Susan Steelman, Mystic, CT.

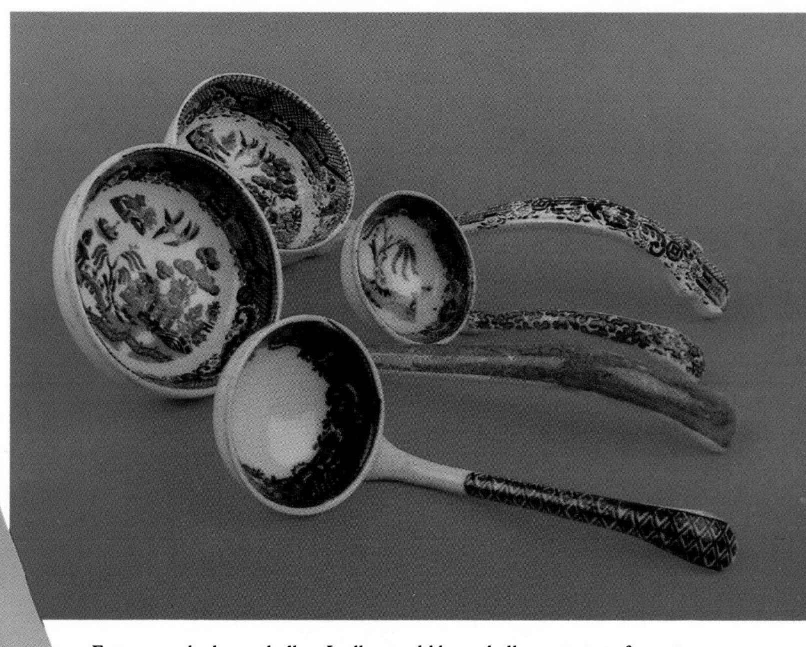

Four unmarked soup ladles. Ladles could be a challenge to transfer-cutters. Courtesy of Rita Entmacher Cohen.

A modern, unmarked ladle with a gold rim. Courtesy of Rita Entmacher Cohen.

The thickness of engraved lines is controlled by hand pressure, making the art of engraving one of great skill and practice.[40] Areas of the engraving that are to be particularly dark can be relined to make the indentations even deeper, after which the 'burr'—bits of leftover metal around the edges of each line—can finally be scaped off. After some samples are printed and fired to make certain the pattern is correct, the copper engraving can be plated with nickel and steel to prevent scratching, and to prolong the life of the plate.[41] When a copper plate is finally retired, it might be 'knocked up'—that is, hammered out to level the engraved face, and then planished until smooth so that a new design could be applied.[42]

Before 1800, blue-printed wares were made from plates engraved solely with line art. After 1800, however, engravers began to use *stippling*—differently-sized dots in varying densities—to give a more shaded, tonal look to the blue-printed pieces. An easy way to date some Willow ware is to look for stippling; if you see dots instead of just lines, you are probably dealing with a piece from after 1800. To do stipple work, engravers struck single etching needles (or several of them bound together) with a hammer to make indentations in the copper, or used a toothed wheel on a handle known as a 'roulette'. They began to achieve great control over contrasting shades and realistic depth, and, as one commentator wrote, "some of their work can only be described as art."[43] The engraving process as used today has changed little since this advance in 1800.

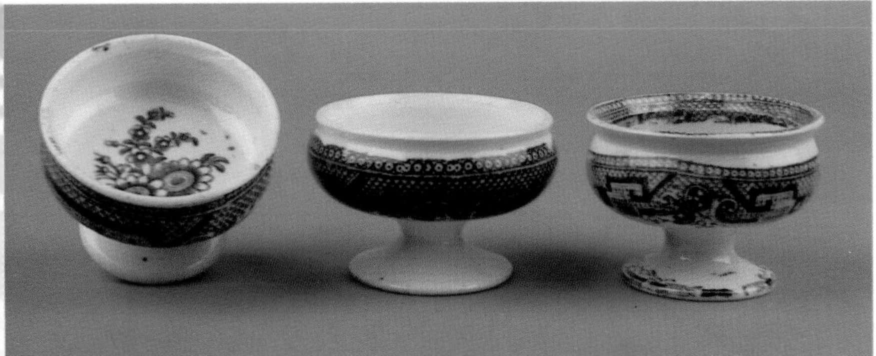

Three open salts, c. 1830, 2" high. Salt on the left has a floral interior. Floral on left, Courtesy of Rita Entmacher Cohen.

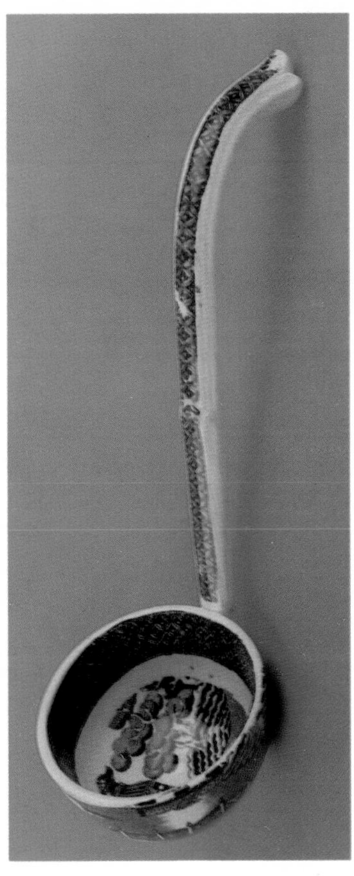

A large ladle with both interior and exterior decoration, 12". Courtesy of Rita Entmacher Cohen.

Notice the limited detail available with line engraving techniques alone.

A close-up of a basket stand, c. 1790, showing the meticulous detail that could be achieved when stippling and crosshatching are added.

As engravers grew more proficient at their craft, they drew business away from the hand-painters, and the demand for engraving services increased dramatically among the potteries. Josiah Wedgwood I's decorators and hand-painters (artisans who were paid more than common transferrers were)[44] began to worry about their jobs, and demanded a promise from him that he would not join the transfer-printing trend. He complied; "I give you my word as a man," he told them, "that I have not made, neither will I make, any Blue Printed Earthenwares."[45] He kept this promise. Not until after his death in 1795 did the Wedgwood factory begin making the blue transfer-printed dinnerwares that were dominating the market, finally entering the extremely lucrative transfer market. Despite the rare hold-outs like Wedgwood, by 1818 there were sixteen engraving establishments mentioned in the Staffordshire area's directory alone, and a decade later there were twenty-eight.[46]

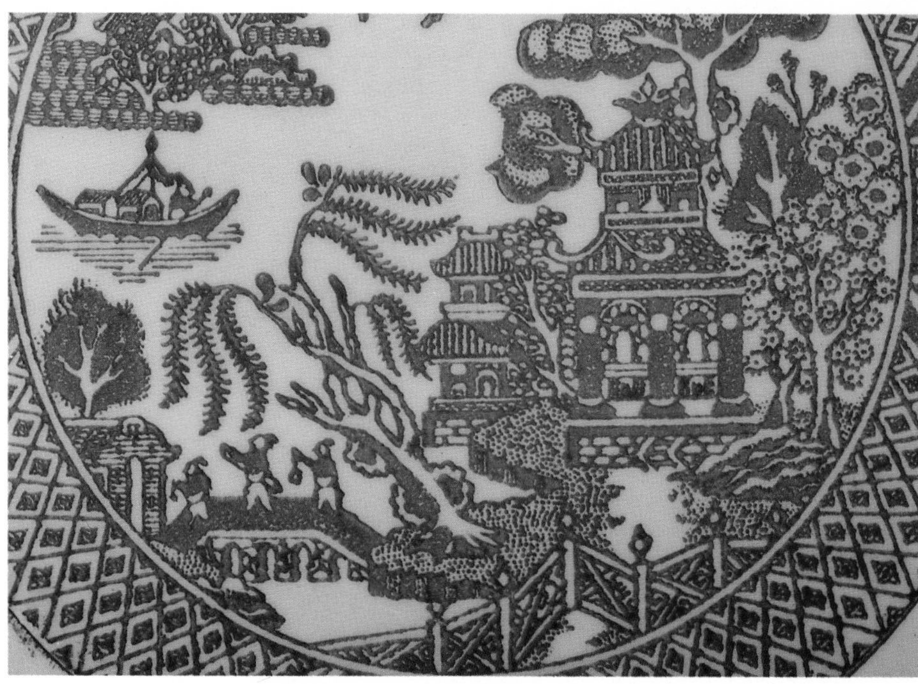

A modern plate; somehow, technological advances have not added more detail to printed wares.

Cobalt Blue

When an engraved copper plate is ready to be used, it is filled with a liquid ink composed of a vibrantly-colored pigment stain and a gummy substance called 'flux', which bonds the color to the ceramic body. The pigment cobaltous oxide (CoO) was found to remain stable even over 800 degrees Celcius, unlike most other pigments, and it quickly became England's most popular (and least expensive) transfer-print color.[47] "It is fortunate," wrote Geoffrey Godden, "that the easiest colour to print with under the glaze is cobalt blue," considering the demand established by Chinese hand-painted wares for the blue and white color scheme. However, cobalt's history in the decorative arts had already spanned several millenia and several continents before making its first appearance on an English transfer-printed plate.

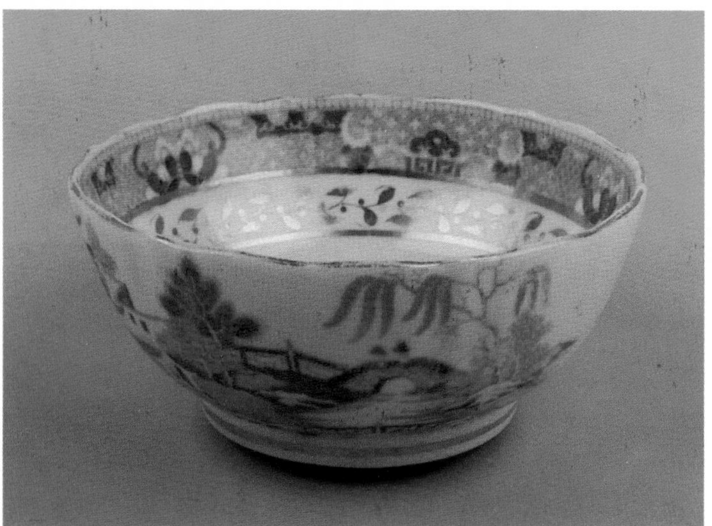

A light blue bowl with gold garland and two borders, c. 1805. As English potters became more experienced with cobalt pigments, they were able to achieve subtle gradations of blue. Courtesy of Rita Entmacher Cohen.

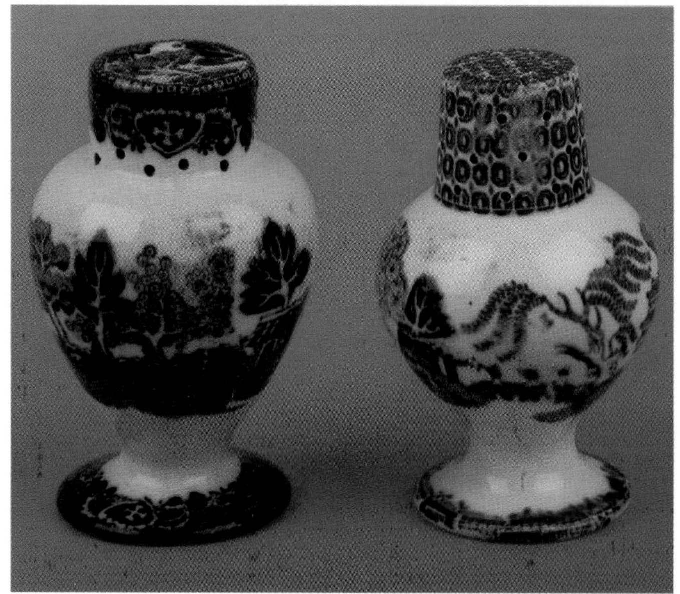

Two pepper pots, with a gold garland over a dark blue rim band. Unmarked. The saucer measures 5.25" diam. Courtesy of Rita Entmacher Cohen.

While Far Eastern pottery made cobalt famous in Europe, its first use must be credited to the Near East. As early as 2680 B.C., cobalt was used to dye the hair on Egyptian statues, and glass beads colored with cobalt have been found in Iran dating back to 2250 B.C.. Cobalt was used in ceramic glazes in Ethiopia, Mycenae, and Tiryns as early as 1200 B.C., long before Muslim merchants began trade caravans to carry the pigment to T'ang dynasty potters in China (A.D. 618-907).[48] Chinese writings indicate that the Far East had no native sources for a pure cobalt blue, so early Chinese potters relied on trade with the Near East for the cobalt ores they called *Su-Ma-ni, Su-ni-po,* and *hui hui ching*—'Mohammedan blue'.[49] Records have been found which specifically mention envoys from Persia arriving with the pigment in 1426, 1430, 1433, and 1434.[50]

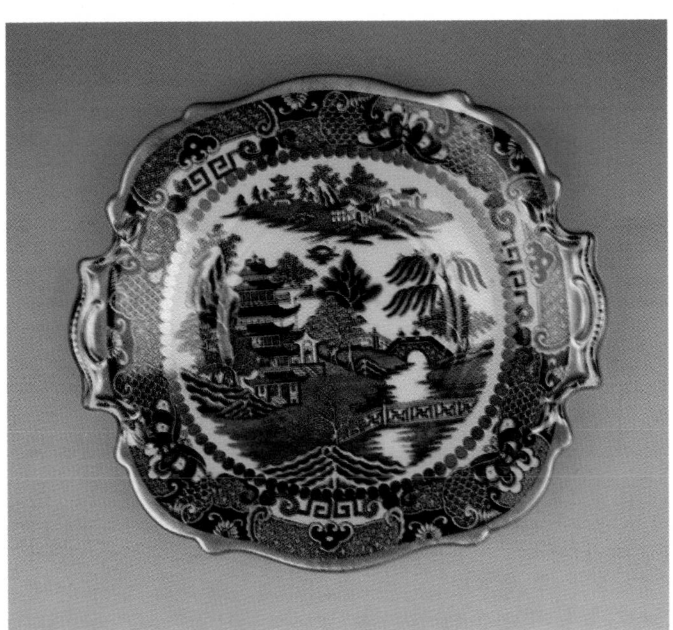

A pearlware dish with two handles, in yet another shade of blue, 10.5" diam. Unmarked. Courtesy of Rita Entmacher Cohen.

During the Ming dynasty several hundred years later, Chinese potters developed methods of removing manganese impurities from ore, and were thus able to extract high-quality cobalt with excellent color from their own local deposits. A Western visitor, T. I. Bowleder, observed the Chinese process in the late 1800s, and wrote in astonishment of the simple methods used by "these ingenious and very peculiar people" to remove iron, nickel, and manganese from the crude cobalt ore.[51]

In 1888, when Bowleder's description was published in *Chemical News* magazine, the English had right to be surprised at any simple, centuries-old method that succeeded in purifying cobalt ore; they had just spent a great deal of time, money, and the best modern technology to discover methods for purifying their own local ore. In 1545 the Germans had discovered a cobalt source in Saxony, and while the best of the Saxon ore was reserved for Meissen, a state pottery, much of the rest was exported to other European countries that had no good local sources of their own, including England.[52] In 1748, England alone imported almost 180,000 pounds of cobalt smalt (cobalt reduced into a glass-like form, easily ground up into a powder pigment), and in 1754, they brought in more than 286,000 pounds.[53] When Saxony became entangled in the Napoleonic Wars between 1756 and 1763, England had to resort to its own sources—but between the lower grade of ore available locally and the inexperienced local processors, the final cobalt product left much to be desired. It varied unpredictably between shades of navy blue, indigo, purple, and violet, making the manufacture of matched sets impossible. When England's Society for the Encouragement of the Arts offered a reward for raw cobalt specimens found in the U.K. in 1764, one Nicholas Crisp took the prize with ore he found in a mine in Cornwall.[54] Then the Society began offering a prize to anyone who could convert this native cobalt ore into five pounds of zaffre (reduced, purified ore) or fifteen pounds of smalt, but the results were so bad that they were forced to lower their demands to a mere one pound of either.[55]

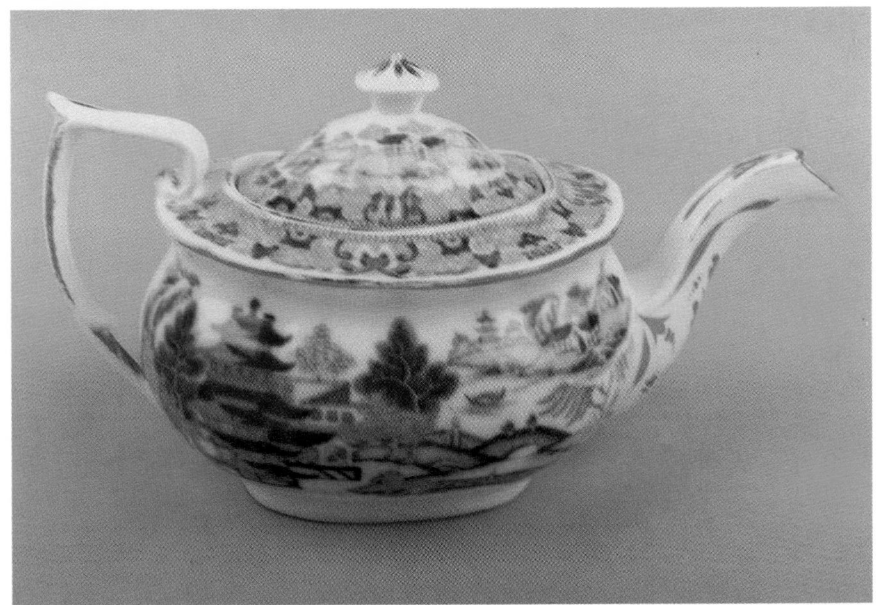

A teapot with gold details by Grainger Worcester, 6" x 11". Marked. Courtesy of Rita Entmacher Cohen.

By 1770, English potters gave up on the domestic products, and began purchasing from Prussians who had confiscated Saxon stores. English refineries kept trying, but only a few mines produced cobalt in any quantity, and several others made less than a ton apiece. Making matters even more difficult, it was found that cobalt frequently occurs in a compound with arsenic, which injured the hands and feet of cobalt miners and could also damage their eyes and lungs.[56] Not until 1820 was an English product—from Copeland—available to match the quality of the Saxon cobalt. Even then, potters seeking the highest-quality cobalt used smalt imported from Scandanavia.[57]

But no matter what its country of origin, cobalt was well-received and well-used by English potters. Years of experience mixing cobaltous oxide with varying formulas of silica (ground quartz), aluminum, and other metallic oxides made them master artisans, connoiseurs of blue. Eventually the potters learned to produce Willow in any shade of blue that could possibly be desired, from the palest periwinkle tint to the deepest midnight blue.

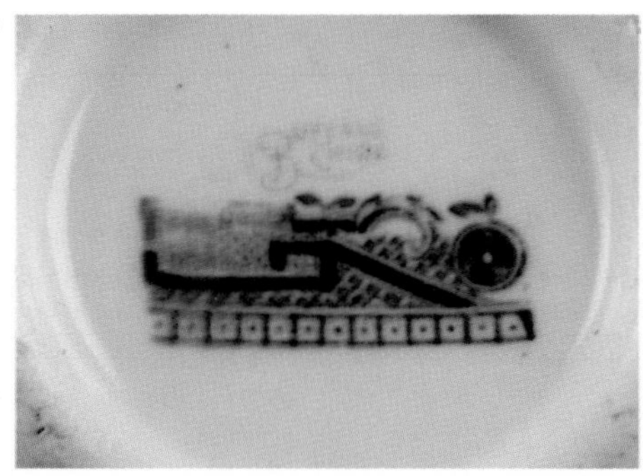

An undated footed bowl from Buffalo China, featuring an unusual mark printed from a scrap of border-pattern. The bowl is 3" high x 6.5" diam. From the collection of Phillip M. Sullivan, South Orleans, MA.

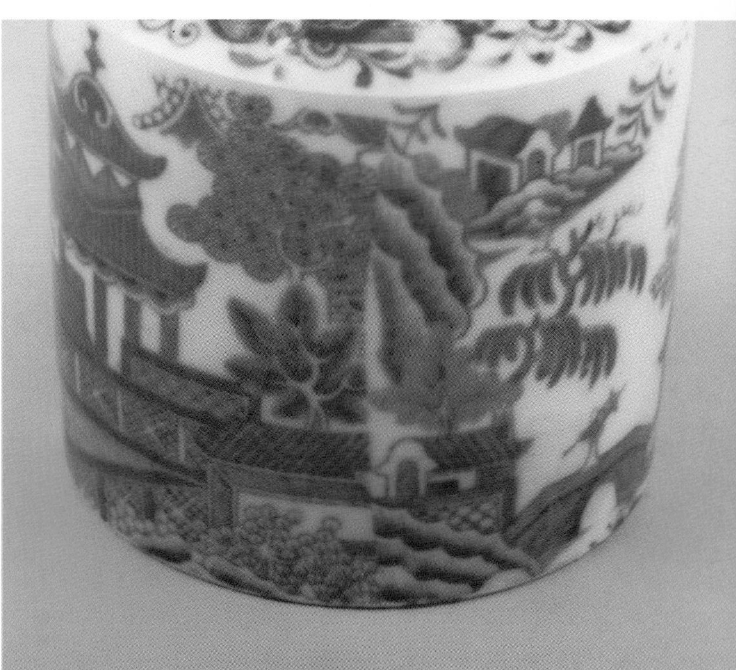

Mismatched transfer-printed lines.

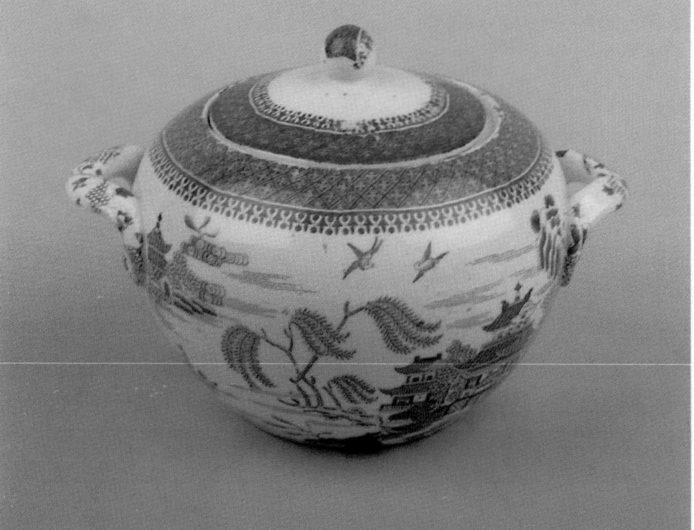

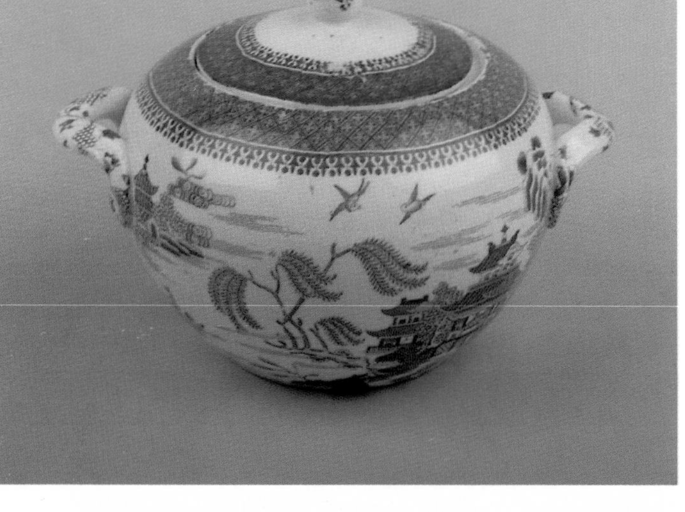

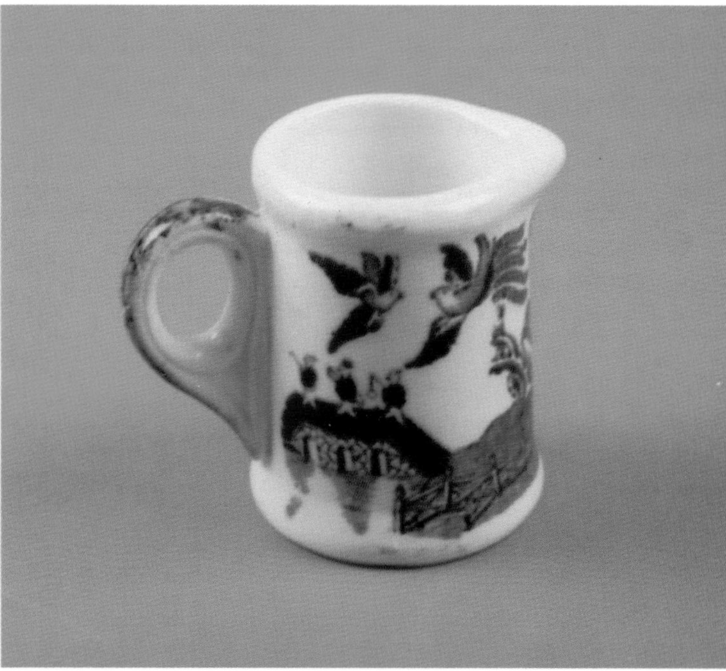

An individual creamer by Buffalo, possibly from 1916 (the mark is blurred), 2.25" high. From the collection of Phillip M. Sullivan, South Orleans, MA.

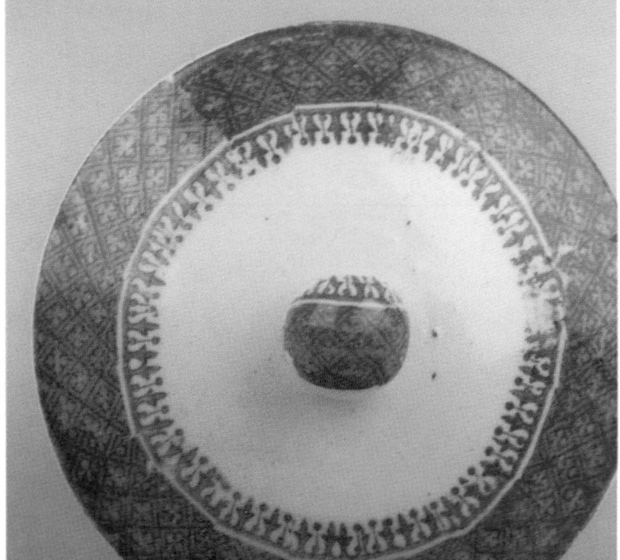

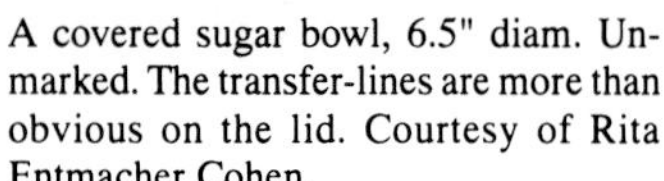

A covered sugar bowl, 6.5" diam. Unmarked. The transfer-lines are more than obvious on the lid. Courtesy of Rita Entmacher Cohen.

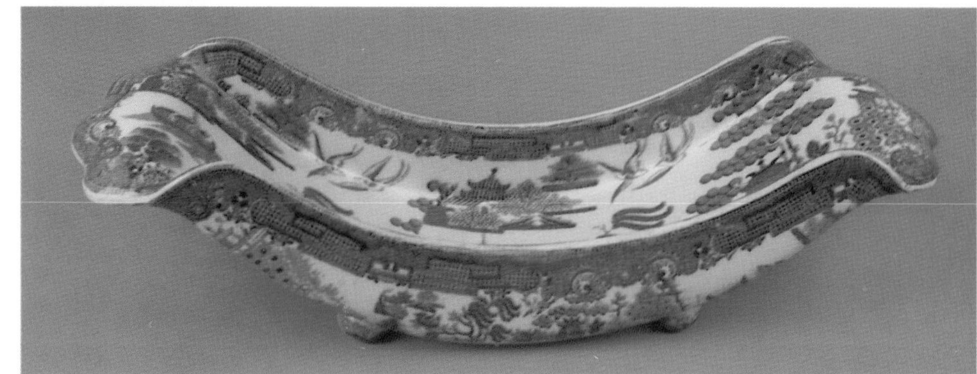

A cheese wheel, 4.25" x 17". Such an intricate shape must have been a challenge for the transferrers. From the collection of Peter and Susan Steelman, Mystic, CT.

Transfer Printing

Of all transfer subjects the Willow pattern has been used the most. It is popular indeed, but, it is likely that the chief reason for its wide use is the fact that almost the entire design consists of straight lines which are much easier to engrave than those required to show a beautiful panorama, a secluded country estate or a national shrine.[58]

Sometimes transfer-printed color smudged or flowed, distorting the details of the original engraving.

When the engraved plate, the unglazed ceramic bodies, and the cobalt ink have been prepared, it is time to apply the pattern to individual ceramic pieces.

The copper plate is warmed on a stove, so that when the ink is spread over it, the pigment will stay fluid on the surface. After the ink is worked into all the crevices, lines, and stipple-dots with a tool called a 'dabber', the excess is removed first with a wooden or metal scraper, and then with a soft corduroy 'boss'. Then a sheet of tissue paper (wet down with a soft, soapy water solution called 'size' to make it easier to work with) is laid down smoothly on top of the inked copper plate. The tissue-covered plate is run through a roller press, which forces the tissue paper to pick up the color from both the deepest engraved trenches and the lightest scratches. Then the paper can be peeled off of the plate, and it is placed face-up while a 'cutter'—usually a young girl—trims away excess paper.

The most delicate of jobs belongs to the actual 'transferrer', who must place the different pieces of inked tissue paper onto the ceramic body, in precise position. In long strips of borders or large center patterns, you can frequently see the matched (or mismatched) lines, where different pieces of tissue paper were laid adjacently. (Flow Blue wares developed as an ingenious way to obscure the tell-tale signs of tissue paper transfer seams.)[59] Once all the papers are properly laid (including the mark on the back), the transferrer rubs them down gently with a felt pad, to set the ink in position. Once that is secure, a stiff brush is used to rub the color down firmly, pressing the color evenly into the porous earthenware. The paper can then be removed in a cold-water wash, and the print is fixed by a low-temperature (680-750 degrees Celcius) firing in a muffle oven. This firing bonds the pigment to the biscuit, and burns off the oils. Once the transfer is complete, the piece can be clear-glazed, and submitted to the final firing.[60]

Glazing and Firing

Clear glazing over transfer-printed blue wares was generally accomplished using a process Enoch Wood had introduced around 1740. The muffle-fired, printed biscuit was dipped into a liquid solution, a suspension of finely-ground glass-forming ingredients. The exact formula of the glaze determined the brilliance of the finished piece, but potters had to undertake a great deal of experimentation to arrive at a viable solution. In general, the more brilliant the glaze, the more likely it was to dissolve some of the cobalt color, making the underglaze design fuzzy and indistinct. It is very rare, writes Robert Copeland, "to find underglaze patterns in cobalt silicate without *any* blurring in the lines and dots, since the intensity of cobalt color shows any hazy edges clearly.[61]

Once they were properly dipped in a suitably brilliant *and* stable glaze, the pieces were stacked in 'saggars' to be placed in the kiln. 'Saggars' are cylindrical drums in which the pieces were carefully arranged to make mass-firings more efficient, while also protecting them from direct contact with the flames of the kiln.[62] Wares were stacked in the saggars in a variety of ways; depending on the quality of the ware, potters went to different lengths in arranging them to minimize the marks left on the faces or backs of the finished pieces.

Pieces made of the best bone china were generally molded with foot-rims on the underside; these allowed them to be stacked in an elaborate set-up of cranks and pins which left only three small unglazed spots on the foot rim (see Figure 1).

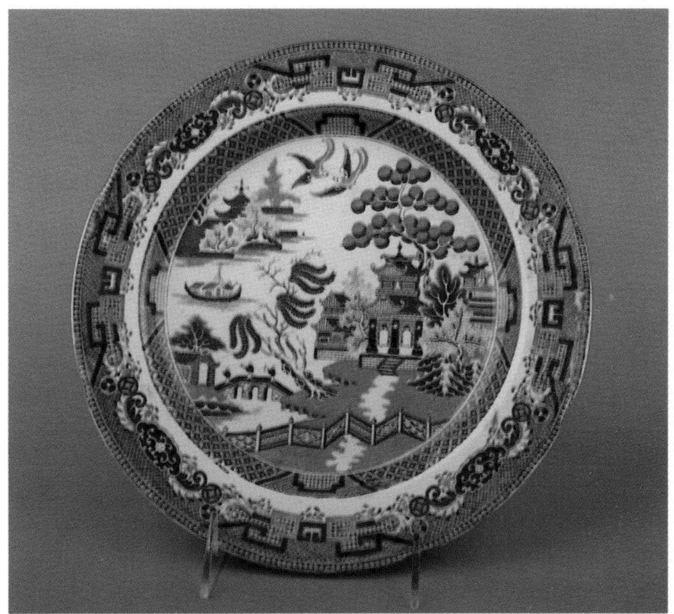

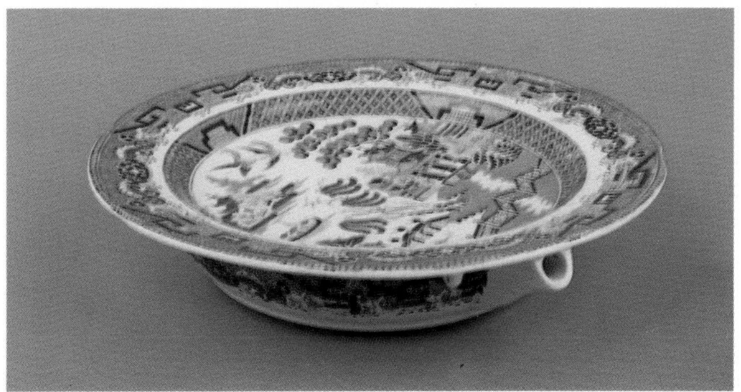

Pearlware hot water plate, 9.875". Unmarked. Courtesy of Rita Entmacher Cohen.

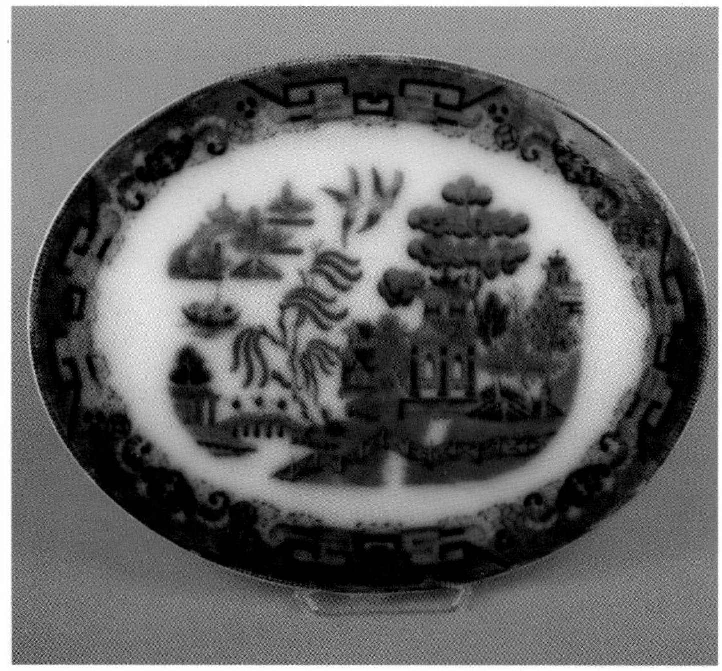

A large, rimless flow blue Willow cheese board by Doulton, 17" x 13". From the collection of Peter and Susan Steelman, Mystic, CT.

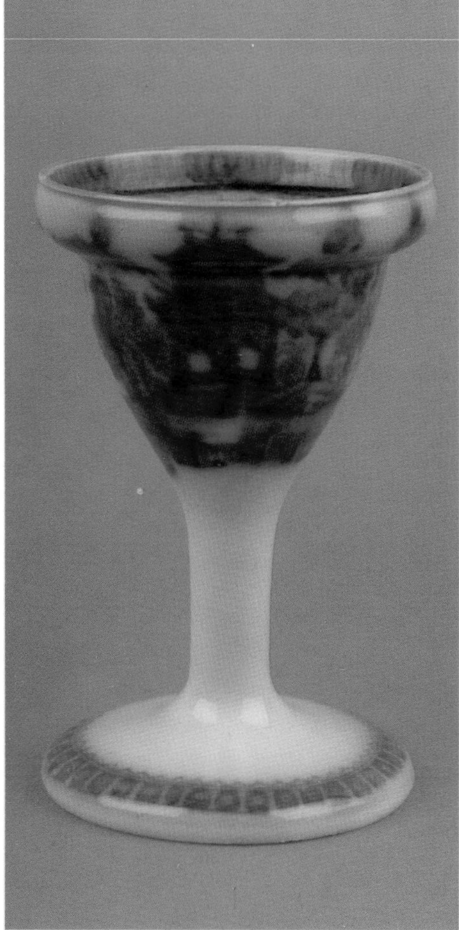

A footed pearlware cup, c. 1800, 3.75". Courtesy of Rita Entmacher Cohen.

Pieces made of the best bone china were generally molded with foot-rims on the underside; these allowed them to be stacked in an elaborate set-up of cranks and pins which left only three small unglazed spots on the foot rim (see Figure 1).

Figure 1

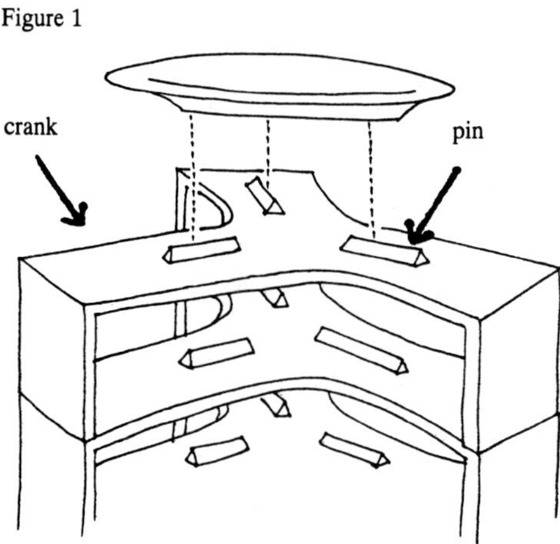

Plates of the best-quality earthenware were stood on edge, supported by two pins on the bottom and a 'thimble' at the top, which left two small spots along the edge of the rim with little or no glaze on them, and a single mark on the back of the rim, with the pattern tending to drip downward a little (see Figure 2).

Figure 2

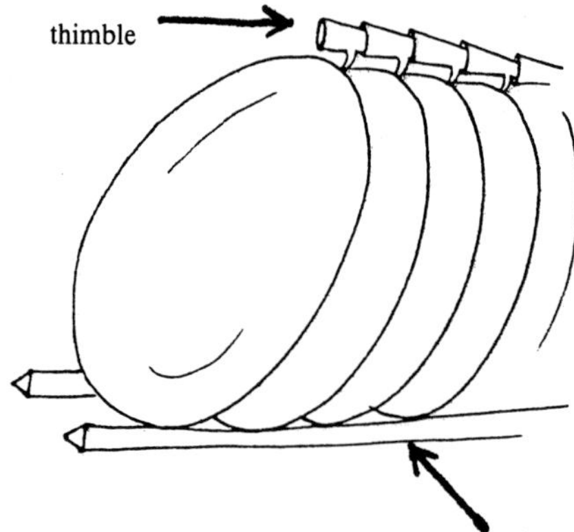

Medium quality earthenware plates were arranged in such a way that there were three marks on the back of each, leaving the face unmarked. Three vertical columns of 'thimbles' were used to support them; a small spur projected from each of the thimbles, on which the plates were rested, face-up, to make a kind of 'floating stack' (see Figure 3).

Figure 3

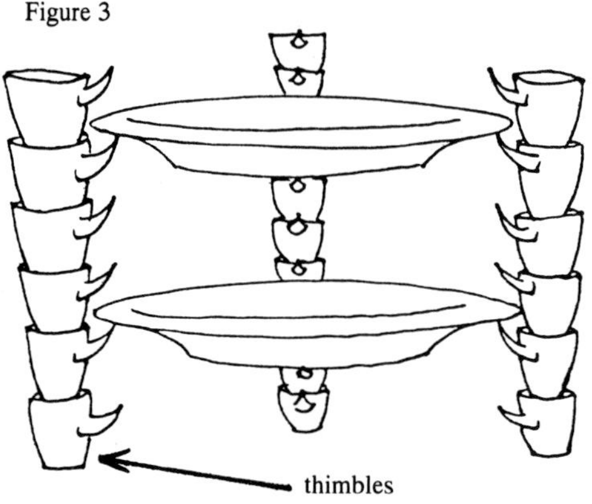

Plates of the lowest grade of earthenware were arranged face-down in stacks, balanced on sets of (usually three) separating spurs. Each spur had three or four pointed feet, and one additional point projecting upward. The three or four feet were rested on the back of the lower plate, and the face of the next plate was rested on the single projecting points of the spurs. Thus these lower-quality plates have three sets of three or four dots each along the the back of the rim, and three single marks on the front of the rim (see Figure 4).

Figure 4

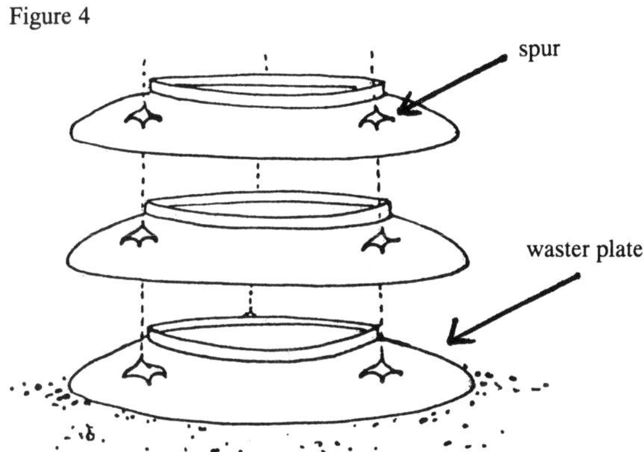

In general, bowls were fired on their feet. Sometimes, to save space, cheap bowls were stacked one inside the other, leaving ugly marks inside the bowl. Large bowls were placed upside-down in a 'dump', which suported them along the rims, one above another, with a small separating space. Cups and other small hollow forms were fired on their feet on saggar shelves (see Figures 5 and 6).

Figure 5

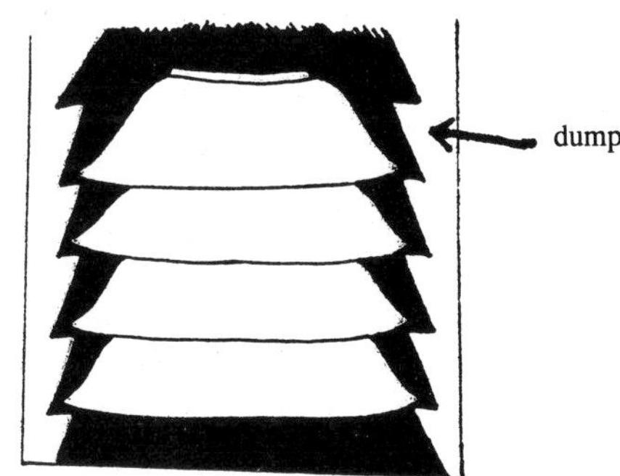

Figure 6

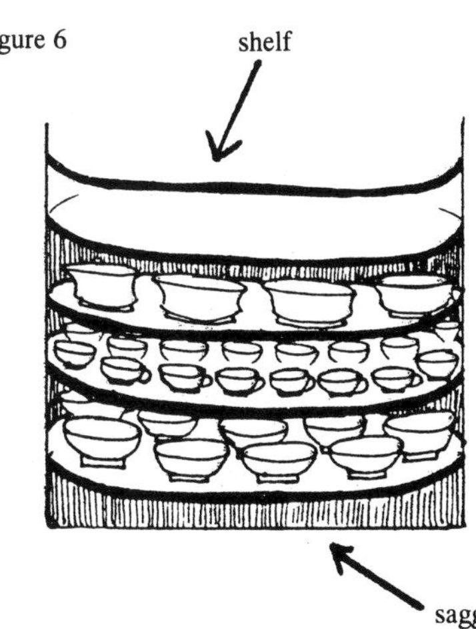

Once the glaze-dipped pieces were appropriately arranged in the saggar, they were re-fired in a 'glost' oven, at approximately 1060-1100 degrees Celcius for earthenware or bone china, and 1350-1400 degrees Celcius for porcelains.[63]

After all the glost-fired pieces were removed from the kiln, they were checked for quality. Only then could the workmen tally up the number of 'good from the oven' pieces for which they were to be paid, by using the workmen's marks they had painted or stamped onto the backs of the pieces.[64] The pieces were then ready for the market.

The Role of Transfer Printing

Clearly, transfer printing was far from a simple process, but it was well worth the effort for potters who wished to keep pace—affordably—with the ever-increasing market for high-quality decorative wares in large quantity. Hand-painted wares had dominated the high end of the blue-and-white market ever since the first Chinese exports reached British shores, but even at the end these were priced beyond the means of most consumers. 'Bat printing', transfer printing's predecessor, was technically suitable only for expensive china, thus pricing it out of the common market as well. Not until the development and perfection of the transfer printing technique was there a suitable method for supplying the middle and professional classes with standardized decorative earthenwares, and the potteries were quick to take full advantage.

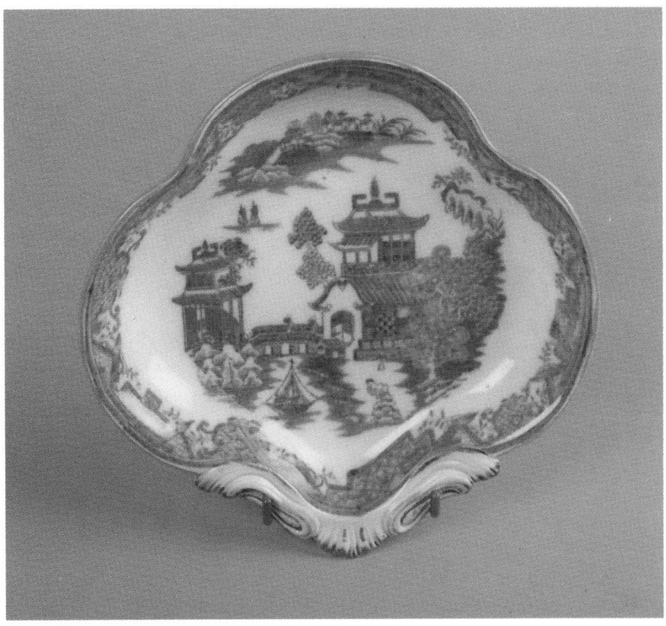

A tri-part pearlware candy dish, unattributed, 8". Courtesy of Charles and Louise Loehr, Louise's Old Things, Kutztown PA.

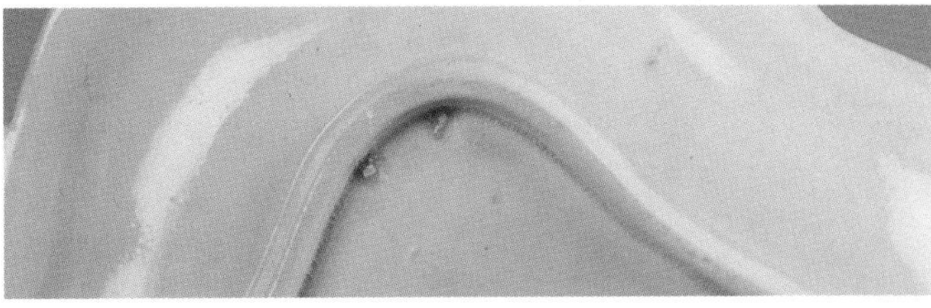

Stilt marks on the reverse of the candy dish. This was probably perched on four-pointed spurs during its firing.

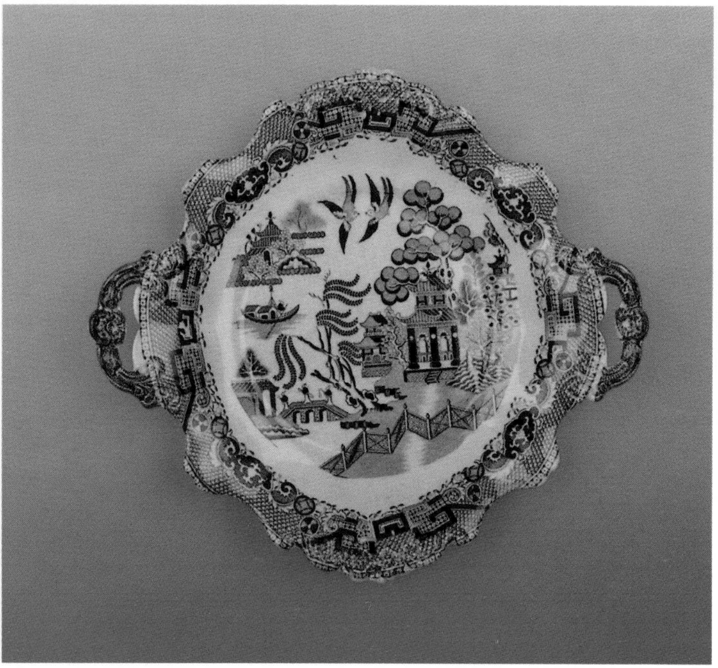

A pearlware dish with two handles, 10.5" diam. Unmarked. Courtesy of Rita Entmacher Cohen.

The transfer-printing revolution was typical of the many changes taking place during this era of technical development. While a greater number of laborers were needed to decorate a single piece of transfer-printed earthenware (bat printing and hand-painting required just a single artisan), transfer printers moved faster, produced more, and were less costly employees. "In short," writes Robert Copeland, "bat printing was a craft process, while transfer printing was an industrial one."[65] Once the copper plates were engraved, there were no limits to the quantity of merchandise a potter could sell. "The potter could decorate in a competent manner a vast array of wares," explains Geoffrey Godden, "using only semi-skilled labour and certainly without the expense of employing trained artists."[66] The process was introduced during the 1750s, and in 1756, the year of their patent, the Sadler & Green pottery in Liverpool testified in an affidavit that they had printed over twelve hundred tiles in less than six hours.[67]

The importance of transfer printing to the pottery industry increased throughout the century, taking a giant leap with the invention of the Fourdrinier paper machine, which made a paper better suited for transfering finer work, including stipple engraving.[68] In 1776, Caughley produced the first truly high-quality, sharp transfer-printed image in underglaze blue,[69] and in 1780 Thomas Turner of Caughley made the first underglaze blue transfer prints on earthenware, in Shropshire. By the end of the 18th century, potters in Staffordshire, Lancashire, Yorkshire, and South Wales were busy making enormous quantities of similar earthenwares with this new, efficient, and extremely effective technique.[70] Though the decoration of the finest china and the most humble crockery continued to depend on painting (either on a wholly artistic level or an utterly slap-dash one), by the beginning of the 19th century, underglaze transfer printing had almost completely eliminated the use of hand-painting on mass-market ceramics of a middle grade.[71]

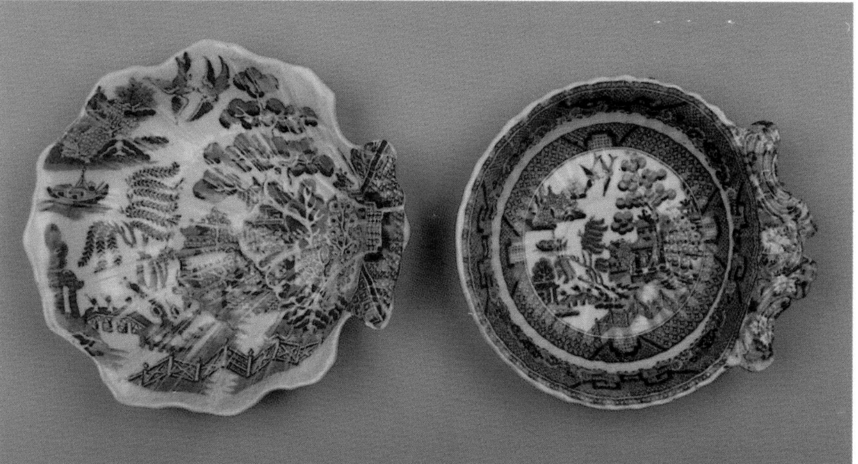

Two shell-shaped pearlware dishes, 1825, 6". Courtesy of Rita Entmacher Cohen.

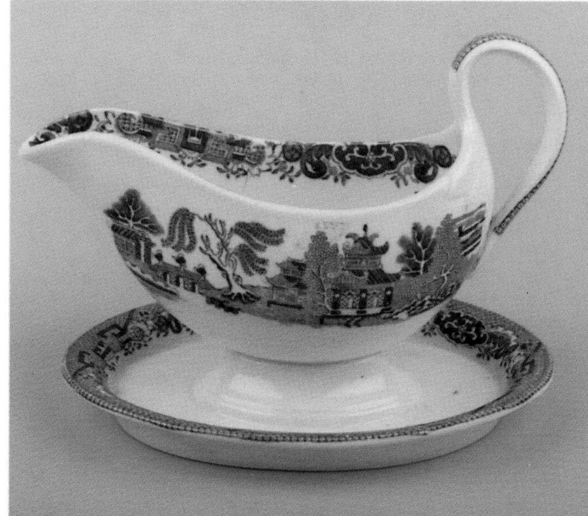

A pearlware sauce boat with an attached tray, c. 1840, 8" wide. Unmarked. Courtesy of Rita Entmacher Cohen.

Five leaf-shaped pickle dishes with pearlware bodies, approximately 5.5" wide. All are unmarked. Courtesy of Rita Entmacher Cohen.

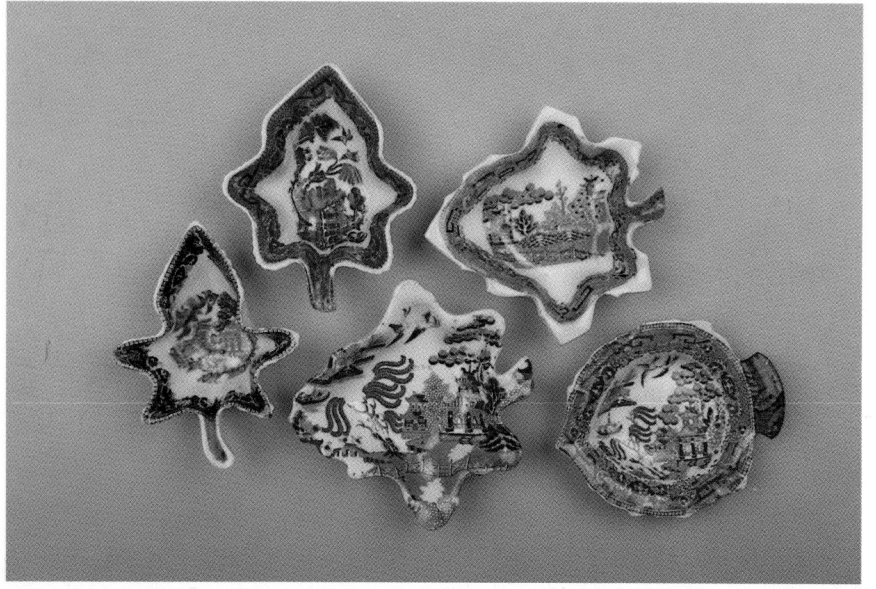

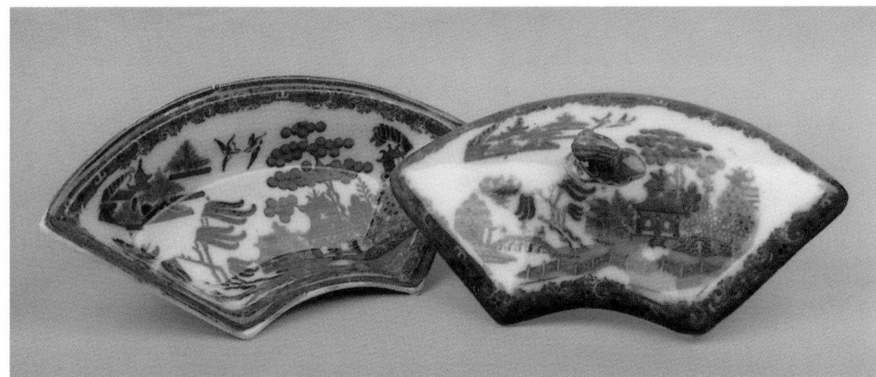

A covered pearlware serving dish, c. 1800, 12" wide, part of a sectional serving set. This piece in unmarked, but may be Spode's 'Willow I' design. Courtesy of Rita Entmacher Cohen.

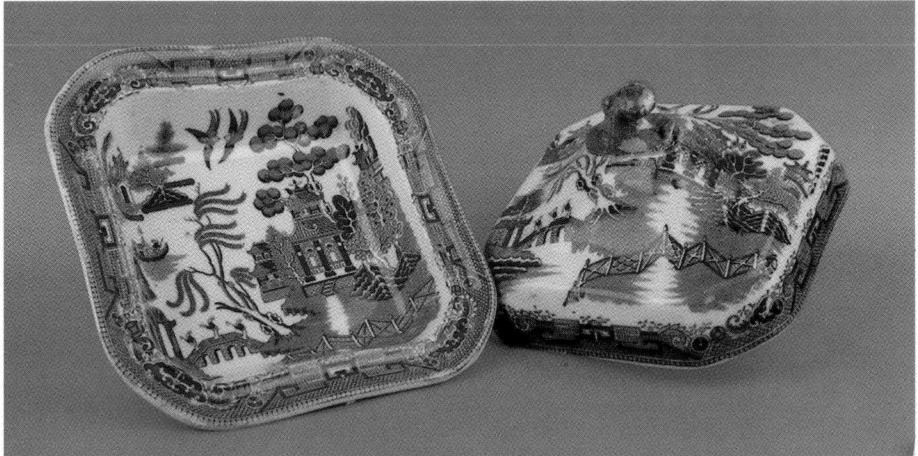

A covered square dish in pearlware, 9". Courtesy of Rita Entmacher Cohen.

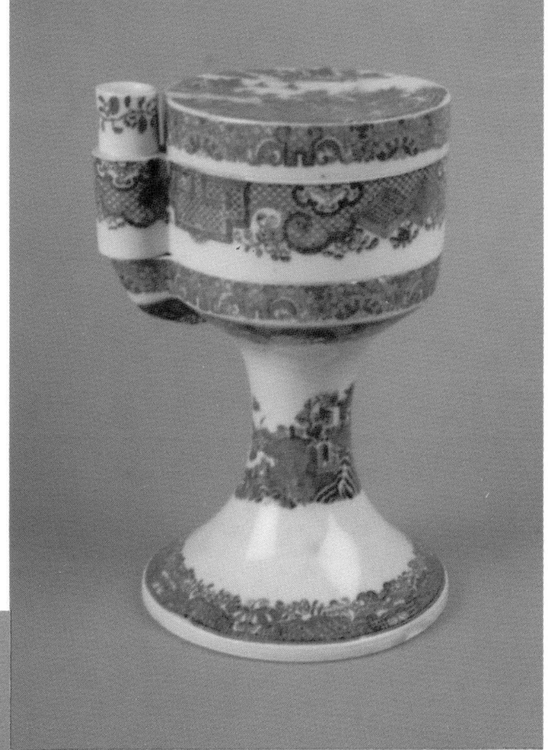

The best guess is that this unmarked pearlware piece is an inhaler. After steaming water was poured into the base, medicinal herbs or powders put into pierced-bottom middle tray, and the lid replaced, the ailing person could inhale from the spout. 8" x 5.5". From the collection of Peter and Susan Steelman, Mystic, CT.

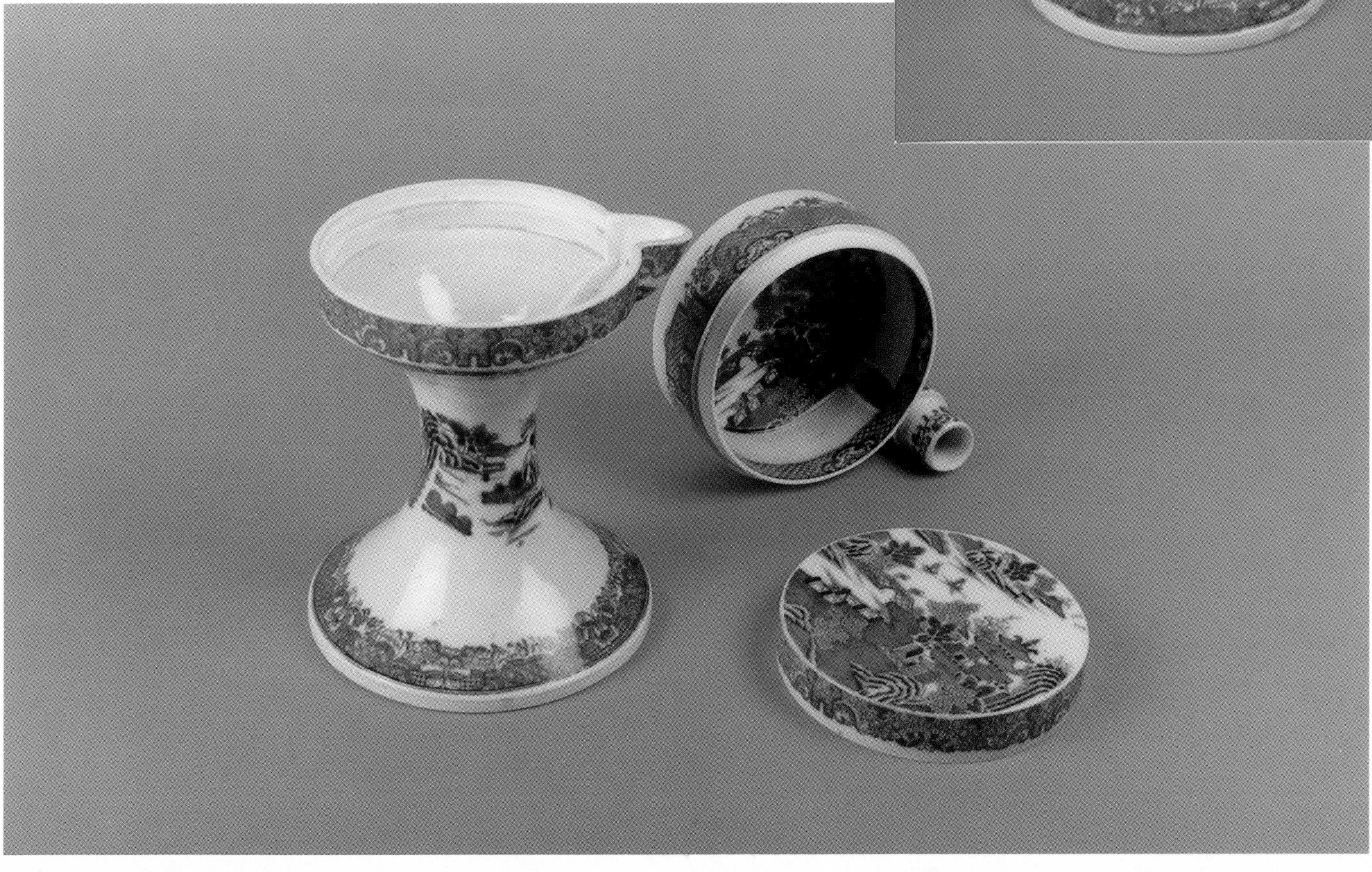

Chapter 5:

The Variants

While this book is primarily concerned with the traditional blue and white Standard Willow pattern, there are many alternative types of ware that show the wide range of chinoiserie products being produced by potters in and around the era of blue transfer-printed Willow manufacture. There are many interesting 'willow-type' chinoiserie designs of interest to Willow enthusiasts despite their substantial deviations from the Standard Willow pattern; many of these are discussed and pictured in Chapter 2. The Staffordshire potters realized that there was a tremendous market for many different patterns with a Chinese appearance, and before Willow's dominance was established they sold patterns like Boy on a Buffalo, Mandarin, Bridgeless Willow, and many others. These patterns have not been included in this chapter on Willow variants, since frequently they grew from the same chinoiserie tradition that inspired Willow, and some are actually the pattern's predecessors. As part of Willow's roots and as lovely designs in their own right, these patterns are much more than mere 'branches' of Willow. However, in this chapter you will see a number of minor pattern deviations—quirks in particular makers' patterns, and peculiarities that are delightful to discover.

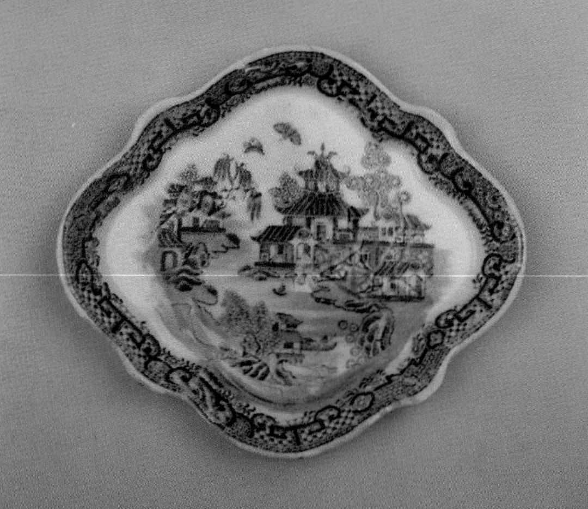

Instead of the usual doves, this Willow-type dish shows flying moths.

Once Willow was properly established as a cultural icon, it began to appear on novelty items as well, with pattern variations both big and small. These lighthearted pieces show how completely and affectionately Willow was taken into the hearts of customers (and designers!) in Britain and the United States.

Eventually, Willow sprung up from its initial development on ceramic wares. In this chapter you will see how Willow has been applied to metals and brass, paper and tin, and a number of other materials that the original potters surely never imagined!

An unforgettable variation from the usual blue and white pattern is the use of color: Willow has been transfer printed in every color under the sun, and on every color background—even luster! Some of the most interesting Willow pieces are polychrome, often decorated with 'clobbering'—hand-painting over a printed design. Parrott & Co. produced a well-known polychrome design, and Buffalo further popularized it with their now-rare Gaudy Willow line. The pictures in this chapter will show a broad cross-section of the color schemes that have been produced in Willow over the decades, from the established series to some one-of-a-kind 'beauties': judge for yourself!

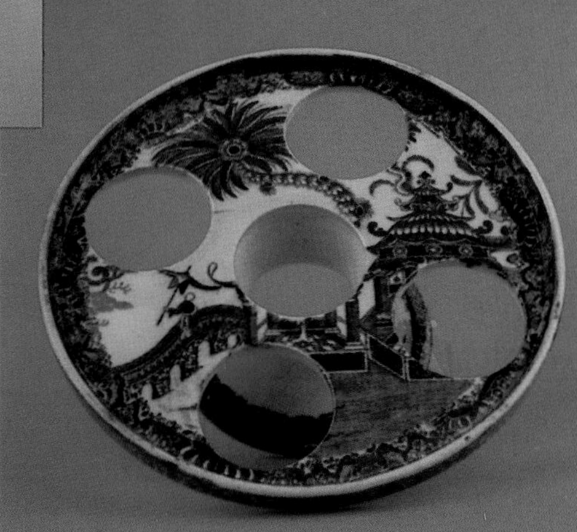

A five-egg stand in the "Curling Palm" pattern, c. 1810, 2.5" x 6.875". Courtesy of Rita Entmacher Cohen.

The Boy on a Buffalo pattern reveals yet another variable—butterfly borders.

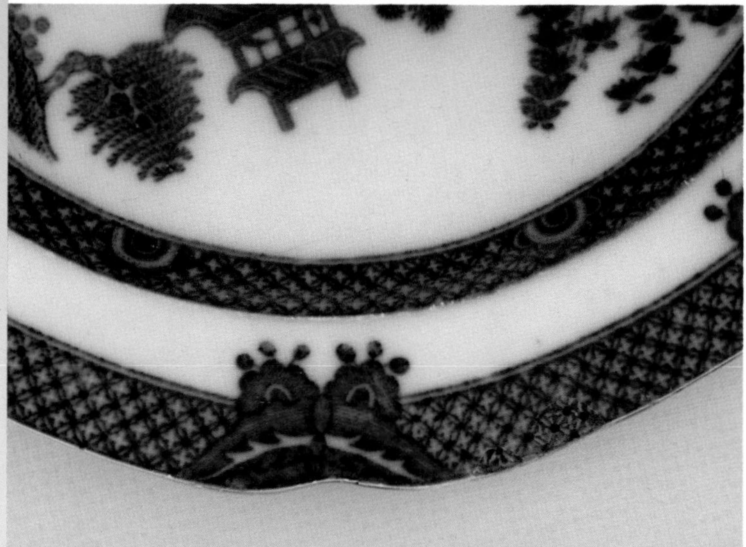

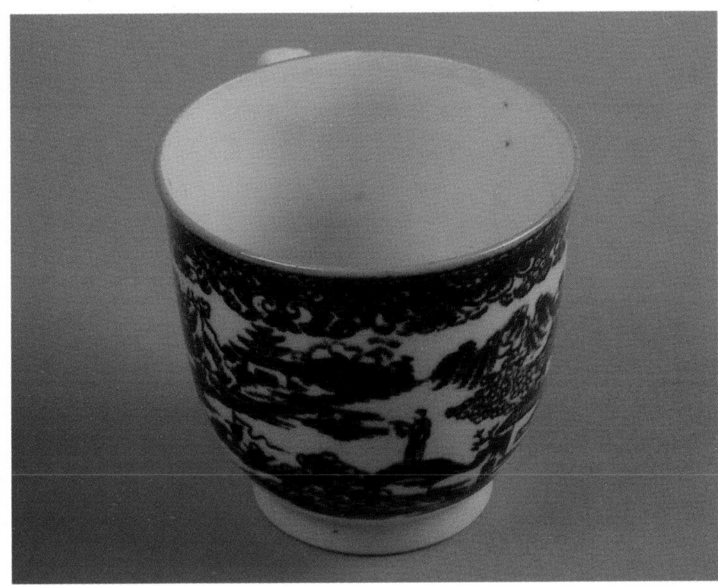

An unmarked teacup, 2.5" high, with an unusual pattern variation—a large man on a very small bridge. Courtesy of Charles and Louise Loehr, Louise's Old Things, Kutztown PA.

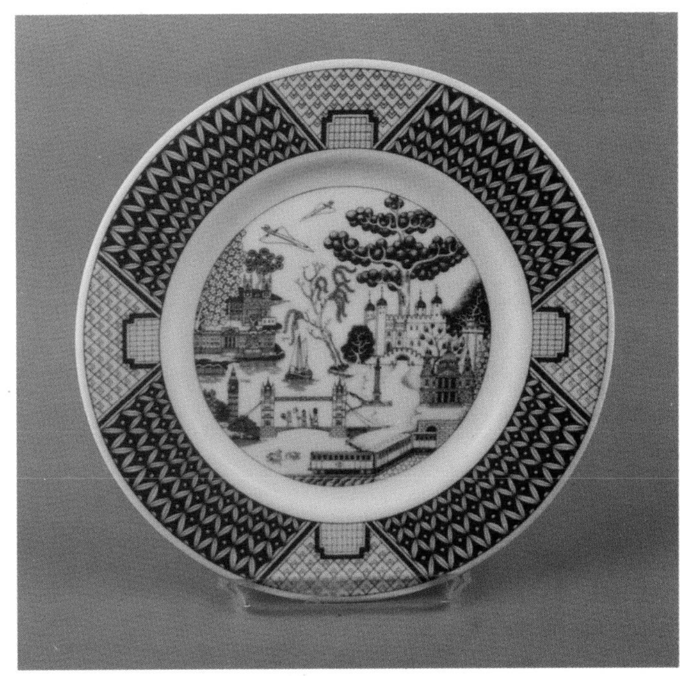

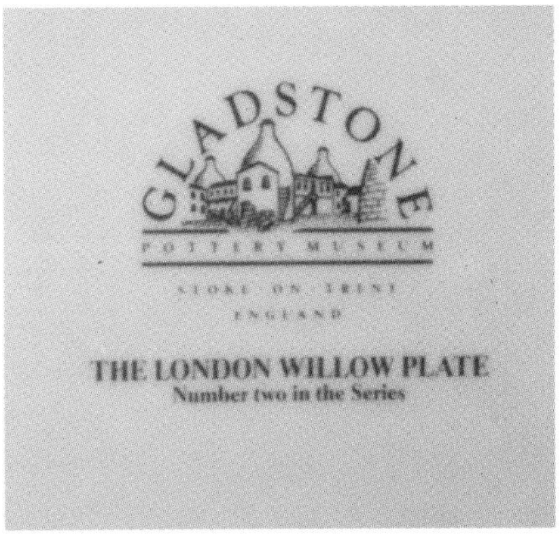

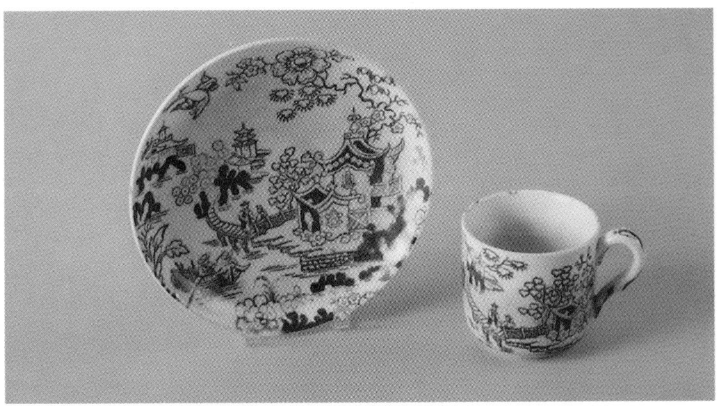

An unmarked demitasse and saucer. From the collection of Jennifer Carpenter and David Arnold.

A plate from 1971, the second in the series of commemoratives produced in Stoke on Trent. 9" diam. From the collection of Peter and Susan Steelman, Mystic, CT.

A plate produced by the Gladstone Pottery Museum in Stoke-on-Trent in 1988. The plate is 9" diam., and features several modern twists to the traditional willow elements. Marked "The Potteries Willow." Courtesy of Rita Entmacher Cohen.

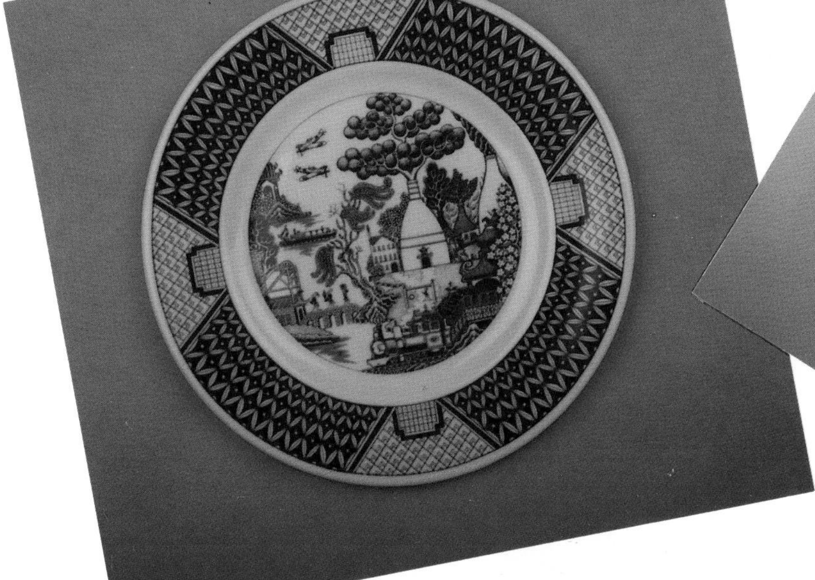

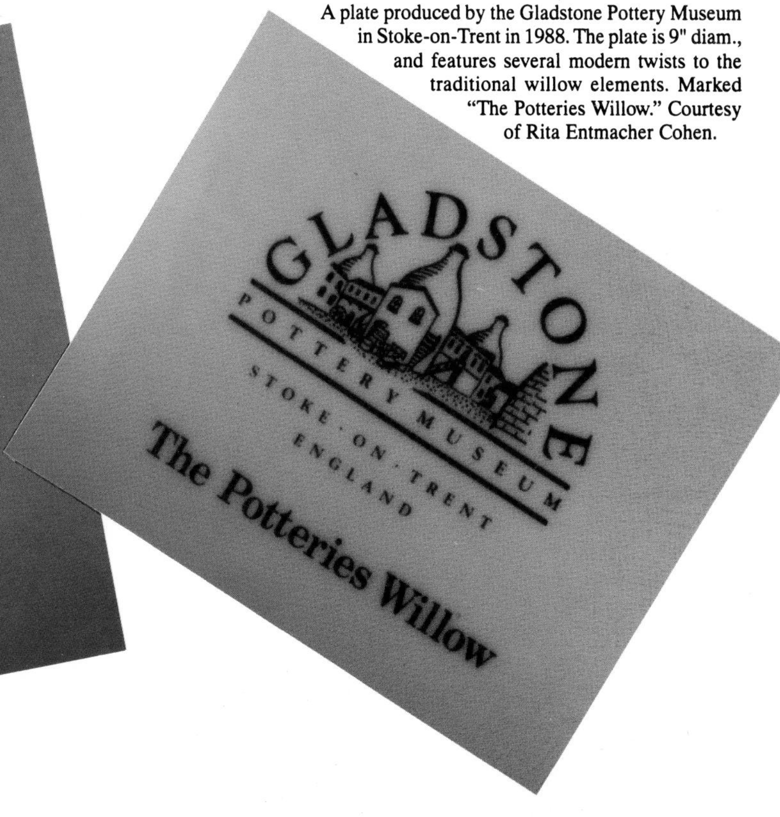

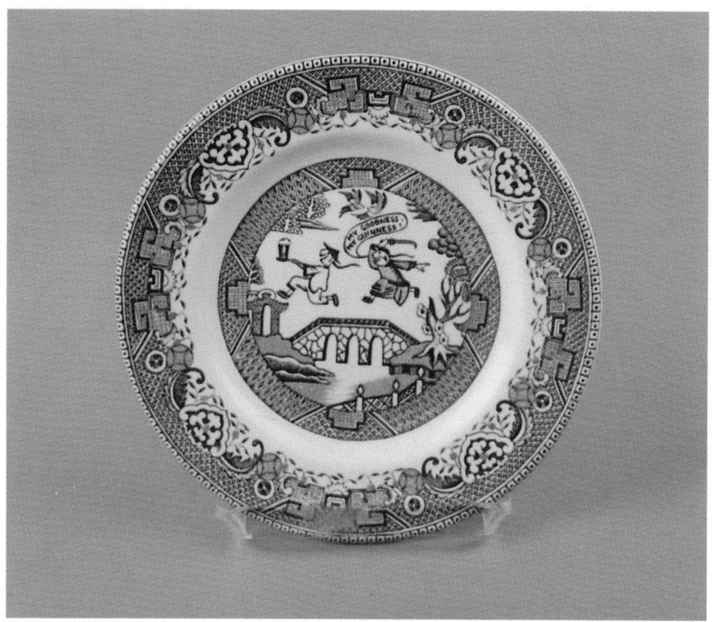

This luncheon plate is Guinness's spoof on the well-loved Willow pattern, 7" diam. From the collection of Peter and Susan Steelman, Mystic, CT.

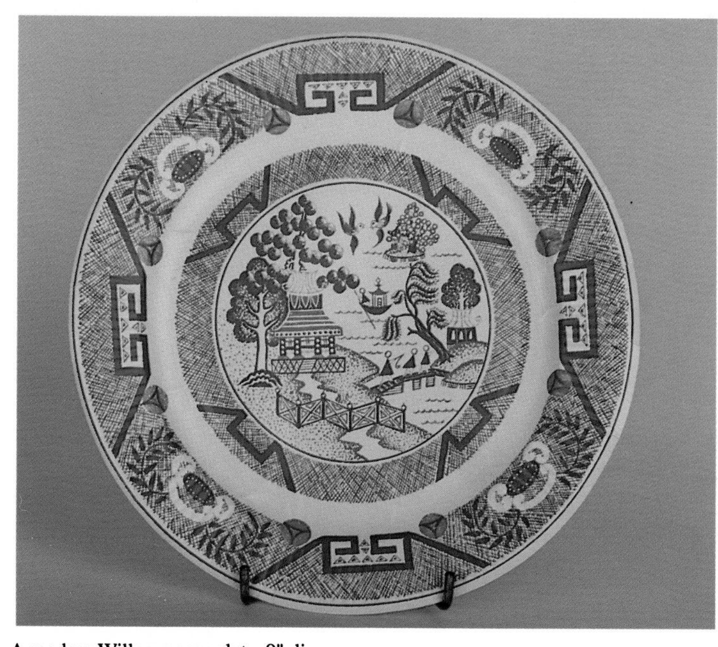

A modern Willow paper plate, 9" diam.

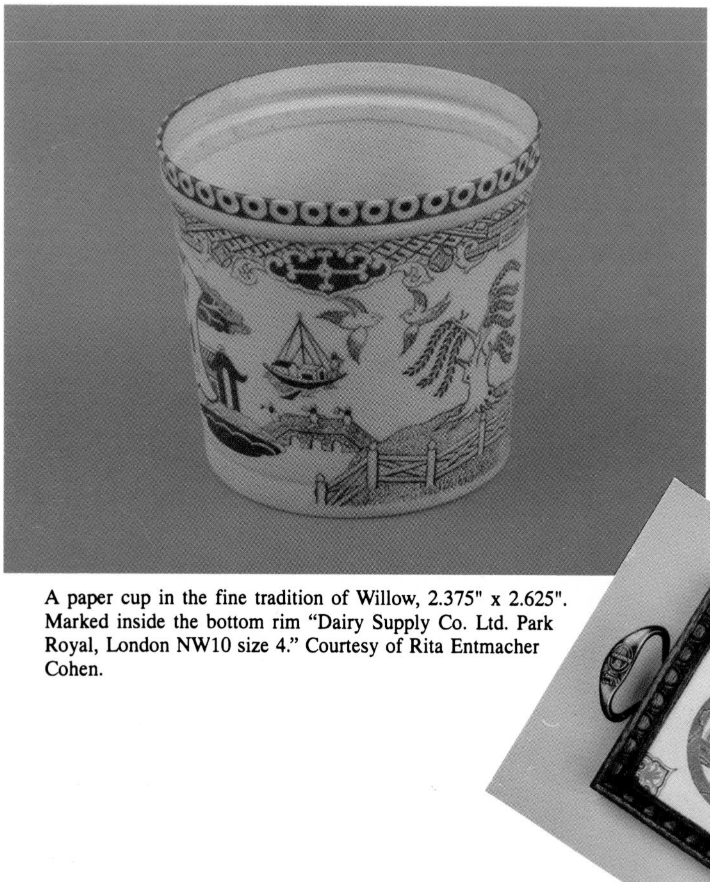

A paper cup in the fine tradition of Willow, 2.375" x 2.625". Marked inside the bottom rim "Dairy Supply Co. Ltd. Park Royal, London NW10 size 4." Courtesy of Rita Entmacher Cohen.

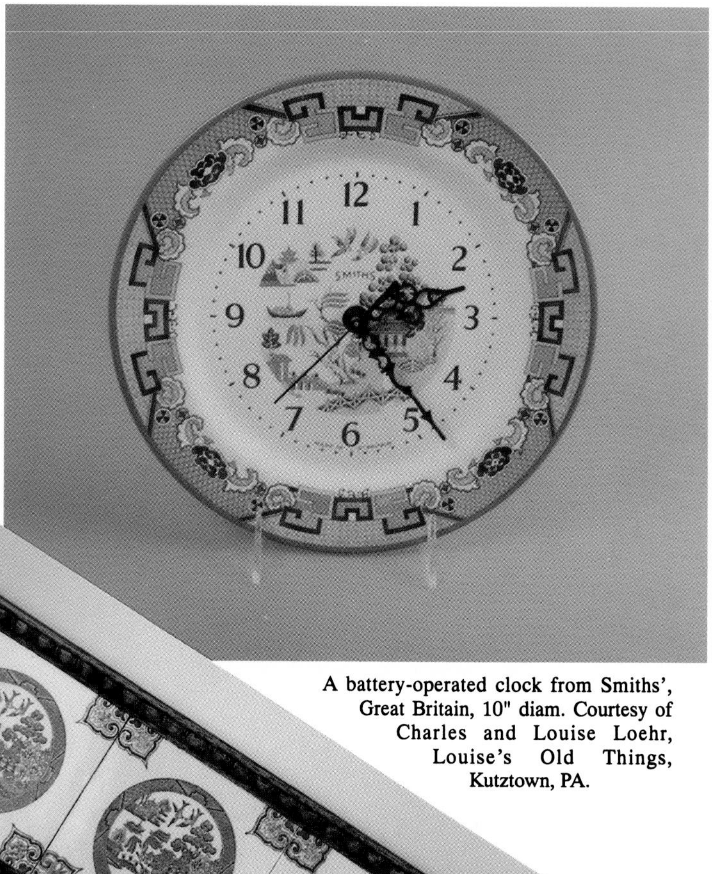

A battery-operated clock from Smiths', Great Britain, 10" diam. Courtesy of Charles and Louise Loehr, Louise's Old Things, Kutztown, PA.

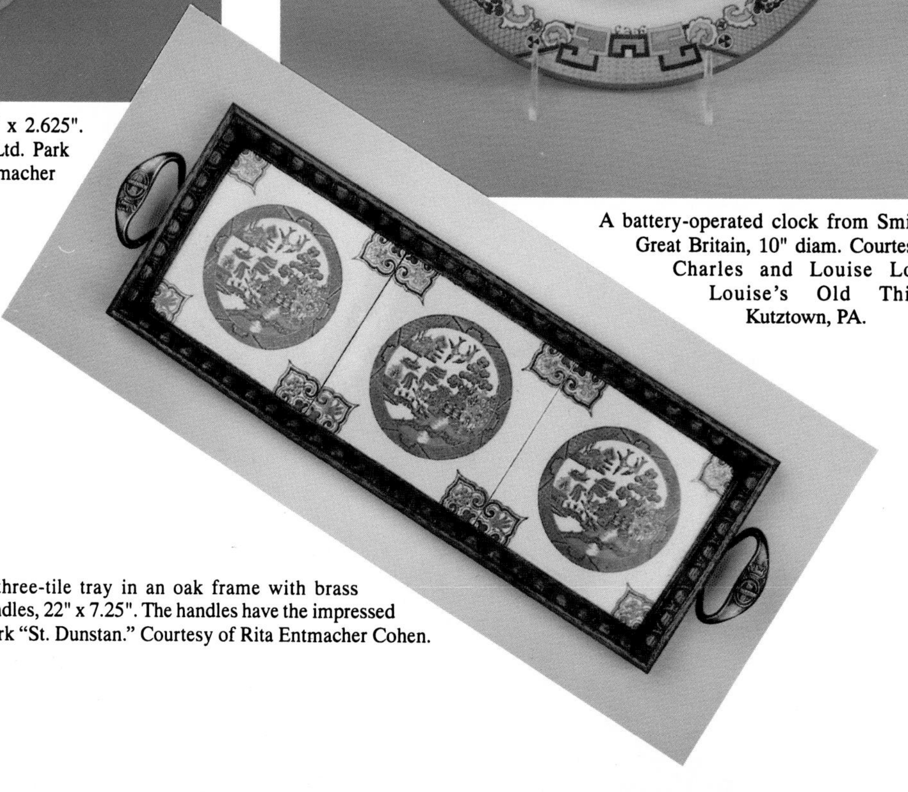

A three-tile tray in an oak frame with brass handles, 22" x 7.25". The handles have the impressed mark "St. Dunstan." Courtesy of Rita Entmacher Cohen.

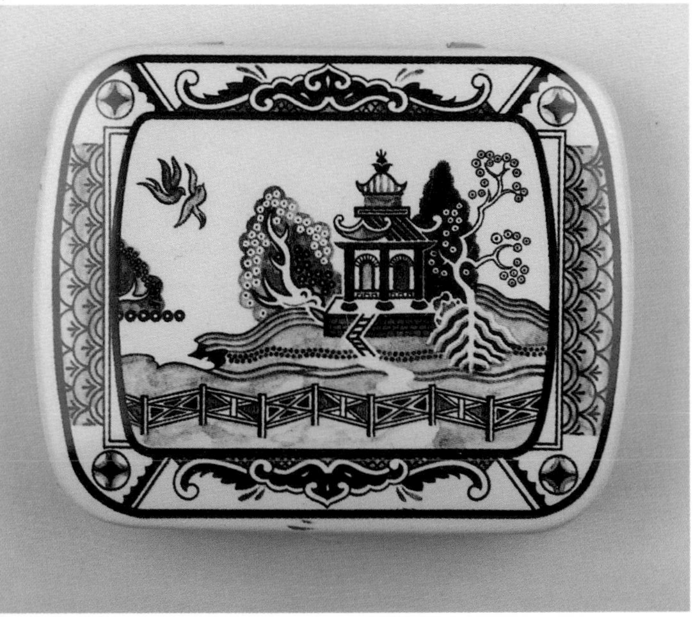

A tin box with Willow elements, rectangular with a hinged top. Courtesy of Rita Entmacher Cohen.

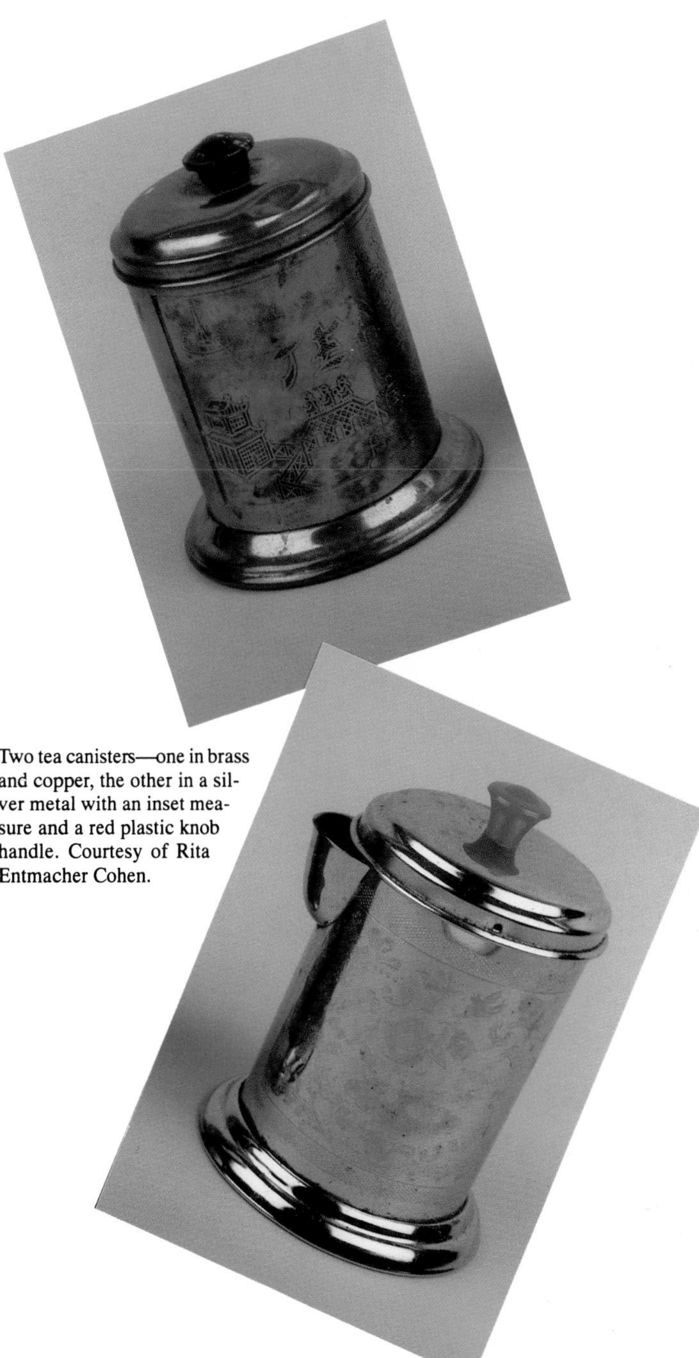

Two tea canisters—one in brass and copper, the other in a silver metal with an inset measure and a red plastic knob handle. Courtesy of Rita Entmacher Cohen.

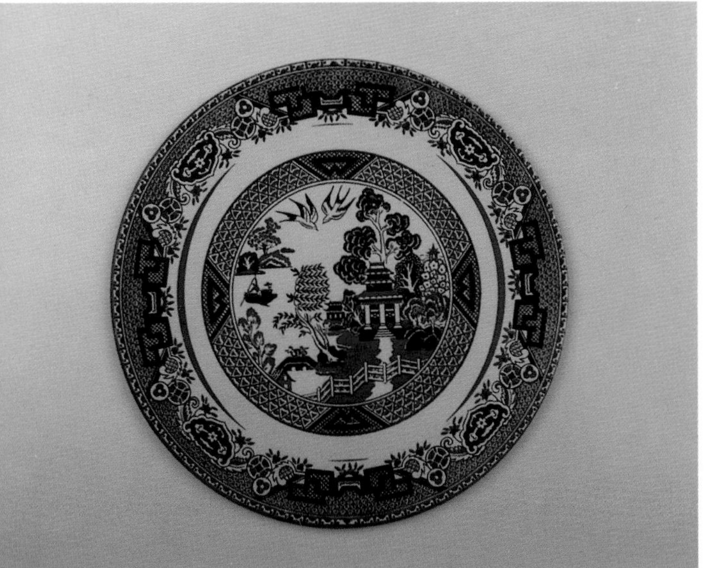

A printed tin-clad trivet with an asbestos back, 6" diam. Courtesy of Rita Entmacher Cohen.

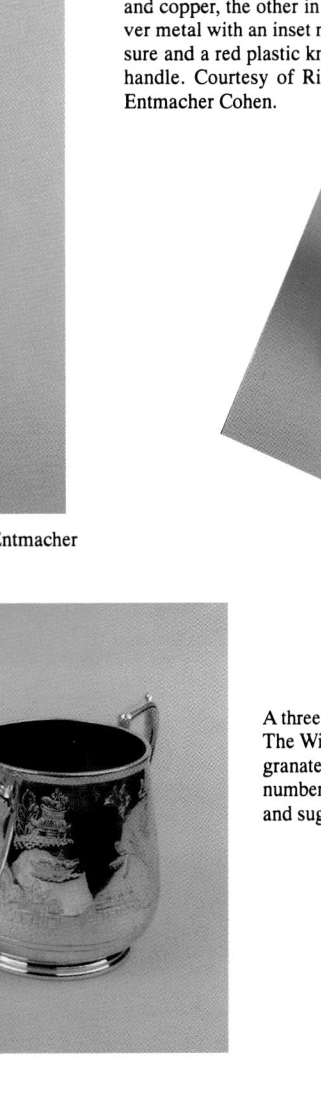

A three-piece tea set in silver-plate by B. Grayson & Son, Sheffield. The Willow pattern appears on all sides, and the pot has a pomegranate finial. The base of the pot is impressed with the pattern number 510, which is also scatched into the bases of both the cream and sugar. Courtesy of Rita Entmacher Cohen.

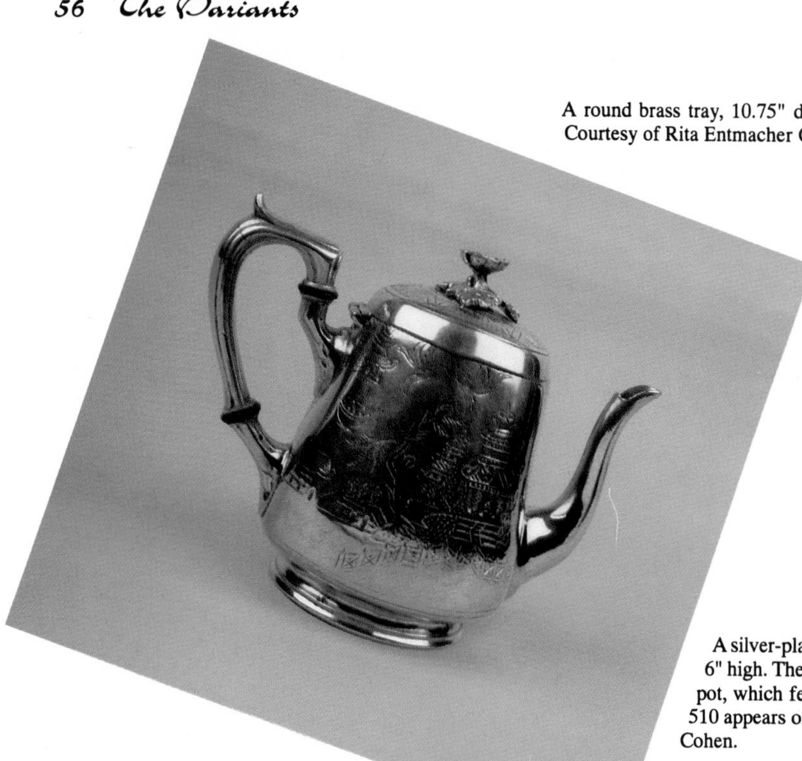

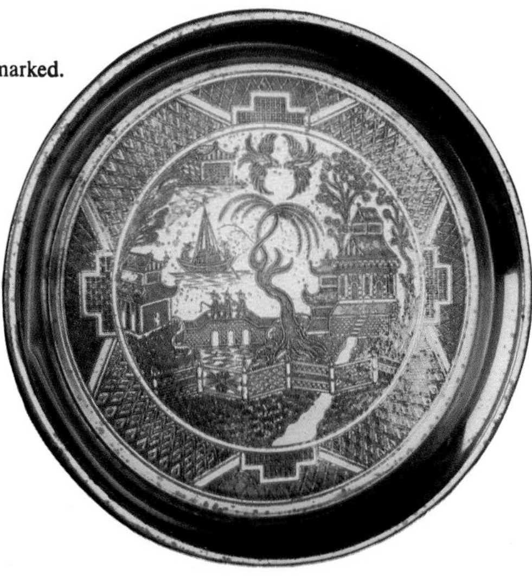

A round brass tray, 10.75" diam. Unmarked. Courtesy of Rita Entmacher Cohen.

A silver-plated teapot by B. Grayson & Son, Sheffield, 6" high. The willow design is etched on all sides of the pot, which features a floral finial. The pattern number 510 appears on the bottom. Courtesy of Rita Entmacher Cohen.

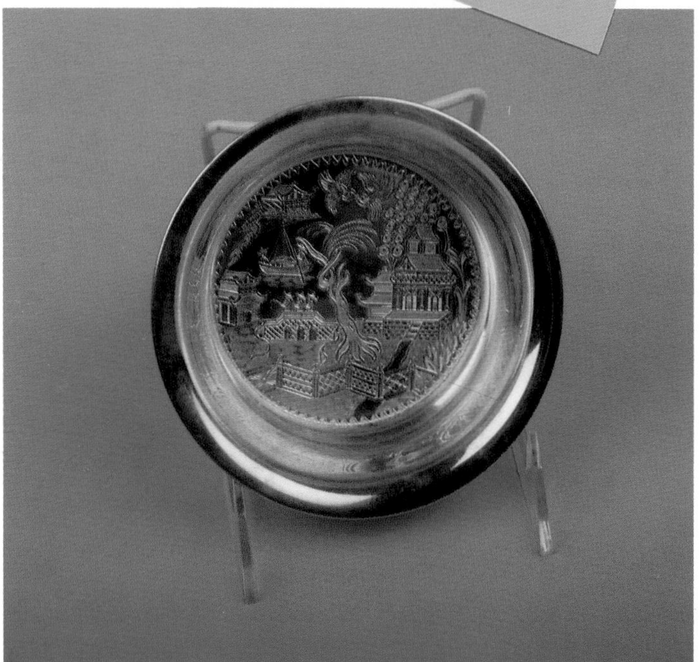

A silver-plated bowl with a Willow design in the base, 5" diam. Marked "SILVER PLATED MADE IN ENGLAND" on the back. Courtesy of Rita Entmacher Cohen.

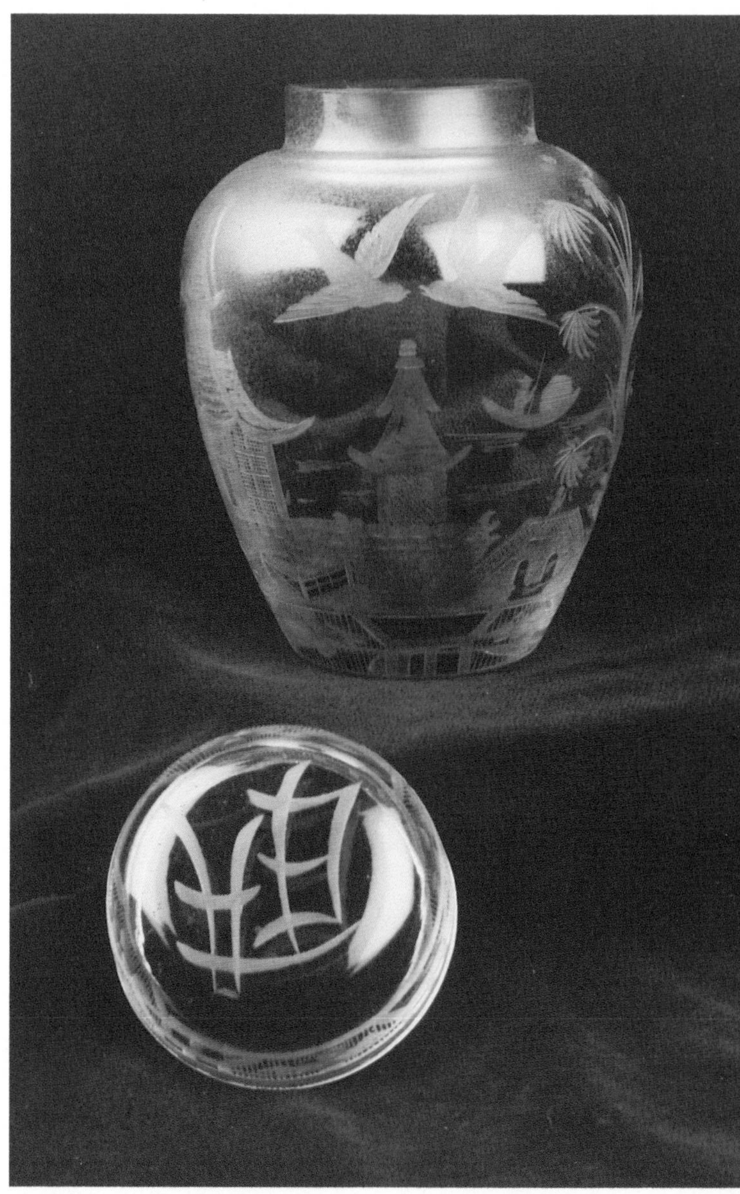

A covered glass jar cut in a Willow pattern, by Hawkes, 5.25" high. Courtesy of Rita Entmacher Cohen.

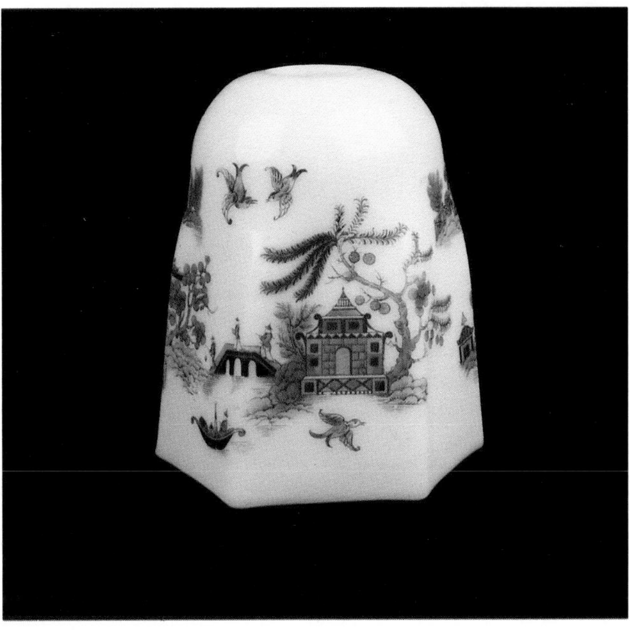

A lampshades in white glass, printed in sepia and decorated in polychrome. Courtesy of Rita Entmacher Cohen.

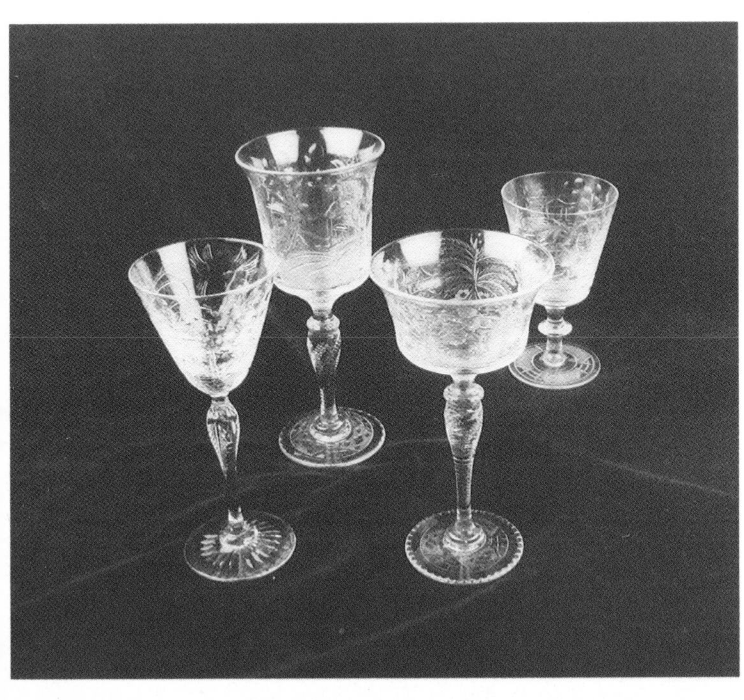

Twentieth century glass stemware cut in a Willow pattern, c. 1920-1940, by Stevens and Williams. Courtesy of Rita Entmacher Cohen.

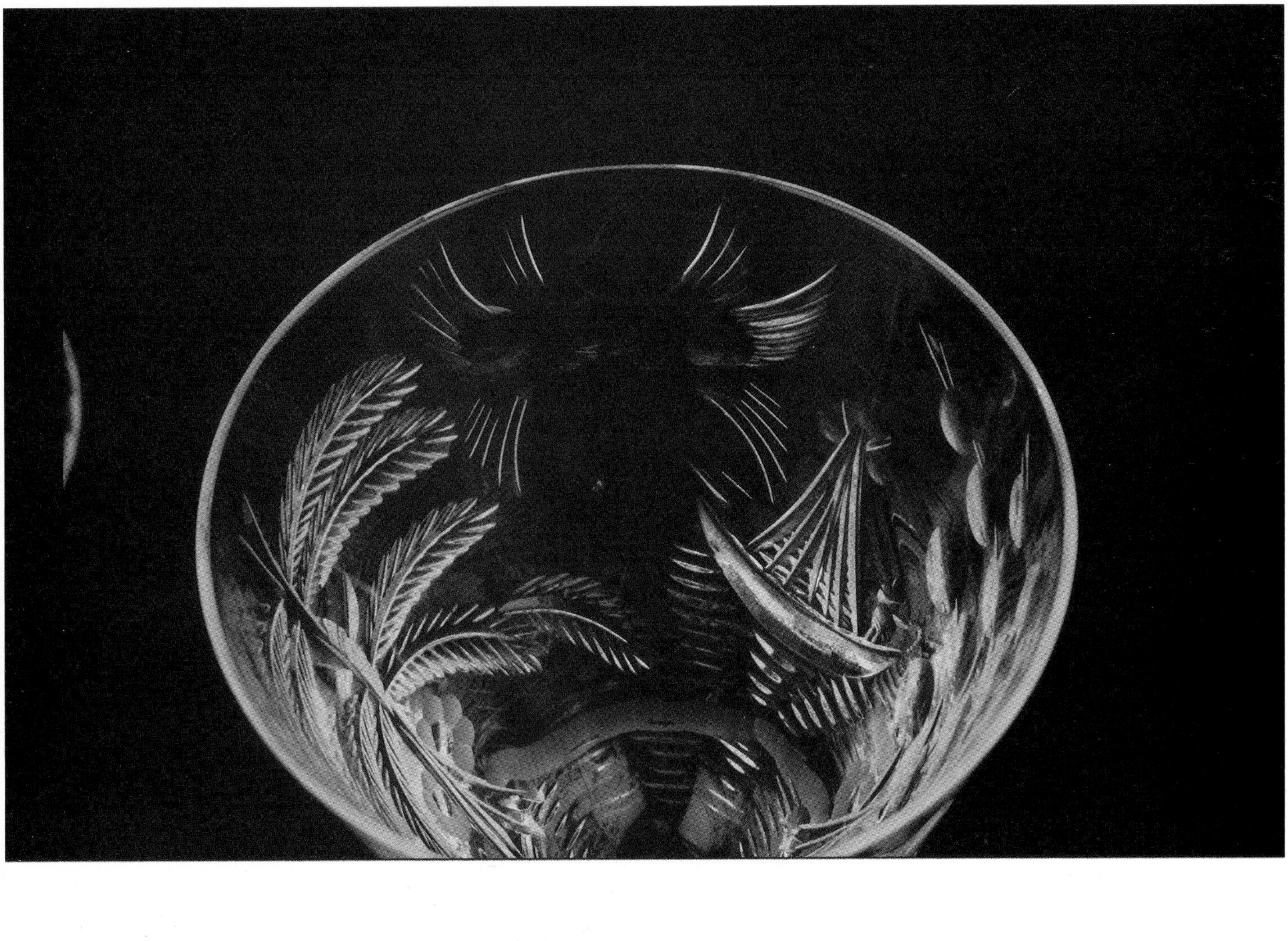

Willow of a Different Color

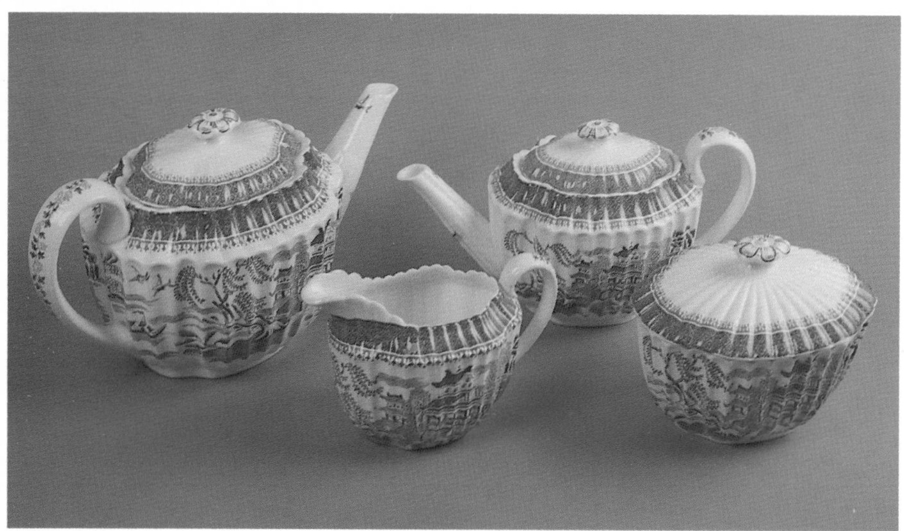

A fluted red tea set. Courtesy of Charles and Louise Loehr, Louise's Old Things, Kutztown, PA.

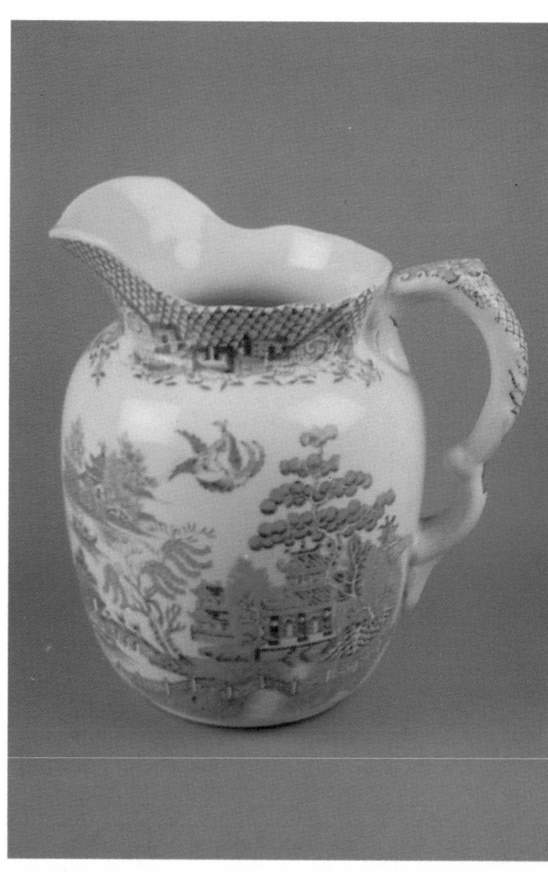

An unmarked Willow pitcher in a light olive green color, 8.5" high. From the collection of Peter and Susan Steelman, Mystic, CT.

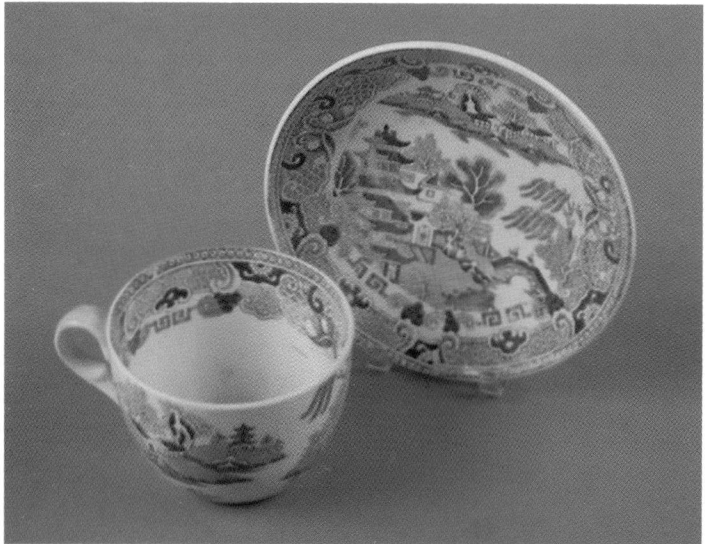

A tea cup and saucer in brown Willow, marked with the words "Semi-China" enclosed in a diamond-shape. From the collection of Peter and Susan Steelman, Mystic, CT.

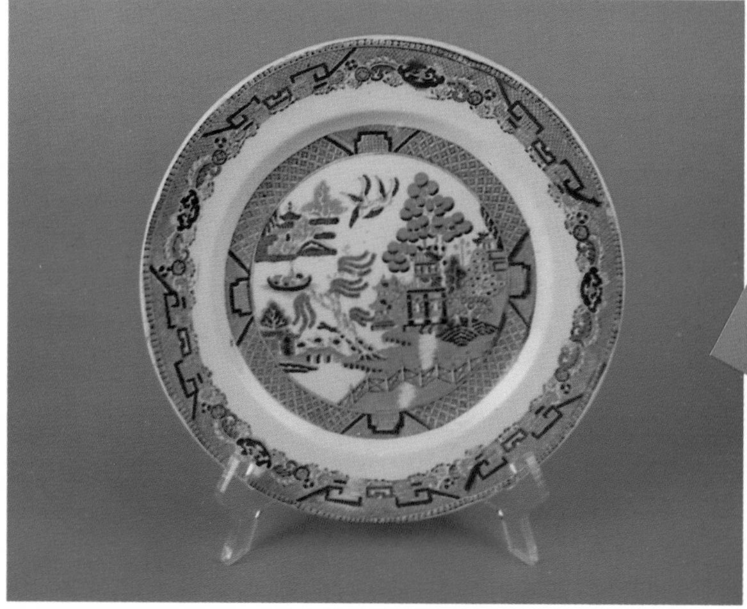

An unmarked purple Willow plate, 8.5" diam. From the collection of Peter and Susan Steelman, Mystic, CT.

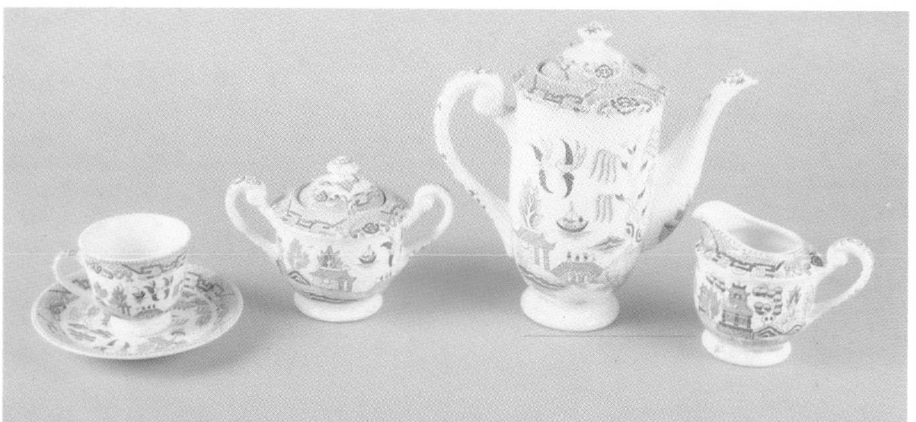

A red tea set, 7.4" high, 1940s, from Japan. Courtesy of Bud & Marguerite Smith, Small World Antiques.

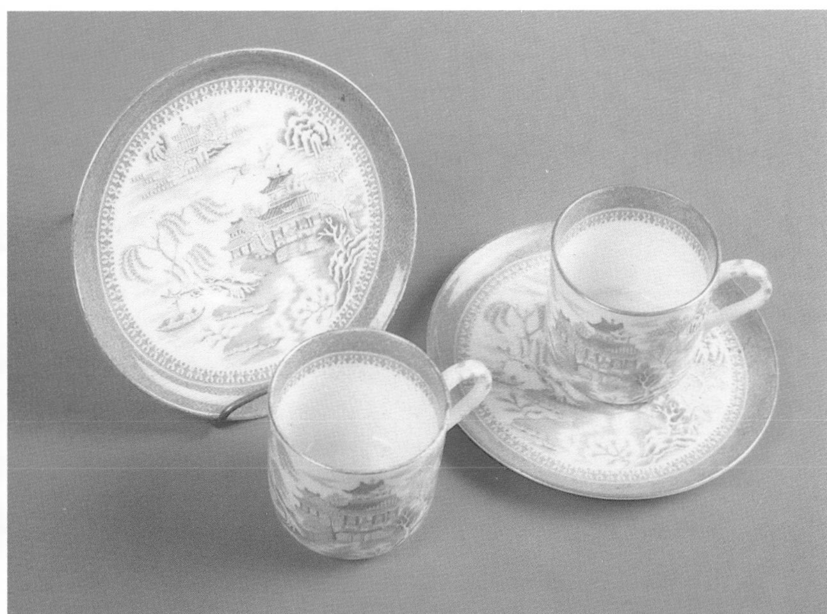

Swinnerton's teacups and saucers in pink Willow. Courtesy of Charles and Louise Loehr, Louise's Old Things, Kutztown, PA.

A green grill plate from Buffalo China, 10/25" diam. Marked "Standard Grill Plate". From the collection of Phillip M. Sullivan, South Orleans, MA.

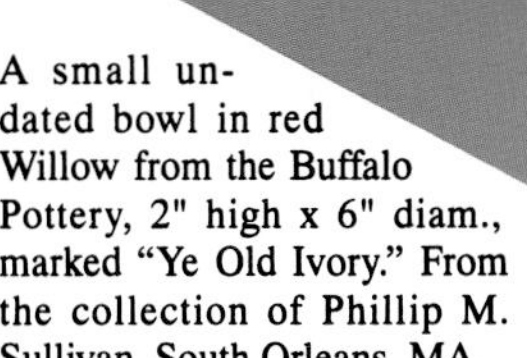

A small undated bowl in red Willow bowl from the Buffalo Pottery, 2" high x 6" diam., marked "Ye Old Ivory." From the collection of Phillip M. Sullivan, South Orleans, MA.

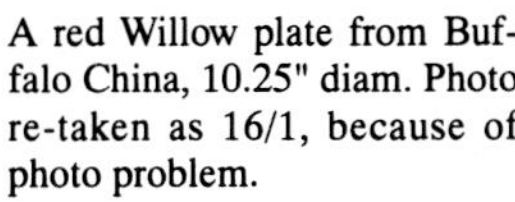

A red Willow plate from Buffalo China, 10.25" diam. Photo re-taken as 16/1, because of photo problem.

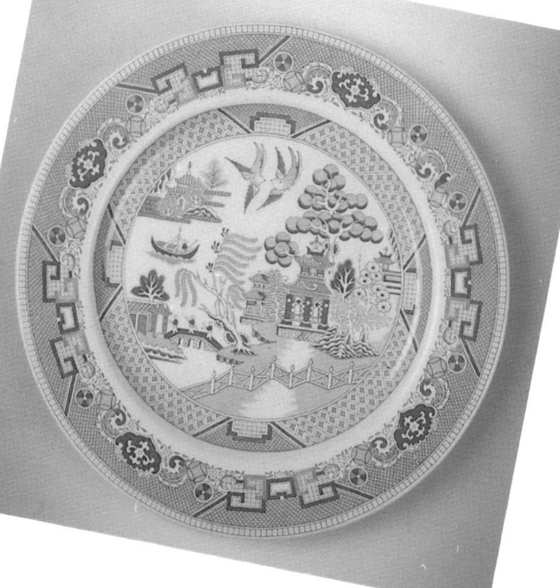

A red Willow plate from Buffalo China, 10.25" diam. From the collection of Phillip M. Sullivan, South Orleans, MA.

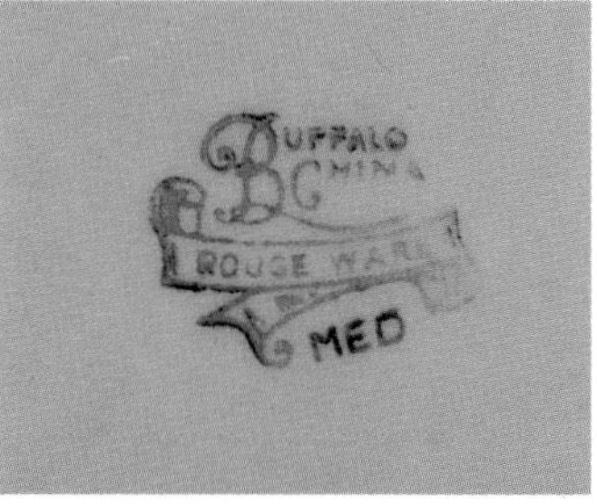

A Buffalo China Rangeware plate in "Rouge Ware," printed in black, 9.25" diam. From the collection of Phillip M. Sullivan, South Orleans, MA.

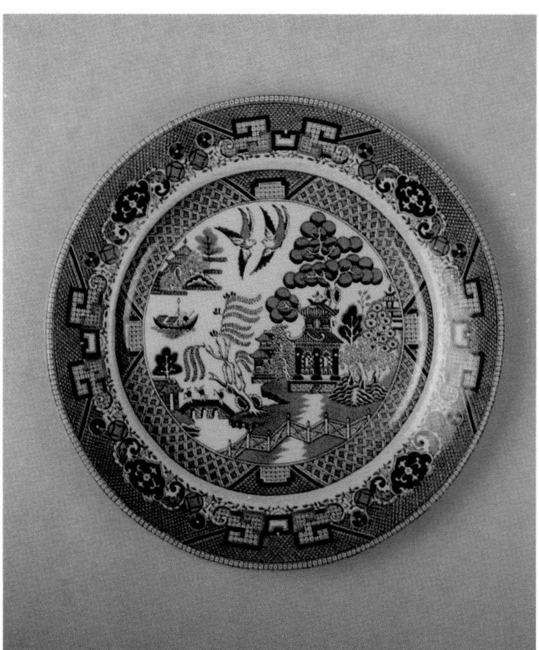

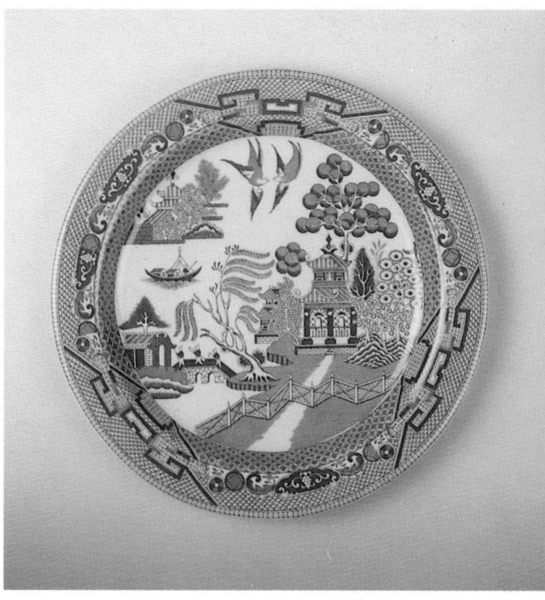

A brown Willow plate from Buffalo China, 11" diam. From the collection of Phillip M. Sullivan, South Orleans, MA.

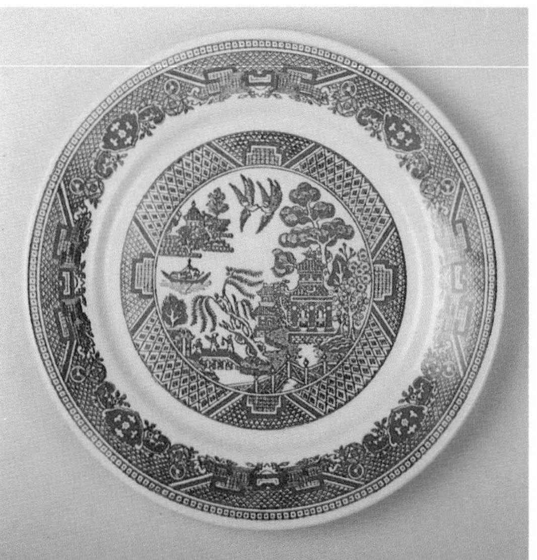

A modern red Willow plate from Buffalo China, 9.5" diam. Marked "BUFFALO CHINA / USA". From the collection of Phillip M. Sullivan, South Orleans, MA.

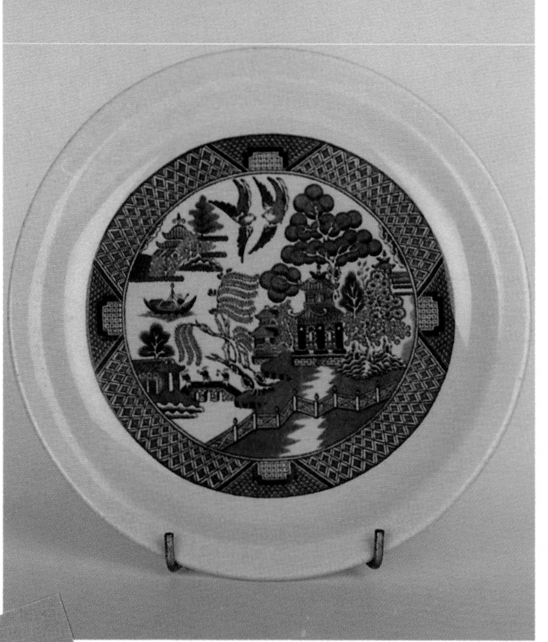

A polychrome tea caddy, missing its lid, 4. 75". Courtesy of Rita Entmacher Cohen.

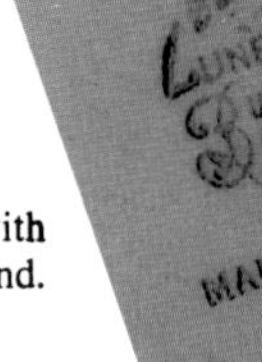

A Buffalo "LuneWare" china plate, with blue printing on a light blue background. From the author's collection.

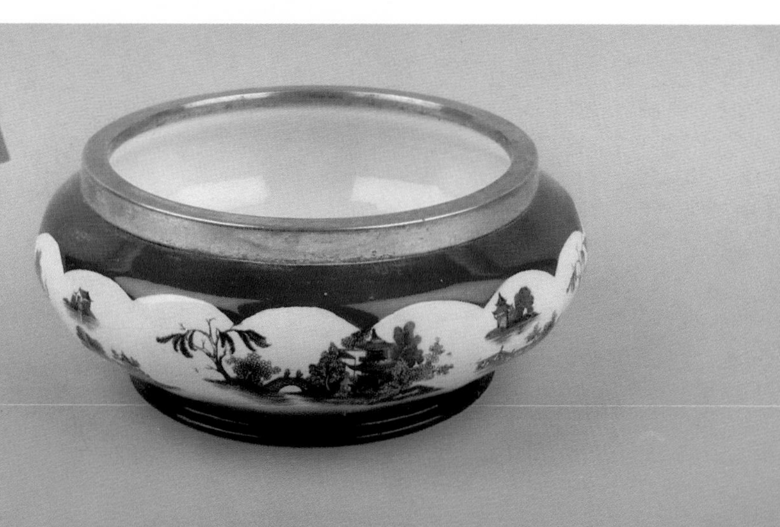

A polychrome salad bowl from L & Sons, Hawley, England, 4" x 8.5". Impressed with the number 180. Courtesy of Rita Entmacher Cohen.

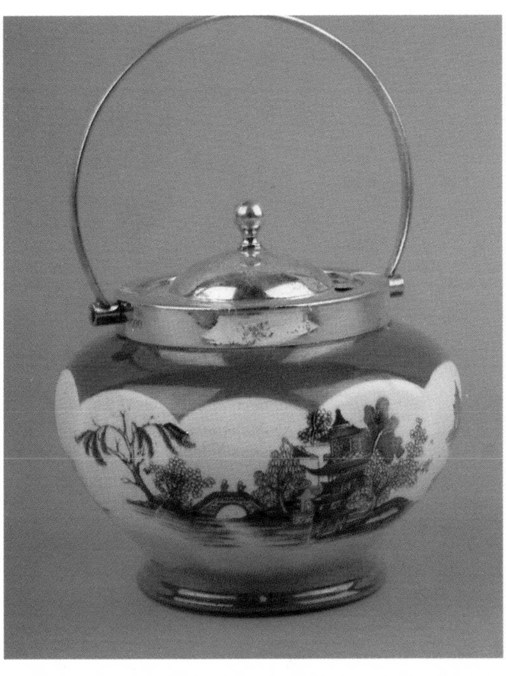

A polychrome lambpot from L+Sons, Ltd., Hawley, England, 3.5". This piece has the impressed numbers "231," and has ten flat sides and an EPNS lid and handle. Courtesy of Rita Entmacher Cohen.

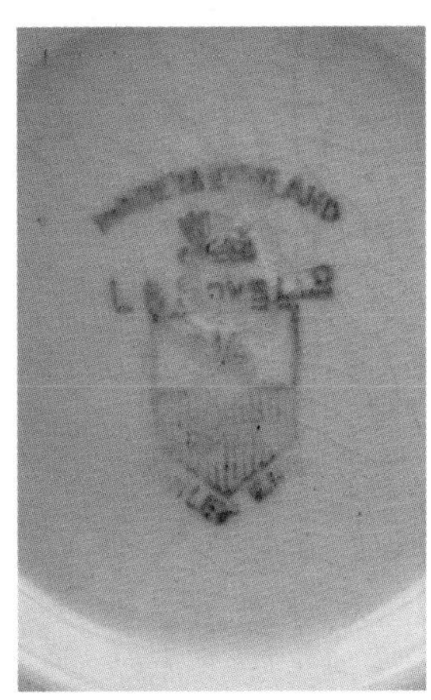

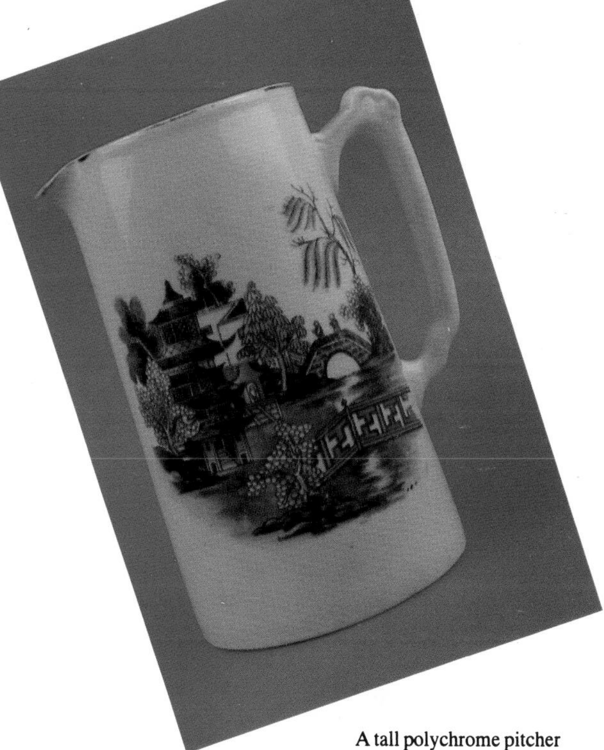

A tall polychrome pitcher or jug, 8" high. Unmarked. Courtesy of Rita Entmacher Cohen.

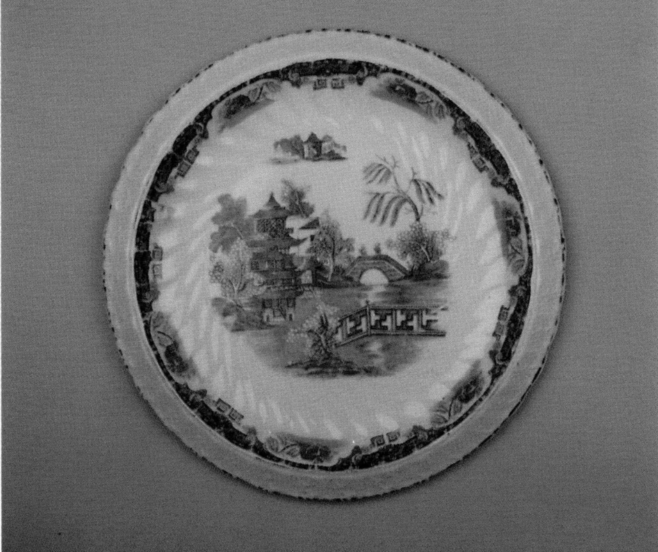

A polychrome bread plate, 10.75". The mark is illegible. Courtesy of Rita Entmacher Cohen.

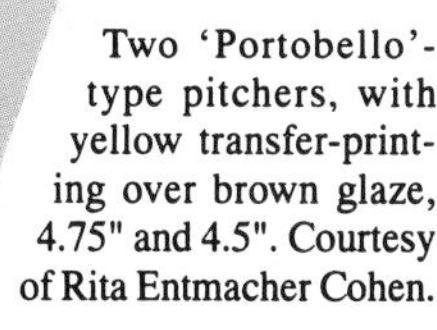

Two 'Portobello'-type pitchers, with yellow transfer-printing over brown glaze, 4.75" and 4.5". Courtesy of Rita Entmacher Cohen.

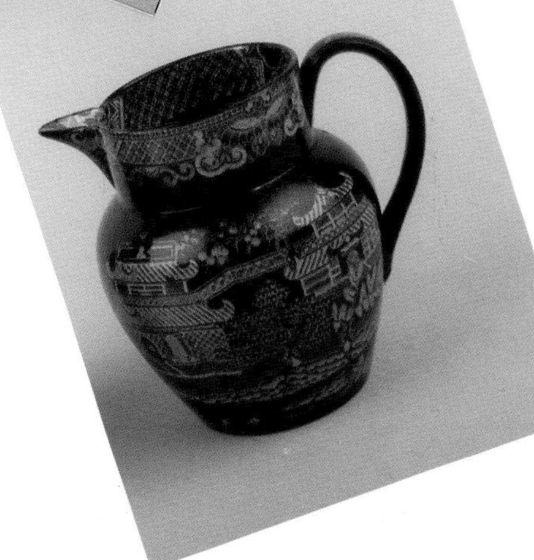

A pearlware teacup and saucer with black transfer-printing, c. 1790. Courtesy of Rita Entmacher Cohen.

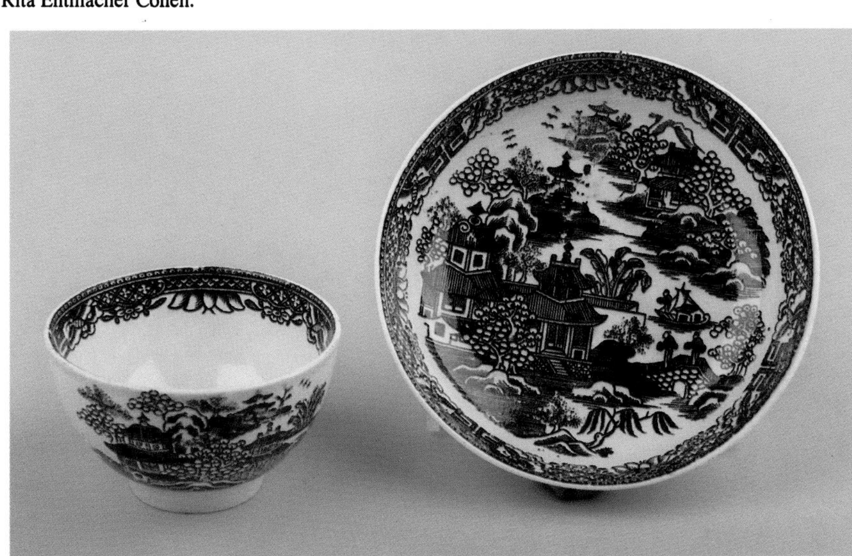

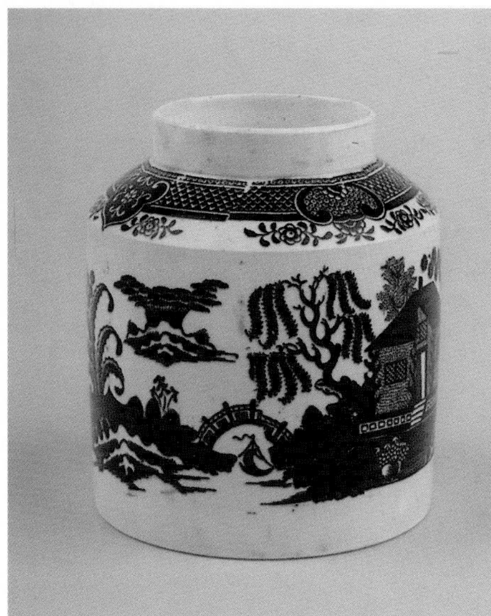

A pearlware tea caddy (lid missing) with the "Bungalo" pattern transfer-printed in black, c. 1790. Courtesy of Rita Entmacher Cohen.

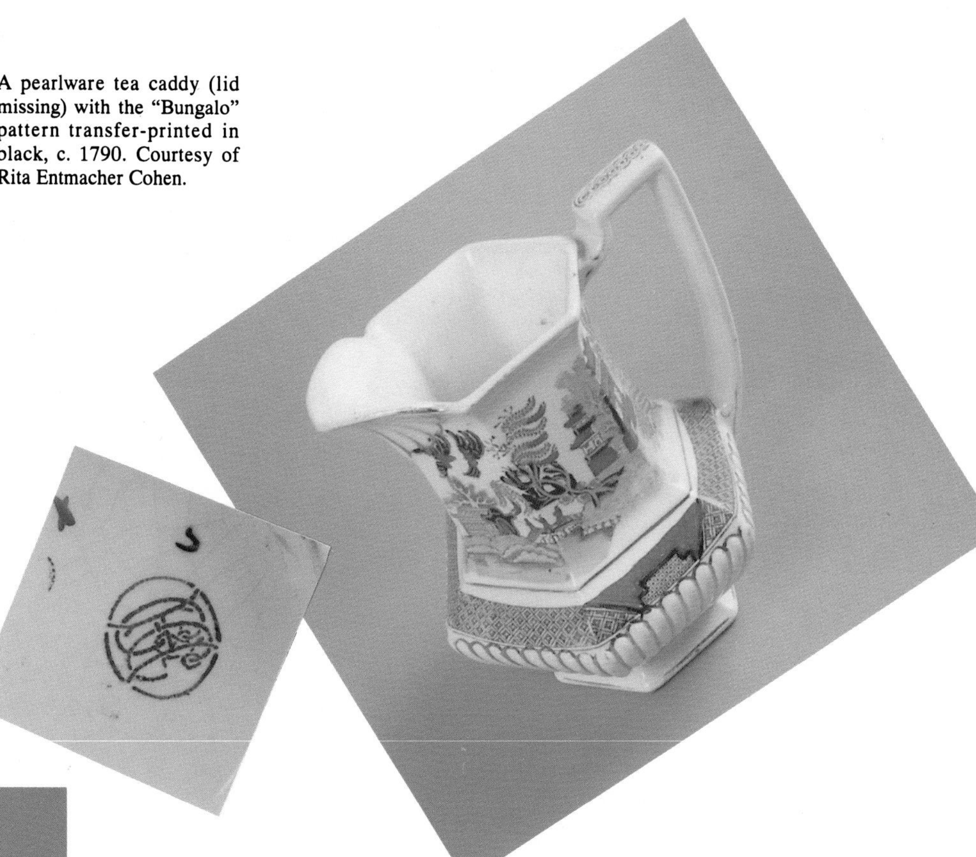

A polychrome Willow pitcher, 6.5" high. Courtesy of Charles and Louise Loehr, Louise's Old Things, Kutztown, PA.

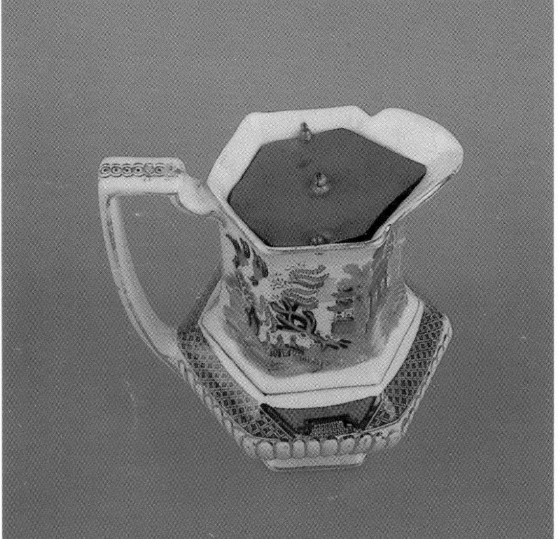

A matching syrup pitcher, with a pewter lid. Courtesy of Rita Entmacher Cohen.

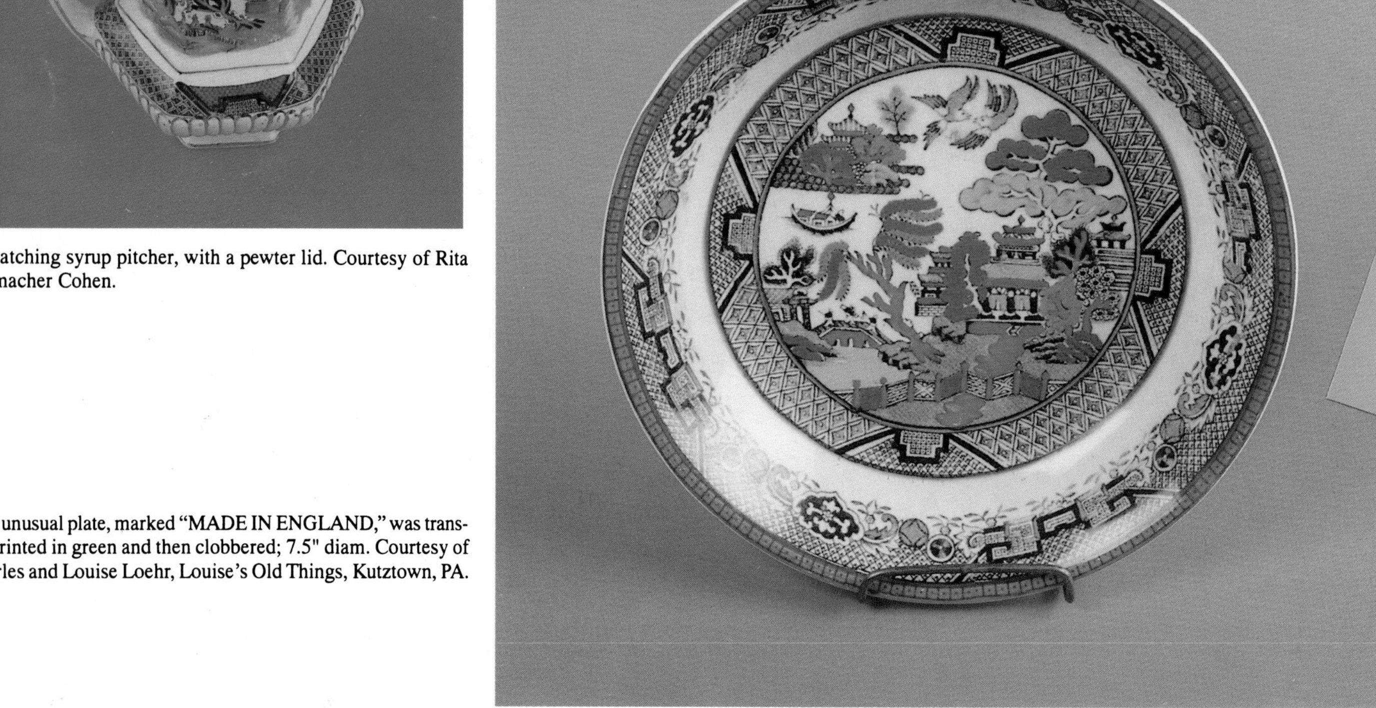

This unusual plate, marked "MADE IN ENGLAND," was transfer printed in green and then clobbered; 7.5" diam. Courtesy of Charles and Louise Loehr, Louise's Old Things, Kutztown, PA.

PLACE
STAMP
HERE

SCHIFFER PUBLISHING LTD
77 LOWER VALLEY RD
ATGLEN PA 19310-9717

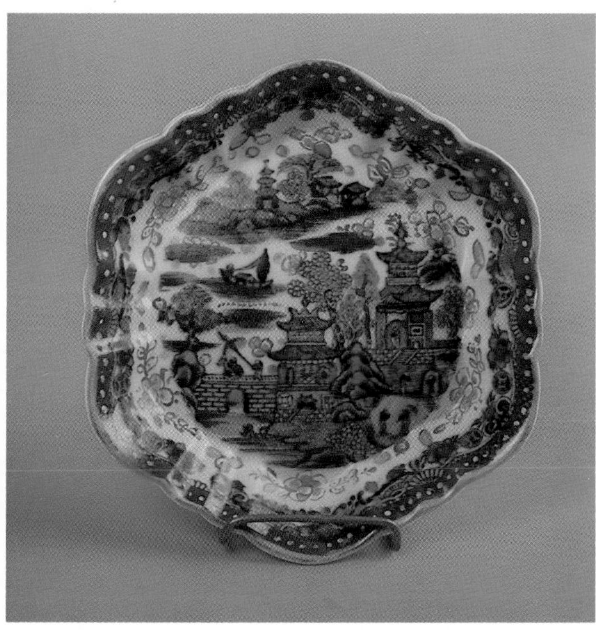

A Gaudy Willow plate with green and orange clobbering, 6" x 6.5". Courtesy of Charles and Louise Loehr, Louise's Old Things, Kutztown PA.

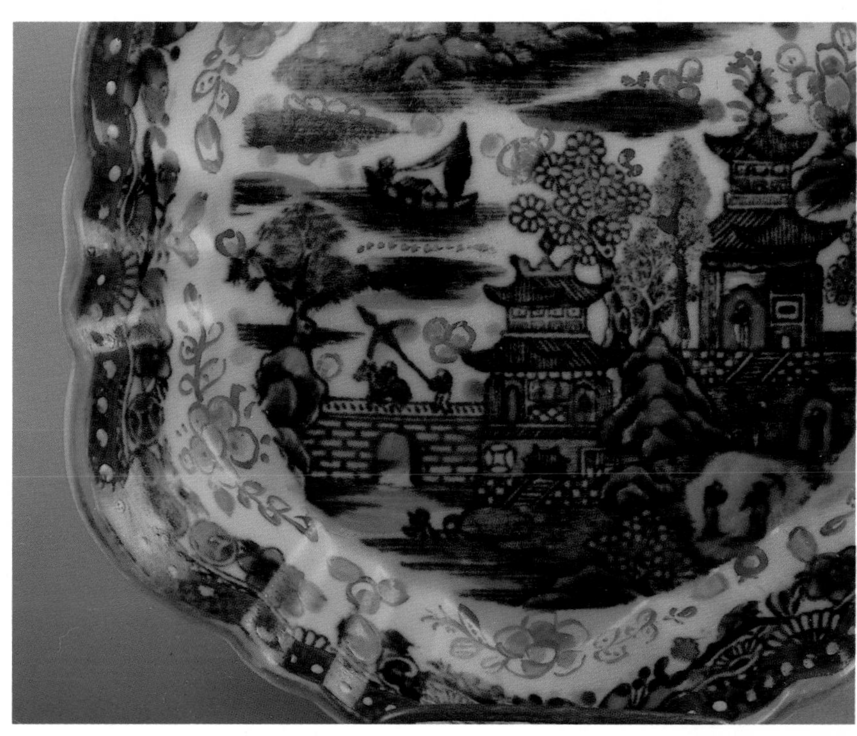

A detail of the clobbering.

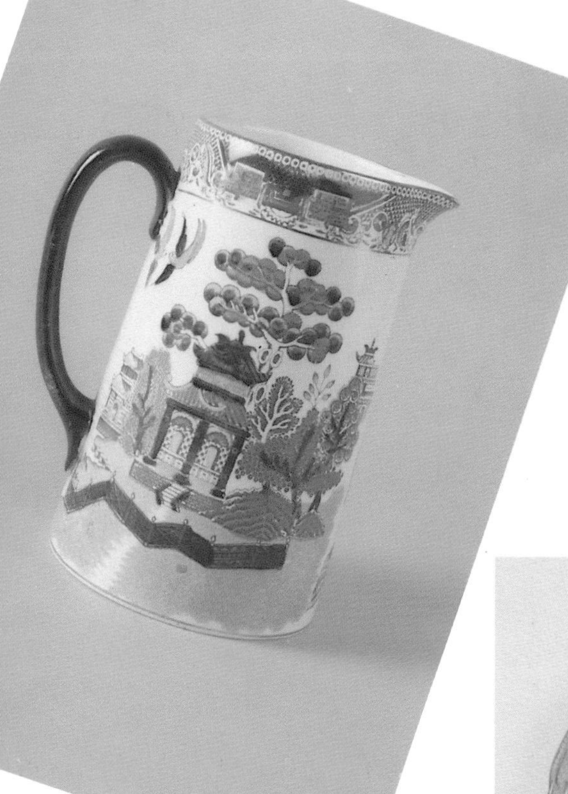

A pitcher in red-transfer printing, with polychrome clobbering, 1880s-1905, 8" high. Courtesy of Loren Zeller, Stoney Hill Antiques & Interiors, Dunstable, Mass.

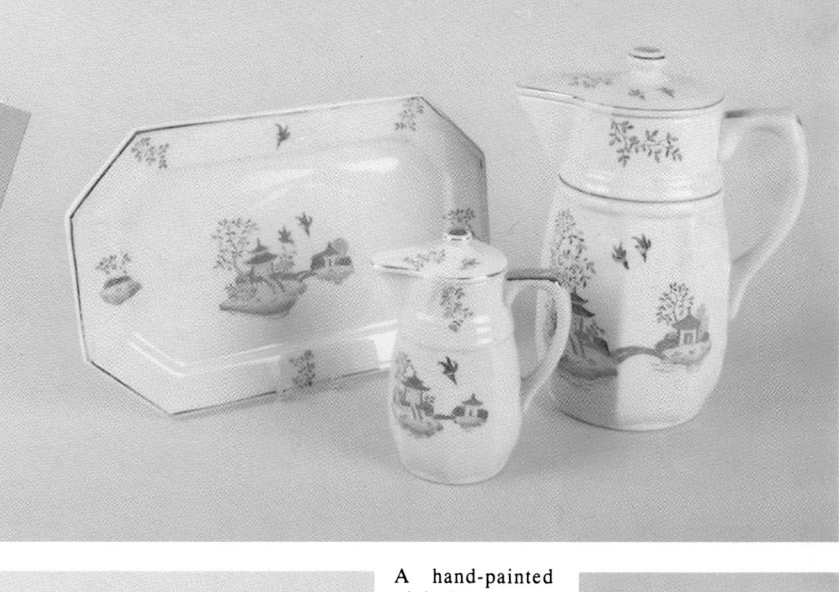

A hand-painted pink batter set, marked "Made in Japan," 1879, 11.25" x 7" (tray), 10" high (large pitcher). Courtesy of Bud & Marguerite Smith, Small World Antiques, MI.

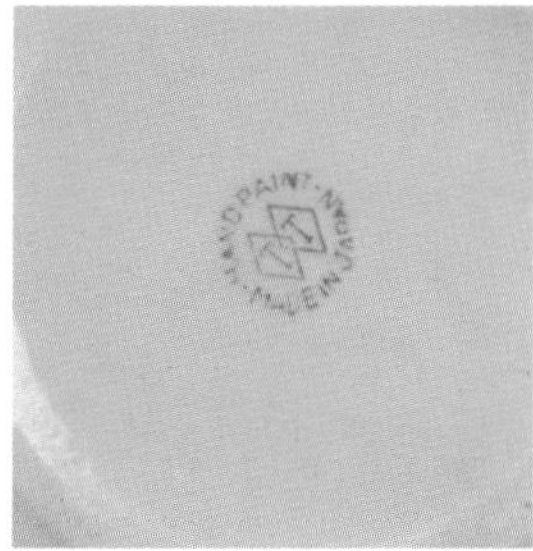

A small scallop-edged luncheon plate in the Gaudy pattern from the Buffalo Pottery, 1907, 7.25" (also comes in 8" and 9.25" sizes). From the collection of Phillip M. Sullivan, South Orleans, MA.

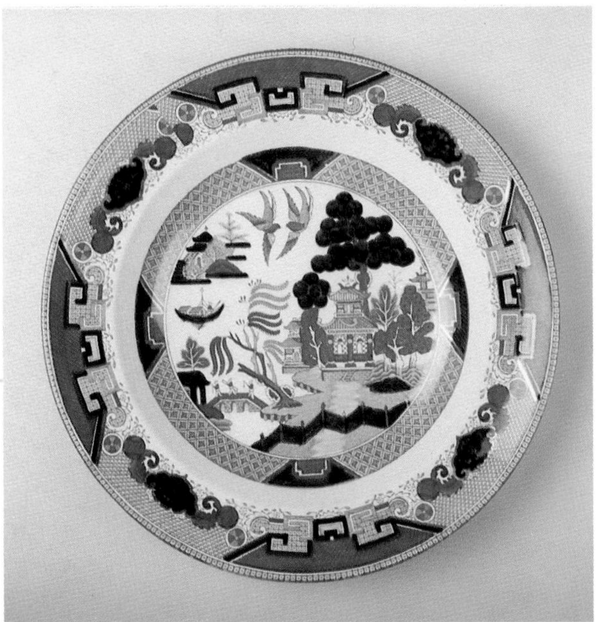

A Gaudy Willow soup plate from the Buffalo Pottery, 1911, 1.5" deep x 9.5" diam. From the collection of Phillip M. Sullivan, South Orleans, MA.

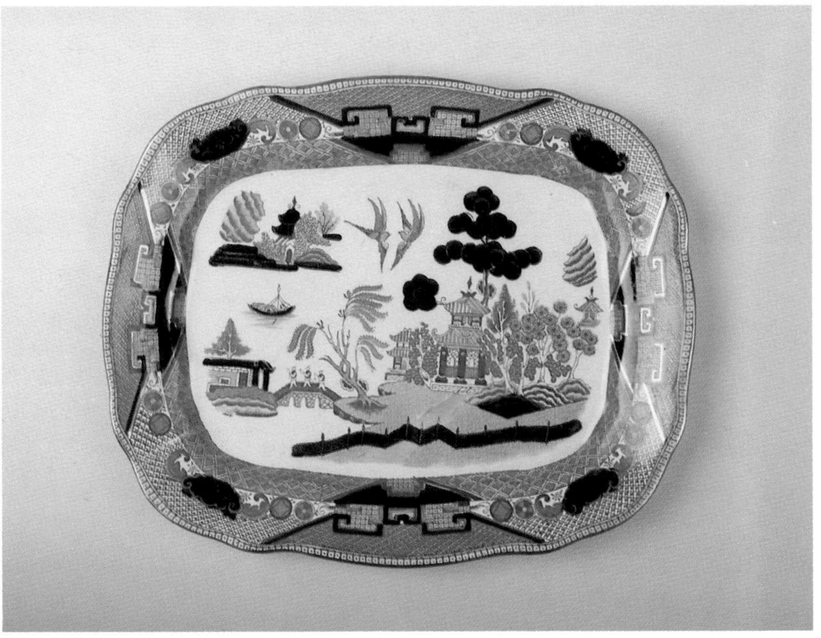

A scallop-edged rectangular platter from the Buffalo Pottery, 1907, 11" x 9". From the collection of Phillip M. Sullivan, South Orleans, MA.

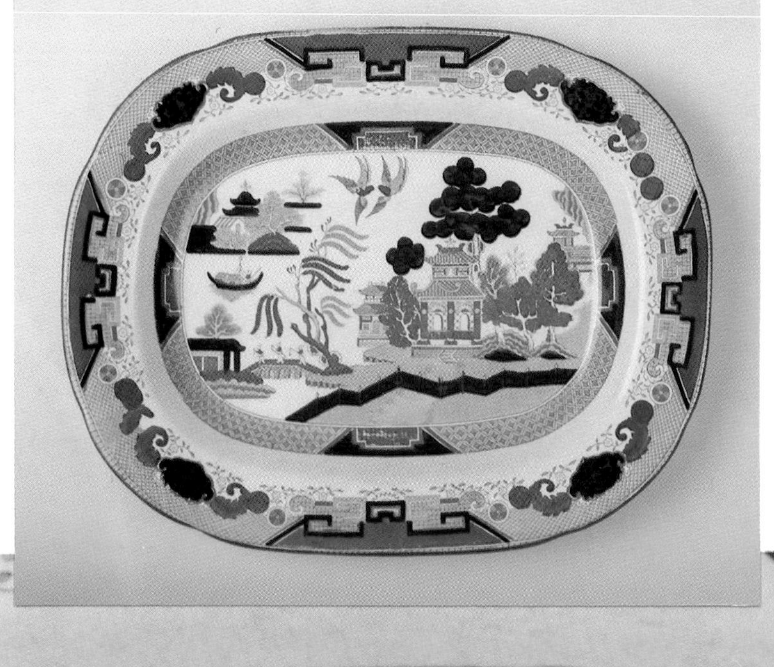

A Gaudy Willow rectangular platter from the Buffalo Pottery, 1909, 9.5" x 12". From the collection of Phillip M. Sullivan, South Orleans, MA.

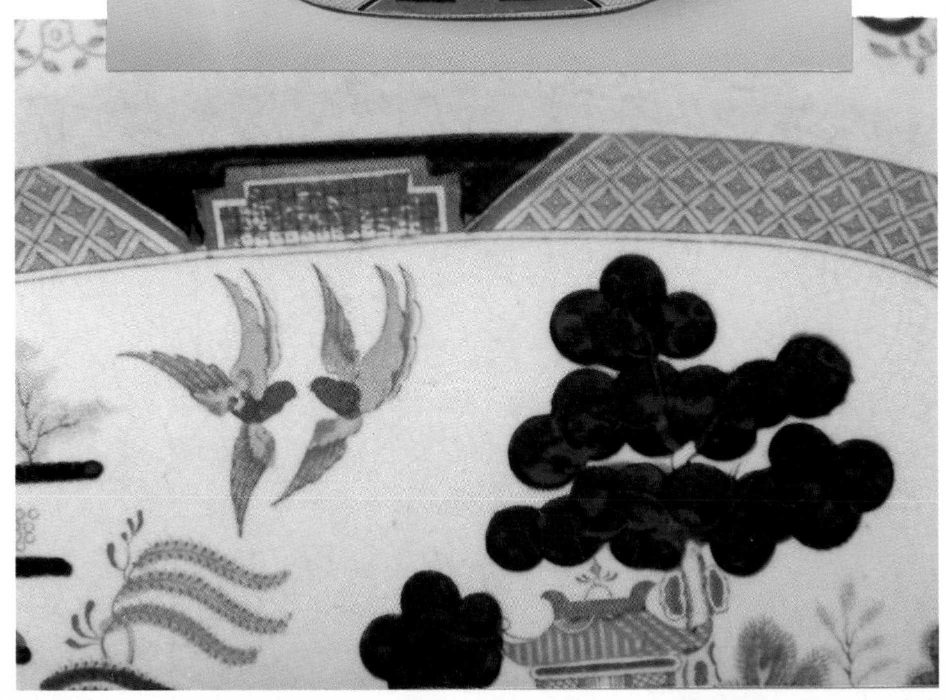

A close up of crazing on Buffalo Pottery's earthenware. As Earthenware ages, it dries, and shrinks slightly. This makes the vitreous, glassy surface of the glaze crack, or 'craze'.

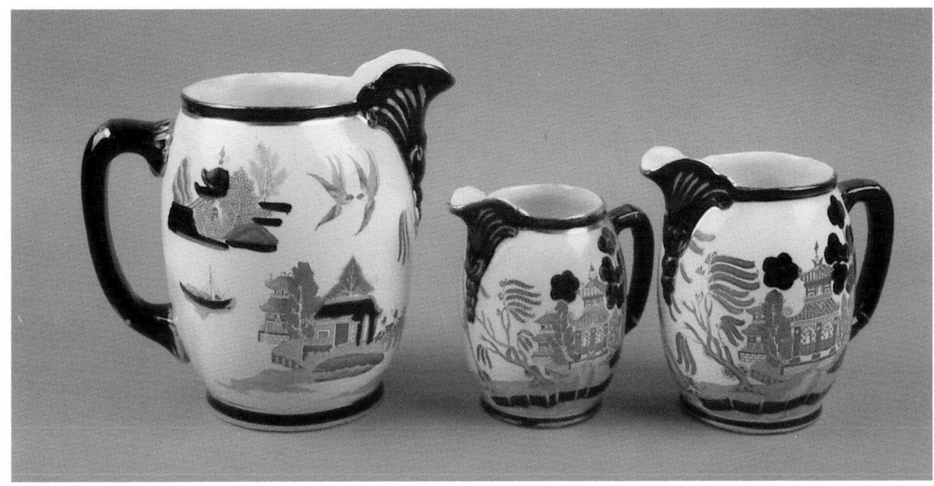

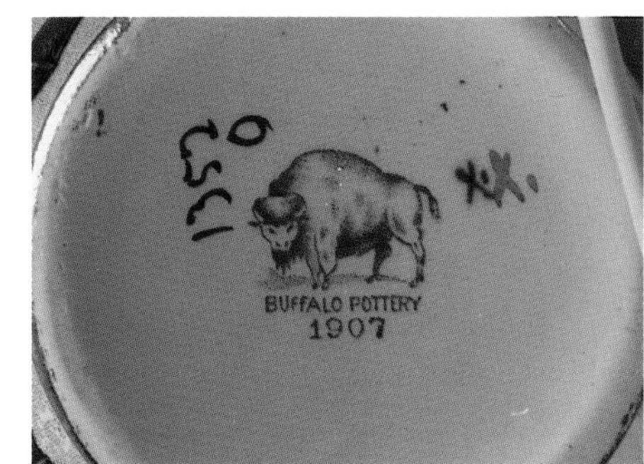

Mark on the mid-sized pitcher

Three Gaudy Willow pitchers from the Buffalo Pottery in 1907. The tallest pitcher stands 7" high. From the collection of Phillip M. Sullivan, South Orleans, MA.

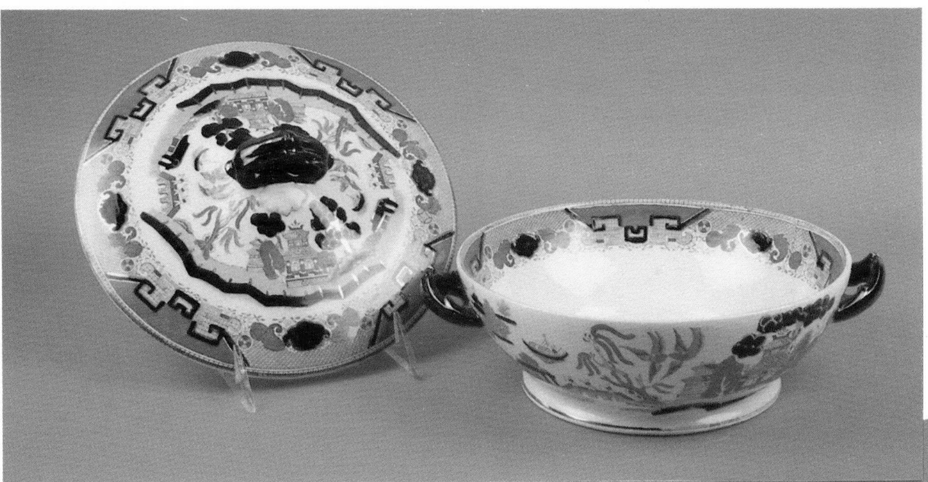

A Gaudy Willow serving bowl from the Buffalo Pottery in 1909, 6" high x 9" diam. From the collection of Phillip M. Sullivan, South Orleans, MA.

A Gaudy Willow teapot from the Buffalo Pottery, 1905, 6" high x 8.75" wide. From the collection of Phillip M. Sullivan, South Orleans, MA.

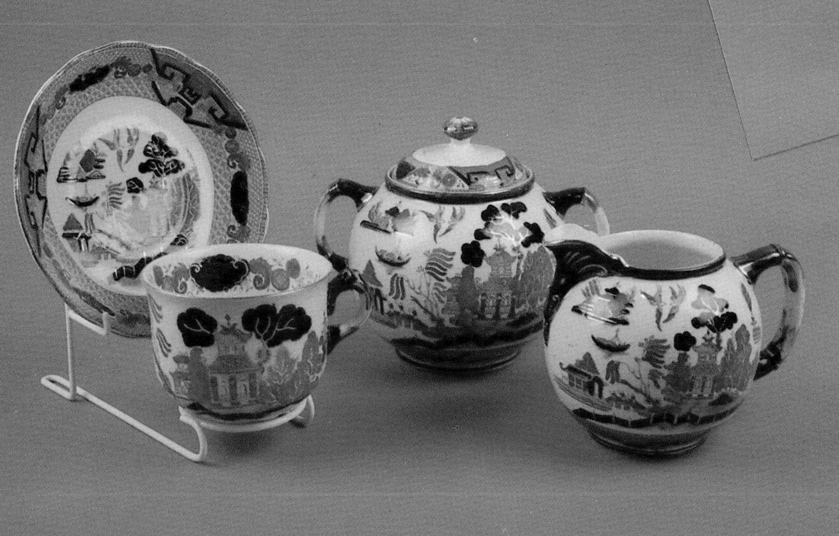

A Gaudy Willow tea set from the Buffalo Pottery, 1905. While most of these pieces were produced for a number of years, the cup and saucer in this form were made only in 1905. All of these pieces except the teacup are marked "First Old Willow Ware" along with the printed mark "Manufactured in America." From the collection of Phillip M. Sullivan, South Orleans, MA.

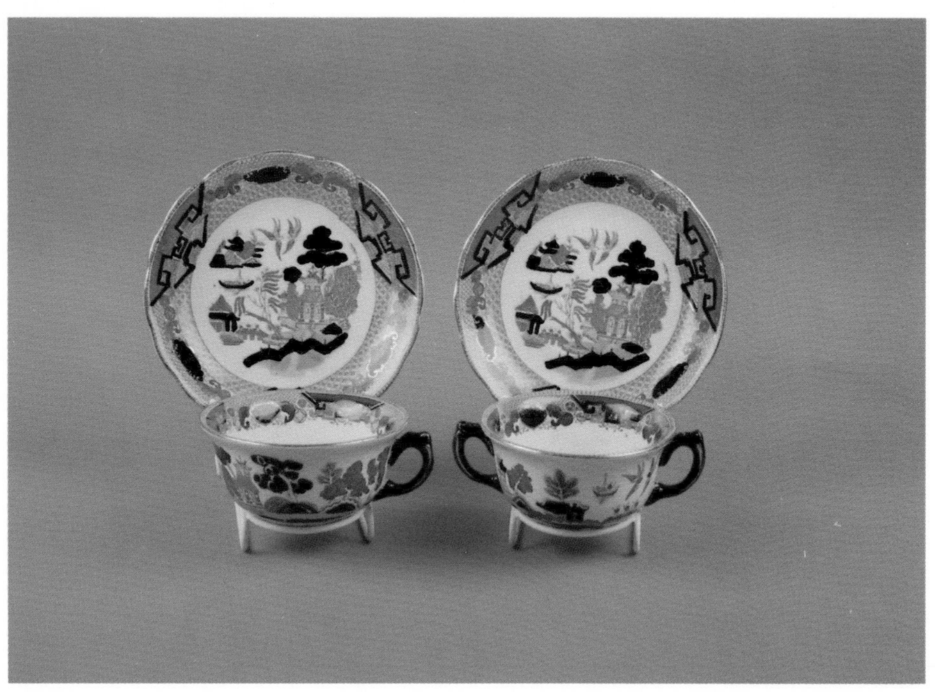

A tea cup and a bouillon cup in Gaudy Willow, both from the Buffalo Pottery, 1911. These pieces are marked with the pottery's standard mark, not as "First Old Willow Ware." From the collection of Phillip M. Sullivan, South Orleans, MA.

Tea pot mark. Same as on the entire tea set. From the collection of Phillip M. Sullivan, South Orleans, MA..

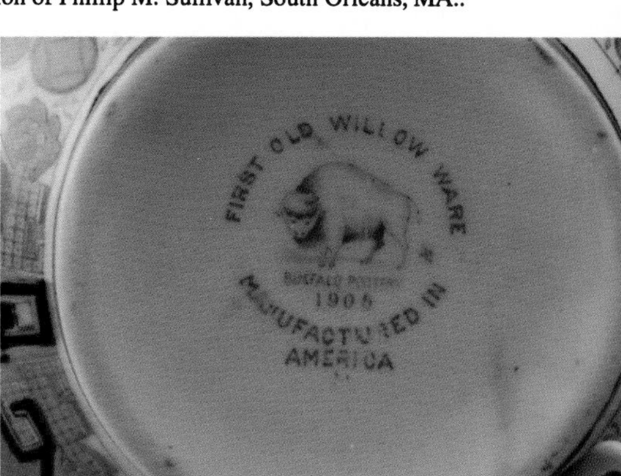

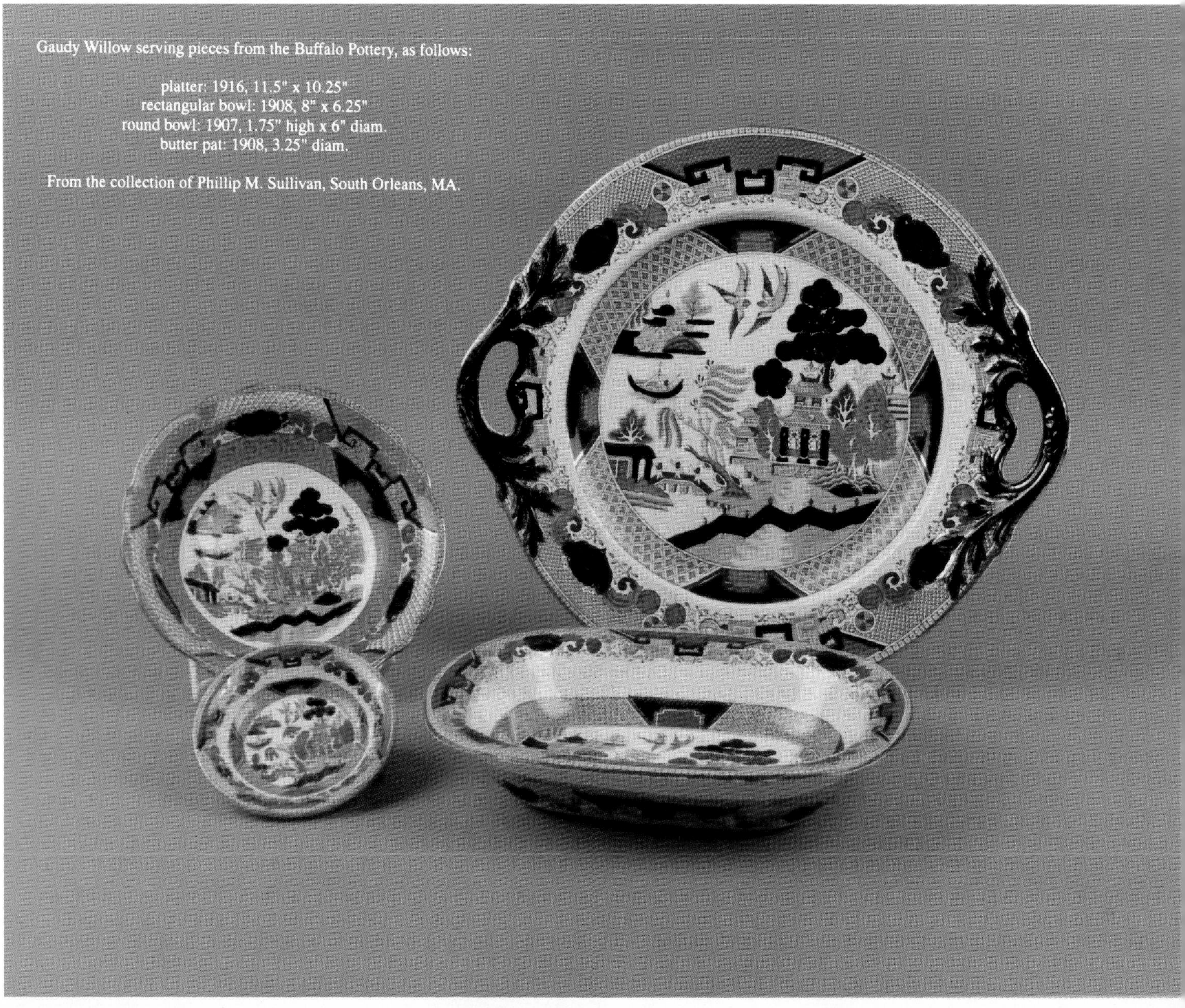

Gaudy Willow serving pieces from the Buffalo Pottery, as follows:

platter: 1916, 11.5" x 10.25"
rectangular bowl: 1908, 8" x 6.25"
round bowl: 1907, 1.75" high x 6" diam.
butter pat: 1908, 3.25" diam.

From the collection of Phillip M. Sullivan, South Orleans, MA.

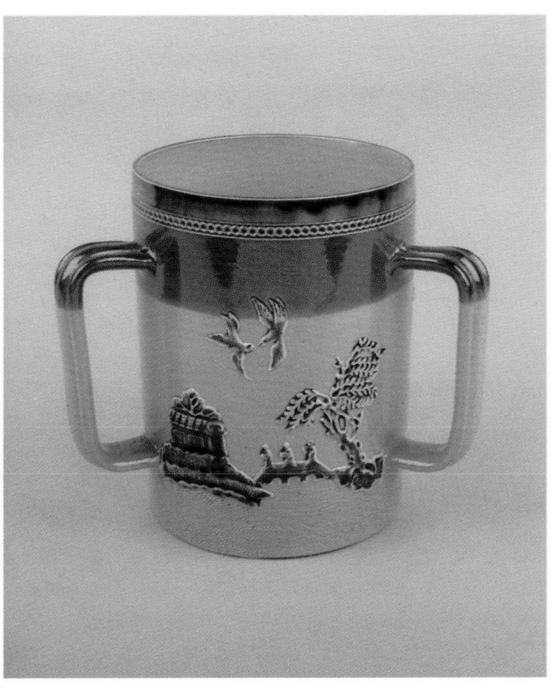

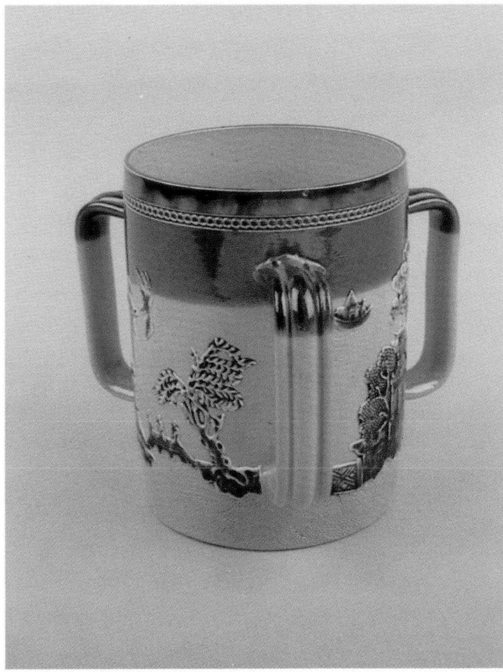

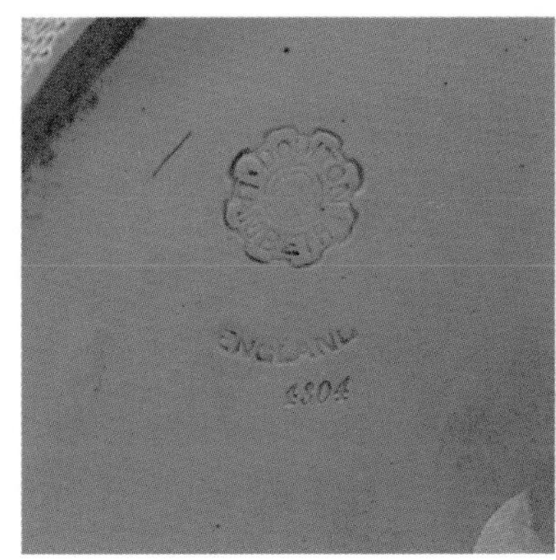

A three-handled mug in brown pottery by Doulton Lambeth, c. 1900, 6.25" high. Courtesy of Rita Entmacher Cohen.

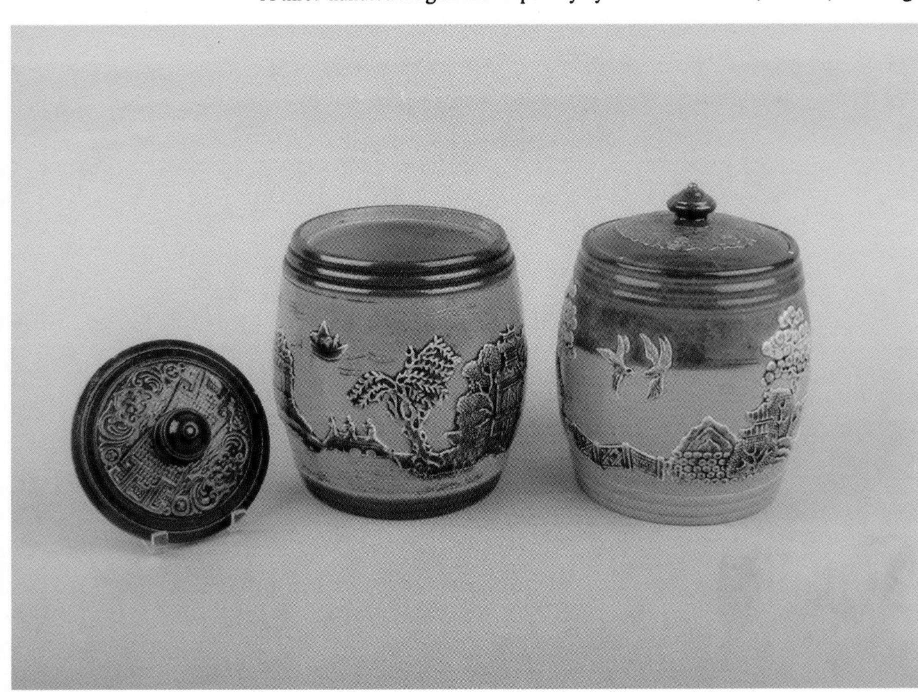

Two covered tobacco jars in brown pottery by Doulton Lambeth, 6" high. The jar with a solid background has a mark (not pictured) identical to that on the matching three-handled mug. The mark shown here appears on the base of the jar with a two-color background. Courtesy of Rita Entmacher Cohen.

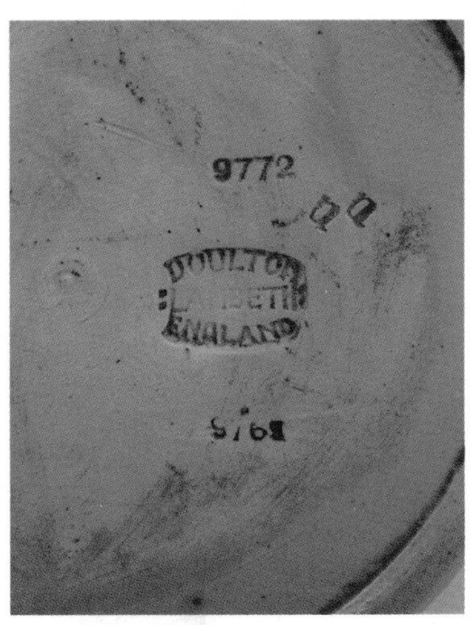

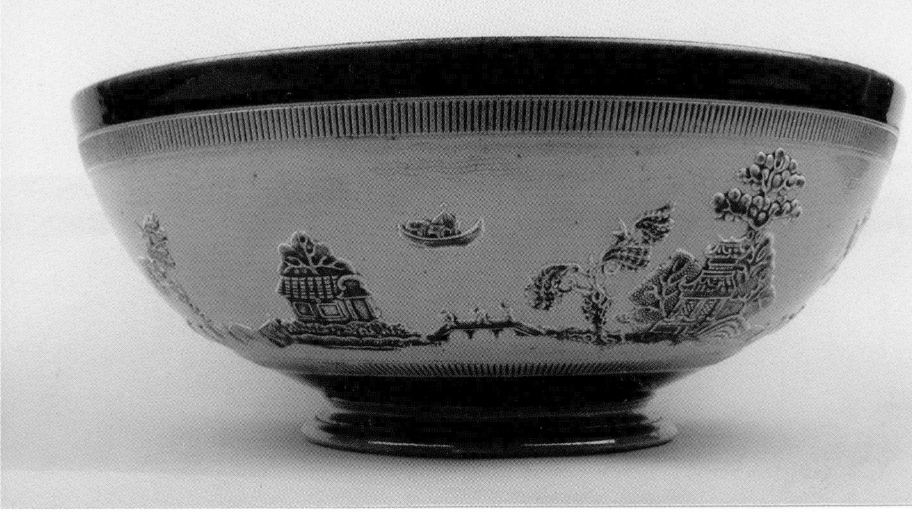

An extremely large pottery bowl by Doulton, 7" high x 17.25" diam. Courtesy of Rita Entmacher Cohen.

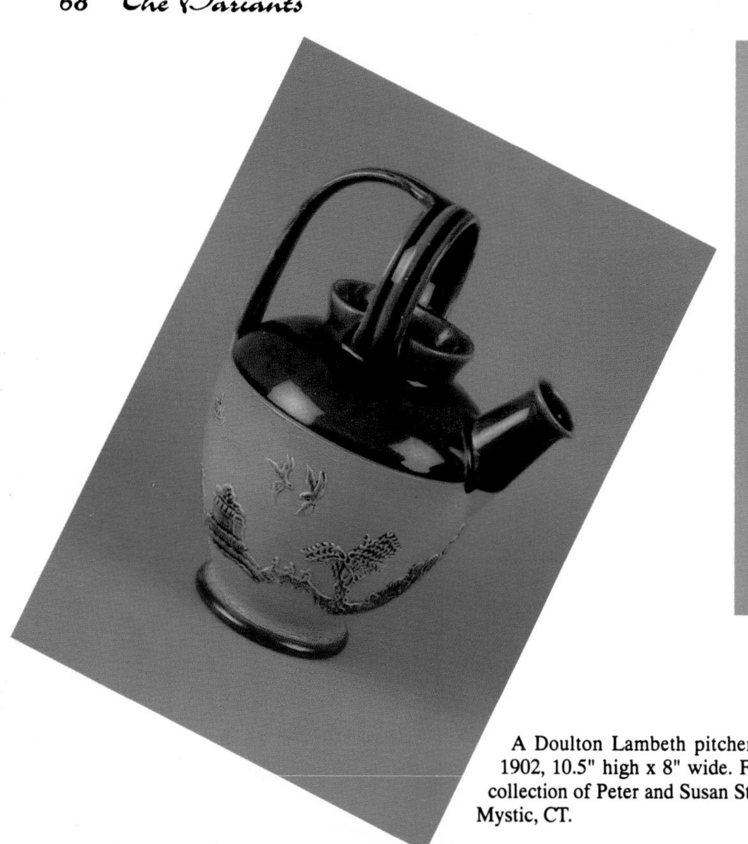

A Doulton Lambeth pitcher, 1899-1902, 10.5" high x 8" wide. From the collection of Peter and Susan Steelman, Mystic, CT.

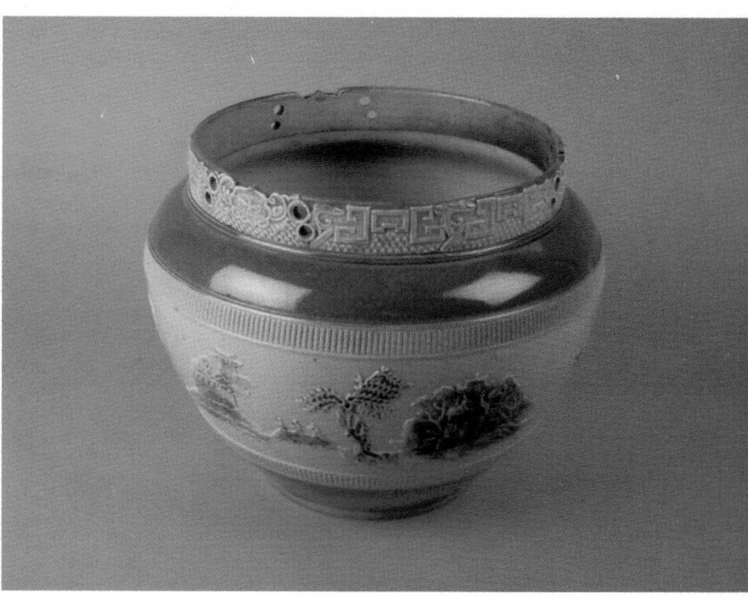

A hanging jardiniere by Doulton Lambeth, 8" high x 10.5". From the collection of Peter and Susan Steelman, Mystic, CT.

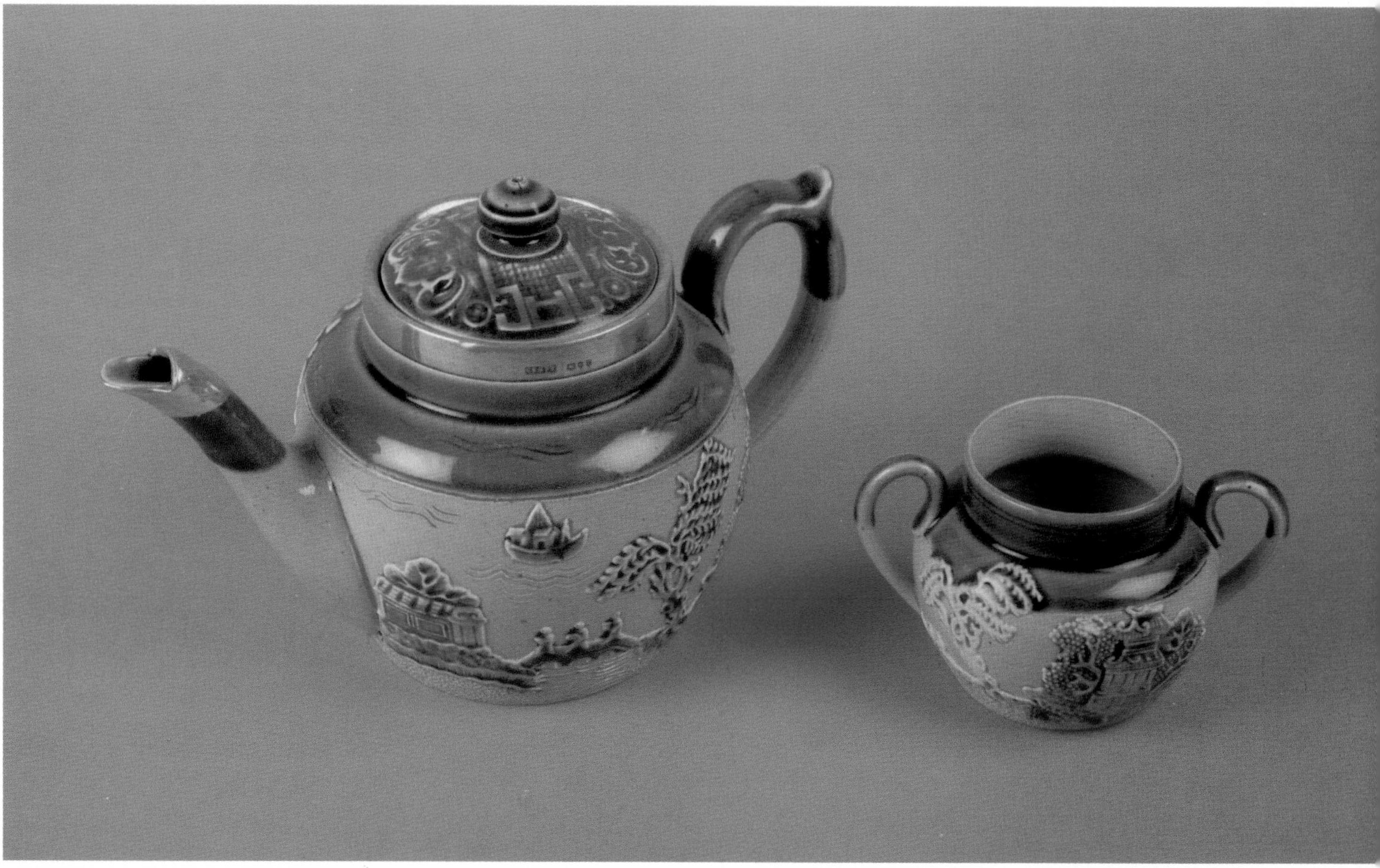

A teapot and lidless sugar from Doulton Lambeth. From the collection of Peter and Susan Steelman, Mystic, CT.

Chapter 6

The Makers:
From England to America, and Beyond

"Consumption is the sole end and purpose of all production; and the interest of the producer ought to be attended to, only so far as it may be necessary for promoting that of the consumer"—from Adam Smith's *Wealth of Nations.*[1]

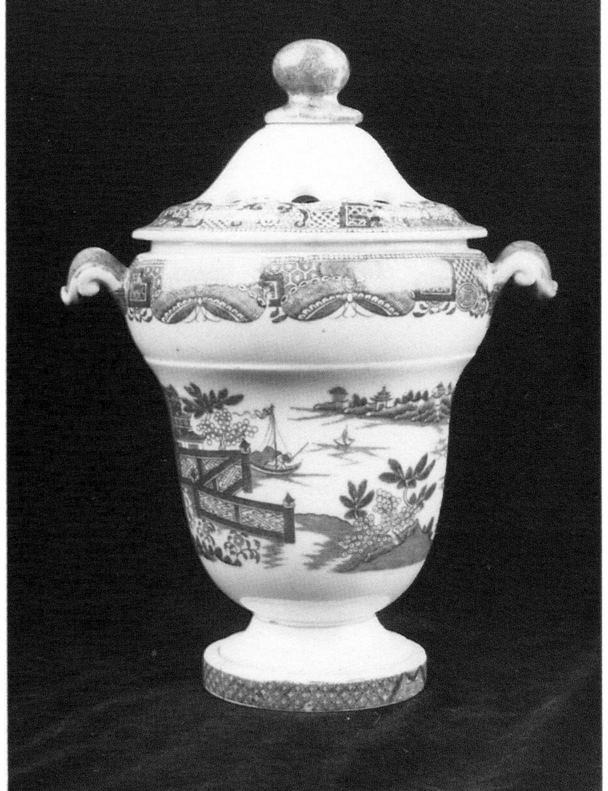

A pearlware potpourri container in three pieces: the finial, the lid, and the bowl. Pieces like this were not made often after the general quality declined. Courtesy of Rita Entmacher Cohen.

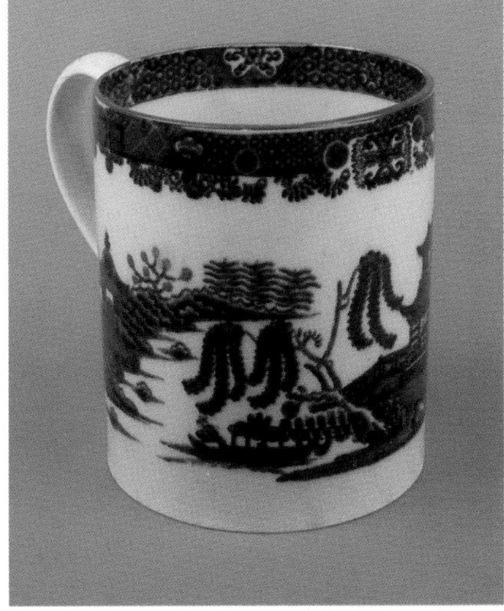

A large pearlware mug, c. 1800, 5.5". Courtesy of Rita Entmacher Cohen.

After well-reputed companies like Copeland/Spode, Caughley and Minton established chinoiserie Willow as the rage in England, the style began to undergo an evolution similar to the one blue-and-white porcelain had undergone in China centuries earlier: the quality of the wares and the social standing of the customers began to drop.

A horde of lesser-known potters began producing their own versions of the Standard Willow pattern. By 1830, there were nearly 200 makers of underglaze blue willow in England,[2] most of them fly-by-night companies that left no records. Because their sales were made by virtue of the pattern's popularity rather than on the strength of the companys' reputations, many of them marked their wares with just a Staffordshire knot, if at all—not much help for identification. Furthermore, because all of these potters were trying to enter an established market by copying the pattern as faithfully as they could, there are not often differences important enough to allow modern researchers to distinguish between the versions decisively. It is almost impossible to attribute a piece of early Standard Willow unless it is marked, or without comparing it to a marked piece.[3]

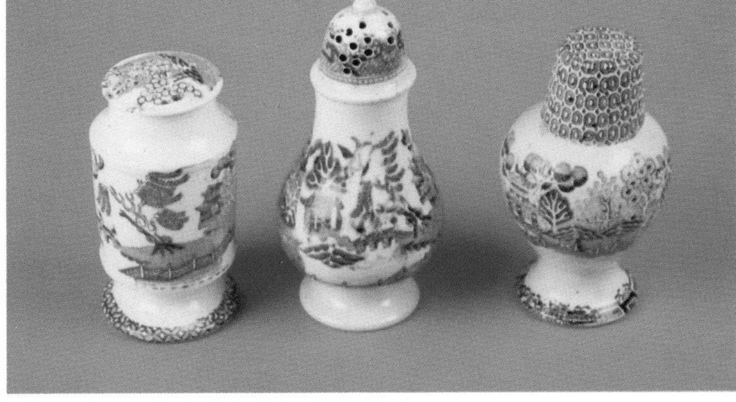

Three different salt & pepper shakers, all unmarked. The cream-colored shaker is overglaze printed. The quality decline is obvious here. From the collection of Peter and Susan Steelman, Mystic, CT.

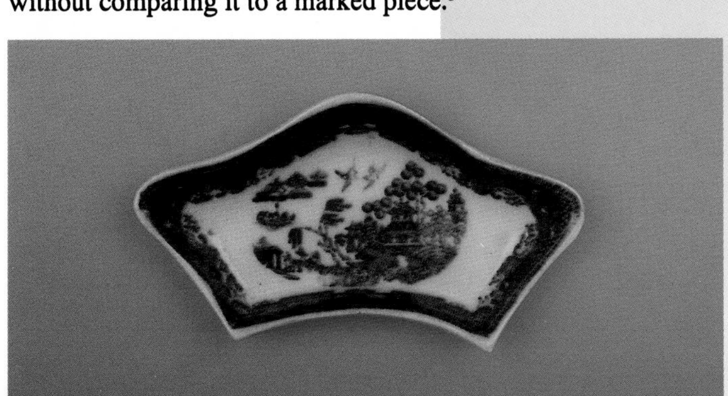

A small dish, 5" wide, from a sectional supper set or condiment service set. Courtesy of Rita Entmacher Cohen.

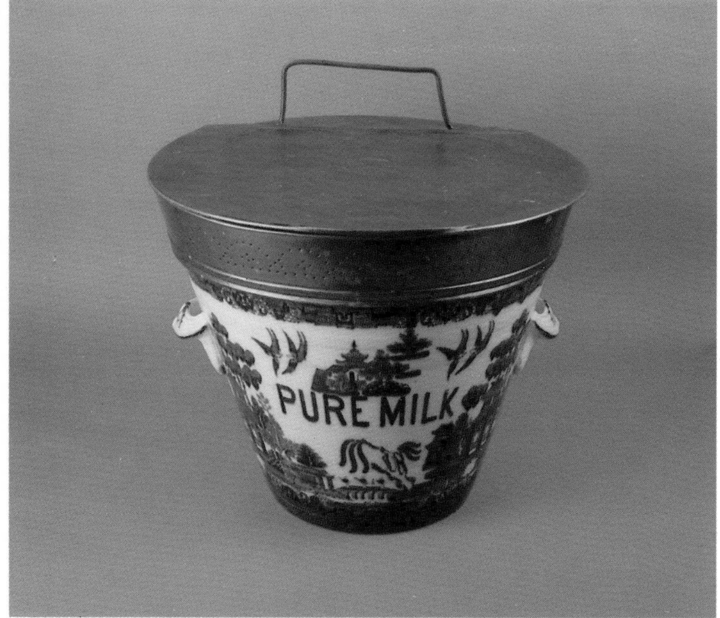

An undated milk pail, 16" high x 12.5" diam. The cover is brass, and the bottom is marked "Dairy Outfit Co Ltd, Kings Crossing." From the collection of Peter and Susan Steelman, Mystic, CT.

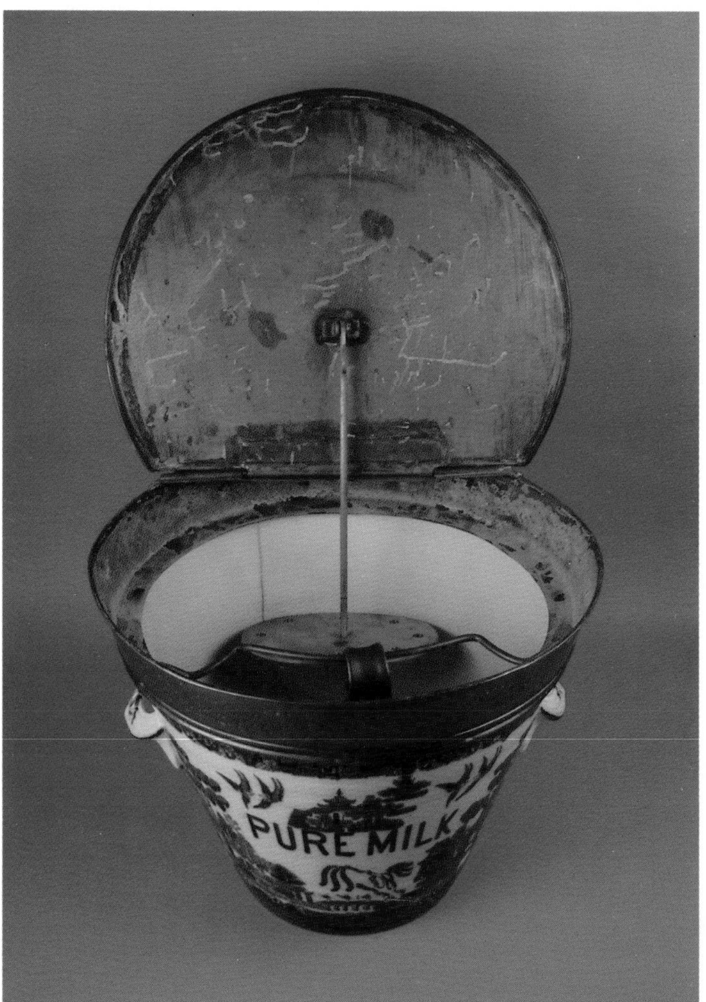

It is important to remember, though, that the original customers of Willow wares did not discriminate between the different manufacturers' marks on the backs of their dishes; they were interested in the design on the front. Indeed, when dishes were advertised, they were listed by type and pattern, not by maker.[4]

As Willow's popularity moved down the social ladder, many customers became similarly indiscriminate about the *quality* of their Willow wares. As Rita Entmacher Cohen told attendees at the 1994 International Willow Collectors convention, "It [was] not out of place in the houses of the rich; it [was] welcome in the houses of the poor." The breadth of the market allowed many potters of varying skill and quality to find their own niches. Wealthy customers who were accustomed to expensive blue and white Chinese exports (and might even be purchasing the English wares to supplement imported sets) demanded fine china, porcelain, and the best earthenwares, but the middle and lower classes were content with less refined lookalikes, which nonetheless smacked of blue-and-white elegance. For these customers, the quality of the wares, like the prestige of the marks, was insignificant; indeed, the hardier, coarser grades of earthenware were even better suited for general everyday use. Because the blue and white Willow pattern appealed to such a broad range of customers, it was guaranteed to remain a perpetual top-seller—but it was also guaranteed that a large quantity of inferior-quality wares would be produced to satisfy the lower end of the market.

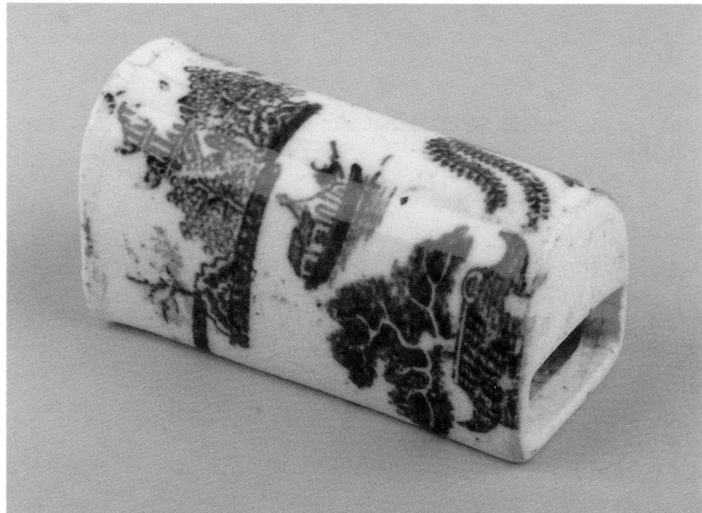

A toothbrush cover, unmarked. Courtesy of Rita Entmacher Cohen.

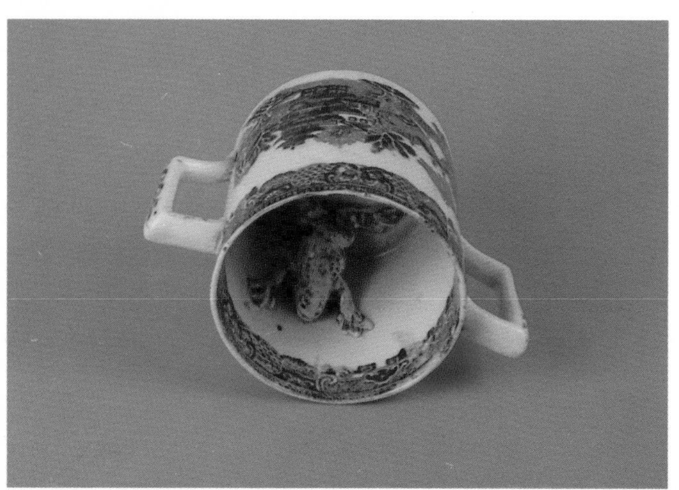

A loving cup with a frog inside, unmarked. 4" x 4". From the collection of Peter and Susan Steelman, Mystic, CT.

Predictably, as the middle and lower classes embraced blue and white chinoiserie, and the inexpensive wares they required flooded the market, the elite began to disown it. While other patterns went in and out of style, Willow maintained a constant share of the market—as the cheapest of the blue-printed wares.[5] This did not endear it to the status-minded and style-conscious upper classes, and by 1835 multi-colored wares were the new trend in genteel circles. They began to consider the blue and white color scheme cheap, common, and unappealing at the worst, and inoffensive at best. This change echoes the original development of blue and white porcelain wares in China in the 14th, 15th, and 16th centuries: when widespread demand and mass-production put blue and white into the hands of China's general population, the aristocracy turned to innovative, bright polychrome wares to distinguish itself.

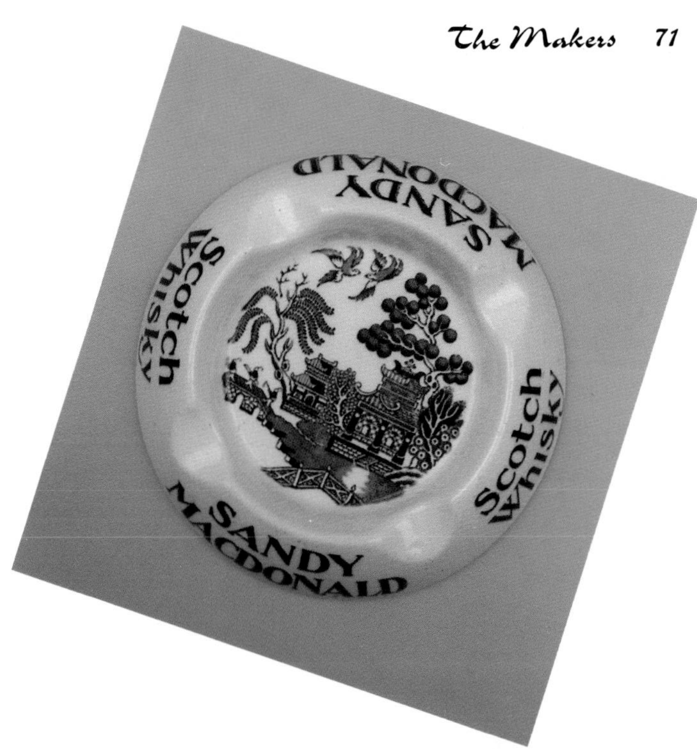

An advertising ashtray made by Minton's, 5.5" diam. Courtesy of Rita Entmacher Cohen.

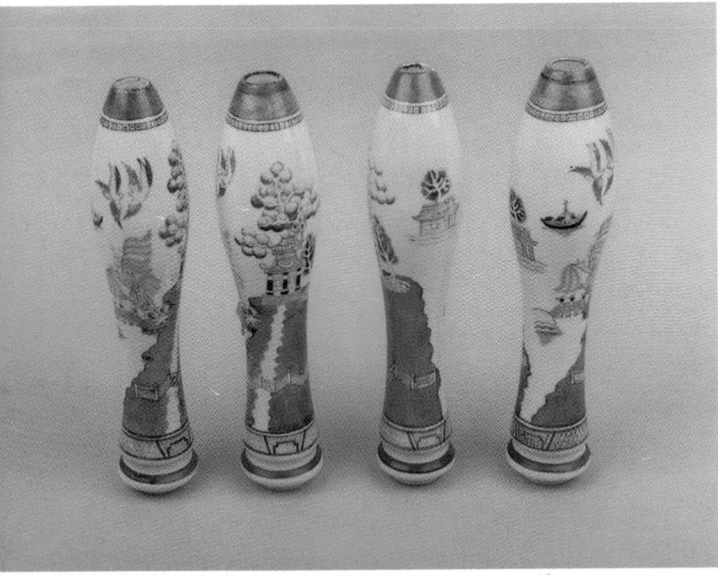

Four bar-pulls (handles for a pub's draft beer dispensers), each 8.75" long. Courtesy of Rita Entmacher Cohen.

Over the years, a string of other English patterns came to the forefront, diminishing both the high- and low-end market for Willow, but never completely displacing the old favorite. As George Gordon (no great admirer of the Willow pattern; see the boxed section) wrote in 1862, "with a general improvement in the design of the middling descriptions of English pottery—and likewise an advance in the general taste—other designs have become common, and the willow pattern has in proportion declined."[6]

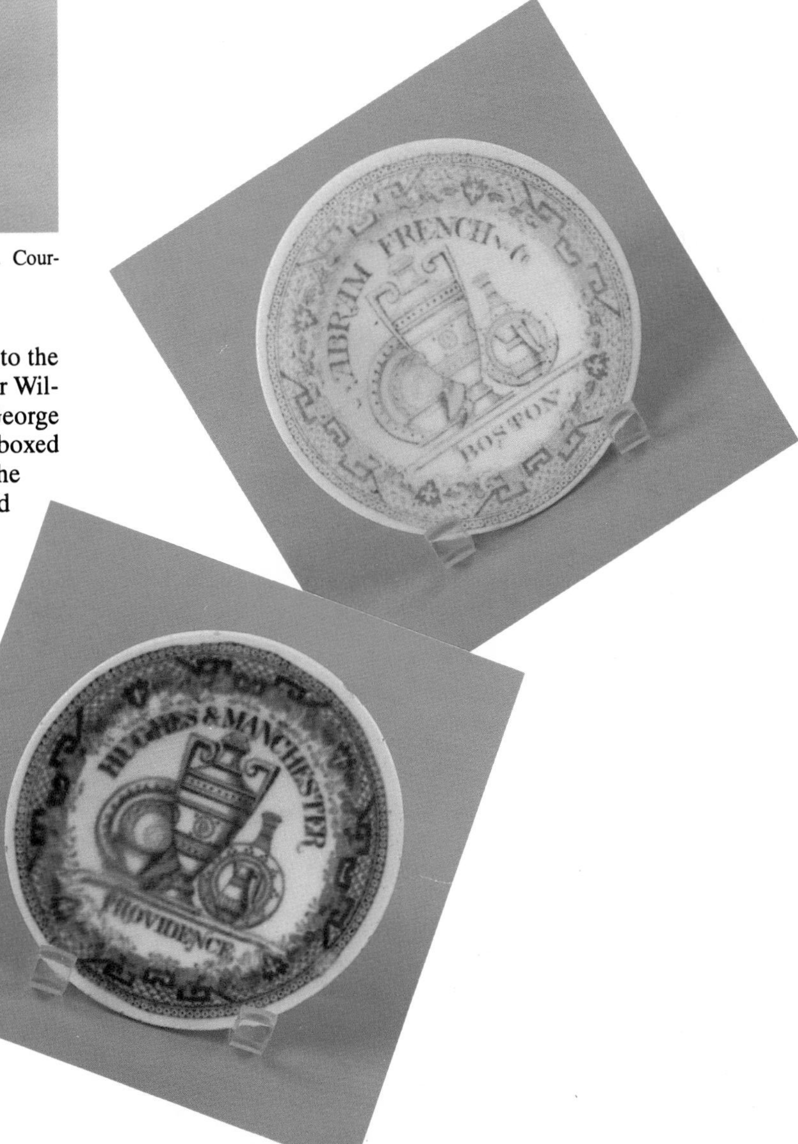

Advertising discs, 2.75" diam. From the collection of Peter and Susan Steelman, Mystic, CT.

A Minute Criticism

An 1862 article by design commentator George Godwin, editor of the weekly journal *The Builder,* provides some insight into the position of Willow in the world of English ceramic decoration throughout the 1800s. He wrote that

> The demand which there has been, for a considerable period, for earthenware decorated with this pattern has been enormous. We have no means of getting any satisfactory statistics, but it is certain that thousands of pieces for table use, decorated in this kind of Anglo-Chinese taste, have long been manufactured and sold yearly. [It has been found] in the houses of the higher and middle classes; in the houses of artists and persons of taste, as well as those who are destitute of accomplishment; and in humble dwellings."

This influential writer, whose readers included Florence Nightingale and Prince Albert over the forty years he edited *The Builder*, speculated about the reasons for Willow's universal appeal. Like many members of the cultural elite during this period, he had little favorable to say:

> It is worth while to consider the cause of this design meeting with such extensive favour...it cannot be truly said that the pattern possesses any claim to consideration for any intellectual qualities which are shown in the pictorial features of the design. There are the steep Chinese bridges; the tall many-storied towers; the peculiar foliage; distant hill; water; and the usual number of stiff ill-drawn figures; the whole having an artificial appearance which we cannot fairly compare with nature, or test by acknowledged rules or principles of art...Without entering into any minute criticism, it may be remarked that the general appearance is clear-looking, and the contrast of the blue and white colours is also agreeable to the eye; besides, at the time of the introduction of this description of ware everything Chinese, even to the pig-tails, was a raging fashion.

To what, then, did Mr. Gordon attribute the seemingly endless market (among the middle and working classes, if not among the upper-crust) for newly-made Willow wares? "In considering the subject," he answered, "we may glance at the other kinds of table pottery which there was then in the market, to be bought for a reasonable price." While he mentions that an effort had been made to improve the decoration of the more expensive English porcelain and high-grade earthenwares, "pictorial art, in conjunction with the ware required for general use, was extremely inferior...colored with dashes done at random from brushes &c...[and] engravings of English figure and landscape subjects which were transferred, and more or less tinted, by boys, girls and women, who were wholly without art-education." These he described as "barbarous in the extreme." Compared to these, he finds Willow a lesser affront to his aesthetic tastes:

> When we think of these, it is not to be wondered at that, besides the prevailing fashion [of chinoiserie], the contrast of the plates and dishes of the willow pattern with the plain common white ones, and those disfigured by the attempts at ornamentation to which we have referred, should have brought them largely into use.

Over the years, the ever-present Willow pattern saw competing patterns rise and fall with regularity. While Willow was not to remain the rage forever, it never lost its place in manufacturers' catalogues, on shopkeepers' shelves, and on customers' tables. Among sceptical commentators, like Mr. Gordon, there is a pragmatic explanation for this:

> When anything is once well-established,—whether is be a gas-lamp, a pewter ale-pot, an omnibus, a locomotive, or fifty other matters that might be mentioned,—the very familiarity and constant view of the objects cause them to be accepted by the great masses of the multitude, without much consideration as regards their artistic beauties or defects."

From *Friends of Blue*, Autumn 1989, contributed by Ruth Richardson.

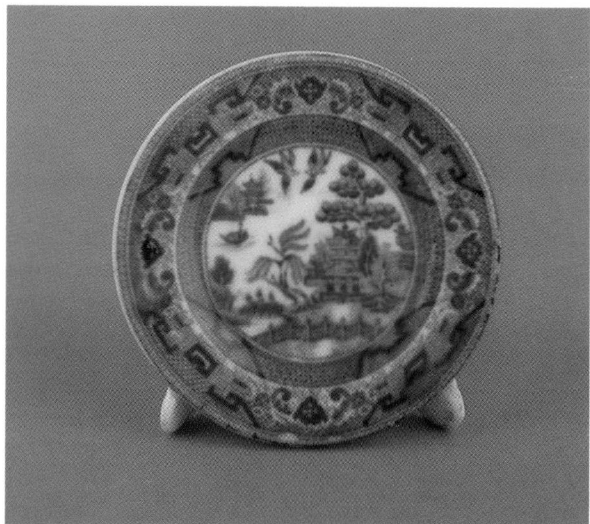

For lovers of the pattern, however, Willow's charming blue and white and graceful chinoiserie scene are sufficient justifications for its lasting popularity.

The decreased demand for Willow on English shores did not put all of the pattern's manufacturers out of business. The English learned the same lesson Chinese potters had over a century ago: when the domestic market dries up, *export*. The export market was especially lucrative for English manufacturers because of their widepread colonization. English tastes and styles circulated all over the globe, accompanying English prisoners to Australia, merchants and administrators to Africa and India, and emigrants to America. As Rita Entmacher Cohen noted, "it is perhaps impossible to go anywhere the British settled without encountering Willow."

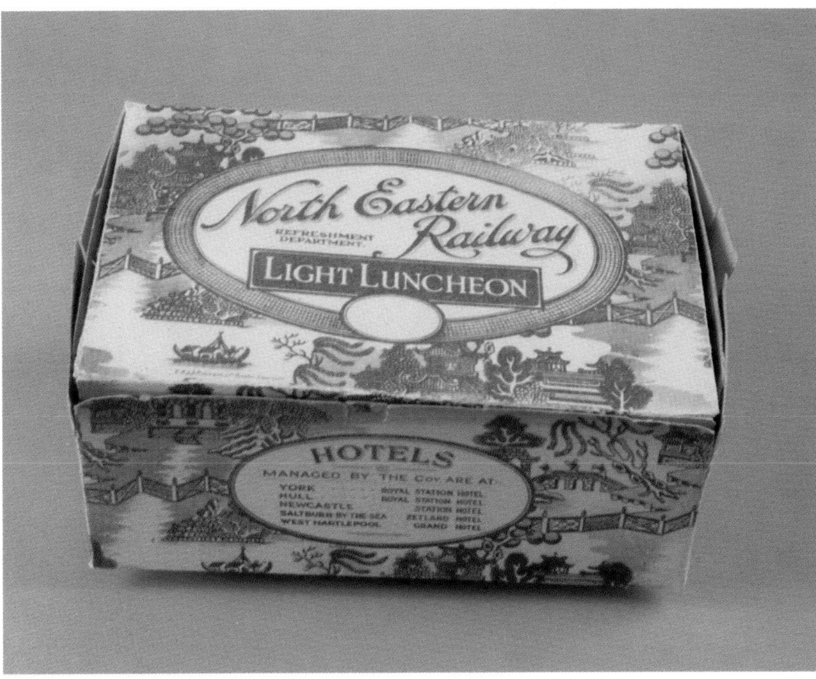

A "light luncheon" box from the North Eastern Railway Refreshment Department. From the collection of Peter and Susan Steelman, Mystic, CT.

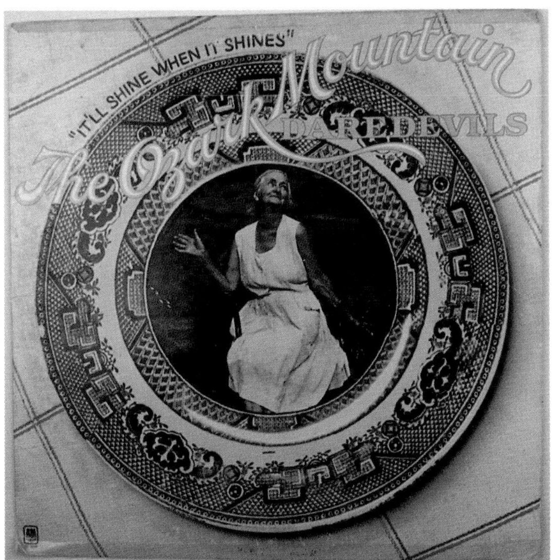

The cover from the Ozark Mountain Daredevil's album "It'll Shine When It Shines," featuring one typical willow border. Courtesy of Rita Entmacher Cohen.

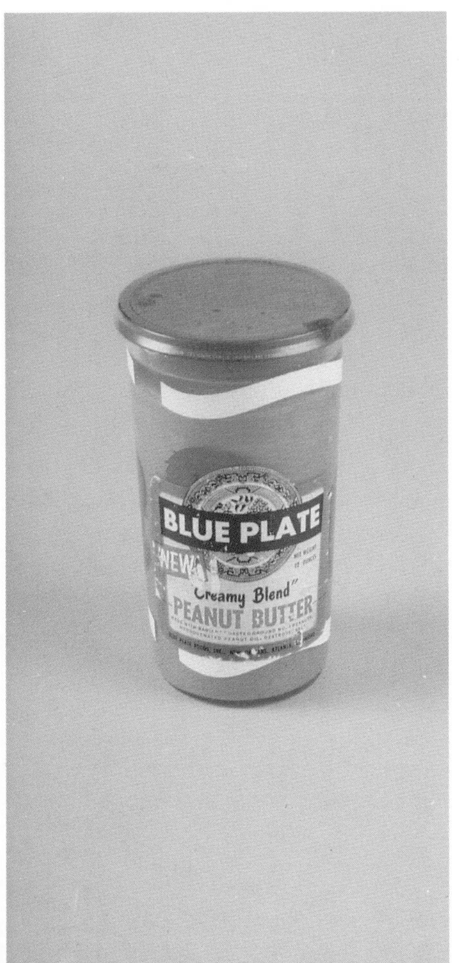

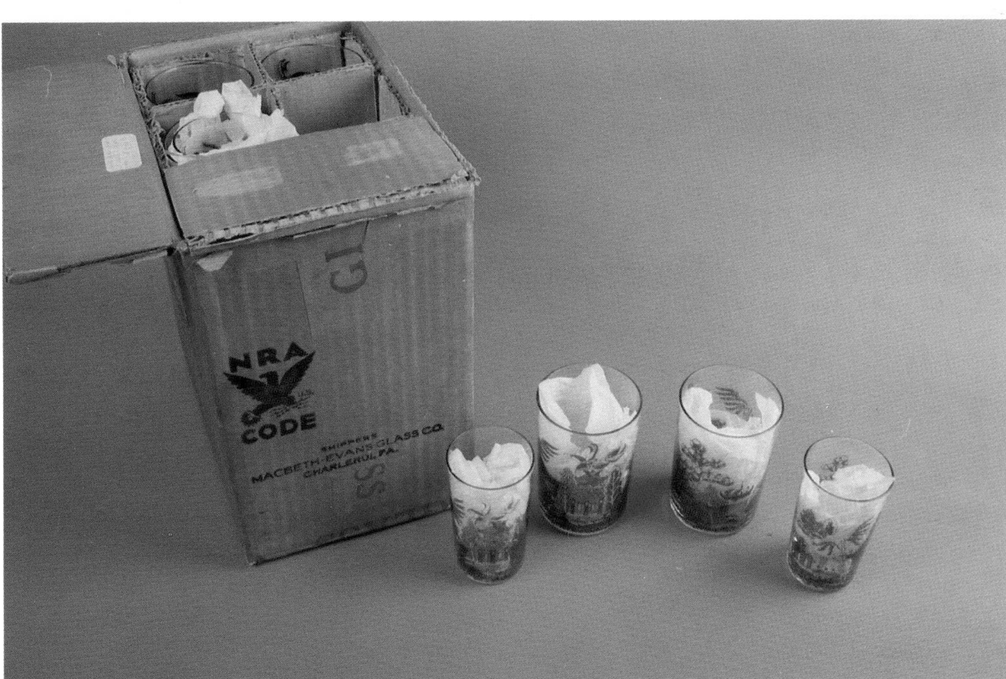

A set of American glasses produced under the National Recovery Act, c. 1930. This original box contains six each of three different sizes. Courtesy of Charles and Louise Loehr, Louise's Old Things, Kutztown, PA.

A 12 oz. jar of Blue Plate peanut butter from the 1950s, 5.25" high. Courtesy of Wendy's Willow.

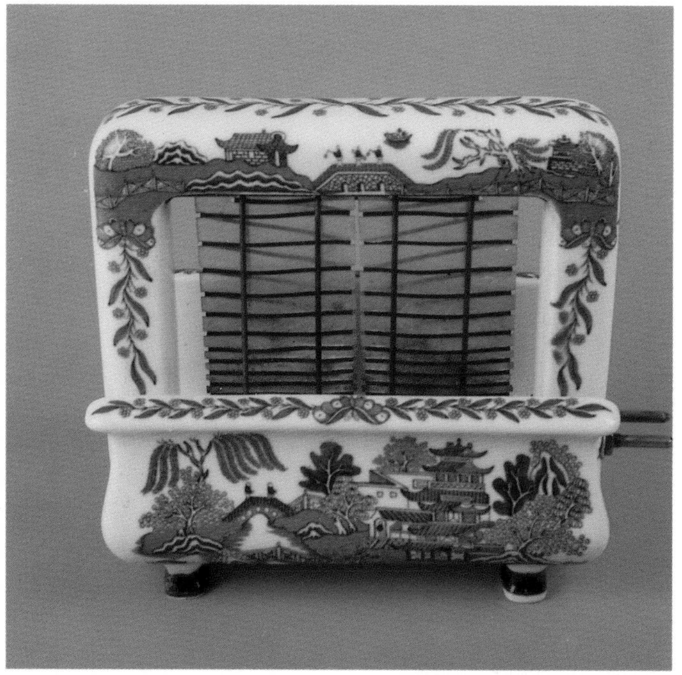

A toaster from 1929, 6.75" high x 7.25" wide. The bottom scene is a reversed version of Two Temples II, while the top is the Standard Willow pattern. The mark reads "TOASTRITE," from Cleveland, originally priced at $9.95. In 1992, an identical piece sold at auction for $2,000. From the collection of Peter and Susan Steelman, Mystic, CT.

America was, and continues to be, an enthusiastic market for Willow wares—perhaps even surpassing the pattern's original home in England. In 1783, just a few short years after the American Revolution, a treaty had already been arranged to increase trade between England and the States. Before the turn of the century, English potteries had made good use of this opening; they began shipping blue and white transfer-printed earthenwares and porcelain across the Atlantic Ocean. By 1810, pearlware had become America's dominant tableware. From 1814 to 1860, the United States was England's best export market for ceramics, receiving 40% to 60% of the potteries' output.[7] The scope of American demand for Willow should come as no surprise—America was a swiftly growing nation, and thus a swiftly growing market. Most of the masses of immigrants arriving on U. S. shores needed goods to establish new households, from beds and bedclothes to tables and tablewares.[7] Often these goods were American-made; but it was not unusual for the newcomers' housewares to have been shipped from Europe, on the same boat on which they had just arrived, or one very similar.

Blue and white pottery was the most popular English export dishware among these immigrants. It was reminiscent of decades of established English tradition—ranking it as 'elegant' for those American-born, and 'homey' for those newly-arrived, who had long seen it used in the kitchens of their mothers and grandmothers.[8] Above all, it was guaranteed to be of good taste. These attitudes were a great boon to English potters, who were quite pleased with the continual growth of the market across the Atlantic.

The growing population of America provided the English with an unprecedented market, but it also presented a huge field of potential competitors. Immigrants made up a seemingly endless workforce of both skilled and unskilled labor, and America began to develop industries to challenge the longstanding British dominance. Potteries began to develop around the Mississippi, the Hudson, and the Ohio Rivers, and near cities with large work forces—and of course, near clay deposits. New York, Ohio, Tennessee, New Jersey, Kentucky, Georgia, North Carolina and West Virginia all had active pottery regions. Eventually, railroad lines became equally crucial to the companies' successful expansion to Western markets.[9]

American potters had a difficult time overcoming English counterparts like Wedgwood, Minton and Spode, since American consumers were steadfastly convinced of the superiority of English china.[10] In addition to the industrial growth necessary to compete in this field, American potters needed a marketing revolution. At the International Willow Collectors convention in 1993, Eugene Ellison quoted commentator Helen Stiles as saying that "in studying antiques, one soon realizes that everything we consider 'Early American' is an echo of something European." This observation summarizes the American potters'plan of attack. Throughout the mid- to late 1800s, American potters took an active role in 'echoing' their English competitors; they decided to create wares that were 'look-alikes' to the most popular English patterns. They were determined to claim their country's loyalty and respect, even if it meant copying English designs. Their situation was no different from that of their British counterparts a century earlier, when Chinese pottery was dominating the English home market. The English potters competed by producing their own 'look-alike' version of Chinese blue and white—transfer-printed pearlware—and carved out their own niche in the market.

It was necessary for the Americans to develop a product of a competitive quality, however, just as it had been necessary for the British. Again, in the realm of blue and white, this was a struggle. Before 1905, they were unable to capture the beautiful whites and deep cobalt blues of English underglaze decoration, and thus were relegated to producing a lower-end product. Eventually, however, the American potters developed methods of producing a ware that could issue a real challenge to the English product. In 1905, the first American-made blue Willow appeared—produced by the Buffalo Pottery of Ohio—and it has been described as "far superior in color, glaze and body to the imported ware."[11] The same author contends that the quality of Buffalo's "semiporcelain willow" was as good as (if not better than) much of the Willow ware coming out of contemporary English potteries.[12]

While Buffalo Pottery's pieces seem to be more aptly described as earthenware, it is likely that this proud description is otherwise accurate. Just as Chinese blue and white had been exported in quantity to England only after it had begun to decline in quality, and had only gotten progressively worse, late English Willow made for export to America was of a lesser quality than that which had been made for domestic sale in previous decades. Buffalo Pottery, poised for the opportunity, made sturdy wares in graceful forms, with a clean white background and vivid cobalt blue printing. The pattern was consistently detailed and clear.

After Buffalo established Willow as a profitable new American tradition, other potters (like Bennett, Homer Laughlin, McNicol, Shenango, Jackson, and Walker) were able to enter the market. These companies maintained Willow's prominence on store shelves, kitchen tables, and restaurant tables across the country, through the prosperity of the turn of the century, the misery of the Depression, the rallying of two World Wars. The market they established remains vibrant even today, as potteries, paper goods manufacturers, textile companies, and other makers of household goods apply the Willow pattern to everything from paper plates and napkins to decorative stove-burner covers, tea towels, and soup-can labels.

Immigrants to America in the 1800s looked upon the Willow pattern as something native to themselves, a tradition that meant comfort, family, and home. After decades of using imported Willow and almost a full century of using the wares made by U.S. manufaturers, it is only right that Americans can now claim Willow with pride, as an equal part of their own rich, vital heritage.

List of Makers

Adams: The Adams family began its pottery enterprise in 1657, and it is still active today. Its first member to do blue-printing was William Adams of Tunstall, who lived from 1746-1805 (between 1800 and 1850 there were three William Adams cousins who worked in Staffordshire). The William Adams who was born in 1745 was apprenticed to Josiah Wedgwood, and operated his own firm from 1779-1805 in Greengates, Tunstall. His son Benjamin Adams took over Tunstall when his father died in 1805, using the mark "B. Adams."

From 1804-1829, a different William Adams operated the Greenfield Works in Stoke-on-Trent, specializing in blue transfer-printed wares of admirable quality for the home market & abroad. This operation stayed in the Adams family until 1863. His son, also named William, opened the Greenfield Works of Tunstall in 1834, with his own sons William & Thomas. This firm passed to the two sons in 1865.

Marks usually use the family name; W. Adams & Sons used "W. A. & S." or the full name. Benjamin used "B. Adams." A variety of backstamps were used, often with trade names, pattern names or body type indicated.

Adams' pink Willow one-piece gravy boat, 9" long, "Warranted Staffordshire". From the collection of Peter and Susan Steelman, Mystic, CT.

An Adams gravy boat marked W. A. & C., Staffordshire, 8" wide. Courtesy of Rita Entmacher Cohen.

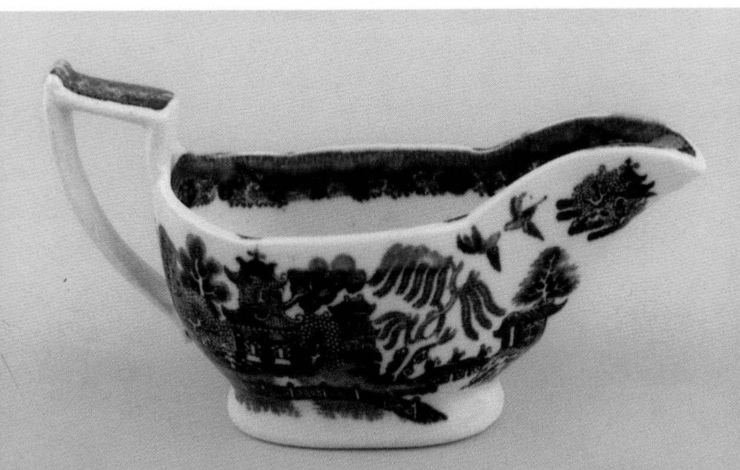

W. A. Adderley & Co.: Active c. 1874-1905, at the Daisy Bank Pottery in Longton, Staffordshire, England. Run by William Alsager Adderley. Produced dark blue-printed wares, bone china, and Willow in various colors. Used a mark of a sailing ship, a printed trademark between 1876-1905, with the initials "W.A.A." between 1876-1885, and "W.A.A. & Co." between 1886-1905.

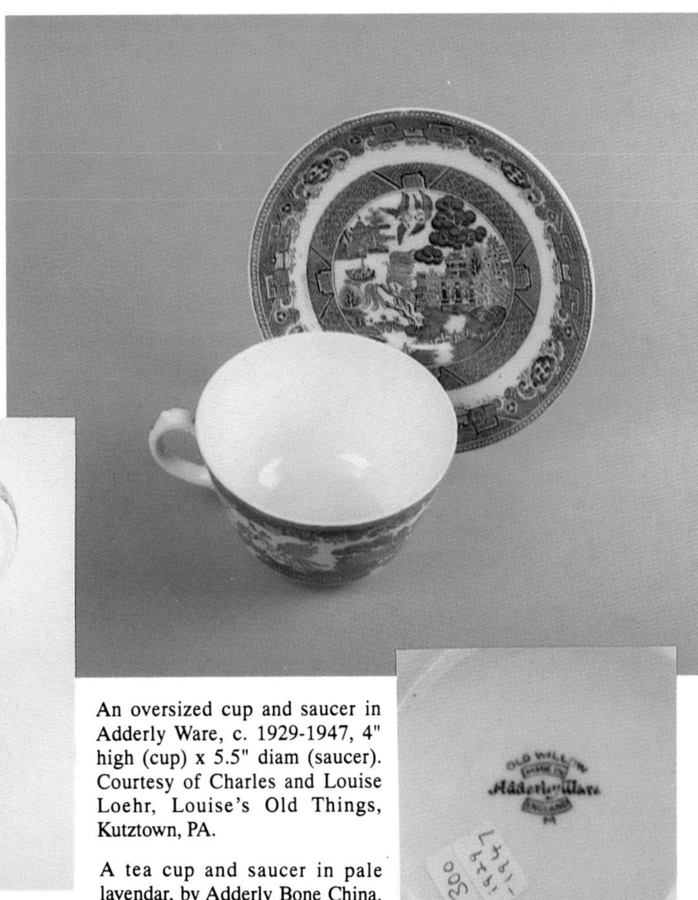

An oversized cup and saucer in Adderly Ware, c. 1929-1947, 4" high (cup) x 5.5" diam (saucer). Courtesy of Charles and Louise Loehr, Louise's Old Things, Kutztown, PA.

A tea cup and saucer in pale lavendar, by Adderly Bone China. From the collection of Peter and Susan Steelman, Mystic, CT.

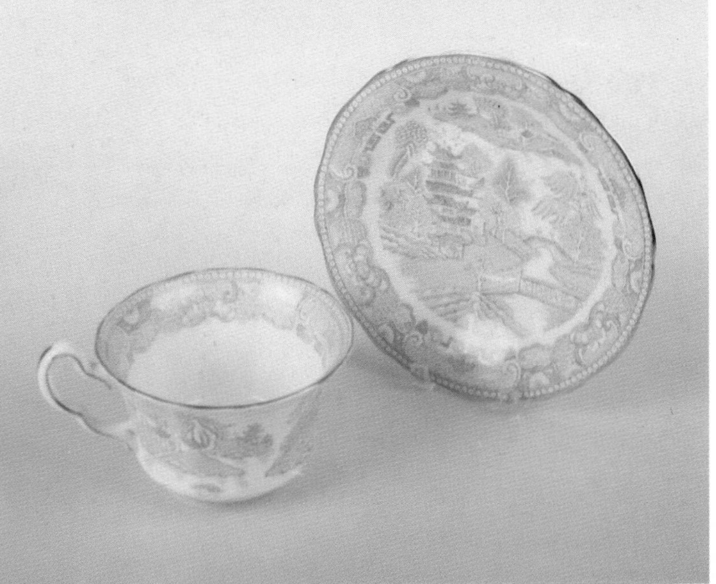

John Allason: Active 1838-1841 at Seaham Harbour Pottery in Sunderland, Durham, England. Used marks of "John Allason/ Seaham Pottery" on blue-printed "Forest" and "Willow" pattern wares.

Allerton: Operated at Park Works, Lane End, Staffordshire. Originally Allerton, Brough & Green (c. 1831-1859), which marked its blue-printed wares A.B. & G., succeeded by Charles Allerton & Sons at the same location. They made great quantities of blue-printed wares, unmarked until 1870-1890. Taken over in 1912 by Cauldon Potteries Ltd., and operated under the name Allerton's Ltd.

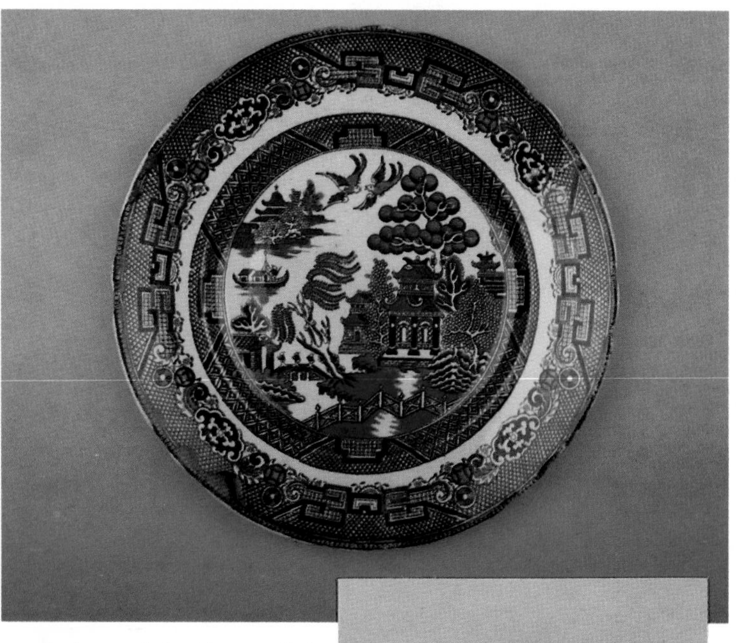

A plate made by Allertons, Ltd., 9.75" diam. Courtesy of Bobbie Jarow Antiques, 142 Main St., Nyack, NY.

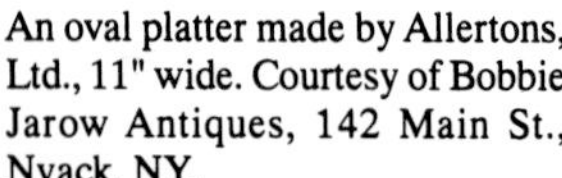

An oval platter made by Allertons, Ltd., 11" wide. Courtesy of Bobbie Jarow Antiques, 142 Main St., Nyack, NY.

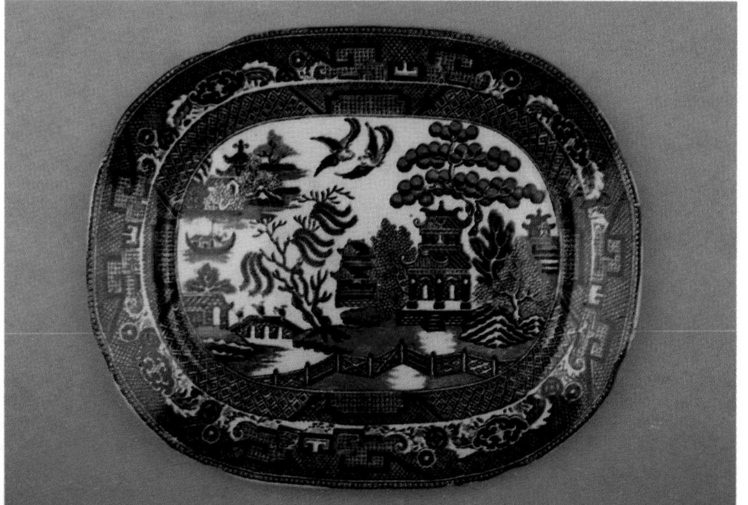

Arklow Pottery: Producing earthenwares since 1934, this current company is located in Co. Wicklow, Ireland.

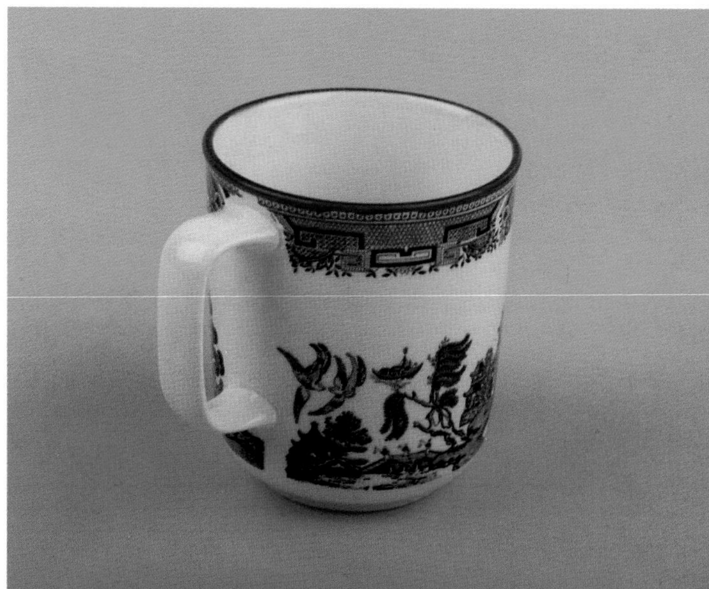

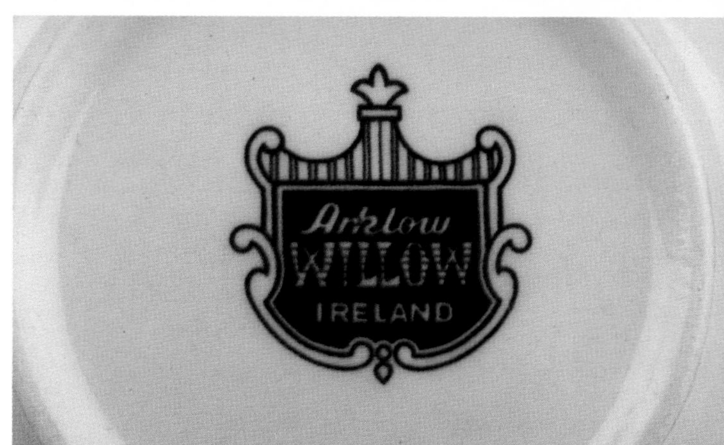

A modern mug from the Arklow pottery in Ireland, 3.75" high. "Willow" mark. Courtesy of Rita Entmacher Cohen.

G.L. Ashworth & Bros.: Active 1862-1883 in Hanley, Staffordshire.

H. Aynsley & Co.: Beginning in 1873, produced earthenwares from the Commerce Works in Longton, Staffordshire. Printed marks include the company name with "Longton," and "H. A. & Co." with or without a Staffordshire knot. "ENGLAND" added to some marks after 1891; "LTD" added after 1932.

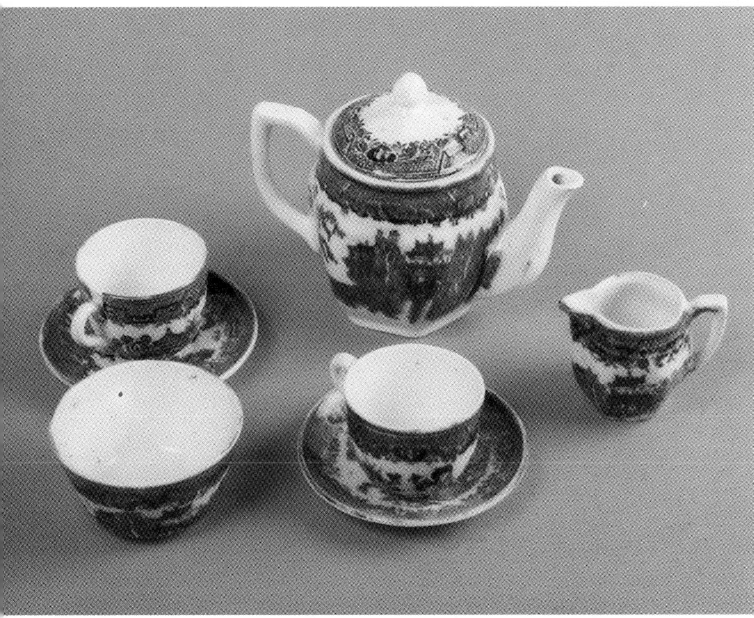

A children's tea set by H. Aynsley & Co., 1891-1931, 4.5" high (teapot). Courtesy of Charles and Louise Loehr, Louise's Old Things, Kutztown, PA.

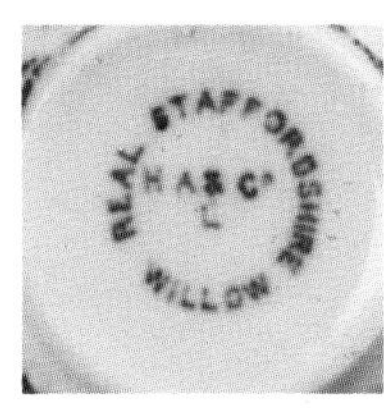

Baker, Bevans & Irwin: Active producing earthenwares between 1813-1838 in the Glamorgan Pottery, Swansea, Wales. Marks include "B. B. & I.," "Baker, Bevans & Irwin," "B.B. & Co." and and "G. P. & Co." (Glamorgan Pottery & Co.).

Samuel Barker & Son: Active 1834-1893 at the Don Pottery in Swinton, Yorkshire. Samuel Barker used a plain name mark or a lion mark with "BARKER" until 1851, when his son joined the company. Thereafter the lion mark read "S. B. & S."

Barker Bros Ltd.: Activity began in 1876 at the Meir Works on Barker Street, Longton, Staffordshire. Used a variety of marks.

Batavian Ware: made at Leeds. A variety of pearlware dipped into brown slip, decorated with underglaze painting, transfer printing, or enamel.

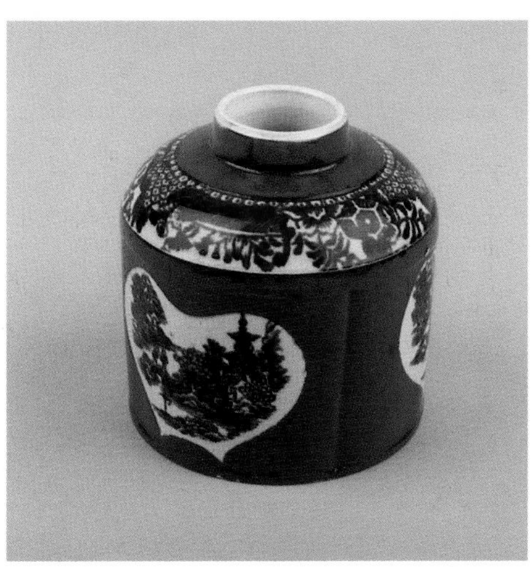

A tea caddy, c. 1780, 3.25" high. "Batavia Ware" with a pearlware body, glazed in brown with white reserves and blue willow decoration. Courtesy of Rita Entmacher Cohen.

Bathwell & Goodfellow: Originally T. & E. Bathwell; often listed as "Bothwell". Produced earthenwares at the Upper House Works in Burslem, Staffordshire, 1818-1823, and at Tunstall from 1820-1822. Used an impressed name mark.

J. & M.P. Bell & Co.: Active 1842-1928 in Glasgow, Scotland, producing earthenwares. Marks include "J.B." (1842-1860), J. & M. P. B. & Co." with a bell or an eagle (1850-1870), and other combinations, using "Ltd" or "Ld" after 1881.

Belle Vue Pottery: Began operations in Hull, Yorkshire c. 1802, under Edward Bell & then W. Bell. Used impressed "BELLE VUE POTTERY, HULL" in a circle, or the name in cursive around a picture of two bells.

Bennett: The Edwin Bennett Pottery Co. was opened by English immigrant Edwin Bennett c. 1846, in Baltimore, Maryland, U.S.A. The pottery closed in 1936. A variety of printed marks were used, generally incorporating the name "BENNETT'S" or the initials "E. B."

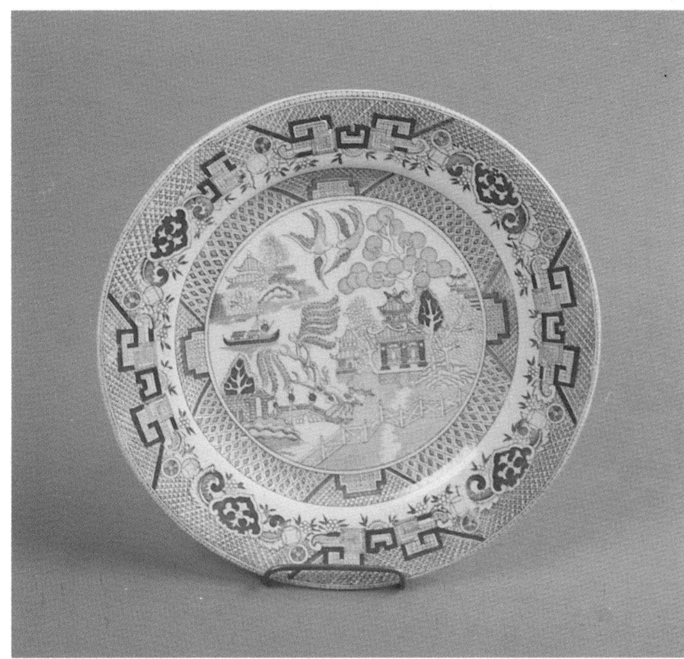

A red Willow plate by Bennett, from Baltimore, 8" diam. Courtesy of Charles and Louise Loehr, Louise's Old Things, Kutztown, PA.

Bishop & Stonier: Operated from various addresses in Hanley, Staffordshire 1891-1939, prodcing earthenwares. Marks use "B. & S.," sometimes also using the abbreviation "BISTO."

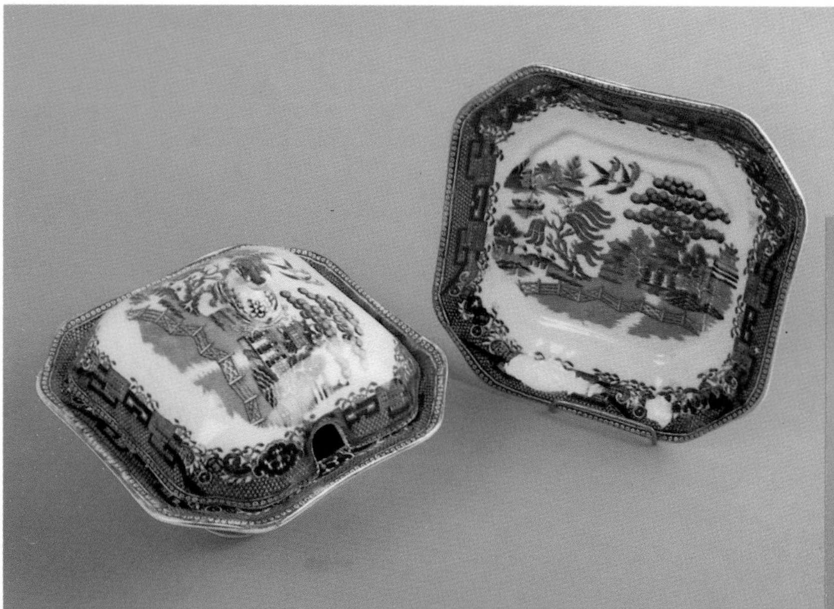

A sauce tureen with a separate tray by Bishop & Stonier, 1916, 5.75" x 7.25". Courtesy of Charles and Louise Loehr, Louise's Old Things, Kutztown, PA.

Booth: Operated in the Church Bank Pottery in Tunstall, Staffordshire. As Thomas Booth & Son (1872-1876) the company used the mark "T. B. & S." Company became Thomas G. Booth (1876-1883), using a script "TGB" inside a circle, surmounted by a crown. Became T. G. & F. Booth (1883-1891), and used the mark "T. G. & F. B." From 1891-1948, the company operated as Booths (Limited), and expanded to include works at the Swan and Soho Potteries in addition to the Church Bank works after 1912, using a variety of marks, generally with the name Booths and a crown logo.

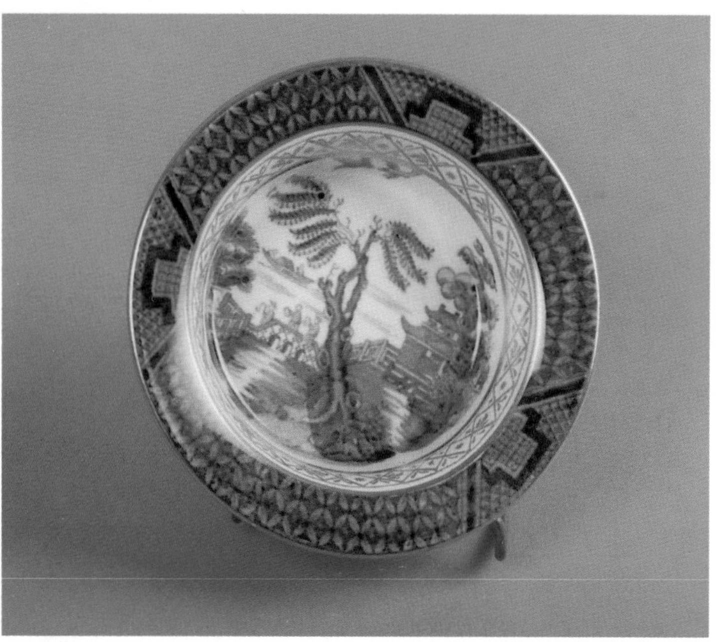

Brameld: From 1787-1806, this pottery was operated in Swinton, Yorkshire by the Leeds firm Hartley, Greens & Co. In 1807 it was taken over by John & William Brameld. After 1826, the firm became known as Rockingham Works. Brameld used name marks in various designs.

Brittania Pottery Co. Ltd.: Operated 1920-1935 in Glasgow, Scotland. A name trademark appears in a circle, with a logo of a person holding a staff and shield.

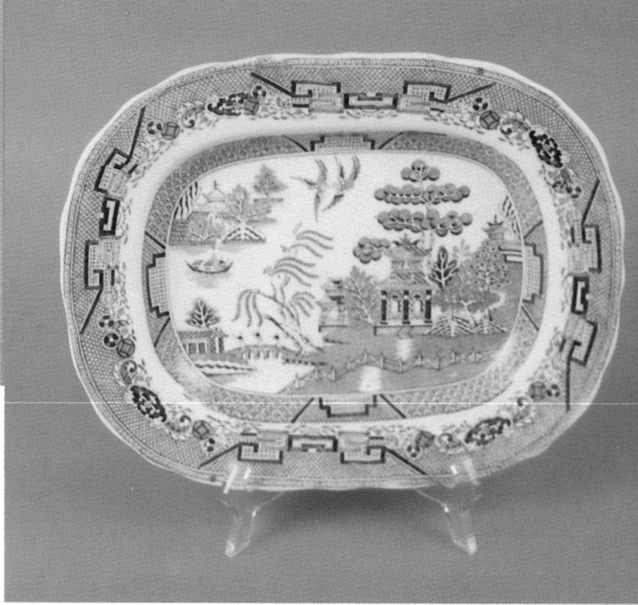

A purple Willow platter with a scalloped edge, "Brittania Pottery Coy Ltd," 11.75" x 9.5". Made in Glasgow, Scotland, imprinted with the mark "IVORY". From the collection of Peter and Susan Steelman, Mystic, CT.

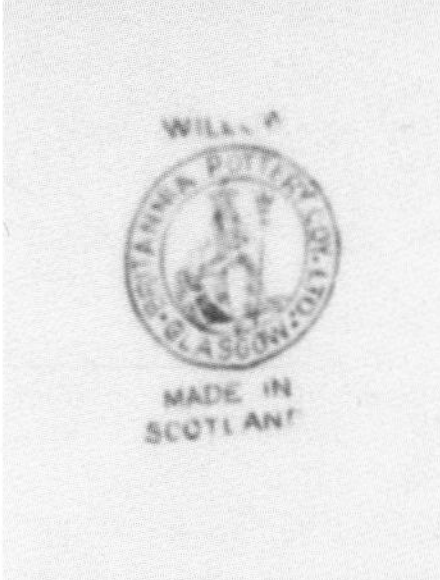

Brown, Westhead & Moore.: From 1862-1904, produced earthenwares and porcelains out of the renowned Cauldon Place Works in Hanley, England, where many other successful firms had been based. The firm employed over a thousand people. They were commissioned by Edward, Prince of Wales in 1876-1877, and by the Imperial Court of Russia, and were prominent in major exhibitions in England and America. In 1904 the company became Cauldon Ltd., and in the 1920s became Cauldon Potteries Ltd. Marks generally spell out the company name, though some use simply the initials "B.W.M" or "B.W.M. & Co.," sometimes using the pottery name, "CAULDON," as well.

A rimmed ramekin from Booths, made of "Silicon China." Courtesy of Charles and Louise Loehr, Louise's Old Things, Kutztown, PA.

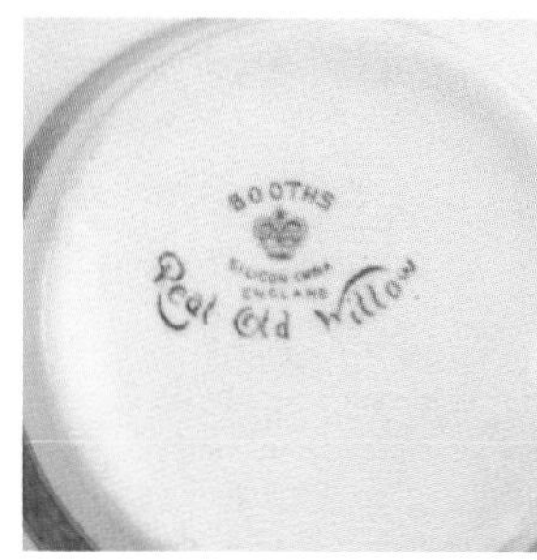

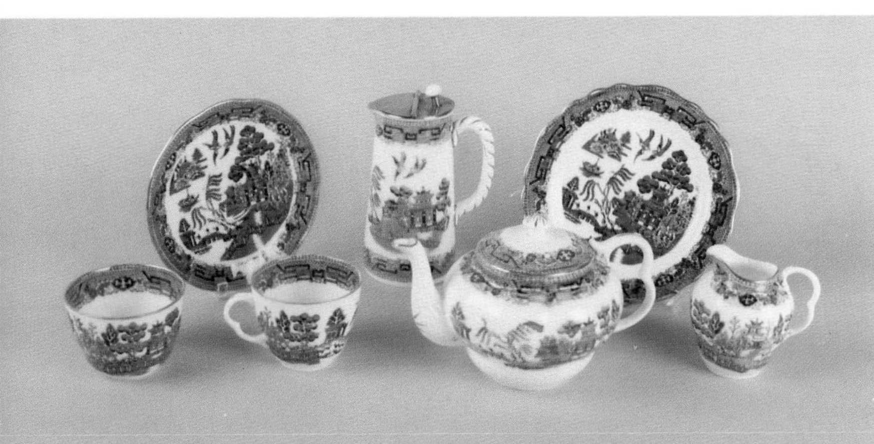

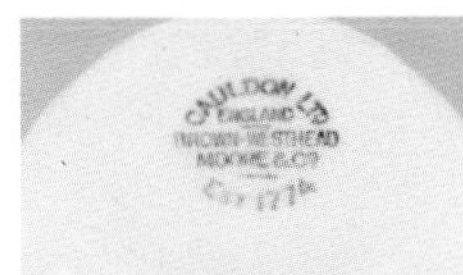

A children's tea set from Cauldon Ltd., 1905-1920, 4.25" high x 7" long (teapot). Marked Brown, Westhead & Moore. Courtesy of Bud & Marguerite Smith, Small World Antiques, Michigan.

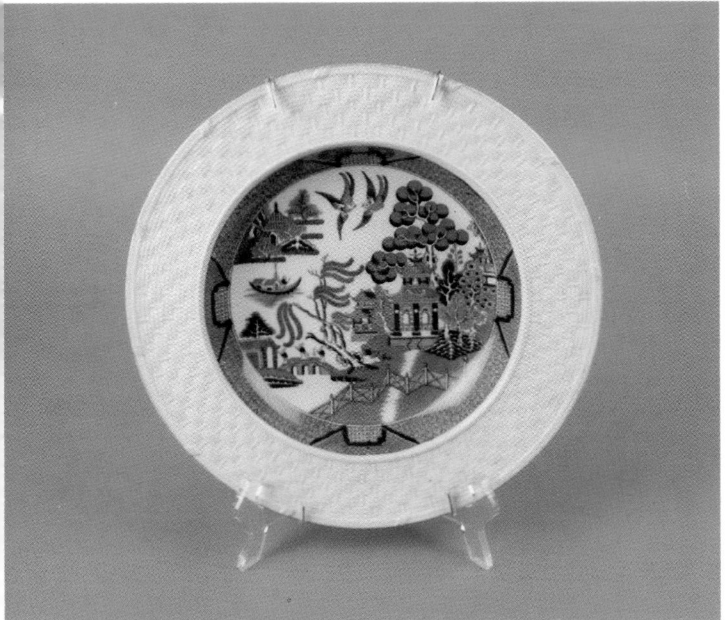

A soup plate with a British registry mark (reading, clockwise from the top, "IV, 4, C, K, ?") and with the impressed mark "Brown, Westhead Moore & Co." and a stamp for the John Mortlock pottery galleries. From the collection of Peter and Susan Steelman, Mystic, CT.

William Brownfield: Operated 1850-1891 in Cobridge, Staffordshire, producing earthenwares and (beginning in 1871) porcelains. Used initial mark, sometimes with a Staffordshire knot, from 1850-1871; impressed mark "BROWNFIELD(S)" beginning in 1860. After 1871, "& SON" or "& S" were added to initial marks. After 1876, "& SON" became "& SONS." From 1871-1891 a printed mark, with two globes and the company name and location, was used.

Buffalo Pottery: The proud originator of the first American Willow line began as an outgrowth of the Larkin Company. This Buffalo (New York)-based firm produced Sweet Home Soap—an ordinary laundry soap—which it marketed with an extensive line of premiums, discussed in detail in Violet and Seymour Altman's *The Book of Buffalo Pottery*. In 1901, owner John Larkin decided that rather than contract with other potteries to make the dishwares he gave out as premiums, he would start his own pottery.

According to American Willow authority Gene Ellison, Larkin believed in "not re-inventing the wheel"—and the already-established popularity of Willow made it the perfect choice for his new production line in 1905. Every piece of Buffalo Willow produced in that year is marked "First Old Willow Ware/Manufactured in America," making it a treasure for collectors (see p. 66). Almost all Buffalo Willow is marked. Before 1916, the company produced earthenwares, and marked their pieces with a variety of "Buffalo Pottery" logos, frequently incorporating the year of manufacture. After 1916, the company became Buffalo China, producing china wares; their marks changed accordingly. Buffalo also produced an extremely rare Gaudy Willow line with clobbering and gilding (see pp. 63-66), as well as colored Willow, sometimes under a "Rouge Ware" or "Lune Ware" title (shown on p. 60). In the 1960s, the company was purchased by Oneida, which still produces a Buffalo line.

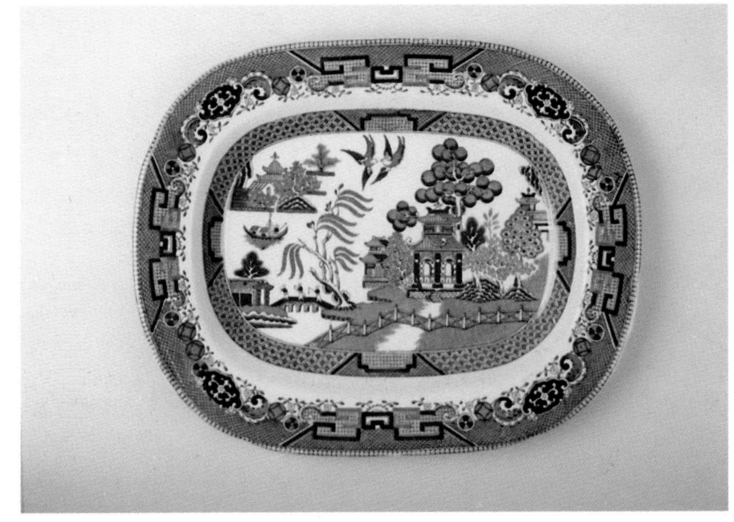

A smooth-edged platter from the Buffalo Pottery, 1916, 12" x 9.5". From the collection of Phillip M. Sullivan, South Orleans, MA.

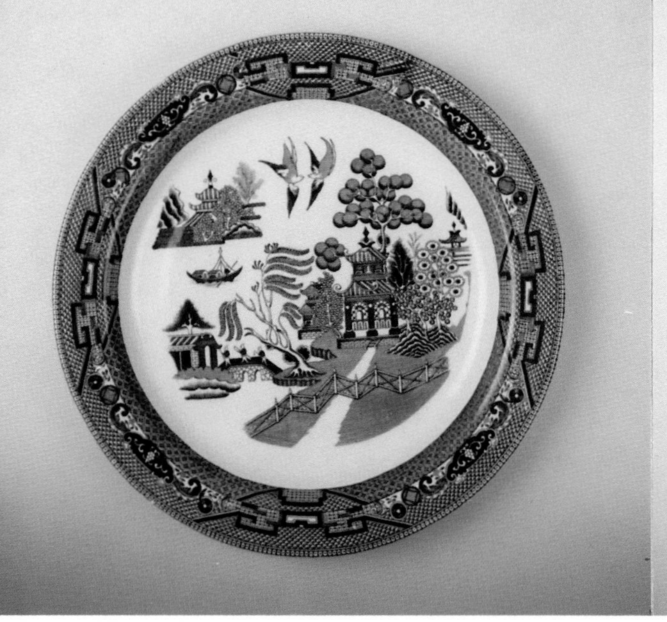

A smooth-edged round "chop plate" (for pork chops) from the Buffalo Pottery, 1908, 13" diam. From the collection of Phillip M. Sullivan, South Orleans, MA.

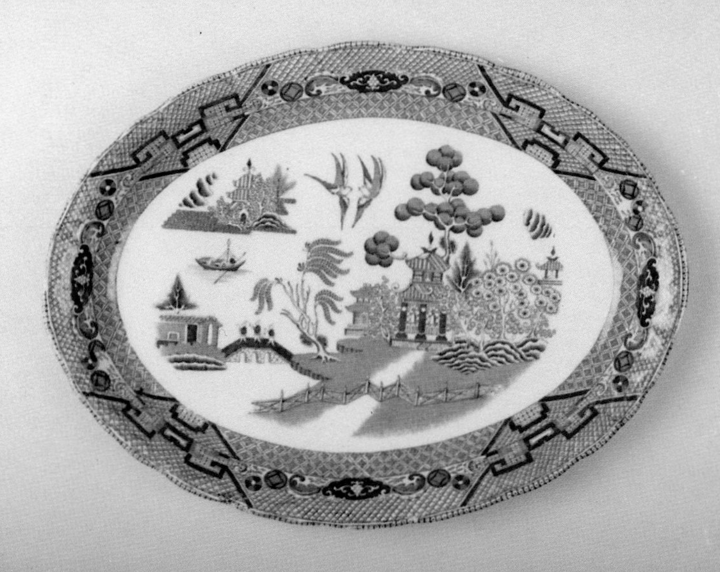

A scallop-edge oval platter from the Buffalo Pottery, 1908, 12" x 8.75". From th collection of Phillip M. Sullivan, South Orleans, MA.

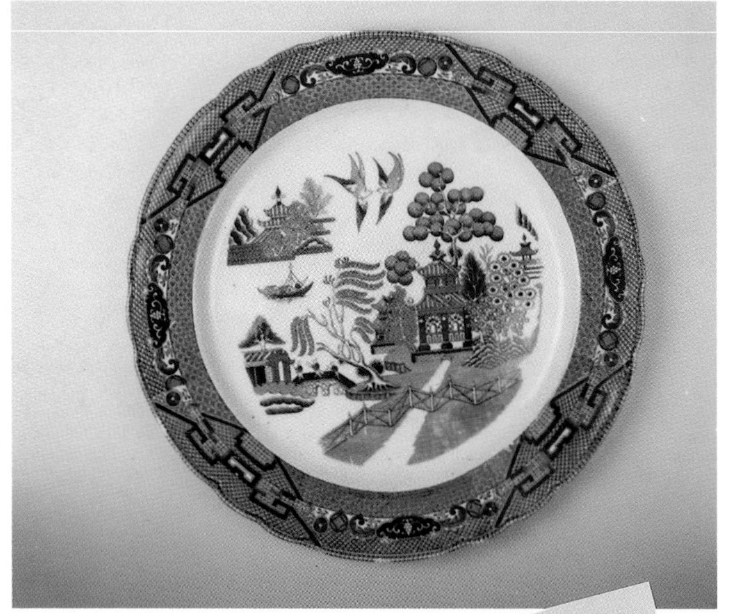

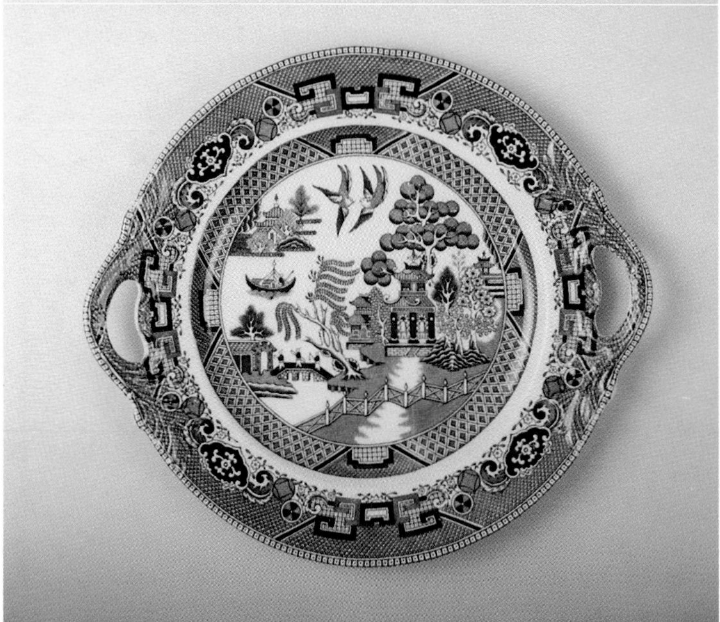

A round platter with handles from the Buffalo Pottery, 1911, 11.25" x 10.25". From the collection of Phillip M. Sullivan, South Orleans, MA.

Above left Photo: A scallop-edged round chop plate from the Buffalo Pottery, 1906, 13.5" diam. From the collection of Phillip M. Sullivan, South Orleans, MA.

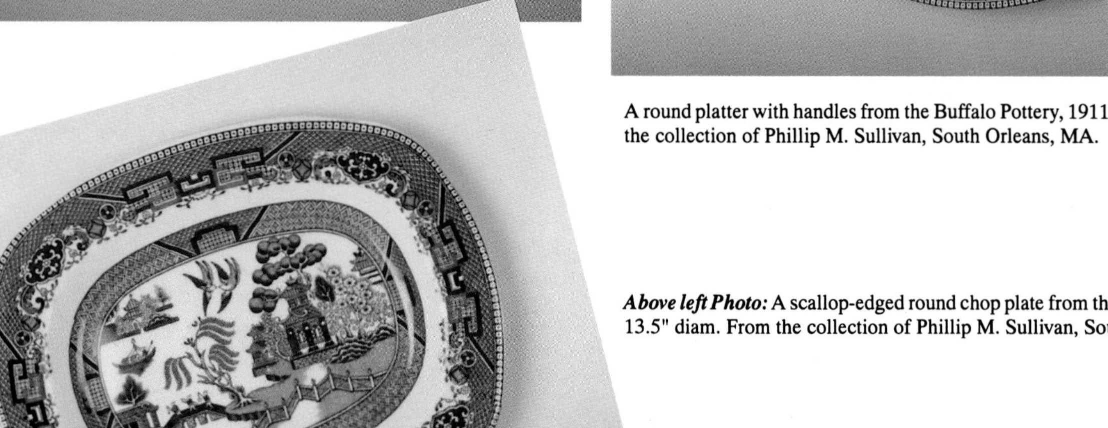

A small rectangular platter from the Buffalo Pottery, 1916, 7" x 6". From the collection of Phillip M. Sullivan, South Orleans, MA.

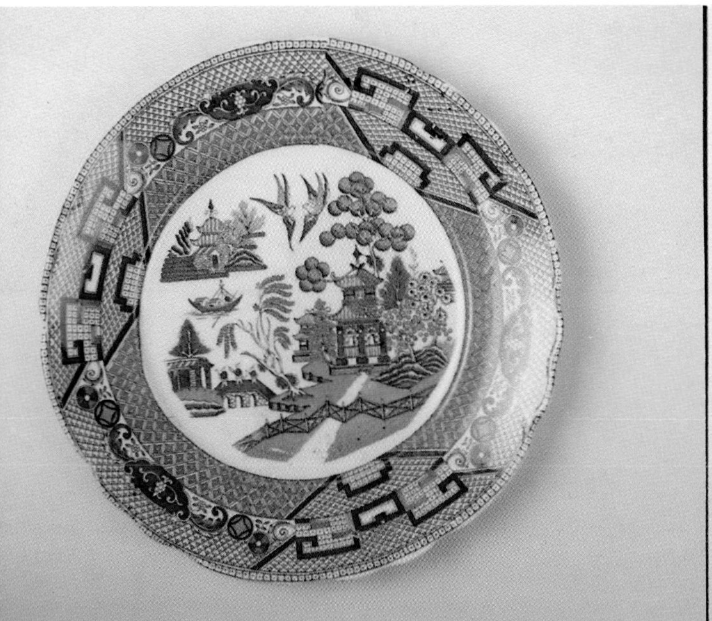

A scallop-edged luncheon plate from the Buffalo Pottery, 1906, 9.25" diam. From the collection of Phillip M. Sullivan, South Orleans, MA.

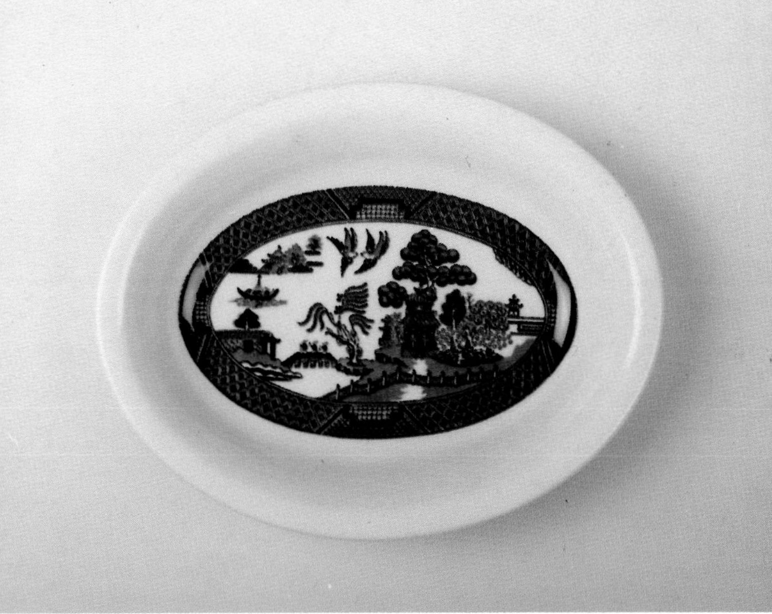

A Buffalo China serving dish, undated, marked "Ye Old Ivory" with lantern mark, 8.75" x 6.75". From the collection of Phillip M. Sullivan, South Orleans, MA.

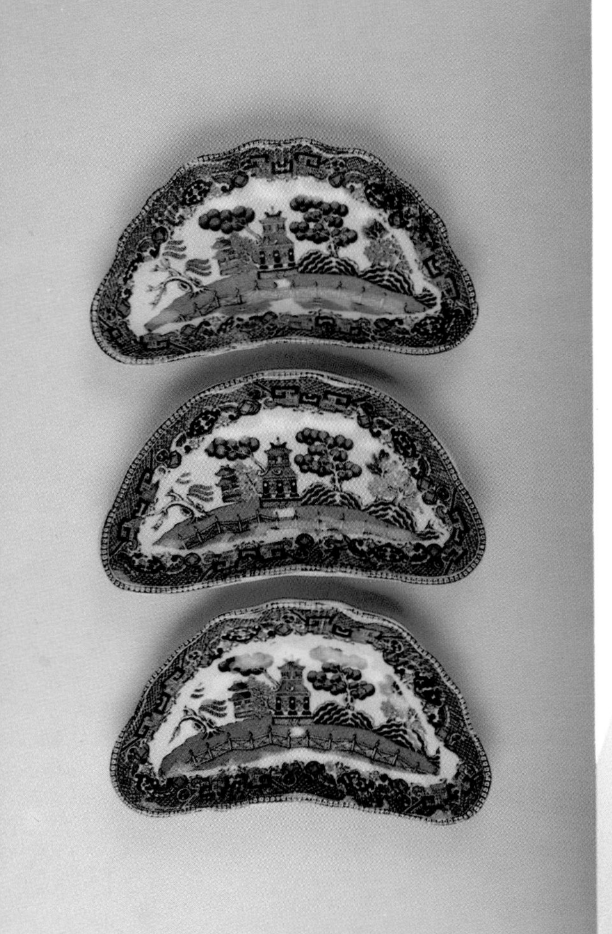

Earthenware dishes for discarded bones, from the Buffalo Pottery, 1909, 6.5" long. From the collection of Phillip M. Sullivan, South Orleans, MA.

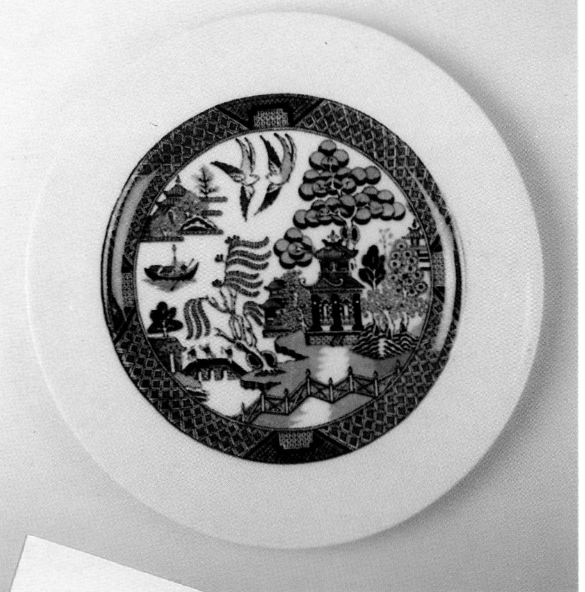

A round undated plate, 9" diam., in the "Ye Old Ivory" style but marked merely as "Buffalo China." From the collection of Phillip M. Sullivan, South Orleans, MA.

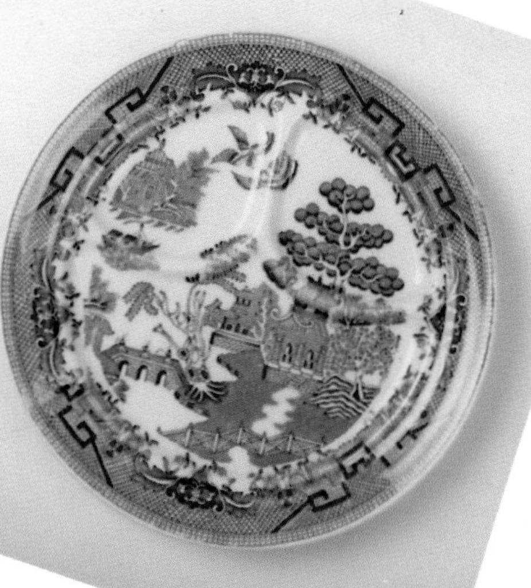

A grill plate, undated, from Buffalo China, 9.5" diam. This piece features the modern large script mark. From the collection of Phillip M. Sullivan, South Orleans, MA.

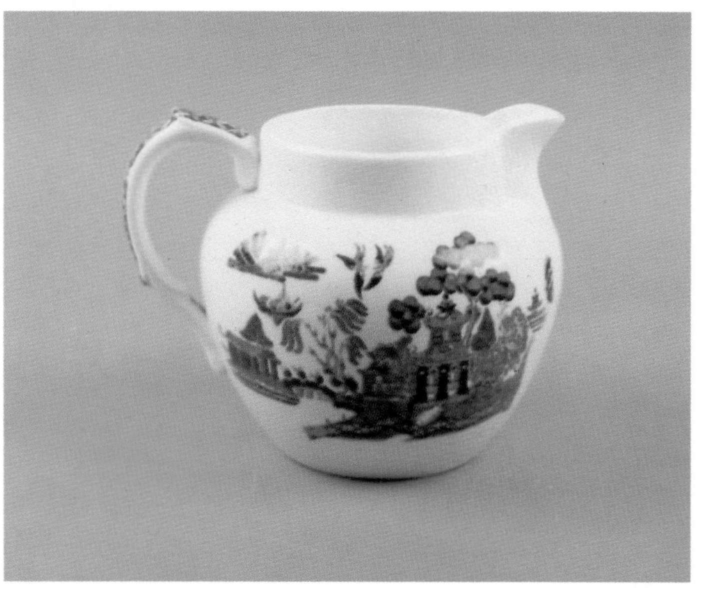

A Buffalo pitcher, 1907, 6" high. The only example of this pitcher found with its border missing. From the collection of Phillip M. Sullivan, South Orleans, MA.

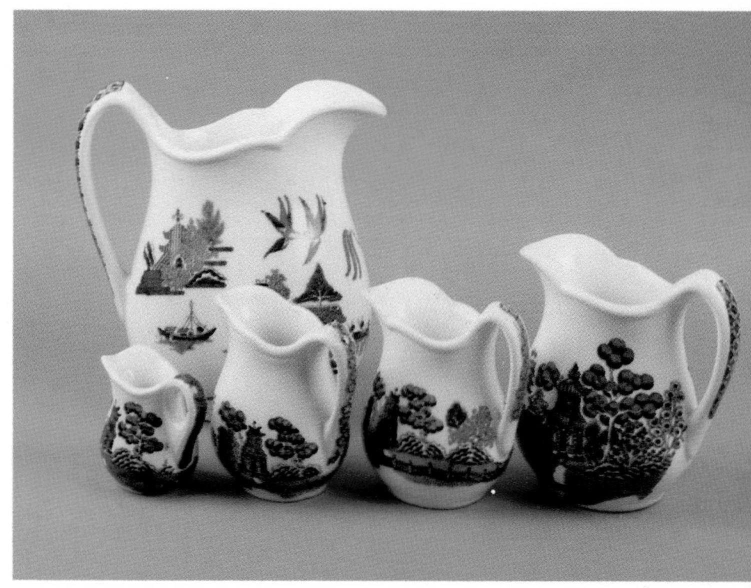

Five Buffalo China pitchers from the 1920s, the largest standing 7.5" high. From the collecti of Phillip M. Sullivan, South Orleans, MA.

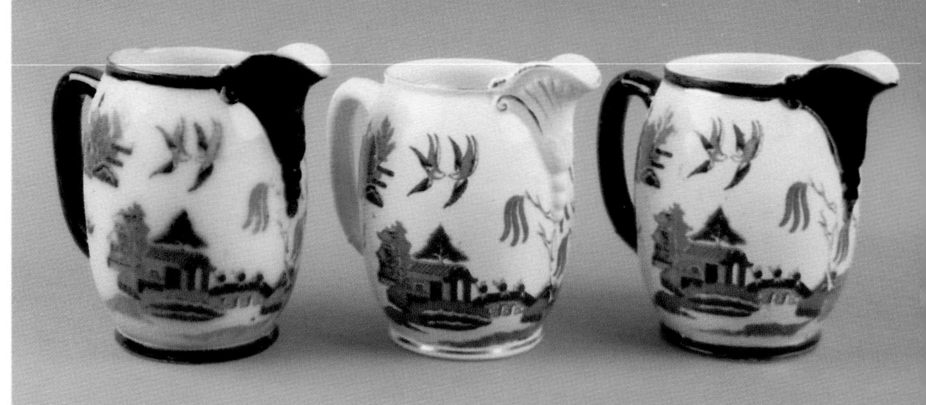

Three 1905 Buffalo pitchers featuring varying decoration on the same ceramic body, 6.7" high. The pitcher with blue border and gilt (on the right) is common; the other two versions are rare. From the collection of Phillip M. Sullivan, South Orleans, MA.

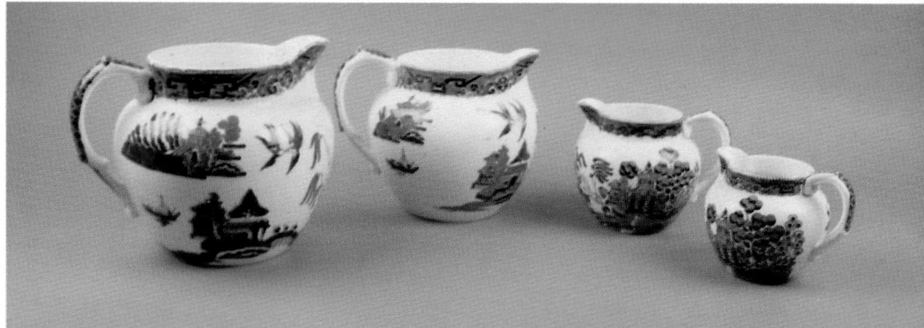

Four pitchers, Buffalo, from 1908, 1909, 1908, 1909. The largest stands 6.5" high. From the collection of Phillip M. Sullivan, South Orleans, MA.

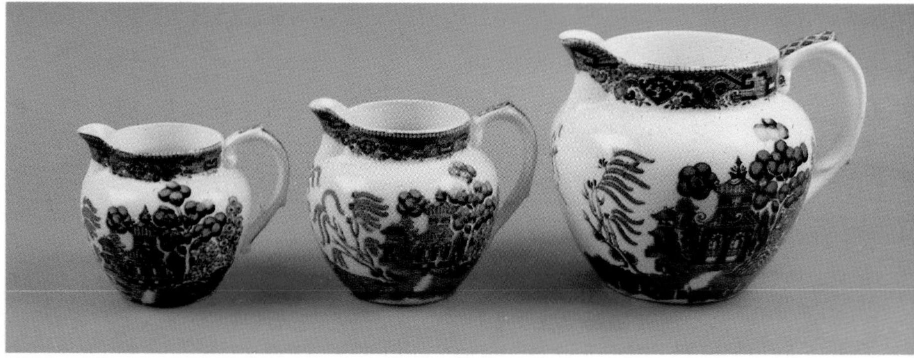

Three Buffalo pitchers, from 1917, 1909, and 1909. The largest stands 5.75" high. From the collection of Phillip M. Sullivan, South Orleans, MA.

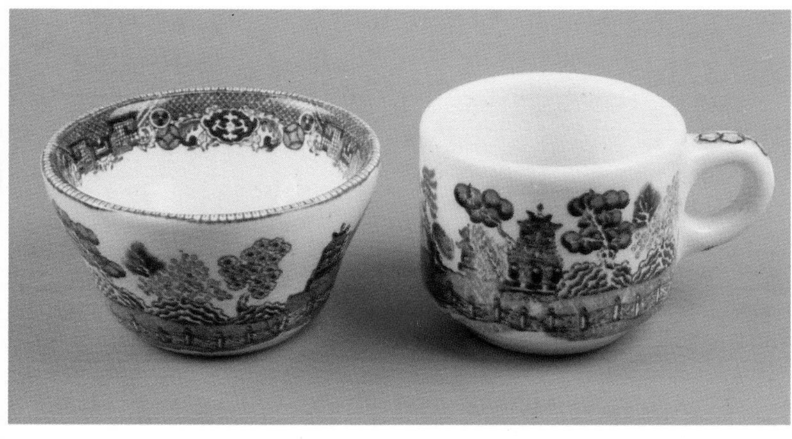

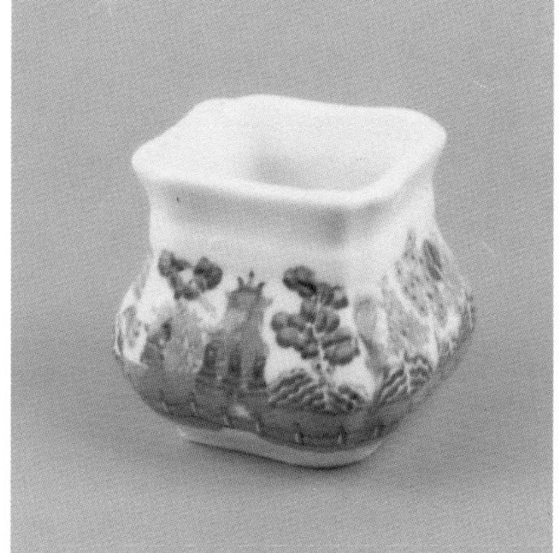

An uncovered sugar bowl from Buffalo China, 2.75" high. From the collection of Phillip M. Sullivan, South Orleans, MA.

A cup and a bowl, undated but probably 1960s or 1970s, embossed "China USA" with a buffalo logo. The cup is 2.75" high x 3" diam., while the bowl is 2.5" high x 4" diam. From the collection of Phillip M. Sullivan, South Orleans, MA.

Syrup pitchers from Buffalo, 1910, 1911, and 1910. The largest is 6.5" high. These can be seen in the Buffalo catalog pages excerpted in Sidney & Violet Altman's book on the company. From the collection of Phillip M. Sullivan, South Orleans, MA.

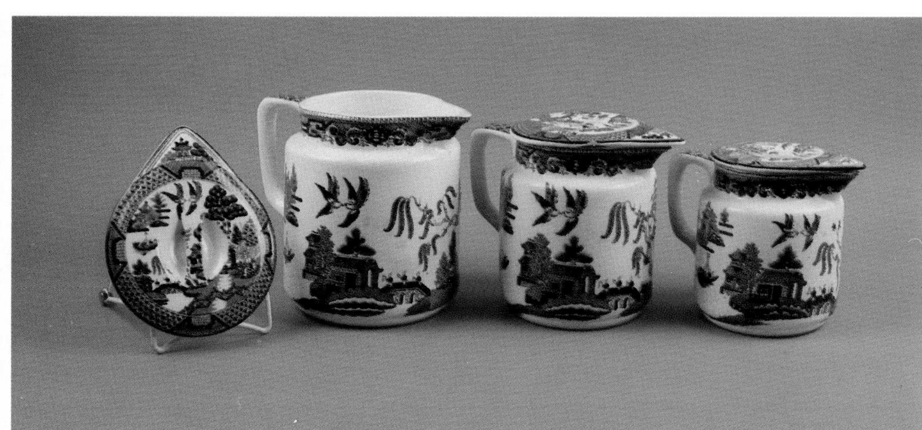

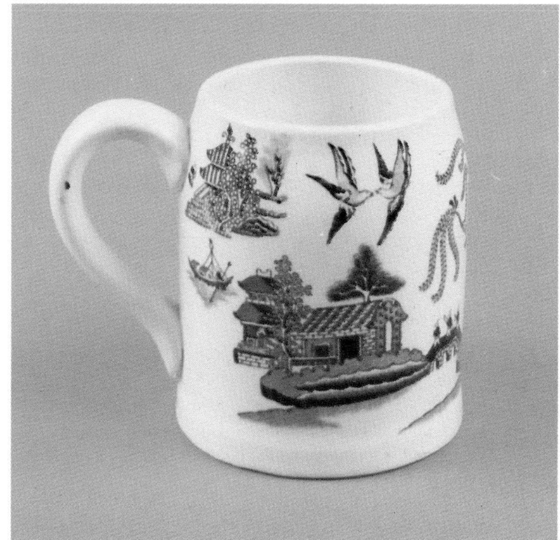

A 1911 Buffalo Pottery handled mug, 4.25" high. From the collection of Phillip M. Sullivan, South Orleans, MA.

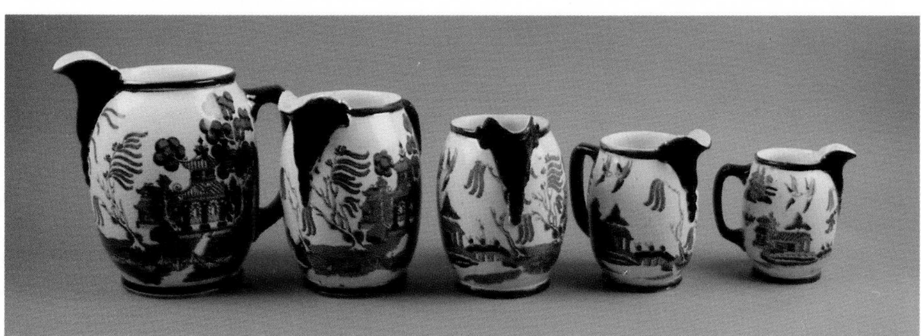

Five "Chicago Jugs" from the Buffalo Pottery, from 1908, 1905, 1906, 1906, and 1907. The tallest stands 7.5" high. From the collection of Phillip M. Sullivan, South Orleans, MA.

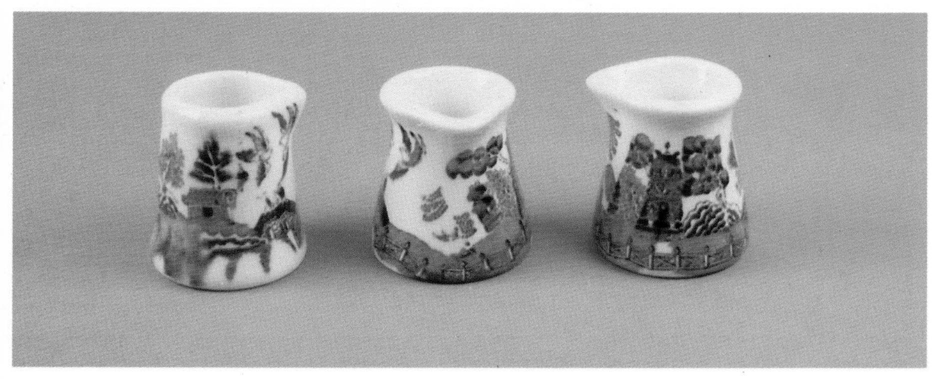

Three individual china creamers from Buffalo China, 2.25" high. The example on the left is undated, but the remaining two creamers are both marked 1925. From the collection of Phillip M. Sullivan, South Orleans, MA.

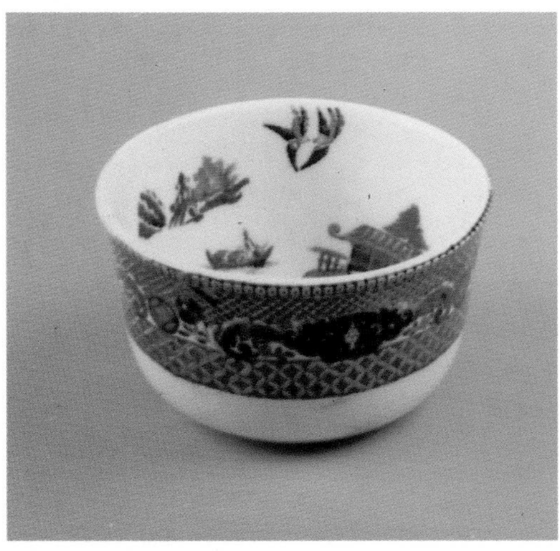

A 1907 Buffalo Pottery waste bowl, 3" high x 4.75" diam. From the collection of Phillip M. Sullivan, South Orleans, MA.

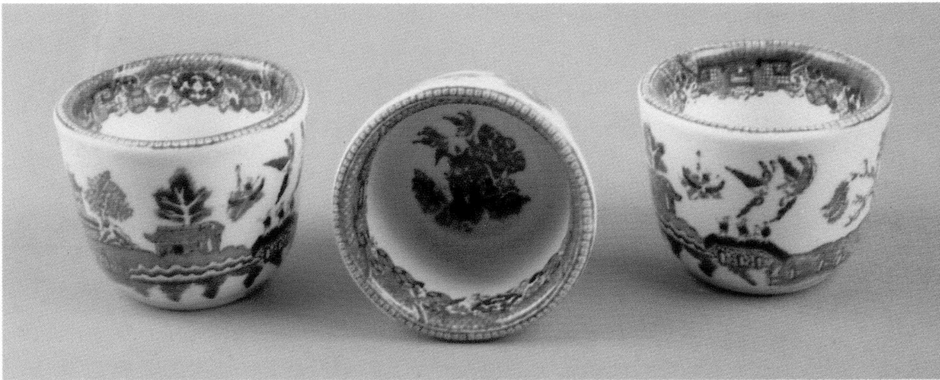

Three china cups from the Buffalo China in 1922, 1925, and 1927, 2.5" high. From the collection of Phillip M. Sullivan, South Orleans, MA.

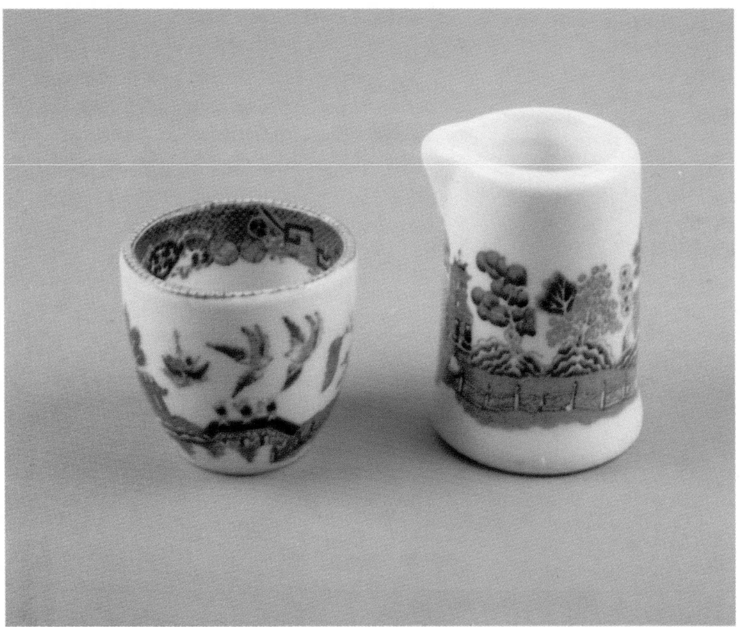

A handle-less china tea cup, dated 1926, and a china creamer, undated, from Buffalo China. The cup stands 2.5" high, the creamer 3.5". From the collection of Phillip M. Sullivan, South Orleans, MA.

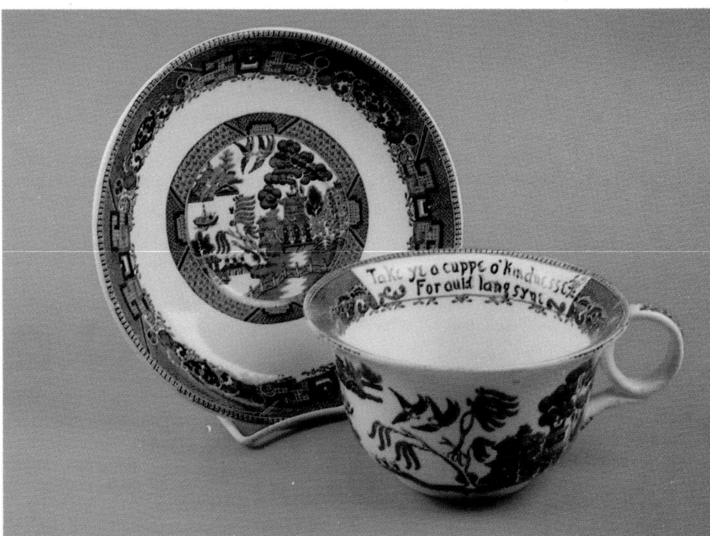

An oversized cup and saucer from the Buffalo Pottery, undated. The cup is 3.5" high, and the saucer is 7.75" diam. From the collection of Phillip M. Sullivan, South Orleans, MA.

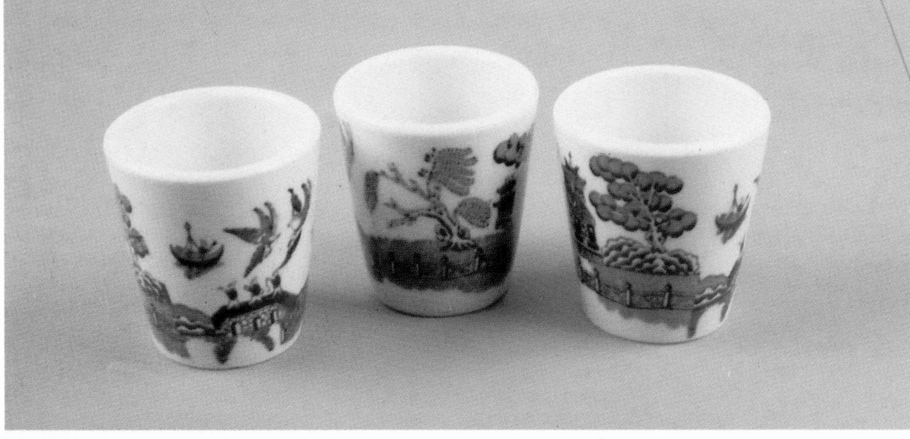

Three handle-less tea cups. From the collection of Phillip M. Sullivan, South Orleans, MA.

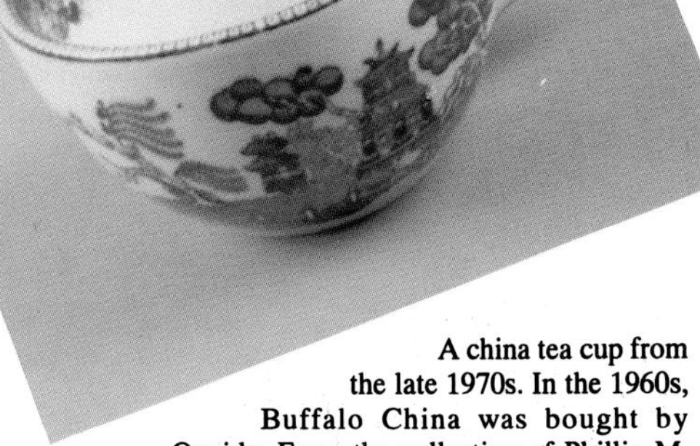

A china tea cup from the late 1970s. In the 1960s, Buffalo China was bought by Oneida. From the collection of Phillip M. Sullivan, South Orleans, MA.

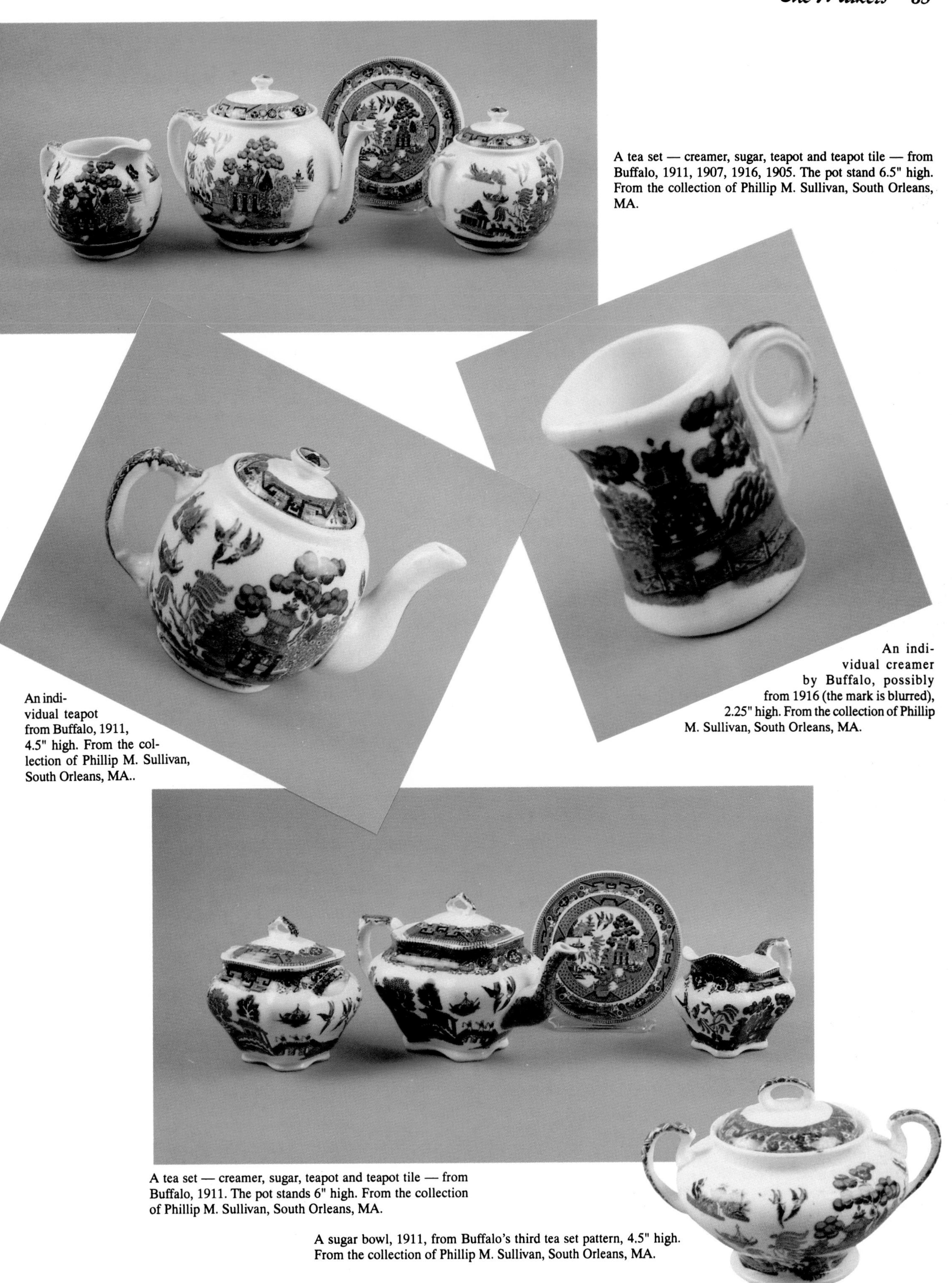

A tea set — creamer, sugar, teapot and teapot tile — from Buffalo, 1911, 1907, 1916, 1905. The pot stand 6.5" high. From the collection of Phillip M. Sullivan, South Orleans, MA.

An individual teapot from Buffalo, 1911, 4.5" high. From the collection of Phillip M. Sullivan, South Orleans, MA..

An individual creamer by Buffalo, possibly from 1916 (the mark is blurred), 2.25" high. From the collection of Phillip M. Sullivan, South Orleans, MA.

A tea set — creamer, sugar, teapot and teapot tile — from Buffalo, 1911. The pot stands 6" high. From the collection of Phillip M. Sullivan, South Orleans, MA.

A sugar bowl, 1911, from Buffalo's third tea set pattern, 4.5" high. From the collection of Phillip M. Sullivan, South Orleans, MA.

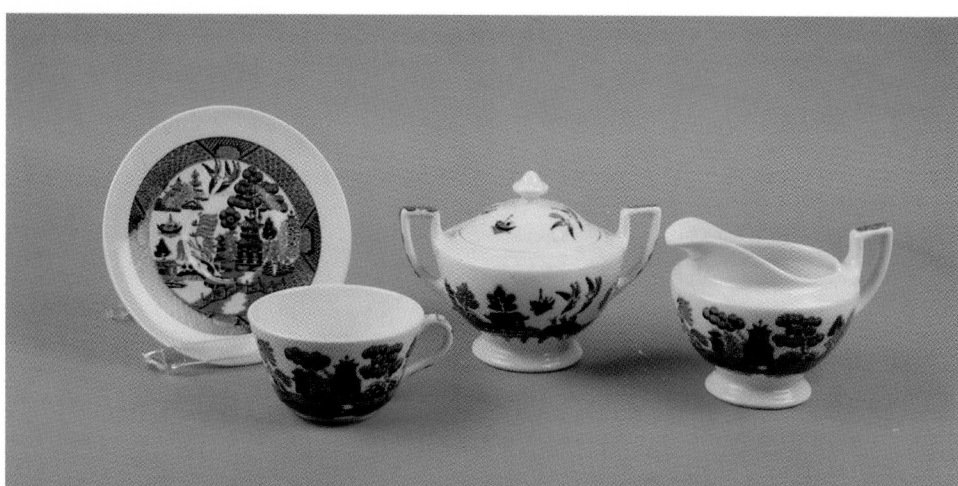

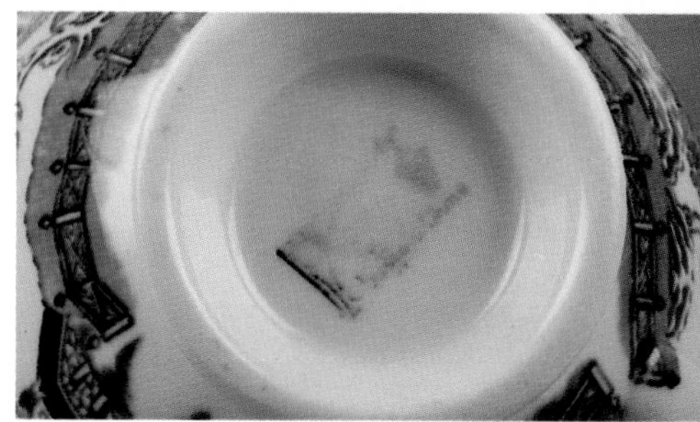

Buffalo China's "Ye Olde Ivory" tea cup and saucer, creamer, and saucer, all from 1930. The creamer and sugar are marked "Ye Olde Ivory." The sugar is 4.5" high x 6.25" diam., the cup is 2.25" high, and the saucer is 5.75" diam. From the collection of Phillip M. Sullivan, South Orleans, MA.

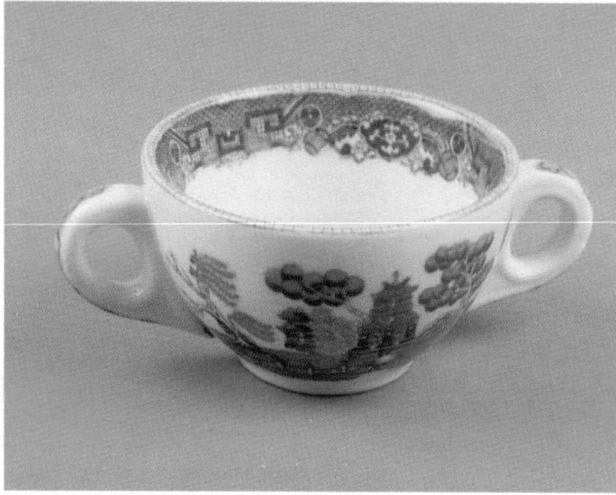

A bouillon cup, undated, from Buffalo China, 2.25" high x 4" diam. From the collection of Phillip M. Sullivan, South Orleans, MA.

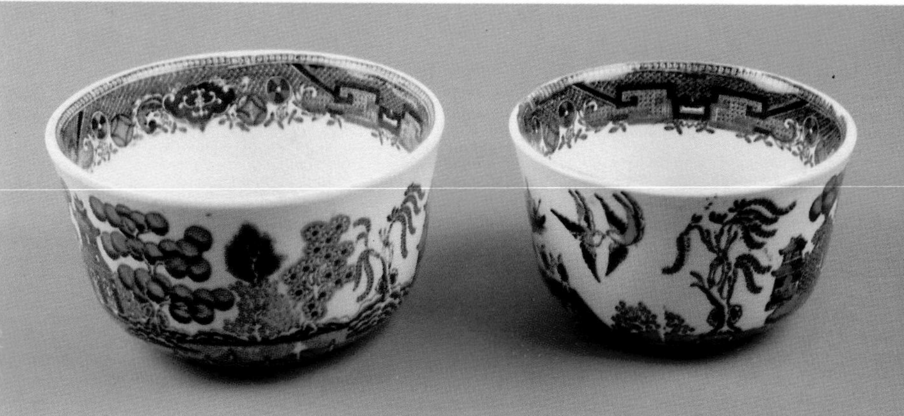

Two waste bowls from the Buffalo Pottery, 1916, with boat and pagoda elements in the center of the bowls. The large example is 3" high x 5.25" diam. From the collection of Phillip M. Sullivan, South Orleans, MA.

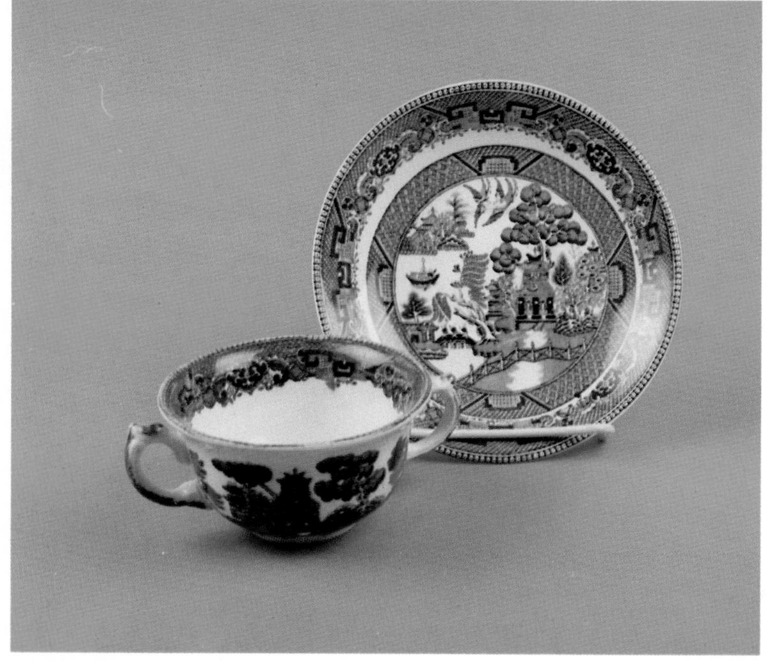

Buffalo Pottery's earthenware bouillon cup and saucer, 1909. The cup is 2" high, the saucer is 6" diam. From the collection of Phillip M. Sullivan, South Orleans, MA.

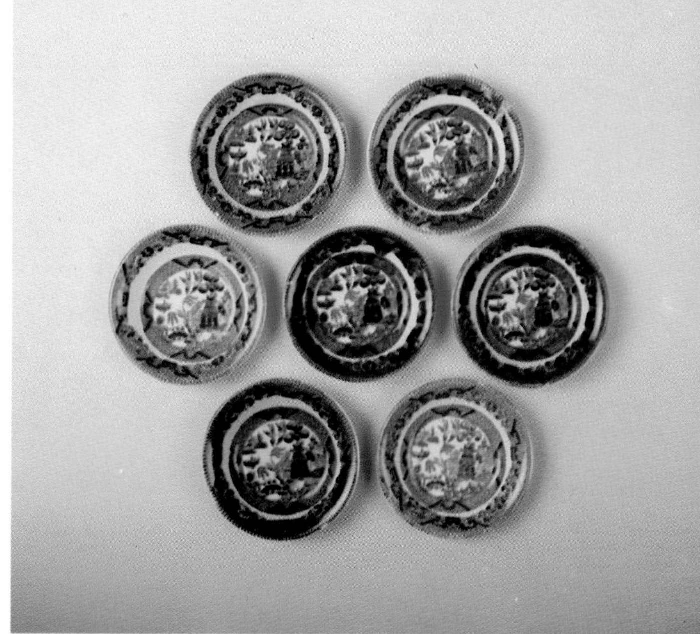

Butter pats made from 1908-1918 by the Buffalo Pottery, each 3.5" diam. From the collection of Phillip M. Sullivan, South Orleans, MA.

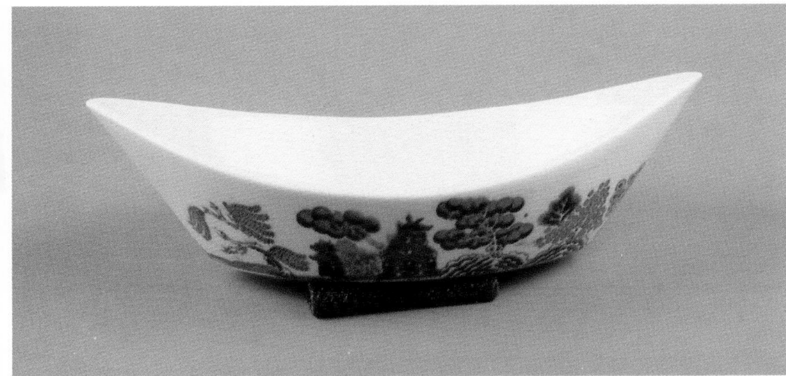

A banana boat from Buffalo China, 1925, 7" long. From the collection of Phillip M. Sullivan, South Orleans, MA.

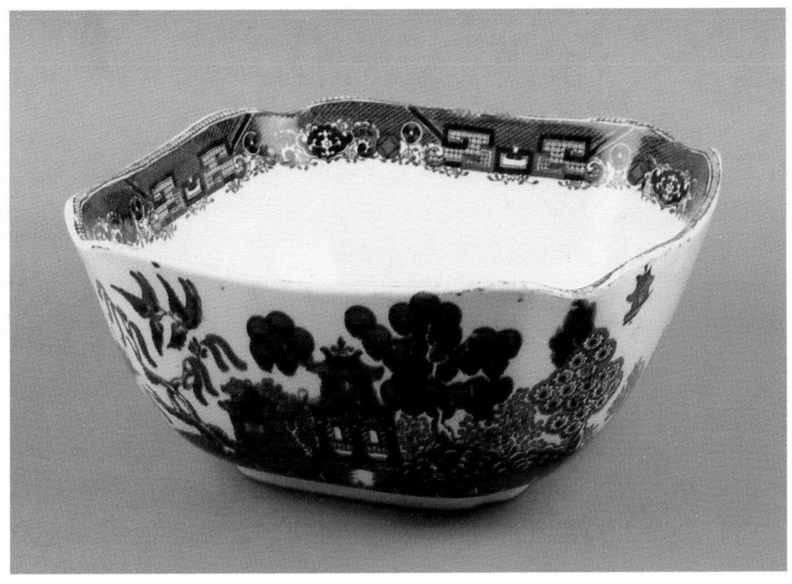

Above and below, a square earthenware salad bowl from the Buffalo Pottery, 1909, 4" high x 9" wide. From the collection of Phillip M. Sullivan, South Orleans, MA.

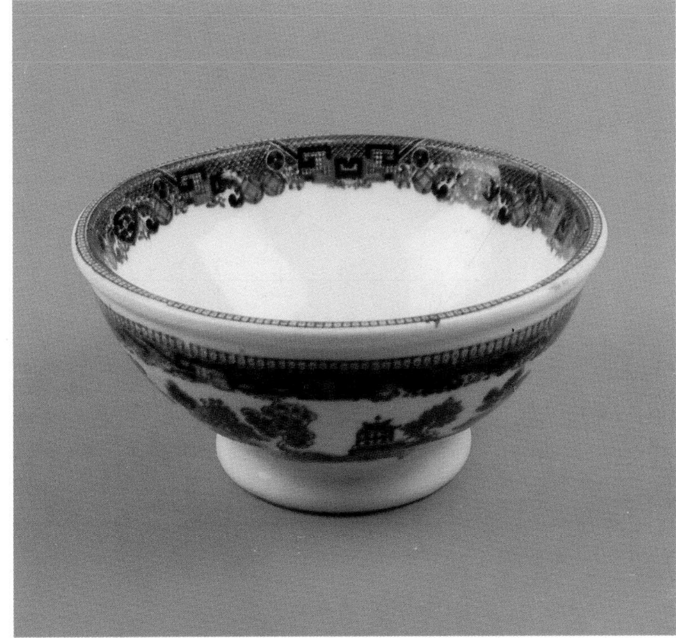

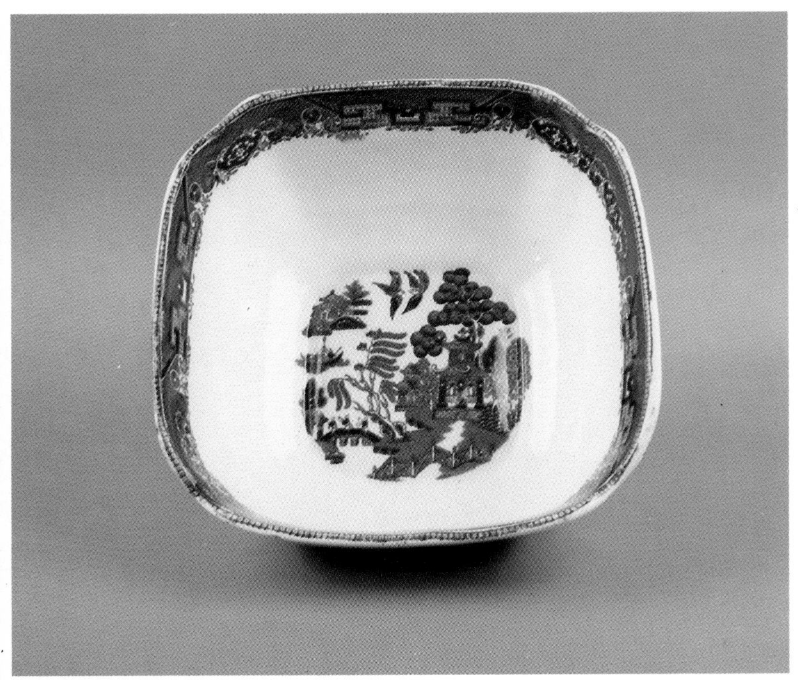

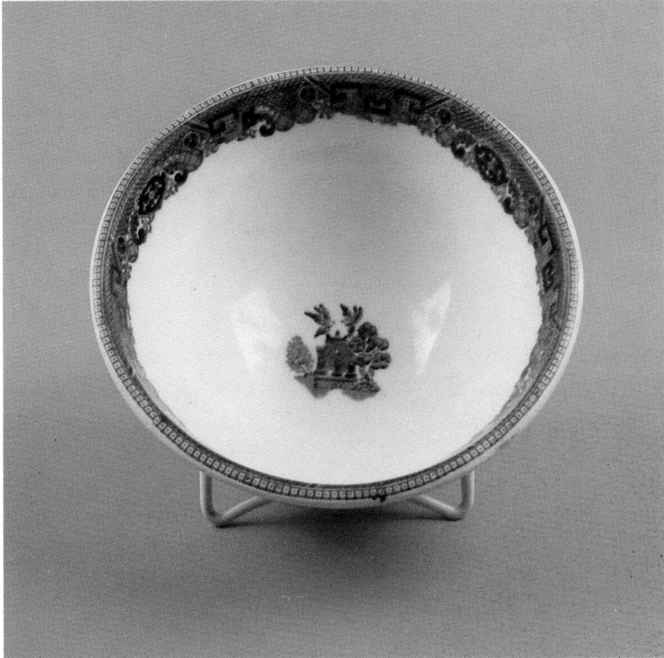

An undated footed bowl from Buffalo China (bearing the unusual mark shown at the top of p. 46), 3" high x 6.5" diam. From the collection of Phillip M. Sullivan, South Orleans, MA.

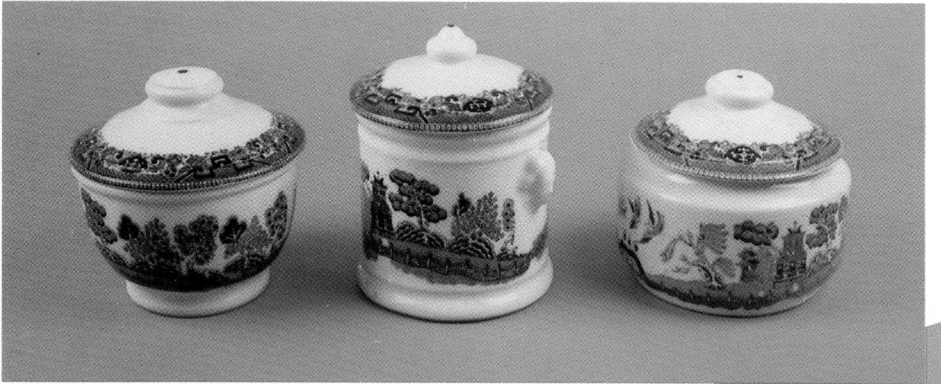

Three sugar bowls: an undated Buffalo China example, 4.5" high; a 1927 Buffalo China example, 5.5" high; a 1960s example marked "Buffalo China Made in USA," 4.25" high. From the collection of Phillip M. Sullivan, South Orleans, MA.

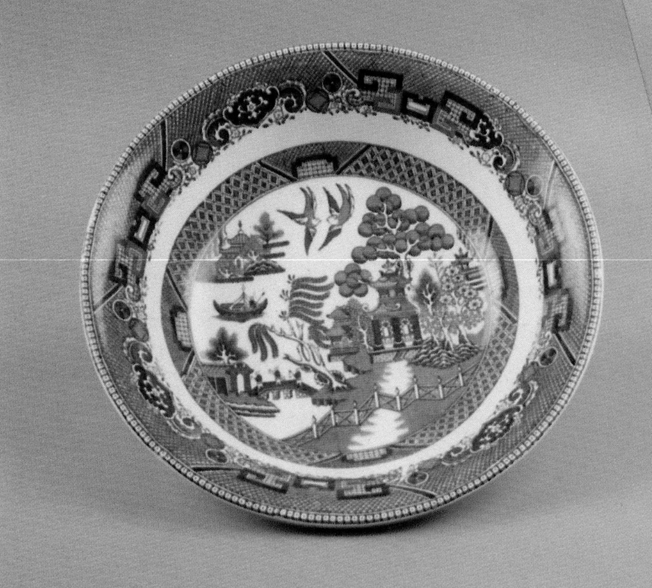

A serving bowl from the Buffalo Pottery, 1909, 9.25" long. From the collection of Phillip M. Sullivan, South Orleans, MA.

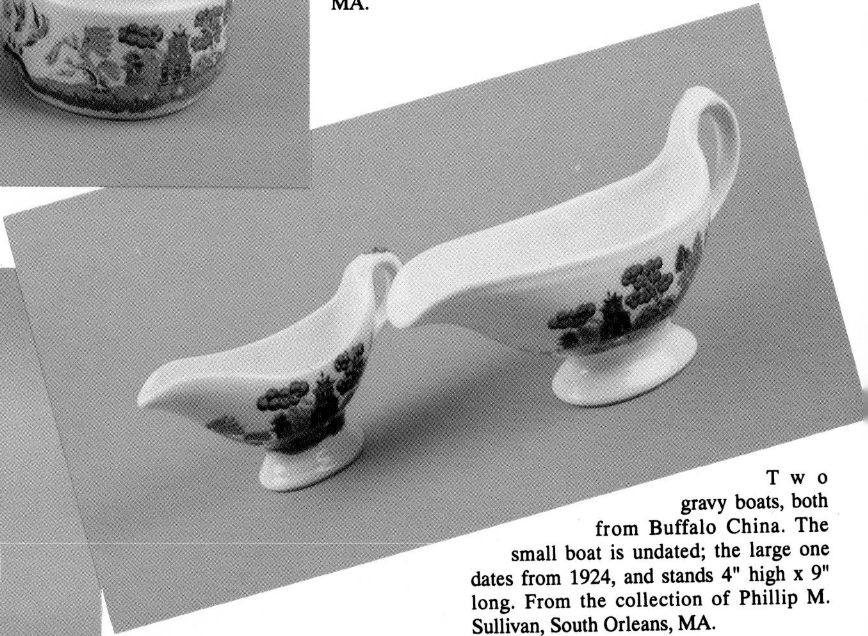

Two gravy boats, both from Buffalo China. The small boat is undated; the large one dates from 1924, and stands 4" high x 9" long. From the collection of Phillip M. Sullivan, South Orleans, MA.

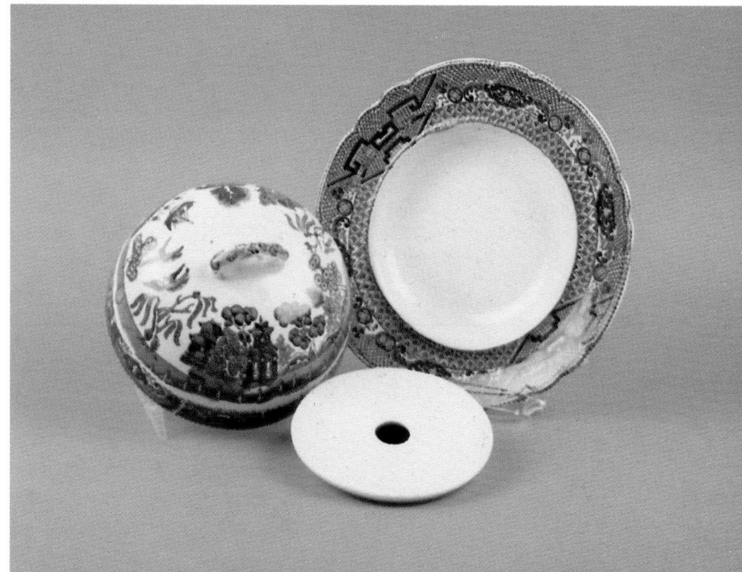

A 1907 Buffalo butter dish, plate 7" long. Note the scalloped rim, indicative of early Buffalo. From the collection of Phillip M. Sullivan, South Orleans, MA.

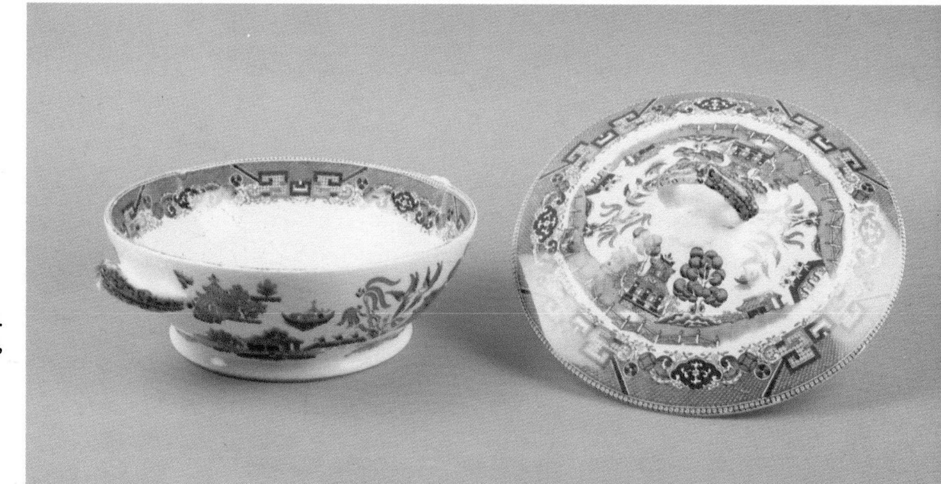

A casserole dish from Buffalo, 1909. This lid is 8.75" diam. From the collection of Phillip M. Sullivan, South Orleans, MA.

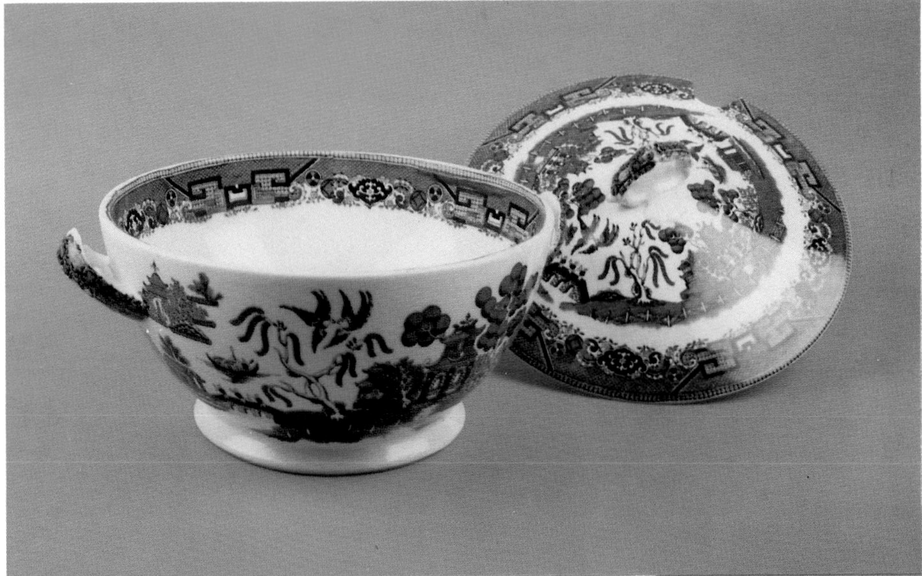

A 1909 Buffalo soup tureen, 4.75" high x 9.5" diam. From the collection of Phillip M. Sullivan, South Orleans, MA.

A smooth-edged butter dish from Buffalo, 1911, 8" diam. From the collection of Phillip M. Sullivan, South Orleans, MA.

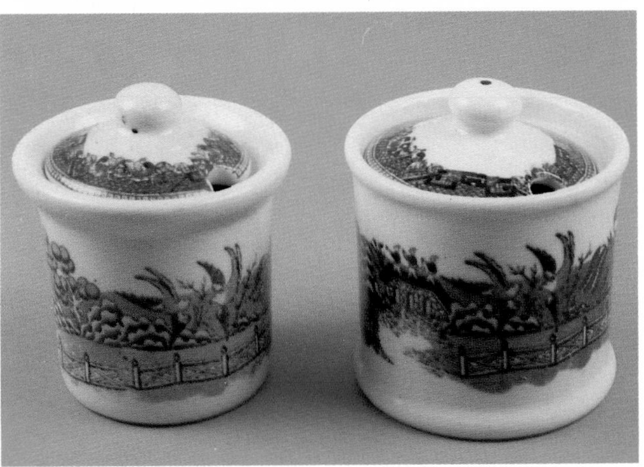

Two mustard pots, both 3.25" high. The larger pot is undated Buffalo China; the smaller pot is marked "Buffalo China 010 Made in USA". From the collection of Phillip M. Sullivan, South Orleans, MA.

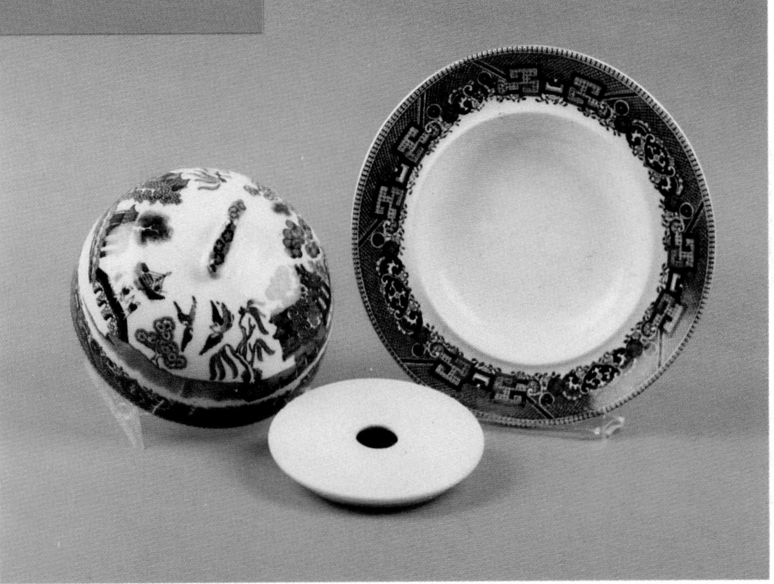

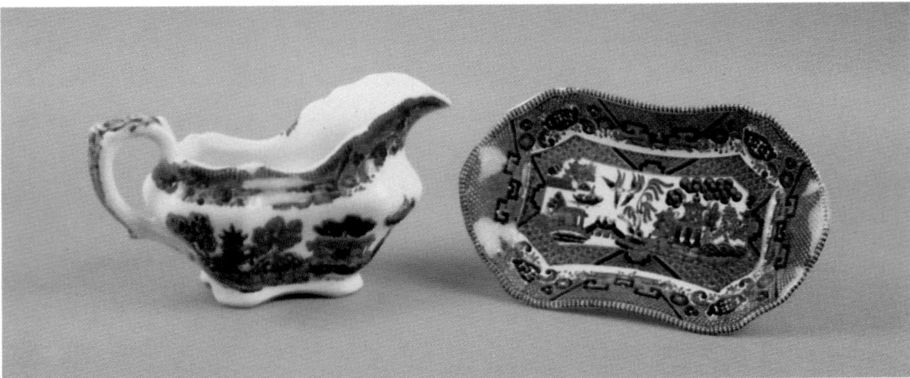

A gravy boat and platter, 1910, 1911, from Buffalo. The platter is 8" long. From the collection of Phillip M. Sullivan, South Orleans, MA.

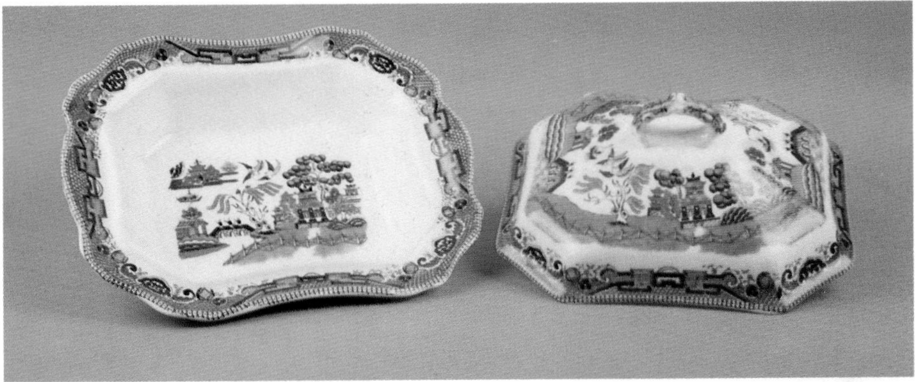

A large vegetable dish, from Buffalo, 1909, 11" x 8.75". From the collection of Phillip M. Sullivan, South Orleans, MA.

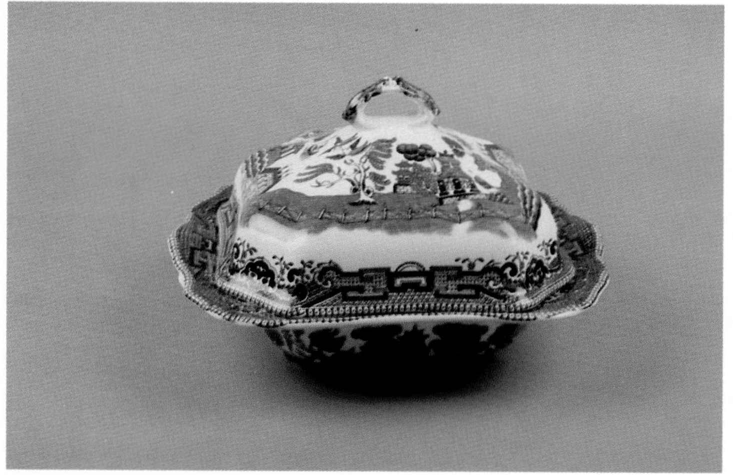

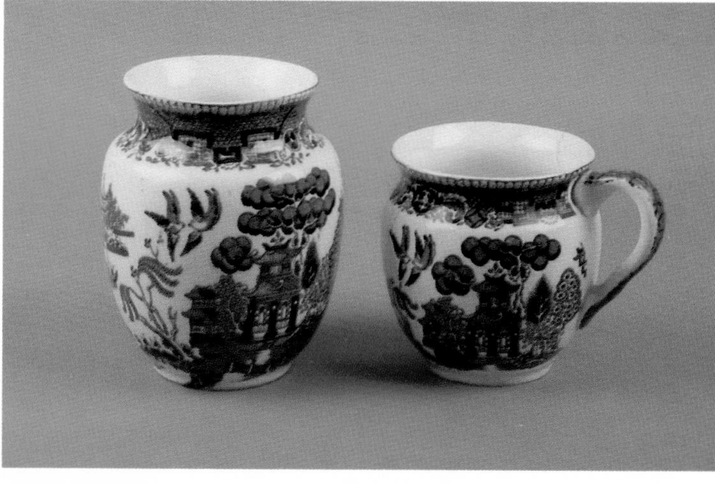

From the Buffalo Pottery bath set: a handled shaving mug and a handle-less toothbrush holder, both 1911. The shaving mug is 5" high x 3.75" diam. From the collection of Phillip M. Sullivan, South Orleans, MA.

At left and above left: a covered vegetable dish from Buffalo, 1911, 5" high x 9". From the collection of Phillip M. Sullivan, South Orleans, MA.

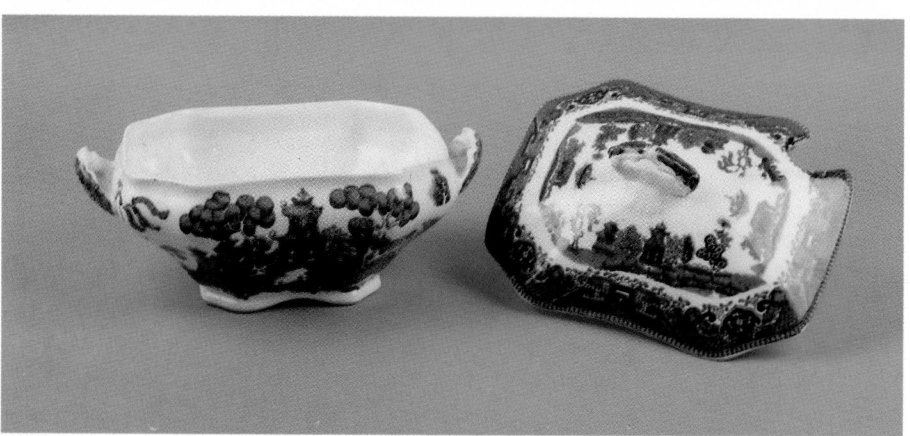

A covered soup tureen from Buffalo. From the collection of Phillip M. Sullivan, South Orleans, MA.

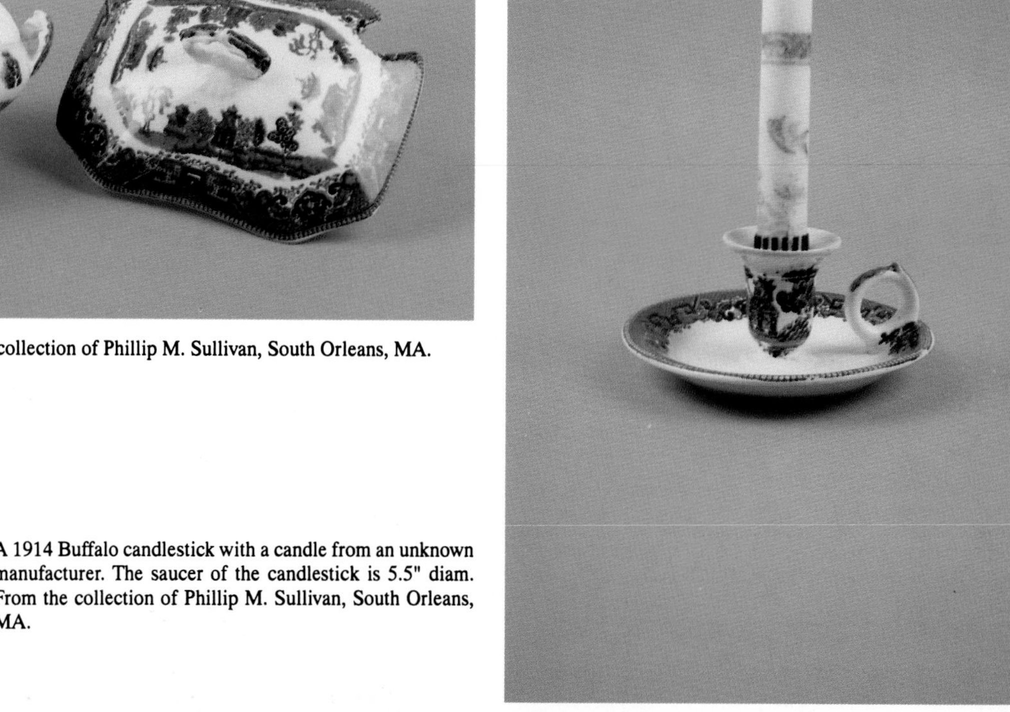

A 1914 Buffalo candlestick with a candle from an unknown manufacturer. The saucer of the candlestick is 5.5" diam. From the collection of Phillip M. Sullivan, South Orleans, MA.

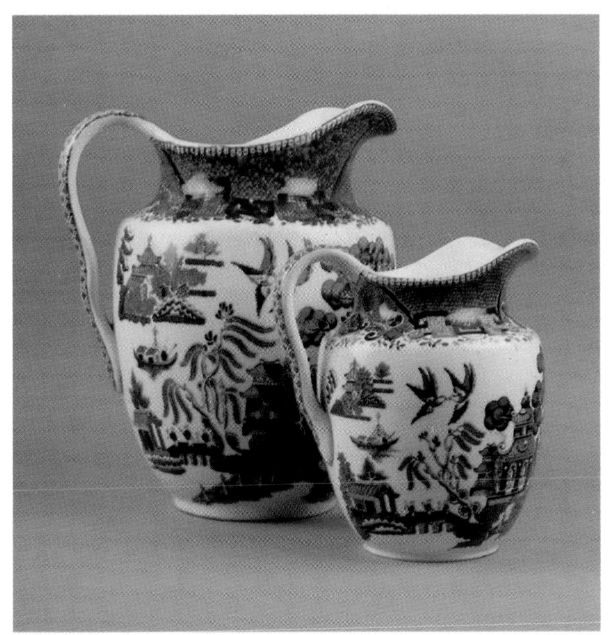

Two pitchers from the Buffalo Pottery bath set: large, 1911, 11.5" high; small, 1910, 7.5" high. From the collection of Phillip M. Sullivan, South Orleans, MA.

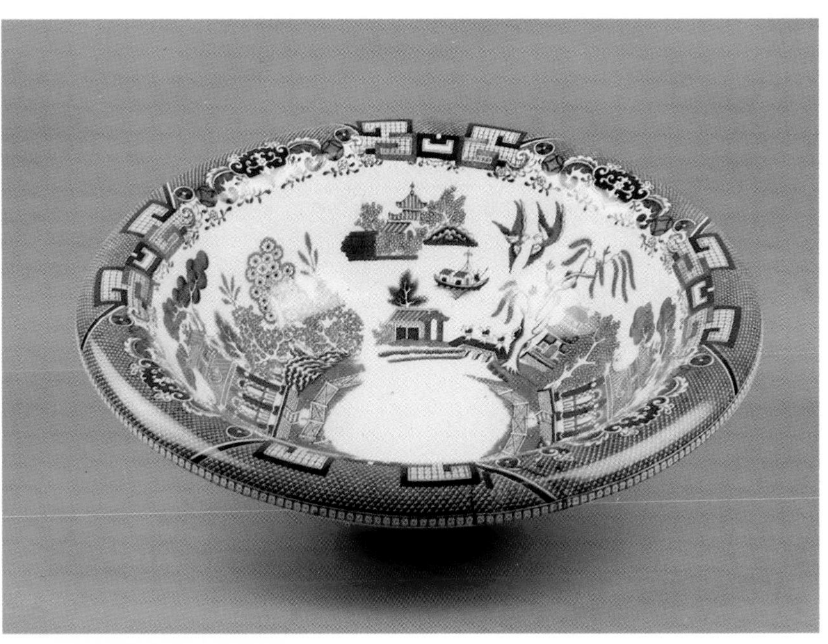

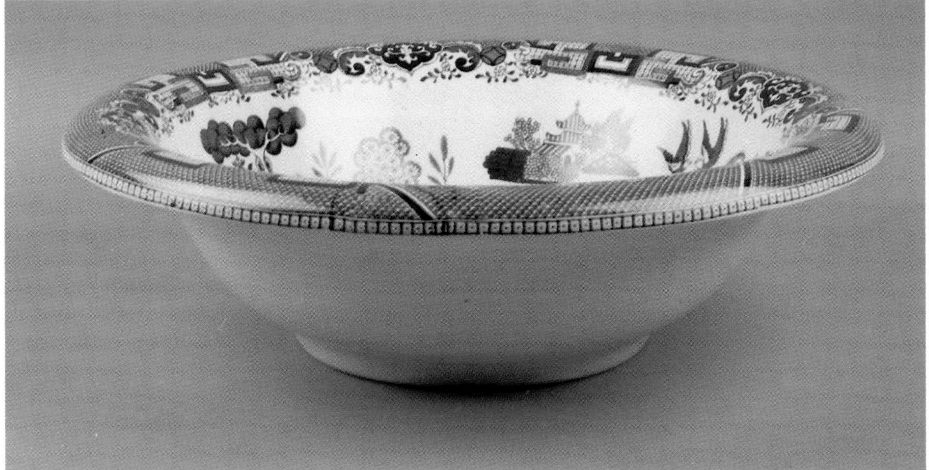

At left and above, the Buffalo Pottery bath set's wash bowl, 1910, 5" high x 16.5" diam. From the collection of Phillip M. Sullivan, South Orleans, MA.

From the Buffalo bath set: a chamber pot, 5.5" high x 9" diam. Undated, originally came with a lid. From the collection of Phillip M. Sullivan, South Orleans, MA.

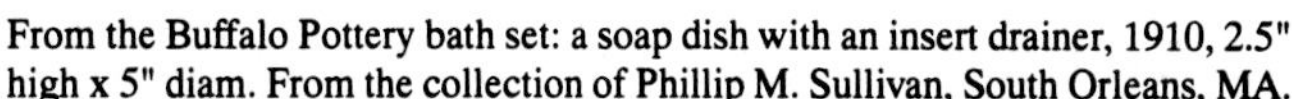

From the Buffalo Pottery bath set: a soap dish with an insert drainer, 1910, 2.5" high x 5" diam. From the collection of Phillip M. Sullivan, South Orleans, MA.

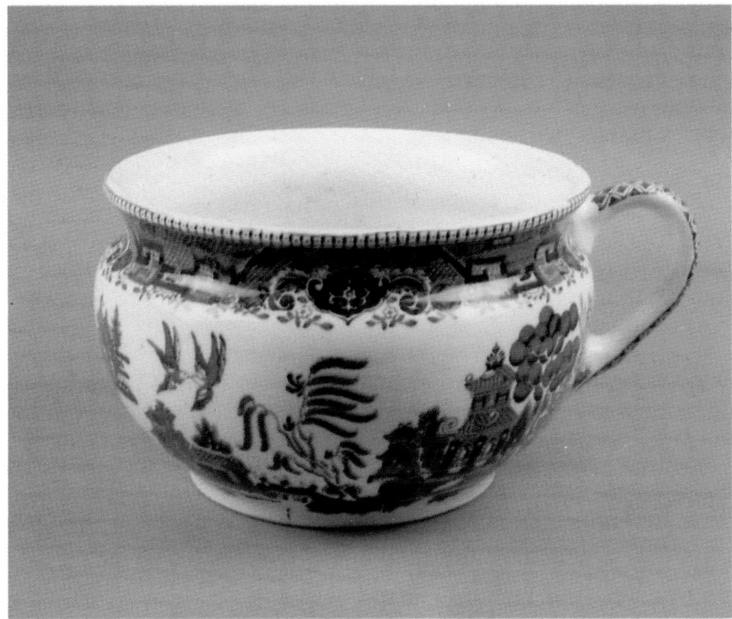

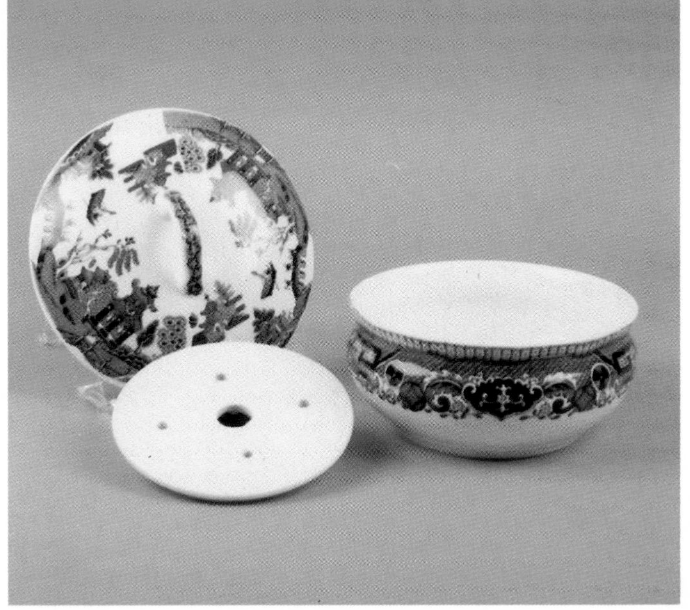

1 2 3

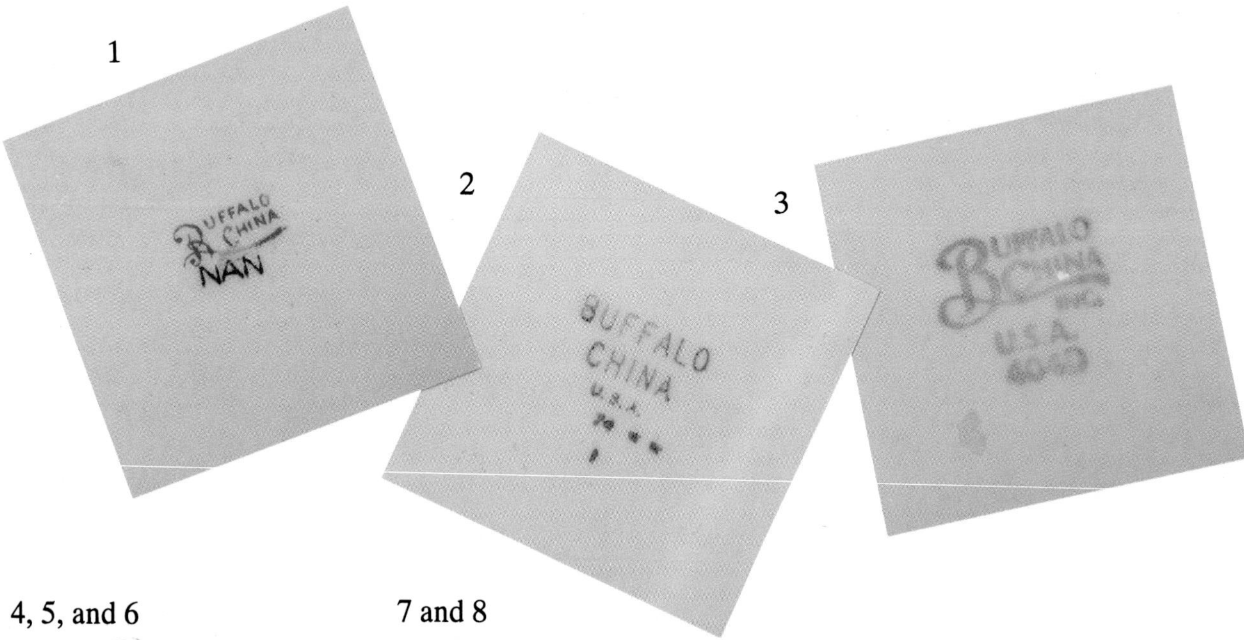

4, 5, and 6

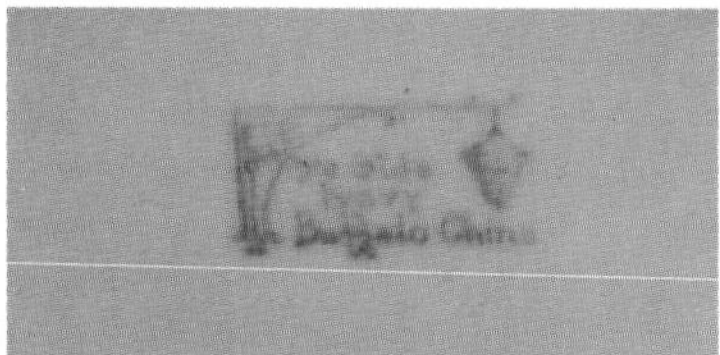

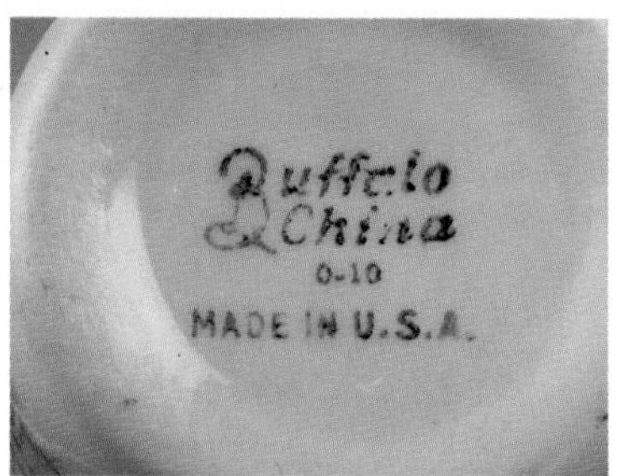

7 and 8

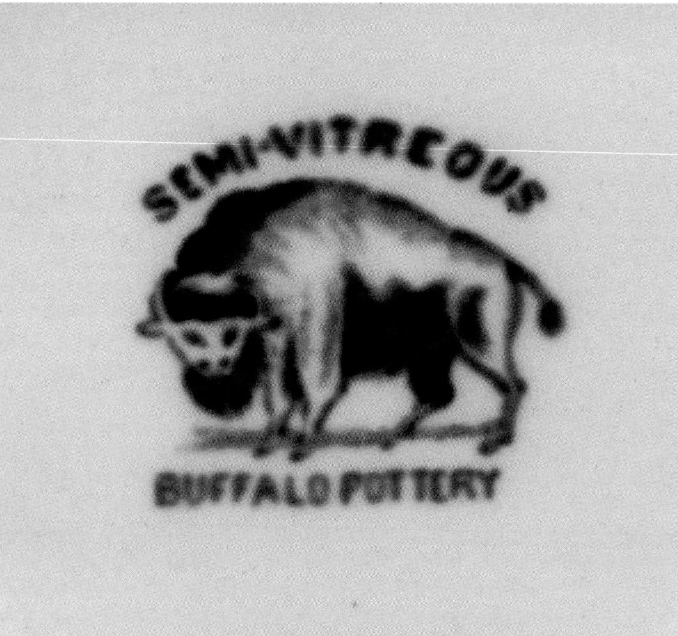

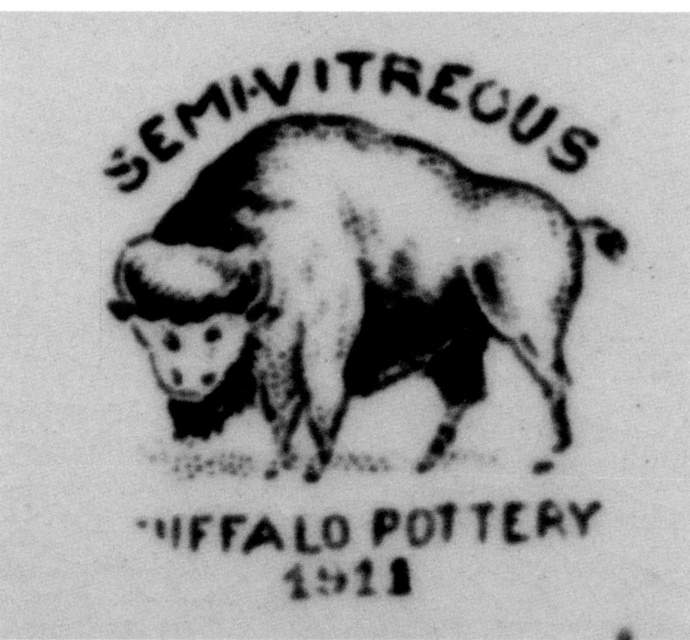

In 1905, the Buffalo Pottery produced its first Willow, and each piece made that year was marked "Ye Olde Willow Ware" (see p. 66). Subsequent runs were marked with the imprinted buffalo mark, with or without a date (see marks 7 and 8, this page). In 1916, the company changed its name to Buffalo China, and stopped making earthenwares in favor of china wares. Their logo reflected this change (see marks 1, 6, and 11, this page).

9, 10, and 11

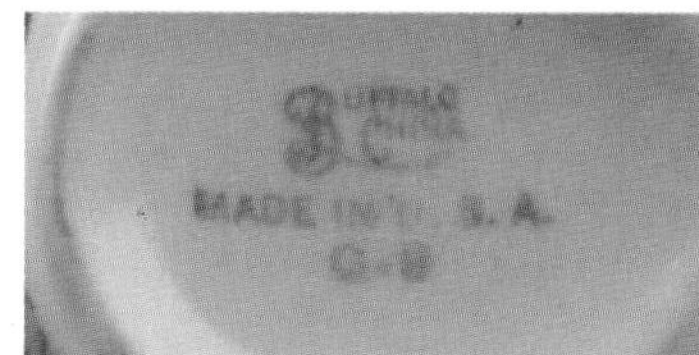

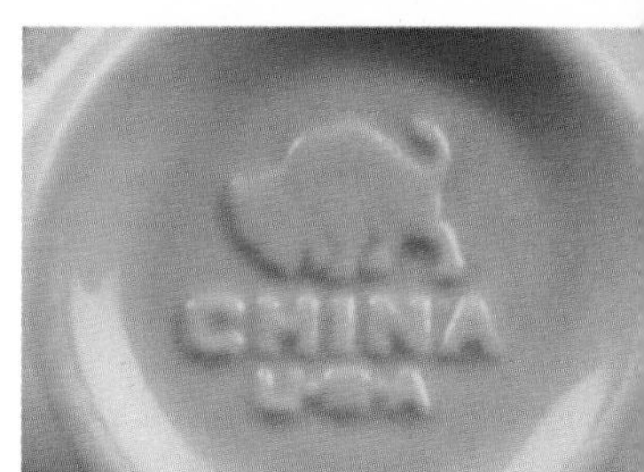

Special design or color lines, like Rouge Ware and Lune Ware (see p. 60), sometimes sported other marks. A "Ye Olde Ivory Buffalo China" mark with a lantern logo was used c. 1930 (see mark 4, this page, and also p. 81).

In the 1960s, Buffalo China was taken over by Oneida. Marks from the 1960s and '70s often include "USA" or MADE IN THE USA" (marks 2, 3, 5, 9, and 10).

Burleigh Ware: A trade name used by Burgess & Leigh Ltd., which began producing earthenwares in the Staffordshire Potteries in 1862. They operated out of the Hill Pottery, 1867-1889, and the Middleport Pottery, c. 1889+, in Burslem. They used a variety of decorative name marks, some including a beehive logo.

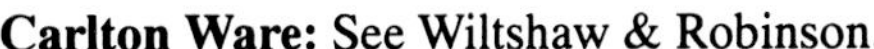

Carlton Ware: See Wiltshaw & Robinson.

Carter Hall Co.: Used a bulldog mark.

Caughley Works: Also known as "Salopian," established near Brosely, Shropshire, England, under Thomas Turner. Active from 1775-1799, producing porcelain. Would later become J. Rose & Co., thereby Coalport. Caughley was a key player in the origins of the Willow pattern; and as one historian wrote, "the production of the willow and other all-over pseudo-oriental patterns set the seal on Caughley's success."[13] Marks include crescent "C" marks and "S" marks in underglaze blue and printed Chinese-style marks made from Arabic numbers (c. 1775-1790).

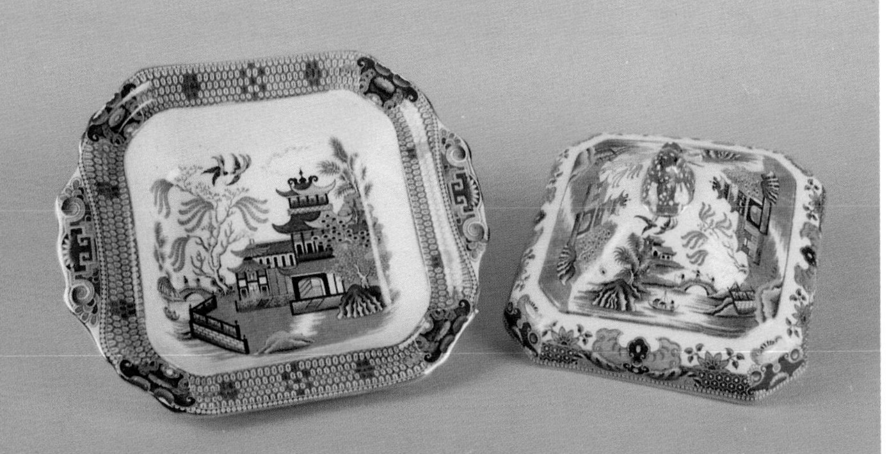

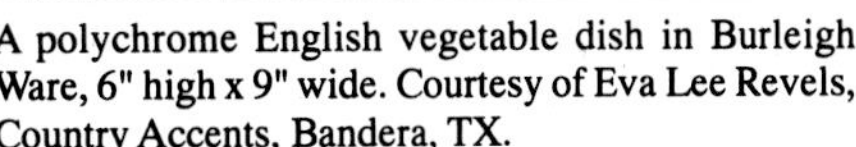

A polychrome English vegetable dish in Burleigh Ware, 6" high x 9" wide. Courtesy of Eva Lee Revels, Country Accents, Bandera, TX.

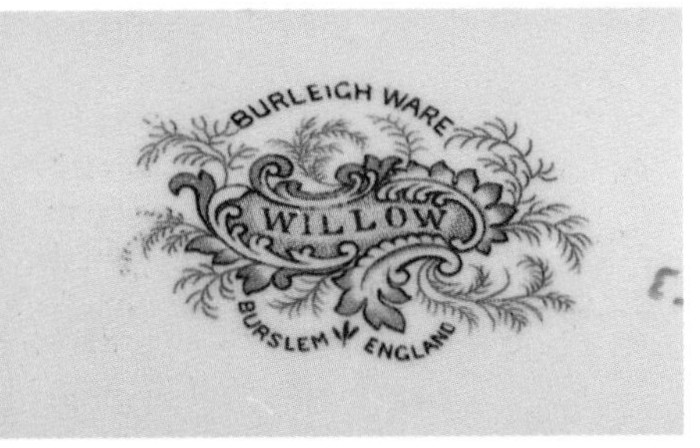

Joseph Burn & Co.: Active from 1852-1860 in Newcastle-upon-Tyne, Northumberland. Used a mark reading "J. Burn & Co."

Caribe: The Puerto Rico division of the Sterling China Co. in Ohio. Marks with a scrawled "Caribe" are c. late 1940s.

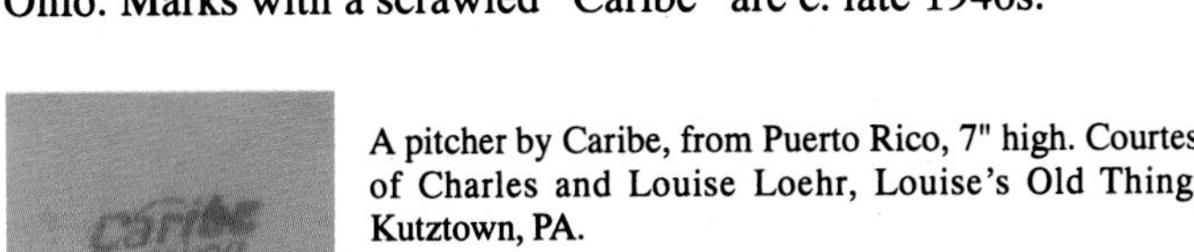

A pitcher by Caribe, from Puerto Rico, 7" high. Courtesy of Charles and Louise Loehr, Louise's Old Things, Kutztown, PA.

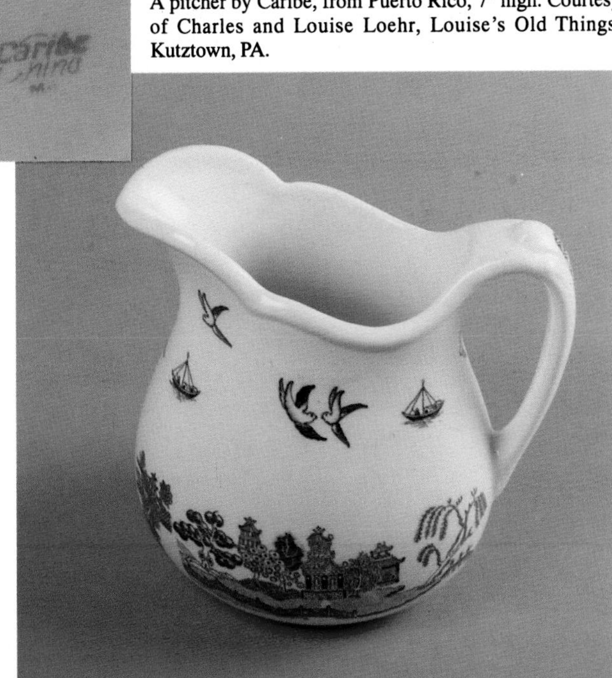

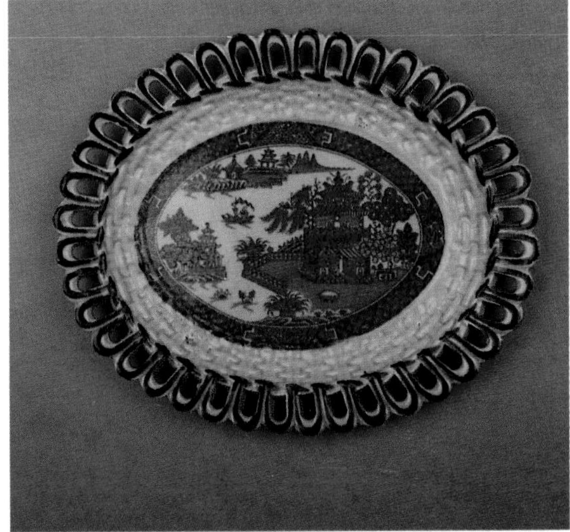

An oval pearlware platter by Turner, c. 1800, 7.75 wide. Courtesy of Rita Entmacher Cohen.

A small plate, c. 1800, 6.5" diam. The Turner mark is impressed on the base. Courtesy of Rita Entmacher Cohen.

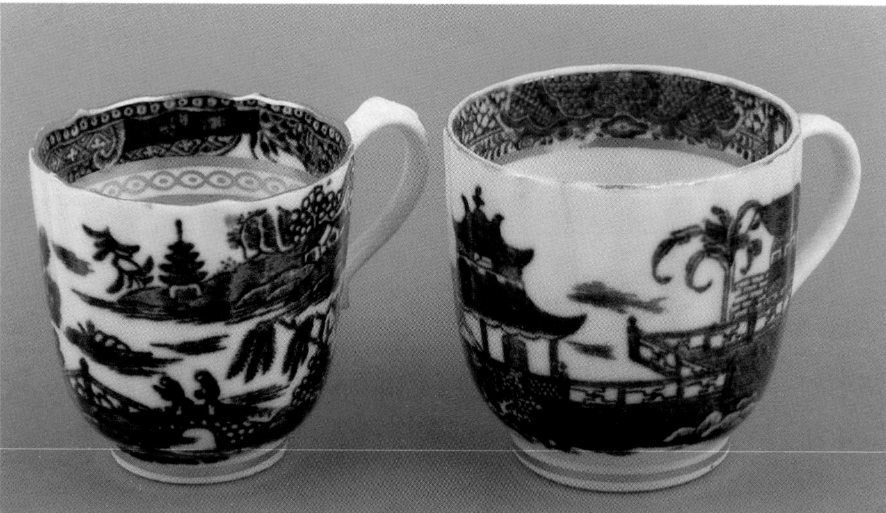

Two pearlware tea cups with gold trim. On the left is a Caughley cup, c. 1785, 2.375"; on the right is a Caughley-Coalport, 2.5", see Godden plate 217. Courtesy of Rita Entmacher Cohen.

Joseph Clementson: Operated from the Phoenix Works in Hanley, Staffordshire, from 1839-1864. In 1865 the name was changed to Clementson Bros. Ltd.

Chambers Jr.: Operated in the mid-1800s.

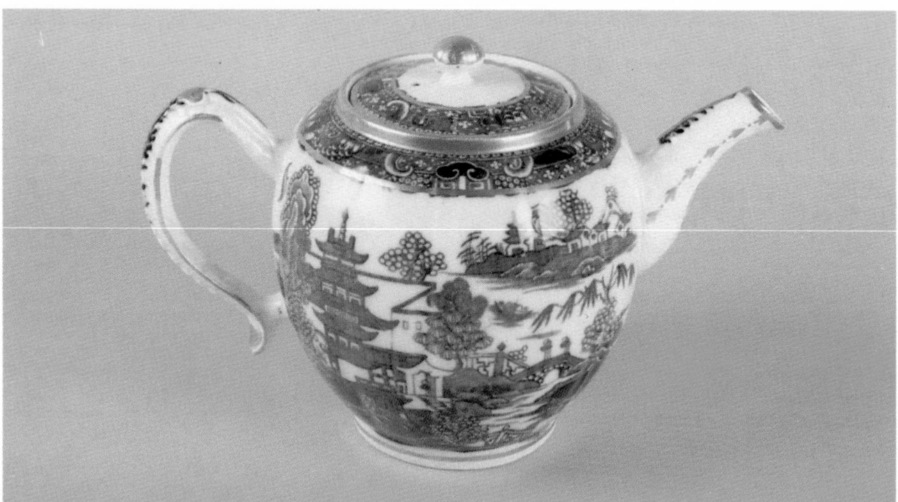

A Caughley teapot, c. 1790, 6" high x 9" wide. Courtesy of Bud & Marguerite Smith, Small World Antiques, Michigan.

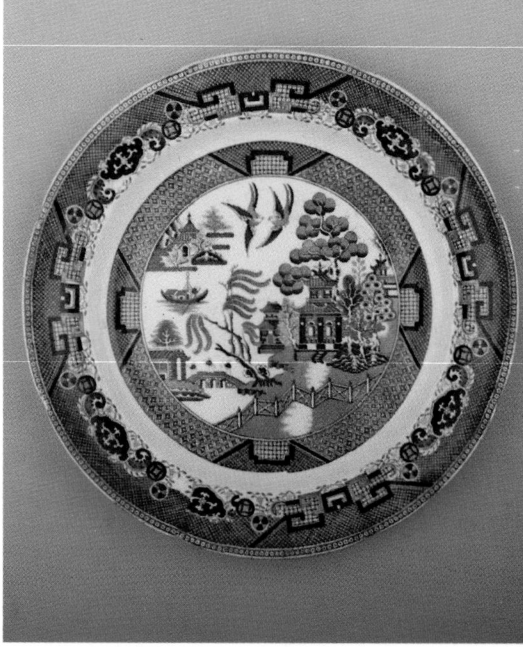

Plate, 1839-1858, 10". Marked with impressed "Chambers Jr." Courtesy of Rita Entmacher Cohen.

Cauldon Ltd Ware: Replaced Brown-Westhead, Moore & Co. at Cauldon Place Works, Hanley in 1905, producing high-quality earthenwares and porcelains. In 1920 the name changed to Cauldon Potteries Ltd.; in 1962, the earthenware division bought by Poutney & Co Ltd, and the porcelain division by E.W. Bain & Co. Ltd. Marks include "Cauldon (Ltd) England". Sometimes Cauldon used old marks from Ridgway and Brown, Westhead & Moore (earlier occupants of the works), with the addition of the Cauldon name.[14]

Clews: James and Ralph Clews rented the Cobridge Works in Staffordshire from William Adams, c. 1815-1817, and worked in the Staffordshire Potteries c. 1817-1834, specializing in high-quality blue transfer wares on earthenwares and china, including the extensive "Dr. Syntax" series. The partnership ended in bankruptcy in 1834. Marks include "CLEWS/WARRANTED/STAFFORDSHIRE" and "R. & J. CLEWS".

Clyde Pottery & Co.: Active from 1857-1872 in Greenock, Scotland. Marks include "CLYDE," "G. C. P. Co." and "C. P. Co."

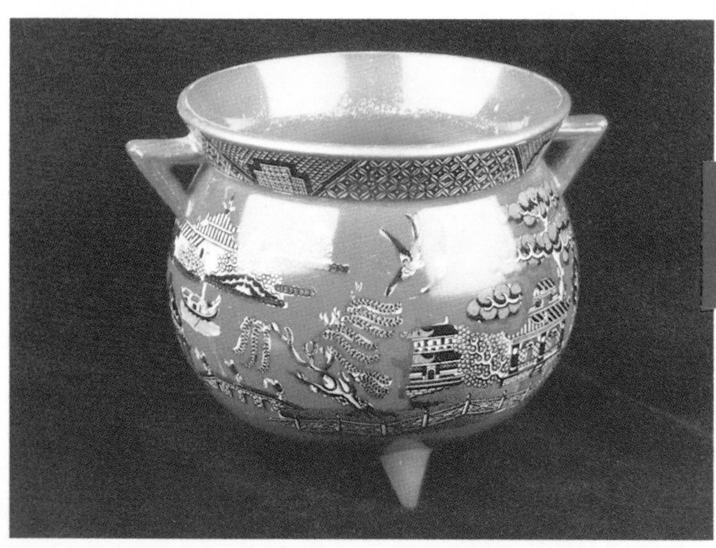

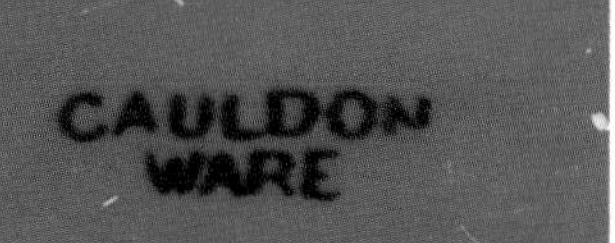

A footed Cauldon Ware bowl with an orange border, 1907-1934, 5.5". Courtesy of Rita Entmacher Cohen.

Coalport: Founded in 1795 by John Rose. Rose had served his apprenticeship at Caughley, and founded his new pottery on the canal bank just opposite the older firm. In 1799, Rose acquired Caughley, and in 1814 absorbed it into the Coalport works. The company made bone china as of 1798 (initially unmarked), and in 1822 began making feldspar porcelain. Until the early 1820s, Coalport's decoration was almost exclusively underglaze blue, either printed (like their Willow line) or painted. From 1815-1828, the company's mark was a painted script "Coalport" in underglaze blue. In 1828 John Rose was succeeded by his son, John Rose II, who immediately gave the company a new name: Colebrookdale, after a renowned neighboring ironworks of the same name. By 1830, the company was recognized as one of the most important potteries in England. Other marks include "J. Rose & Co." "Colebrookdale," "C. D.," "C. Dale," and a script "CBD" monogram. From the late 1700s through 1881, one mark read "COALPORT A D 1750;" from 1881-1885, a crown was added. Marks with a printed or impressed "ENGLAND" are post-1894.

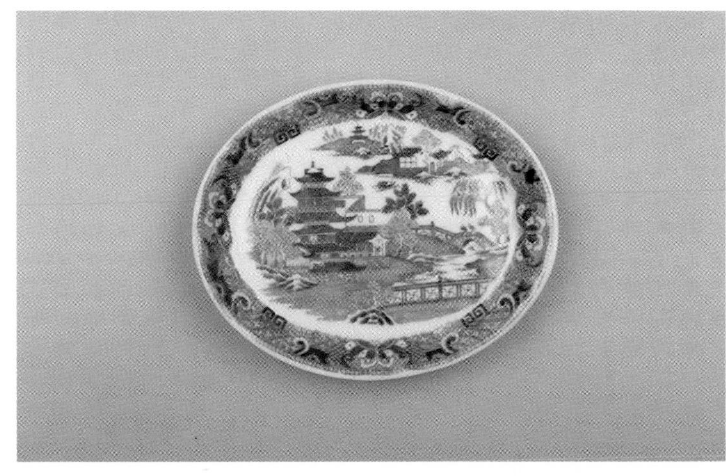

A light blue oval dish from Jon Rose, Coalport, 6.625" wide. Courtesy of Rita Entmacher Cohen.

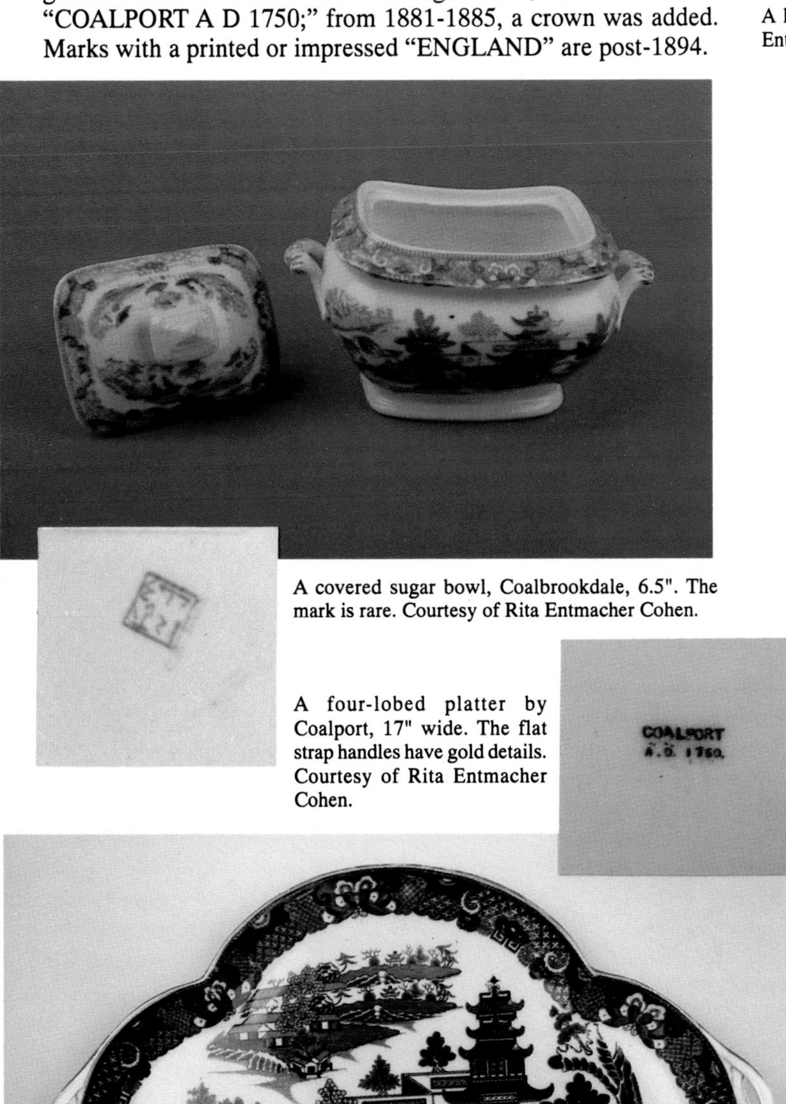

A covered sugar bowl, Coalbrookdale, 6.5". The mark is rare. Courtesy of Rita Entmacher Cohen.

A four-lobed platter by Coalport, 17" wide. The flat strap handles have gold details. Courtesy of Rita Entmacher Cohen.

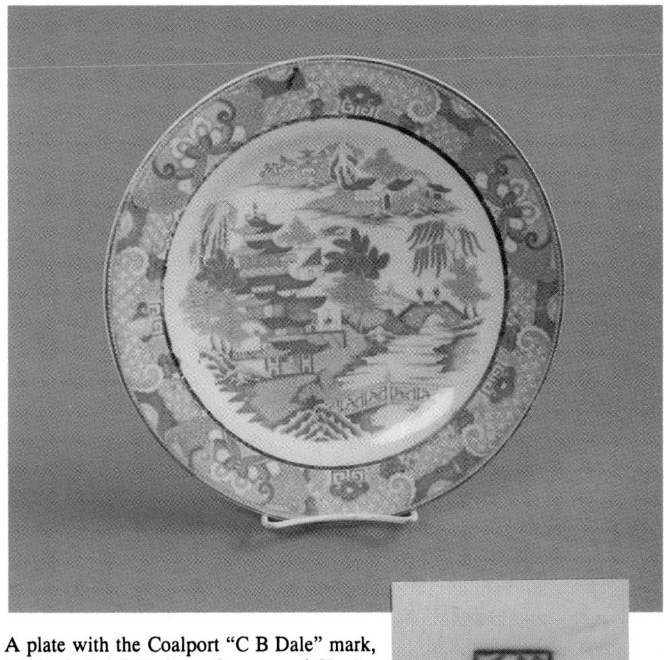

A plate with the Coalport "C B Dale" mark, 1810-1815, 9.25" diam., Courtesy of Charles and Louise Loehr, Louise's Old Things, Kutztown, PA.

C.B. Dale (Coalport) mark.

Robert Cochran & Co.: Active from 1846-1918 at the Verreville Pottery in Glasgow, Scotland, producing earthenware, stoneware, and (until 1856) china. Marks include "R. C. & Co." beginning in 1846; "COCHRAN, GLASGOW" starting in 1875; and "R. Cochran & Co." in a variety of designs beginning in 1918.

Cockson & Harding: Active from 1856-1862, succeeding various Hackwood partnerships and W. & J. harding at the New Hall Works in Shelton, Staffordshire. Marks include "C. & H.," sometimes with the addition of "LATE HACKWOOD".

Copeland Spode: In 1733, Josiah Spode I was born. He apprenticed at Whieldon, and in 1770 took over the Turner & Banks pottery. By 1776 he was producing wares under his own name from the Spode Works in Stoke, Staffordshire. In the early 1780s, the company perfected their underglaze transfer-printing techniques, prompting the eventual development of the first Willow pattern (see Chapter 2). Their transfer-printed lines became so successful that Spode established a London warehouse, managed by William Copeland. When Spode began producing quantities of bone china in 1796, the warehouse made tremendous profits in selling it, and within a year Spode made Copeland a partner, renaming the enterprise "Spode, Son & Copeland."

When Josiah Spode I died in 1797, he was succeeded by his son, Josiah Spode II. Likewise, William Copeland was succeeded by his son, W. T. Copeland, in 1826. In 1827, Josiah Spode II died, but his son Josiah Spode III filled his shoes. When Josiah III died in 1829, W. T. Copeland was left as sole proprietor of the works.

Under W. T. Copeland's direction, the pottery grew immensely, inspiring him to take Thomas Garrett into partnership in 1833. They operated under the name "Copeland & Garrett," in the original Spode Works. Marks included "C & G" "COPELAND & GARRETT," and "LATE SPODE," sometimes with the pattern name or body type. Thomas Garrett retired in 1847, but the company continued to manufacture respectable-quality export earthenwares and high-quality porcelain, under the new name of "W. T. Copeland." By 1861 they employed 800 workers, and were considered to be Minton's biggest rival. They enjoyed royal patronage, and participated in all major international exhibitions. In 1867 Copeland was joined by his sons, and the company became "W. T. Copeland & Sons." In that year, the "LATE SPODE" mark was discontinued in favor of "W. T. COPELAND & SONS."

The company thrived in the 1800s, and maintained its reputation through the present century. In 1970, the company resumed the use of the Spode name.

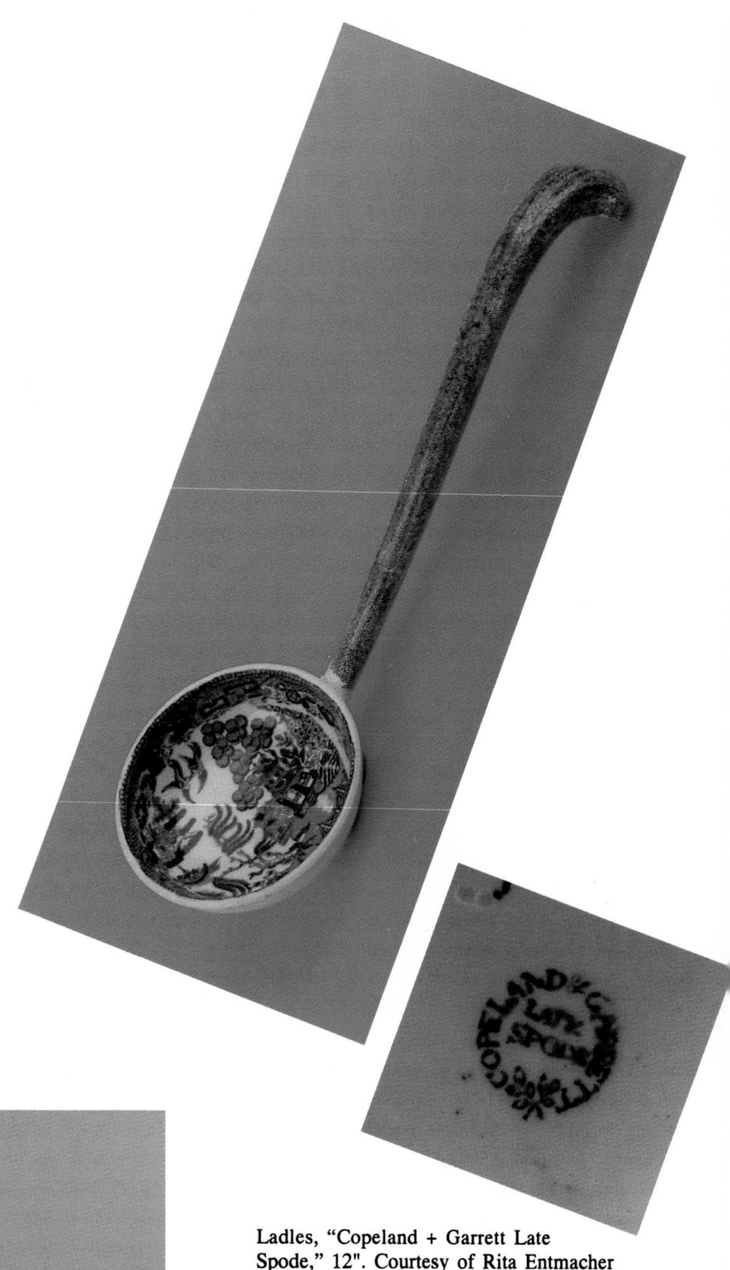

Ladles, "Copeland + Garrett Late Spode," 12". Courtesy of Rita Entmacher Cohen.

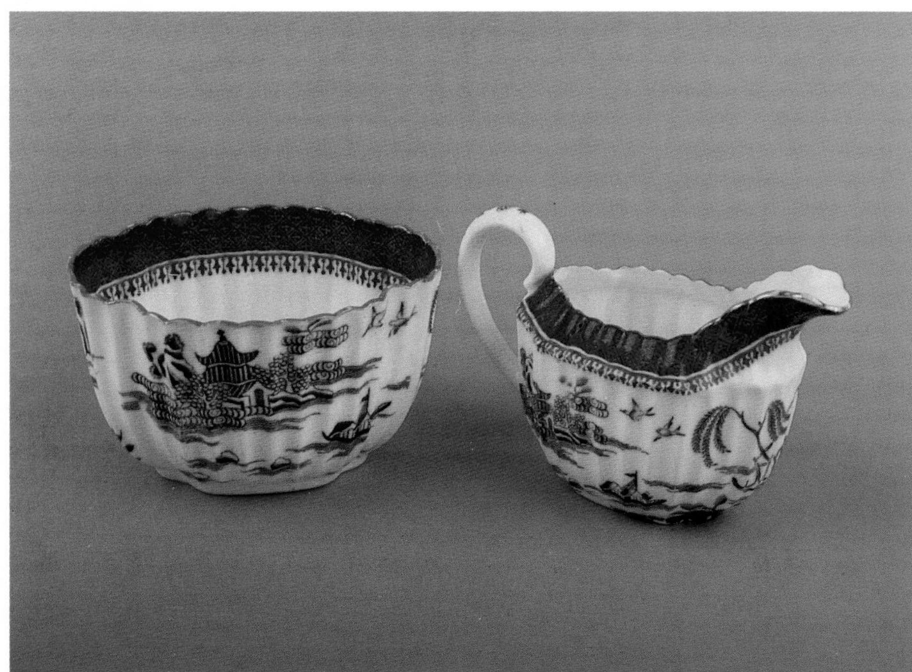

A fluted cream and sugar set with gold trim, 1851-1855, 3". With Copeland's printed mark. Courtesy of Rita Entmacher Cohen.

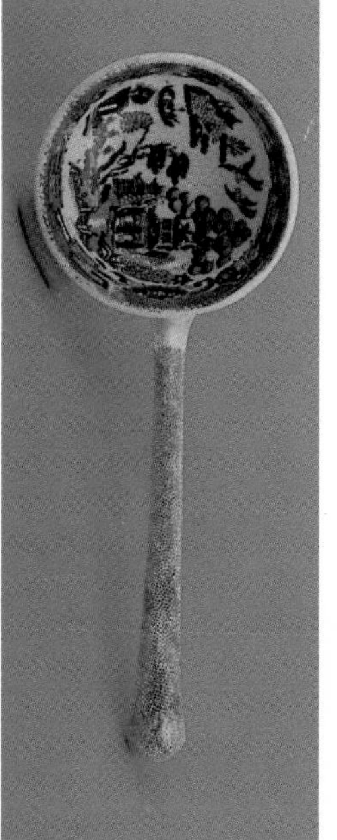

A small Copeland ladle, 1880. Courtesy of Rita Entmacher Cohen.

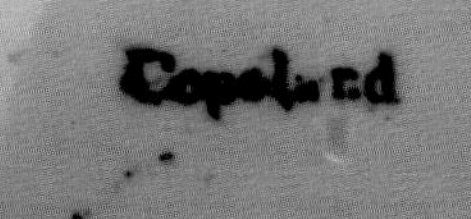

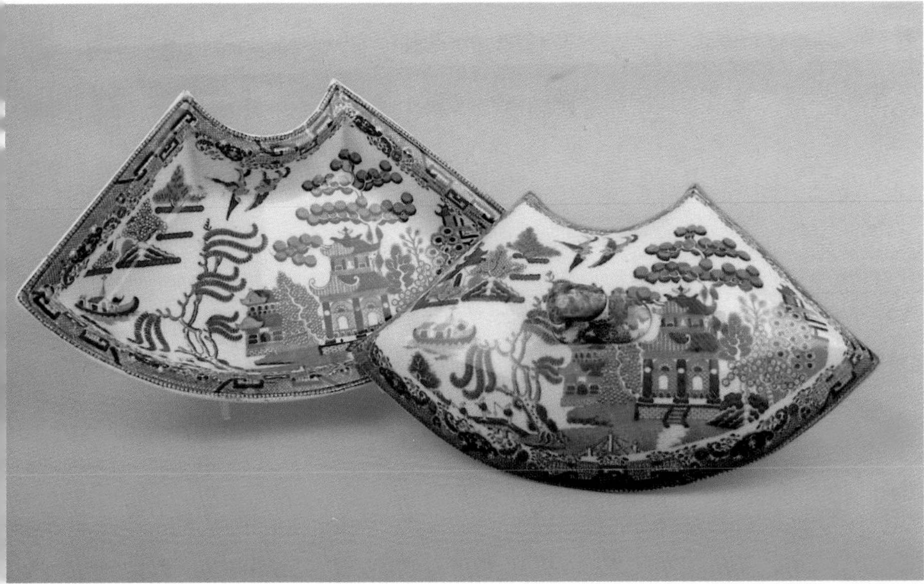

A covered pearlware serving dish, c. 1800, 12" wide, part of a sectional serving set. This piece in unmarked, but resembles Spode's 'Willow I' design. Courtesy of Rita Entmacher Cohen.

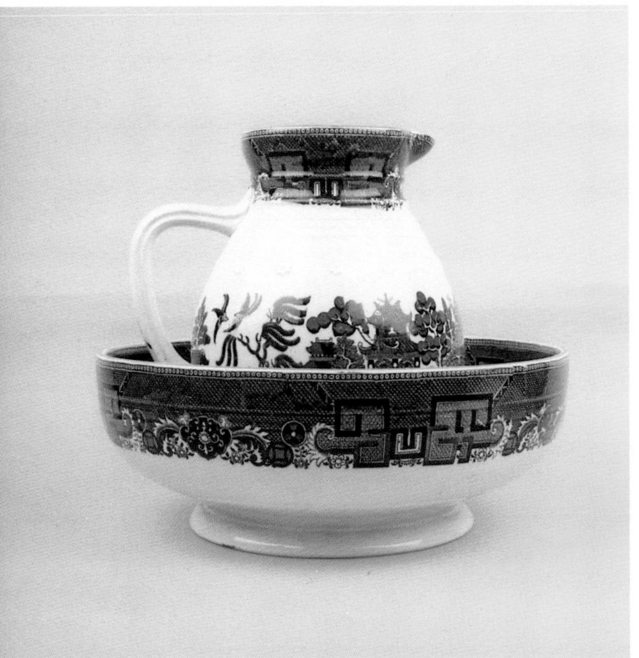

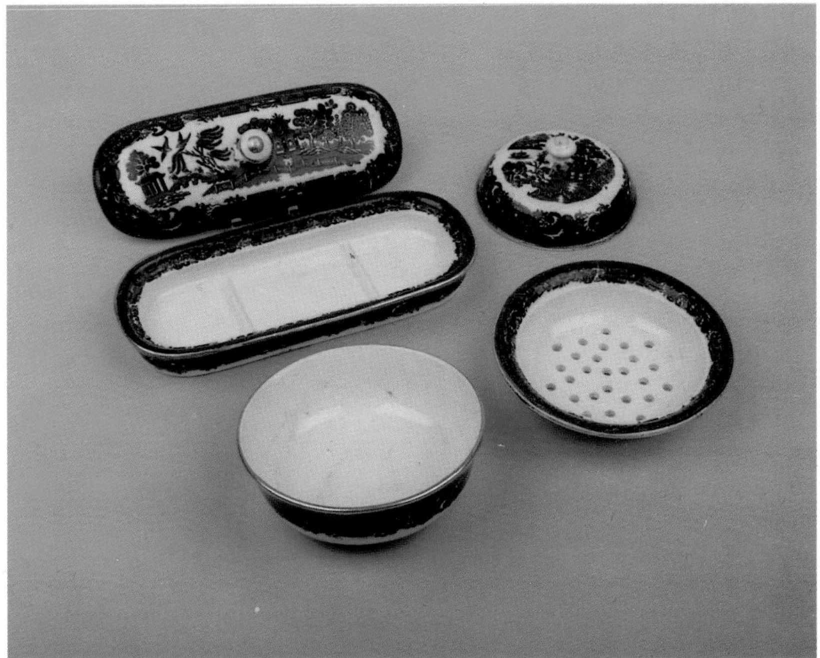

A bath set from 1877. The pieces have gold rim bands, and were made by Copeland. Courtesy of Rita Entmacher Cohen.

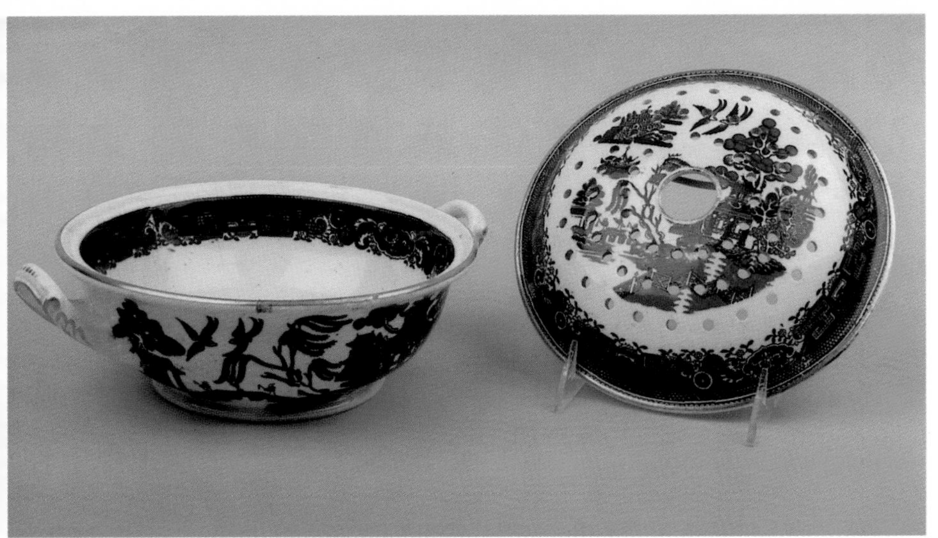

A platter with a removable drainer in the "Forest" pattern,

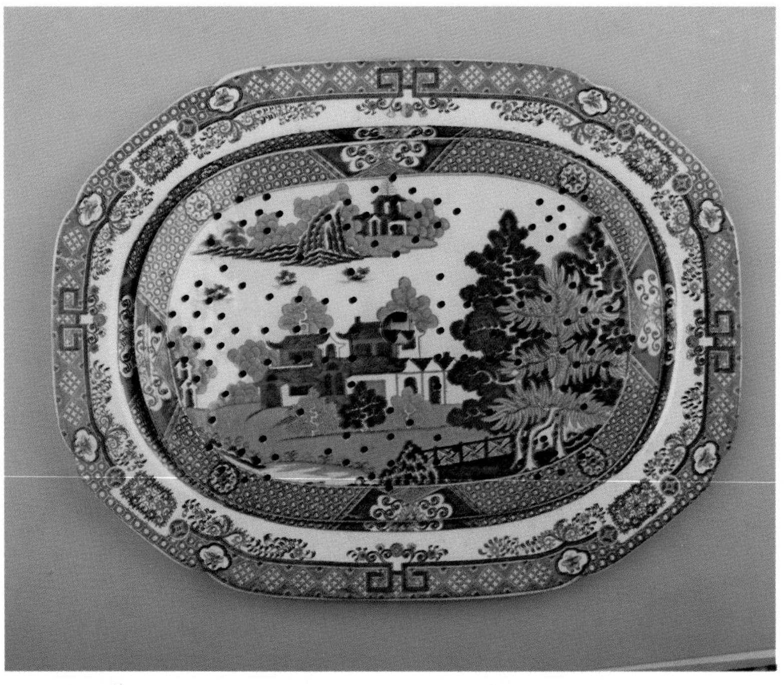

A platter with a removable drainer in the "Forest" pattern, 19" x 14.25". Courtesy of Rita Entmacher Cohen.

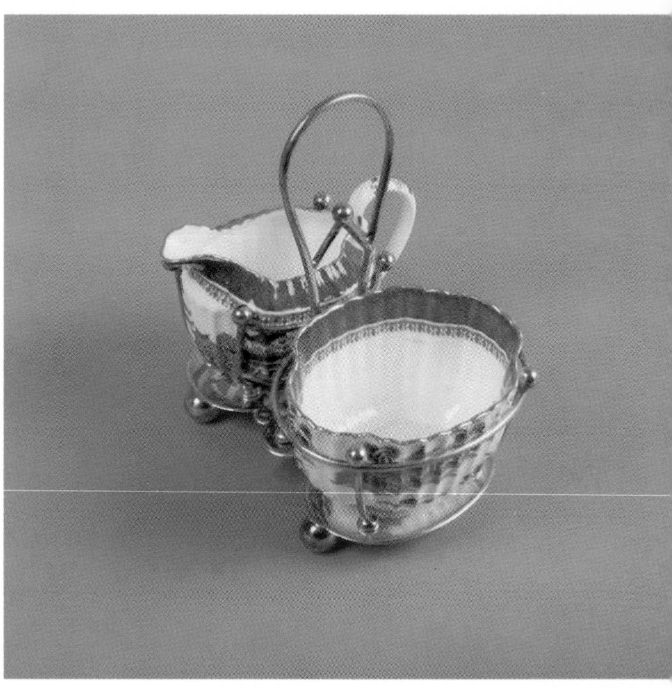

A cream and sugar set by Copeland, 1879-1890. Courtesy of Charles and Louise Loehr, Louise's Old Things, Kutztown, PA.

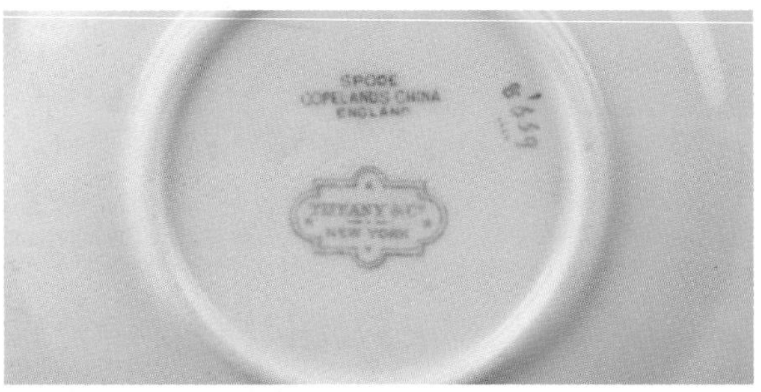

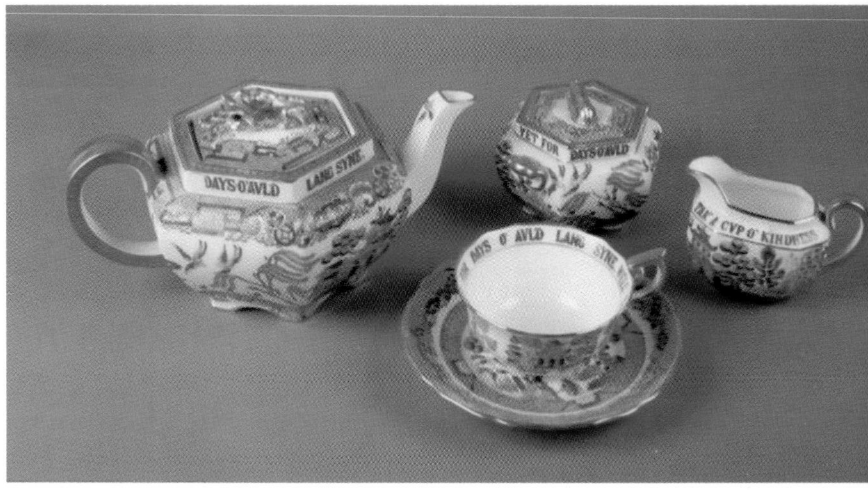

A tea pot, creamer, sugar, cup and saucer, from Spode Copeland through Tiffany. Reads "We'll Take A Cup O' Kindness Yet For Days O' Auld Lang Syne". From the collection of Peter and Susan Steelman, Mystic, CT.

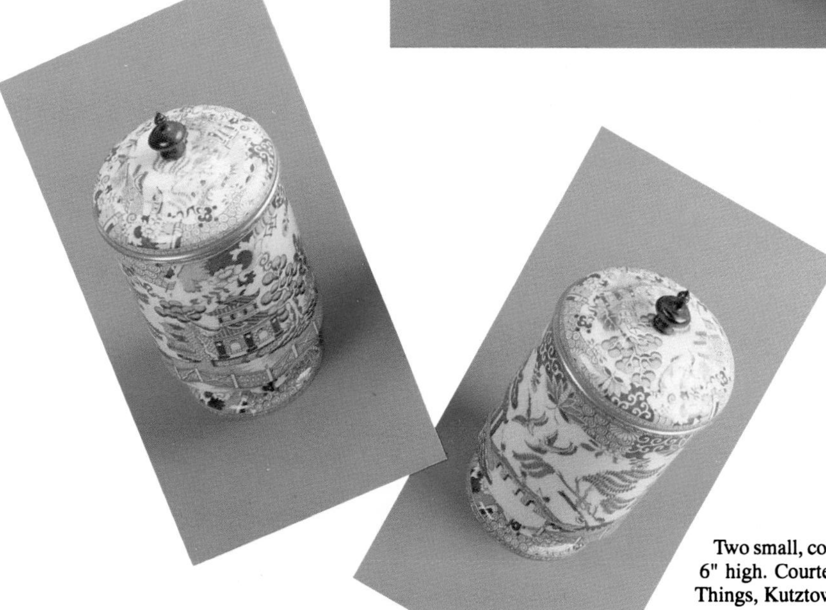

Two small, covered, porcelain vases by Copeland, 1851-1885, 6" high. Courtesy of Charles and Louise Loehr, Louise's Old Things, Kutztown PA.

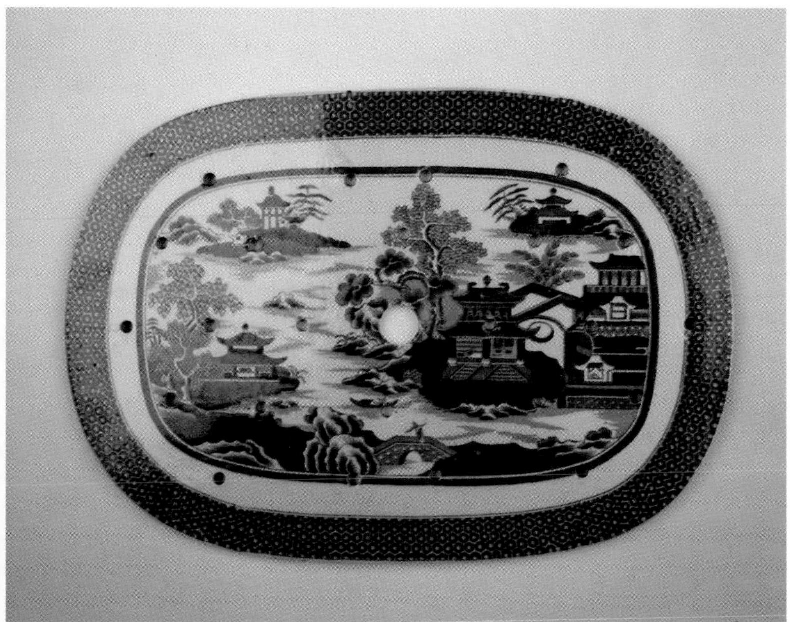

A drainer, 14.5" wide, from Spode's New Stone line. Courtesy of Rita Entmacher Cohen.

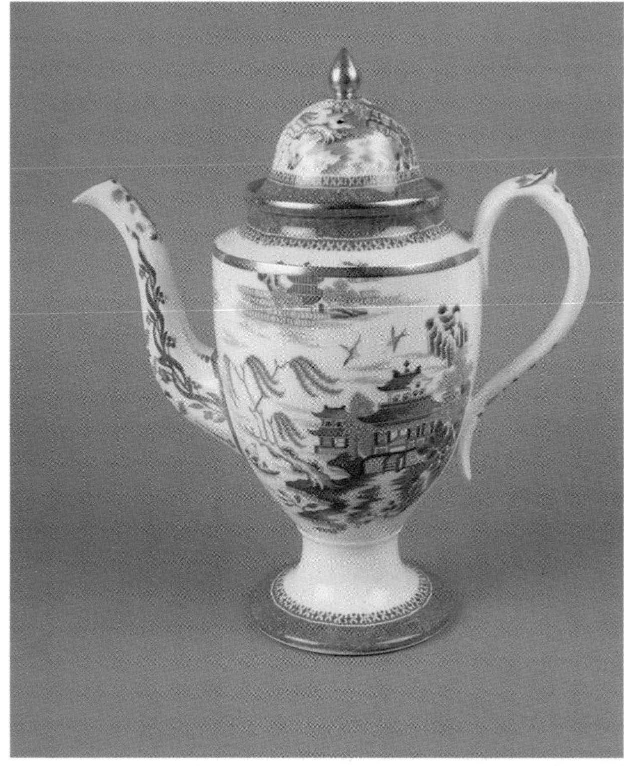

A Spode coffee pot in the Mandarin pattern, with that pattern's characteristic dagger border, 12" high. Marked on bottom with the printed mark "Spode" (not all caps). From the collection of Peter and Susan Steelman, Mystic, CT.

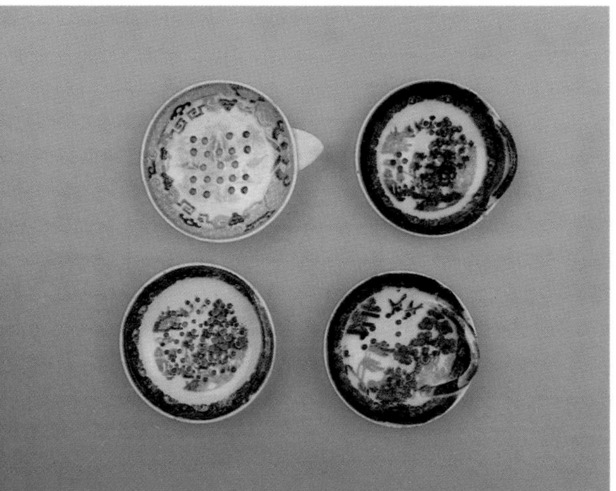

A Spode mark from c. 1900-1910.

Four milk seives ('Milseys'), c. 1800, 1810, and 1820. One is marked SPODE. Courtesy of Rita Entmacher Cohen.

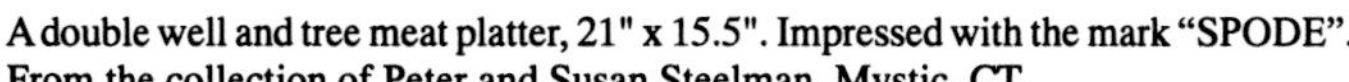

A double well and tree meat platter, 21" x 15.5". Impressed with the mark "SPODE". From the collection of Peter and Susan Steelman, Mystic, CT.

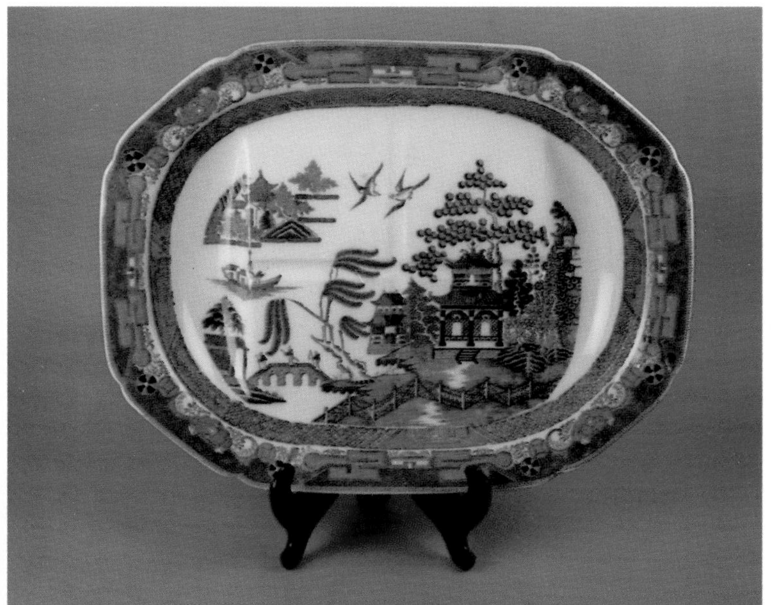

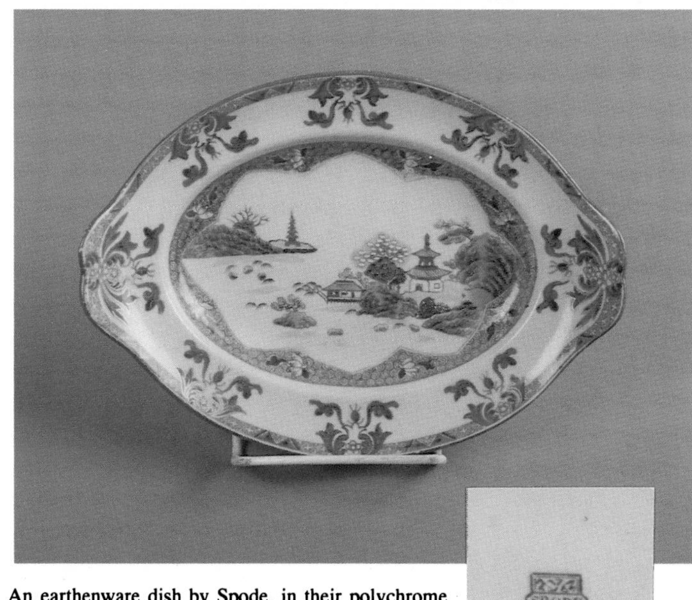

An earthenware dish by Spode, in their polychrome "Landscape" variant, 1812-1833, 8.5" wide. Courtesy of Charles and Louise Loehr, Louise's Old Things, Kutztown PA.

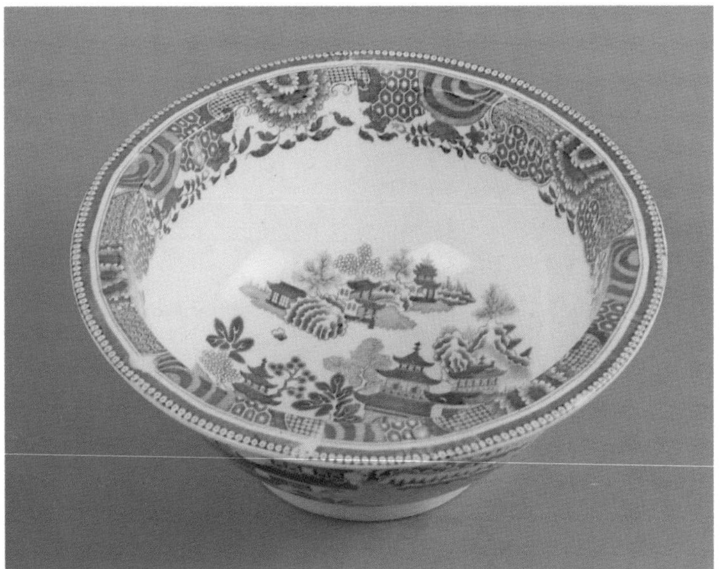

A Spode bowl, with the impressed "SPODE" mark on the bottom, 3.5" high x 8.5" diam. Courtesy of Charles and Louise Loehr, Louise's Old Things, Kutztown, PA.

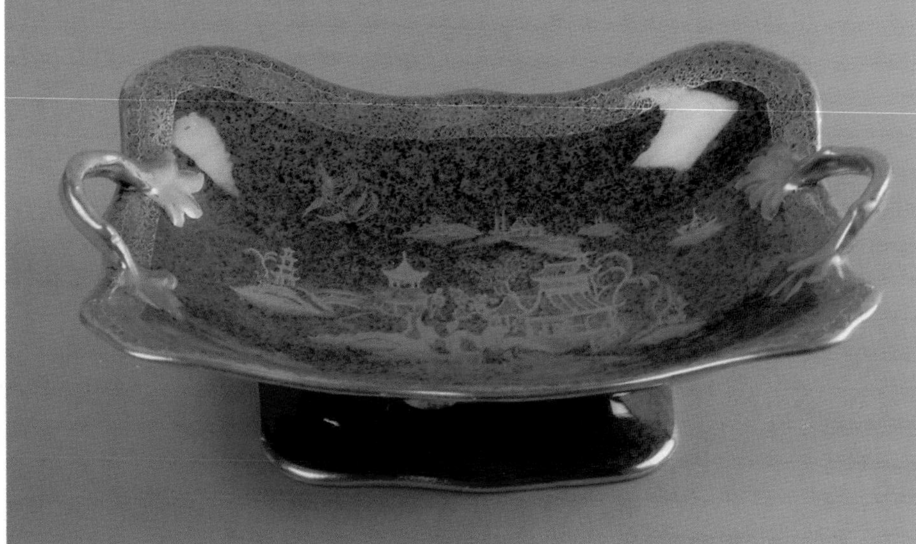

A Spode gold-on-blue Willow server, 4" high. Courtesy of Charles and Louise Loehr, Louise's Old Things, Kutztown, PA.

Corona Ware: see S. Hancock & Sons

Crown Pottery: see John Tams (& Son) (Ltd.)

Crown Staffordshire: Active 1889-1962 at the Minerva Works in Fenton, Staffordshire, under the name Crown Staffordshire Porcelain Co., Ltd. (formerly T. A. & S. Green). In 1948 the name was changed to Crown Staffordshire China Co., Ltd. Marks included a crown with leaves, printed with the word "STAFFORDSHIRE" (1889-1912), printed marks with "ENGLAND" or "AD 1801" added (1905+), the printed mark "CROWN STAFFORDSHIRE" (1930), and a variety of printed trademarks (throughout the 1930s).

Crown Clarence: The Co-operative Wholesale Society Ltd. produced earthenwares out of the Crown Clarence Pottery in Longton, Staffordshire, starting in 1946. Marks of various printed designs include the pottery name and "MADE IN ENGLAND."

Davenport: Established at Unicorn Bank Works in Longport, Staffordshire by John Davenport in 1793. Initially, the company made earthenwares, later adding stone china, at first unmarked. Around 1805 they began producing porcelain. Early 19th century wares were marked with an anchor under an arching "Davenport," which was changed to an anchor above "DAVENPORT/ LONGPORT/STAFFORDSHIRE" in 1806. A variety of marks were transfer-printed beginning in 1810; the anchor was topped by a crown as of 1830, and a semi-circular ribbon banner was added in 1850. Sometimes the anchor is flanked by the last two digits of the manufacturing year. When John Davenport retired in 1832, his pottery employed 1400 workers. The company began exporting in earnest in 1815, and manufactured great quantities of ironstone for the American market until the 1880s. The firm was operated under Davenport's sons until 1887.

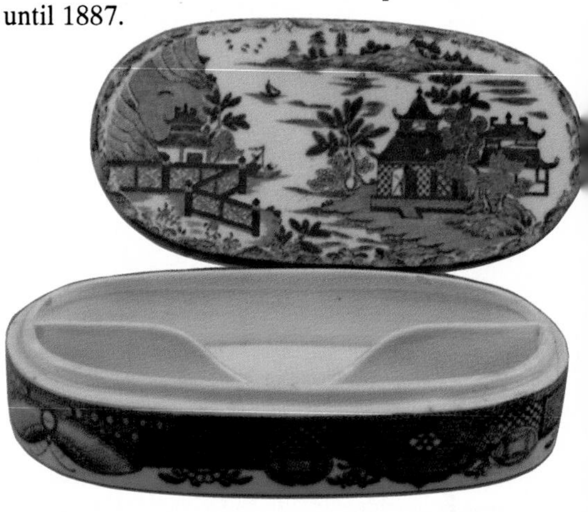

A covered oval box by Davenport, c. 1810. The inside is divided into two compartments, and it is decorated with the bridgeless design. Courtesy of Rita Entmacher Cohen.

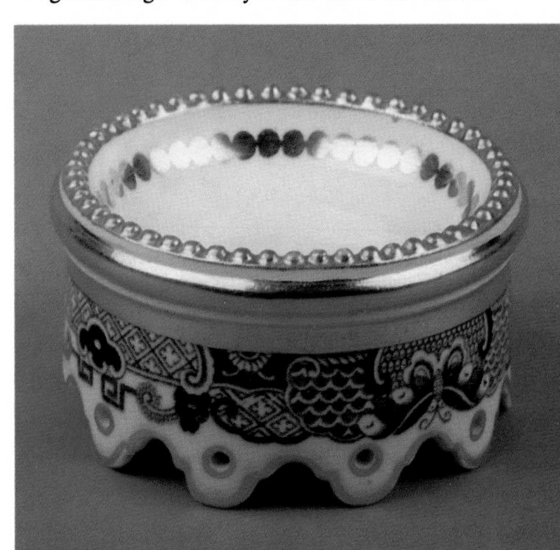

An open salt by Davenport, 3". Trimmed in gold, with a pierced and cut-out foot. Courtesy of Rita Entmacher Cohen.

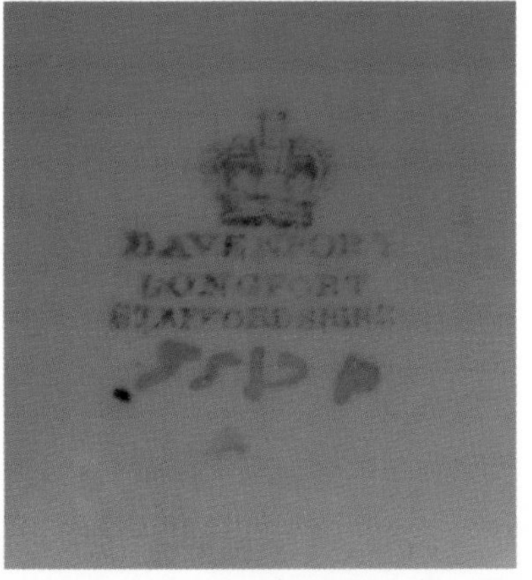

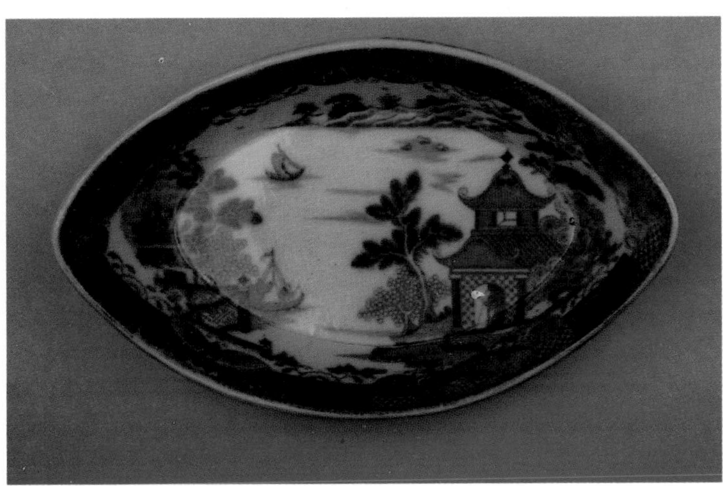

An oval pearlware dish in Davenport's "Bridgeless Willow" pattern, 7.5" wide. Courtesy of Rita Entmacher Cohen.

Davison & Sons: Operated out of Bleak Hill Works in Burslem, Staffordshire, producing earthenwares from 1898-1952. No early marks known. A printed trademark was used c. 1948: a shield with a mountain, under which is a banner reading "DAVISON & SON LTD., BURSLEM, ENGLAND."

Richard Davies & Co.: Tyne Main Pottery, Salt Meadows, Gateshead, active 1833-1844, probably exporting wares to Norway. Used a mark reading "DAVIES & CO".

Dillwyn: see Swansea.

Thomas Dimmock & Co.: Active from 1828-1859 in Shelton and Hanley, Staffordshire, producing earthenwares. The company used the initial "D" to mark their works, a script monogram, or a crown with the name of the pattern and "STONEWARE D".

Double Phoenix: A Japanese company active and producing Willow both before and after World War II.

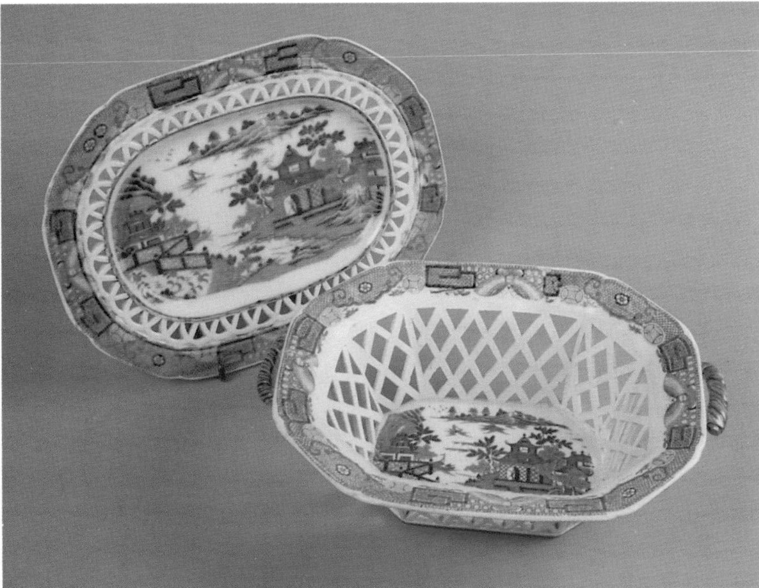

A two-piece pearlware chestnut dish attributed to Davenport, c. 1810, 3" high (bowl) x 10" wide (plate). Courtesy of Charles and Louise Loehr, Louise's Old Things, Kutztown PA.

A crumpet comport attributed to Davenport, c. 1810, 6.5" high x 7.5" diam. Courtesy of Charles and Louise Loehr, Louise's Old Things, Kutztown PA.

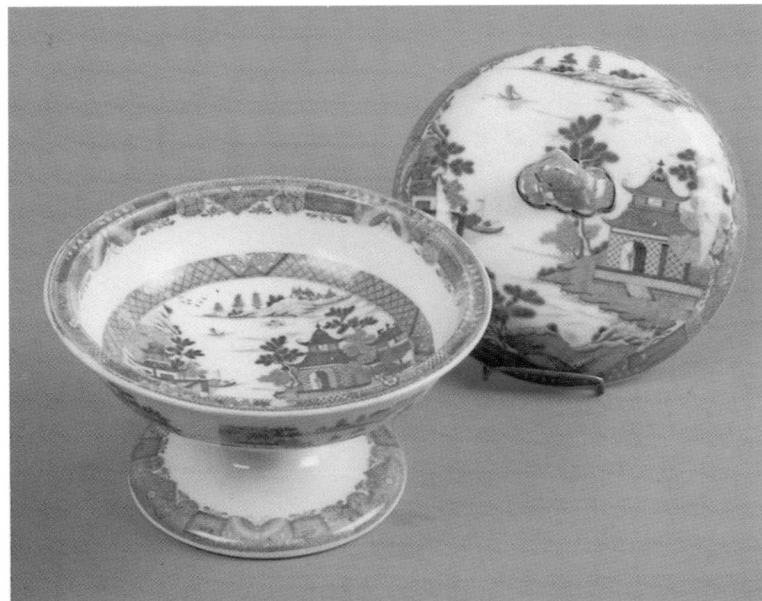

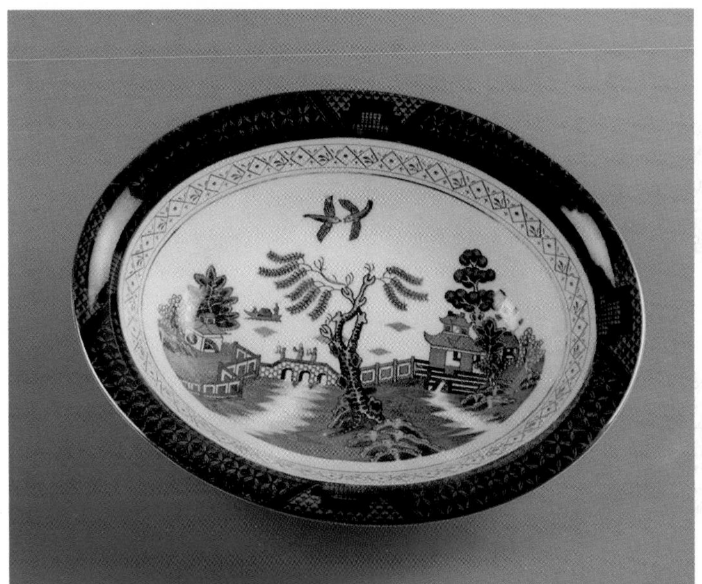

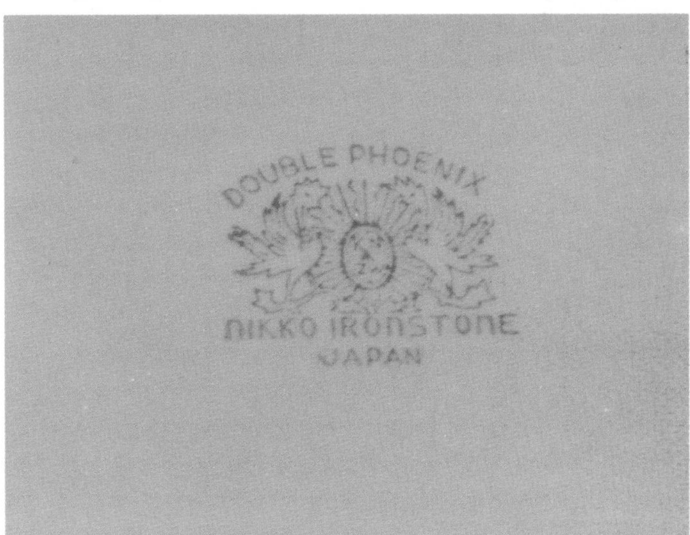

A Japanese oval serving bowl imitating Booth, this one pre-Occupation (before 1945), by the Double Phoenix company. Note the simplified design of the Willow pattern here. 2.75" high x 10.25" diam. Courtesy of Charles and Louise Loehr, Louise's Old Things, Kutztown, PA.

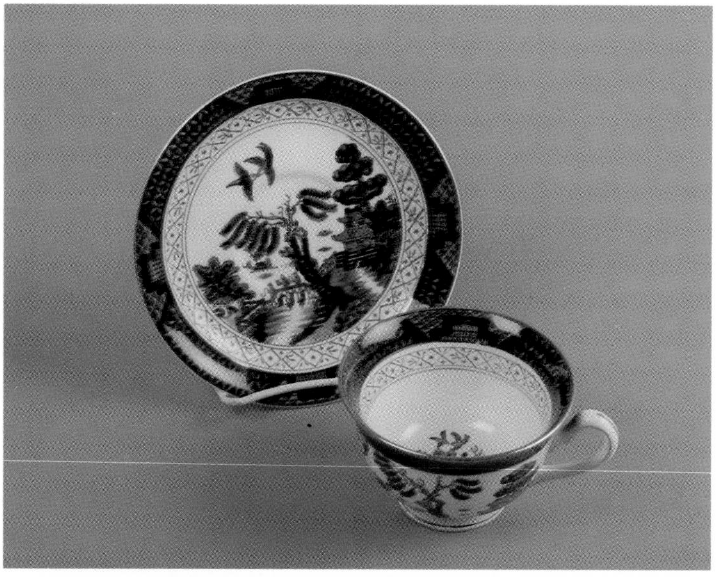

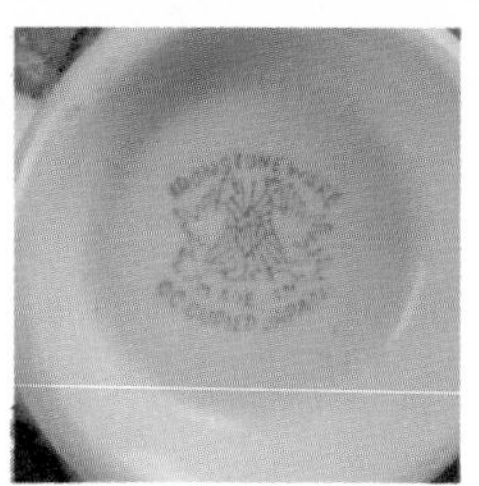

While this ironstone teacup and saucer may look like Booth, they are actually imitations, made by Double Phoenix in Occupied Japan between 1945-1952. The cup is 2.25" high and 3.75" diam. Courtesy of Charles and Louise Loehr, Louise's Old Things, Kutztown, PA.

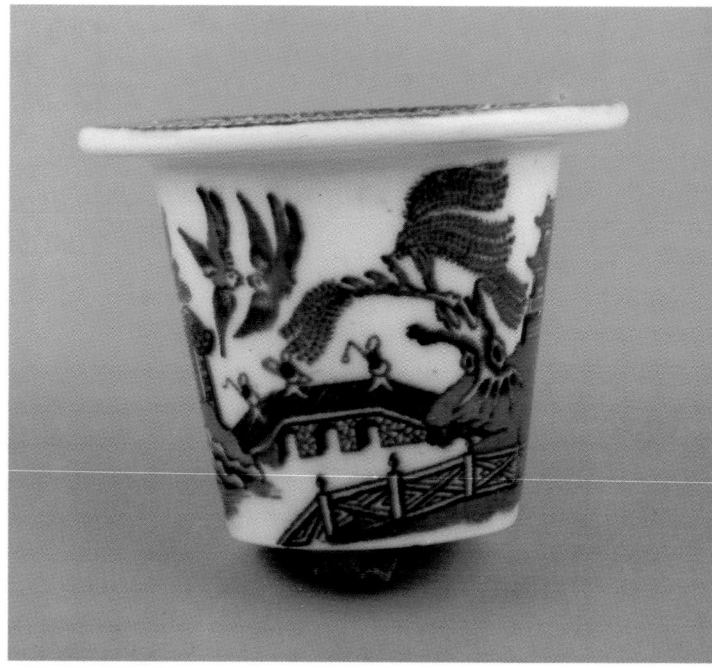

A horseradish dish by Doulton, 2.75" x 3.5". Courtesy of Rita Entmacher Cohen.

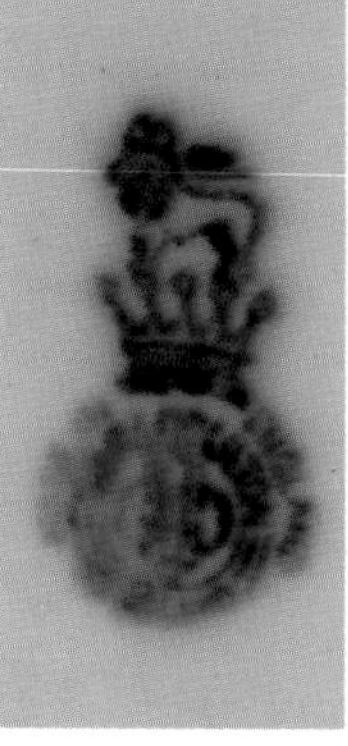

Doulton: This well-known pottery was established by John Doulton as Doulton & Watts at Vauxhall c. 1815-1818, but moved to Lambeth in the mid-1850s after the initial operation closed. From the start, they made practical stonewares, adding earthenwares to their line after 1872. Around 1882 they opened a second pottery in Burslem, on the former Pinder, Bourne & Co. site, and began to produce superior-quality earthenwares, including Willow in flow blue. A commentator from 1887 wrote that their chinoiserie designs were "imbued with the quaint ideas of the Japanese artists, rendered more graceful and acceptable by the refinement of feeling of the English mind."[15] Marks include the printed or impressed words "Doulton Lambeth" on wares from that site, and "Doulton Burslem" in a variety of designs for Burslem products. "ENGLAND" was added to marks in 1891, "Made in England" c. 1930. A mark with the words "Royal Doulton" arched around four interlaced script D's, often with a lion and a coronet, began in 1902.

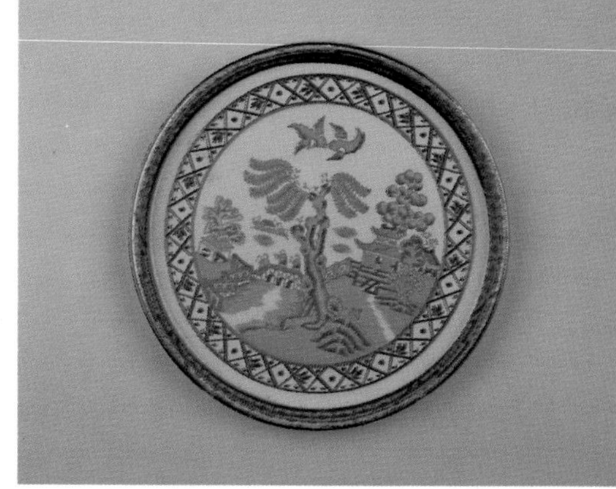

A "Rustic Willow" decanter stand, copyright 1989 by Royal Doulton, 5.375" diam. Courtesy of Rita Entmacher Cohen.

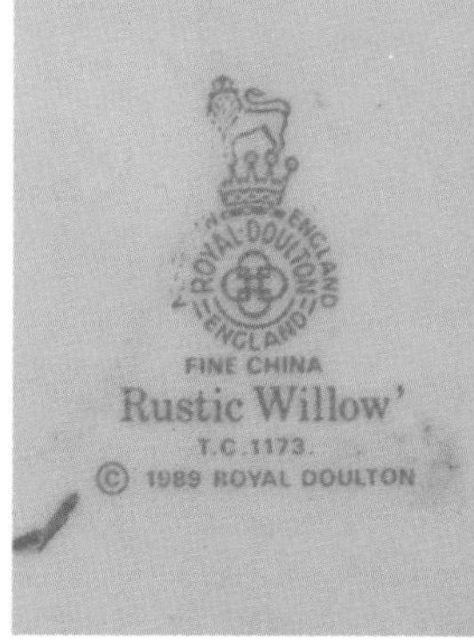

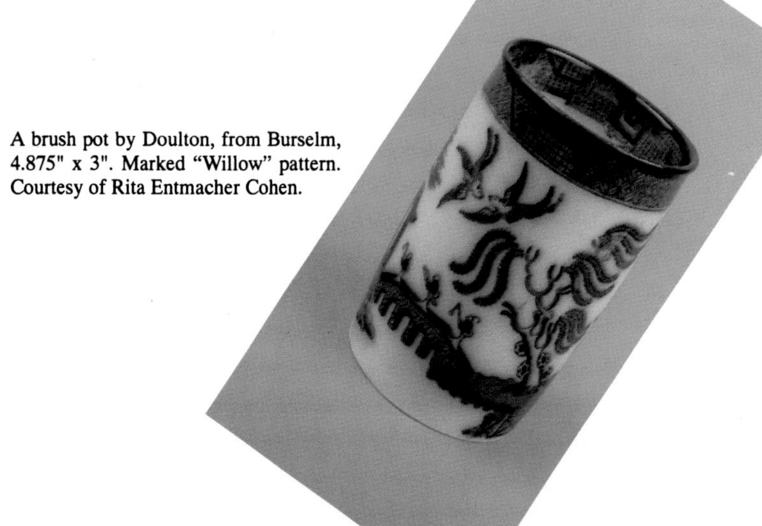

A brush pot by Doulton, from Burselm, 4.875" x 3". Marked "Willow" pattern. Courtesy of Rita Entmacher Cohen.

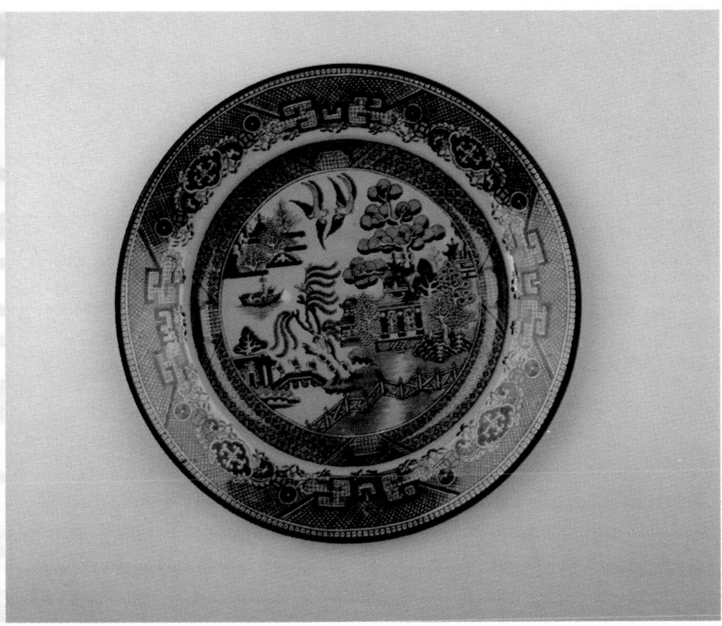

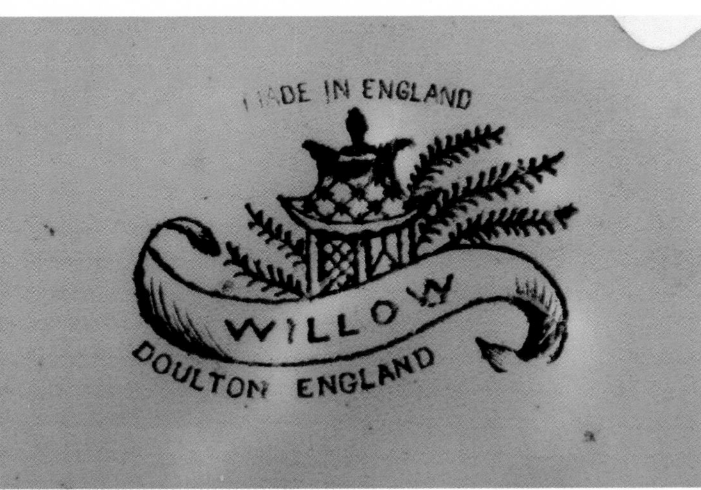

A yellow and black willow plate, c. 1900, 9.5" diam., made by Doulton. Courtesy of Rita Entmacher Cohen.

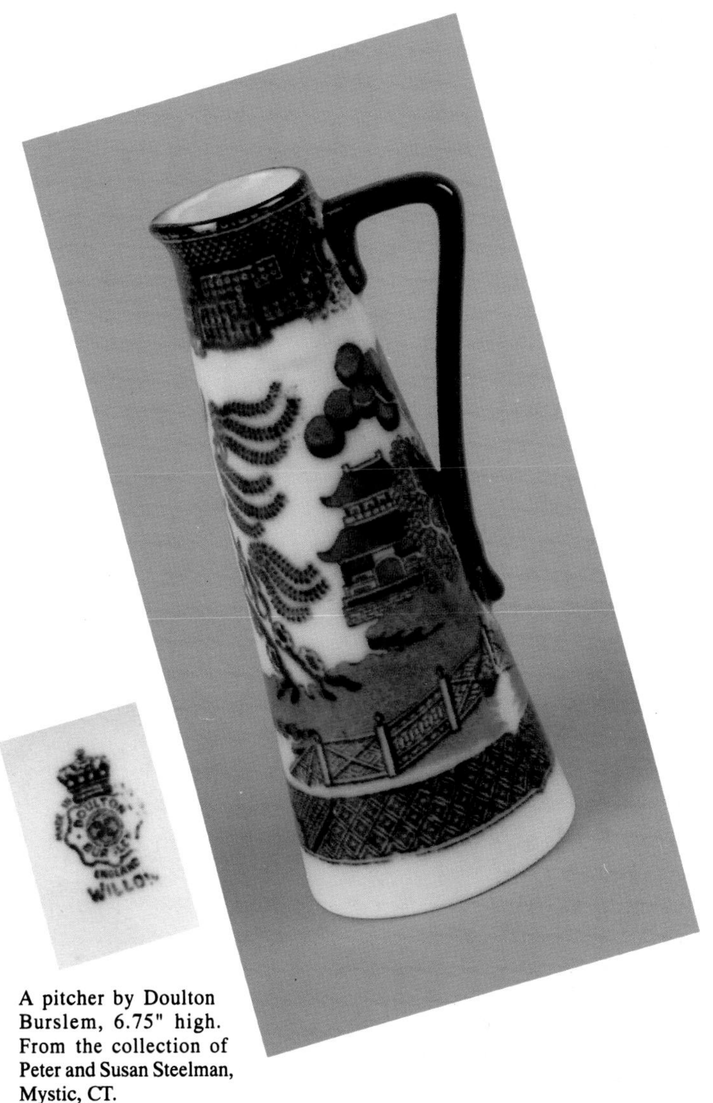

A pitcher by Doulton Burslem, 6.75" high. From the collection of Peter and Susan Steelman, Mystic, CT.

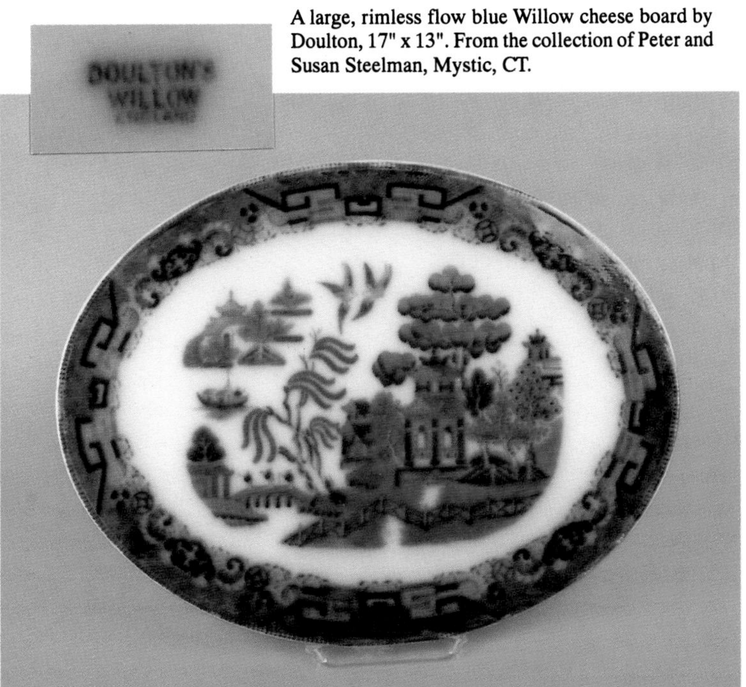

A large, rimless flow blue Willow cheese board by Doulton, 17" x 13". From the collection of Peter and Susan Steelman, Mystic, CT.

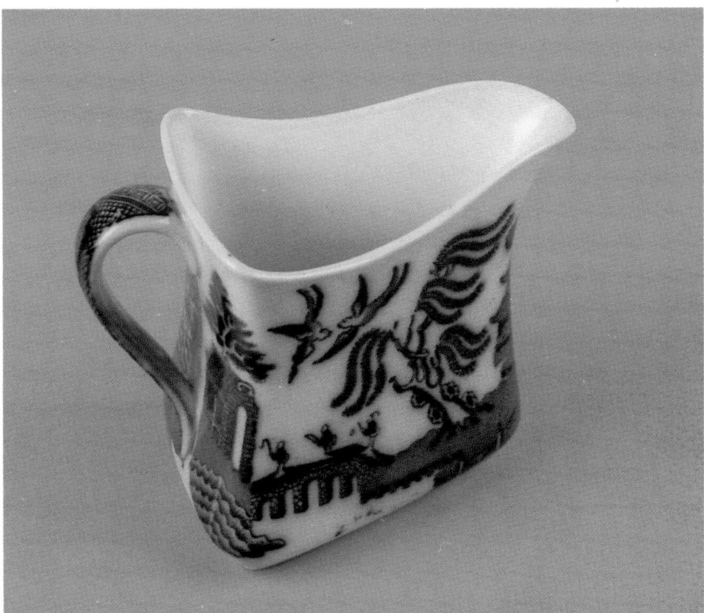

A triangular pitcher, 5" high, marked Doulton Burslem. Either the pottery body or the glaze has an unusual orange tinge. From the collection of Peter and Susan Steelman, Mystic, CT.

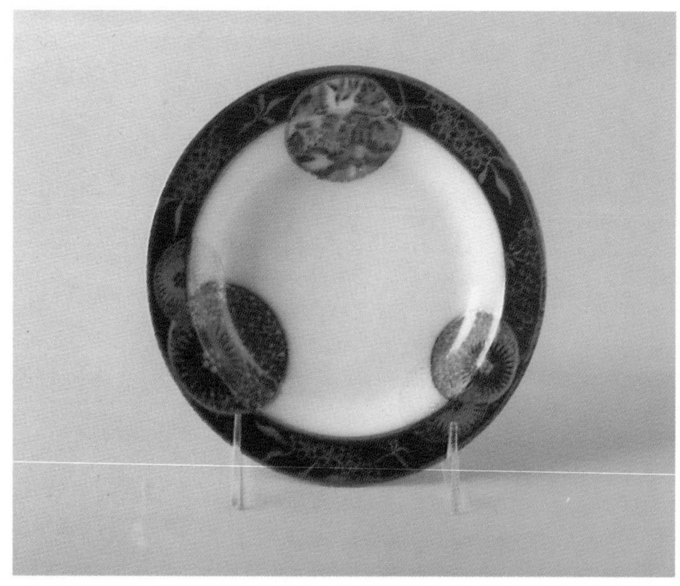

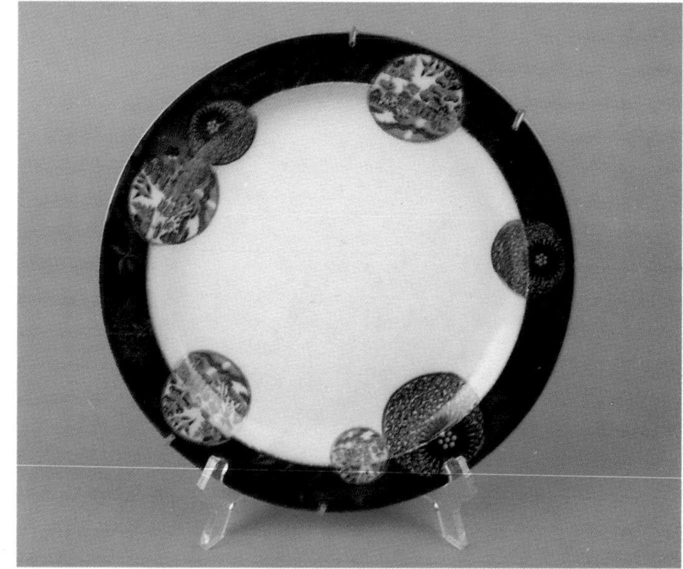

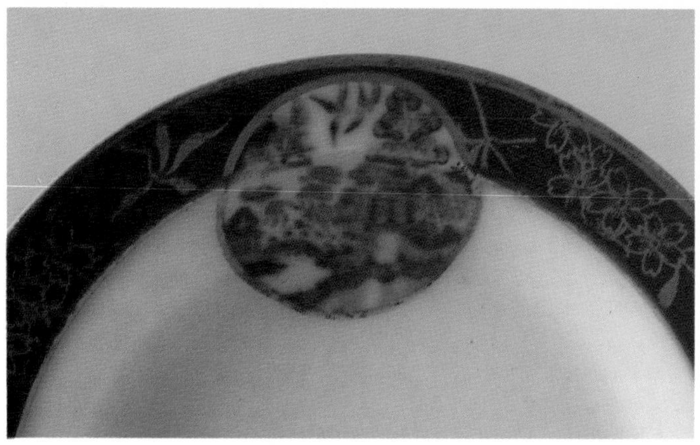

A Doulton "Persian Spray" pattern flow blue plate with a Willow medallion, 7" diam. Courtesy of Eva Lee Revels, Country Accents, Bandera, TX.

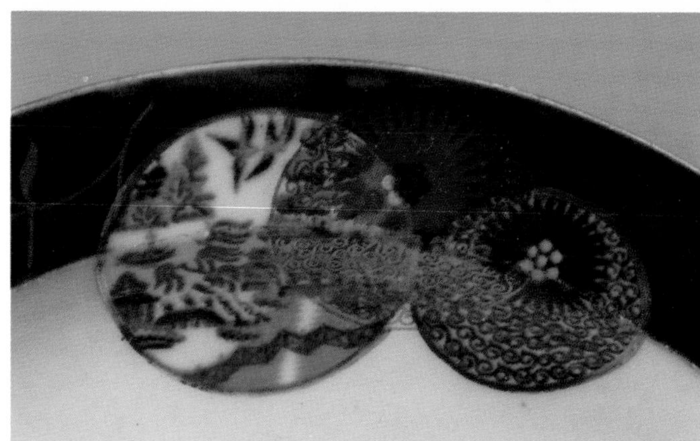

A Doulton plate in the "Persian Spray" design, incorporating willow-pattern medallions into its design. From the collection of Peter and Susan Steelman, Mystic, CT.

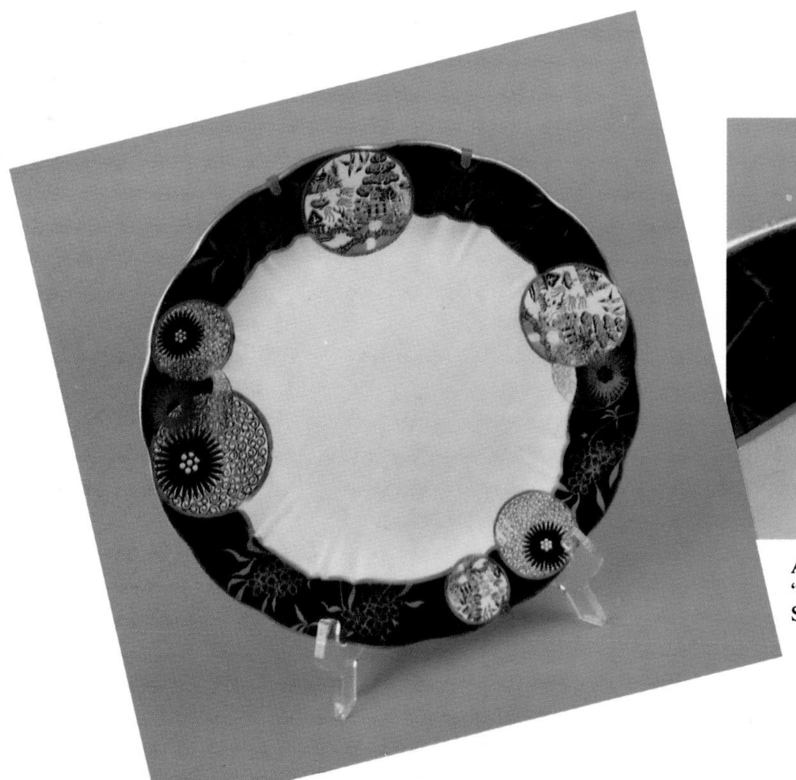

A "Persian Spray" plate, 9.5" diam., with impressed Doulton mark, "Doulton's Willow + ASTEP." From the collection of Peter and Susan Steelman, Mystic, CT.

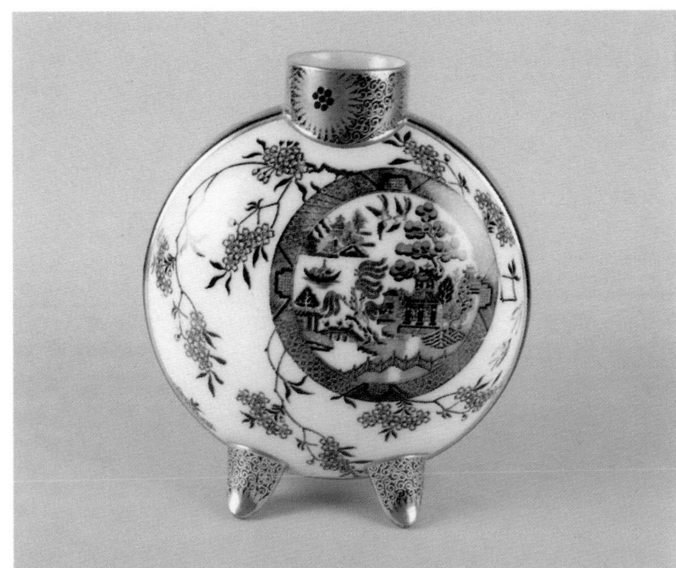

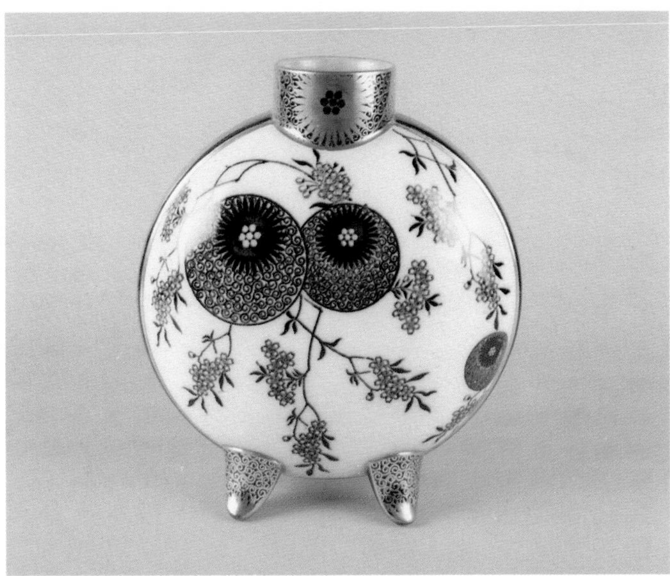

A Doulton pillow vase from the 1880s, 11.75" high. Courtesy of Wendy's Willow.

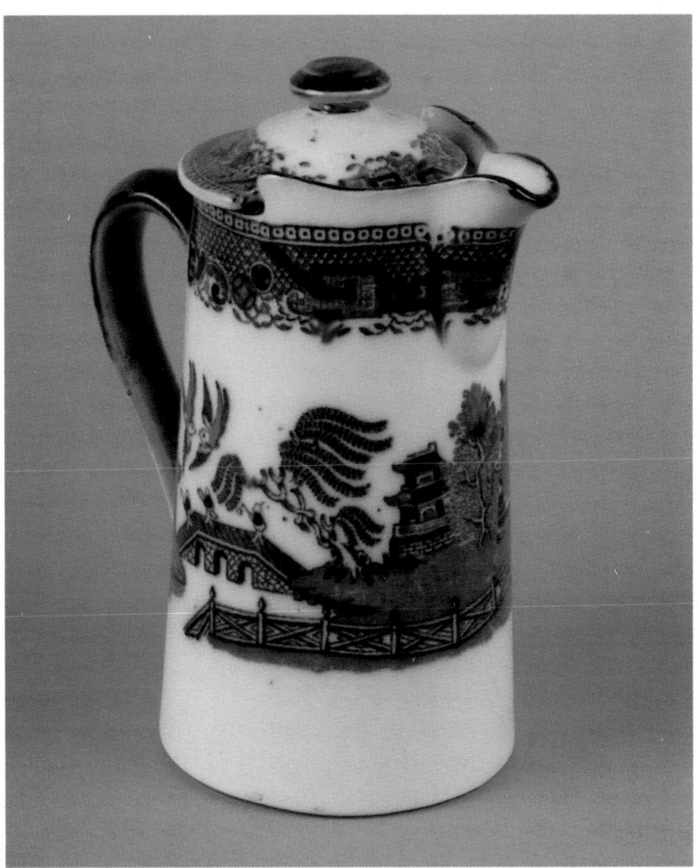

A pitcher, 6.25" high, with an interesting catch on the lid. Marked with the impressed words "Willow" and "Patent 11-4107." From the collection of Peter and Susan Steelman, Mystic, CT.

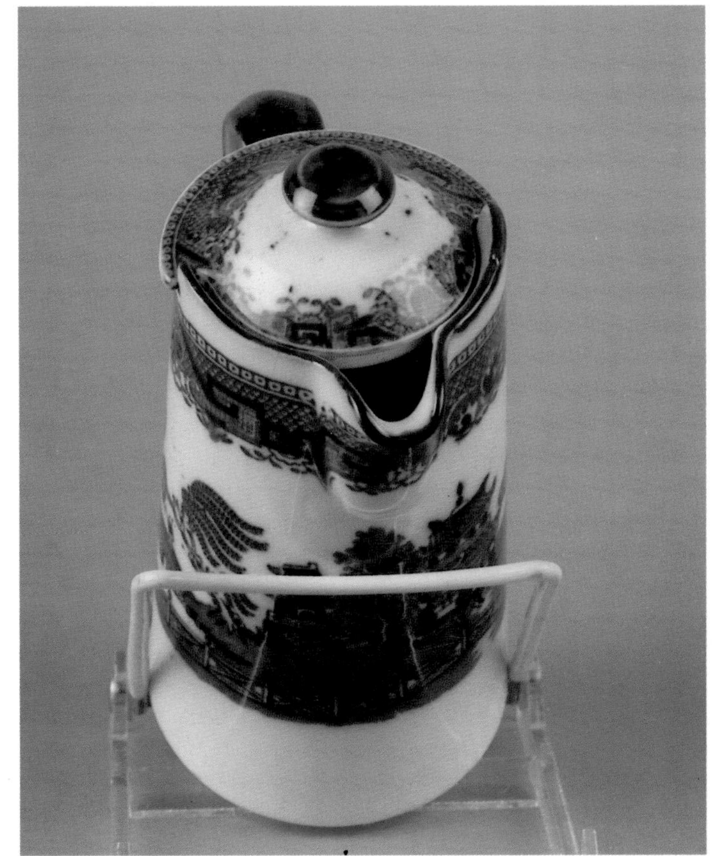

Dudson, Wilcox & Till Ltd.: Active between 1902-1926 at the Britannic Works in Hanley, Staffordshire, producing earthenwares. They used the lion & unicorn Royal Arms mark, and printed or impressed marks sometimes including "DUDSON, WILCOX & TILL LTD. HANLEY ENGLAND".

Dunstan: no information available.

William & Samuel Edge: operated in Lane Delph, Staffordshire, producing earthenwares from 1841-1848. Their mark, "W. & S. E.," sometimes included the name of the pattern.

Edge, Malkin & Co.: Active in earthenware production at the Newport and Middleport Potteries in Burslem between 1871-1903. Printed marks read "EDGE, MALKIN & CO." or "E. M. & CO.," sometimes on a banner beneath a seated dog. "LTD." may appear on wares produced after 1899.

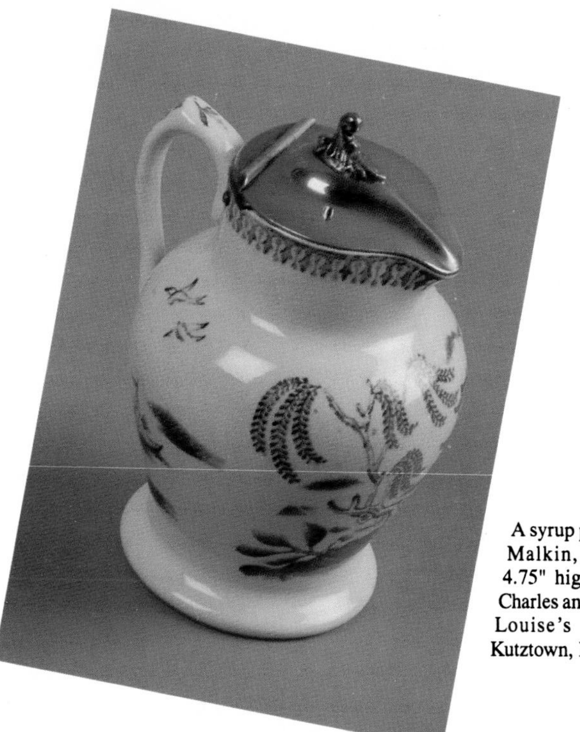

A syrup pitcher by Edge Malkin, 1873-1890, 4.75" high. Courtesy of Charles and Louise Loehr, Louise's Old Things, Kutztown, PA.

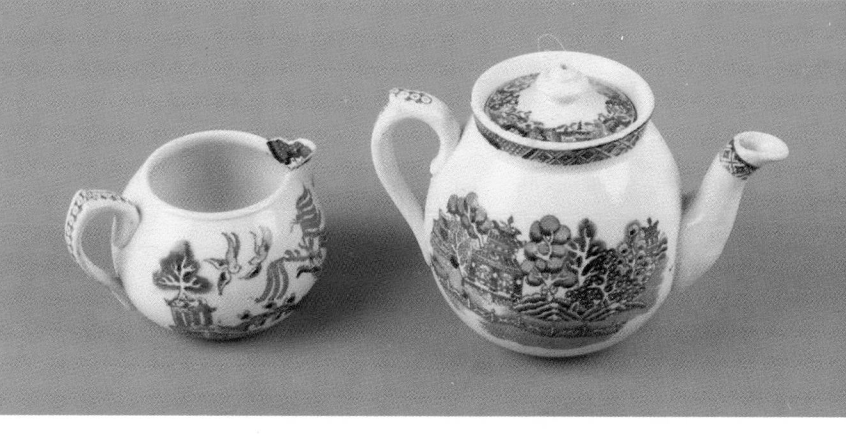

Edge Malkin's small teapot and an irregular creamer, 4" high, with identical mark: an illustration of a dog and the trademark "E. M. & Co. / B / Willow". From the collection of Peter and Susan Steelman, Mystic, CT.

Elkin & Newbon: Operated in Longton, Staffordshire, producing earthenwares from 1844-1845, with a printed mark reading "E. & N."

D. J. Evans & Co.: see Swansea.

Evans & Glasson: see Swansea.

Thomas Fell & Co.: Operated out of St. Peter's Pottery in Newcastle-upon-Tyne, Northumberland, from 1817-1890, producing earthenwares and creamwares. Until 1830 their mark read "FELL." After 1830, they used an "F" with an anchor symbol, "F & CO.," "FELL & CO." with an anchor, "T. F. & CO.," and "T. FELL & CO."

Alfred Fenton & Sons: Operated out of Brook Street, Hanley, Staffordshire, between 1887-1901. Their marks included the initials "A. F. & S." with several impressed or printed designs.

Foley: E. Brain & Co., Ltd., formerly Robinson & Son, worked out of the Foley China Works in Fenton, Staffordshire beginning in 1903. Their mark closely resembles the Minton globe mark, with the name "FENTON" replacing "MINTON" on the banner.

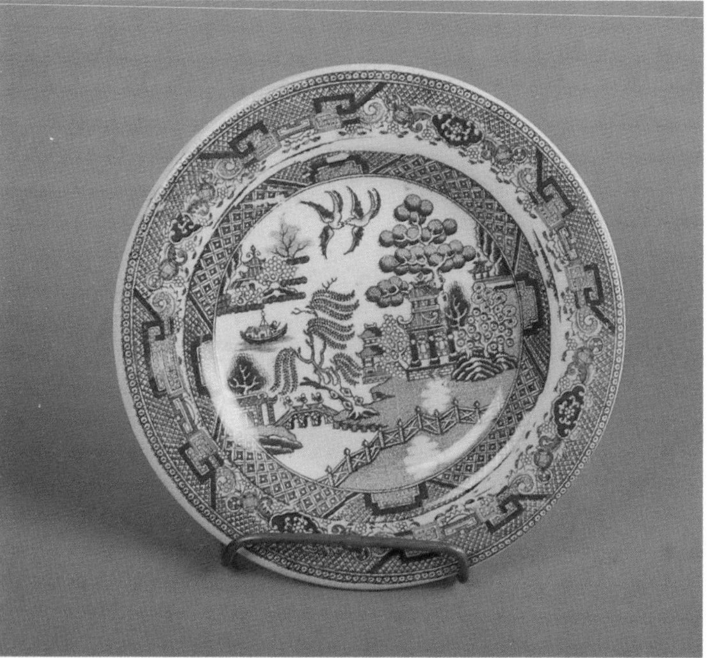

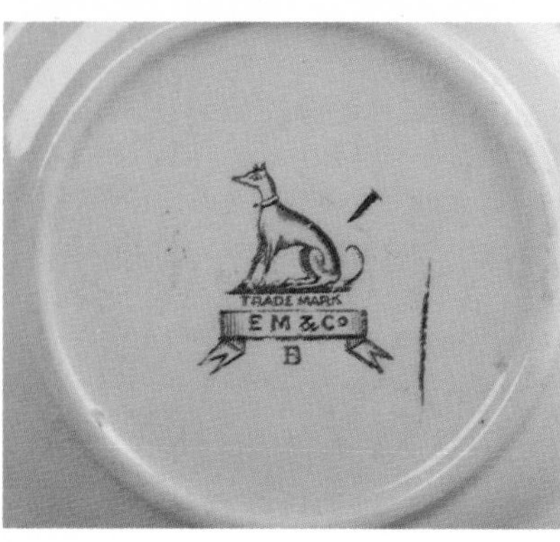

A saucer by Edge Malkin, 1873-1890, 5" diam. Courtesy of Charles and Louise Loehr, Louise's Old Things, Kutztown, PA.

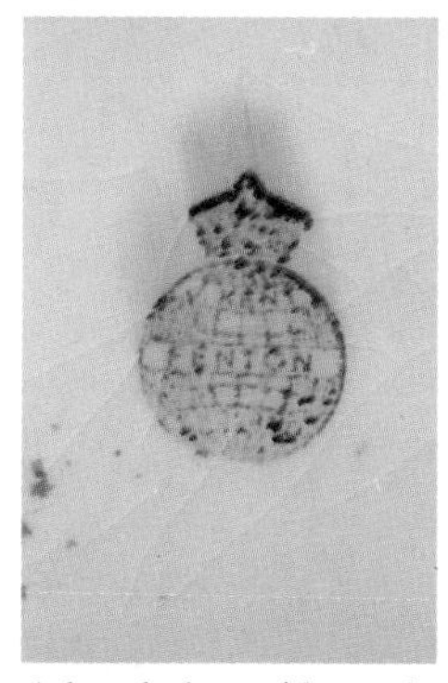

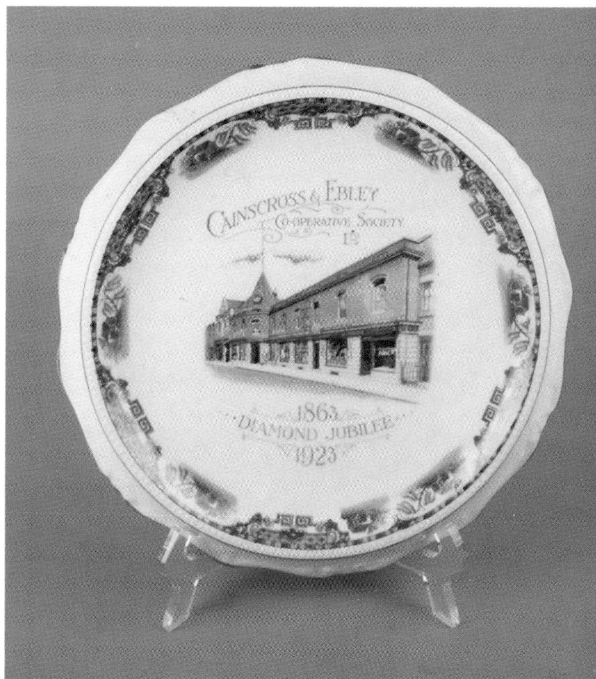

A bread plate with a polychrome willow-scene border and a Foley mark. From the collection of Peter and Susan Steelman, Mystic, CT.

Ford, Challinor, & Co.: Active 1865-1880, producing earthenwares in Tunstall, Staffordshire. Their printed marks incorporated the initials "F. C." or "F. C. & Co."

Thomas Forester & Sons: Active at the Phoenix Works in Longton, Staffordshire, 1883-1959, producing china and earthenwares. Marks included the intials "T. F. & S." (1883-1891), with the addition of "Ltd" or "Ld" and a flying bird logo (1891-1912). Beginning in 1912 through 1959, the mark included the initials on a winged globe logo, with "Phoenix China" in an arch above and "England" below.

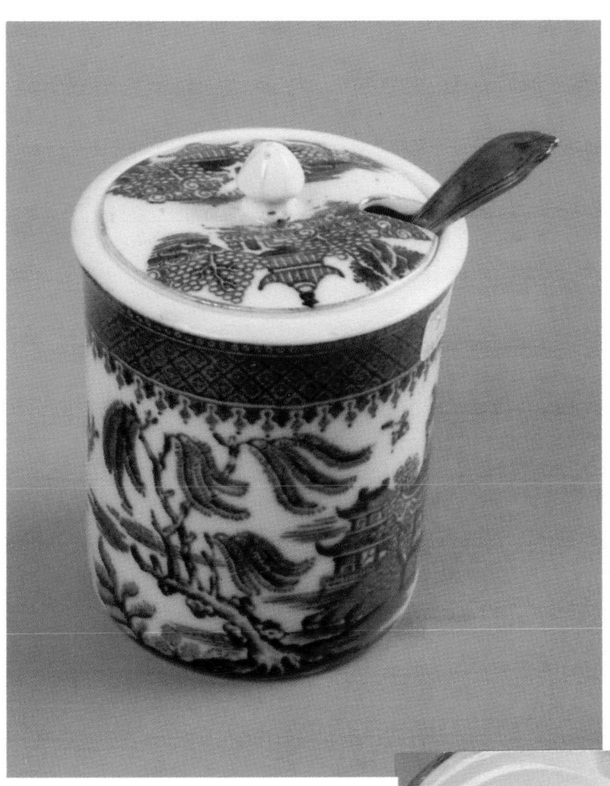

A condiment server by Foley, 3.5" high. Courtesy of Charles and Louise Loehr, Louise's Old Things, Kutztown, PA.

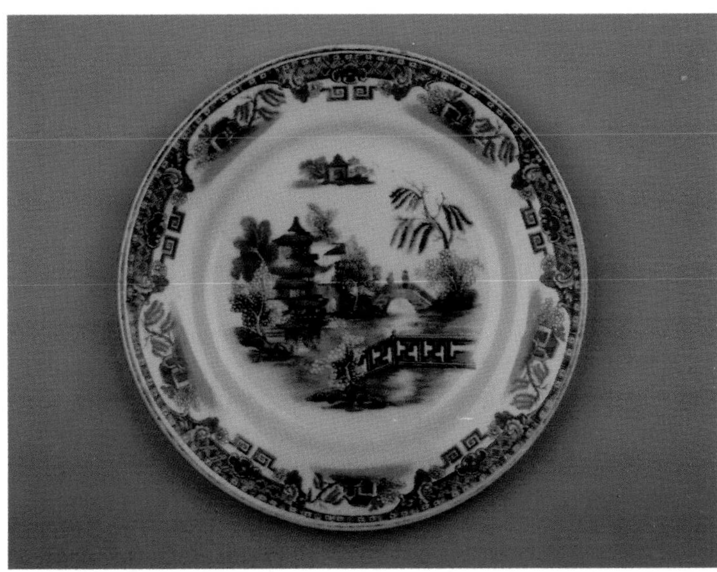

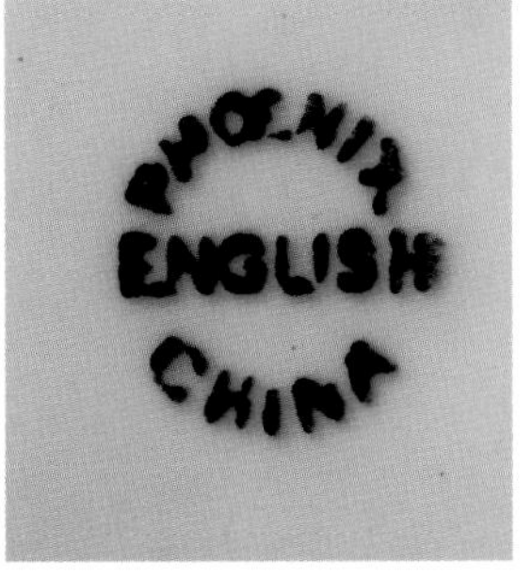

A polychrome plate from Thomas Forester & Sons, Staffordshire, 1884-1888, 6.875" diam. Marked "Phoenix China." Courtesy of Rita Entmacher Cohen.

Charles Ford: Operated out of Hanley, Staffordshire, from 1879-1909, producing china wares. Formerly T. & C. Ford, the works was sold to J. A. Robinson & Sons, Ltd. in 1904. The company used an impressed or printed monogram mark from 1874-1904, and a swan mark from 1904-1909.

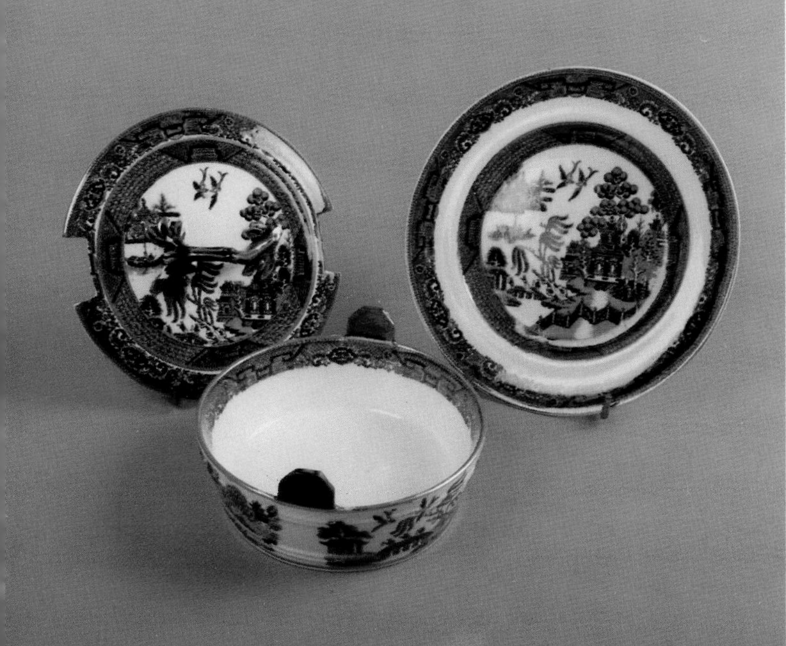

A butter server from Charles Ford, 1874-1890, 7.25" diam. Courtesy of Charles and Louise Loehr, Louise's Old Things, Kutztown, PA.

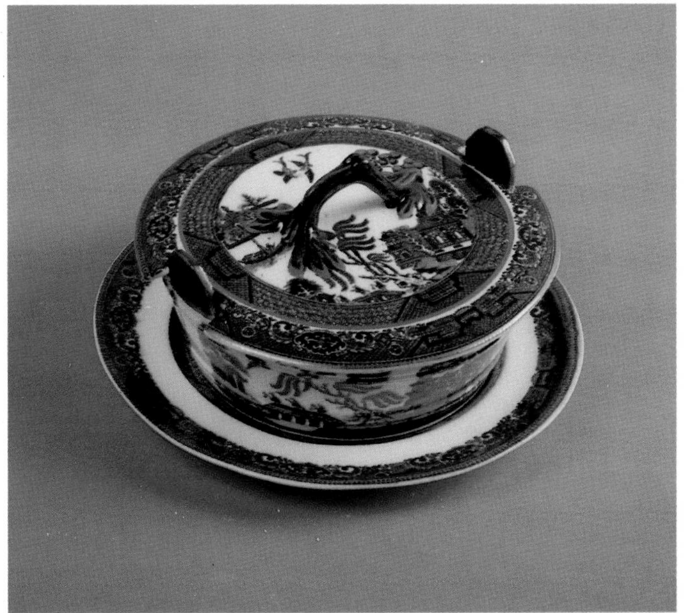

Garrett: See Copeland/Spode.

Garrison Pottery: Operated by various Dixon partnerships between 1813-1865 in Sunderland, Durham.

Gibson & Sons, Ltd.: Active at the Albany & Harvey Pottery in Burslem, producing earthenwares beginning in 1885. Marks in the early twentieth century include the initials "G. & S. LTD" in several differently designed printed marks (1905), "H. P. Co./ BURSLEM/ENGLAND" in a handled vase logo (1904-1909), and other designs incorporating the Gibson name or initials through 1950.

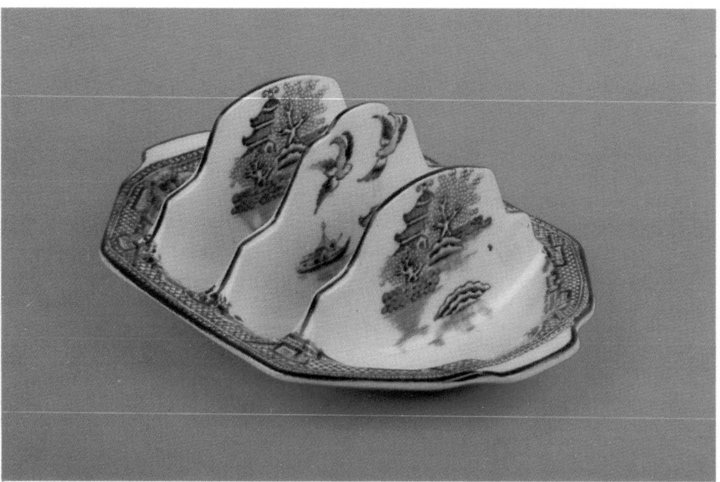

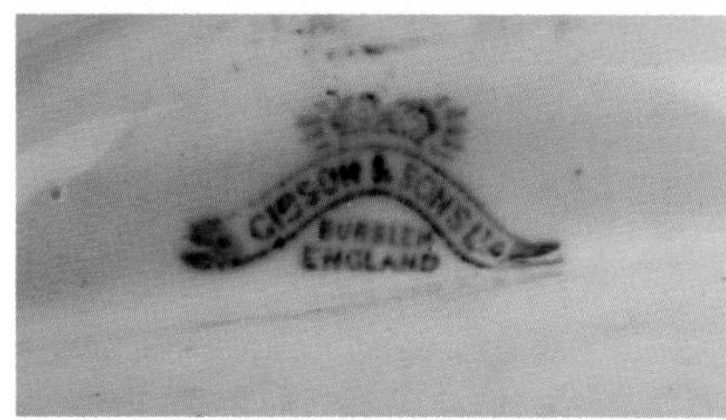

A toast rack, from Gibson & Sons, Ltd., Burselm, c. 1912, 6.5". Courtesy of Rita Entmacher Cohen.

Globe Pottery: Produced earthenwares in Cobridge beginning in 1914, and at Shelton after c. 1934. Marks generally include the "Globe Pottery" name with a number of different globe logos.

Godwin, Rowley & Co.: Active between 1828-1831 in Burslem, Staffordshire. Marks used the initials "G. R. & Co." in several designs, also incorporating "STAFFORDSHIRE STAR CHINA" on a scroll below a crown.

Thomas Godwin: Active in earthenware production between 1834-1854 in Burslem, Staffordshire, formerly Thomas & Benjamin Godwin (q.v.). Marks include the initials "T. G." or the full company name; sometimes "THOS GODWIN/BURSLEM/ STONE CHINA," "THOS GODWIN/NEW WHARF," or "OPAQUE CHINA/T GODWIN/WHARF." A logo mark reading "MEDINA/T.G." has also been attributed to Thomas Godwin.

Thomas & Benjamin Godwin: Operated at the New Wharf and New Basin Potteries in Burslem, Stafforshire between 1809-1834, producing earthenwares and creamwares. Marks included the initials "T. & B. G." and "T. B. G.", as well as "T. & B. GODWIN/NEW WHARF."

Thomas Goodfellow: Active from 1828-1859 from the Phoenix Works in Tunstall, Staffordshire. Printed marks usually incorporate the potter's full surname and pattern names.

George Gordon: Operated out of the Gordons Pottery in Prestonpans, Scotland, from the early 1700s through 1832. Very seldom were any wares marked, but sometimes an impressed "GORDON" or printed pattern names with "G. G." can be found.

Grafton Bone China: A. B. Jones & Sons operated out of the Grafton Works in Longton beginning in 1900, producing china and earthenwares. A variety of marks incorporate the Grafton name, though some use only the company name, "A. B. J. & S.," "A. B. J. & SONS," or "A. B. JONES & SONS."

Grainger, Lee & Co. of Worcester: Established in 1801 by Thos Grainger as Grainger, Wood & Co. at the Royal China Works in Worcester. In 1812 the company became Grainger, Lee & Co. By 1815 they were producing a good soft porcelain, but by 1820 had switched to bone china. In 1889 they were absorbed by Worcester Royal Porcelain Co., Ltd. Marks generally include the Grainger name and the location "WORCESTER," though between 1812-1820 "NEW CHINA WORKS" or "ROYAL CHINA WORKS" sometimes took the place of the company name.

B. Grayson & Son: Sheffield, England.

Thomas Green: Active producing earthenwares and china at the Minerva Works in Fenton, Staffordshire between 1847-1859. They produced transfer patterns in a variety of colors, including blue, black, brown, green, and pink. Marks include "T.G." "T. GREEN, FENTON POTTERIES" and "T.G., FENTON" with a Staffordshire knot beneath a crown. After 1859, the company's name became M. Green & Co., producing earthenwares and china until 1876. Marks during this period include the name "M. GREEN & CO."

Griffiths, Beardmore & Birks: Formerly Thomas Griffiths & Co., this company operated in Lane End, Staffordshire, producing earthenwares in 1830, after which the name changed to Beardmore & Birks. In *British Pottery & Porcelain* (p. 292), Godden mentions a willow dish with a large printed mark bearing the initials "G. B. & B." with the Royal Arms and "STAFFORDSHIRE IRONSTONE CHINA."

Grimwades: Operated as Grimwade Bros. from 1886-1900 and as Grimwades Ltd. from 1900 through the 20th century, working in potteries in Winton, Hanley, Upper Hanley, Elgin, and Stoke. Grimwade Bros. marked their wares with a circular printed logo, reading "STOKE ON TRENT/STAFFORDSHIRE ENGLAND" around a central logo of a six-pointed star with the trademark "[large] G [small] Bros." inside. Grimwades Ltd. used a wide variety of marks, generally incorporating the family name, and frequently the name of the pottery site. A mark similar to the Grimwades Bros. circular mark was in use c. 1906, differing in that the outside text reads "GRIMWADES/STAFFORDSHIRE ENGLAND," the printing inside the star reads "UPPER HANLEY POTTERY," and the outline of the circle is nubbed.

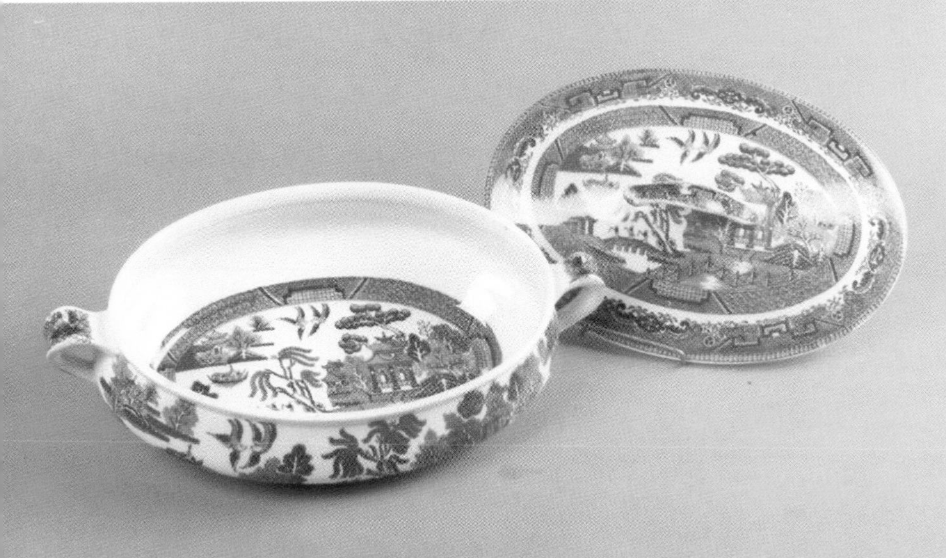

A covered vegetable server by Grimwades, 5" high x 11.5" long. Courtesy of Charles and Louise Loehr, Louise's Old Things, Kutztown, PA.

William Hackwood & Son: Formerly Hackwood & Co. (1807-1827), then William Hackwood (1827-1843), then William & Thomas Hackwood, in Hanley, Staffordshire. From 1846-1849, William Hackwood & Son (Thomas) operated from the New Hall Pottery in Shelton. Marks from this period frequently include the initials "W. H. & S." After William's death in 1849, Thomas continued the business until 1853.

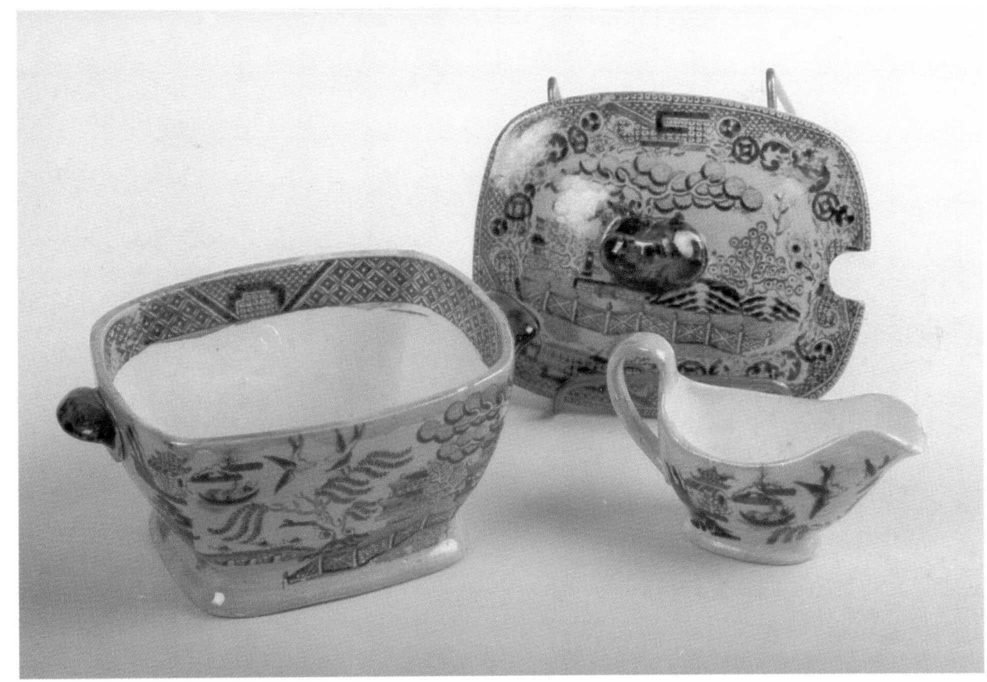

A tureen and a creamer from a children's pink lustre set, 4.5" long (tureen). Impressed "HACKWOOD" on bottom of both pieces. Courtesy of Charles and Louise Loehr, Louise's Old Things, Kutztown PA.

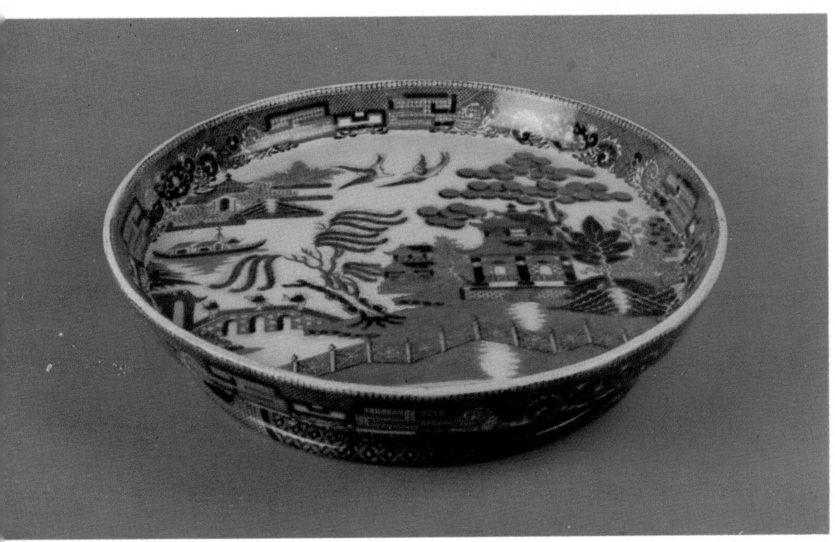

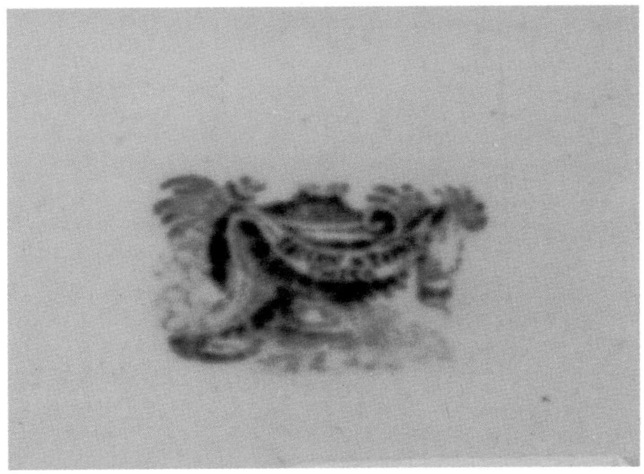

A cheese platter, Hackwood Ironstone, 1830-1840. 2.5" x 11.75". From the collection of Peter and Susan Steelman, Mystic, CT.

S. Hancock & Sons: Active frm 1912-1937 at the Corona Pottery in Hanley, producing "Corona Ware." Marks include "ROYAL CORONA WARE/S. HANCOCK & SONS/STOKE ON TRENT/ENGLAND" with a crown logo, and from 1935-1937 "S. HANCOCK & SONS LTD./CORONA POTTERY, HANLEY."

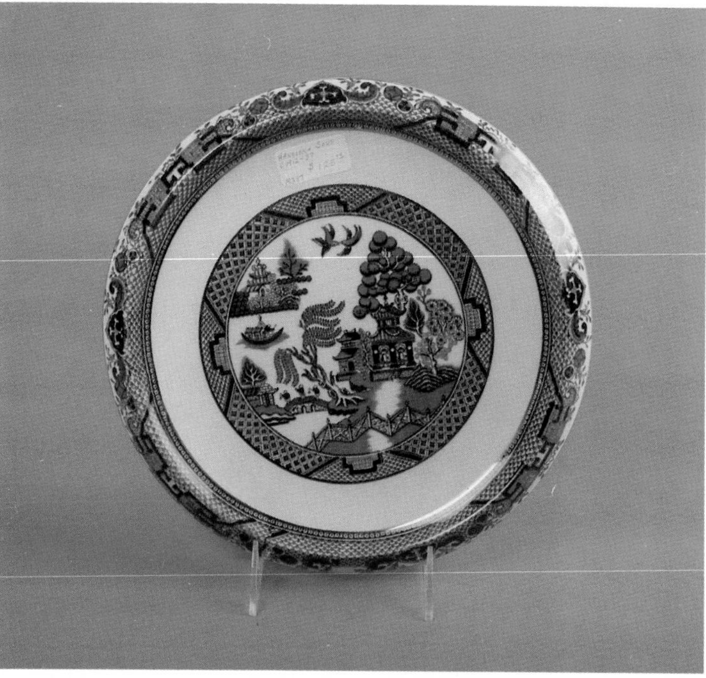

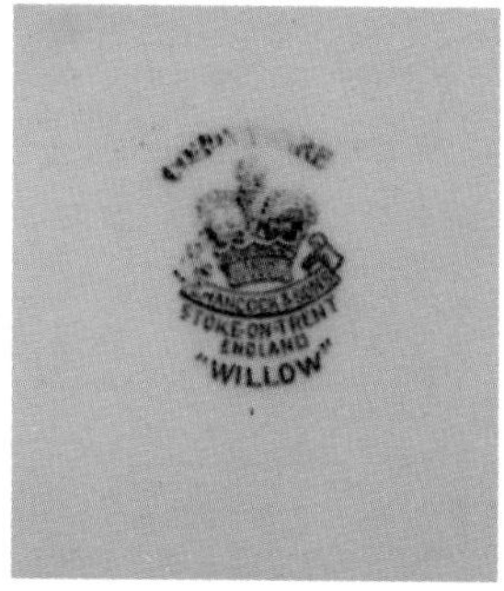

A Corona Ware bread platter from Hancock at Stoke-on-Trent, 1912-1937, 10.25" diam. Courtesy of Charles and Louise Loehr, Louise's Old Things, Kutztown, PA.

Joseph Harding: Operated in Burslem, producing earthenwares from 1850-1851. Several marks were used, with various designs incorporating the name "J. HARDING."

Hawkes: no information available.

Herculaneum Pottery: Active c. 1793-1841 in Liverpool, Lancashire, producing earthenwares and porcelains. Marks include the name "HERCULANEUM" in a variety of crown logos, and the word "LIVERPOOL" arched over an anchor (all c. 1796-1833), the impressed name "HERCULANEUM/POTTERY" (1822+), and printed or impressed "Liver bird" logos with or without the company name (1833-1836).

Robert Heron & Son: Active c. 1850-1929 in Kirkcaldy, Scotland, producing earthenwares. Initials "R H & S" frequently appear on their works, as does the company's full name.

Thomas & John Hollins: Active in Shelton, Hanley, c. 1795-1820. Used an impressed mark reading "T. & J. Hollins."

J.T. Hudden: Active 1859-1885, producing earthenwares in Longton, Staffordshire. Marks read "J. T. H." or "J. T. HUDDEN."

Ideal: see McNicol

Jackson (Vitrified) China: A currently active Falls Creek, Pennsylvania company that opened in 1917, primarily making vitrified china. Marks bear the Jackson name.

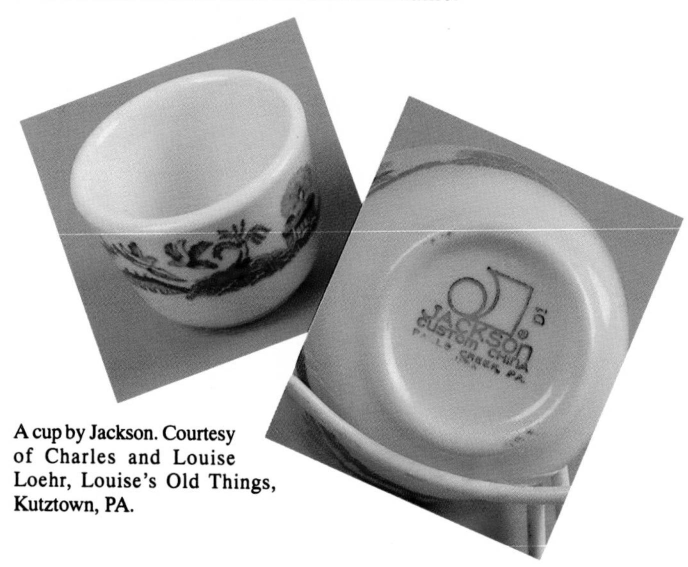

A cup by Jackson. Courtesy of Charles and Louise Loehr, Louise's Old Things, Kutztown, PA.

James Jamieson & Co.: Active from 1836-1854 in Bo'ness, Scotland. Impressed marks included the name and location of the company.

George Jones: Produced earthenwares c. 1854 in Staffordshire, most notably majolica wares. Willow pattern wares impressed with "GEORGE JONES" mark.

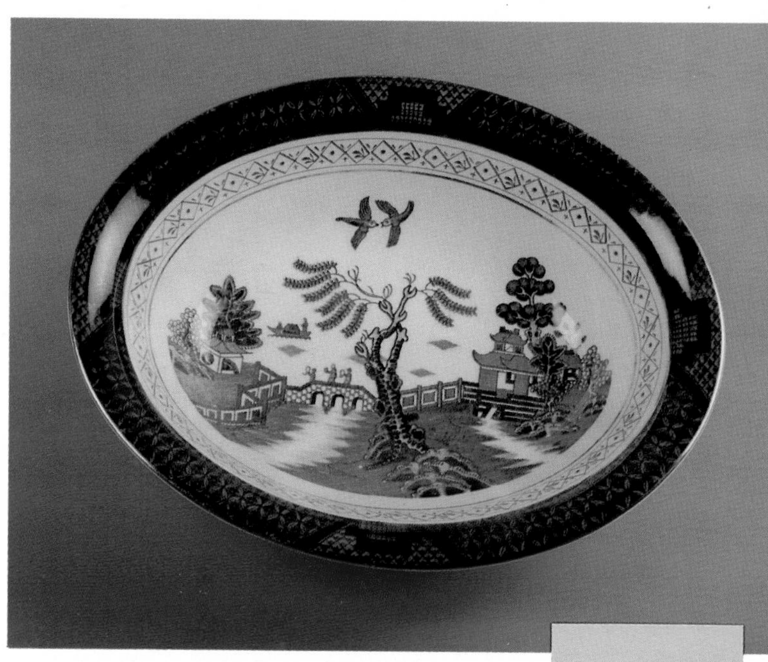

A George Jones serving bowl, 1874, 2.5" high x 9" x 12". Courtesy of Charles and Louise Loehr, Louise's Old Things, Kutztown, PA.

Johnson Bros., Ltd.: Operated in Hanley beginning in 1883 through the mid-20th century, and in Tunstall c. 1899-1913, producing earthenwares and ironstone. Various marks include pattern names with "JOHNSON BROS." name.

Kakusa: A Japanese firm.

R.A. Kidston & Co.: Active from 1838-1846 in Glasgow, Scotland, makring their wares with the initials "R. A. K. & Co."

J.K. Knight: John King Knight worked out of Fenton, Staffordshire, 1846-1853, producing earthenwares. Marks frequently included pattern names, the name "J. [or I.] K. KNIGHT," and occasionally the name of the pottery works, "FOLEY."

Lancaster & Sons: Operated out of the Dresden Works in Hanley, England, 1900-1944, producing earthenwares. Marks include initials "L. S." in different designs (1900-1906), with "& Sons" or "& S" after 1906, and "Ltd" on most marks after 1906.

Homer Laughlin: Established in East Liverpool, Ohio, U.S.A. in 1874, and won a prize for the best whiteware in the 1876 Philadelphia Centennial exhibition. Expanded across the Ohio River to Newell, West Virginia. Though most famous for their Fiesta Ware line, Homer Laughlin produced a widely-known line of Willow, primarily for restaurant and hotel use.

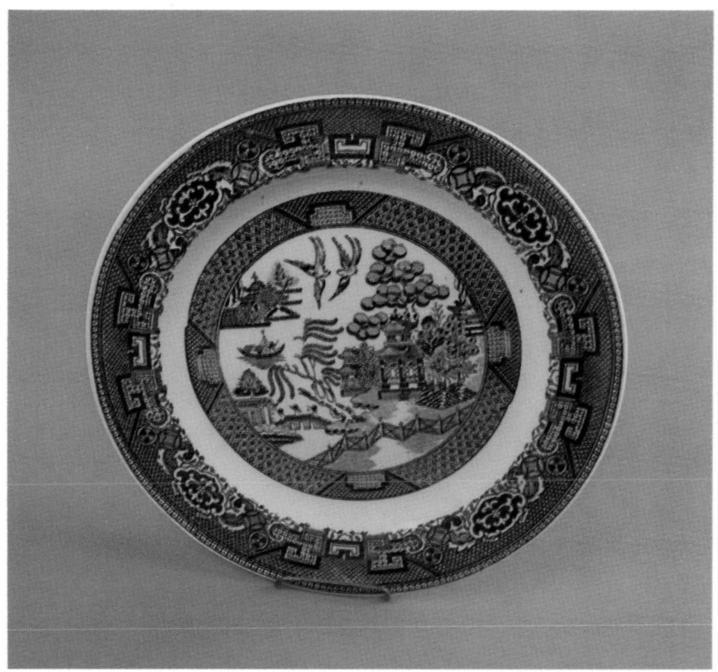

A Homer Laughlin dinner plate, 1940, 10" diam. Courtesy of Charles and Louise Loehr, Louise's Old Things, Kutztown PA.

The Homer Laughlin mark reveals the year of manufacture—1945.

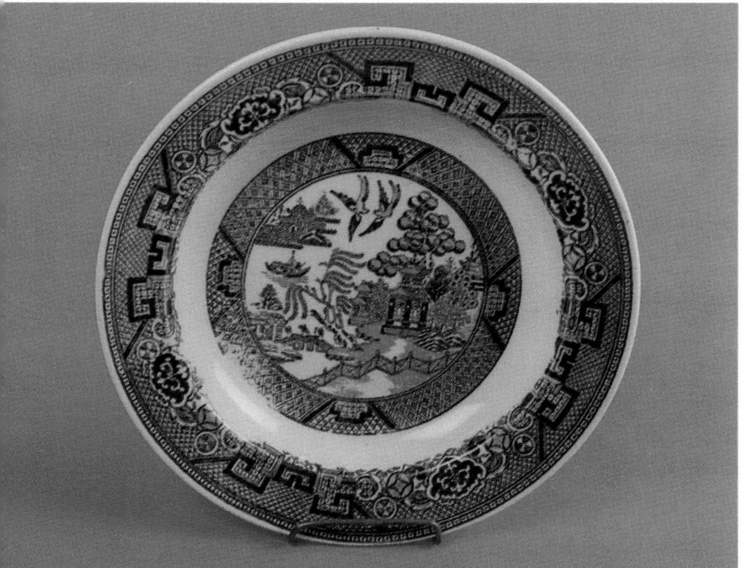

A Homer Laughlin soup plate, 1945, 7.75" diam. Courtesy of Charles and Louise Loehr, Louise's Old Things, Kutztown PA.

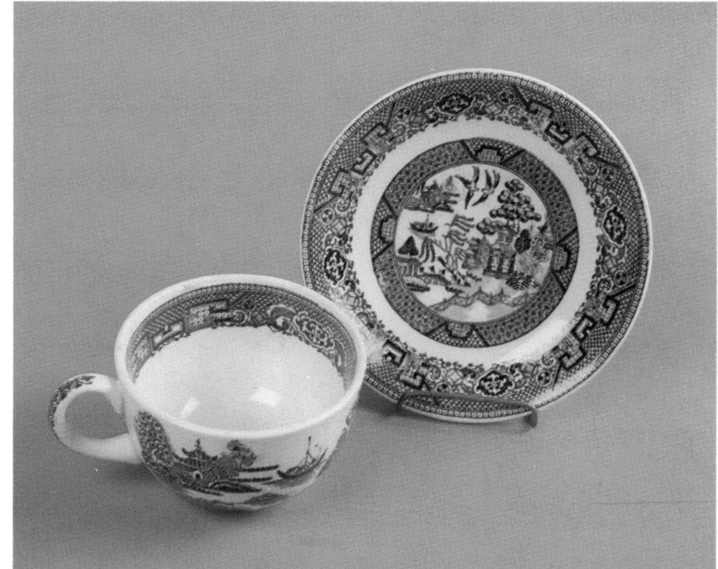

A Homer Laughlin teacup and saucer set, 1954, 6" diam. (saucer). Courtesy of Charles and Louise Loehr, Louise's Old Things, Kutztown PA.

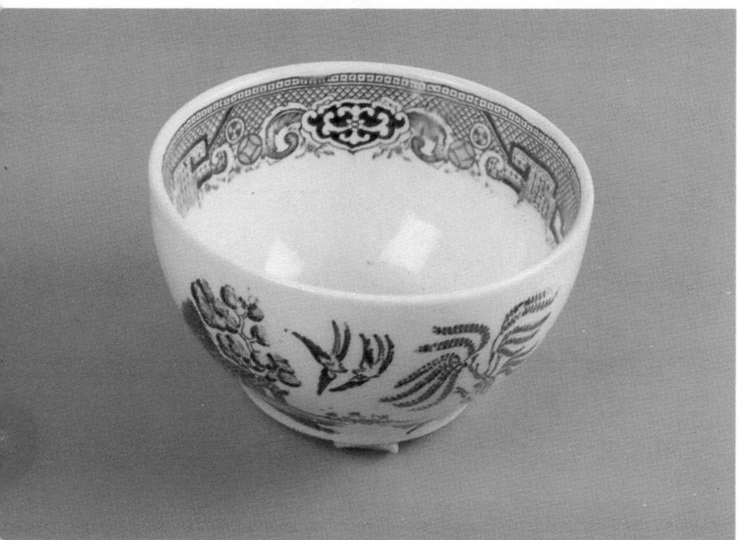

An unmarked Homer Laughlin oatmeal bowl, 2.25" high x 4.75" diam. Courtesy of Charles and Louise Loehr, Louise's Old Things, Kutztown PA.

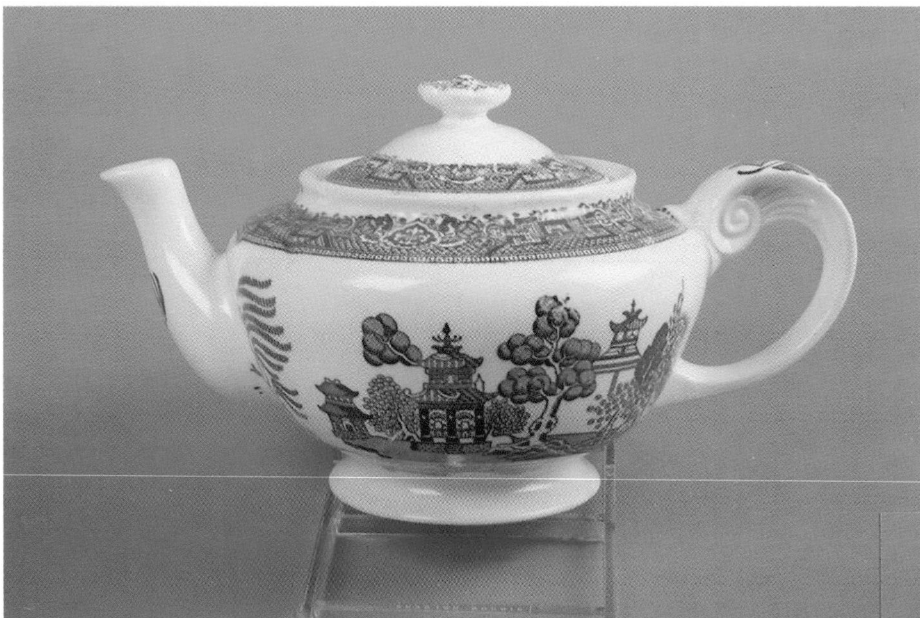

An unmarked Homer Laughlin teapot, 6.5" high x 10" long. Courtesy of Charles and Louise Loehr, Louise's Old Things, Kutztown PA.

This handle pattern is one good way to identify a piece as Homer Laughlin.

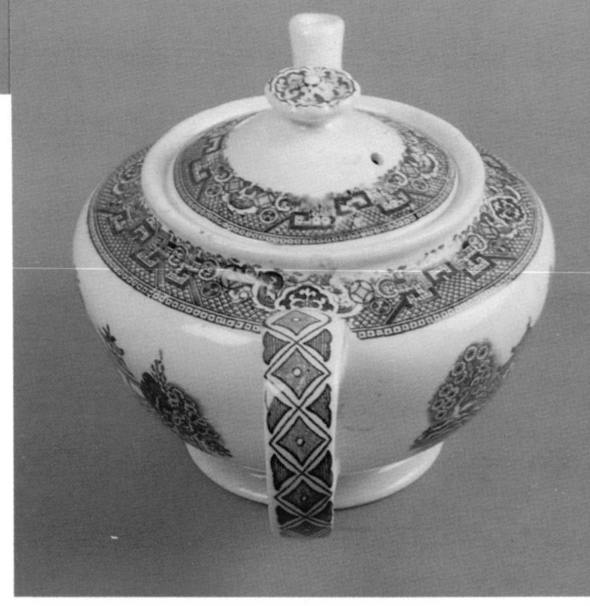

William Lowe: Operated out of Longton, Staffordshire.

John Maddock: A Burslem firm, previously known as Maddock & Seddon. Maddock operated independently from 1842-1855, and in 1855 entered into a partnership with his sons, changing the name to John Maddock & Sons. In 1896, "Ltd." was added to the name. The firm remained active during 20th century. They produced a variety of earthenwares, ironstone, and granite wares, often for the U.S. market. Marks for Madddock & Seddon include the initials "M & S" with the names of the ware. John Maddock used "M" or "MADDOCK" in several printed markswhen he operated alone, sometimes including the type of ware. Maddock & Sons (Ltd.) used many printed or impressed marks, from the full name of the firm to the surname only, adding "LTD." after 1896.

A plate by John Maddock & Sons, England, 1896-1921, 9" diam. This design is the "Royal Willow" pattern, and here is done in polychrome with gold accents. Courtesy of Rita Entmacher Cohen.

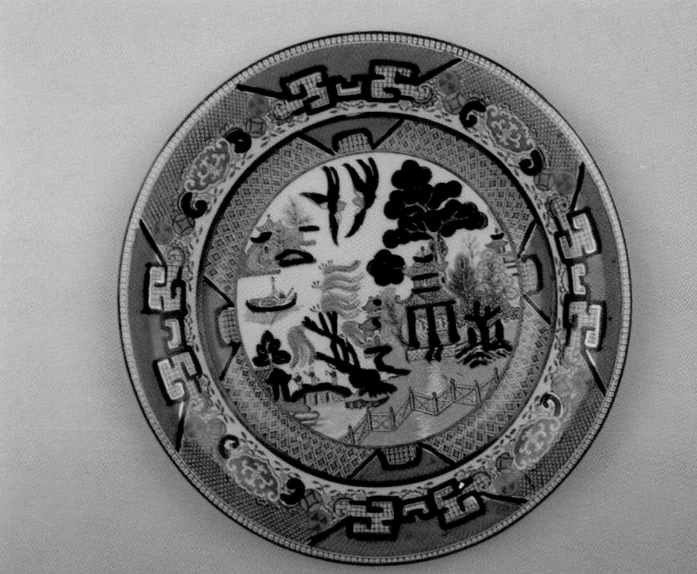

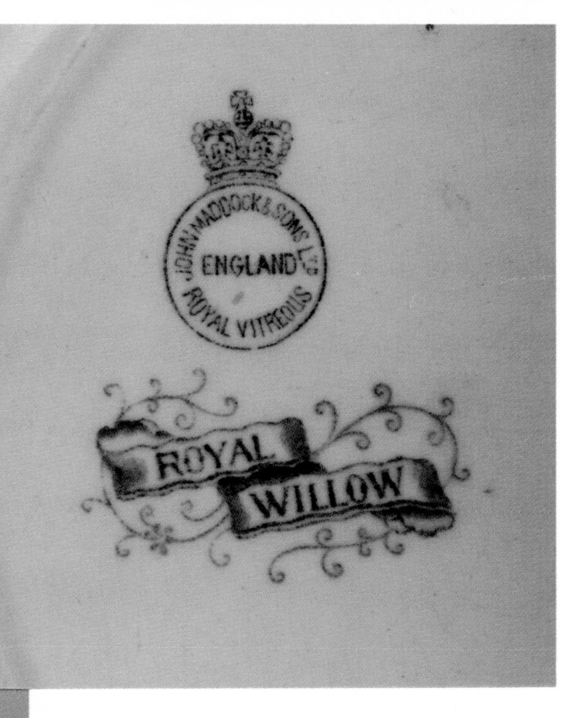

C.T. Maling: A Newcastle-on-Tyne, Northumberland company; used a crown or crown in wreath mark.

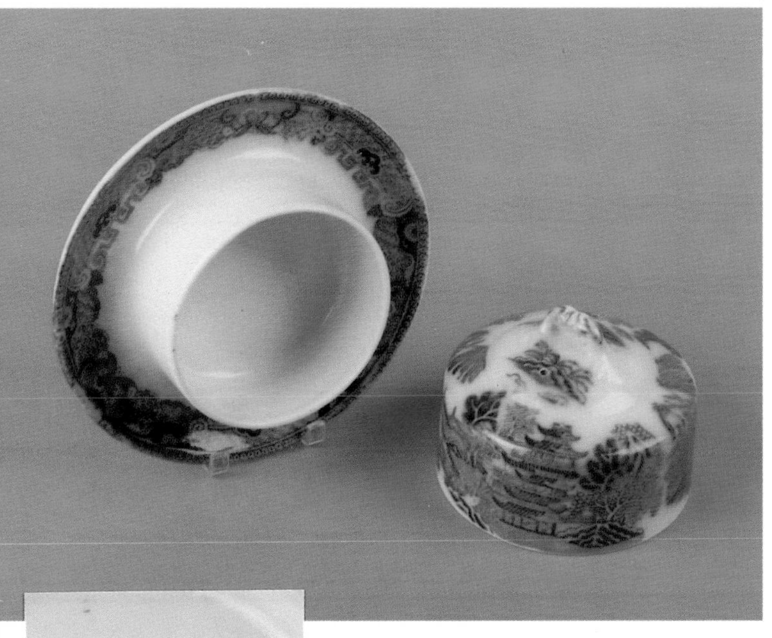

An onion keeper from Maling, 3.5" high x 5.75" diam. From the collection of Peter and Susan Steelman, Mystic, CT.

Mandarin Blue: A Japanese company active in the twentieth century.

Bowls by Mandarin Blue, a Japanese company, 1940s or 1950s, 7.25" diam. Courtesy of Charles and Louise Loehr, Louise's Old Things, Kutztown, PA.

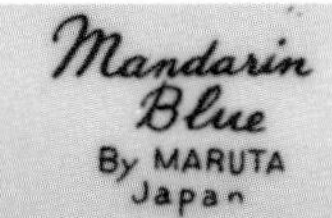

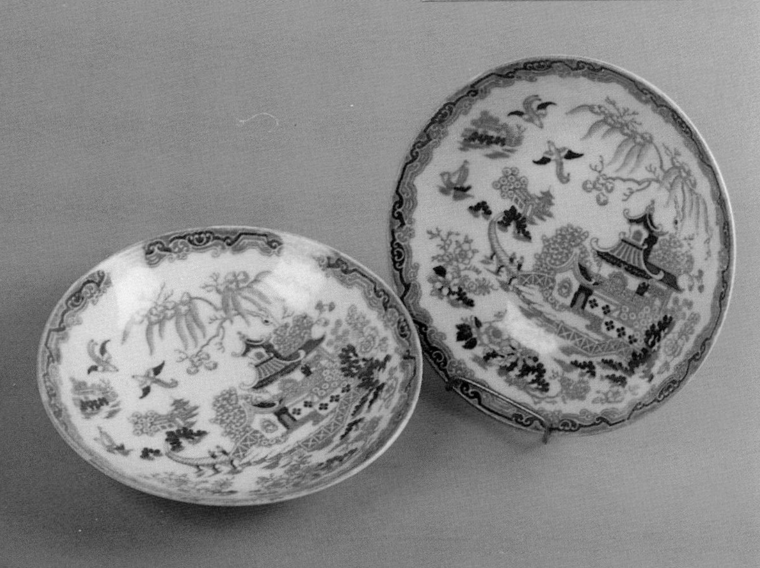

Marutyama: A firm active in Occupied Japan.

The Mason family: Miles Mason began the family's pottery interests c. 1792-1816 when taxation on imported china became prohibitively high. The company produced porcelain in various works in Lane Delph, Staffordshire, and used a printed square with Chinese-looking hashmarks to mark Willow and other chinoiserie designs. In 1804 the company began to produce an early version of stone china, which they transfer printed. In 1813, Miles' son Charles J. Mason was granted a patent to make Ironstone china, through his 1813-1829 company G. M. & C. J. Mason in Lane Delph. Initials or name marks were used, as were many mark designs indicating that the wares were "PATENT IRONSTONE." Mason's Ironstone was produced under various family designations until the middle of the 18th century (c. 1854).

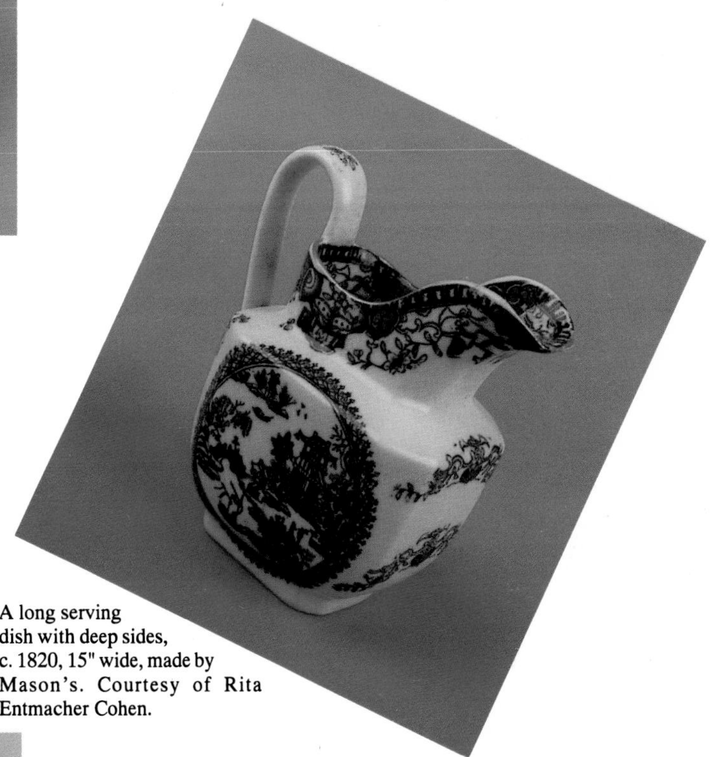

A long serving dish with deep sides, c. 1820, 15" wide, made by Mason's. Courtesy of Rita Entmacher Cohen.

An ironstone polychrome plate made by Mason's, 10.25" diam. Courtesy of Rita Entmacher Cohen.

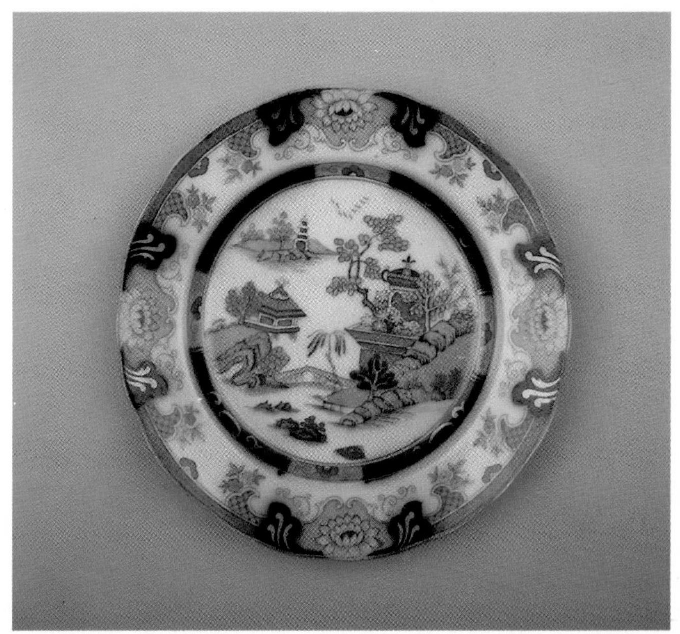

A long serving dish with deep sides, c. 1820, 15" wide, made by Mason's. Courtesy of Rita Entmacher Cohen.

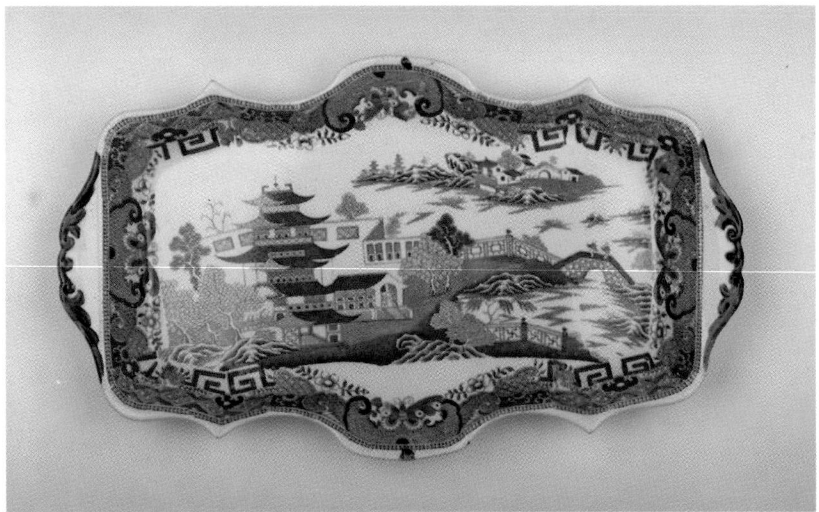

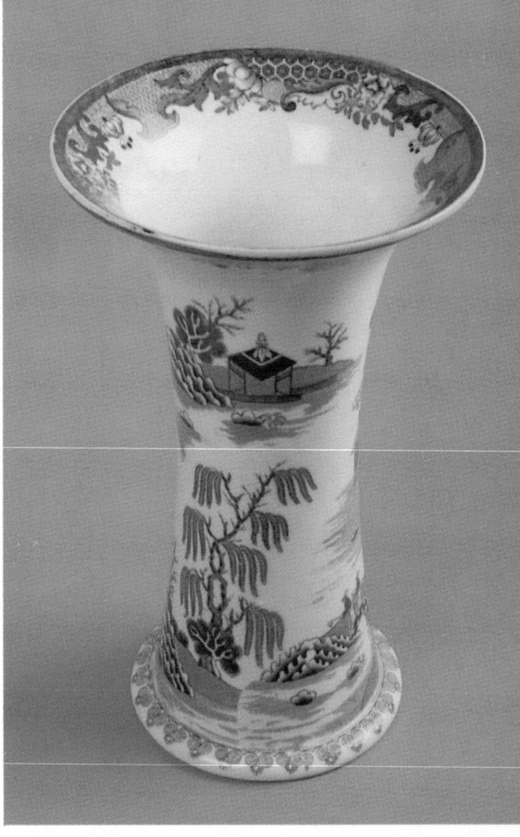

A spill vase for used tapers and matches, made by Mason's Ironstone, 10" high. Courtesy of Charles and Louise Loehr, Louise's Old Things, Kutztown PA.

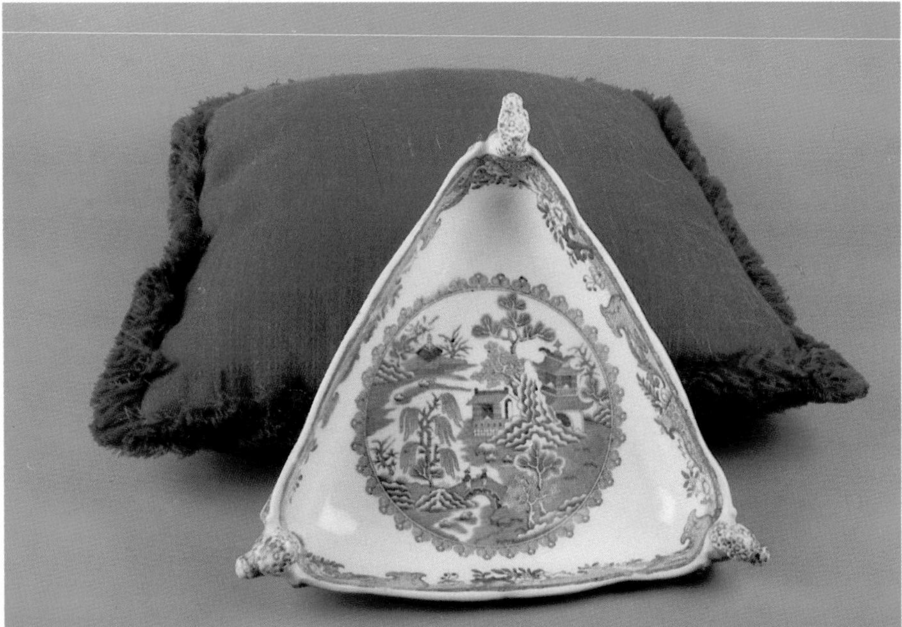

A triangular bowl, Mason's, painted ironstone. From the collection of Peter and Susan Steelman, Mystic, CT.

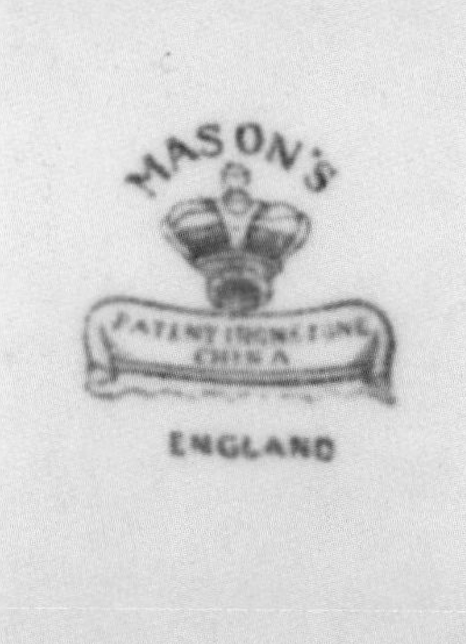

A serving dish with a scalloped edge, made by Mason's. Courtesy of Charles and Louise Loehr, Louise's Old Things, Kutztown, PA.

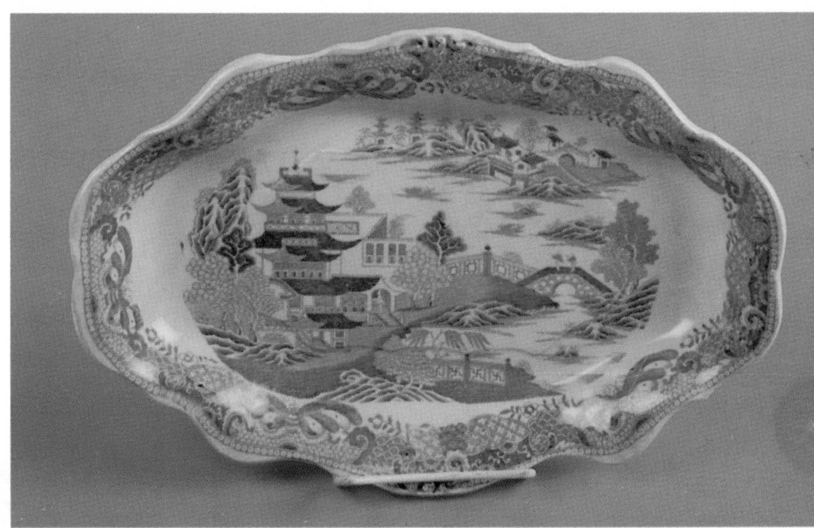

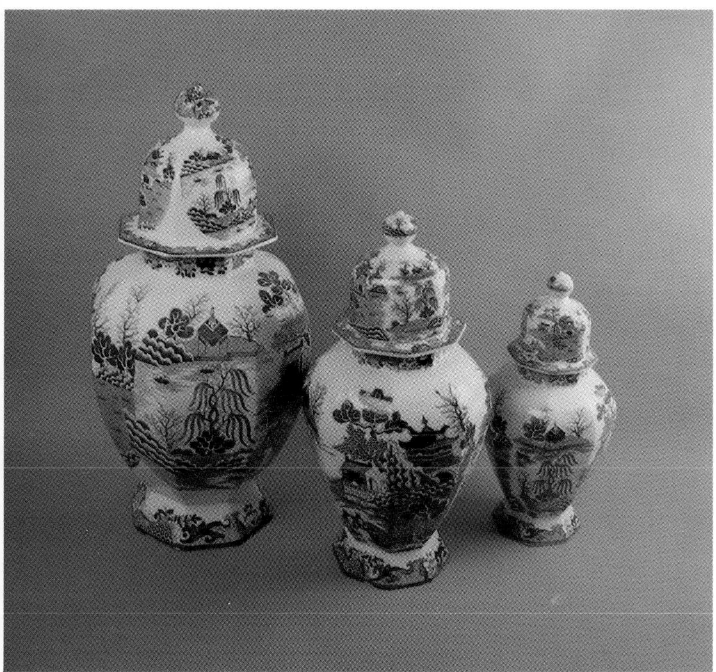

Three large covered vases from Mason's Ironstone, the smallest of which is 12" high. They bear the same Mason's mark as the spill vase. Courtesy of Charles and Louise Loehr, Louise's Old Things, Kutztown PA.

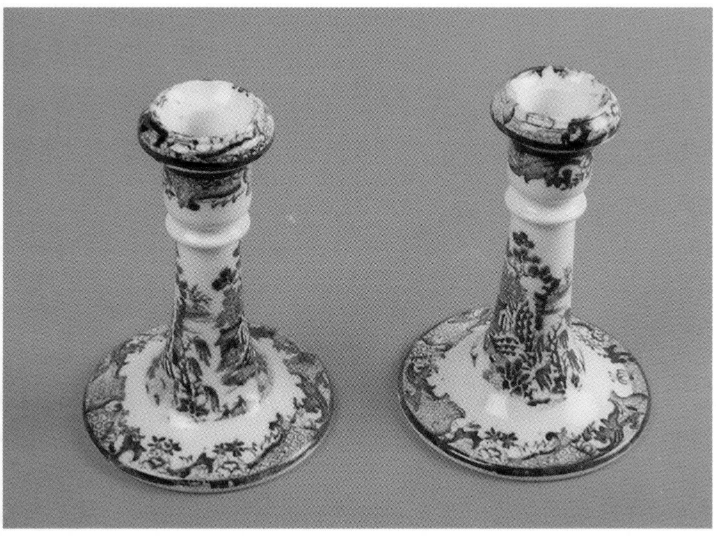

Candlesticks by Mason's, 5.25" high. Courtesy of Charles and Louise Loehr, Louise's Old Things, Kutztown, PA.

Mayer: Brothers Thomas, John, and Joseph produced well-regarded earthenwares & china from Burslem from 1843-1855. They participated in the exhibitions of 1851, 1853, and 1855, taking home a medal in 1851. Marks include "Mayer Bros." or "T. J. & J. Mayer".

Thomas Mayer: Thomas Mayer operated the Cliff Bank Works at Stoke, Staffordshire, c. 1826-1835, and another works in Longport, Staffordshire, c. 1826-1838. He exported blue transfer wares to the USA. Marks included "T. MAYER" and, before 1836, "T. MAYER/STOKE."

The Mayer China Co.: In 1880, Joseph & Arthur Mayer arrived in the United States from England, moved to Beaver County, Pennsylvania, and established J. & E. Mayer Potteries Co, Ltd. It was later incorporated as Mayer China Co, and is still active. Around 1914-1915, the began producing a wide range of wares in white graniteware and semi-vitreous china, focusing solely on hotel wares. The company grew substantially, and in 1901 employed 145 workers for white granite alone. Marks included "J. & E. Mayer" and later "Mayer China."

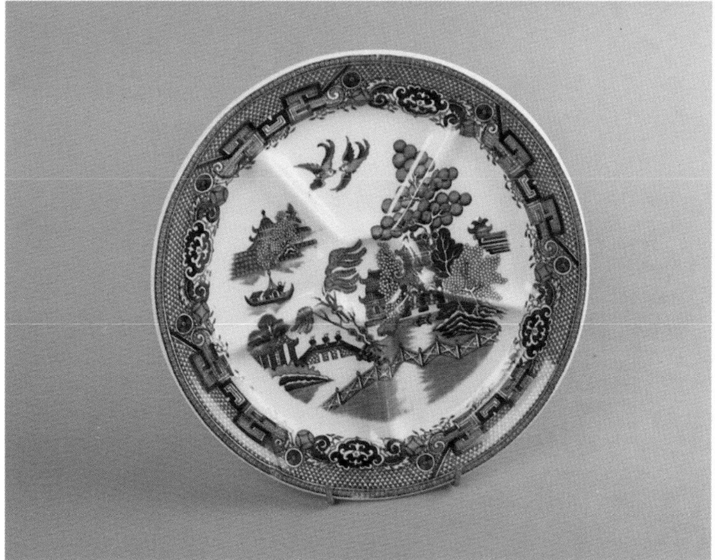

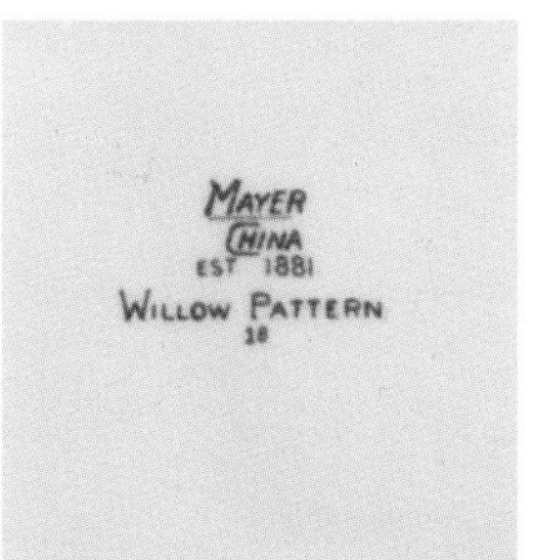

An oyster plate by Mayer, 10" diam. Courtesy of Charles and Louise Loehr, Louise's Old Things, Kutztown, PA.

McCoy Pottery: Opened in 1899 in Roseville, Ohio, U.S.A., and began production the following year. The company expanded to Zanesville, Ohio in 1912. In 1925, the firm's name was changed to the Brush Pottery. Impressed marks read "McCOY," and a mark reading "MITUSA" (Made In The USA) may be found.

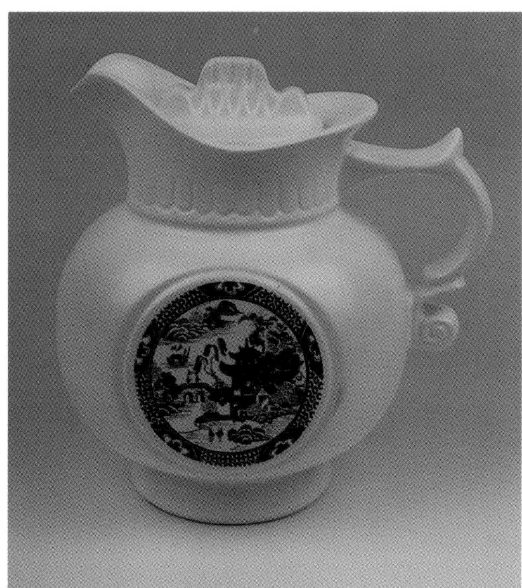

Though it looks like a covered pitcher, this pottery piece is actually a cookie jar, 9" high. This jar is completely white except for a single willow-motif medallion in overglaze transfer, and was made by McCoy in the United States. Courtesy of Rita Entmacher Cohen.

D.E. McNicol Pottery Co.: A firm operating out of East Liverpool, Ohio, from 1892-1954. The "Ideal" trade name was used c. 1905. A mark reading "McNICOL CHINA" in a crest above "CLARKSBURG, W.VA." was in use c. 1930-1954. A mark reading simply "D. E. McNICOL" appeared c. 1915-1929, and one reading "McNICOL CHINA" appeared c. 1935-1950.

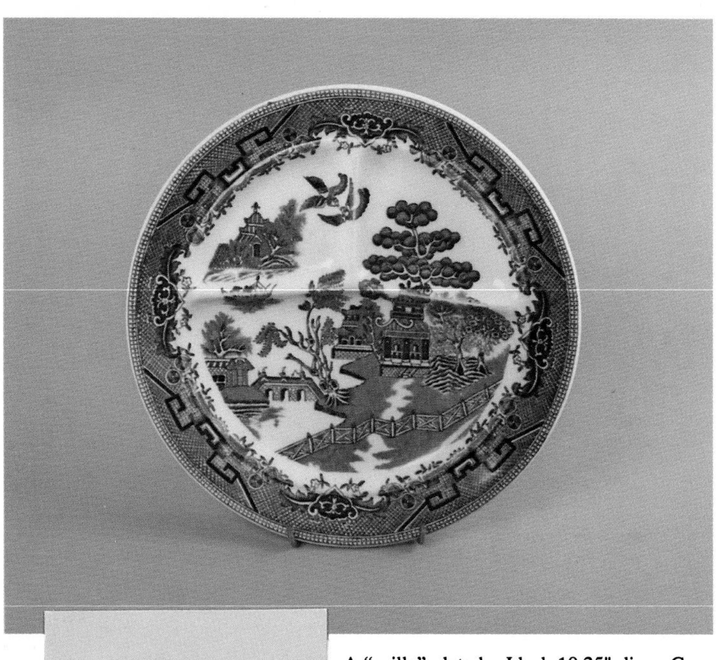

A "grille" plate by Ideal, 10.25" diam. Courtesy of Charles and Louise Loehr, Louise's Old Things, Kutztown, PA.

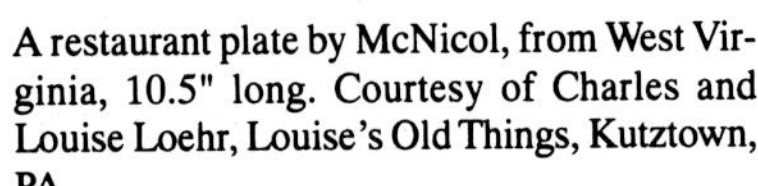

A restaurant plate by McNicol, from West Virginia, 10.5" long. Courtesy of Charles and Louise Loehr, Louise's Old Things, Kutztown, PA.

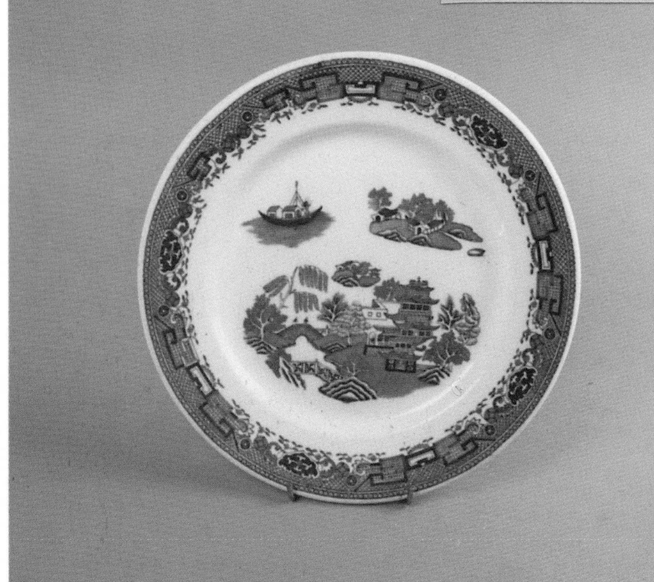

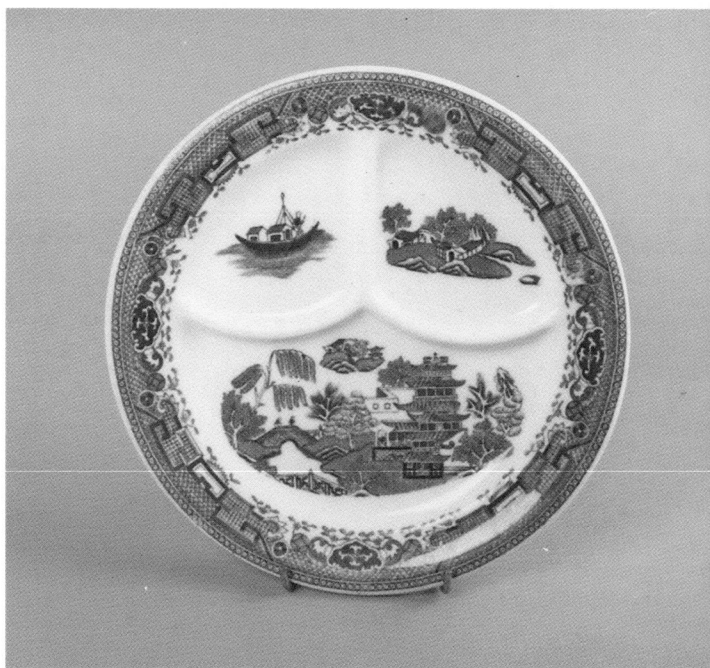

A grill plate by McNicol, 9.5" diam. Courtesy of Charles and Louise Loehr, Louise's Old Things, Kutztown, PA.

Alfred Meakin: Produced earthenwares at Tunstall, beginning in 1875. A variety of printed and impressed marks with the company name also incorporate Royal Arms and crown logos. After 1897, "LTD." was added to the name on marks; it was dropped after 1930. A "Willowette" line was produced c. 1937.

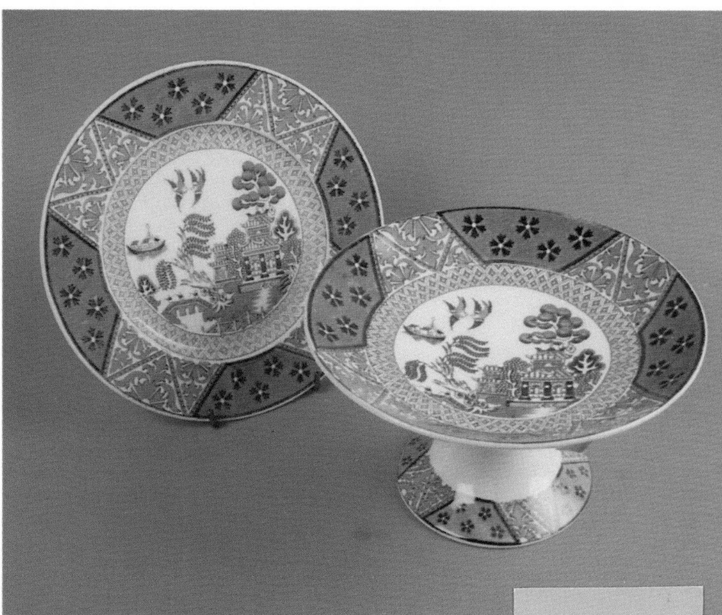

A doughnut stand and a plate in Alfred Meakin's "Border" pattern, 5.25" high x 9" diam. (doughnut stand), 9.5" diam. (plate). Courtesy of Charles and Louise Loehr, Louise's Old Things, Kutztown, PA.

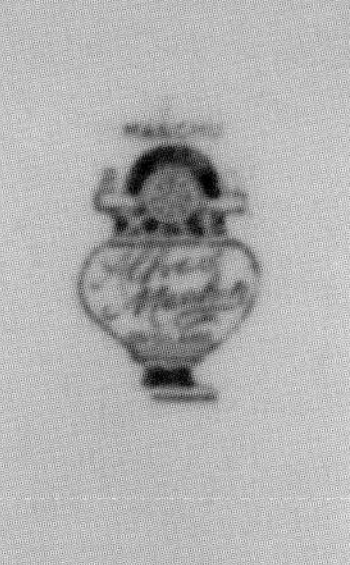

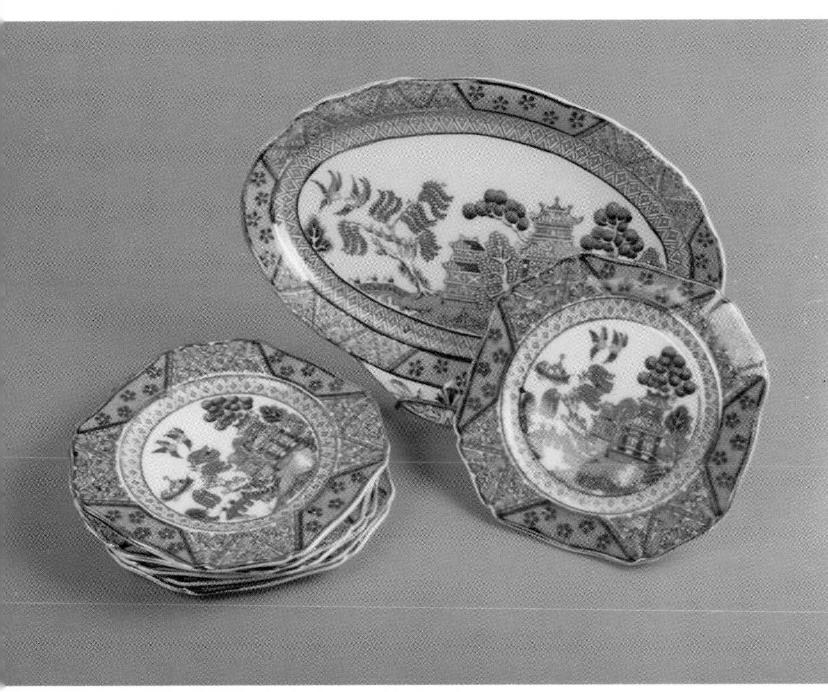

An ice cream set in Alfred Meakin's "Border" pattern. Courtesy of Charles and Louise Loehr, Louise's Old Things, Kutztown, PA.

David Methven & Sons: This potter produced earthenwares in Kirkcaldy, Scotland from the first half of the 19th century through c. 1930. The early wares were usually unmarked, but after c. 1875 name and initial marks were applied.

Middlesbrough Pottery: Operated in Yorkshire, 1834-1844, producing earthenwares and creamwares. In 1844 the name was changed to Middlesbrough Earthenware Co., and continued production through 1852. Marks include the Middlesbrough name, sometimes printed as "MIDDLESBRO'," or the initials "M. P. Co." or "M. E. & CO.," often with an anchor logo.

W. R. Midwinter: Operated out of Burslem, Staffordshire, after its establishment in c. 1910. Its earthenwares were generally unmarked at first, but simple pre-World War II marks include the W. R. Midwinter name, "Burslem" and "[MADE IN] ENGLAND." Post-war marks began to incorporate crown logos. Some of their willow is said to bear a pagoda and willow tree mark.

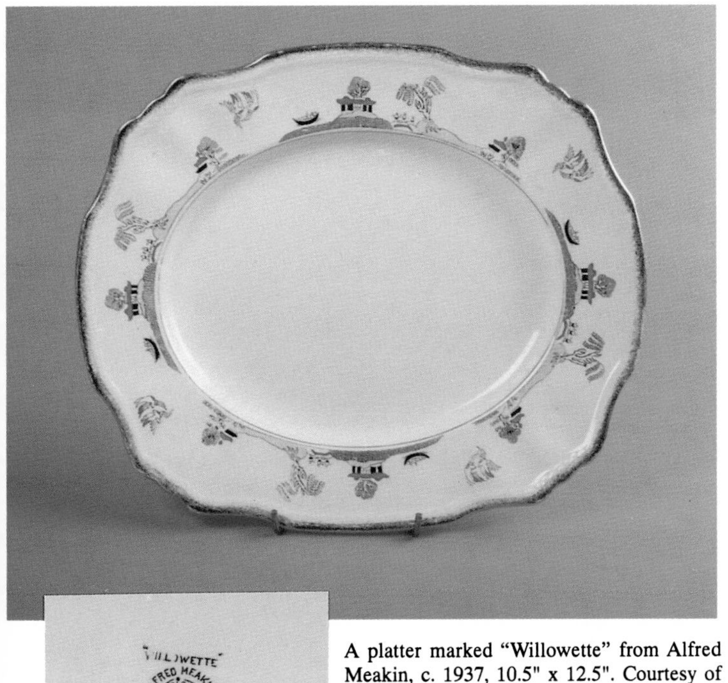

A platter marked "Willowette" from Alfred Meakin, c. 1937, 10.5" x 12.5". Courtesy of Charles and Louise Loehr, Louise's Old Things, Kutztown, PA.

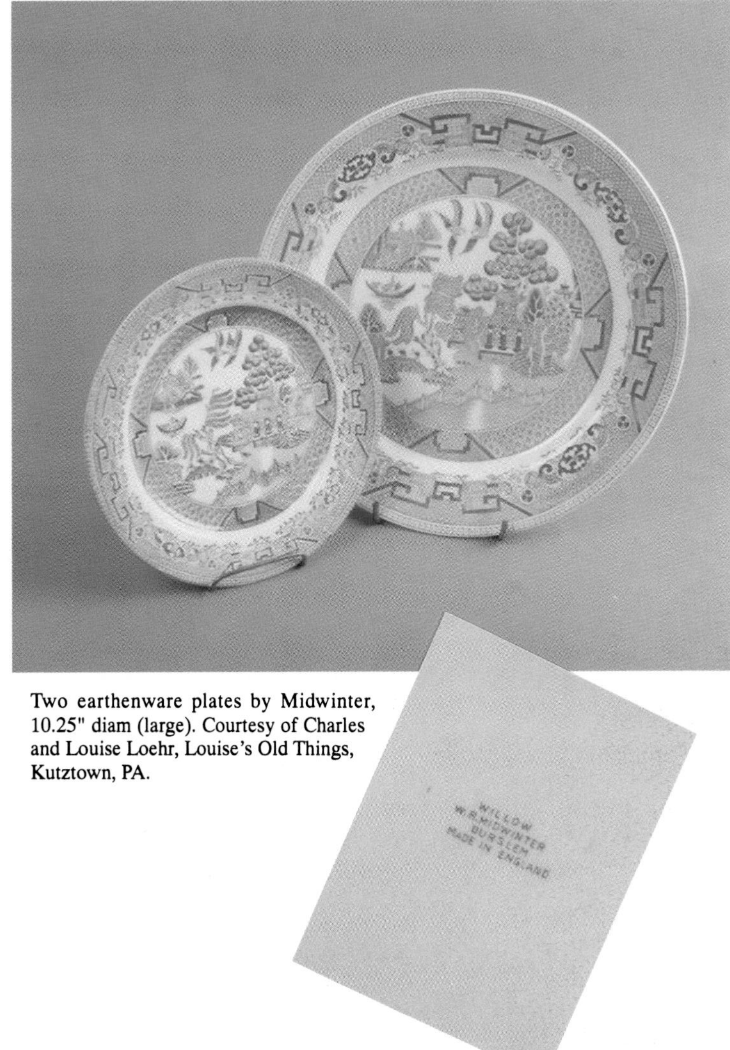

Two earthenware plates by Midwinter, 10.25" diam (large). Courtesy of Charles and Louise Loehr, Louise's Old Things, Kutztown, PA.

John Meir: This maker of earthenwares operated under his own name at Greengates Pottery in Tunstall, Staffordshire, from c. 1812-1836; from 1837-1897, the company was known as John Meir & Son. Marks read "J.M." or "I.M." before 1837, and afterwards "J. M. & S.," "I. M. & S.," "J. M. & SON," "J. MEIR & SON," and "MEIR & SON."

Minton: Founded in Stoke, Staffordshire in 1793 by Thomas Minton, who had first apprenticed as an engraver at Caughley. He had gone on to work for Spode's warehouse in London, and then moved to Stoke-on-Trent to open an engraving workshop. At first the company made earthenware, but when Thomas' son Herbert took over the works between 1836-1858, the company added semi-porcelain, ironstone, white earthenware, and bone china to its repertoire. The firm competed and took high honors at international exhibitions regularly. Herbert Minton use advanced techniques to produce blue transfer-printed wares of high quality at a time when most potters' transfer-print quality was in decline. Changing partnerships in the Minton concern proceeded as follows: Thomas Minton (1793-1817), Thomas Minton & Sons (1817-1836), Minton & Boyle (1836-1841), Minton & Co. (1841-1873), Minton & Hollins (Minton's Patent Tile Works in Stoke; the name appears sporadically between 1845-1868), and Mintons (1873-). Wares were not marked before the 1820s; then, the first marked blue-printed wares bore a scroll cartouche with the pattern name or number and a cursive letter "M". Beginning in 1842, cyphers were impressed on most wares to indicate the year of production (see Coysh & Henrywood, vol. I). Among other marks used by the firm are the impressed initials "B.B." ("Best Body," used in the mid-19th century); "MINTON" (impressed, c.1862-1871, with impressed year cypher); "MINTONS" (impressed, after 1871); "MINTON" in the printed globe trademark (c. 1863-1872), later crowned or with an added "S"; and "MINTONS" (impressed, after 1871 or 1873). A revised globe mark, topped with a crown, reading "MINTONS" was used from c. 1873 onwards, with "ENGLAND" added after 1891, and "Made in England" c. 1902-1911; the crown was omited on some earthenwares produced beginning in 1901. "MINTONS ENGLAND" appeared c. 1890-1910, and a further revised globe trademark reading "MINTONS/EST. 1793/MADE IN ENGLAND," with globe, crown, and surrounding laurels, was in use from c. 1912-1950.

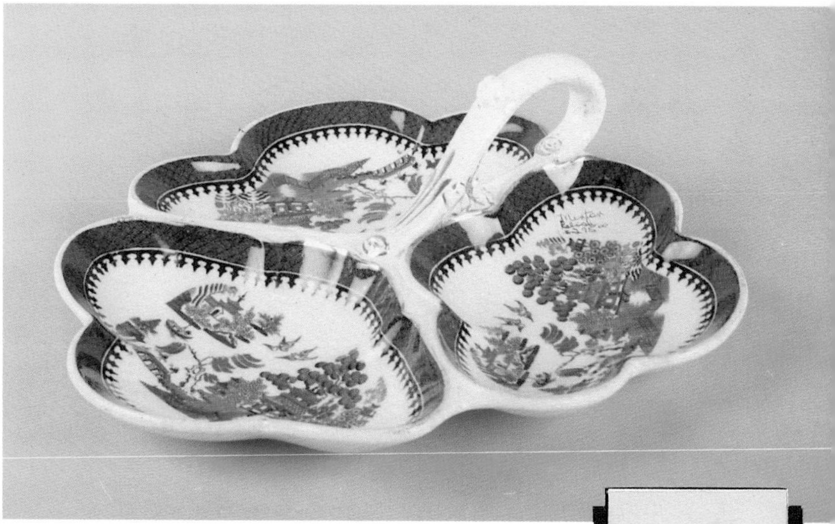

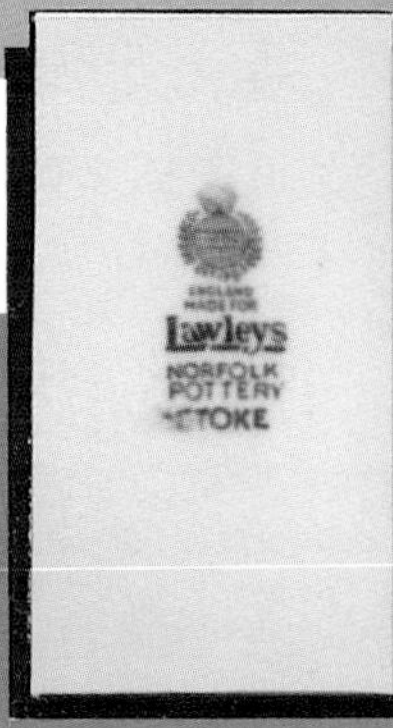

Relish dish by Minton for Lawleys, 10.5" wide. Courtesy of Eva Lee Revels, Country Accents, Bandera, TX.

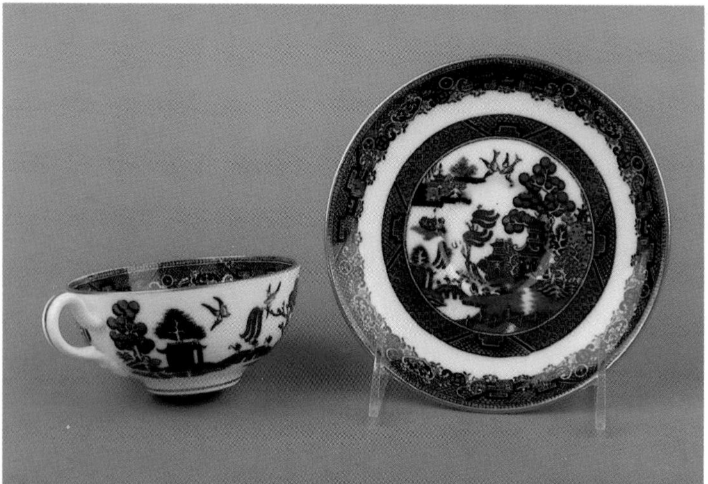

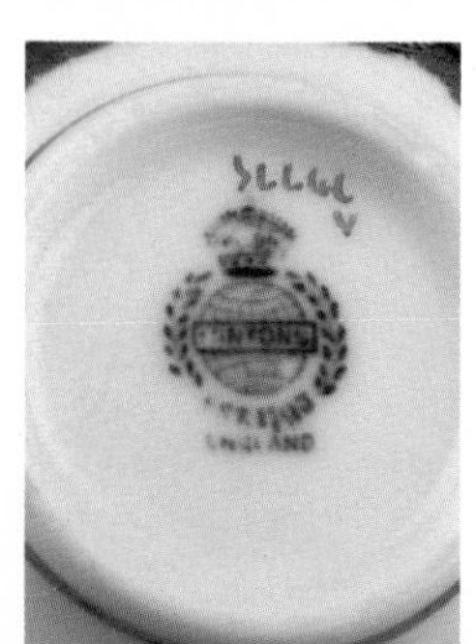

A gold-trimmed cup and saucer in bone china porcelain, by Minton; saucer is 5.625" diam. Courtesy of Rita Entmacher Cohen.

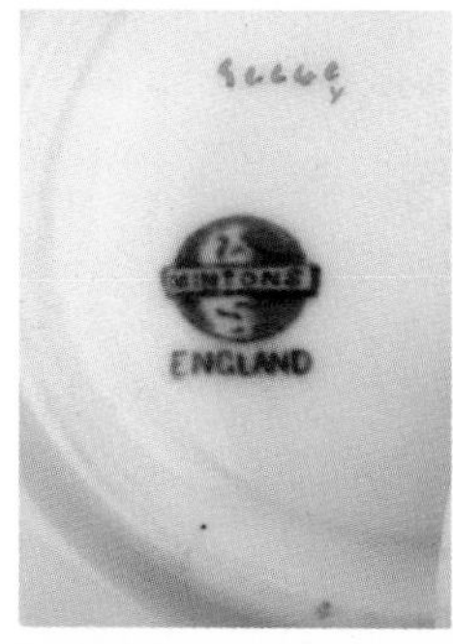

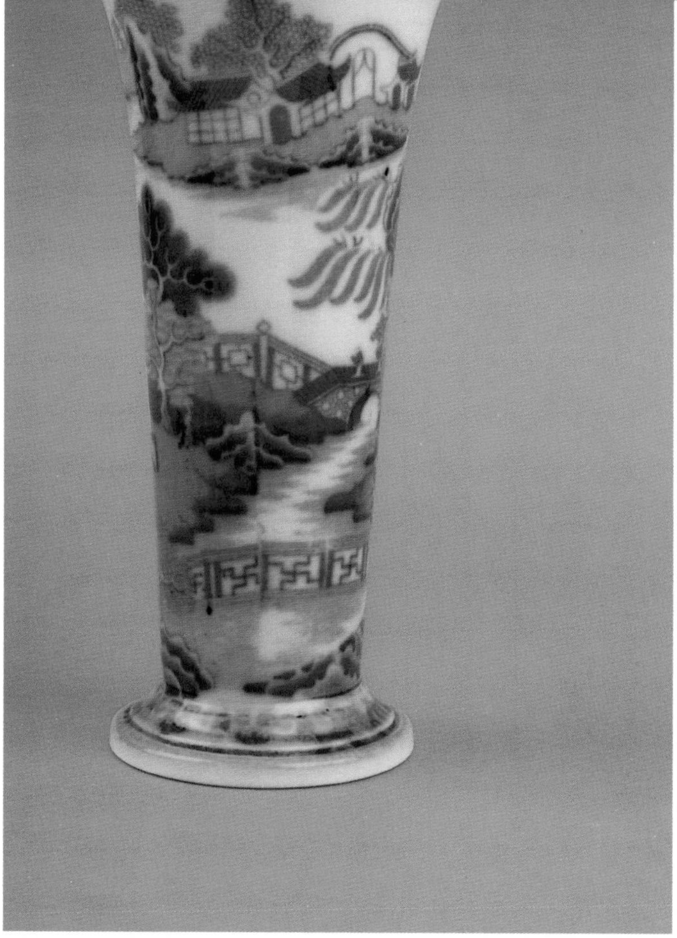

A round vase from Minton, 7.5". Courtesy of Rita Entmacher Cohen.A tri-part

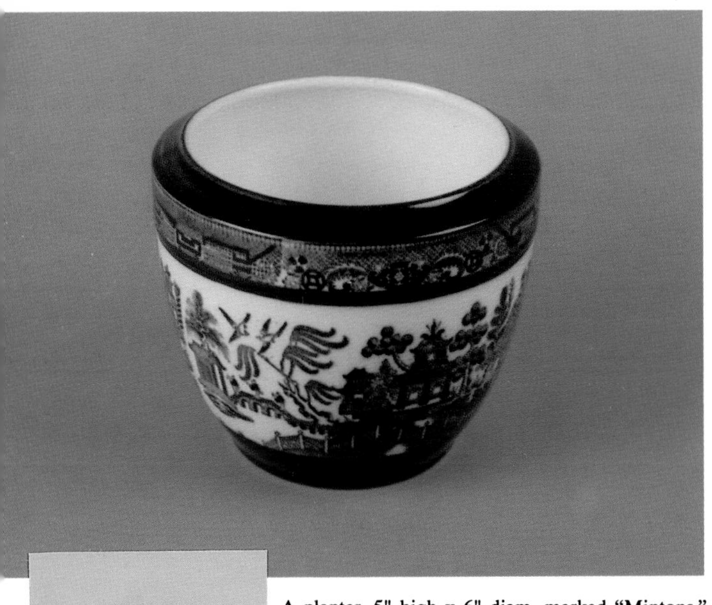

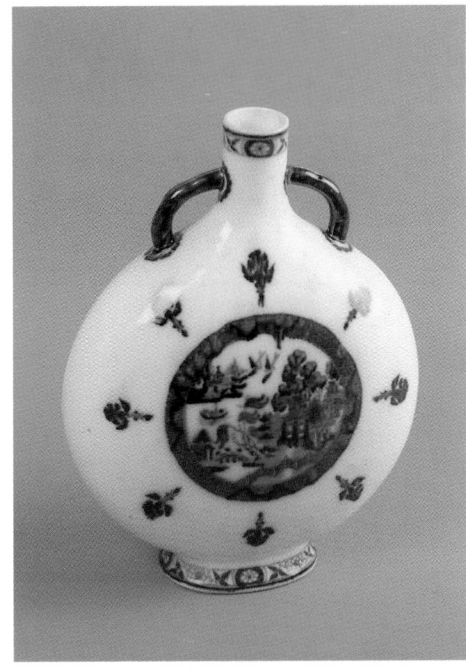

A pillow vase by Minton, 1875, 11.5" high. This shape is also called a pilgrim vase. Courtesy of Charles and Louise Loehr, Louise's Old Things, Kutztown PA.

A planter, 5" high x 6" diam, marked "Mintons." From the collection of Peter and Susan Steelman, Mystic, CT.

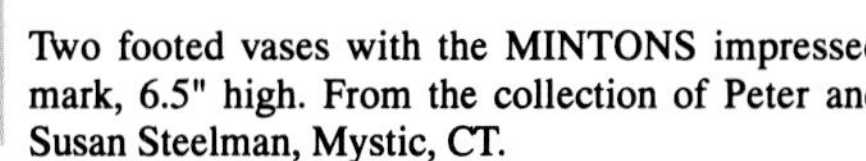

Two footed vases with the MINTONS impressed mark, 6.5" high. From the collection of Peter and Susan Steelman, Mystic, CT.

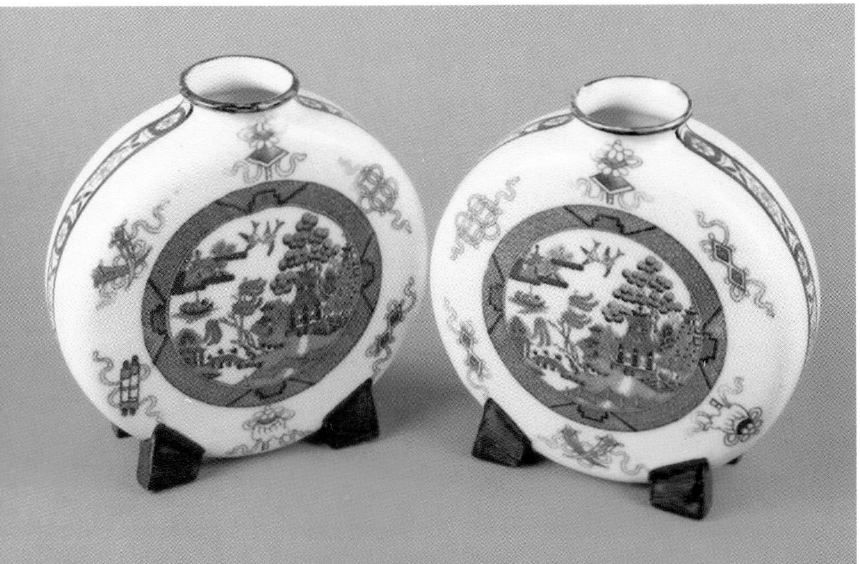

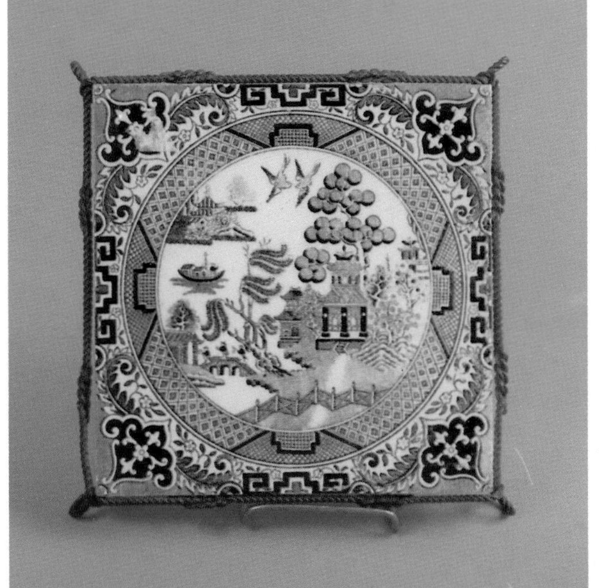

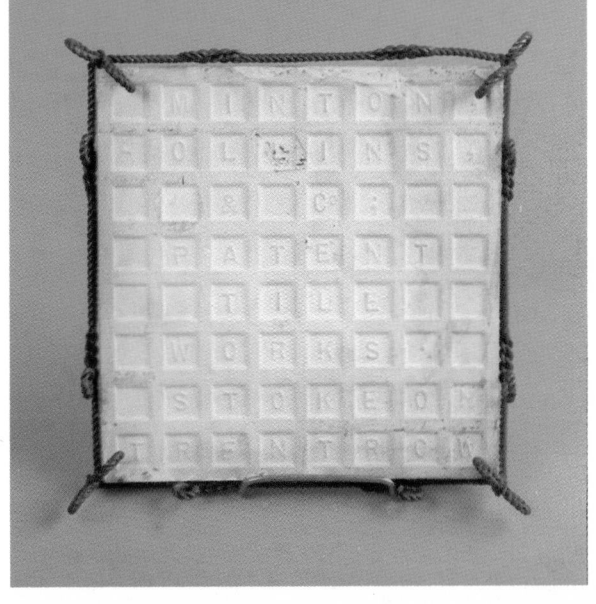

Right, Above Right: A tile from Minton Hollins, 1868, 6.5" square. Courtesy of Charles and Louise Loehr, Louise's Old Things, Kutztown, PA.

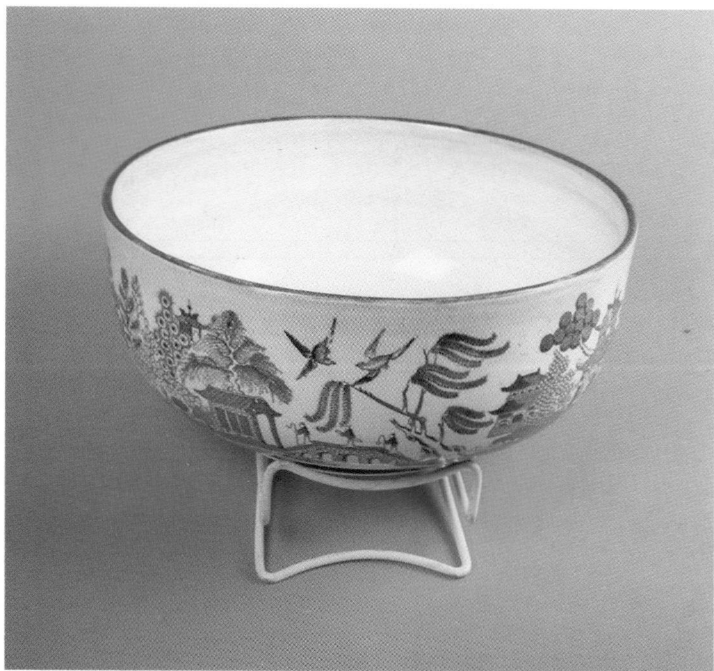

A Minton bowl with painting, 3.25" high x 8" diam. Courtesy of Charles and Louise Loehr, Louise's Old Things, Kutztown, PA.

Mopiyama: A firm active in Occupied Japan.

Andrew Muir & Co.: Active between 1816-1840 in Greenock, Scotland. The pottery made blue-printed wares, and exported to Canada. Marks include the initials "A.M."

Myott Son & Co.: Produced earthenwares out of Stoke (1898-1902), Cobridge (1902-1946), and Hanley (beginning in 1947). The company was known to use a crown mark, with the company name or the initials "M. S. & Co."

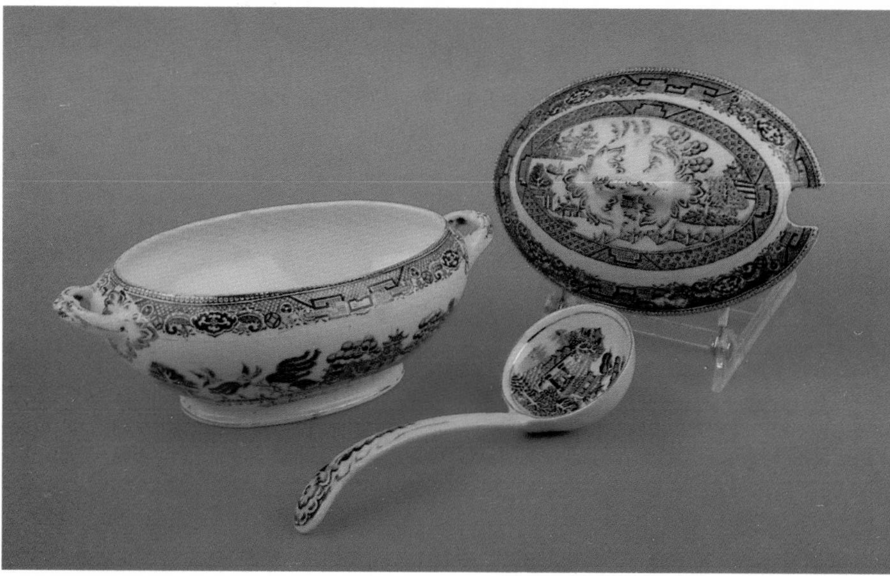

A sauce tureen and ladle in Imperial semi-porcelain, by Myott Son & Co., c. 1901. Courtesy of Rita Entmacher Cohen.

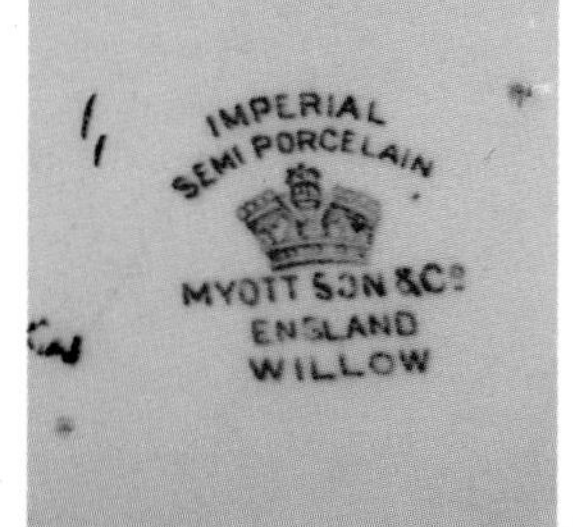

Sterling China Co.: E. Liverpool, Ohio, 1917-present. Marks frequently bear the company name and location. See Caribe.

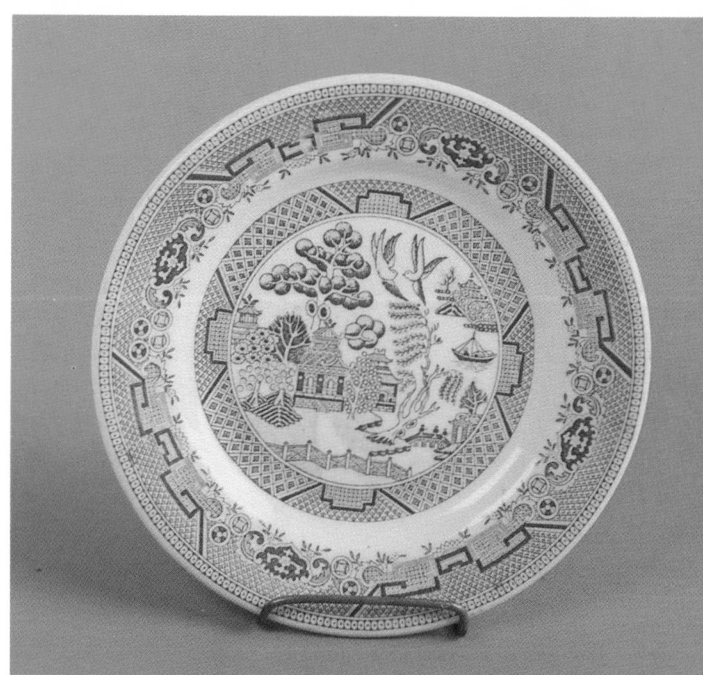

A plate made by the New York pottery Sterling, 5.75" diam. Courtesy of Charles and Louise Loehr, Louise's Old Things, Kutztown, PA.

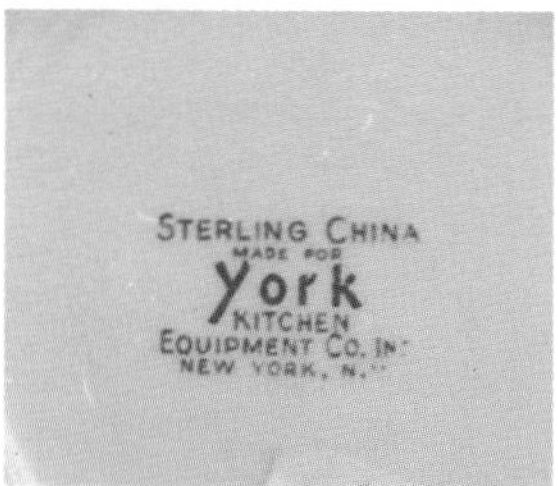

Mark for plate by Sterling

New Hall Porcelain Works: This company was run by a number of partnerships in Shelton, Hanley, Staffordshire between 1781-1835. They initially produced hard-paste porcelain, from patent rights they had acquired from the Plymouth & Bristol discovery. By 1810, they switched to bone china. A printed mark bearing the New Hall name in script inside two concentric circles was used only on the company's bone china line, c. 1812-1835.

Nikko: A Japanese manufacturer.

North Staffordshire Pottery Co.: This twentieth-century company produced earthenwares from 1940-1952, first out of the Globe Pottery in Cobridge, and then in Hanley. The pottery was then taken over by Ridgway, which continued to use its trade name. Marks include circle seals with a cliff logo. The cliff was surmounted by the words "STRONG AS A ROCK" (trademark registered in 1944), and encircled by "N. S. POTTERY CO LTD/COBRIDGE/ENGLAND" (c. 1945-1952; the bottom of this circular seal was closed with a Staffordshire knot). After Ridgway's acquisition in 1952, the name "NORTH STAFFORDSHIRE POTTERY" was spelled out in full, and the words "VITROCK" and "ENGLAND" were added to the mark.

Paden City Pottery Co.: A firm from Sisterville, W. Virginia, in operation from 1914-1963.

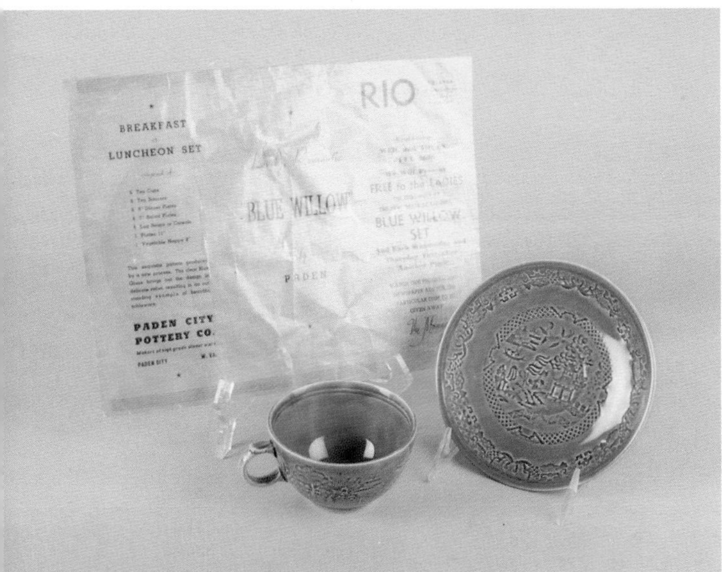

Paden Pottery's earthenware Willow. This set was offered as a premium to theater attendees. Courtesy of Wendy's Willow.

Parrott & Co.: Active beginning in c. 1921 in Burslem, Staffordshire. Produced earthenwares, including the well-known polychrome "Parrott Willow" line. Their printed trademarks show a parrot inside a crest, reading "PARROTT & COMPANY/ BURSLEM/REGISTERED TRADE MARK/[MADE IN ENGLAND]." The mark was redrawn in 1935, after which it sometimes included "CORONET WARE."

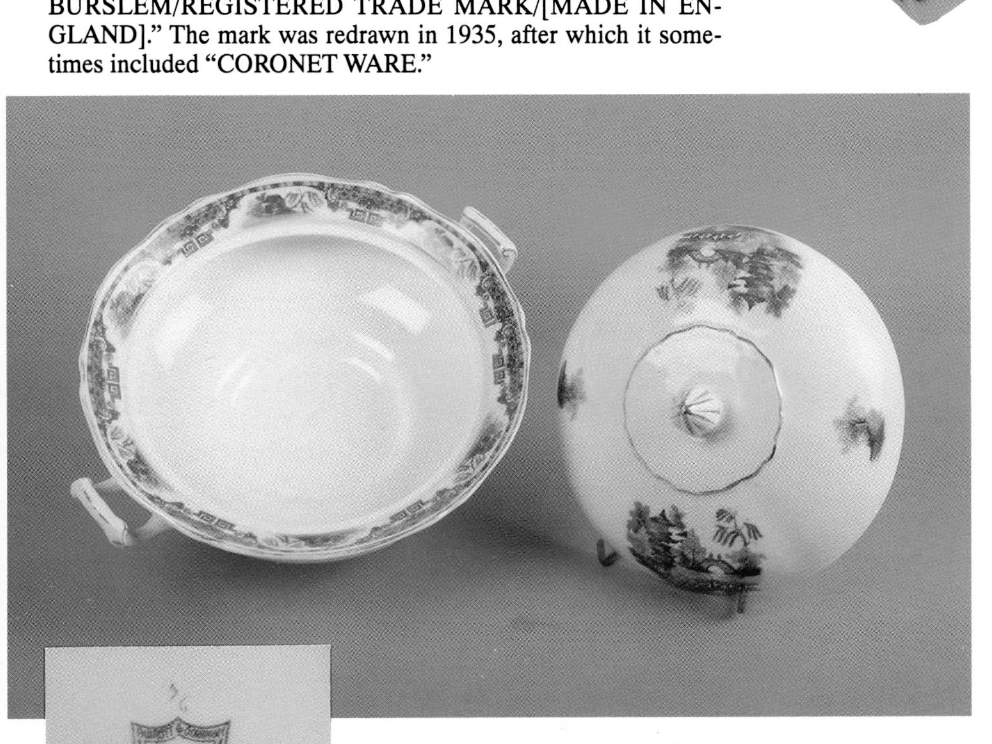

A bowl in Parrott Willow, 1935, 5.5" high x 10" x 9". Courtesy of Charles and Louise Loehr, Louise's Old Things, Kutztown, PA.

The Parrott & Co. mark.

Patterson: Several companies operating in Gateshead, Durham may have used this name. Among them are Thomas Patterson & Co., which worked at the Tyne Pottery from 1827 until at least 1835, and Jackson & Patterson, which worked at Sheriff Hill Pottery between 1833-1838. Other firms using the Patterson name continued until the 1890s.

Edward & George Phillips: Longport, Staffordshire, 1822-1834; then, George Phillips, c. 1834-1848. As a partnership, the company produced several blue-printed patterns; on his own, George Phillips produced many such designs. George is known to have marked his wares with printed marks reading "G. PHILLIPS." He also used a Staffordshire knot, with the impressed name "PHILLIPS" above and "LONGPORT" below (with an inverted "N"). The earlier partnership may also have used a mark of this description.

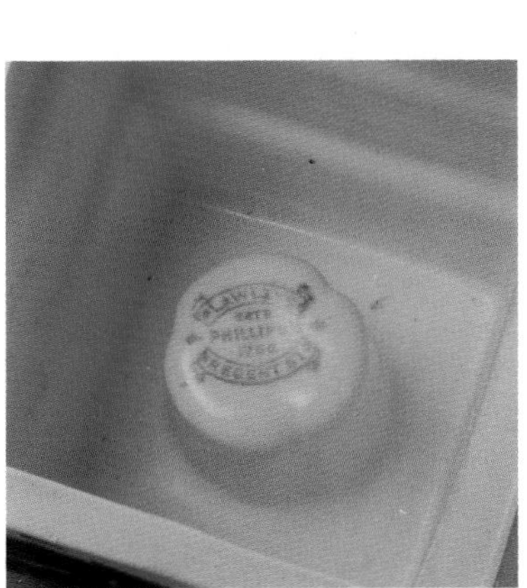

Candlesticks by Phillips, 3.5" high. Courtesy of Charles and Louise Loehr, Louise's Old Things, Kutztown, PA.

Thomas Phillips & Son: A short-lived enterprise from Burslem, Staffordshire, 1845-1846. Marks read "T. PHILLIPS & SON/BURSLEM."

Phoenix Pottery Co.: Ouseburn, Northumberland.

Pinder Bourne & Company: Previously Pinder, Bourne & Hope (1851-1862), the company produced earthenwares bearing the "& Company" tag in Burslem beginning in 1862. The firm was purchased by Doultons in 1878, but maintained the Pinder, Bourne & Co. name until 1882. Marks bear the company name or initials, sometimes in triangle or circle marks, and sometimes with the Royal Arms.

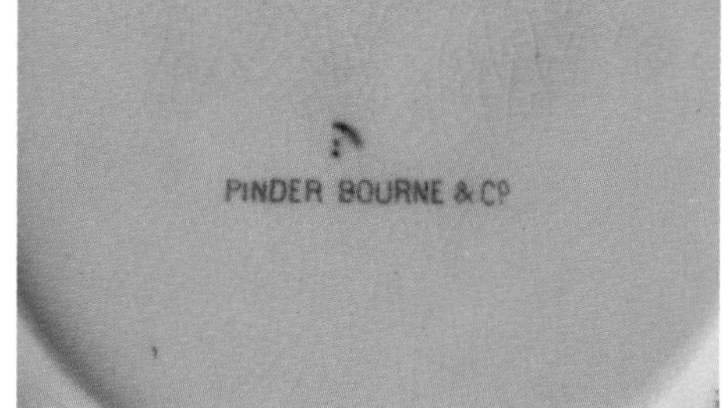

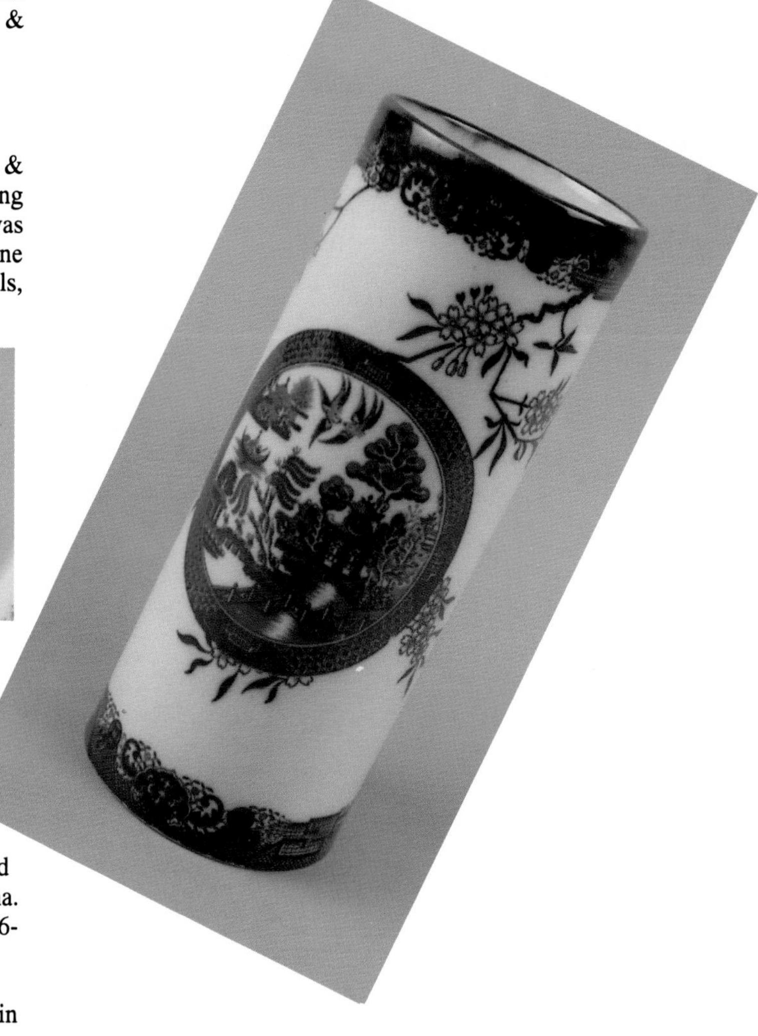

A pearlware vase, 11" high, marked on the bottom "Pinder Bourne & Company." From the collection of Peter and Susan Steelman, Mystic, CT.

Podmore Walker & Co: Opened in Tunstall, Staffordshire in 1834 as Podmore, Walker & Company, and operated until 1859. Enoch Wedgwood became a partner c. 1856. From 1856-1859 the firm used a mark reading "P.W. & W"—Podmore Walker & Wedgwood. Enoch Wedgwood took over in 1859 and changed name to Wedgwood & Company, using the marks "WEDGWOOD" and "WEDGWOOD & CO." They produced earthenwares called Pearl Stone Ware and Imperial Ironstone China. Marks included "P. W. & Co." (1834-1859), and "P. W. & W." (1856-1859).

Poutney: Operated from 1816-1835 as Poutney & Allies in Bristol, using several printed or impressed marks bearing the name in a horseshoe-and-cross mark, or reading ""P," "P & A," "P. A.," "B. P.," or "P. A./BRISTOL." Coysh and Henrywood note in their first volume that a Poutney plate in the Willow pattern was found with a printed mark reading "IMPROVED STONE CHINA," with an illustration of three bottle kilns. The firm operated as Poutney & Goldney between 1836-1849, using name marks and "BRISTOL." From 1849 through 1958, the company was called Poutney & Co., using "P. & CO." and name marks, adding "LTD" after 1889.

Powell & Bishop: Operated in Hanley from 1876-1878, marking its wares with its full name or the initials "P. & B." The company was succeeded by Powell, Bishop & Stonier.

Preston Pan [or Prestonpans]: A Scottish pottery known to have made Toby-type figurals with Willow decoration.

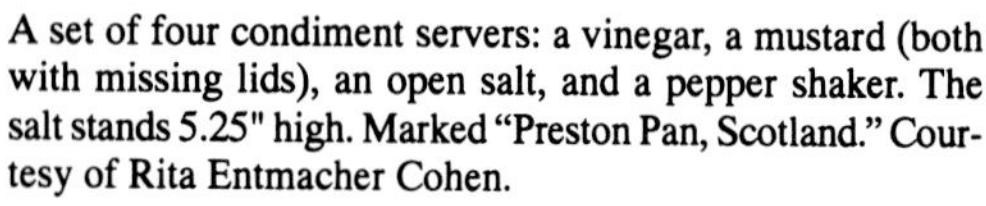

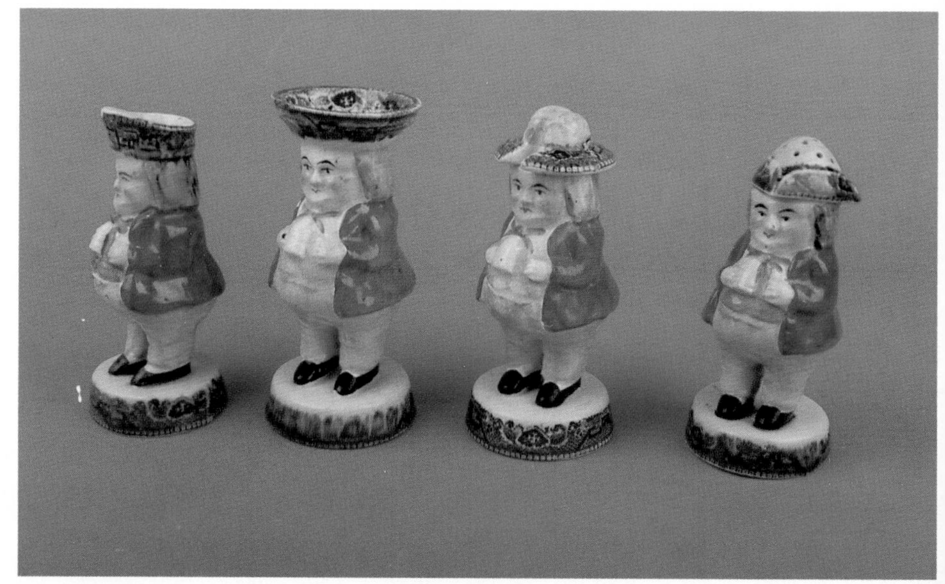

A set of four condiment servers: a vinegar, a mustard (both with missing lids), an open salt, and a pepper shaker. The salt stands 5.25" high. Marked "Preston Pan, Scotland." Courtesy of Rita Entmacher Cohen.

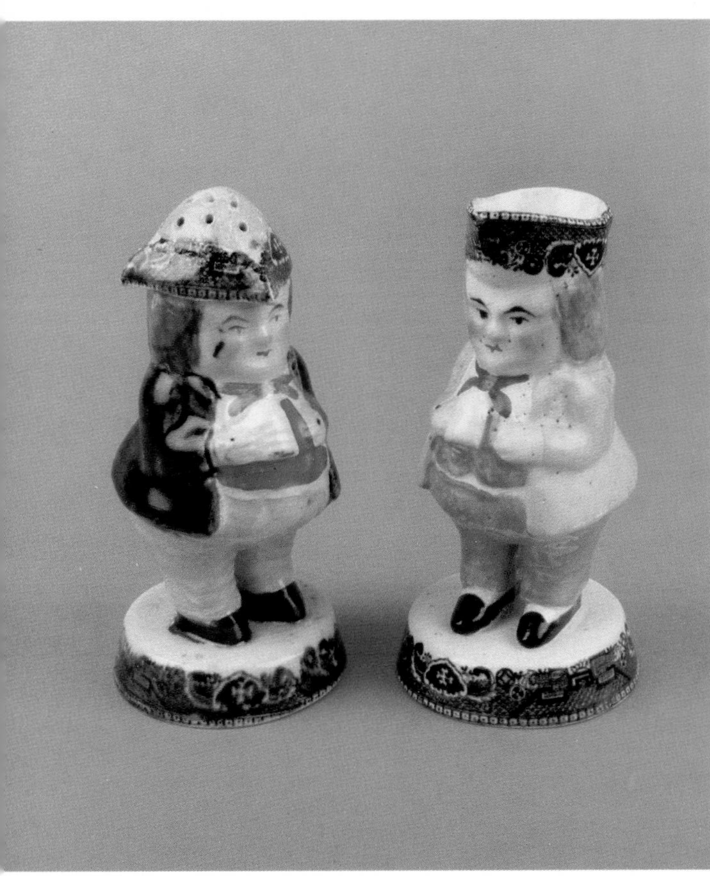

A vinegar server (in yellow) and a pepper shaker (in blue), 5.125". Marked "Preston Pan." Courtesy of Rita Entmacher Cohen.

William Ratcliffe: Operated in the New Hall Works in Hanley, c. 1831-1840, producing earthenwares. They used a mark reading "R/HACKWOOD," with a horizontal dividing line, and the initial "R" inside a sunburst trademark.

Thomas Rathbone & Co.: This Portobello, Scotland company was active c. 1810-1845, producing earthenwares. Marks read "T. R. & CO." and "T. RATHBONE/P."

Read & Clementson: Shelton, Staffordshire, 1833-1835. Used marks reading "R. & C.," sometimes including a pattern name and "STONEWARE."

William Reid: Musselburgh, Scotland, 1800-1839. Marks include a printed "W. REID."

Ridgway: This pottery family made high-quality earthenwares, porcelains, and stonewares, participated in international exhibitions, and won a number of medals. In 1792, brothers Job & George Ridgway began at the Bell Works in Hanley, Staffordshire. In 1802 Job built his own works at Cauldon Place, Hanley, and between 1814-1830, Job worked with his sons John & William. From 1830 to c. 1855, John ran the Cauldon Place Works. Brown-Westhead, Moore & Co. took over Cauldon in 1862; Cauldon Ltd. took it in 1905. The Ridgway family used a number of printed and impressed marks, regularly featuring the surname or initials. From c. 1830-1845, William Ridgway used "W. RIDGWAY" or intials. Around 1841 his son joined him, using the mark "W RIDGWAY, SON & CO." "RIDGWAYS" appears on wares from the Bedford Works in Hanley, 1879-1920. A quiver & bow logo was registered to the company in 1880. After 1891 the company re-issued old marks with initials "J & WR" and "W.R.," featuring a flower in one mark, and an urn and beehive in another. Later a square mark was used, and in the 20th century they used a crown design.

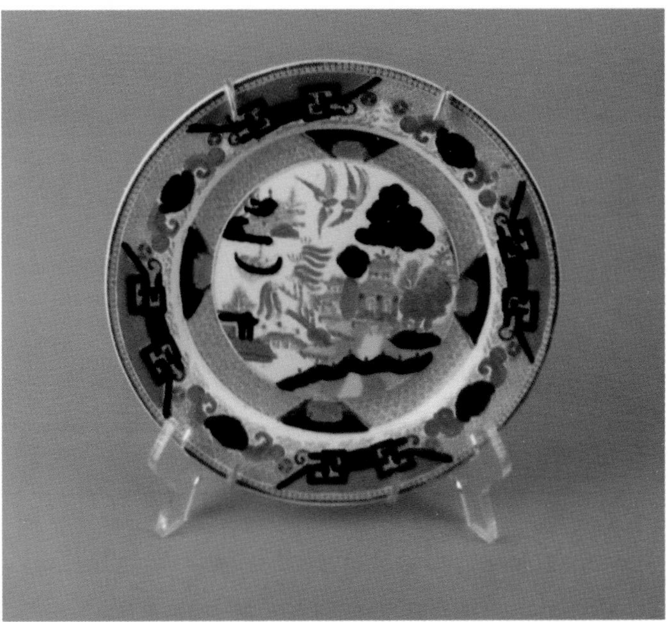

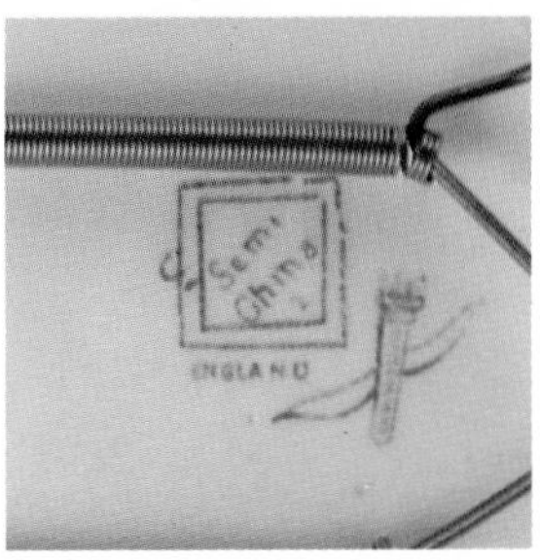

A 7.5" luncheon plate from Ridgway, indistinguishable from Buffalo's Gaudy Willow were it not for the mark. From the collection of Peter and Susan Steelman, Mystic, CT.

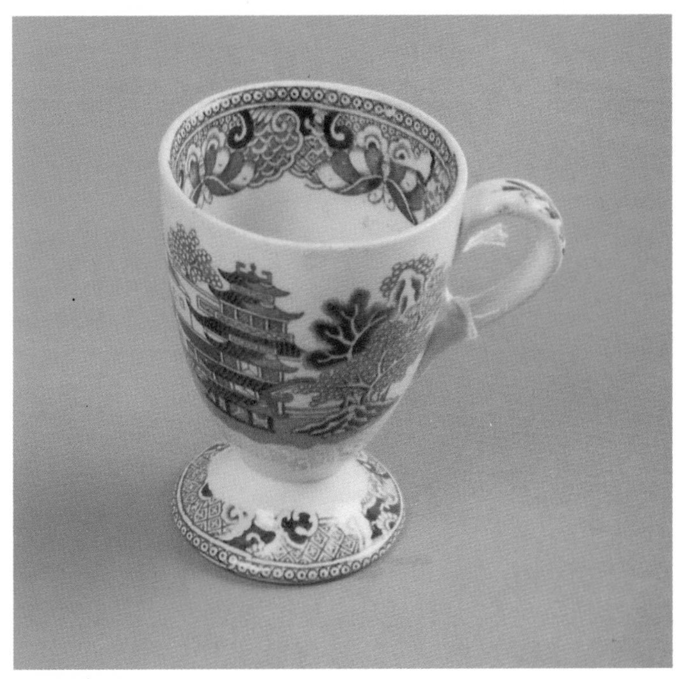

A punch cup by Ridgway, 3.5" high. Courtesy of Charles and Louise Loehr, Louise's Old Things, Kutztown, PA.

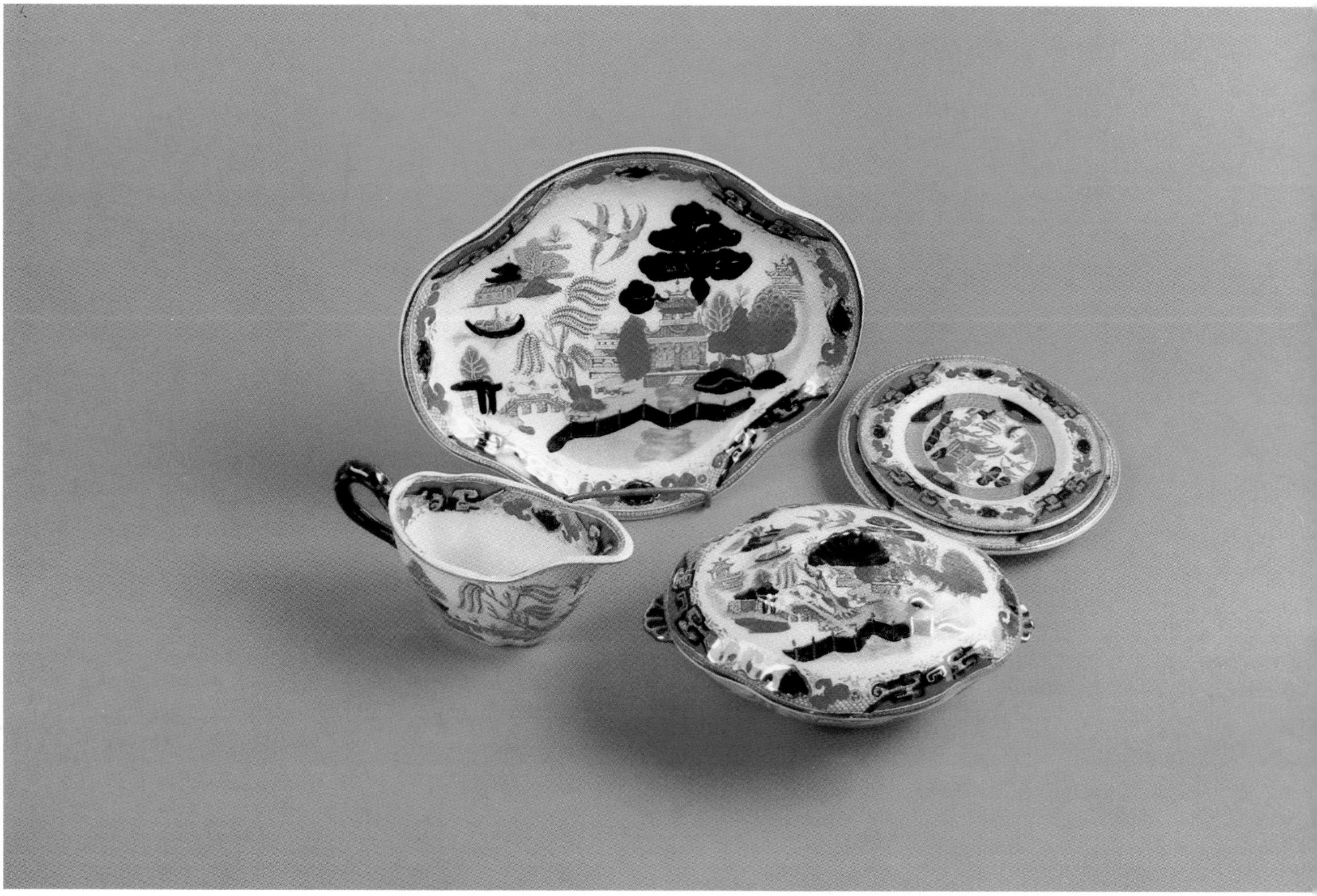

A children's dinner set in Gaudy Willow by Ridgway, 1890-1908, 6" long (platter). A full set includes three graduated platters, six large plates, six small plates, two covered vegetables, and a sauce/gravy boat. Courtesy of Charles and Louise Loehr, Louise's Old Things, Kutztown, PA.

John & Richard Riley: Operated from 1802-1828 in Burslem, Staffordshire. Marks included "RILEY" and initials.

Rington Ltd. Tea Merchants: A North Staffordshire company known to have used a pagoda mark.

Rockingham Works: Operated by varous owners, this pottery was active between 1745-1842 near Swinton, Yorkshire, producing earthenwares and, after 1826, porcelains. A wide range of marks, usually incorporating the Rockingham name, were used over the years.

John Rogers & Son: John Rogers and son Spencer were active in Longport, c 1814-1836. They produced good-quality wares out of Dale Hall, largely made for English market. Marks include the impressed "ROGERS" name.

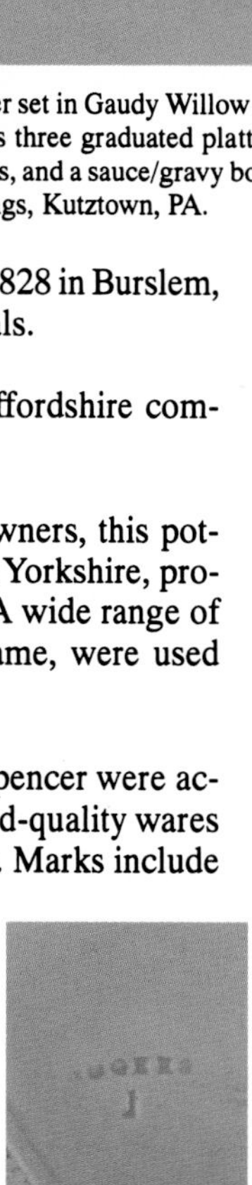

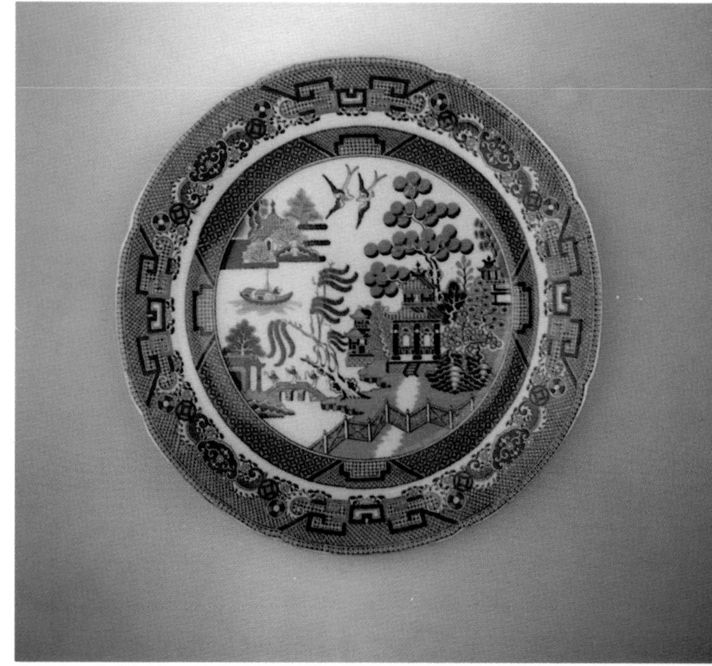

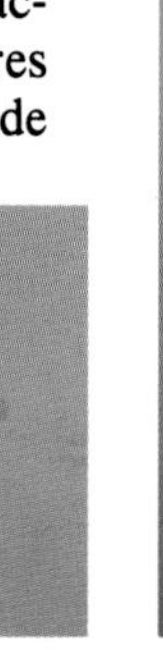

Pearlware plate by Rogers, 1800-1820, 10". Impressed mark. Courtesy of Rita Entmacher Cohen.

Royal Doulton: see Doulton & Co., Ltd.

Royal Grafton: A. B. Jones & Sons, Ltd. operated out of Grafton Works and other sites in Longton, Staffordshire, beginning in 1900. Name and initial marks were used in the early years, with the Grafton name appearing in marks beginning in c. 1913: a circle reading "A. B. JONES & SONS/H.C.E./ENGLAND" with a bar reading "GRAFTON CHINA," c. 1913+; an eagle with a teacup in his beak and a plate (reading "A. B. J. & S.") under his feet, above the words "GRAFTON CHINA," c. 1920+; a sheild with the Staffordshire knot, underneath a rising sun, reading "ENGLAND/GRAFTON CHINA/[in the knot] A B J/& Sons," c. 1930+; "GRAFTON CHINA" with a small sunrise logo, reading "A. B. J." in the center of the sun, and "MADE IN ENGLAND" below, c. 1935+; a diamond shape with a crown reading "ROYAL GRAFTON BONE CHINA," c. 1949+; "ROYAL GRAFTON BONE CHINA," c. 1950+, etc.

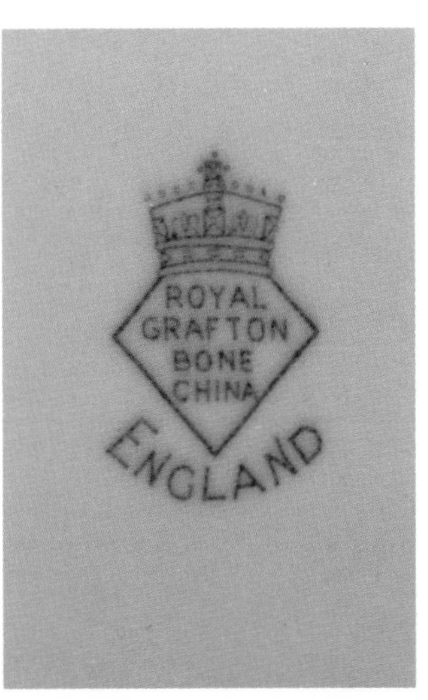

A Royal Grafton cake plate, cup, and server, 8.25" x 9.75" (cake plate). Courtesy of Bud & Marguerite Smith, Small World Antiques, MI.

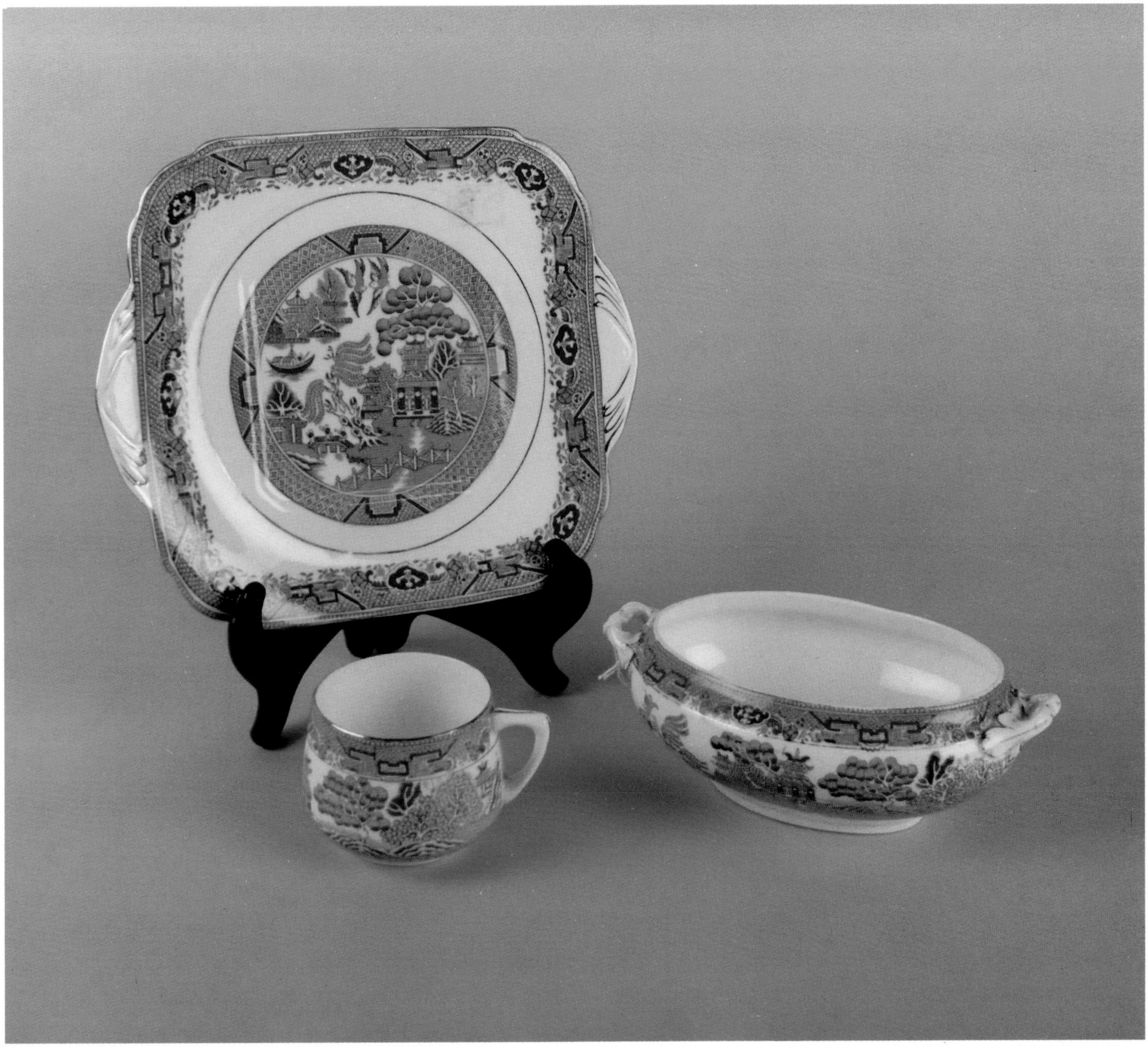

Royal Worcester: see Worcester.

Royal China Co.: A Sebring, Ohio company in business from 1933 to the present which made willow for mail-order houses.

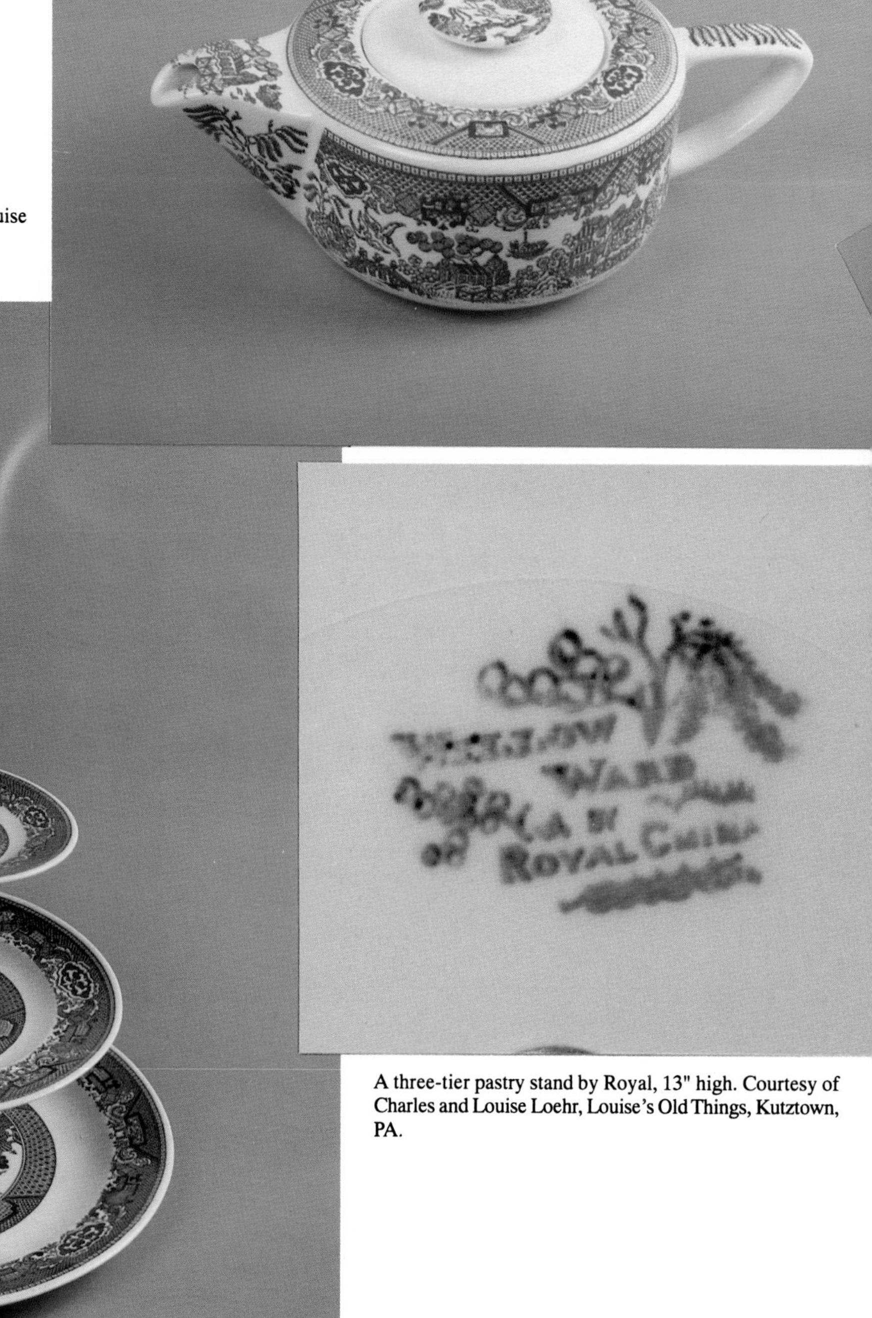

A teapot from Royal, 10.25" wide. Courtesy of Charles and Louise Loehr, Louise's Old Things, Kutztown, PA.

A three-tier pastry stand by Royal, 13" high. Courtesy of Charles and Louise Loehr, Louise's Old Things, Kutztown, PA.

Sadler & Green: A Liverpool firm established in 1756 as transfer-printers on tile, later on earthenwere & porcelain. Held the original patent for over-glaze transfer printing.

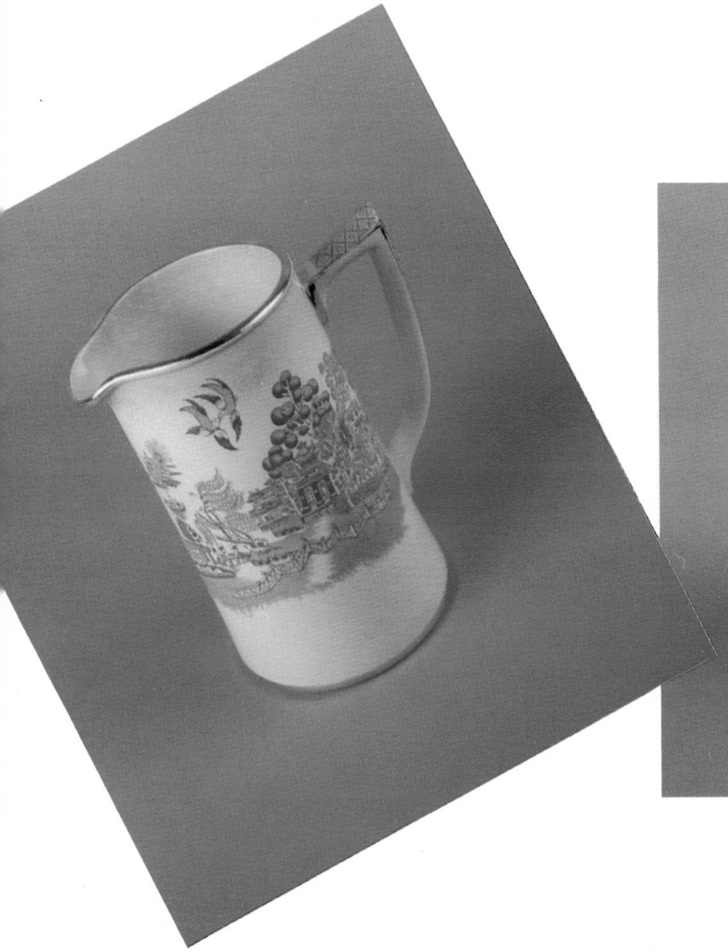

A red or pink Willow pitcher from Sadler, made in England, 7" high. From the collection of Peter and Susan Steelman, Mystic, CT.

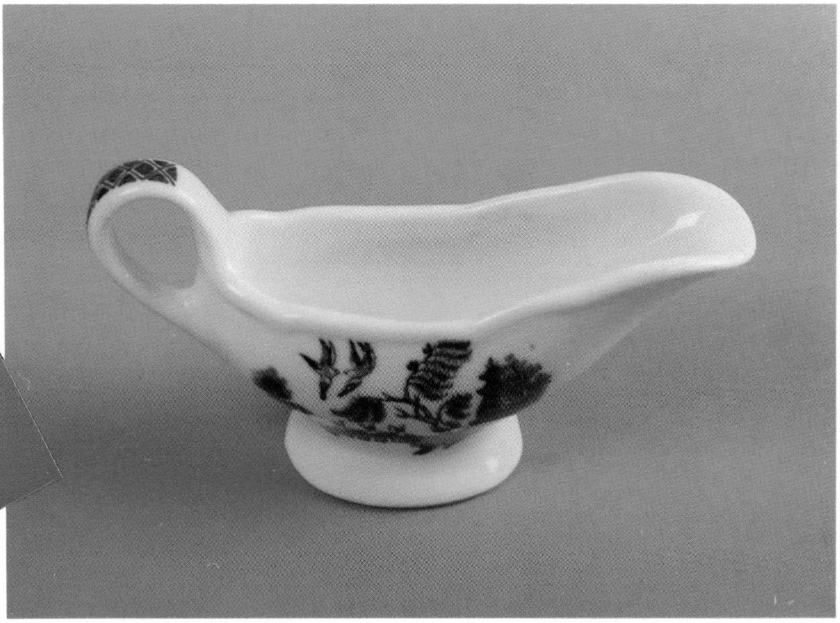

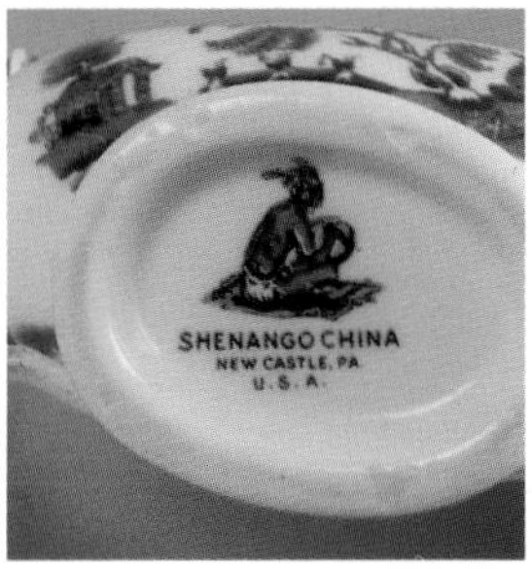

Individual sauce boat by Shenango, 6" high x 3.5" long. Courtesy of Charles and Louise Loehr, Louise's Old Things, Kutztown, PA.

Shenango mark; unusual, in color.

Sewell & Donkin: Impressed mark used by St. Anthony's Pottery in Newcastle-upon-Tyne, Northumberland, betweem 1828-1852.

Anthony Shaw: A firm active in Tunstall, Staffordshire from 1851-1856, and in Burslem, Staffordshire from 1858-c. 1900. Marks include the name Shaw, sometimes with the initial "A" or the name Anthony, in a number of different printed or impressed marks. Around 1882-1898, "& SON" was added to the mark; this was changed to "& CO." around 1898-1900.

Shenango China: A Newcastle, Pennsylvania company, founded in 1901, that made willow for Marshall Field & Co. of Chicago. In 1979, the firm became Anchor Hocking, which still uses Shenango's famous seated Indian mark.

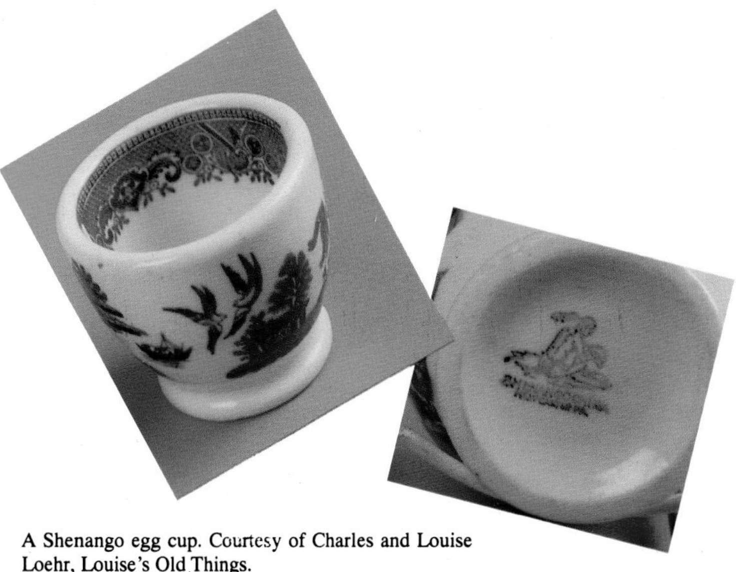

A Shenango egg cup. Courtesy of Charles and Louise Loehr, Louise's Old Things.

Simpsons (Potters) Ltd.: Active in earthenware production at the Elder Works in Cobridge, Staffordshire, beginning in 1944.Marks bear the Simpsons name, along with trade names including "Ambassador Ware," "Solian Ware" (both c. 1944+), and "Mei Kuei [with Chinese lettering]" (c. 1951+), among others.

Samson Smith: Longton, c. 1881.

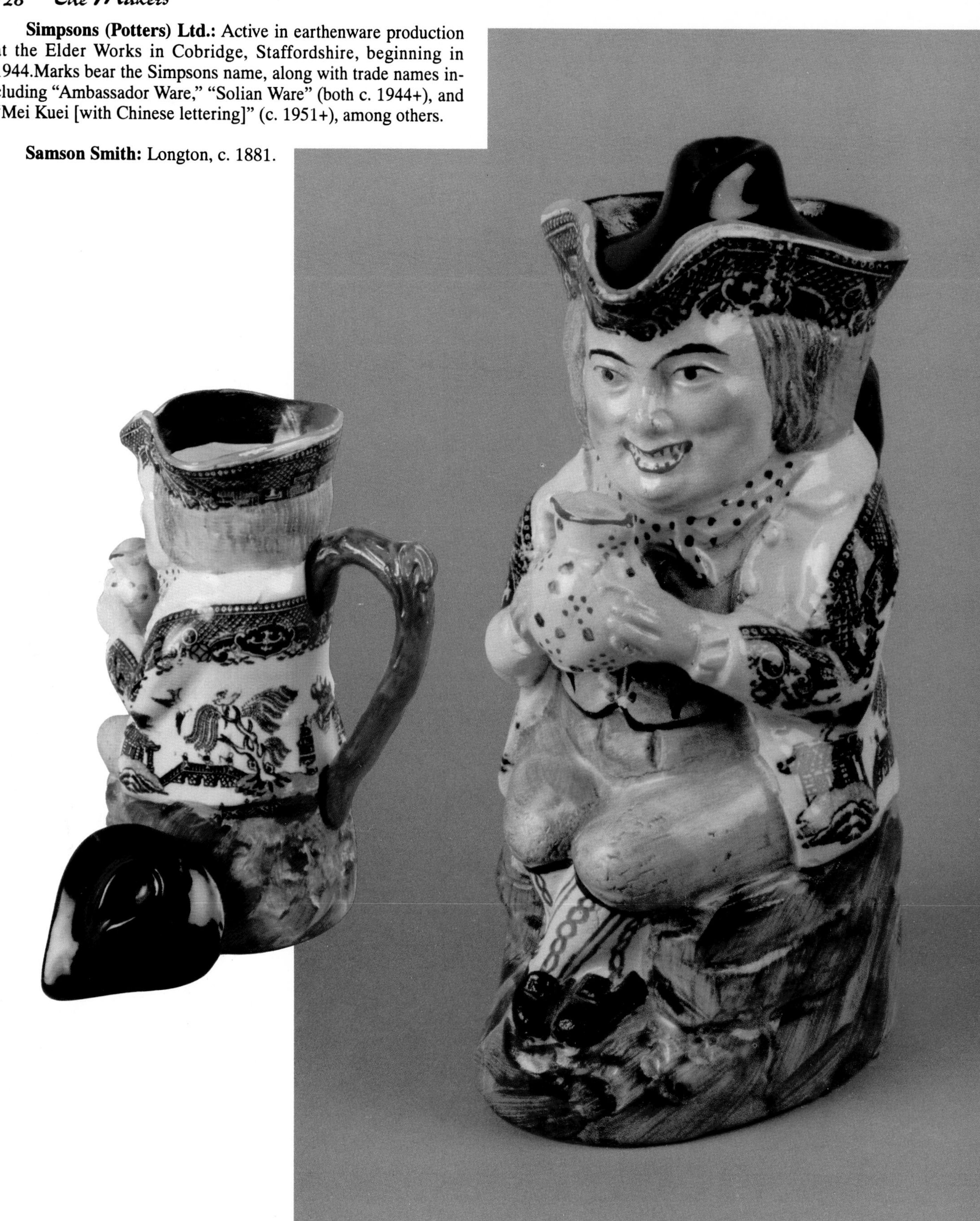

A Toby jug, 1881, 8.5" high. It is unusual to find a Toby that still has its hat-shaped lid. This one has the embossed bottom-mark "Samson Smith Longton 1881". From the collection of Peter and Susan Steelman, Mystic, CT.

William Smith (& Co.): Occupied the Stafford Pottery in Stockton-on-Tees, Yorkshire, c. 1825-1855, producing earthenwares. Marks frequently include the impressed initials "W. S. & CO." In *British Pottery & Porcelain* (pp. 583 and 734), Godden notes that they are notorious for using "WEDGWOOD," "WEDGEWOOD," and even "VEDGWOOD" impressions as well, with or without the qualifying "W. S. & Co's."

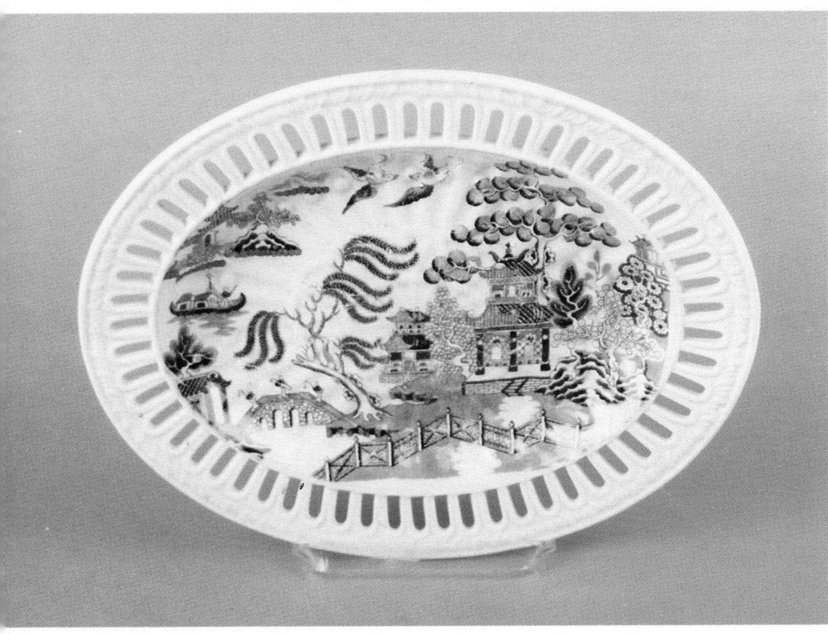

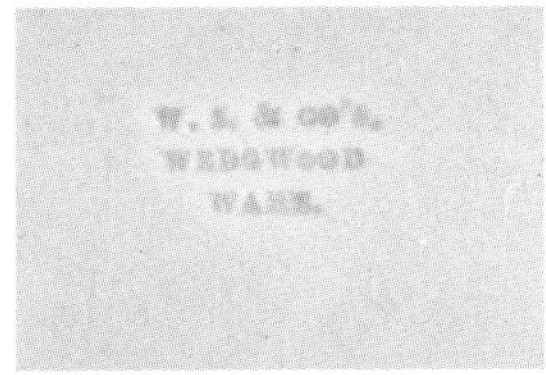

An oval platter in black-printed pearlware, 10.5" x 8.25", marked "W S & Co's Wedgwood Ware". From the collection of Peter and Susan Steelman, Mystic, CT.

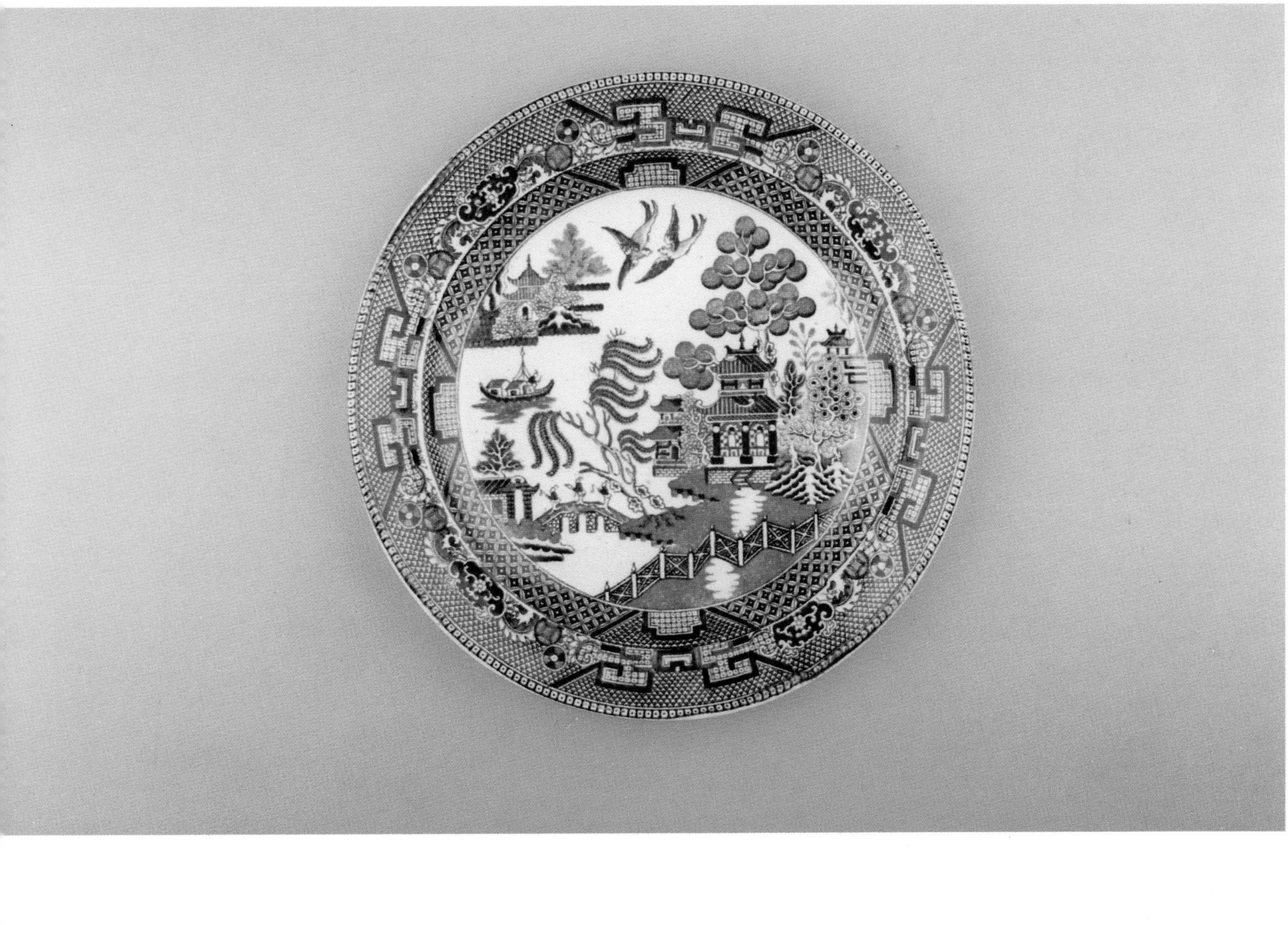

Pearlware plate by Wm. Smith & Co. Marked with impressed "Wedgwood" and "W. S. & Co's." The rim has a transfer-printed mark reading "Stafford Stone China No. 11." Courtesy of Rita Entmacher Cohen.

Société Cérámique: Produced porcelain in Maestricht, Holland, from 1863 until after 1887.

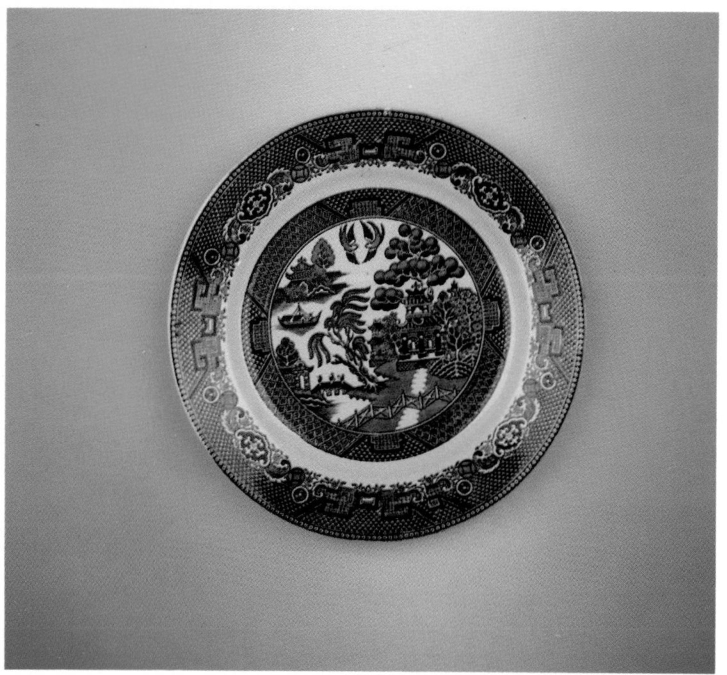

A plate, 9.375" diam., from the Société Cérámique, Maestricht, Holland. Courtesy of Rita Entmacher Cohen.

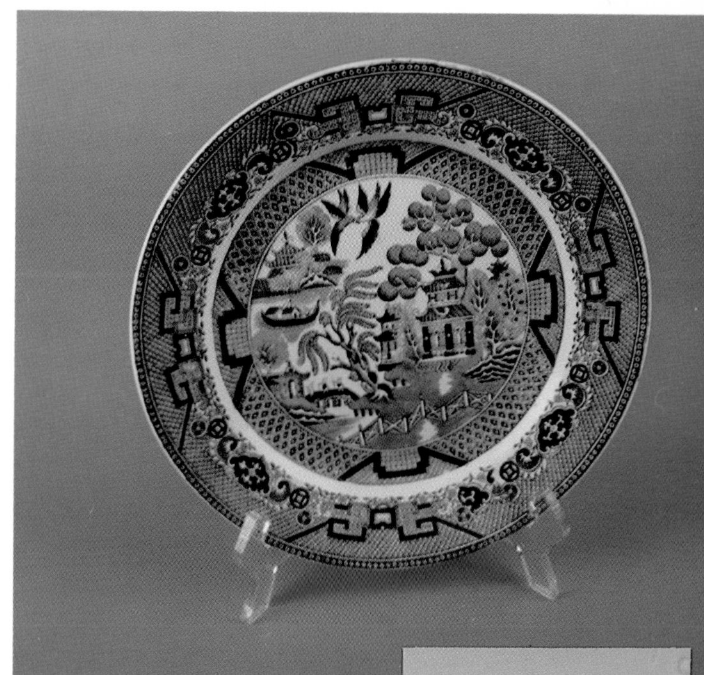

A green Willow plate made by the Société in Maestricht, Holland, 9" diam. From the collection of Peter and Susan Steelman, Mystic, CT.

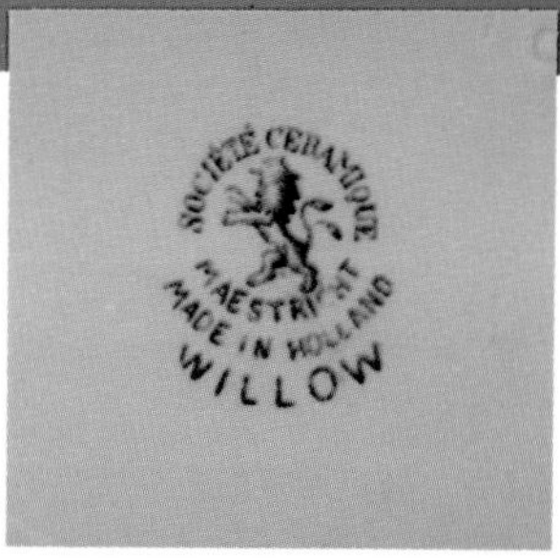

A covered server by Maestricht, 5" high x 11" wide. Courtesy of Charles and Louise Loehr, Louise's Old Things, Kutztown, PA.

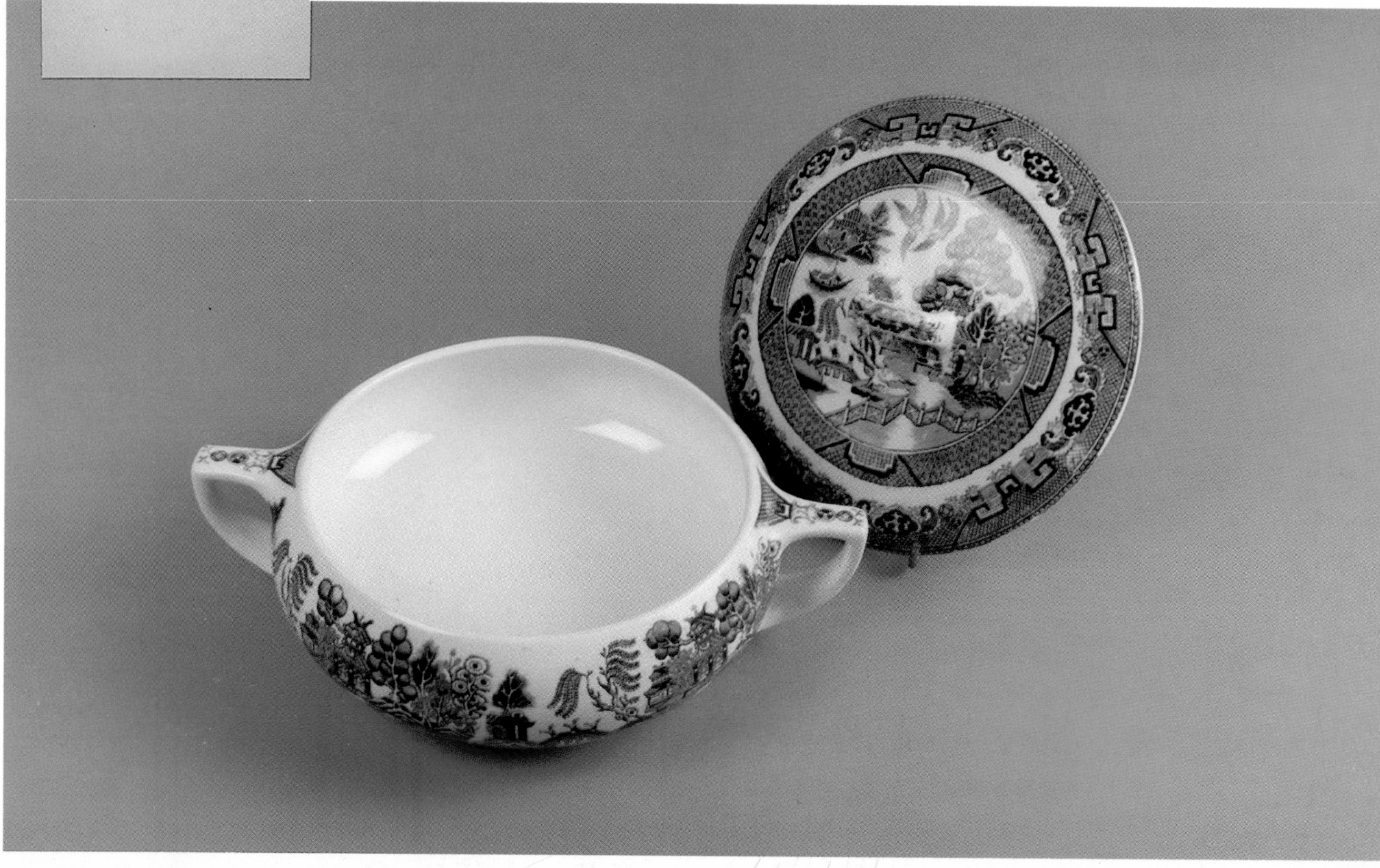

The Southern Potteries, Inc.: Operated from 1920-1957 in Erwin, Tennessee, producing wares in their "Blue Ridge" line. The company marked most of their works, and made a Willow pattern with a small central design and no border.

Spode: see Copeland/Spode

St. Amand: A French pottery manufacturer which marked its wares with a variety of crown and shield motifs.

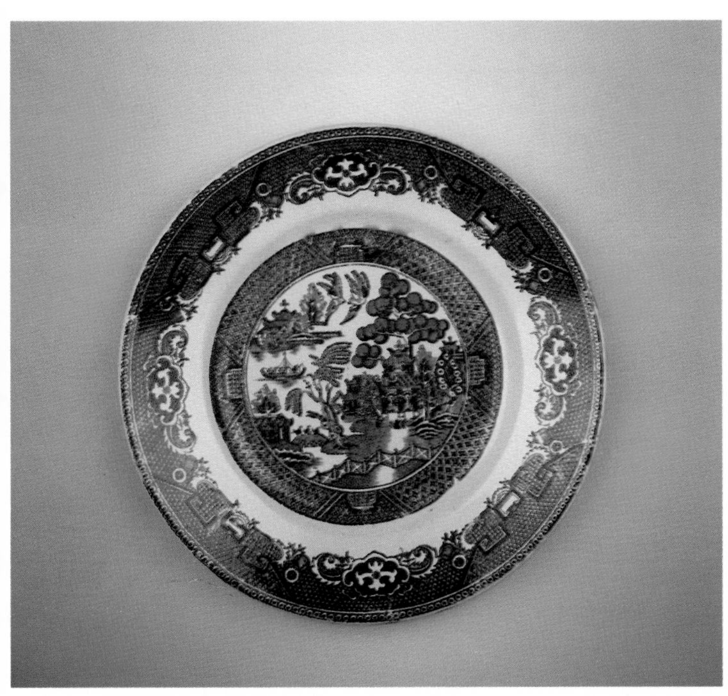

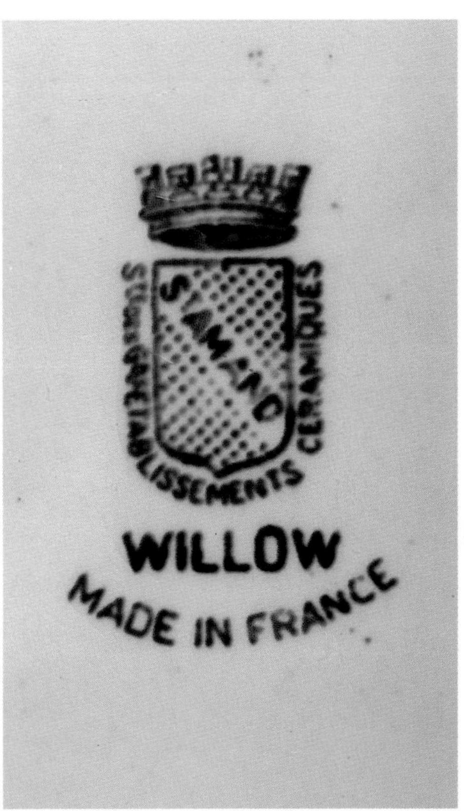

A willow-pattern plate from St. Amand, France, 9.5" diam. Courtesy of Rita Entmacher Cohen.

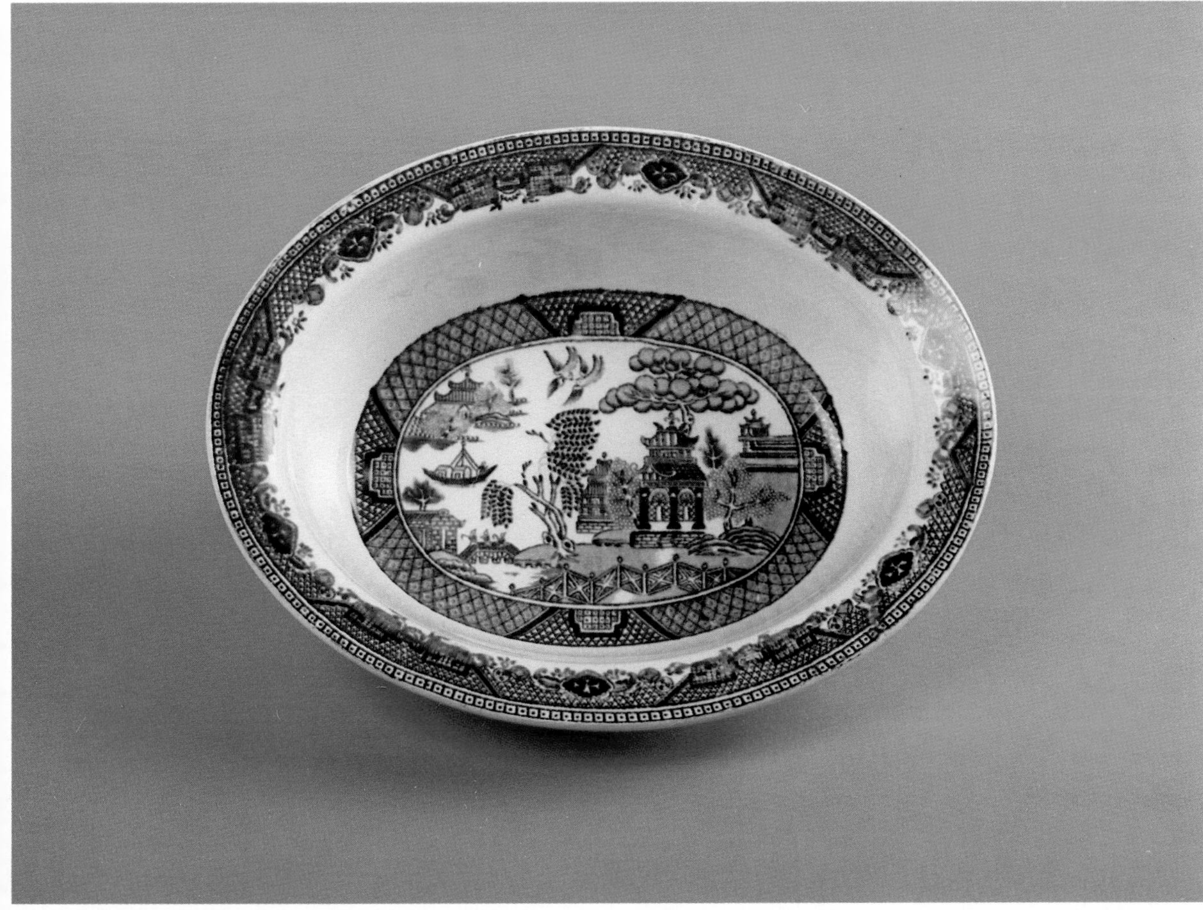

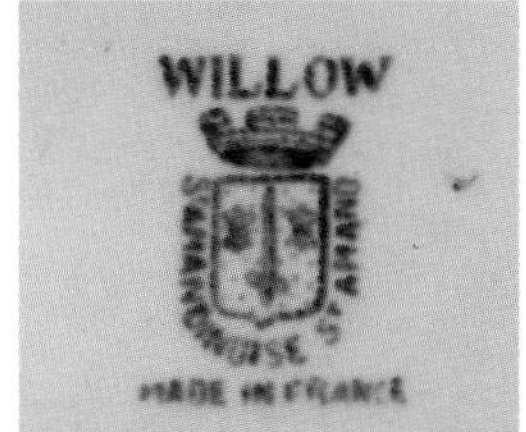

A French bowl by St. Amand, 2" high x 9" wide. Courtesy of Charles and Louise Loehr, Louise's Old Things, Kutztown, PA.

Star China Co.: Active at the Atlas Works and other addresses in Longton, Staffordshire, c. 1900-1919. A variety of marks all contain a star logo, the initials "S. C. Co." or monogram "C.S.C.," or the trade name "Paragon."

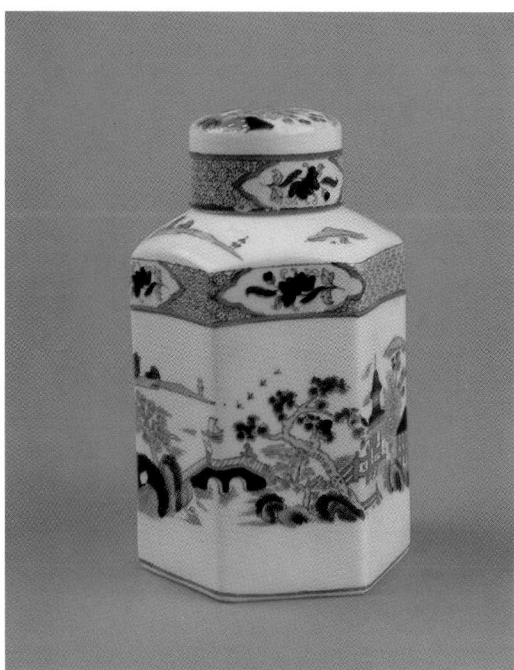

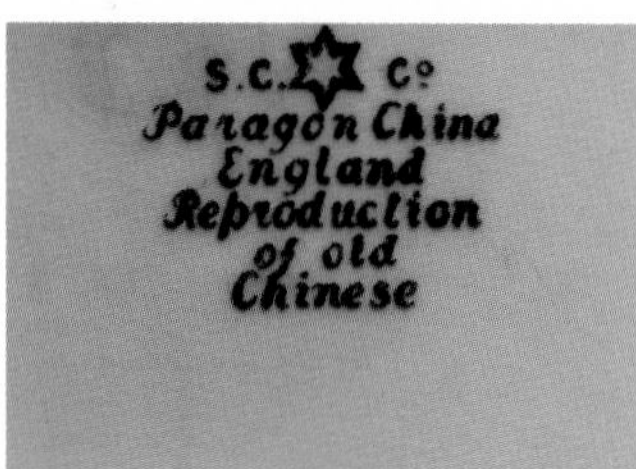

A polychrome tea caddy, made by Star China Co., Atlas Works, Longton, Staffordshire, 1900-1919, 4.625". Marked "Paragon China, England. Reproduction of old Chinese." Courtesy of Rita Entmacher Cohen.

Andrew Stevenson: A potter working in Cobridge, Staffordshire, c. 1816-1830. Marks frequently read "STEVENSON" or "A. STEVENSON,", sometimes with an impressed galleon logo or encircled crown. Blue printed wares used a printed banner and crown logo reading "Nankeen Semi China."

R. Stevenson, Alcock & Williams: A Cobridge, Staffordshire pottery opened c. 1825 to produce earthenwares. They used printed name marks for their wares.

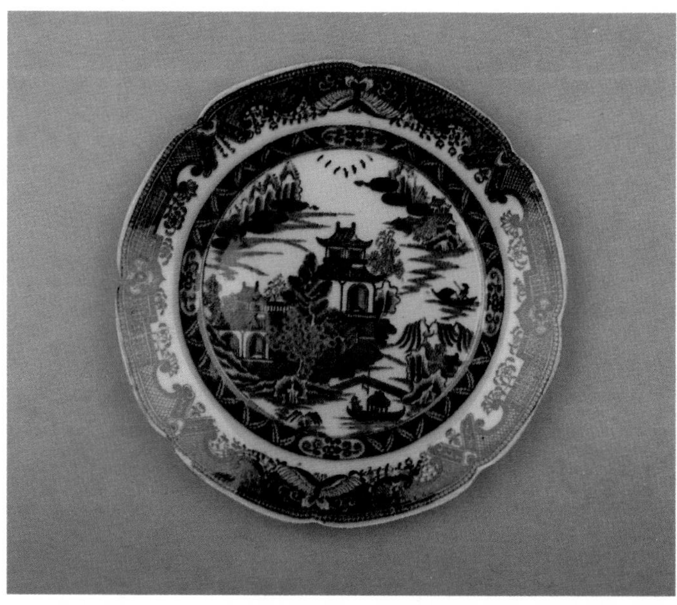

A small pearlware plate by Stevenson's, c. 1795, 6.5" diam. Courtesy of Rita Entmacher Cohen.

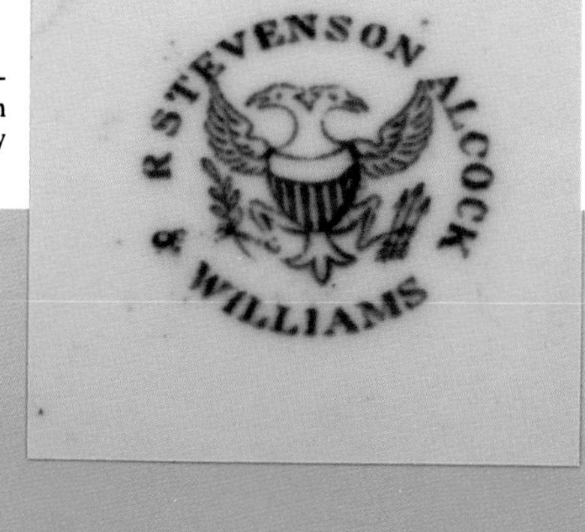

A cup (no handle) and saucer, from R. Stevenson Alcock & Williams. Courtesy of Rita Entmacher Cohen.

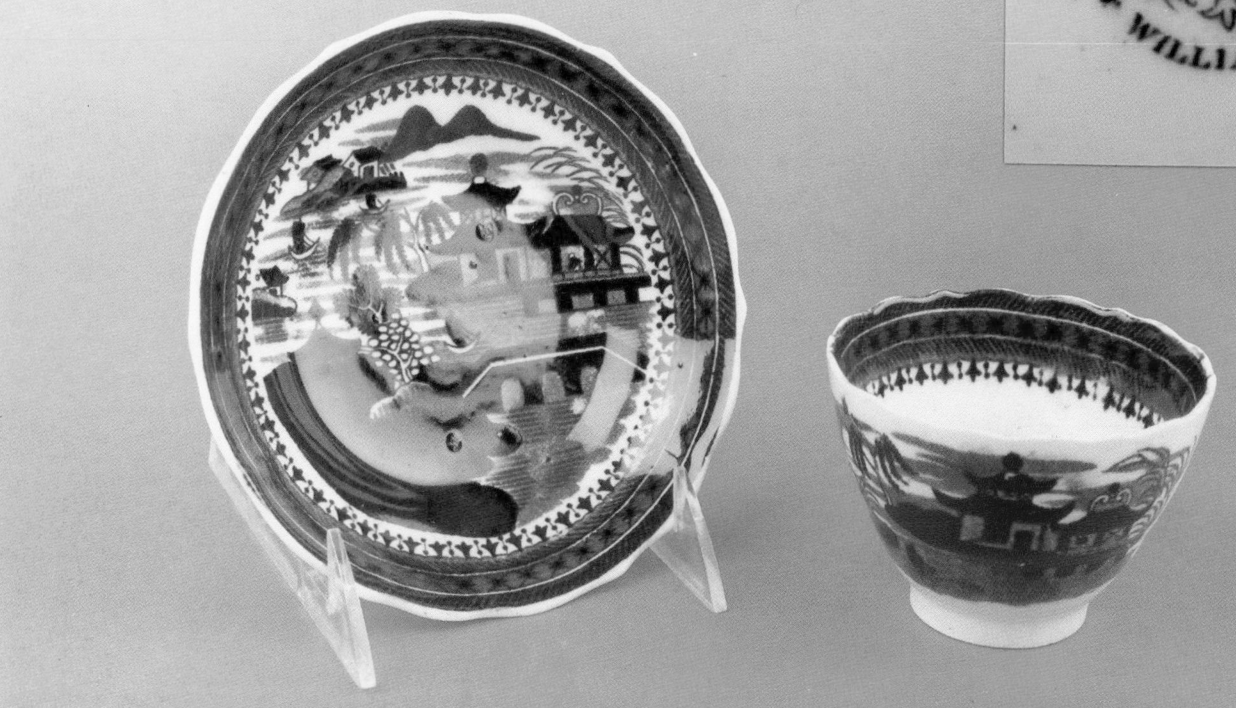

John Steventon & Sons, Ltd.: Operated in the Royal Pottery in Burslem, Staffordshire, from 1923 through the present (though no longer producing dishware). Wares are marked with a crown logo, the company's full name and location, and the trade name "VENTON WARE" or "ROYAL VENTON WARE."

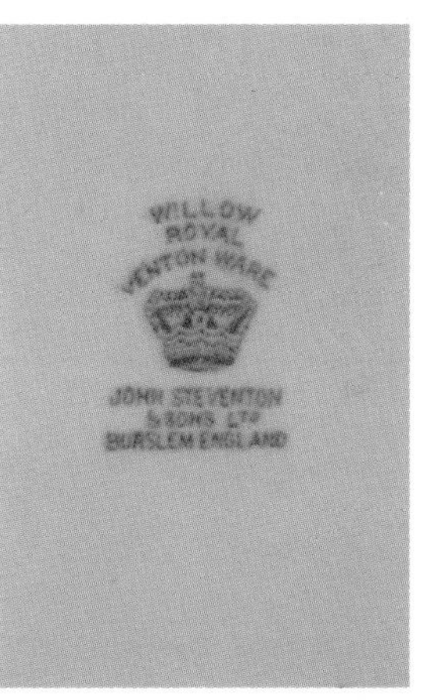

A light green, rectangular "Venton Ware" platter, 11" x 19", from John Steventon & Sons, Ltd, Burselm, England. Willow Royal Venton Ware. From the collection of Peter and Susan Steelman, Mystic, CT.

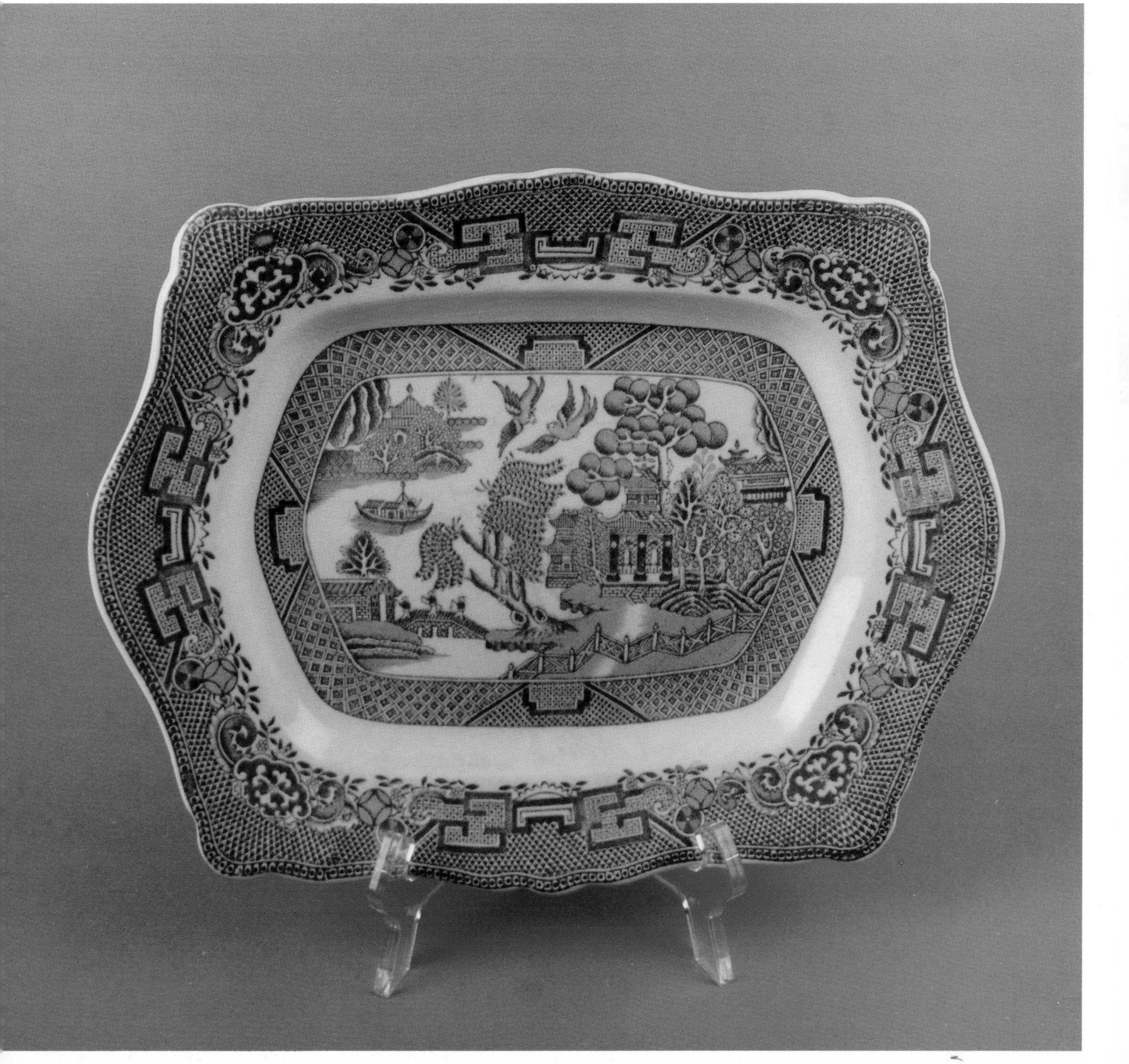

Sunderland: An area to the south of Durham, important in English pottery from the 18th century. In the 19th century they became a major potting district, with more than 15 potteries in operation, including Deptford or Ball's Pottery, Low Ford or Dawson's Pottery, North Hylton Pottery, Southwick Pottery, and Sunderland or Garrison Pottery. The area's wares bore a great deal of transfer printing. Maling and Phillips are among the potteries of this district that produced marked Willow.

Swansea: The Cambrian Pottery (1783-1870) and the Glamorgan Pottery (1813-1838) operated in this Welsh town, with significant interaction and many changes of ownership (and therefore company names). Transfer printing began here in the 1790s.

At the Cambrian Pottery, "SWANSEA" was initially impressed on the wares. From 1802-1810, Haynes & Lewis Dillwyn marked their Cambrian wares "DILLWYN & CO." In 1811, Timothy Bevington joined Dillwyn, and much blue-printed ware was manufactured, some bearing the "DILLWYN & CO." mark, occasionally with "SWANSEA" as well. In 1817, Bevington took over, trading under the name T. & J. Bevington & Co. In 1821 the "& Co." was omited. In 1824, Dillwyn returned, and "Dillwyn & Co." was reinstated. In 1850, the company was acquired by Evans & Glasson. In 1862, the name was changed to "D. J. Evans & Co.," under which name it operated until the pottery closed in 1870.

The Glamorgan Pottery was founded in 1813 by Baker, Bevans & Irwin, under which name they conducted business. In 1819 the company began to trade under the Glamorgan Pottery name, until they closed in 1838. Marks include "BAKER, BEVINS & IRWIN," "B. B. & I.," and "B. B. & Co.," and later "G. P. & Co."

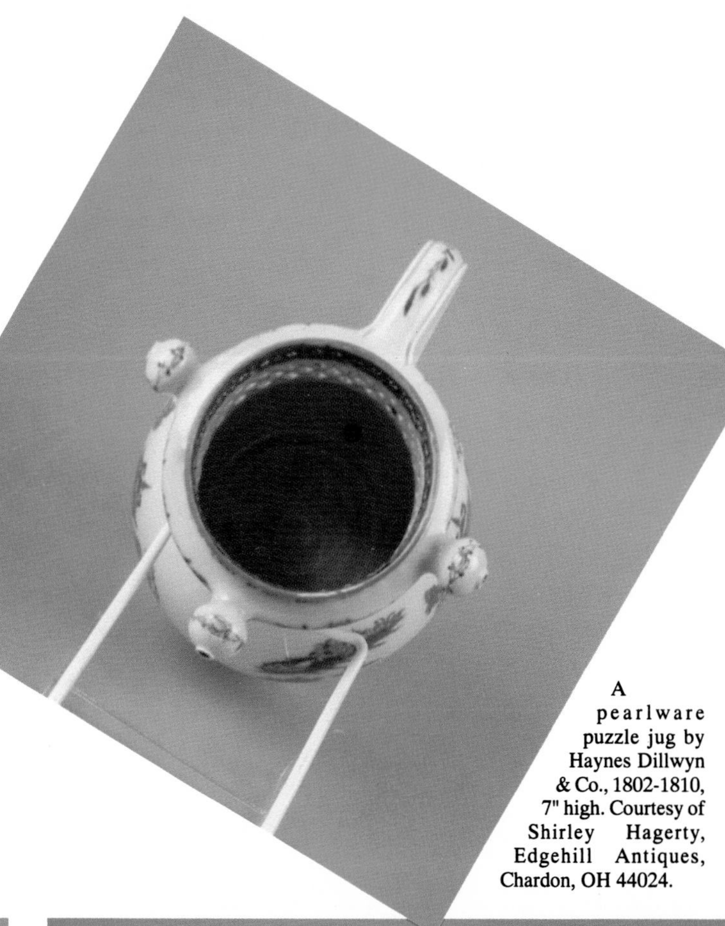

A pearlware puzzle jug by Haynes Dillwyn & Co., 1802-1810, 7" high. Courtesy of Shirley Hagerty, Edgehill Antiques, Chardon, OH 44024.

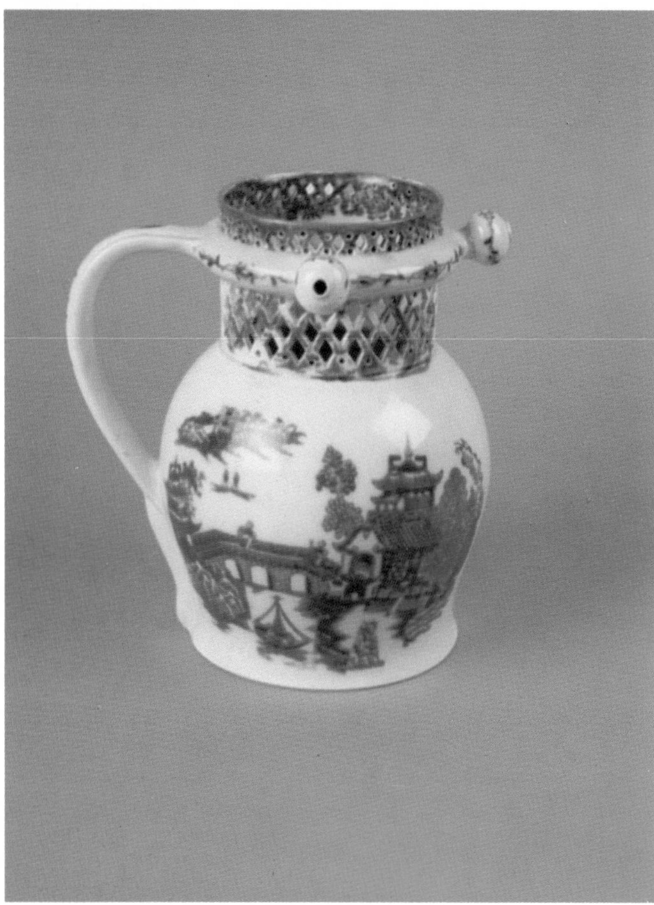

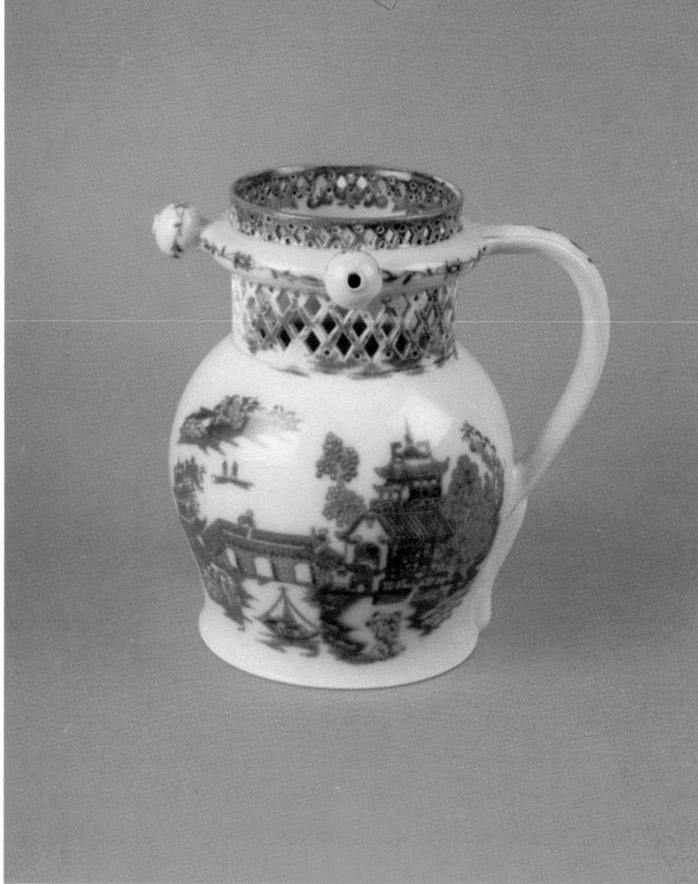

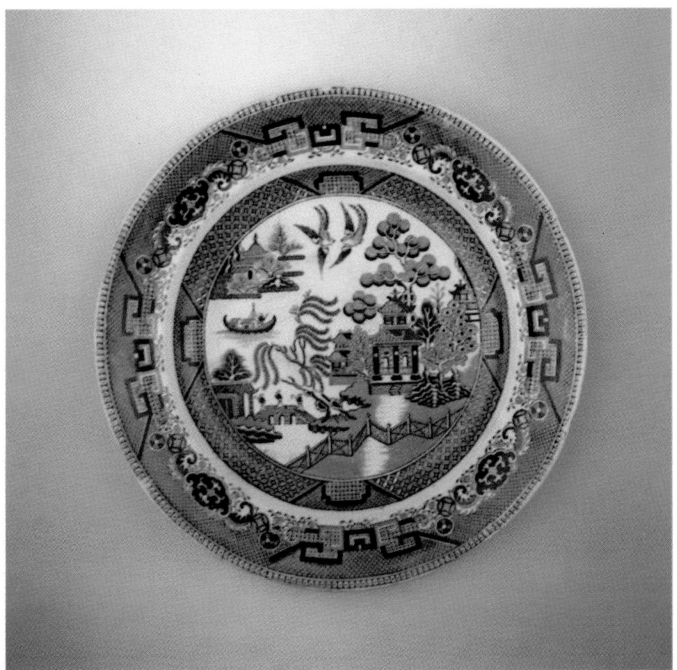

Pearlware plate by Dillwyn, 1824-1850, 9". Marked "Dillwyn, Swansea." Coutesy of Rita Entmacher Cohen.

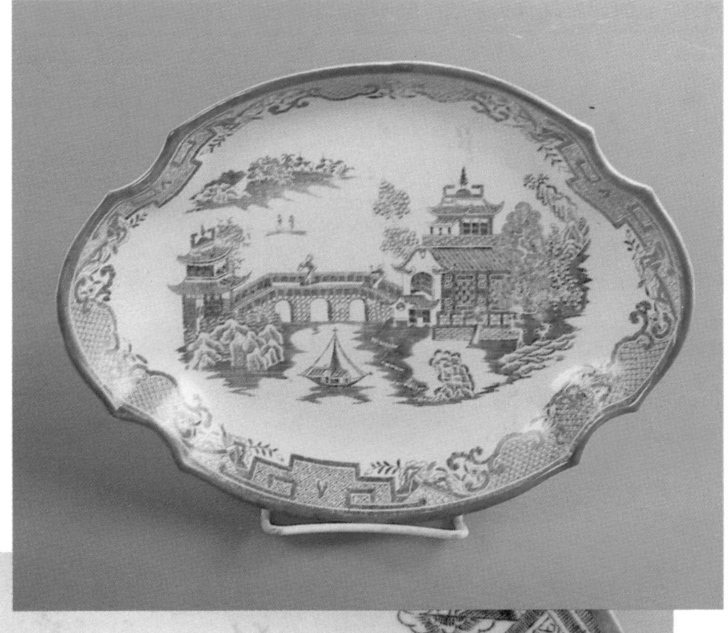

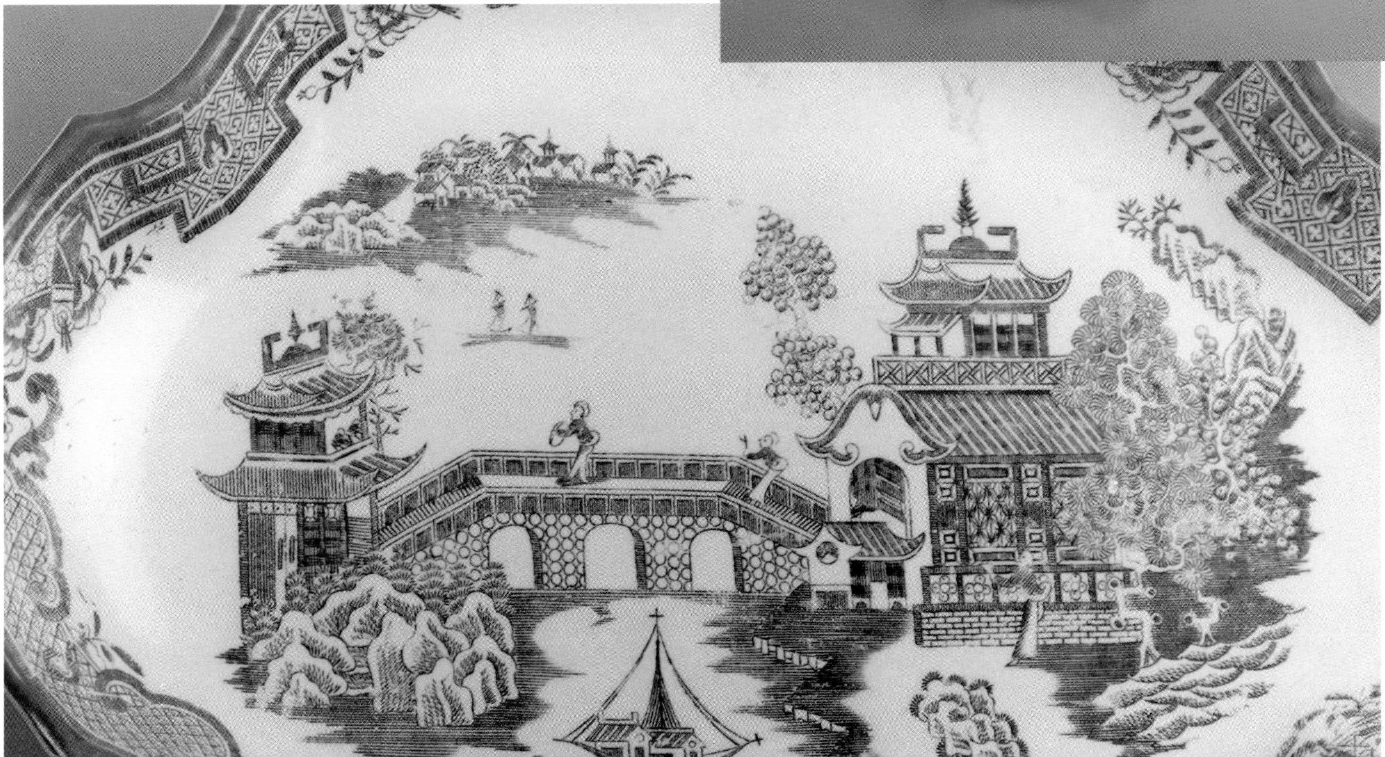

An oval serving dish by Swansea, c. 1800, 9.75" wide. The printing, though brown, was nonetheless done on blue-tinged pearlware. Courtesy of Charles and Louise Loehr, Louise's Old Things, Kutztown PA.

Swinnertons Ltd.: Active at various addresses in Hanley, Staffordshire from 1906. Most marks bear the Swinnerton's name.

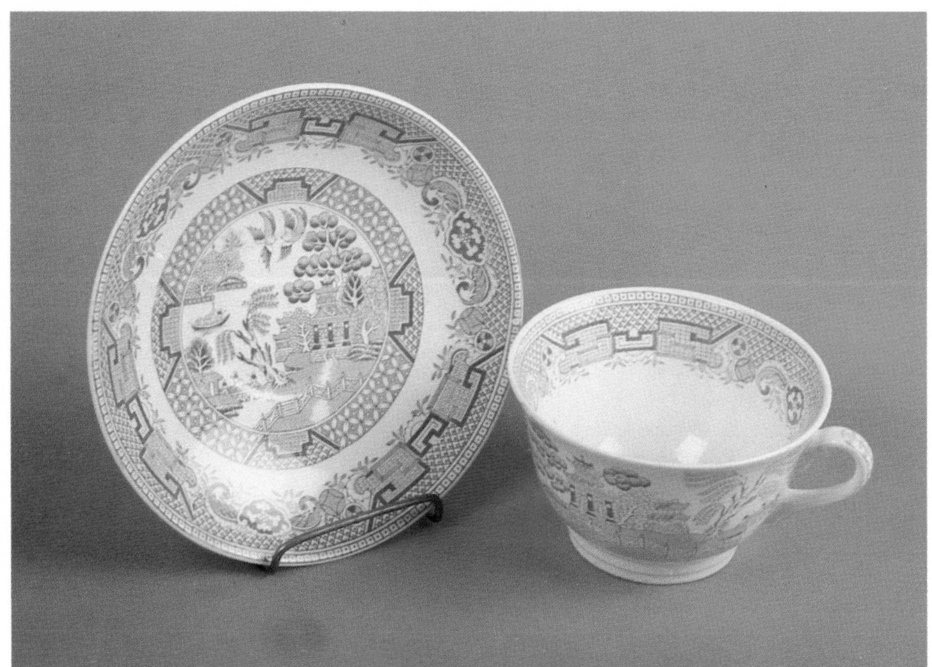

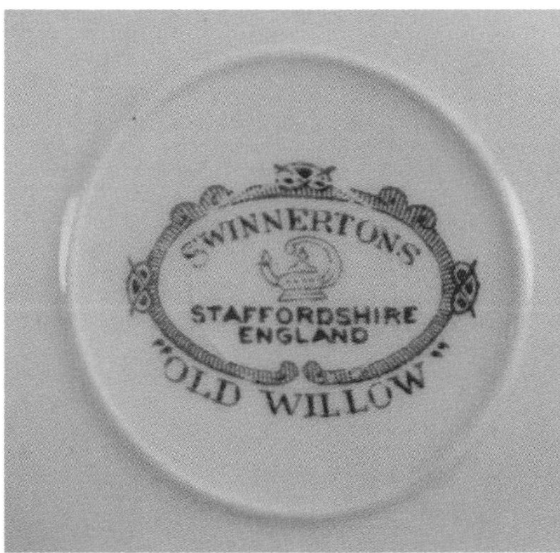

Swinnerton's teacups and saucers in pink Willow. Courtesy of Charles and Louise Loehr, Louise's Old Things, Kutztown, PA.

John Tams (& Son) (Ltd.): Operated in Longton, Staffordshire at the Crown Pottery starting in 1875, producing earthenwares. Marks included a trademark with the initials "J. T." or "J. Tams," becoming "J. T. & S." between 1903-1912, when the company was John Tams & Son. In 1912, the company was re-named John Tams Ltd., and various marks were used.

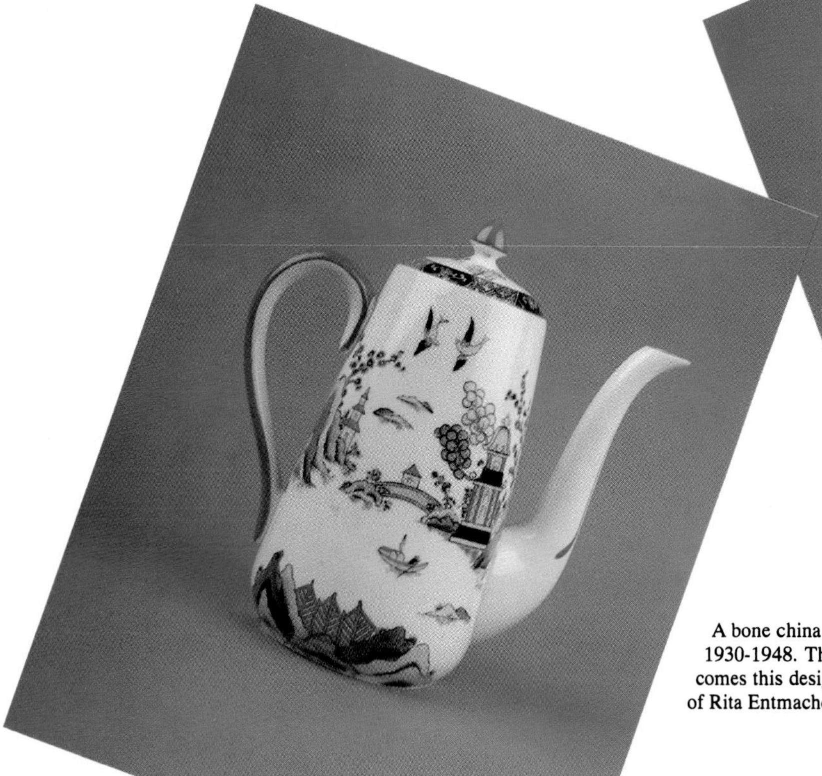

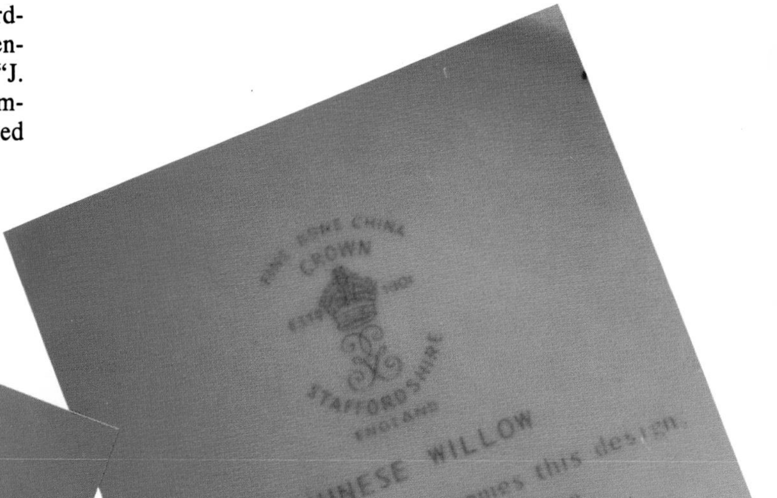

A bone china coffee from the Crown Pottery, Staffordshire, 1930-1948. The bottom mark reads: "From Ancient China comes this design symbolic of love and the home." Courtesy of Rita Entmacher Cohen.

A Crown Ware egg cup, 2.5". With a silver screw-on lid. Courtesy of Rita Entmacher Cohen.

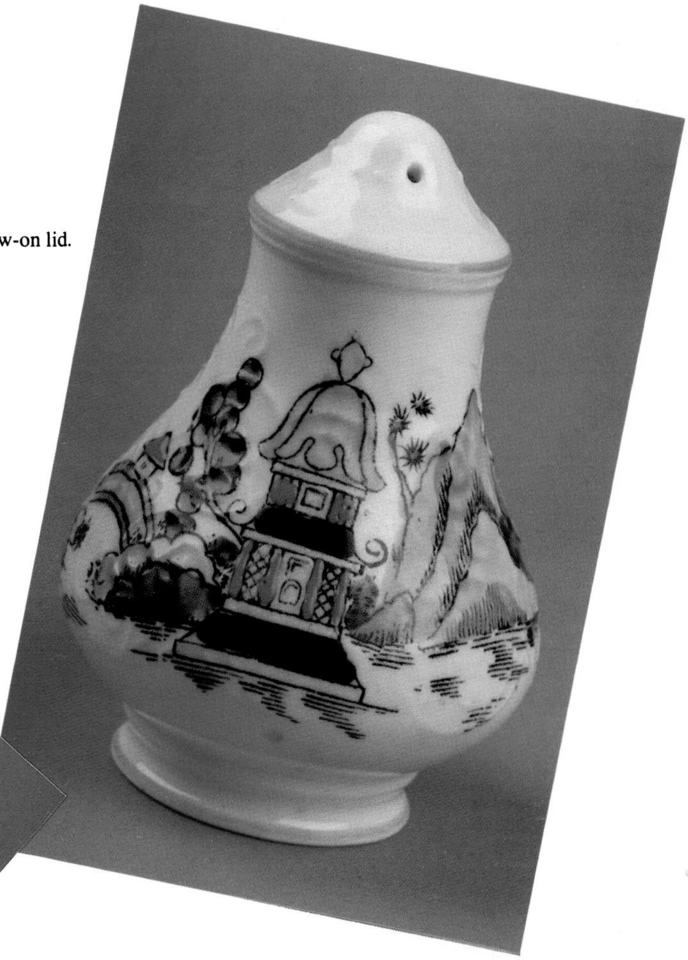

A polychrome pitcher from the Crown Pottery, 1930-1948, 4.5". Courtesy of Rita Entmacher Cohen.

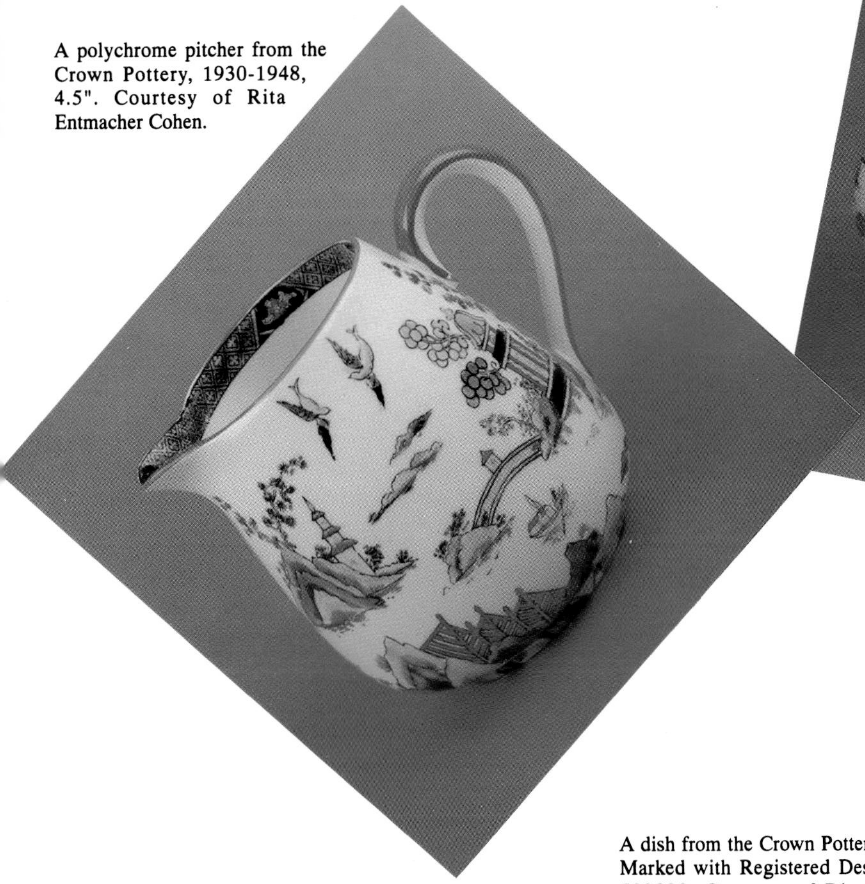

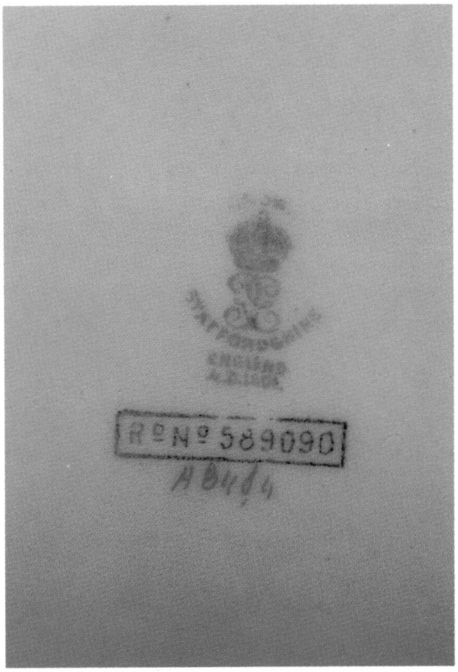

A dish from the Crown Pottery, 10" wide. Marked with Registered Design number 589090. Courtesy of Rita Entmacher Cohen.

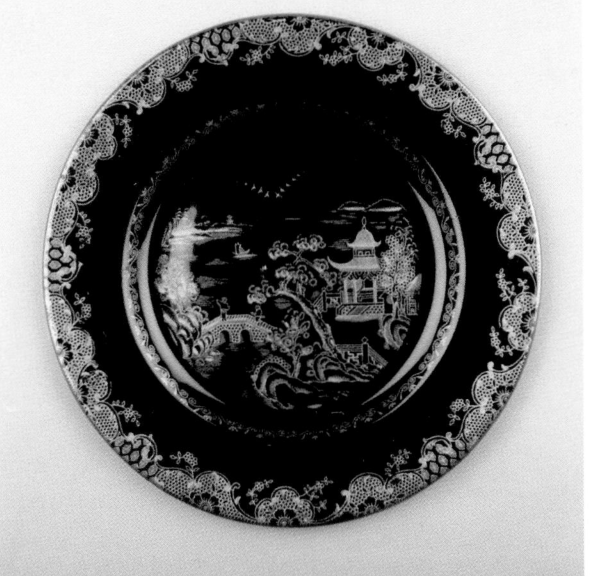

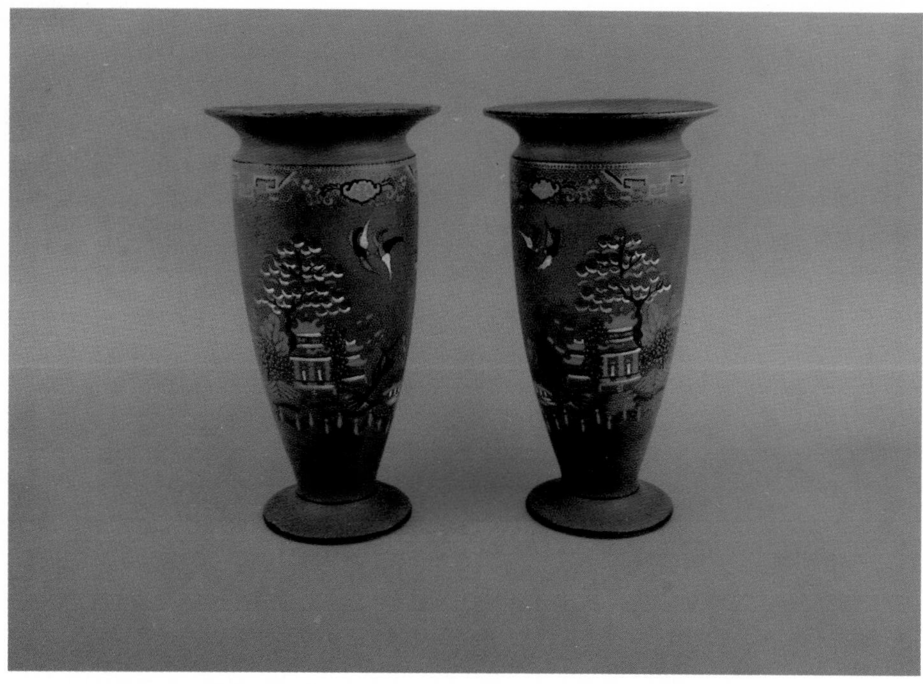

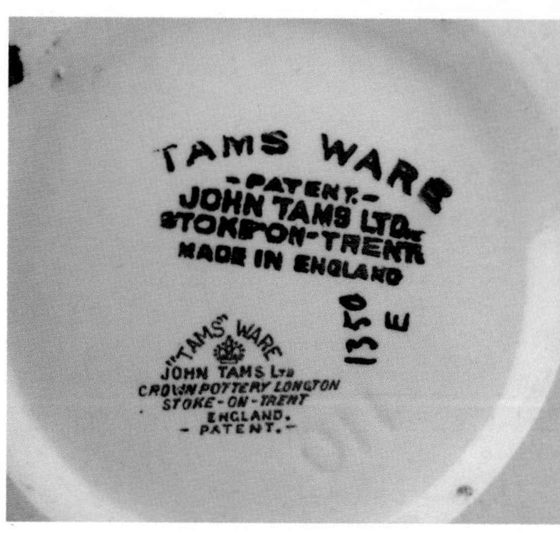

A pair of vases by John Tams, Ltd., from the Crown Pottery, Longton, Stoke-on-Trent, England, yellow transfer-printing and polychrome paint on a blue backgound, 10" high. Marked "Tams Ware, Patent," and impressed "110". Courtesy of Rita Entmacher Cohen.

Taylor & Tunnicliffe: Operated by Michael Tunnicliffe in Tunstall, Staffordshire. The firm made earthenware figures from 1828-1835. Noted is a mark reading "TUNNICLIFF TUNSTALL."

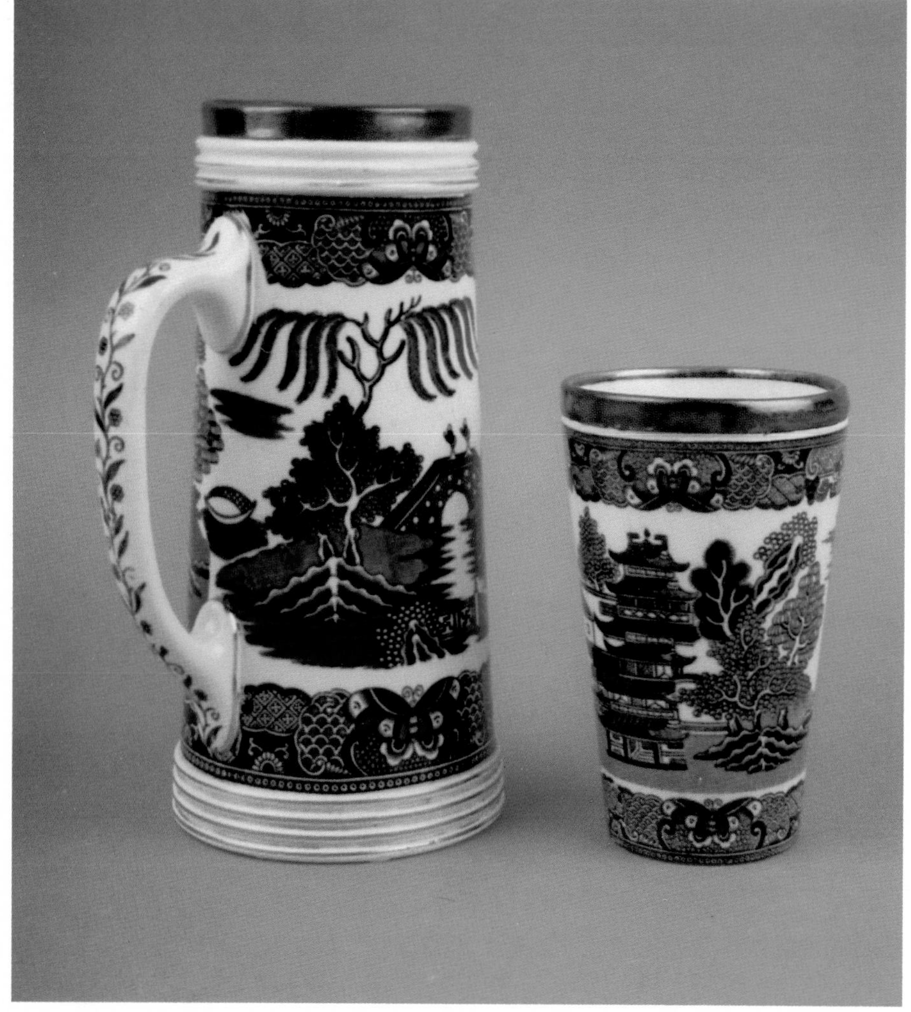

A cup and stein (two-piece) by Taylor & Tunnicliffe, c. 1870, 8.25". Monogram mark on back. Courtesy of Rita Entmacher Cohen.

John Thomson: A Glasgow, Scotland firm, active in the Annfield Pottery from c. 1816-1884 (or 1896). Marks read "J. T.," "J. T./ANNFIELD," "J. T. & SONS" (after 1866), "J. T. & SONS/ GLASGOW," or "J. THOMSON & SONS/GLASGOW."

George Townsend: Active at several addresses in Longton, Staffordshire, c. 1850-1864, producing earthenwares. Wares are marked "G. TOWNSEND."

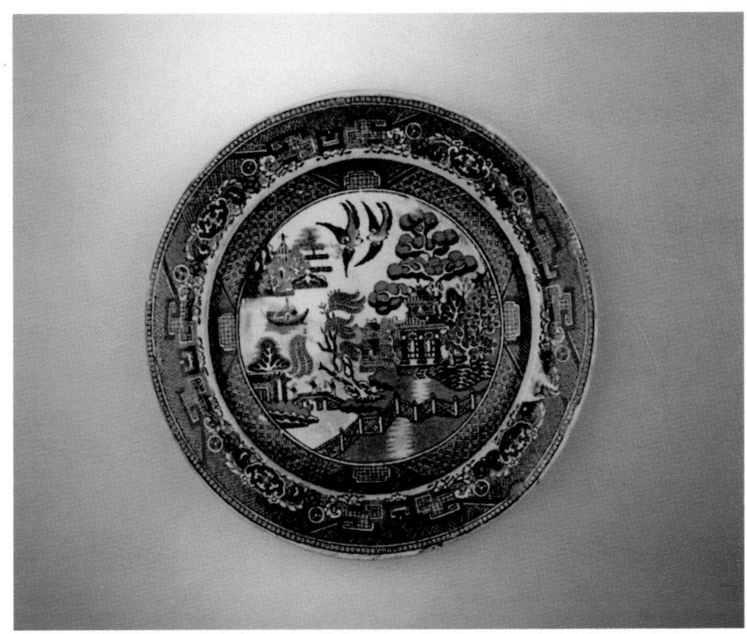

Earthenware plate from G. Townsend, Longton, 1850-1864, 9.125". Courtesy of Rita Entmacher Cohen.

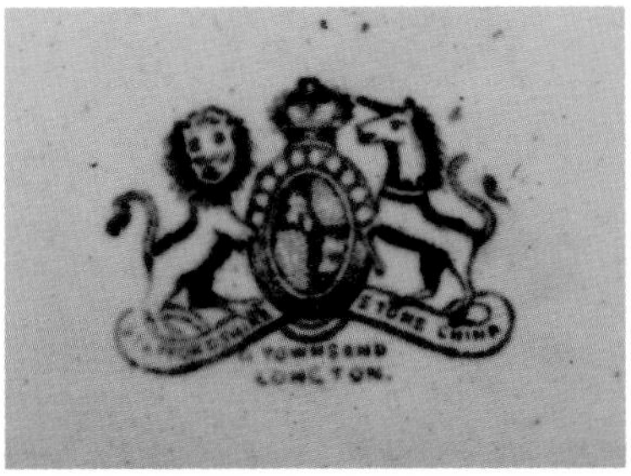

Tremblese Godley: no information available.

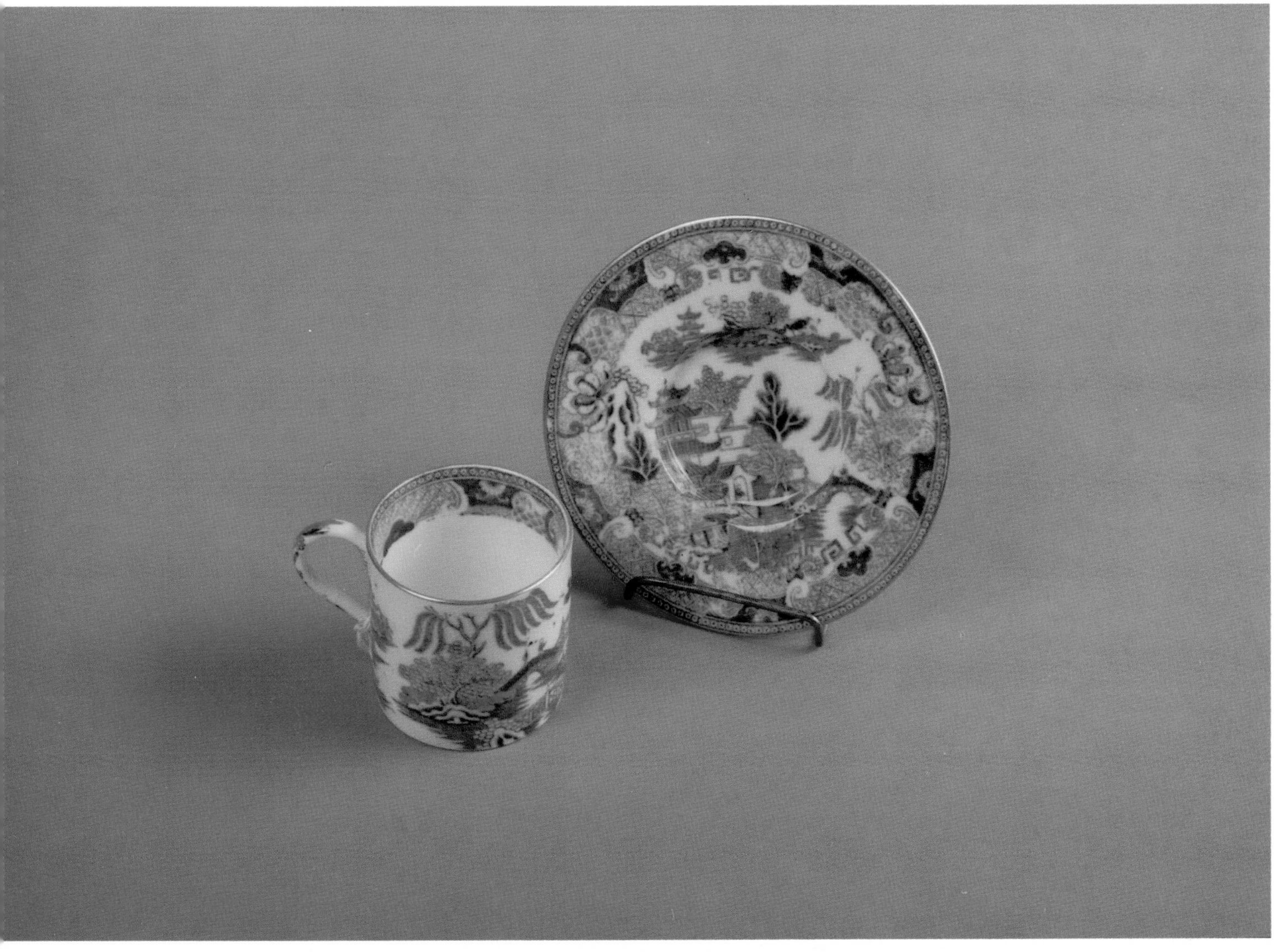

A demitasse cup and saucer by Tremblese Godley, c. 1850, 2.25" high x 4.75" diam. (cup). Impressed "GODLEY" on the bottom of the saucers. Courtesy of Charles and Louise Loehr, Louise's Old Things, Kutztown, PA.

Venton Ware: see John Steventon & Sons

James Vernon: Active in Burslem, Staffordshire, from 1860-1880, producing earthenwares. Marks generally bear the "J. V." initials; after c. 1875, "& S[on]" was added.

Walker China Co.: A Bedford, Ohio company that has produced vitreous porcelain and tablewares with its script "Walker China/VITRIFIED" mark from 1923 until the present.

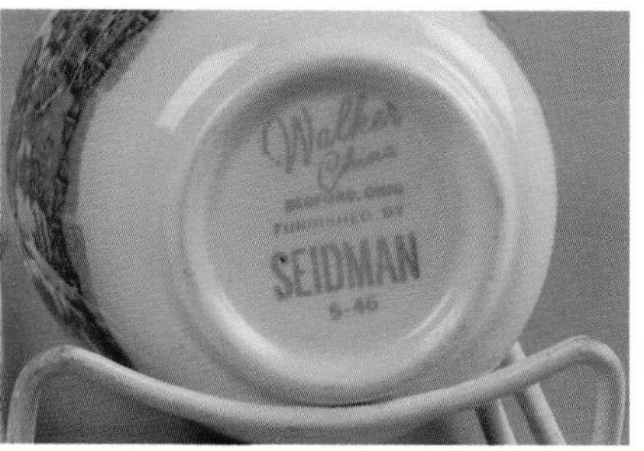

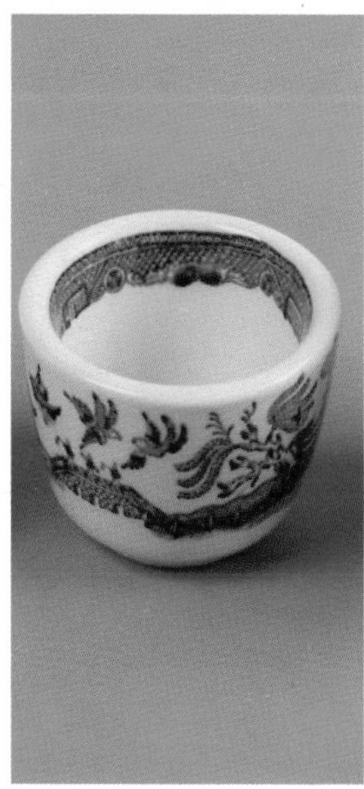

A small cup by Walker. Courtesy of Charles and Louise Loehr, Louise's Old Things.

Wallace China: A Los Angeles pottery; made wares marked "Ye Olde Willow."

A brown Willow plate by Wallace, a Los Angeles potter, marked "Ye Olde Willow," 9" diam. Courtesy of Charles and Louise Loehr, Louise's Old Things, Kutztown, PA.

John Warburton: Active at Hot Lane, Cobridge, Staffordshire from c. 1802-1825, producing earthenwares, creamwares, etc. Used an impressed "WARBURTON" mark.

Wardle & Co.: Operated out of the Washington Works, Hanley, Staffordshire, 1871-1935. Around 1871, they began using an impressed "WARDLE" mark; after 1891, "ENGLAND" was added to this. Other later marks were generally printed, not impressed.

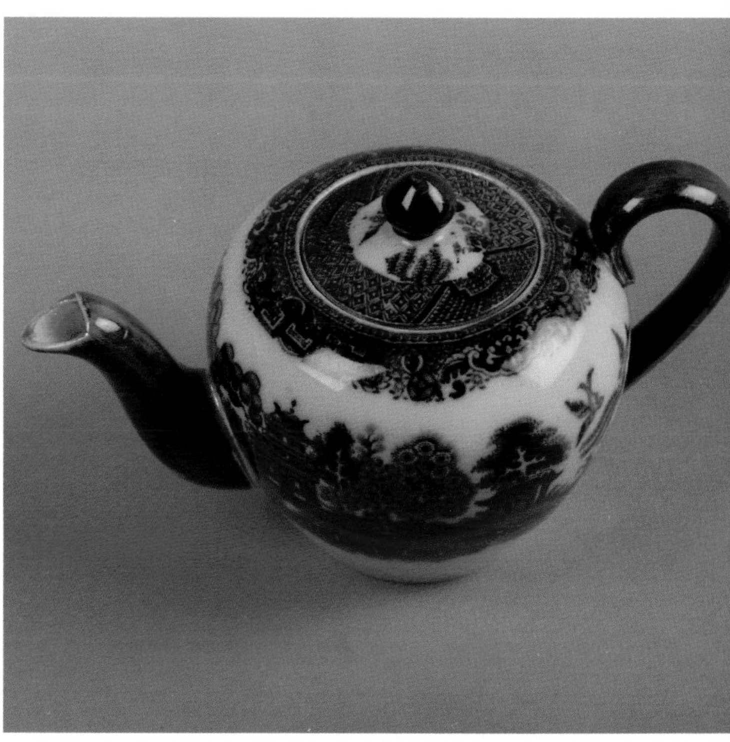

A miniature teapot by Wardle, impressed "MADE IN ENGLAND," 1821, 3.5" high x 6" long. Courtesy of Charles and Louise Loehr, Louise's Old Things, Kutztown, PA.

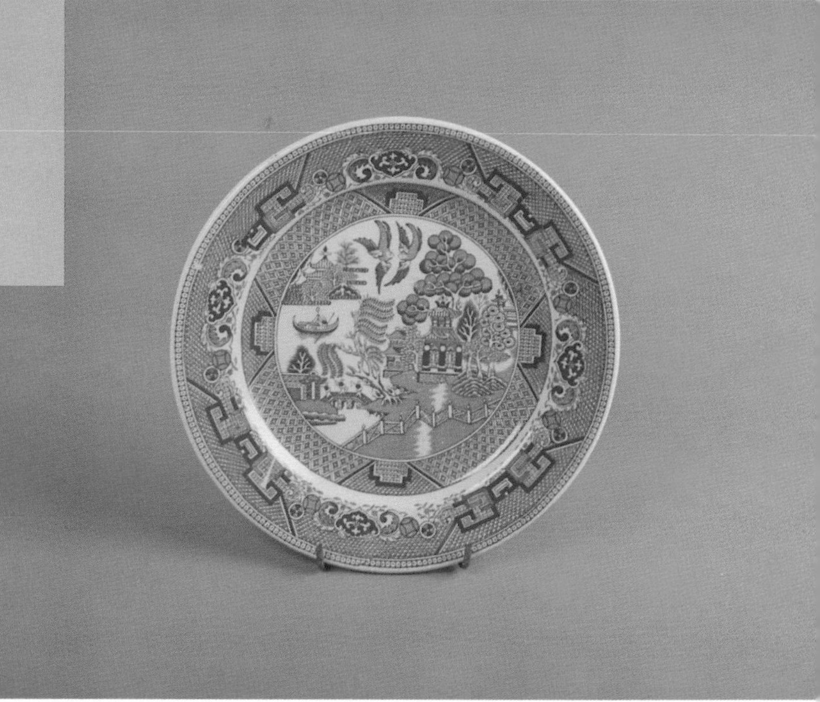

Washington: A Willow pattern was produced under this label, marked with a cabin between two trees.

J.H. Weatherby & Son: Began activity in 1891 at the Falcon Pottery in Hanley, England. Marks include "J. H. W. & SONS," frequently with a pattern name, the name of the Falcon works, and (beginning in 1936) a scroll reading "WEATHERBYWARE."

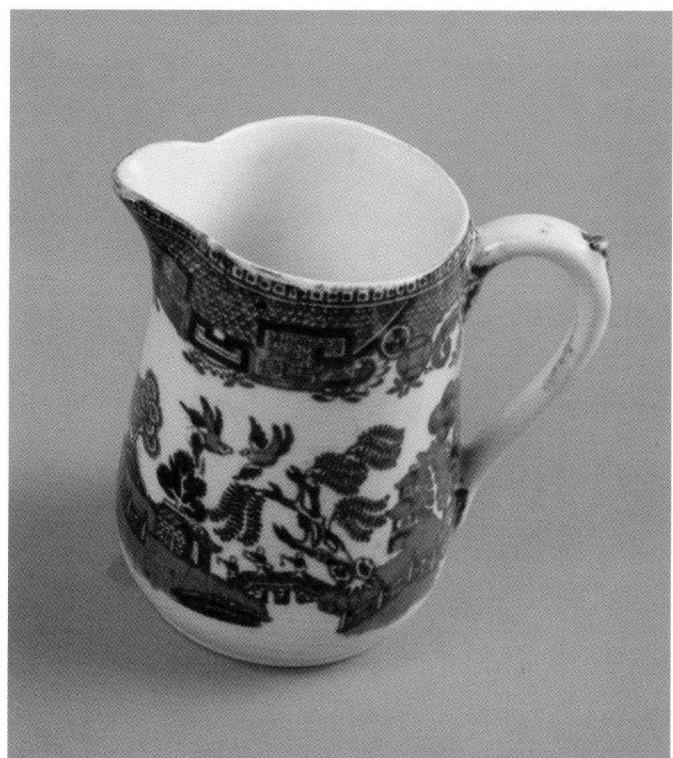

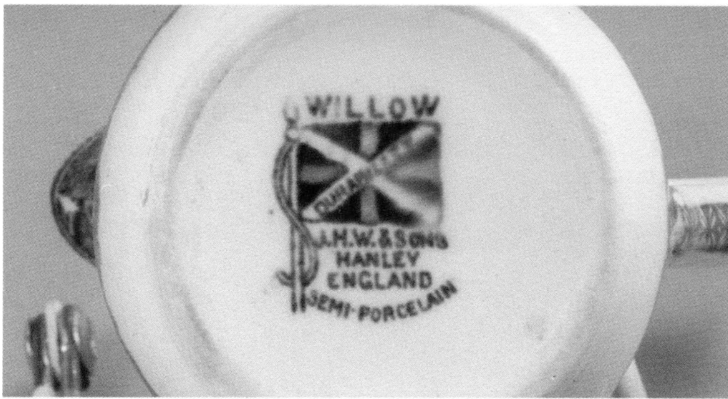

A creamer by J.H. Weatherby & Son, c. 1892, 3/75" high. Courtesy of Charles and Louise Loehr, Louise's Old Things, Kutztown, PA.

Wedgwood & Co. Ltd: The famous Wedgwood & Co. was founded by Josiah Wedgewood in 1759, in Burslem, Staffordshire; in 1769 he opened the works in Etruria. In the early years, Wedgwood did not participate in the Willow fray, since Josiah had assured his painters that their jobs were safe from the threat of the transfer-printing trend. After Josiah I's death in 1795, however, successor Josiah II made up for lost time in joining the wave of transfer-printing potteries. Josiah II relinquished control of the company to his sons Josiah III and Francis in 1842; they controlled it until 1870. The company remained in family hands until 1967.

Wedgwood & Co. ws very careful to mark its wares. Nearly all pieces have been marked with an impressed "WEDGWOOD," to which "ENGLAND" was added in 1892, and "MADE IN ENGLAND" in 1911. The marks varied over the years, and between the different pottery facilities. Beginning in 1860, the company marked pieces with a three-letter code to indicate manufacturing details. Year Ccodes are as follows: O 1860, P 1861, Q 1862, R 1863, S 1864, T 1865, U 1866, V 1867, W 1868, X 1869, Y 1870, A 1871, A 1872, B 1873, C 1874, D 1875, E 1876, F 1877, G 1878, H 1879, I 1880, J 1881, K 1882, L 1883, M 1884, N 1885. In 1886, the sequence began again.[4]

See also William Smith & Co.

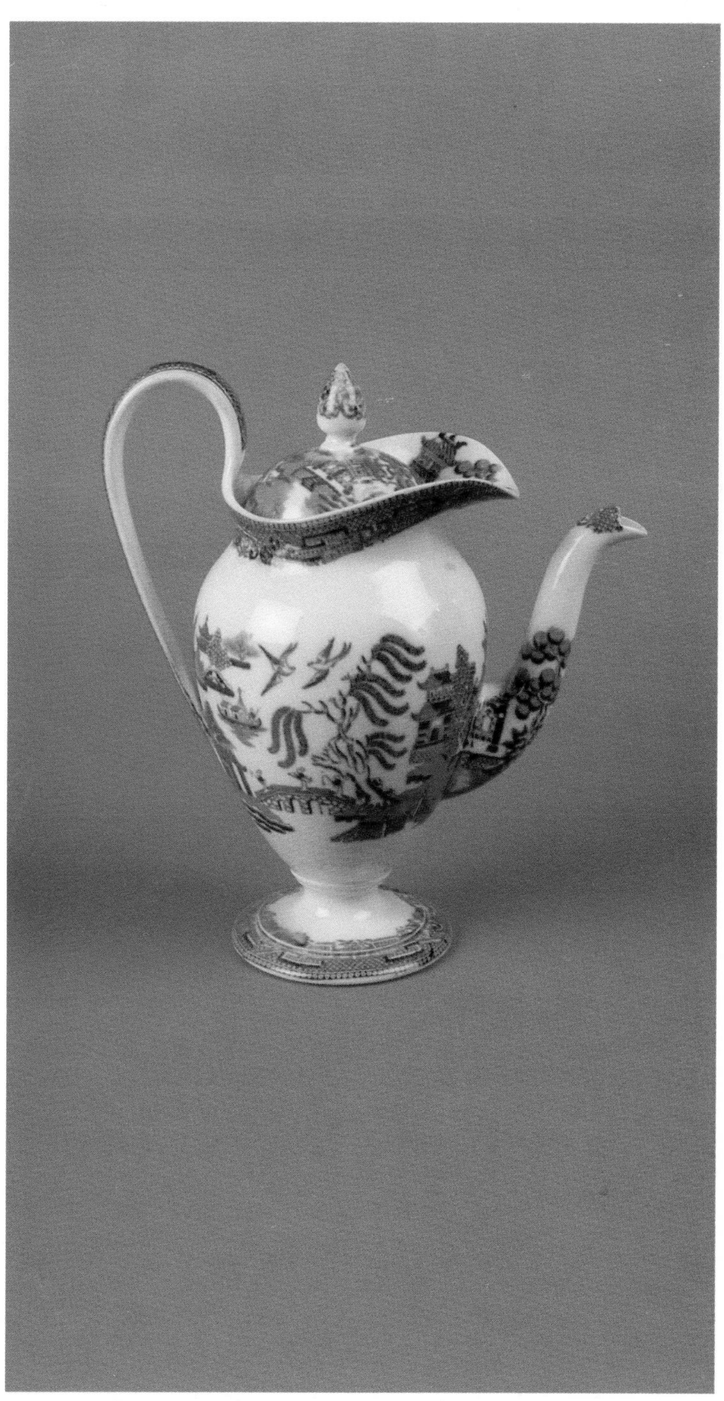

A teapot with an impressed Wedgwood mark, 8" high. From the collection of Peter and Susan Steelman, Mystic, CT.

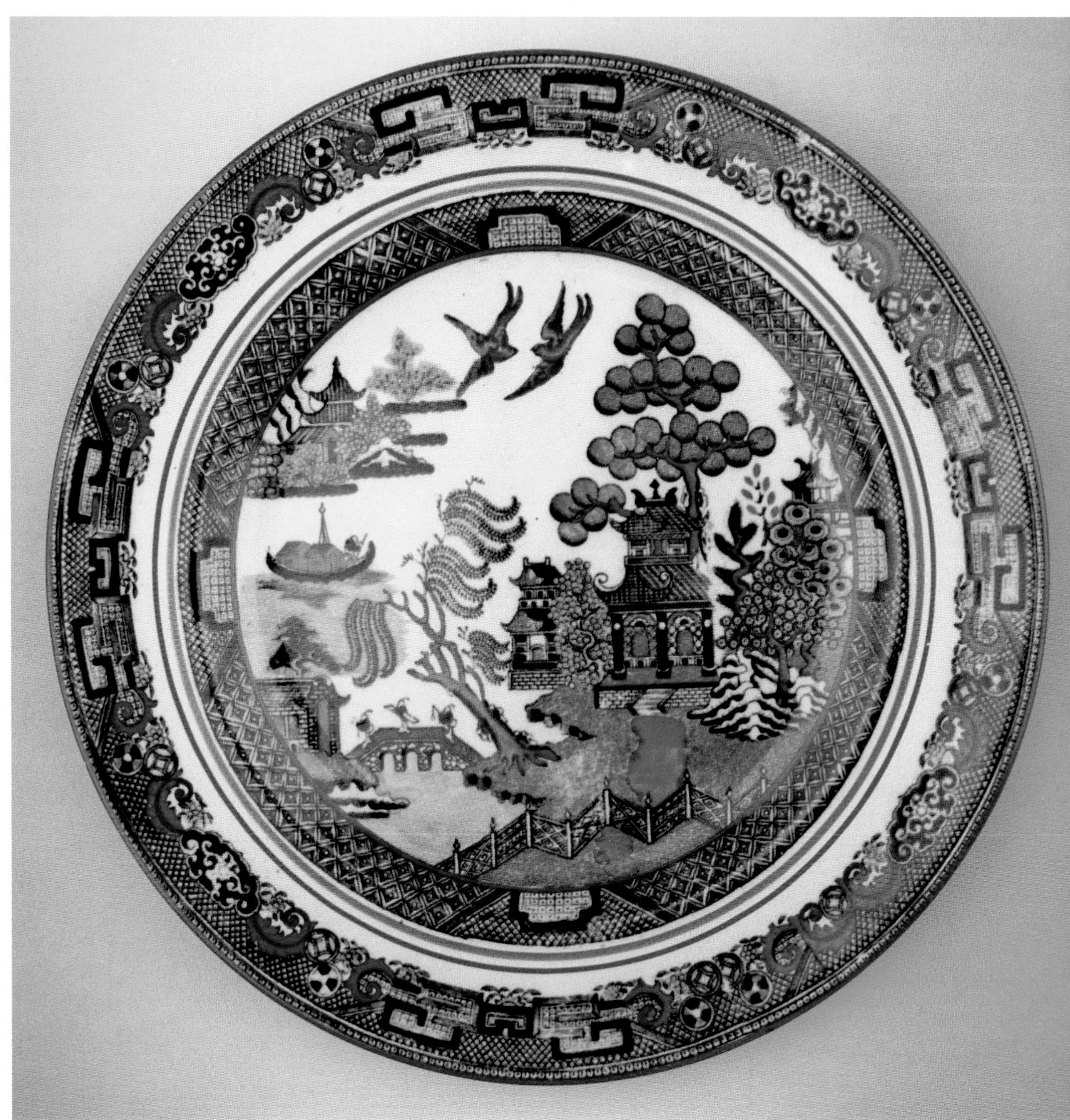

Wedgwood Etruria plate, with color added, 10.375". Both impressed and printed marks. Courtesy of Rita Entmacher Cohen.

WILLOW
WEDGWOOD
ETRURIA ENGLAND

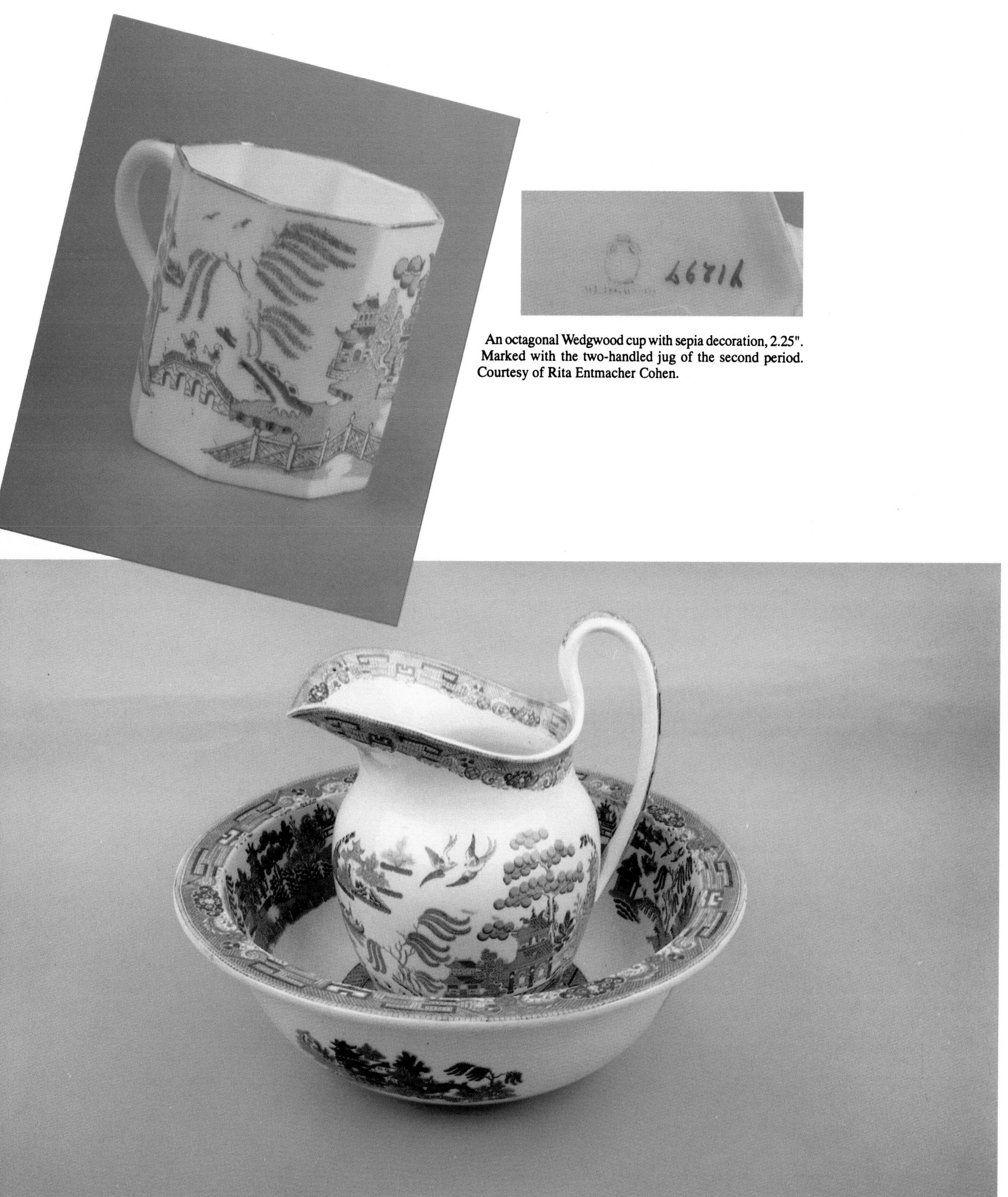

An octagonal Wedgwood cup with sepia decoration, 2.25". Marked with the two-handled jug of the second period. Courtesy of Rita Entmacher Cohen.

Wedgwood's wash basin and pitcher, 16" x 5.5" and 11.5" respectively. The bases of both pieces are marked "Willow" in underglaze blue; the pitcher has the impressed base-mark "Wedgwood." Courtesy of Rita Entmacher Cohen.

A round trivet by Wedgwood & Co., 6" diam., with the full willow pattern and border. The back of this piece bears the Wedgwood unicorn mark. Courtesy of Rita Entmacher Cohen.

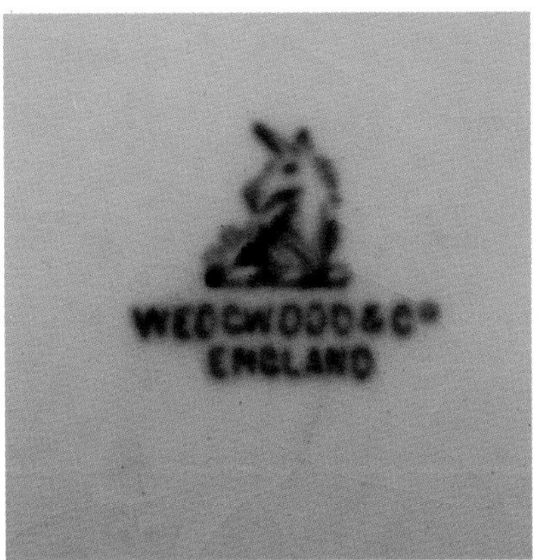

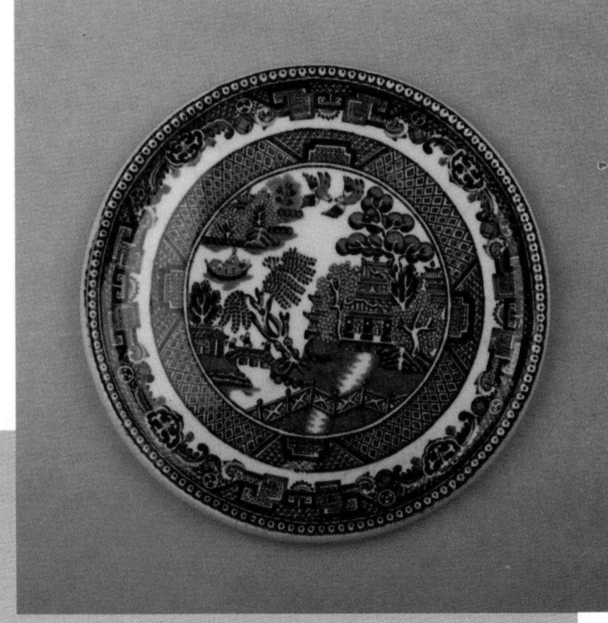

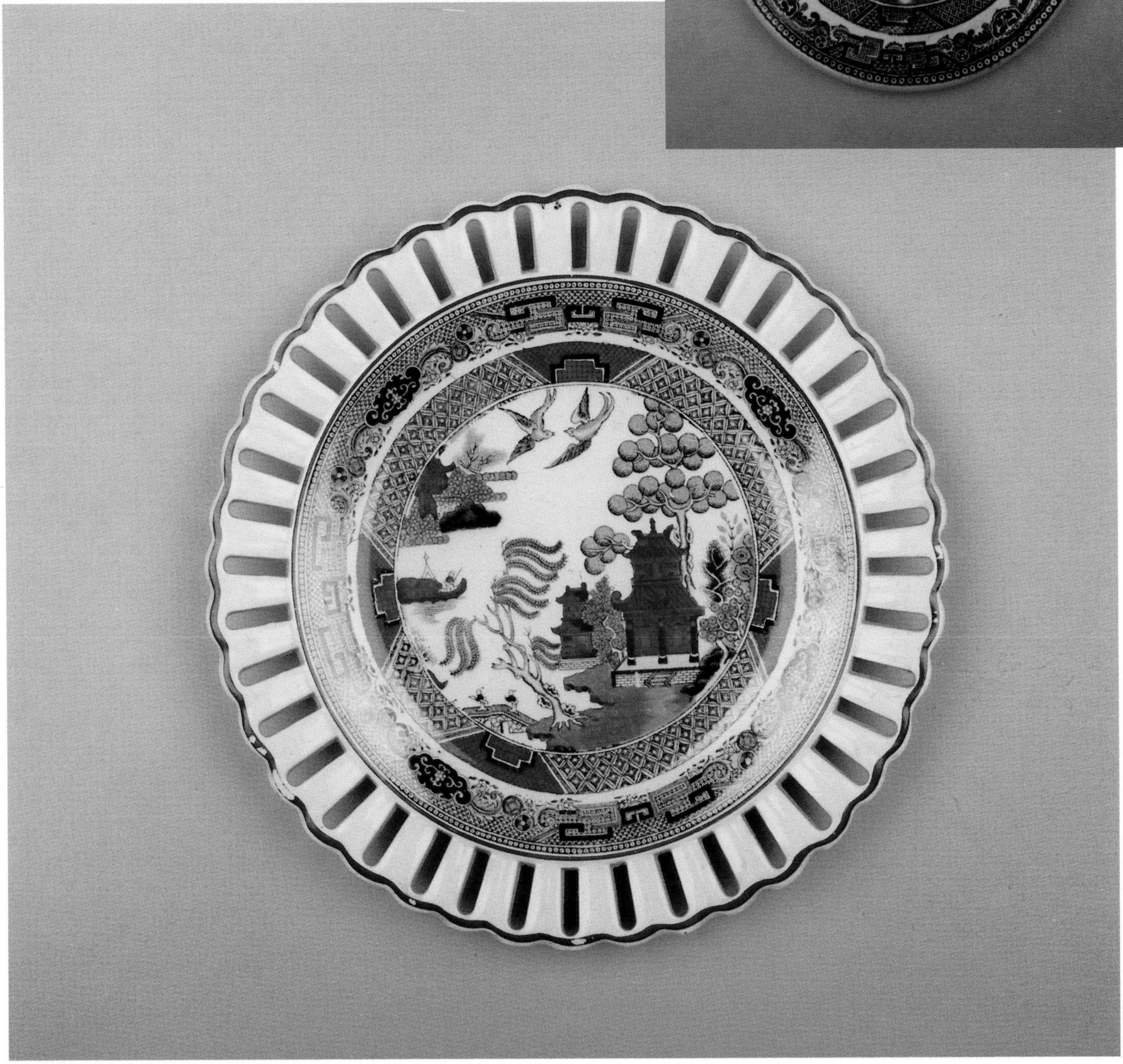

A polychrome Etruria plate from Wedgwood, with a pierced rim, 8.75" diam. "Wedgwood 3FT" is impressed in the bottom. Courtesy of Rita Entmacher Cohen.

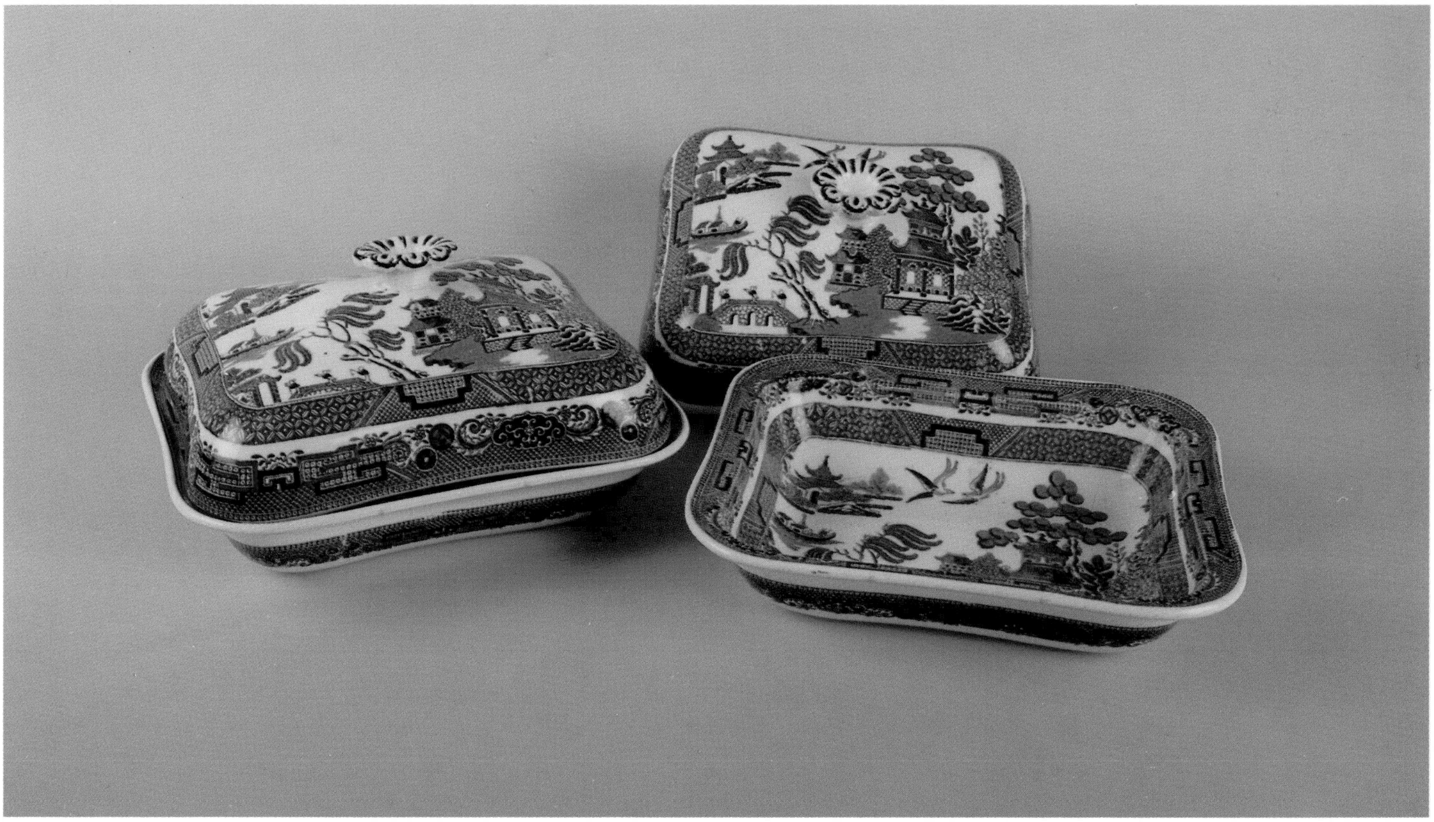

A pair of vegetable dishes by Wedgwood, c. 1891, 5" high x 9" long. Courtesy of Eva Lee Revels, Country Accents, Bandera, TX.

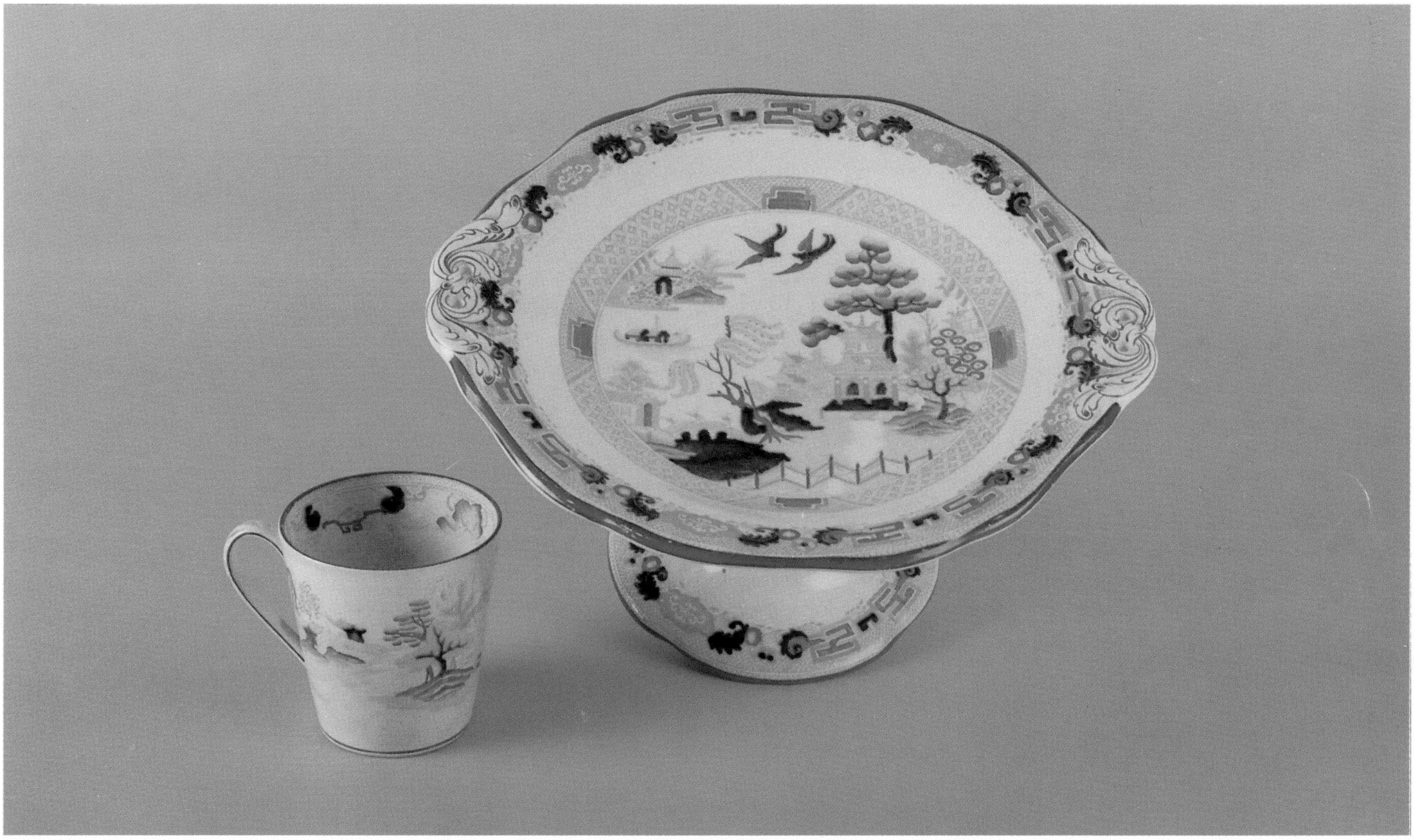

A early Wedgwood cake plate and cup; the plate is 4.5" high x 9" diam. The cup is especially rare. Courtesy of Wendy's Willow.

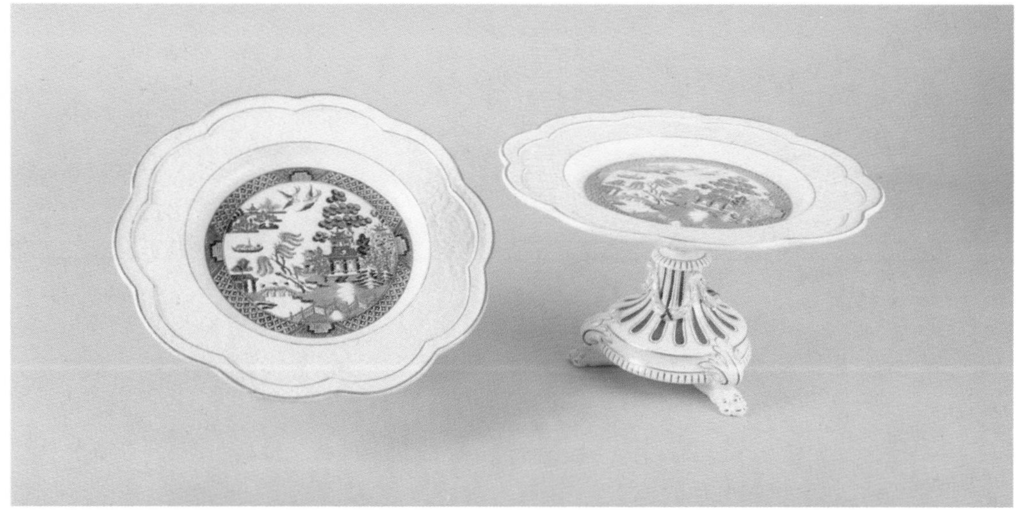

A pair of Wedgwood cake plates in brown transfer printing, 5.5" and 3" high, 9.25" diam. Courtesy of Wendy's Willow.

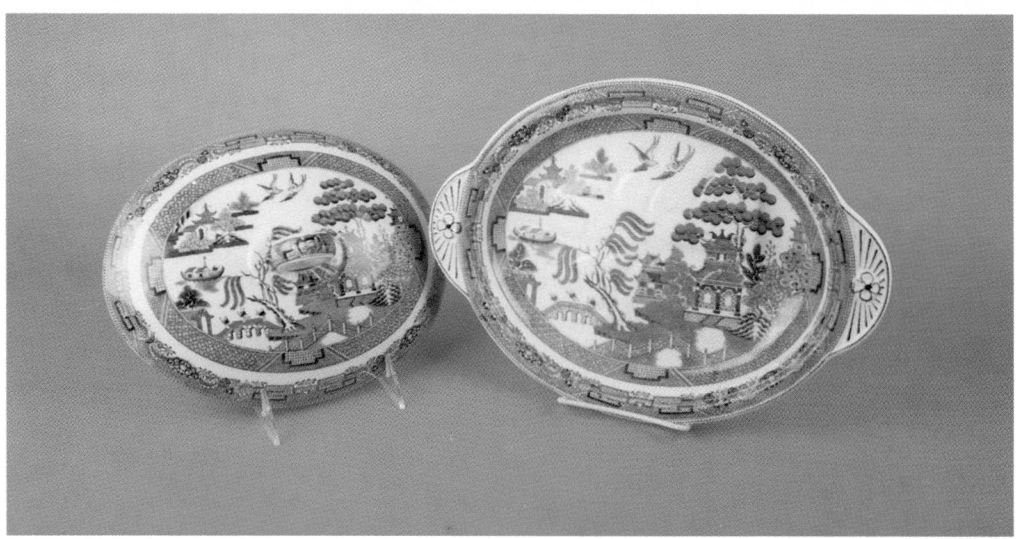

A covered well-and-tree platter from Wedgwood's Etruria line, 12.25" x 9". From the collection of Peter and Susan Steelman, Mystic, CT.

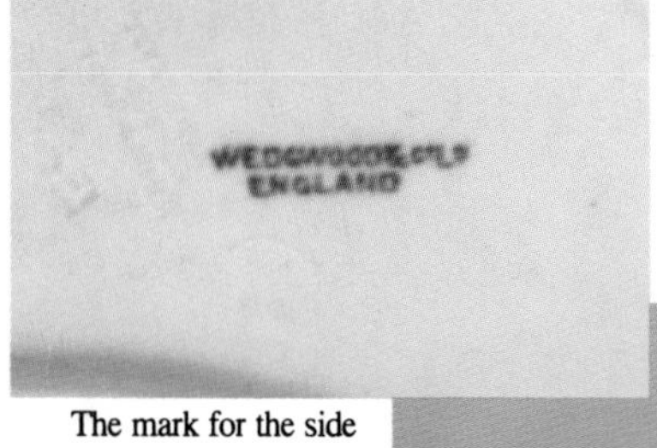

The mark for the side plate. From the collection of Peter and Susan Steelman, Mystic, CT.

An advertising luncheon plate marked "W & C" and an advertising side plate by Wedgwood. Luncheon plate is 7.75" diam, the side plate is 8.75" wide. From the collection of Peter and Susan Steelman, Mystic, CT.

The mark for the luncheon plate, "Stoneware W & C". From the collection of Peter and Susan Steelman, Mystic, CT.

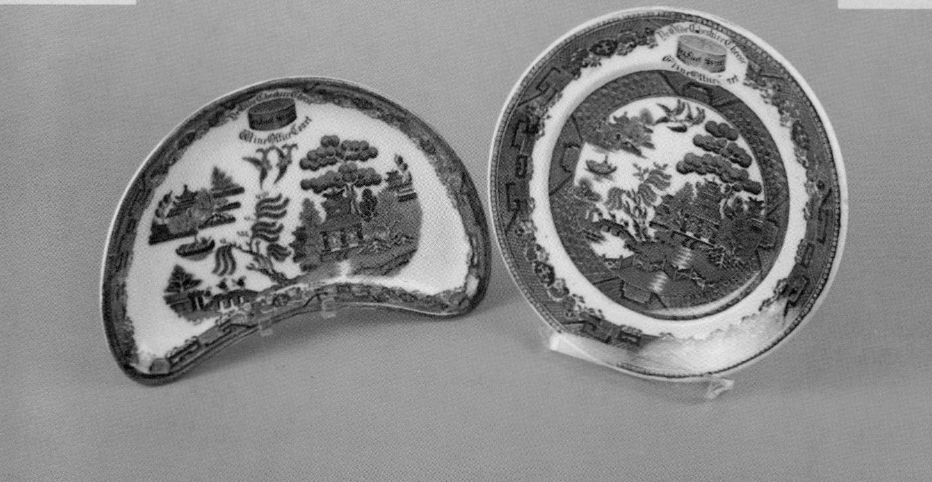

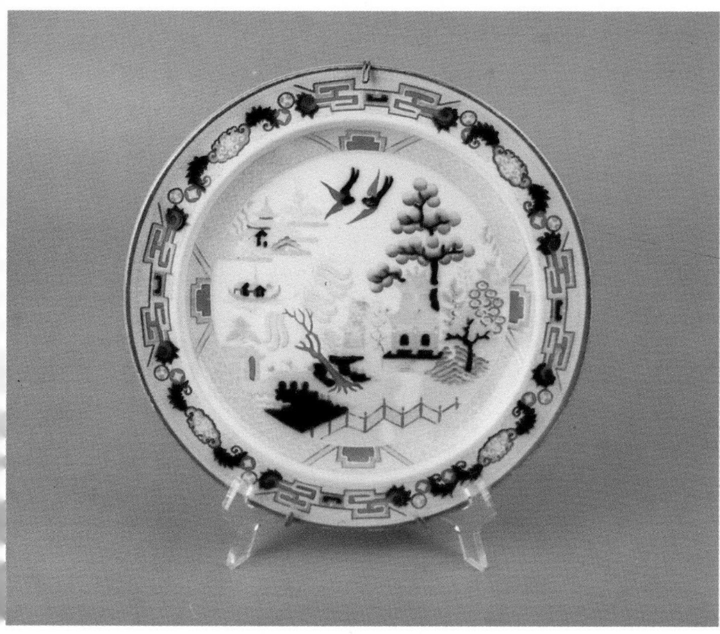
A Wedgwood plate, 10.25" diam. The back bears an impressed Wedgwood mark and another printed in yellow reading "Wedgwood Etruria, England". From the collection of Peter and Susan Steelman, Mystic, CT.

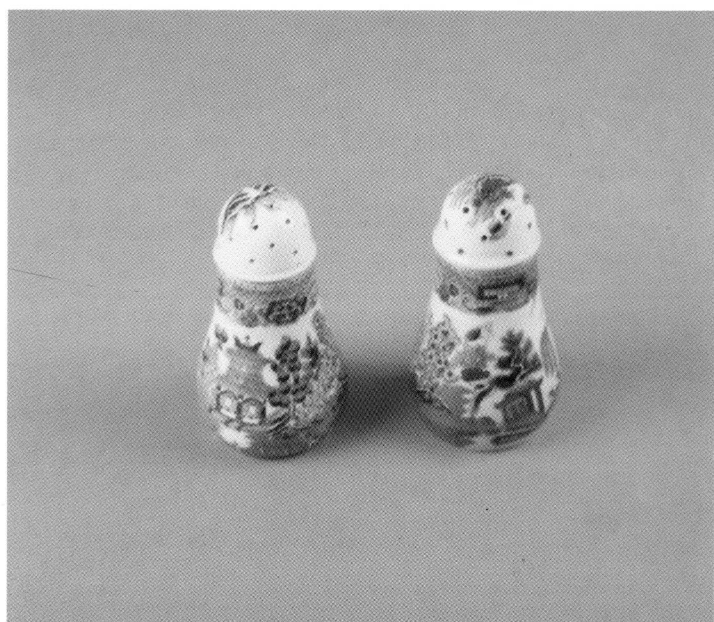
Salt and pepper shaker set from "Willow Wedgwood". From the collection of Peter and Susan Steelman, Mystic, CT.

Arthur J. Wilkinson (Ltd.): A Burslem, Staffordshire potter who began operations in 1885 to produce earthenwares and ironstone, etc. From 1891, a crown and crest mark reading "WILKINSON'S/ENGLAND/ROYAL SEMI-PORCELAIN" was used; c. 1896 a Royal Arms mark was used reading "ROYAL IRONSTONE CHINA/A. J. WILKINSON Ltd./ENGLAND" (earlier marks omitted the "Ltd."); and from 1907, a crown mark with a rampant lion and a banner reading "ROYAL STAFFORDSHIRE POTTERY" was used, with or without "IRONSTONE CHINA." In the 1930s, the Clarice Cliff name would appear on the Wilkinson marks as well.

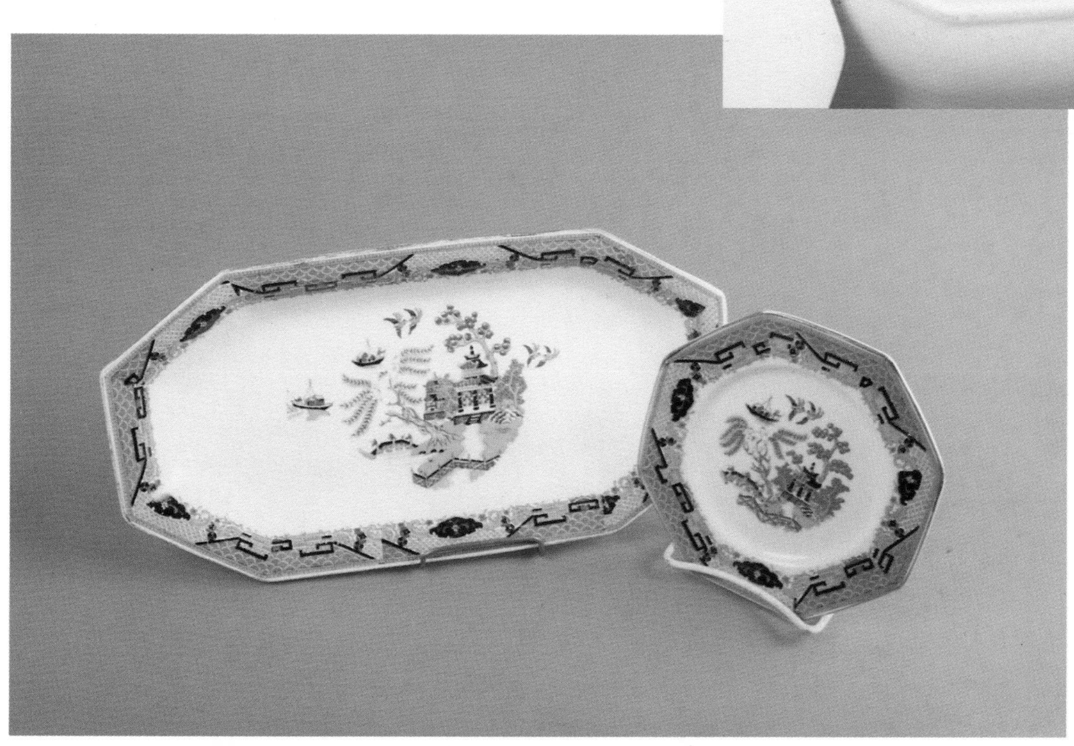
A Gaudy Willow platter and plate made by Wilkinson, distributed by Hampton & Son, London, c. 1910. Courtesy of Charles and Louise Loehr, Louise's Old Things, Kutztown, PA.

Wiltshaw & Robinson: Active 1890-1957 at the Carlton Works, in Stoke-on-Trent, producing earthenwares and china. In 1958, the company was renamed Carton Ware Ltd. Beginning in 1894, marks used include a flying swallow inside a circle, with "W. & R." above and "STOKE-ON-TRENT" below, also enclosed in a circle. This is surmounted by a crown, and "CARLTON WARE" is printed below. After 1906, "CARLTON WARE" was replaced by "CARLTON CHINA". The "Carlton Ware" swallow mark was resumed by Carlton Ware Ltd. after 1958.

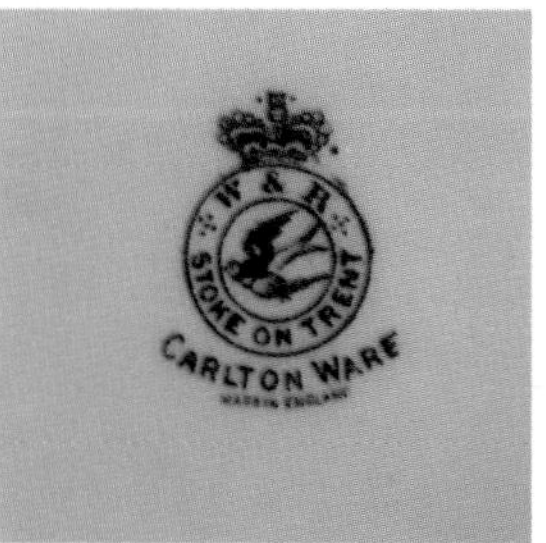

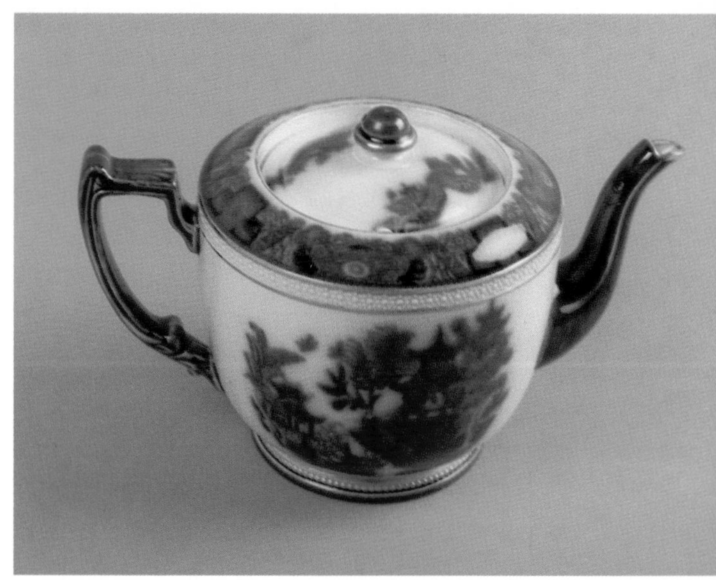

A flowed Carlton Ware teapot, c. 1894, 5.5" high x 9" long. Courtesy of Charles and Louise Loehr, Louise's Old Things, Kutztown PA.

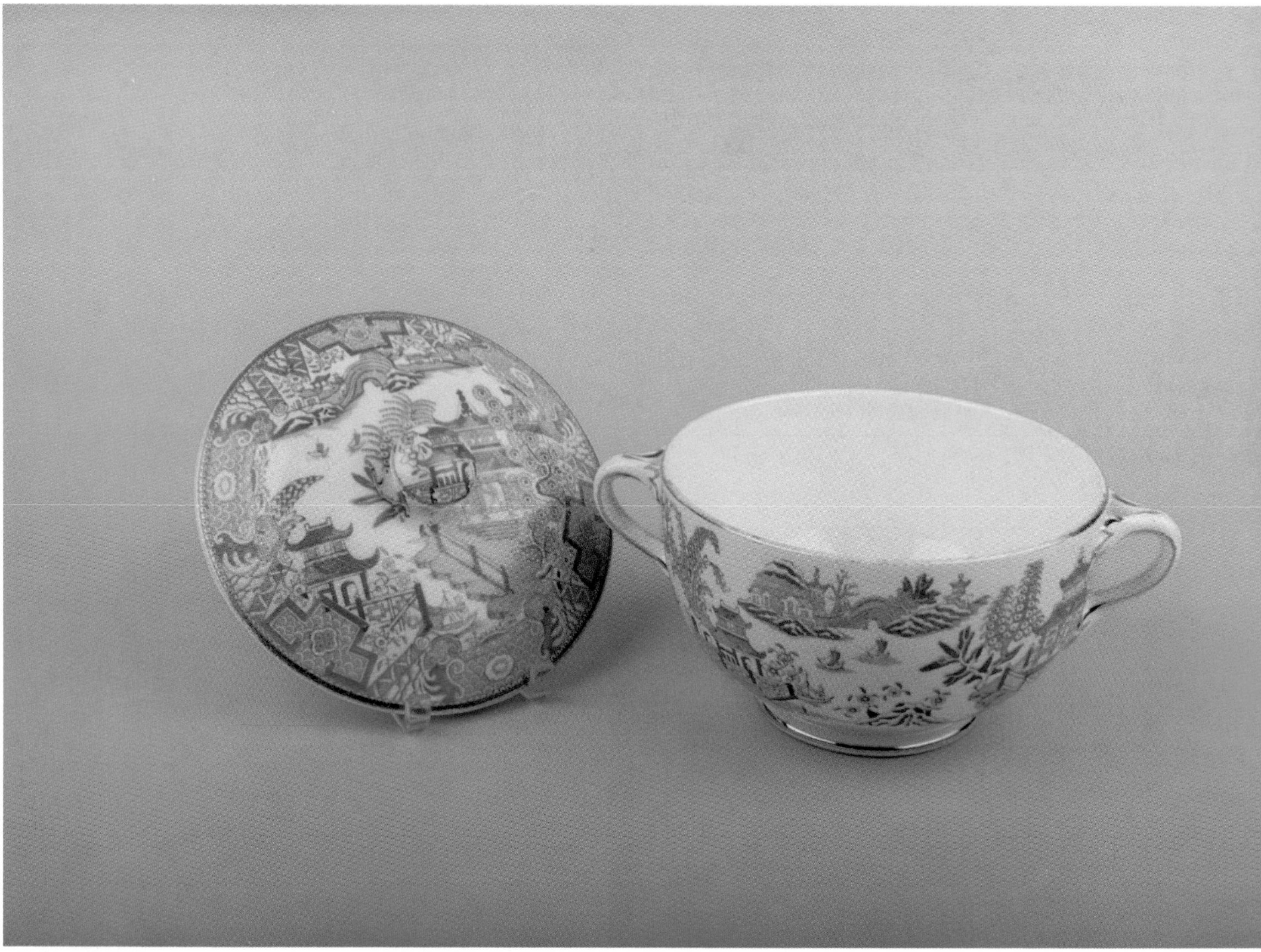

A covered sugar bowl, 4.75" diam, in the Carlton Ware line from the W & R pottery in Stoke-on-Trent—light blue with a gold trim. Courtesy of Rita Entmacher Cohen.

Isaac Wilson & Co.: A Middlesbrough, Yorkshire company active from 1852-1887, producing earthenwares. Marks include "I. W. & CO.," with our without "MIDDLESBROUGH" beneath, and a crown mark reading "MIDDLESBROUGH POTTERY" with an anchor.

Thomas Wolfe: Active in Stoke, Staffordshire, c. 1784-1800 and c. 1811-1818. A quantity of his wares were exported. Wares were marked with an impressed "W", "WOLFE," or (c. 1800-1811) Wolfe & Co., when Thomas was in a partnership with Robert Hamilton.

Enoch Wood & Sons: The firm was founded by Enoch Wood and his cousin Ralph in 1783 at Fountain Place, Burslem. In 1790 they were joined by James Caldwell, and traded as Wood & Caldwell. After 1819, the Woods bought out Caldwell's interest, and traded as Wood & Sons. The company used a name mark from 1783 until it went out of business in 1846-1847. Over the years, marks included "WOOD & CALDWELL," "ENOCH WOOD & SONS," and (with eagle and shield) "ENOCH WOOD & SONS, BURSLEM."

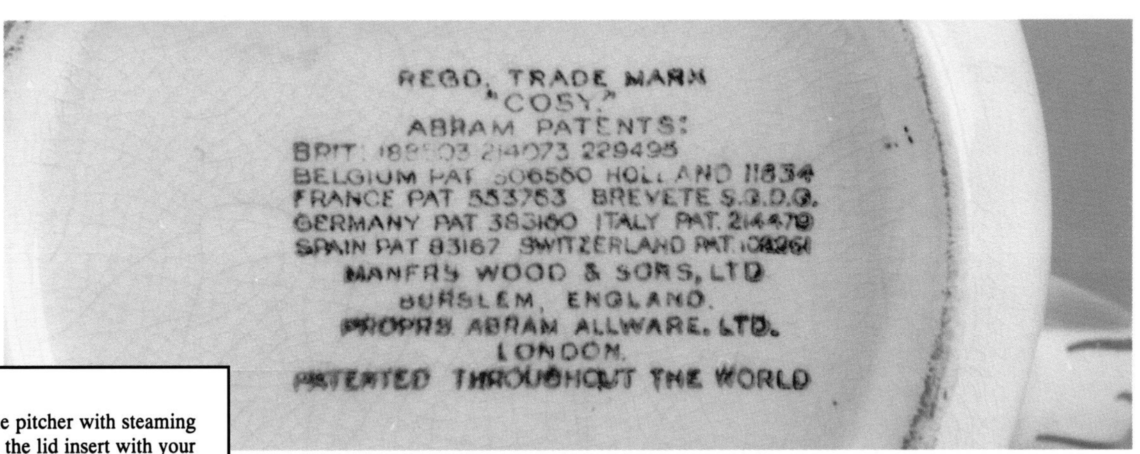

Fill the pitcher with steaming water, the lid insert with your medicinal powders or herbs, and inhale through the spout. This piece is extensively patented.

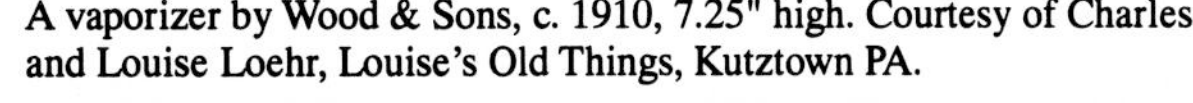
A vaporizer by Wood & Sons, c. 1910, 7.25" high. Courtesy of Charles and Louise Loehr, Louise's Old Things, Kutztown PA.

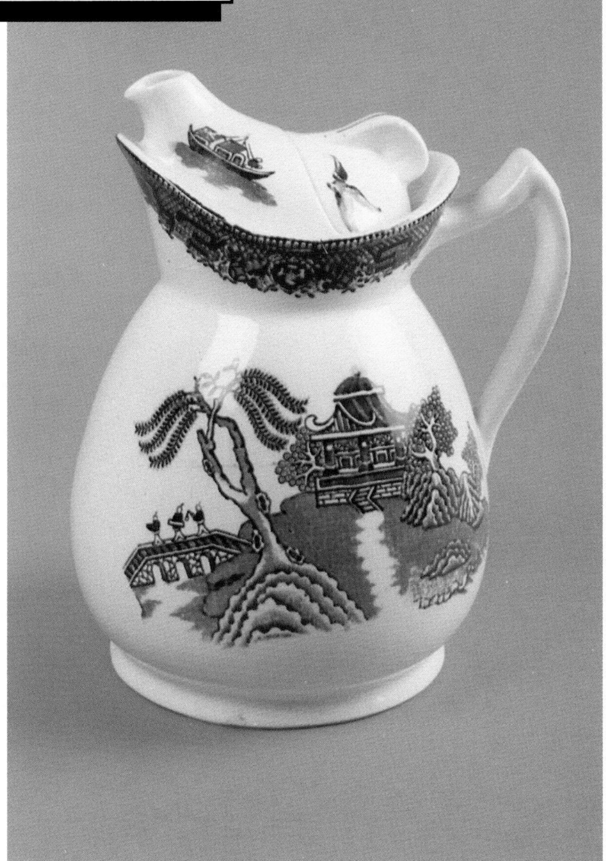

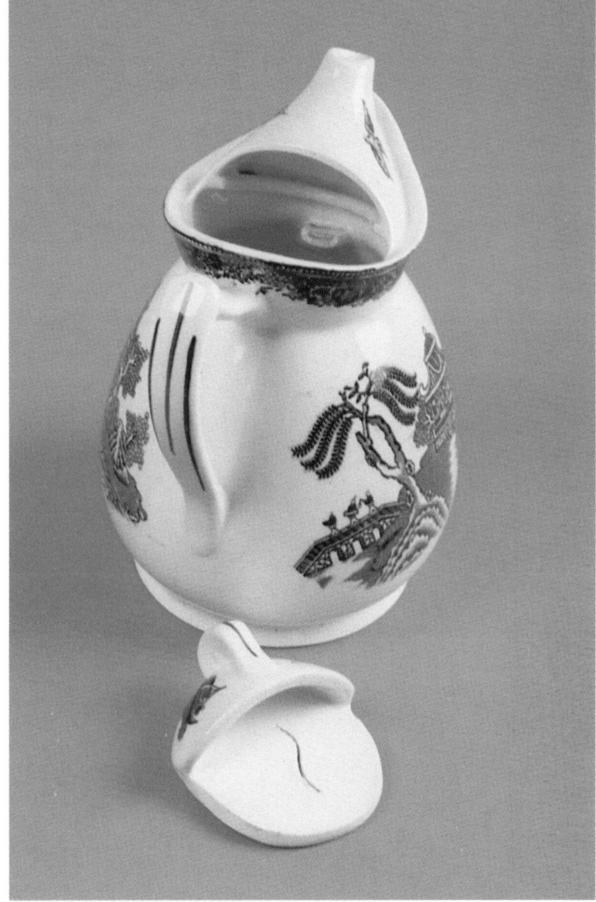

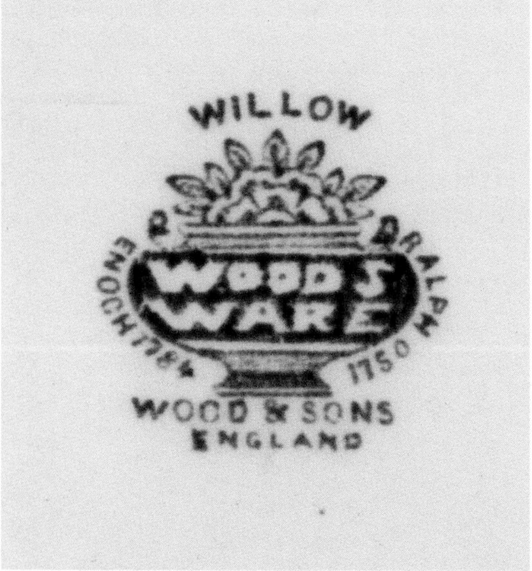

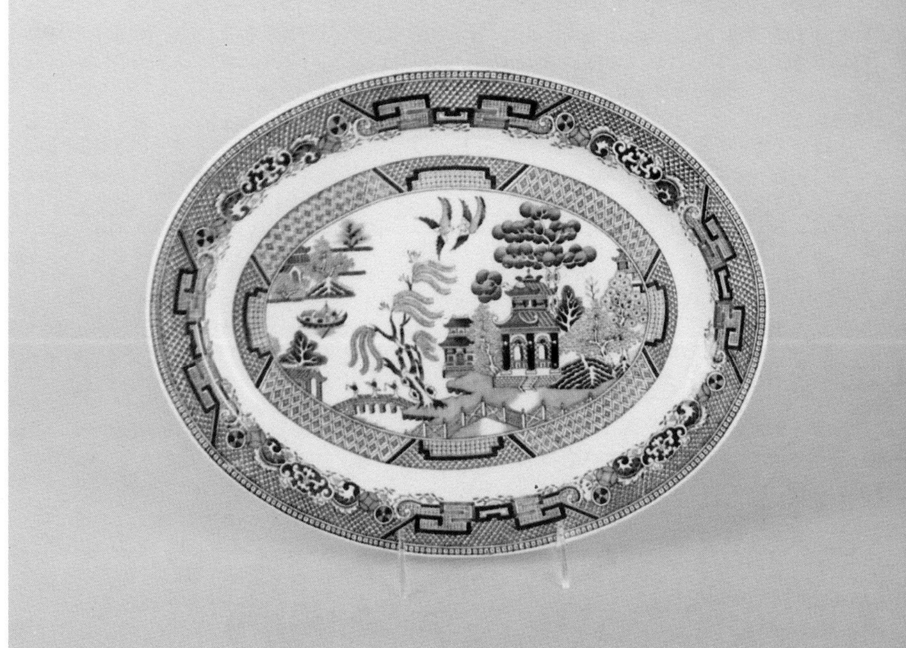

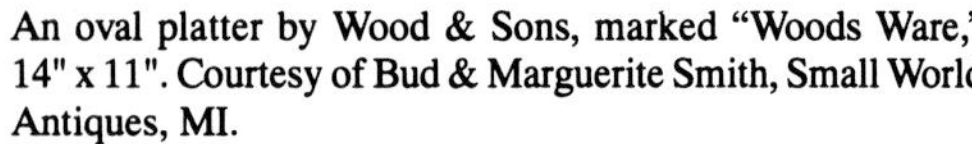
An oval platter by Wood & Sons, marked "Woods Ware," 14" x 11". Courtesy of Bud & Marguerite Smith, Small World Antiques, MI.

Wood & Brownfield: A Cobridge, Staffordshire firm active c. 1838-1850, producing earthenwares. Look for the "W. & B." mark.

Woods Ware: Enoch & Ralph Wood's operated Wood & Sons in England, active betweemn 1750-1784.

Worcester: Established c. 1751 at the main factory in Worcester, and still active today. Worcester's marks are numerous and widely varied. Worcester Willow most often appears with a variation of their standard mark, however—four script "W"s arranged in a circle, printed or impressed, in use since c. 1852. This mark was topped with a crown in 1862, and a coding system was used to indicate exact years. In 1891 the words "ROYAL WORCESTER ENGLAND" were added, and another coding system was implemented, carrying it through 1963.

A mustache cup with gold details by Grainger Worcester, 6" x 11". Marked. Courtesy of Rita Entmacher Cohen.

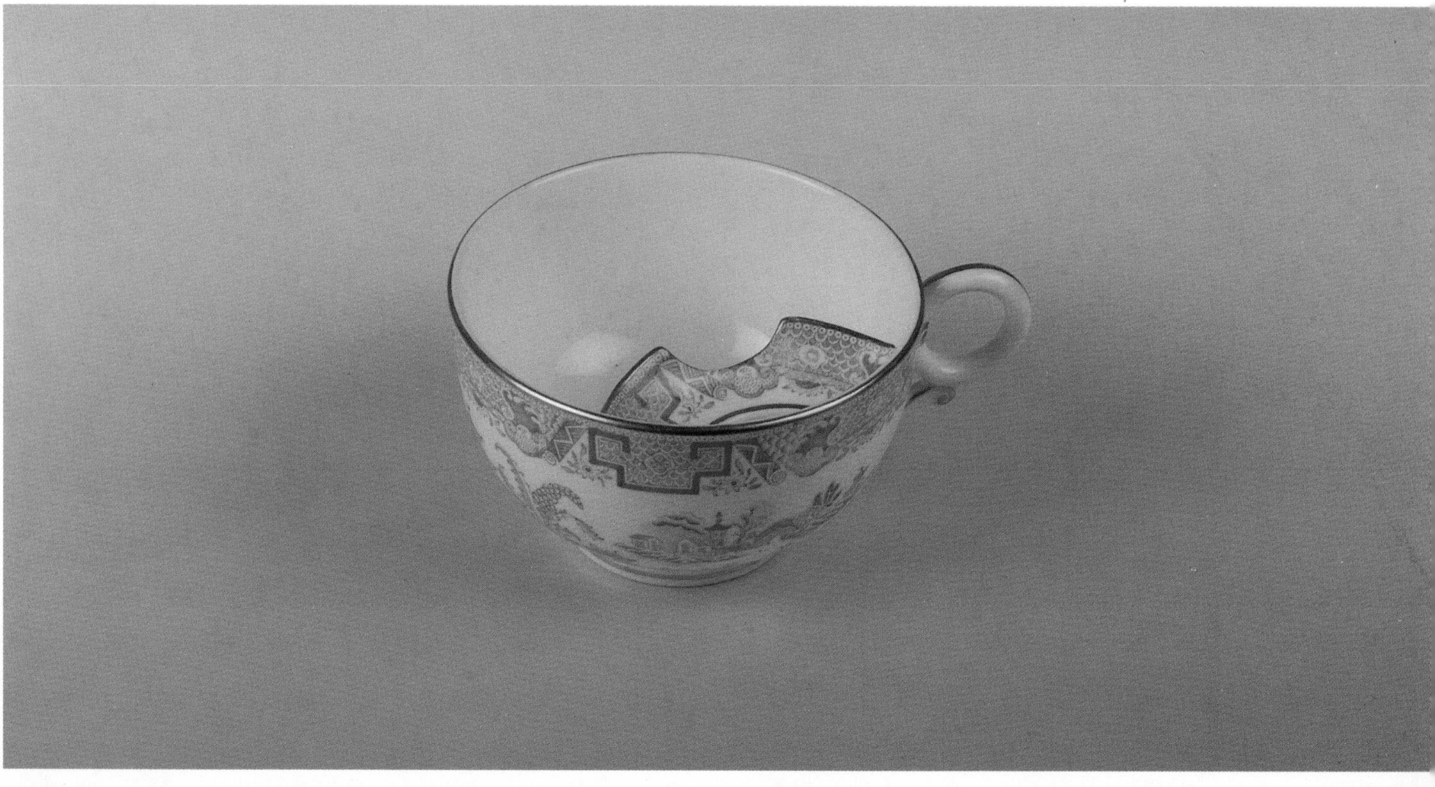

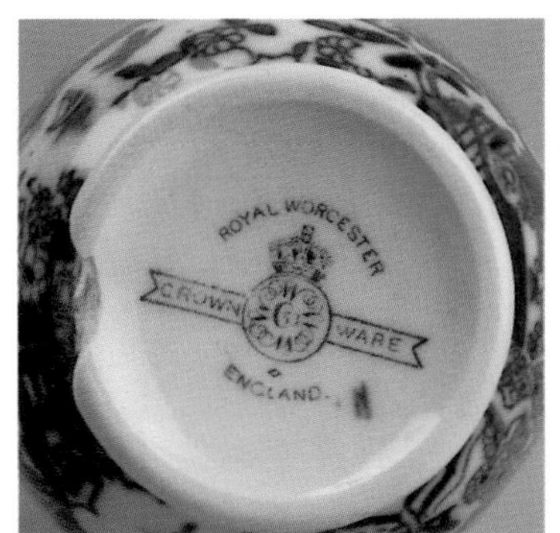

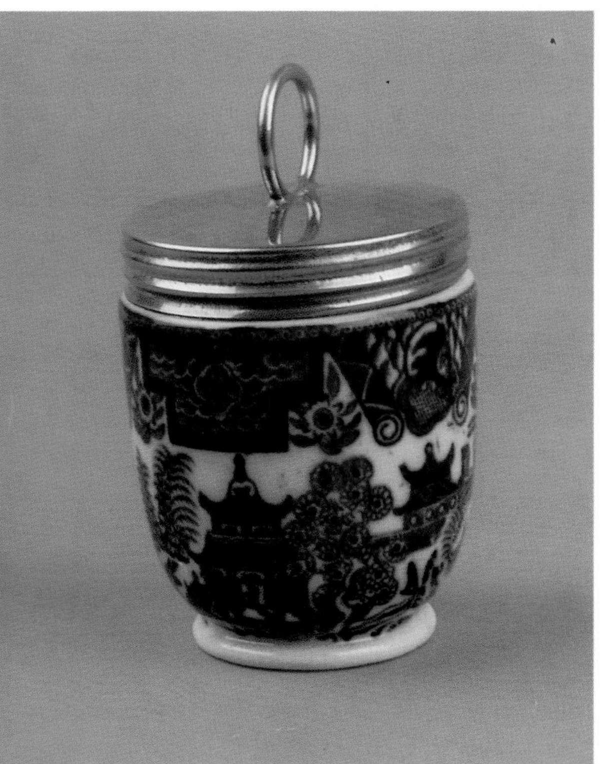

A Crown Ware egg cup by Royal Worcester, 2.5". With a silver screw-on lid. Courtesy of Rita Entmacher Cohen.

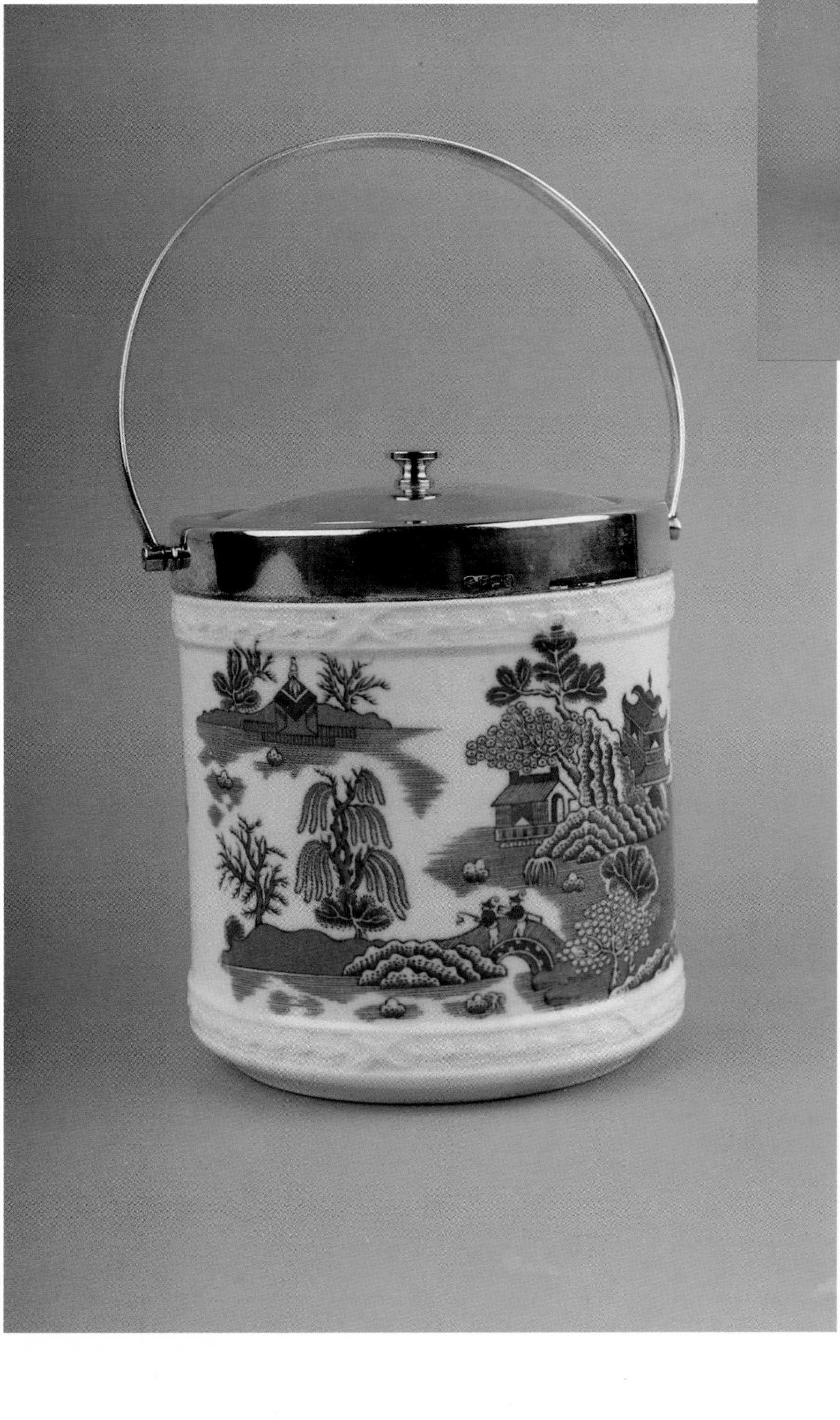

A biscuit barrel from Royal Worcester, in the Crown Willow pattern, 5.25". The handle and lid of this piece are made of Electro Plated Nickel Silver (EPNS). Courtesy of Rita Entmacher Cohen.

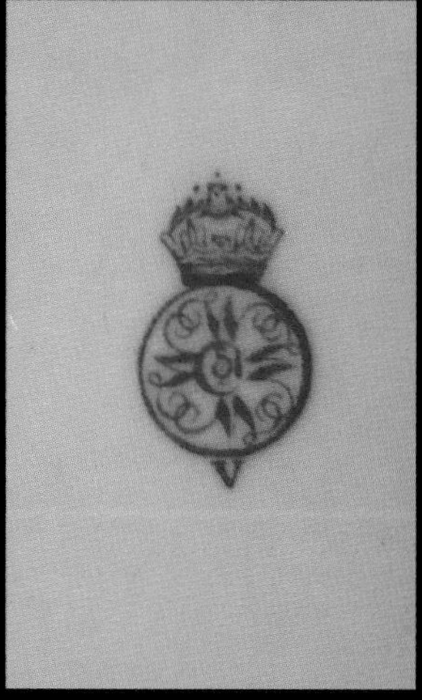

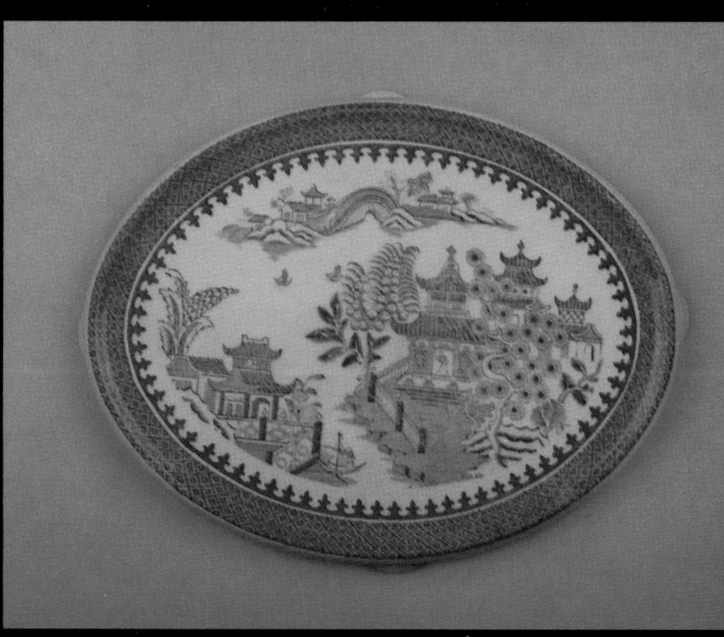

An oval trivet by Royal Worcester, 7.5" wide. Courtesy of Rita Entmacher Cohen.

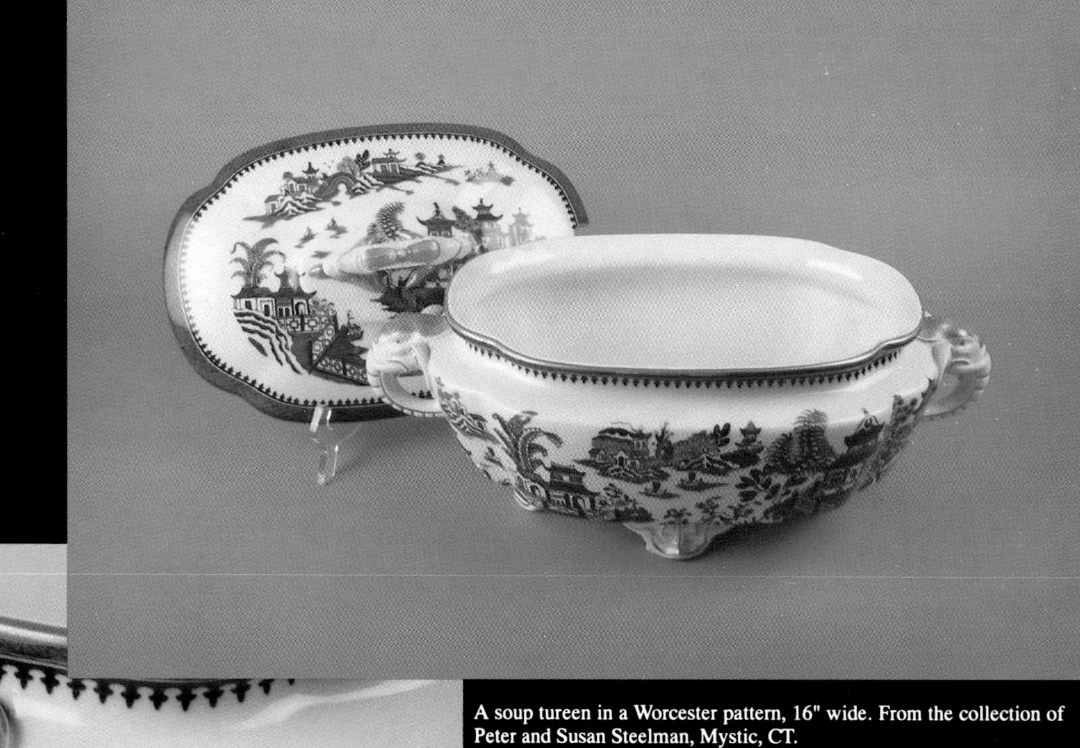

A soup tureen in a Worcester pattern, 16" wide. From the collection of Peter and Susan Steelman, Mystic, CT.

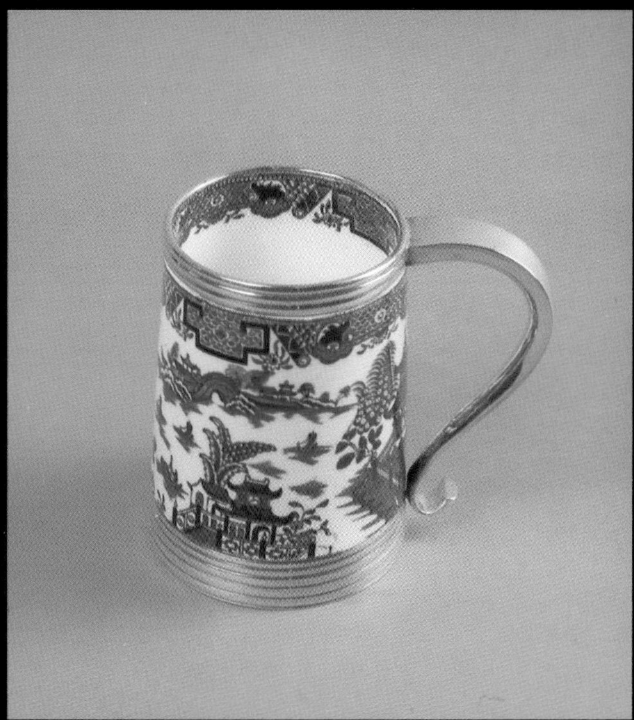

A Worcester tankard with silverplate decoration, 1881, 5" high. Marked on the bottom. Courtesy of Charles and Louise Loehr, Louise's Old Things, Kutztown, PA.

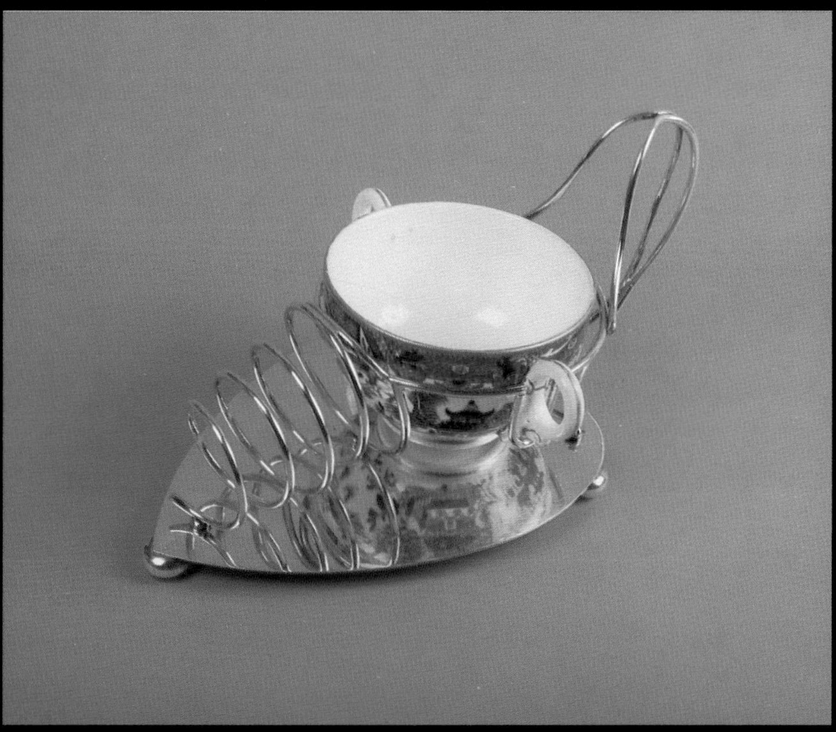

A combination bouillon cup/toast rack, a clever combination, though not guaranteed to keep your toast warm for long. The porcelain cup was made by Worcester, the silverplated stand by Mappin & Webb. Courtesy of Charles and Louise Loehr, Louise's Old Things, Kutztown, PA.

Endnotes

Introduction

1 Jensen, *The First International Book of Willow Ware,* 5.
2 Ibid., 13.
3 Detweiler, *American Presidential China,* 33.
4 Robert Hughes, *The Fatal Shore,* 203-204.
5 Jensen, 5.
6 Ibid., 59.
7 Altman, *The Book of Buffalo Pottery,* 33.
8 Richardson, "Garden China," 11-12.
9 Coysh, *Blue and White Transfer Ware,* 42.
10 Godden, *British Pottery & Porcelain,* 150.
11 Richardson, 11-12.

Chapter 1

1 Pearce, "Chinese Export Porcelain," 30-31.
2 Rust, *Collector's Guide of Antique Porcelain,* 106.
3 Medley, "Patterns of Chinese Taste in Porcelain," 70.
4 Ibid., 70.
5 Ibid., 70.
6 Ibid., 68.
7 Ibid., 70.
8 Ibid., 70.
9 Ayers, "Blanc-de-Chine," 20.
10 Grun, *Timetables of History,* 293.
11 Medley, "Patterns of Chinese Taste," 61.
12 Ibid., 74.
13 Spence, *The Search for Modern China,* 134.
14 Ibid., 134.
15 Savage, 77.
16 Spence, 128.
17 Pearce, 21.
18 Spence, 188-121.
19 Spence, 121.
20 Bortone and Camusso, *Ceramics of the World,* 219.
21 Copeland, *Spode's Willow,* 4.
22 Jensen, 6.
23 Macintosh, *Chinese Blue and White Porcelain,* 109.
24 Ibid., 117.
25 Ibid., 117.
26 Pearce, 21.
27 Medley, "Patterns of Chinese Taste," 61
28 Pearce, 21.
29 Sheaf, "Geldermalsen Cargo," 83
30 Pearce, 21-26; Copeland, 4-5.
31 Pearce, 21.
32 Ibid., 21.
33 Spence, 149.
34 Ibid., 121-149.
35 Copeland, 4-5.
35a Godden, *British Porcelain: An Illustrated Guide,* 22.
36 Pearce, 30-31.
37 Medley, "Patterns in Chinese Taste," 79.
38 Ibid., 79.
39 Copeland, 4.
40 Pearce, 30-31.
41 Ibid., 30-31.
42 Copeland, 11.
43 Ibid., 45.
44 Ibid., 4, 10.
45 Ibid., 13.
46 Cohen, 1994 IWC Convention.
47 Cohen, 1994 IWC Convention.
48 B. & T. Hughes, *The Collector's Encyclopaedia,* 148.
49 Jensen, 9.
50 Copeland, 13.
51 Coysh, 7.
52 B. & T. Hughes, 8-9, 36-37, 41, 163.

Chapter 2

1 Coysh, 10.
2 B. & T. Hughes, 157-158.
3 Copeland, 39.
4 B. & T. Hughes, 157-158.
5 Cohen, 1994 Convention lecture.
6 Copeland, 45.
7 Ibid., 45.
8 Ibid., 50.
9 Ibid., 33.
10 Ibid., 33.
11 Ibid., 33-35.
12 Ibid., 33.
13 Cameh, *Blue-China Book,* 288.
14 Coysh and Henrywood, *The Dictionary of Blue and White Printed Pottery, 1780-1880,* volume I, 402-403.
15 Coysh, 14.
16 Copeland, 35.
17 Ibid., 33.
18 Ibid., 33.

Chapter 3

1 Cameh, 287.
2 Bergeson, "Pantomime Scene," 5.
3 *Inventors & Discoverers: Changing Our World,* 174.
4 Cameh, 287.
5 Bergeson, "The Willow Pattern Plate," 12.
6 Coysh & Henrywood, vol. I, 403.
7 Worth, *Willow Pattern China,* 5-6.
8 International Willow Collectors pamphlet, 1993.
9 Altman, 34-37.

Chapter 4

1 Cohen, 1994 Convention lecture.
2 Bortone, 219.
3 Grun, 55.
4 Rust, 15.
5 Bernard & Therle Hughes, 15.
6 Ibid., 125.
7 Godden, *British Porcelain: An Illustrated Guide,* 21.
8 B. & T. Hughes, 124-125.
9 Grun, 255.
10 B. & T. Hughes, 125.
11 Ibid., 126.
12 Rust, 15.
13 Grun, 326.
14 Godden, *British Porcelain: An Illustrated Guide,* 21.
15 Ibid., 21
16 Bortone, 22.
17 Godden, *British Porcelain: An Illustrated Guide,* 25.
18 Bortone, 222.
19 Copeland, 3.
20 Ibid., 45.
21 *Creamware & Pearlware,* 11 and 45.
22 Seidel, "'China Glaze' Wares on Sites from the American Revolution," 86.
23 *Creamware & Pearlware,* 46.
24 Ibid., 46.
25 Ibid., 46.
26 Ibid., 46
27 Cohen, 1994 Convention lecture.
28 Godden, *British Porcelain: An Illustrated Guide,* 25.
29 Ibid., 25.
30 Copeland, 175.
31 Cohen, 1994 Convention lecture.
32 Newman and Savage, *An Illustrated Dictionary of Ceramics,* 175.
33 Ibid., 158
34 B. & T. Hughes, 108-109.
35 Copeland, 173.
36 Cohen, 1994 Convention lecture.
37 Rust, 107.
38 Copeland, 21.
39 Copeland, 21.
40 Coysh & Henrywood, vol. I, 219.
41 Copeland, 21-22.
42 Ibid., 8.
43 Coysh & Henrywood, 350.
44 Cohen, 1994 Convention lecture.
45 Coysh & Henrywood, vol. I, 396.
46 Cohen, 1994 Convention lecture.
47 Godden, *British Pottery: An Illustrated Guide,* 229.
48 Copeland, 17.
49 Garner, *Oriental Blue & White,* 5.
50 Ibid., 15.
51 Ibid., 5.
52 Bernard & Therle Hughes, 45.
53 Copeland, 18.
54 Cohen, 1994 Convention lecture.
55 Copeland, 18.
56 Ibid., 18-19.
57 Bernard & Therle Hughes, 45.
58 Laidacker, *Anglo-American China, part II,* xiii.
59 Snyder, *Flow Blue: A Collector's Guide to Pattern, History & Values,* 16.
60 Coysh, 7; Godden, *British Pottery: An Illustrated Guide,* 228; Copeland, 23-24; Snyder, *Flow Blue: A Collector's Guide,* 15-16.
61 Copeland, 19-24.
62 Ibid., 3, 24, 174.
63 Ibid., 173.
64 Copeland, 166.
65 Ibid., 30.
66 Godden, *British Pottery: An Illustrated Guide,* 228.
67 Savage, 77.
68 Coysh, 7.
69 B. & T. Hughes, 36-37.
70 Coysh, 7.
71 Godden, *British Pottery: An Illustrated Guide,* 149.

Chapter 6

The list of makers was compiled from a wide variety of sources, including the aforementioned texts by Jensen, Coysh & Henrywood (volumes I & II), Bernard & Therle Hughes, Snyder (*Flow Blue* and *Historic Flow Blue*), Bockol & Snyder, Cushion, Godden (*British Pottery & Porcelain*), Altman, and Copeland.

1 Pearce, 26.
2 B. & T. Hughes, 157-158.
3 Jensen, 13.
4 Cohen, 1994 Convention lecture.
5 Ibid.
6 Richardson, 11-12.
7 Cohen, 1994 Convention lecture; Ellison, 1994 Convention lecture.
8 Ellison, 1994 Convention lecture.
9 Ibid.
10 Bockol & Snyder, 44.
11 Altman, 33.
12 Ibid., 26.
13 Hughes, 36.
14 Coysh & Henrywood, vol, I, 396-397.

Price Guide

This price guide has been compiled with the gracious help of Rita Entmacher Cohen, Phillip M. Sullivan, and the many dealers and collectors who contributed their items for illustration. Please keep in mind that many factors, especially condition, affect the value of any particular piece. Prices vary from one region to another and from one year to another, so keep your wits about you, and always rely on your own best judgement. The prices here (given in U.S. dollars) are provided only as a general guide, and should be used as such.

Page	Item	Price ($)
5	plate	65-90
7	tin box	90
	tea cannister	300
	large cup	100
9	Chinese strainer	200
	pearlware drainer	275
	four plates	195-225 ea.
10	square drainer	125-145
	oval drainers	285-325 ea.
	tea caddies	550-650 ea.
	relish set (c. 1805)	1100
11	Canton plate	395
	Nankin basket	850
14	round dish	200
	oval dish	150
15	"Swag" plate	325
	basket stand	245
17	puzzle jug	2500
	tureen	385
	potpourri keeper	1400
18	trivet	90
19	"Mandarin" platter	325
	"Willow I" platter	325
	early English platter	325-375
20	"Conversation" plate (c. 1800)	150
	"Queen Charlotte" plate (c. 1908)	150
21	"Stag" mug	400
	brown-edge "Long Bridge"	125
	pierced-rim "Long Bridge"	325
	rectangular "Long Bridge"	345
	tea caddy	395
22	oval footed bowl	125
	scalloped dish	245
	"Boy/Buffalo" plate	150
	Swansea "Long Bridge"	325
23	giraffe/camel cheese platter	475
	Spode cup & saucer	195
24	Two Temples I plate	150
	Two Temples II platter	145
	Ridgway Standard Willow	175
25	H. H & M. plate	65
	knife rests	125 ea.
	asparagus dishes	185 ea.
26	vase	250
	cheese trowel	125
27	soup dish	95
	"Best Goods"	65
	fluted rim plate	55
28	Doulton story plate	300
34	Podmore Walker plate	20
	perfume bottle	400
35	three painted plates	350 ea.
36	5 children's service platters	125 ea.
	chestnut basket & stand	975
37	loving cup	395
	polychrome plate	165
38	Royal vegetable server	75
39	engraving plates	495 ea.
40	The Dome	3500
42	cow figurine	2200
	cow cream pitcher (left)	125
	cow cream pitcher (center)	575
	cow cream pitcher (right)	575
	modern ladle	55
	dog figurine	400
	man figurine	700
	4 unmarked ladles	225-275 ea.
43	open salts	150 ea.
	large ladle	275
44	pepper pots	150 ea.
	light blue bowl	125
45	two-handled dish	150
	teapot	495
46	covered sugar bowl	125
	cheese wheel	2500
47	hot water plate	250
48	flow blue cheese board	225
	footed cup	175
49	tri-part dish	275
50	two-handled dish	245
	shell dishes	125 ea.
	leaf-shaped pickle dishes	125-165 ea.

	sauce boat	135
51	covered sectional dish	345
	covered square dish	145
	inhaler	3500
52	five-egg stand	265
53	demitasse & saucer	10-15
	Gladstone plate (1988)	75
54	paper cup	40
	Smith's clock	145
	tile tray	145
55	tin box	4
	tim trivet	15
	brass/copper tea cannister	60
	silver-colored cannister	45
	silver-plated tea set	350
56	brass tray	75
	silver-plated teapot	175
	silver-plated bowl	45
	glass jar	575
57	lampshade	95
	glass stemware	200/stem
60	polychrome tea caddy	135
	L & Sons salad bowl	125
61	L & Sons lambpot	95
	polychrome pitcher	95
	polychromew bread plate	185
	black-printed teacup & saucer	185
	"Portobello"-type pitchers	500 ea.
62	"Bungalo" tea caddy	325
	syrup pitcher	165
	green-printed, clobbered plate	75
63	Gaudy plate	165
	pink tea set, Japanese	195
67	three-handled mug	450
	covered tobacco jars	475
	large bowl	1200
68	pitcher	600
	hanging jardiniere	400
	teapot	450
	lidless sugar	275
69	potpourri (c. 1820)	1600
	mug	495
	salt & pepper shakers	165
	small dish	75
70	milk pail	3800
	toothbrush cover	95
	frog cup	395
71	bar-pulls	450/set
	ashtray	125
	advertising disks	125
73	record album	45
	NRA glasses	275
75	Adderly oversize cup	45
	Adams gravy boat	75
76	Arklow mug	6
77	Aynsley children's set, with 4 cups and saucers	450
	Bennett red Willow plate	10
	tea caddy	385
79	children's tea set	575

79-92 Because of the wide variety of Buffalo pieces made, this section of the price guide will refer to forms in general, not to particular items pictured unless noted.The prices listed here apply to smooth-edged pieces of blue-printed Willow from years after 1905. As a general rule, pieces marked 1905 (the first year of production) are priced 150% higher than the prices listed here. The scalloped pieces made between 1905 and 1908 are priced one-third higher than the prices listed here. Buffalo's Gaudy Willow was produced with the same set of molds that Blue Willow was, so prices can be compared. Prices for Gaudy pieces corresponding to *inexpensive* Blue pieces tend to be six times higher; prices for the Gaudy versions of *expensive* Blue pieces are usually three times higher.

	Buffalo Willow:	
	baking dishes (5.5" to 9.5")	60-85
	baking dishes (10.25" to 11.75")	125-150
	bone dish, crescent-shaped (p. 81)	60
	bowl (1, 1.5, or 2 pints)	50-75
	bowl, footed (1 or 1.5 pints, p. 87)	65-75
	bowl, square salad (9", p. 87)	275
	bowl, soup	25-40
	bowl, soup with rim	25-35
	butter, covered (p. 88)	170
	butter, individual (p. 86)	20-25
	cake plate	135
	candlestick (p. 90)	175
	casseroles	150-175
	compote(p. 38)	40
	creamers, individual or toy (1 to 3 oz., pp. 83, 85)	50
	creamers, full-size	75-100
	cup, bouillon (p. 85)	60
	cups, coffee	25
	cup, jumbo coffee (p. 84)	125
	cup, tea	25
	cup, egg	60
	gravy boat, square	60
	gravy boat, with attached platter	100
	jug, Buffalo (.75 pints to 4 pints, p. 82)	125-200
	jug, Chicago (.875 pints to 4.5 pints, p. 83)	125-200
	jugs, vitrified, scalloped rim (2.75" to 8.5")	50-75
	jugs, vitrtified, scalloped rim (10")	100
	mustards, covered (p. 89)	60
	pickle dish	50
	plates	25-40 ea.
	plate, chop	100-150
	platter (7.25")	160
	platter (8.75" to 14")	100-125
	platter (16")	160
	platter (18")	200
	ramekin	25
	saucer	15
	stein mug (p. 83)	100
	sugar bowls (individual, round and square, p. 88)	90-100
	syrup pitchers, covered (1 pint to 3.5 pints)	250-300
	tea tile	125
	teapots	250-350
	tureen (9.5")	475-500
	toilet set (p. 91):	
	toothbrush holder	125
	chamber pot w/ lid	300
	large pitcher	700
	small pitcher	350
	shaving mug	125
	slop jar w/lid	200
	soap dish w/ lid	250
	wash basin	350
85	individual teapot, 1911	265
93	Turner platter	325
	small Turner plate	150
94	two teacups	75 ea.
	Caughley teapot	485
	Chambers plate	85
	footed bowl	95
95	oval dish	145
	sugar bowl	225
	round plate	125
	four-lobed platter	385

96	ladle	250
	fluted set	135
	small ladle (1880)	145
97	covered sectional serving dish	325
	bath set	1500
98	"Forest Landscape" platter	850
	cream & sugar set	265
99	drainer	425
	milk seives	185
	coffee pot	475
	double well & tree platter	495
100	covered box	295
	open salt	150
101	"Bridgeless Willow" dish	95
	2-pc. chestnut dish	950
	crumpet comport	345
	serving bowl	60
102	horseradish dish	75
	"Rustic Willow"	25
	brush pot	95
103	yellow & black Willow plate	125
	flow blue cheese board	175
	tall pitcher	225
	trangular pitcher	185
104	"Persian Spray" plate (bottom)	150
105	pillow vase	675
	pitcher	245
106	Edge Malkin saucer	45
	bread plate	225
107	Forester polychrome plate	45
	Ford butter server	240
108	toast rack	175
109	cheese platter	275
110	bread platter	125
	Jackson cup	15
	G. Jones serving bowl	185
111	Laughlin teacup & saucer	10
113	Mandarin Blue bowls	15 ea.
	Mason's polychrome plate	185
114	long Mason's serving dish	425
115	three covered vases	750-1250 ea.
	candlesticks	750/pr.
	oyster plate	65
	cookie jar	45
116	Meakin doughnut stand	195
	Meakin plate	25
117	Midwinter plate (large)	20
	Midwinter plate (small)	12
118	relish dish	295
	vase	225
119	planter	525
	two footed vases	900
	pillow vase	350
	tile	85-110
120	Sterling plate	6-10
	Myott & Son sauce tureen	245
121	Parrott bowl	180
122	vase	450
	condiment servers (set)	1100
123	vinegar server	275
	pepper pot	275
	Ridgway plate	100
	punch cup	95
124	plate	85
125	cup	20
	cake plate	60
	server	60
126	teapot	75
	pastry stand	75
127	sauce boat	65
	egg cup	30
128	Toby jug	1200
129	black-printed platter	275
	round plate	95
130	plate	25
	covered server	150
131	plate	25
	bowl	45
132	tea caddy	125
	plate	85
	cup & saucer	65
134	puzzle jug	2500
135	Dillwyn plate	95
137	salt shaker	25
	pitcher	100
	dish	125
138	vases (pair)	250
	cup & stein	245
139	plate	65
	demitasse & saucer	75
140	cup	15
	miniature teapot	295
	brown Willow plate	20
141	teapot	475
	creamer	50
142	plate	125
143	octagonal cup	65
	basin & pitcher	700
144	trivet	95
	polychrome plate	95
147	Wilkinson Gaudy (in a 7-pc. set)	225
148	teapot	575
	covered sugar bowl	80
149	vaporizer	245
150	mustache cup	125
151	egg cup	95
	biscuit barrel	175
152	soup tureen	575
153	tankard	245
	bouillon cup/toast rack	475

Bibliography

Altman, Seymour and Violet. *The Book of Buffalo Pottery.* West Chester, Pennsylvania: Schiffer Publishing, 1987.

Ayers, John. "Blanc-de-Chine: Some Reflections." *Transactions of the Oriental Ceramics Society, 1986-1987.* London: Sotheby's Publications, 1988.

Bergesen, Victoria, contributor. "The Willow Pattern Plate" by Horace Hutchinson, 1912. *Friends of Blue* 71 (Spring 1991): 12.

Bergesen, Victoria. "The Pantomime Scene, January 1890." *Friends of Blue* 66 (Winter 1989-1990): 5.

Bockol, Leslie and Jeffrey B. Snyder. *Majolica: American and European Wares.* Atglen, Pennsylvania: Schiffer Publishing, 1994.

Bortone, Sandro and Lorenzo Camusso, eds. *Ceramics of the World from 4000 B.C. to the Present.* New York: Harry N. Abrams, 1991.

Cameh, Ada Walker. *The Blue-China Book: Early American Scenes and History Pictured in the Pottery of Time.* New York: Dover Publications, 1971.

Clark, Garth, ed. *Ceramic Art: Comment & Review 1882-1977.* New York: E.P. Dutton, 1978.

Cohen, Rita Entmacher. *It Must Be Blue Willow in Any Pattern.* International Willow Collectors Convention, June 18, 1994.

Copeland, Robert. *Spode's Willow Pattern and Other Designs After the Chinese.* Longton, England: Studio Vista, 1990.

Coysh, A.W. *Blue and White Transfer Ware, 1780-1840.* London: David & Charles, 1974.

Coysh, A. W. and R. K. Henrywood. *The Dictionary of Blue and White Printed Pottery, 1780-1880,* vol. I. Suffolk, UK: Antique Collectors' Club, 1982.

Coysh, A. W. and R. K. Henrywood. *The Dictionary of Blue and White Printed Pottery, 1780-1880,* vol. II. Suffolk, UK: Antique Collectors' Club, 1989.

Coysh, Bill. "Standard Willow." *Friends of Blue* 75 (Spring 1992); 4.

Creamware and Pearlware. From the Fifth Exhibition of the Northern Ceramic Society, Stoke-on-Trent City Museum and Art Gallery: Prince George Street Press Ltd., 1986.

Cushion, John P. *Pottery and Porcelain Tablewares.* New York: William Morrow & Co., 1976.

Detweiler, Susan G. *American Presidential China.* Washington D.C.: Smithsonian Institute, 1975.

Ellison, Eugene. *American Pottery Practices.* International Willow Collectors Convention, June 18, 1994.

Garner, Sir Harry. *Oriental Blue and White.* London: Faber & Faber, 1964

Godden, Geoffrey A. *British Porcelain: An Illustrated Guide.* London: Barrie and Jenkins, 1974.

Godden, Geoffrey A. *British Pottery & Porcelain,* 1780-1850. London: Arthur Baker Ltd., 1963.

Godden, Geoffrey A. *British Pottery: An Illustrated Guide.* London: Barrie & Jenkins, 1974.

Godden, Geoffrey A. *Encyclopedia of British Pottery and Porcelain Marks.* Exton, Pennsylvania: Schiffer Publishing, 1964.

Grun, Bernard. *The Timetables of History.* New York: Simon & Schuster, 1979.

Henzke, Lucile. *Art Pottery of America.* Exton, Pennsylvania: Schiffer Publishing, 1982.

Honey, W. B. *English Pottery & Porcelain,* 5th edition. London: Adam & Charles Black, 1962.

Hughes, Bernard and Therle. *The Collector's Encyclopaedia of English Ceramics.* London: Abbey Library, 1968.

Hughes, Robert. *The Fatal Shore.* New York: Alfred A Knopf, 1987.

Ifert, Barbara. *Made in Japan Ceramics, 1921-1941.* Atglen, Pennsylvania: Schiffer Publishing, 1994.

Inventors & Discoverers: Changing Our World. Washington, D.C.: The National Geographic Society, 1988.

Jensen, Veryl M. *The First International Book of Willow Ware.* Myrtle Creek, Oregon: The Mail Printers, 1975.

Laidacker, Sam. *Anglo-American China, part II.* Bristol, Pennsylvania: published by Sam Laidacker, 1951.

Lehner, Lois. *Lehner's Encyclopedia of U.S. Marks on Pottery, Porcelain, and Clay.* Paducah, Kentucky: Schroeder Publishing Company, 1988.

Macintosh, Duncan. *Chinese Blue and White Porcelain.* Rutland, Vermont: Charles Tuttle Co. Publishing, 1977.

Martin, Jean. "A Ceramic Legacy of Asia's Maritime Trade." *Transactions of the Oriental Ceramics Society, 1986-1987.* London: Sotheby's Publications, 1988.

Medley, Margaret. "Blue and White and the Qing Dynasty." *Transactions of the Oriental Ceramics Society, 1986-1987.* London: Sotheby's Publications, 1988.

Medley, Margaret. "Patterns of Chinese Taste in Porcelain." *Transactions of the Oriental Ceramics Society, 1987-1988.* London: Sotheby's Publications, 1989.

Newman, Harold and George Savage. *An Illustrated Dictionary of Ceramics.* London: Thames & Hudson, 1985.

Niblett, Kathy. "What is Pottery?" *Friends of Blue* 56 (Summer 1987): 4.

Palmer, Marjorie. "New Life for Old Willow." *Friends of Blue* 47 (Spring, 1985): 12.

Pearce, N. J. "Chinese Export Porcelain for the European Market: The Years of Decline, 1770-1820." *Transactions of the Oriental Ceramic Society, 1987-1988.* London: Sotheby's Publications, 1989.

Pusheng, Zhang. "New Discoveries from Recent Research into Chinese Blue and White Porcelain." *Transactions of the Oriental Ceramics Society, 1991-1992.* London: Azimuth Editions Limited, 1993.

Richardson, Ruth. "Garden China." *Friends of Blue* 70 and 71 (Winter 1990/1991 and Spring 1991).

Richardson, Ruth, contributor. "A Victorian View of Transfer Ware." Friends of Blue 65 (Autumn 1989).

Rust, Gordon A. *Collector's Guide of Antique Porcelain.* New York: Viking Press, 1973.

Savage, George. *English Pottery and Porcelain.* London: Oldbourne Press, 1961.

Seidel, John L. "'China Glaze' Wares on Sites from the American Revolution: Pearlware Before Wedgwood?" *Journal of the Society for Historical Archaeology* (24:1) 1990.

Sheaf, Colin. "The Geldermalsen Cargo." *Transactions of the Oriental Ceramics Society 1986-1987.* London: Sotheby's Publications, 1988.

Snyder, Jeffrey B. *Historic Flow Blue.* Atglen, Pennsylvania: Schiffer Publishing, 1994.

Snyder, Jeffrey B. *Flow Blue: A Collector's Guide to Pattern, History and Values.* Atglen, Pennsylvania: Schiffer Publishing, 1992.

Spence, Jonathan D. *The Search for Modern China.* New York: W.W. Norton, 1990.

Weibull, Jörgen. "Recent Chinese Reseach on the European Trade in the Eighteenth Century." *Transactions of the Oriental Ceramic Society, 1990-1991.* London: Soltheby's Publications, 1992.

Morley-Fletcher, Hugo. *Investing in Pottery and Porcelain.* New York: Clarkson N. Potter Inc. Publishing, 1968.

Worth, Veryl Marie. *Willow Pattern China.* Fuller Printing Company, 1979.

Index

International Willow Collectors

The International Willow Collectors organization provides a forum for enthusiasts to share their discoveries, insights, and love of blue and white chinoiserie. Founded in 1967, the group now has approximately 500 members, holds a fantastic annual convention, and helps to keep everyone up to date on the latest Willow activities. For information about the organization or other Willow inquiries, please contact

President: Eva Lee Revels
Country Accents
HC02—Box 200, Highway 16
Bandera, TX 78003

Vice President: Nancee L. Blaney
836 Moss Hill
Ashland, OH 44805

Officers: Barbara Stevens
86 N. Portwine Rd.
Roselle, IL 60172

Franklin Ladner
2407 Westwood Dr.
Arlington, TX 76012

Mary Lina Berndt
808 Glynn Oaks
Arlington, TX 76010

Mary Lina Berndt also publishes the *Willow Word,* an invaluable newsletter full of current happenings. Contact her for subscription information.